Charles Rieu

Supplement to the Catalogue of the Persian Manuscripts in the British Museum

Charles Rieu

Supplement to the Catalogue of the Persian Manuscripts in the British Museum

ISBN/EAN: 9783337310882

Printed in Europe, USA, Canada, Australia, Japan

Cover: Foto ©ninafisch / pixelio.de

More available books at **www.hansebooks.com**

SUPPLEMENT TO THE CATALOGUE

OF THE

PERSIAN MANUSCRIPTS

IN

THE BRITISH MUSEUM

SUPPLEMENT TO THE CATALOGUE

OF THE

PERSIAN MANUSCRIPTS

IN

THE BRITISH MUSEUM

BY

CHARLES RIEU, PH.D.

PRINTED BY ORDER OF THE TRUSTEES

London:

SOLD AT THE BRITISH MUSEUM;

AND BY

MESSRS. LONGMANS & CO., 39, PATERNOSTER ROW; B. QUARITCH, 15, PICCADILLY, W.; A. ASHER & CO., 13, BEDFORD STREET, COVENT GARDEN; KEGAN PAUL, TRENCH, TRÜBNER & CO., PATERNOSTER HOUSE, CHARING CROSS ROAD; AND HENRY FROWDE, OXFORD UNIVERSITY PRESS, AMEN CORNER.

1895.

LONDON:
PRINTED BY GILBERT AND RIVINGTON, LIMITED,
ST. JOHN'S HOUSE, CLERKENWELL, E.C.

PREFACE.

The present Supplement deals with four hundred and twenty-five Manuscripts acquired by the Museum during the last twelve years, namely from 1883, the year in which the third and last volume of the Persian Catalogue was published, to the last quarter of the present year.

For more than a half of these accessions, namely, two hundred and forty volumes, the Museum is indebted to the agency of Mr. Sidney J. A. Churchill, late Persian Secretary to Her Majesty's Legation at Teheran, who during eleven years, from 1884 to 1894, applied himself with unflagging zeal to the self-imposed duty of enriching the National Library with rare Oriental MSS. and with the almost equally rare productions of the printing press of Persia. By his intimate acquaintance with the language and literature of that country, with the character of its inhabitants, and with some of its statesmen and scholars, Mr. Churchill was eminently qualified for that task, and he availed himself with brilliant success of his exceptional opportunities.

His first contribution was a fine illuminated copy of the Ẓafar Nāmah, or rhymed chronicle, of Ḥamdullah Mustaufi (no. 263), no other MS. of which is known to exist. His last was a rich collection, including original Firmans of the Sovereigns of Persia from the Aḳ-ḳuyunlu dynasty to the present Shah (nos. 401-2); numerous autographs of celebrated statesmen, scholars and poets (nos. 400, 403); and, finally, portraits of Nāṣir ud-Dīn Shāh and some of his ministers (no. 412).

Mr. Churchill's MSS. abound in rare, or altogether new, materials for the study of Eastern, and more especially Persian, history. The following are a few of the most valuable: The general histories of Elchi e Niẓāmshāh and of Ḥaidar Rāzi (nos. 32, 33); Rauẓat uṣ-Ṣafaviyyah, a history of the Safavi dynasty, written by a follower of Shāh

'Abbās I., and brought down to the accession of Shāh Ṣafi (no. 58); three works, treating chiefly of the reign of Shāh Ṭahmāsp, and respectively written by Amir Maḥmūd, son of Khwāndamir (no. 53), by Ḥasan Beg Rūmlu (no. 55), and by an anonymous writer, whose work is entitled Afẓal ut-tavārikh (no. 56); Khuld i Barin, an official record of the reigns of Shāh Ṣafi and 'Abbās II. (no. 34); Gulshan i Murād, a history of Karim Khān Zand and his immediate successors (no. 66); two contemporary accounts of the reign of Fatḥ 'Ali Shah, one by his son, Mahmūd Mirza, the other by his secretary, Fazlullah Khāvari (nos. 70, 71); a history of 'Abdullah Khān Uzbek, by Ḥāfiẓ Tanish (no. 73); local histories of Ḳum, of Baihaḳ, and of the conquest of Kirman by Malik Dinār (nos. 88—90); geographical works, with historical notices, by Zain ul-'Ābidīn Shirvāni (nos. 139—141); lastly, the best copy known of Ta'rikh i Jadid, the history of the Bābis, lately translated by Mr. E. G. Browne (no. 15).

Poetry will be found to be still more largely represented than history. Mr. Churchill's collection is especially rich in Tazkirahs, a favourite branch of Persian literature, combining biographies of poets with more or less extensive specimens of their compositions. It contains one of the earliest works quoted under that head, the Chahār Maḳālah of Niẓāmi 'Arūẓi (no. 390); a large volume of the rare Khulāsat ul-Ash'ār, by Taḳi Kāshi (no. 105); three otherwise unknown works of the same class, entitled Bazm-ārāi, Maikhānah, and Khair ul-Bayān (nos. 106—8); and a whole host of later Tazkirahs, illustrating the revival of Persian poetry under the Ḳajār dynasty (nos. 115, 118—129). Early copies of the Divans, or collected works, of ancient poets will be found under nos. 211, 220, 222, 240, 243, 246; and those of modern poets described under nos. 340—373 were almost exclusively supplied by Mr. Churchill. Nor should we leave unnoticed the unique "Mu'ajjam" of Shams i Ḳais (no. 190), the earliest treatise extant on Persian metres.

Not the least curious of Mr. Churchill's acquisitions consisted of eight MSS. written in Persian, but in the Hebrew character. Two of them, being transcripts of Muslim works, have found place in this Supplement (nos. 230, 272). The others, belonging more properly to Jewish literature, have been reserved for the Hebrew Catalogue now in course of preparation.

Having concluded this brief sketch of the Churchill MSS., we now proceed to enumerate, in chronological order, the main sources from which the remainder of the present collection has been derived.

A number of Oriental MSS. brought together by the genial author of "Histoire des religions et des philosophies dans l'Asie centrale," Comte de Gobineau, during his residence as French Envoy at the Persian Court, were sold by auction, after his death, in Paris in the year 1885. Nine of the most valuable were secured for the British Museum. These included the gem of the collection, a finely written and tastefully illuminated volume comprising the best text known of Asadi's Garshāsp Nāmah, and three other epic poems hitherto scarcely known by name (no. 201); further, a volume of the great historical work of Ḥāfiẓ i Abrū (no. 27); the Persian translation of Narshakhi's history of Bukhara (no. 87); the history of Tabaristan, by Ibn Isfandiyar (no. 92); and Iḥyā ul-Mulūk, a curious and otherwise unknown history of Sistān (no. 97).

In the same year eleven Persian MSS. were purchased of the sons of the Rev. Henry Aaron Stern, who had acquired them during his missionary journeys in Persia in the years 1847—52. The only one that calls for a special notice here is a copy of the Shāhnāmah in two large folios (nos. 196-7), containing a number of additional episodes and later poems grafted on the original text of Firdausi.

Eleven MSS. acquired at the same date originally belonged to a distinguished Persian scholar, the late Nathaniel Bland. Besides a copy of the Ātashkadah, a Biography of Poets, which he had been the first to make known in Europe, they include the Yūsuf u Zulaikhā of Firdausi (no. 200), the only copy of that rare poem which contains the full text of the prologue; the history of the Moghols, by Rashīd ud-Dīn (no. 25); an early MS. of the Khamsah of Niẓāmi (no. 226); and a profusely illuminated copy of the Ḥamlah i Ḥaidari (no. 336).

The collection of Alfred von Kremer, purchased in 1886, is essentially Arabic, and has been described in the Preface to the Arabic Supplement. The most interesting of the nine Persian MSS. which it includes is a volume containing a large collection of letters written by Bahā-ullah, the late head of the Bābis, to his followers in Persia (no. 13).

At the sale of the MSS. of the late Thomas Fiott Hughes, Secretary to the British Embassy at Constantinople, which took place in London in the year 1890, the Museum became possessed of seven choice MSS. remarkable either for their early dates or their exquisite calligraphy. The Risālah of Ḳushairi (no. 16) and the Akhlāḳ i Nāṣiri (no. 147) are dated respectively A.H. 601 and 680. A Gulistān (no. 249) and a

TABLE OF CONTENTS.

THEOLOGY 1
Shī'ah works 4
Bābī books 6
Sufism 9
Appendix to Theology 13

LAW 13

HINDUISM 14

HISTORY. *General history* 15
Muḥammad and the Imams . . . 29
Moghols 33
Muzaffaris 33
Timur 33
Safavis 34
Nādir Shah 43
Zands 43
Kajars 45
Uzbeks 49
Afghans 51
India 51
Local histories 58

BIOGRAPHY 68
Lives of Sufis 70
Tazkirahs or Lives of Poets . . . 71
Memoirs and Travels . . 96

COSMOGRAPHY AND GEOGRAPHY 98

SCIENCES. *Encyclopædias* 102
Ethics and Politics 105
Astronomy 110
Mineralogy 112
Medicine 113
Farriery 114
Music 114

PHILOLOGY. *Persian Lexicography* . . 116
Arabic Lexicography and Grammar. 120
Various Lexicographical works . . 120
Rhetoric and Insha 121
Prosody 123
Riddles 126

POETRY 127
Anthologies 232

TALES AND FABLES 238
Collections of Anecdotes 243

LETTERS, STATE PAPERS AND AUTOGRAPHS . 253
PAINTINGS 260
INSCRIPTIONS 263
MSS. OF MIXED CONTENTS 264
LATEST ACCESSIONS 270
ALPHABETICAL INDEX OF TITLES . . . 275
INDEX OF PERSONS' NAMES 285
CLASSED INDEX OF WORKS 299
NUMERICAL INDEX 305

SUPPLEMENT TO THE

CATALOGUE OF THE PERSIAN MANUSCRIPTS.

THEOLOGY.

1.

Or. 4379.—Foll. 384; 12¾ in. by 8¼; 27 lines, 6 in. long; written in Neskhi by two hands, apparently in the 17th and 18th centuries. [Wallis Budge.]

مواهب عليه

The Persian commentary of Ḥusain Vā'iẓ Kāshifī upon the Coran. See the Persian Catalogue, p. 9 *b*, and Ethé, Bodleian Catalogue, nos. 1805—8.

The MS. contains the first part of the work. It breaks off in the middle of Sūrat ul-A'rāf, vii., v. 149.

The latter part of the volume, foll. 132—384, contains a portion of the Arabic commentary entitled Ma'ālim ut-Tanzīl. See the Supplement to the Arabic Catalogue, no. 1266.

2.

Or. 2983.—Foll. 550; 12 in. by 7¾; 20 lines, 4¾ in. long: written in small, neat and close, Nestalik; dated Thursday, 20 Rabi' II., A.H. 1085 (A.D. 1674). [H. A. Stern.]

The first volume of an extensive Shī'ah commentary upon the Coran, without title or author's name.

It is imperfect at the beginning, commencing abruptly in the middle of comments on the first words of the Fātiḥah as follows: الرحمن الرحيم اشتقاق هر دو از رحمتست و رحمت نعمت باشد كتاب خودرا رحمت خواند و تفسير او بارادت خير وترك عقوبت درين معنى داخل است

The commentary upon Sūrat ul-Baḳarah begins, fol. 4*a*, as follows: سورة البقره اين سوره دويست وهشتاد و شش آيتست بعدد كوفيان وآن عدد امير المومنين على ابن ابى طالبست عليه السلام وسوره جمله مدنى است و بروايت ديكر الا يلك آيه كه در حجة الوداع آمد

The next-following Surahs begin respectively as follows: Āl 'Imrān, fol. 125*a*; al-Nisā, fol. 186*b*; al-Mā'idah, fol. 231*a*; al-An'ām, fol. 275*b*; al-A'rāf, fol. 312*a*; al-Anfāl, fol. 360*a*; al-Taubah, fol. 367*b*; Yūnus, fol. 410*b*; Hūd, fol. 430*b*; Yūsuf, fol. 448*b*; al-Ra'd, fol. 469*b*; Ibrāhīm, fol. 478*b*; al-Ḥijr, fol. 485*b*; al-Naḥl, fol. 492*a*; Bani Isrā'il, fol. 506*a*; and al-Kahf, fol. 529*b*.

The commentary includes the text of the Coran in rather long passages consisting of one or more verses, followed by a Persian paraphrase. It deals chiefly in traditions and legends. Although quite distinct from the Khulāṣat ul-Manhaj by Fatḥ-ullah B. Shukr-ullah Kāshāni (see the Persian Catalogue, pp. 12*a* and 1077*b*), it contains much matter in common with it. The Shi'ah character of the work is shown by frequent references to the interpretations of the Imams, such as تفسیر اهل البیت and اجماع اهل البیت

The title written on the outer edge, both at the side and at the bottom, is الجلد الاول من المواهب. It is probably due to a confusion of the present work with that contained in the preceding MS.

Copyist: محمد جعفر بیك ابن قیاس المازندرانی ساروی

3.

Or. 3208.—Foll. 55; 8¼ in. by 5; 12 lines, 3½ in. long; written in Nestalik, apparently in India; dated Monday, 29 Jumada I., in the sixth year (of Aurangzib's reign) and A.H. 1072 (A.D. 1661).

[Kremer, no. 211.]

سراج القلوب

Answers of Muḥammad to questions put to him by the Jews.

Beg. الحمد لله رب العالمين ... العالم الحكيم المدبر القديم ذى الملك والبقا الحمد لله والثنا خالق كل شى ورازق كل حي

No author is named in the present copy; but the contents agree substantially, notwithstanding some variations, with those of the MS. noticed in the Persian Catalogue, p. 17*b*, in which the work is ascribed to Sa'īd B. Muḥammad al-Ḳaṭṭān al-Ghaznavī. The same author is named in a Berlin MS., Pertsch, no. 219.

The first question is: خبر کن یا محمد مارا که خدای تعالی این جهانرا بچند روز آفریده است.
The last, fol. 45*a*, is: خبر کن یا محمد مارا که بر کور سلیمان علیه السلام رفتند تا خاتم بدست آرند الخ
The answer to this last consists of the Story of Balūḳiyā, foll. 45*a*—74, which concludes the work. For other copies see Pertsch, no. 218.

4.

Or. 2842.—Foll. 246; 8 in. by 5¼; 10 lines, 2¾ in. long; written in large and elegant Nestalik, with 'Unvān and ruled margins; dated Dār us-Salṭanah (Teheran), Sunday, 15 Ṣafar, A.H. 1221 (A.D. 1806).

[Sidney Churchill.]

شرعة الاسلام الفارسی تحفة الخاقانی

A translation by Mūsa B. Ayyūb B. Aḥmad Naṣrapūri of the Shir'at ul-Islām, a treatise on religious duties and rules of life founded on the precepts and example of the Prophet. See the Arabic Supplement, no. 178.

Beg. اجناس حمد وسپاس واصناف شکر بیقیاس آفریدکاریرا سزد که نوع بنی آدم را ... وبعد چنین کوید حقیر قلیل البضاعة موسی ابن مخدوم ایوب ابن مخدوم احمد نصرپوری که این کتابیست نفیس متضمن بر سنن سید الانام ... وبمنزله ترجمه کتاب شرعة الاسلام تالیف کرده شد

The preface of the translator includes a dedication to Amir Khusrau Khān and a long panegyric upon him in prose and verse. The work consists of a Bāb, or introductory chapter, on the duty of following the Sunnah, and of fifty-nine sections (Fuṣūl) fully enumerated in the preface. The contents agree with the analysis of the original work given by Krafft, no. 929.

Copyist: محمد علی بن مهرعلی افشار

5.

Or. 4507.—Foll. 186; 8½ in. by 6; 17 lines, 3⅜ in. long; written in fair Nestalik; dated 10 Ṣafar, A.H. 1034 (A.D. 1624).

[Raverty.]

تذكرة الابرار

A controversial treatise against heresies, by the great champion of Sunni orthodoxy among the Afghans, Shaikh Darvīzah Ningarhāri. See the Persian Catalogue, pp. 28 and 1078*a*, and Raverty's Pukhto Grammar, 2nd edition, p. 33.

This copy wants about three pages at the beginning. The first words extant, تاراج یابد عیاذا بالله و یا آنکه بعد از فراغ مصنف متدین و متقی, are found at fol. 4*a*, line 9, of the previously described MS., Or. 222. Two leaves are lost after fol. 184. The lacuna corresponds with foll. 197—199 of the latter MS. The missing text has been imperfectly supplied by an inserted leaf in a later hand, and the passage which gives the date of composition, A.H. 1021, is wanting. In the colophon the work is called تذكرة الابرار والاشرار.

Major Raverty writes on the fly-leaf: "This very old copy was obtained at Haiderabad, in India, from the descendants of a disciple of the Ākhund."

6.

Or. 4380.—Foll. 89; 8 in. by 5¼; 15 and 17 lines, 3 in. long; written in Neskhi and in Nestalik, apparently in the 17th century.

[Wallis Budge.]

هداية السعدا فى جلوة الشرفا

A work treating of the holiness and prerogatives of the descendants of the Prophet, imperfect at beginning and end, without author's name.

The first page contains the last two lines of the doxology, and the beginning of the preface, which commences thus: اما بعد عرضه میدارد بنده درگاه نبوی و مولای هم پایگاه مصطفوی که این رساله معتبر و فضاله مختصر منقولست از درون سیصد کتب

After dwelling at length on the duty incumbent on every believer to love and honour the descendants of the Prophet, the author states that the work comprises fourteen sections called Hidāyah, subdivided into chapters termed Jilwah, a table of which concludes the preface.

The MS. contains only the first of those fourteen Hidāyahs and a portion of the second. The first treats of the pre-eminence of the Prophet's descendants, and has the following heading: الهداية الاولى وفضالة العلى فى سيرة مذهب الباب التقى وتفضيل اولاد السيد المصطفى تصديقا ويقينا فى اجلاله

It is divided into eighteen Jilwahs, enumerated at the beginning, fol. 7*a* (there are only seventeen in the body of the volume). Of the second Hidāyah (فى معرفة اولاد الرسول وبيان الايمان والدين), which is divided into seven Jilwahs, the MS. contains only the first three and the last two, foll. 78—89.

The author purposely suppressed his name, lest it should be placed before those of the holy Sayyids, as he states himself: اسم و نام خود ذکر کرده نشد ازانکه چون این کتاب در بیان فضل سادات است روا نداشته که نام مولف مقدم بر بیان ایشان شود. That he was a Sunni is abundantly proved by the contents. He devotes a whole chapter, foll. 32—45, to the refutation of the Rāfiḍis or Shī'ah, and in another passage, fol. 8*b*, he says that whosoever places 'Ali above Abu Bakr and 'Omar is a heretic, and whosoever denies their claim to the Khilāfat and abuses them is a Kāfir, or unbeliever. He cannot have lived earlier than the 8th century of the Hijrah; for he quotes Sa'di, and Khulāṣat us-Siyar, the author of which died A.H. 694.

The margins contain miscellaneous notes and extracts in a later hand.

Shi'ah Works.

7.

Or. 2971.—Foll. 114; 9¾ in. by 5¼; 25 lines, 3½ in. long; written in clear Neskhi; dated Ardabil, 26 Rajab, A.H. 1096 (A.D. 1685). [Sidney Churchill.]

تبصرة العوام

An account of the tenets of various religions and of the sects of Islām, considered from a Shī'ah standpoint, by Sayyid Murtaẓa 'Alam ul-Huda, who lived about A.H. 653. See the Persian Catalogue, pp. 140, 1081*a*.

Beg. حمد و سپاس خدای را عز وجل که جملهٔ موجودات را از عدم بوجود آورد

The work has been lithographed, together with Ḳiṣaṣ ul-'Ulamā, Teheran, A.H. 1304. For MSS. see Rehatsek, Mulla Firuz Library, p. 188; Pertsch, Berlin Catalogue, no. 228; and Ethé, Bodleian Catalogue, no. 1766. In the last two works the Persian headings are given in full.

Copyist: احمد بن بیك احمد خلخالی

In a note written at the end, S. Churchill states that in the colophon of another copy the author was called Sayyid Murtaẓa Rāzī.

8.

Or. 2812.—Foll. 164; 8¼ in. by 5; 14 lines, 2¾ in. long; written in elegant Nestalik, with 'Unvān and gold-ruled margins; dated Monday, 17 Rabī' I., A.H. 1092 (A.D. 1681). Bound in painted and glazed covers.

ترجمه مفتاح الفلاح

A collection of prayers, handed down by tradition from the Imams, and appointed for stated times of day and night, translated from the Arabic work Miftāḥ ul-Falāḥ, of Bahā ud-Din Muḥammad al-'Āmili (died A.H. 1030), with explanations and additions, by Jamāl ud-Dīn Muḥammad B. Ḥusain Khwānsāri.

Beg. مفتاح فلاح دنیا و عقبی و مقدمه نجاح آخرت واولی حمد و ثنای بارگاه کبریای کریمیست

The work is divided into six Bābs, according to the appointed times of prayer from the rise of dawn to the hours after midnight. The text of the prayers is Arabic, with an interlinear Persian version. The preface concludes with a wordy and stilted panegyric upon Shāh Sulaimān Ṣafavi. The present MS. was transcribed from the original draft of the translator, who is spoken of in the colophon as being still alive. Copious marginal notes.

The Miftāḥ ul-Falāḥ is mentioned, as well as the translation of Aḳā Jamāl Khwānsāri, in a full notice of Bahā ud-Din 'Āmili, Ḳiṣaṣ ul-'Ulamā, pp. 174—84. See also Samā un-Nujūm, pp. 26—34, and Majma' ul-Fuṣaḥā, vol. ii., p. 8. Aḳā Jamal Khwānsāri was one of the disciples of Mulla Muḥammad Taḳi Majlisi, who was himself a disciple of Shaikh Bahā ud-Din 'Āmili and died A.H. 1070. See Ḳiṣaṣ ul-'Ulamā, p. 172.

9.

Or. 2993.—Foll. 281; 9 in. by 4¾; 20 lines, 2½ in. long; written in small and neat Nestalik; dated 1 Zulḥijjah, A.H. 1060 (A.D. 1650). [Sidney Churchill.]

کوهر مراد

A treatise on metaphysics and Shī'ah

theology, by 'Abd ur-Razzāḳ B. 'Ali B. al-Ḥusain al-Lāhiji.

Beg. کوهر مرادی که غواص فکرت را از دریای حیرت درکف اندیشه آید

The author, an eminent disciple of Mulla Ṣadrā Shīrāzi, lived in Ḳum under Shāh Ṣafi and 'Abbās II. See the Persian Catalogue, p. 32; Nujūm us-Samā, p. 87; Majma' ul-Fuṣaḥā, vol. ii., p. 27; and Gobineau, Religions de l'Asie, p. 92. The present copy contains a fuller text than the previously described MS., Add. 26,289, and has annotations written by another hand in a cursive character on the margins and on inserted slips. Foll. 39—52 have been supplied by the same hand to fill up a lacuna of the original MS.

Copyist: ابن اسمعیل ابو تراب الحسینی القمی

Foll. 268—280, written in the cursive character above mentioned, contain two additions, namely: 1. A Persian tract on the fate of souls after death, and on the Day of Judgment; being the original draft of the anonymous author, dated Ṣafar, A.H. 1100; imperfect at the beginning. 2. An Arabic tract on the question whether Ruḳayyah and Zainab, wives of 'Uṣmān, were daughters of Muḥammad; also anonymous; beginning (fol. 274b) as follows: بعد حمد من عم لطفه المطیع والعاصی ... اما بعد فهذه رسالة کتبت جوابا عن سوال اشیر الیه من خدمة قائل

10.

Or. 4183.—Foll. 243; 9½ in. by 4½; 23 lines, 2¾ in. long; written in small and neat Neskhi, with red-ruled margins; dated 1 Zulhijjah, A.H. 1073 (A.D. 1663).

[Sidney Churchill.]

تقدیس الانبیا وتمجید الاوصیا

A Shi'ah work tending to establish the immunity from sin of the Prophets and the Imams, by Muḥammad B. Sayyid Aḥmad al-'Alavi al-'Āmili, commonly called 'Abd ul-Ḥasīb al-Ḥusaini al-Fāṭimi.

سر هر نامه است نام خدا بهتر از هر سخن کتاب خدا ... شکر بیقیاس و سپاس با اساس ذاتی را سزد که دوایر سموات و ارضین از قدرت صنع او شمه

The work is divided into a Fātiḥah, or introduction, and twenty chapters called Taḳdis, subdivided into sections termed Tamjid. The contents are as follows:

Fātiḥah treating of the necessity of Prophets and of their attributes. Taḳdis I. Impeccability of Prophets and Imams, fol. 8a. Refutation of doubts and objections arising from apparent sins ascribed to the following fifteen Prophets, to each of whom a special chapter (Taḳdis) is devoted, viz.: Taḳdis II. Adam, fol. 17a. III. Nūḥ, fol. 27a. IV. Ibrāhim, fol. 33a. V. Ya'ḳūb, fol. 45a. VI. Yūsuf, fol. 46a. VII. Ayyūb, fol. 65b. VIII. Shu'aib, fol. 66b. IX. Mūsa, fol. 67b. X. Dā'ūd, fol. 88b. XI. Sulaimān, fol. 92b. XII. Yūnus, fol. 97a. XIII. Lūṭ, fol. 100b. XIV. Zakariyyā, fol. 103a. XV. 'Īsa, fol. 104b. XVI. Muḥammad, fol. 105b. XVII. Evidences of the Imamship of 'Ali, fol. 114a. XVIII. Evidences of the legitimacy of the Imams, fol. 195b. XIX. Refutation of doubts raised by the Sunnis as to the impeccability of the Imams, fol. 211a. XX. The fundamental points of the creed and the Day of Judgment, fol. 221a.

The author refers incidentally to two other works of his, entitled سدرة المنتهی and مناهج الشارعین

Copyist: ابن حیدر محمد امین النایبی

11.

Or. 2813.—Foll. 98; 9¼ in. by 5; 15 lines, 2⅞ in. long; written in fair Persian Neskhi, with gold-ruled margins; dated 1st Rabi' II., A.H. ١٢٧, probably for 1127 (A.D. 1715).

[Haji Khan.]

A short guide to prayers and religious obligations, according to Shī'ah practice, by Muḥammad Bāḳir B. Muḥammad Taḳi, with the heading: هذا رسالة وجيزة الشهير بالزائده زاد المعاد

Beg. الحمد لله رب النور والظلام ... اما بعد بنده خاطی محمد باقر ابن محمد تقی

The author, Shaikh ul-Islām Mulla Muḥ. Bāḳir Majlisi, who died in Ispahan A.H. 1110 (see the Persian Catalogue, p. 20), extracted this manual, as stated in the preamble, from his previous work, Zād ul-Ma'ād (Persian Catalogue, p. 21, and Pertsch, Berlin Catalogue, no. 210) for the benefit of such persons as could not procure the larger treatise. It is divided, according to the preface, into five Bābs and a Khātimah; but in the body of the volume there are four Bābs and two Khātimahs. The contents are as follows: Bāb I. Observances for each month, fol. 2a. Bāb II. Visitation of (the tombs of) Muḥammad and the Imams, fol. 6b. Bāb III. Prayers not appointed for special days or months, fol. 29b. Bāb IV. Ordinances relating to the dead, fol. 46b. Khātimah: Laws relating to tithes (زکوة و خمس) and to religious retreat (اعتکاف), fol. 76b. Second Khātimah, treating of expiations (کفارات), fol. 91a.

The author states at the end that he wrote the work in Ispahan, in the months of Sha'bān and Ramazān, A.H. 1107.

Copyist: محمد بن عبد الله بن ابو القاسم الخوزستانی

Babi Books.

12.

Or. 2819.—Foll. 166; 8½ in. by 5; 19 lines, 3 in. long; written in neat Neskhi; dated A.H. 1299 (A.D. 1882).

[Sidney Churchill.]

A Babi book without title or author's name.

Beg. بسم الله الامنع الاقدس

تسبیح و تقدیس بساط قدس عز مجد سلطانی را لایق که لم یزل ولا یزال بوجود کینونیت ذات خود بوده وهست

It is the work known as the Persian Bayān, بیان فارسی, the last of the Bāb's writings, and the most complete exposition of his teaching. The author, Mirza 'Ali Muḥammad Shirāzi, suffered martyrdom A.H. 1266.

The present MS. has been noticed and the doctrines and tendency of the work have been set forth by Dr. E. G. Browne in the Journal of the Royal Asiatic Society, 1889, pp. 911—933. The contents have been fully stated by Baron V. von Rosen in "Collections Scientifiques de l'Institut," iii., pp. 1—32. Two other MSS. are noticed by Dr. Browne in the above Journal, 1892, pp. 450 and 698, and extracts in text and translation have been given by the same scholar in his "Traveller's Narrative," vol. ii., pp. 218—26, 347—49.

The present copy is due to the pen of the Bābi poet Nabil, who writes at the end: تمت علی ید الفقیر وحرره المسمی بنبیل قبل علی تغمده الله فی لجه غفرانه بجوده وفضله وعنایته سنه ١٢١١

13.

Or. 3116.—Foll. 127; 8¾ in. by 7¼; 14 lines, 4¼ in. long; written in cursive and rather indistinct Shikesteh, in the latter part of the 19th century. [Kremer, no. 126.]

I. Foll. 1—67. The Īḳān, by Bahā-ullah (Mirza Ḥusain 'Ali, who died A.H. 1309). See the supplement to the Arabic Catalogue, no. 222, and p. 935*a*.

II. Foll. 67—77. An epistle treating at length, and in true Sufi spirit, of mystical love and of the seven degrees by which the devotee سالك rises to complete detachment from self and from the world, and finally obtains perfect union with the Beloved.

Beg. الحمد لله الذی قد اظهر الوجود من العدم وارقم علی لوح الانسان من اسرار القدم وعلمه من البيان ما لا يعلم كتابا مبينا لمن آمن واستسلم

From the Arabic introduction, which occupies the first two pages, it appears that the author, whose name is not given, wrote this epistle in answer to a disciple already advanced in spiritual life, whom he addresses in the course of the work sometimes as brother, sometimes as son. The doxology includes the usual blessings invoked upon Muḥammad and his family. The Persian text begins as follows: مراتب سير سالكان را از مسكن خاكی بوطن الهی هفت رتبه معين نموده اند چنانچه بعضی هفت وادی و بعضی هفت شهر ذكر كرده اند و كفته اند كه سالك تا از نفس هجرت ننمايد و اين اسفار را طی نكند به بهر قرب وصال وارد نشود و از خمر بی مثال نچشد

It ends, fol. 77*a*, with these words: چون قلم در وصف اينحالت رسيد هم قلم بشكست و هم كاغذ دريد والسلام ای حبيب من

The next page contains a letter addressed to a Shaikh not named, and alluding to impending persecution and martyrdom. It begins as follows: اينغزال صحرای احديه را كلابی چند در پی و اين بلبل بستان صمديه را منقاری چند در تعاقب .... ای شيخ همت را زجاج كن كه شايد اين سراج را از بادهای مخالف حفظ نمايد

The last words are: للحب راحته عنا فاوله سقم و اخره قتل والسلام علی من اتبع الهدی

After this comes an explanation of the mystic meaning conveyed by the letters composing the word كنجشك: انچه از بدايع فكر در معنی طير معروف كه بفارسی كنجشك مينمايند

III. Foll. 78—127. A collection of Persian letters by Bahā-ullah. They are mostly letters of admonition or encouragement written to followers of both sexes; a few others are addressed to outsiders or opponents, with the object of convincing them of the truth of the new revelation. They generally begin with a formula which contains an allusion to the writer's name, بسم الاقدس الابهی or هو الاقدس الاعظم الابهی. In several instances, however, the heading is باسم محبوب عالميان.

The letters are too numerous to be individually noticed. The beginnings of the first seven are as follows:

Fol. 78*a*. هو الناظر من الافق الاول

بشنويد ندای الهی را و به بصر حديد وقلب منير در كلمات بديعش نظر نمائيد و تفكر كنيد كل اسماء در قبضهٔ قدرت او بوده و خواهد بود

Fol. 79*a*. بسم الله البهی الابهی

اهل انصاف را اقتضا نه كه باحبای الهی و قاصدانحرم رحمانی كه لحب الله كاس بلا نوشيده اند تعرض نمائيد اين اوراق را ارياح مشيت ربانی از وطن و ديار ظاهره حركت داده و بوطن باقيه الهيه كشانده

Ib. بنام دوست

ربيع رحمت رحمانی در اين ايام ظاهر و شمس عنايت سبحانی از افق سجن طالع بعضی در قربش واصل و جمعی در بعدش آمل

Fol. 79*b*. بسم الله الاقدس الابهى

فانيان بهر الهى را لازم كه در كل جهان عباد را بشطر رحمن بخوانند چه كه هر نفسيكه از خود فانى شد ببقاى حق فائز خواهد شد

Fol. 80*a*. بسم الله الاقدس الابهى

اى كنيز من و فرزند كنيز من جميع عباد و آماء را امروز خلق فرموديم چه كه مقصود عالميان اليوم ظاهر و بر عرش عظمت مستوى و در كل جهان مناديان الهى ناس را بشطر رحمن ميخوانند

Ib. بسم الله الاعز الامنع الابهى العليم

اكثرى از رجال از شطر ذو الجلال محروم مانده اند از فضل الهى ميشايد كه بر امرش قيام نمايند و بذكرش ناطق شوند و بامرش متوجه كردند اى كنيز حق الخ

Fol. 80*b*. بسم الله الاعظم الابهى

اى دوستان امروز روزى است كه هر يك از محبان بنصرت رحمن بر خيزند چه كه اكثر من على الارض در اطفاء نار الله و نور او سعى مينموده اند

Further on, foll. 87—89, is a long letter, addressed to one of the Persian 'Ulamā, in which the writer gives his proper name, Ḥusain 'Ali. It is an urgent appeal to his correspondent to accept the new faith. It begins: هذا كتاب من لدى المظلوم الذى يسمى بحسين قبل الى [على] اليك يقربك الى الله المهيمن القيوم لا تكن من الذين تمسكوا بالعلوم اذ جائهم المعلوم من لدى الله العزيز الودود وان اخرق حجاب الاكبر باذن الله مالك القدر ثم اقبل الى المنظر الاكبر انه خير لك مما عندك من العلوم

A similar, but shorter, appeal is addressed further on, fol. 104*a*, to the father of the writer. It begins: اى پدر قلم اعلى ميفرمايد در حال پير فكر كن و ببصر اطهر بمنظر اكبر ناظر باش آخر هر گلى را بوئى و هر نورى را اشراق و ظهورى بوده تفكر نما كه پسرت را چه نارى مشتعل نموده و چه نورى جذب كرده الخ

There is at fol. 116*b* an important passage, in which Bahā enjoins on his correspondent the duty of collecting and reading the previously revealed Persian letters: آنجناب بايد الواح پارسيه كه از سماء مشيت احدى نازل شده بقدر مقدور جمع نمايند وقراءت كنند

The last letter begins as follows:

هو الله تعالى جلت عظمته

كتب عديدةٌ الجناب لدى الوجه حاضر و تمام ان عبد [عند] خاطر مذكور داشت انچه در وصف احباى ان ارض نوشته بوديد نشهد لهم كما شهدت ولاكن نوصيهم بتقوى الله ربك ورب العالمين

The names of the persons to whom the letters are addressed are rarely given. We have only noticed the following: Riẓā, fol. 101*b*; 'Abdullah, foll. 103*b*, 116*a*; Yūsuf, fol. 105*a*; Muḥammad 'Ali, محمد قبل على (probably the poet Nabīl), fol. 106*b*; 'Ali Akbar, على قبل اكبر, fol. 110*a*. One of the letters, fol. 82*a*, is addressed to the writer's cousin, پسر عم.

14.

Or. 3115.—Foll. 30; 7 in. by 4¼; written in Neskhi and Nestalik, in the latter half of the 19th century. [Kremer, no. 125.]

Letter of Bahā-ullah to the Shah, written in Arabic with passages in Persian. See the Supplement to the Arabic Catalogue, no. 224.

15.

Or. 2942.—Foll. 177; 8 in. by 5; 16 lines, 2¾ in. long; written in neat minute Nestalik; dated Rajab, A.H. 1298 (A.D. 1881). [Sidney Churchill.]

تاريخ جديد

A history of the Bāb and of his early disciples, by Mīrza Ḥusain Hamadānī, who died A.H. 1299.

Beg. خرده بينان خردمند بفرّ فراست دريافت كنند و دانشمندان بصير بعين اليقين بينند وهوشمندان خبير بنور كياست دانند كه الخ

The "New History" is based upon a contemporary account due to Ḥāji Mirza Jāni, of Kāshān (who died as a martyr A.H. 1268), a copy of which was brought home by Comte de Gobineau, and is now in the Paris Library. The present work, which differs from the original by excisions, alterations, and considerable additions, bears no author's name. It is known, however, to have been written, at the request of the Pārsi Mānakji, son of Limji Hūshang, who died about A.D. 1890, by Mirza Ḥusain Hamadānī, who submitted it for correction to one of the earliest disciples of the Bāb, Sayyid Jawād Karbalā'i (d. about A.H. 1301). Mirza Abu 'l-Fazl Muḥammad, of Gulpāigān, wrote the preface, and Mānakji several additions.

An English translation, under the title "The Ta'ríkh-i-Jadíd, or New History of Mirza 'Ali Muḥammad the Báb," was published by Dr. Edward G. Browne, Cambridge, 1893. A full account of the composition of the work will be found in the preface, pp. xxxv.—xliii., and in the Journal of the Royal Asiatic Society, 1892, pp. 440—44. The present MS., on which Dr. Browne's translation is principally based, was described by him in "A Traveller's Narrative," vol. ii., pp. 192—97. Another copy is noticed by Baron v. Rosen, Collections Scientifiques, vol. vi., p. 244.

On the first page is written: "Tarikh i Jedid. Henry L. Churchill. 1882."

Sufism.

16.

Or. 4118.—Foll. 280; $9\frac{1}{2}$ in. by $6\frac{1}{4}$; 15 lines, 5 in. long; written in large bold Neskhi; dated Baghdad, 5 Zulhijjah, A.H. 601 (A.D. 1205). [T. Fiott Hughes.]

الرسالة القشيرية

A Persian translation of the celebrated Sufi work known as Tazkirat ul-Kushairi, by Abu 'l-Kāsim 'Abd ul-Karim B. Hawāzin al-Kushairi, who died A.H. 465. See the Arabic Supplement, no. 227.

The following title is prefixed by the hand of the transcriber: كتاب الرسالة القشيرية تاليف الشيخ الامام العالم الزاهد السالك المحقق ابى القسم عبد الكريم بن هوازن القشيرى رضى الله عنه

Beg. لحمد لله الذى تفرد بجلال ملكوته وتوحد بجمال جبروته

After the Arabic doxology, which is simply transcribed from the original text, the translation begins as follows: بدانيد رحمكم الله كى اين رسالتى است كى بندهٔ محتاج برحمت خذاى تعالى ابو القسم عبد الكريم ابن هوازن القشيرى رضى الله عنه بجماعت صوفيان شهرها اسلام نبشت در سنه سبع وثلثين واربع مايه وكفت بدانيد رحمكم الله كى ايزد سبحانه وتعالى اين طايفه را بركزيذكان اوليا خويش كرد و فضل ايشان بيدا كردانيذ بر جمله بندكان خويش

The headings of the chapters and the poetical quotations are left in the original language. The order of the chapters has been partly interverted. Their ordinal numbers, which have been added by a later hand, go from the first (باب التوبه) to the fiftieth. In the following table of headings the word باب has been, for brevity's sake, omitted: فى ذكر مشائخ هذه الطريقه وما يدل من سيرتهم واقوالهم

على تعظيم الشريعه, fol. 12a; تفسير الفاظ يدور بين هذه الطائفه وبيان ما يشكل منها, fol. 51a; التوبه, fol. 78b; المجاهده, fol. 63b; الخلوة والعزلة, fol. 87a; التقوى, fol. 90a; الورع, fol. 93b; الزهد, fol. 96a; الصمت, fol. 99a; الخوف, fol. 103a; الرجا, fol. 107b; الحزن, fol. 111a; مخالفة النفس وذكر عيوبها, fol. 112a; الفتوة, fol. 113a; الفراسة, fol. 116b; الخلق, fol. 124b; الجود والسخاء, fol. 127b; الغيره, fol. 133a; الولاية, fol. 135b; الدعاء, fol. 139a; الفقر, fol. 140b; التصوف, fol. 149a; الادب, fol. 152a; احكامهم فى السفر, fol. 155b; الصحبه, fol. 162a; التوحيد, fol. 165b; احوالهم عند الخروج من الدنيا, fol. 180a; المعرفه, fol. 186b; المحبه, fol. 190b; الشوق, fol. 197b; حفظ قلوب المشايخ وترك الخلاف عليهم, fol. 204a (here a folio is missing; the lacuna corresponds with p. 196, line 9, to p. 197, line 5, of the Bulak edition, A.H. 1284); السماع, fol. 205a; اثبات كرامات الاوليا, fol. 211b; رويا القوم, fol. 220a; الحسد, fol. 227a; الغيبه, fol. 228a; القناعه, fol. 230a; التوكل, fol. 231b; الشكر, fol. 237a; اليقين, fol. 240a; الصبر, fol. 242b; المراقبه, fol. 245b; الرضا, fol. 247a; العبوديه, fol. 251b; الاراده, fol. 253b; الاستقامه, fol. 258a; الاخلاص, fol. 259b; الصدق, fol. 261a; الحيا, fol. 262b; الحريه, fol. 265a; الذكر, fol. 266b; الوصيه للمريدين, fol. 277a.

The author states at the end that the dictation of the Risālah was completed at the beginning of A.H. 438.

Copyist: محمد بن عمر القزوينى

Three pages at the beginning of the volume and two at the end are occupied by a Sufi tract of 'Abdullah Anṣāri, من فوايد شيخ ... عبد الله الانصارى, written in a very cursive and crowded character of nearly the same date as the Risālah. The first few words are partly obliterated. The next passage reads الهى اين چه فضلست كه با دوستان خود كردى. The first section begins as follows: باب ازبراى مال و جاه كار مخاطره مكن احر كه بدين كار بكند سخنش مشنو

The first of the above passages is the beginning of the Munājāt. See Pertsch, Berlin Catalogue, no. 2, 4.

17.

Or. 3242.—Foll. 132; $9\frac{1}{2}$ in. by 7; 23 lines, $5\frac{3}{4}$ in. long; written in large, distinct Neskhi; dated Rustāḳ Kajūr, in Rūyān, Saturday, 20 Muḥarram, A.H. 779 (A.D. 1377).

[Sidney Churchill.]

مرصاد العباد

A treatise on Sufism by Najm ud-Dīn Ibn Shāhāvar, called Dāyah, who died A.H. 654. See the Persian Catalogue, p. 38b.

This copy has lost the first leaf. It begins abruptly with this passage of the preface: حضرت خداوندبست جنانك داود عليه السلام برسيد يا رب لماذا خلقت الخلق, which is found at fol. 3b, line 4, of Or. 258.

In the epilogue the author calls himself Abu Bakr 'Abdullah B. Muḥammad Shāhāvar al-Asadi al-Rāzi, and says that he completed the work in Sivās, on Monday, the first of Rajab, A.H. 620.

A copy is mentioned by Ethé, Bodleian Catalogue, no. 1248, and an abridged Arabic version is described by Ahlwardt, Berlin Catalogue, no. 3006.

Copyist: ابو سليمن محمد بن على بن عمر بن يعقوب بن محمد بن قاسم بن ابرهيم الرودبارى الاورى

18.

Or. 3547.—Foll. 219; 9½ in. by 5; 17 lines, 2⅓ in. long; written in neat Nestalik; dated Thursday, in the last decade of Shavvāl, A.H. 1077 (A.D. 1667).

[Sidney Churchill.]

دقائق الحقائق

A Sufi work consisting of religious precepts exemplified by anecdotes in prose and verse, chiefly derived from the works of Maulānā Jalāl ud-Dīn, by Aḥmad Rūmi.

Beg. الحمد لله رب العالمين والعاقبة للمتقين ... هذا رسالة من كلام احمد الرومى اضعف العباد من عباد السلطان المحققين ... جلال الملة جمال الاسلام والمسلمين

This is the work contained in Or. 251 (Persian Catalogue, p. 39) under an inverted form of the above title, حقائق دقائق. In a preface, not found in the latter copy, the author gives a short notice of Jalāl ud-Dīn, son of Maulānā Muḥammad Balkhi, and says that, some Faḳīrs having applied to him for some words conducive to salvation in the next world, كلمهٔ چند از براى نجات آخرت, he wrote for them the present work, under the above title, in eighty Faṣls. The date of composition, A.H. 720, is given in the epilogue in the following verse, omitted in the other copy:

بود عشرين سبعمائة سال تمام
كين رساله درعوض شد انتظام

Copyist: شيخ على الظاهرى الاسدى المازندرانى

For another copy see Aumer, no. 329.

19.

Or. 3649.—Foll. 177; 8½ in. by 5½; 17 lines, 2¾ in. long; written in neat Nestalik, with red-ruled margins, apparently in the 17th century.

[Sidney Churchill.]

العروة لاهل الخلوة والجلوة

A treatise on theology and Sufism, by 'Alā ud-Daulah Aḥmad B. Muḥ. al-Simnāni, who died A.H. 736. See the Persian Catalogue, p. 413a, and Haj. Khal., vol. iv., p. 197.

Imperfect at the beginning, commencing abruptly with the latter part of the preface, as follows: اتممت عليكم نعمتى ورضيت لكم الاسلام دينا وفى آية اخرى ادع الى سبيل ربك بالحكمة والموعظة الحسنى

The preface concludes with a full table of the contents. The work is divided into six Bābs, with the following headings:

I. در ثابت كردانيدن وجوب وجود حق تعالى Fol. 3b.

II. در توفيق دادن ميان اقوال مختلفه كه واقع كشته ميان خلايق در الهيات Fol. 20b.

(Here the author expounds and discusses seventy-seven tenets of various sects with regard to God's nature and attributes, to Creation, &c.)

III. در تقسيم چيزها از روى حصر وچكونكى ظهور ان ممكنات بر ترتيبى كه حق تعالى افريده Fol. 81a.

IV. در تنزيه خداوند واجب الوجود ... و باطل كردانيدن اتحاد و حلول و تناسخ Fol. 111a.

V. النبوات والولايات Fol. 118b.

VI. در بيان صراط مستقيم Fol. 128b.

This last Bāb is divided into four Faṣls and a Khātimah. It includes in the first Faṣl the autobiography of the author, and an interesting account of his early struggles between the whisperings of Satan and the voice from above, before he finally renounced the world and entered upon the true path of religious life. From it we learn that the author served in his youth under the Moghul sovereign Arghūn, and was engaged, A.H. 683, at the age of four and twenty, in a battle fought before Ḳazwīn. After a severe illness he retired, A.H. 685, to his native place Simnān, gave up his worldly possessions and founded a monastery called Khānaḳāh i Sakkākiyyah, after Shaikh Ḥasan Sakkāki, a contemporary of Abu Sa'īd Abu 'l-Khair.

The title of the work appears in the colophon. The author, who there calls himself احمد بن محمد بن احمد بن محمد البيابانكى السندى محتدا السمنانى منشاء ومولدا المعروف بعلاء دولت, states that he completed the work on Monday, the 23rd of Muḥarram, A.H. 721, in Ṣūfiyābād, being then sixty-two years of age. He adds that he subsequently wrote with his own hand a second and a third copy with additions, the last for his son (ولد) Abu 'l-Barakāt Taḳi ud-Dīn 'Ali ad-Dausi as-Simnāni, A.H. 722.

A Cambridge MS., Palmer, p. 116, no. 20, contains strictures of 'Abd ur-Razzāḳ al-Kāshi upon the above work and the author's reply. See also Guyard, Journal Asiatique, 1873, i., pp. 131-34.

20.

Or. 4381.—Foll. 73; 8 in. by 5; 17 lines, 2½ in. long; written in fair Neskhi, apparently in the 17th century. [Wallis Budge.]

A Persian commentary upon a collection of Aurād, or Litanies, without author's name; imperfect at the beginning.

It commences abruptly with this passage of the preface: صادق و برهانيست ناطق بر جزالت حال كلمات طيبات او و بر جلالت و كمال بركات و خاصيات او

In the extant portion of the preface, the author, after expatiating on the sanctity of the Aurād, relates, as an instance of their efficacy, a vision which came to his Shaikh, Ḳuṭb ul-Aḳṭāb 'Imād ud-Dīn, while thrown into an ecstatic state by their recital.

The Arabic text of the Aurād is included in the commentary. It begins as follows: استغفر الله العظيم الذى لا اله الا هو الحى القيوم واتوب اليه

It concludes with some prayers for Muḥammad, the last of which begins: اللهم صل على سيدنا محمد فى الاولين وصل على سيدنا ونبينا محمد فى الاخرين

The author of the Aurād is the famous Saint, Sayyid 'Ali Hamadāni, who died A.H. 786, and the commentator appears to have been an orthodox Sufi of the Sunni sect. The commentary bears a marked Sufi character; but the Hadiths quoted are taken from the canonical books of the Sunnis. The latest authorities cited are Shaikh Nūr ud-Dīn Ja'far, a disciple of Sayyid 'Ali Hamadāni, and the work entitled Faṣl ul-Khiṭāb, apparently that of Khwājah Pārsā Naḳshabandi, who died A.H. 822.

The Aurād, which are entitled اوراد فتحيه, have been lithographed at Lahore, A.H. 1289, and at Cawnpore, A.D. 1876.

The commentary, which is the work of Muḥammad Ja'far Ja'fari, has been lithographed at Lucknow, A.D. 1876. It begins as follows: الحمد لله الفتاح الذى فتح على المستفتحين ابواب الفتوح وجعل الاوراد الفتحيه اورادا الخ

For other copies of the Aurād see Loth, nos. 368-9.

21.

Or. 4382.—Foll. 45; 8 in. by 5½; 13 lines, 3¾ in. long; written in small and neat Nestalik; dated Saturday, 25 Zulhijjah, A.H. 1154 (A.D. 1742). [Wallis Budge.]

در مکنون

A collection of Sufi sayings and anecdotes, in prose intermixed with verses, by 'Aziz-ullah B. Sayyid Asad-ullah al-Ḥasani al-Ḥusaini al-Hindi.

Beg. شروع بنام خدائی که بی نشان آمد
کره کشای طلسمات جسم وجان آمد

... وبعد می کوید فقیرترین مفلسان ومحتاج ترین بیکسان ... عزیز الله بن سید اسد الله لحسنی لحسینی الهندی احسن الله تعالی امره وارضاه

The author, who in his verses designates himself by the Takhalluṣ 'Aziz, says that he began this work A.H. 1151, being then thirty-six years of age. The work is divided into seventeen Bābs. The headings of the first eight are as follows: 1. در بیان لا اله الا الله محمد رسول الله; 2. در بیان نماز; 3. در بیان زکوة; 4. در بیان روزه; 5. در بیان حج; 6. در بیان بخل; 7. در بیان سخاوت; 8. در بیان فقر. Many of the anecdotes relate to Indian Saints, as Shaikh Kabīr, Mu'īn ud-Dīn Chishti, Dārā Shikūh, lastly to the author's own Shaikh, 'Abd ur-Rasūl B. Muḥammad Khān al-Bījāpūri. Most paragraphs begin with the heading شطح, a word in use with the Sufis to designate an ecstatic thought or inspired utterance.

It would appear from the following colophon that the MS. was written by the author: بتمام رسید این نسخه مسماه درمکنون بیدا حقر الغربا تراب اقدام العرفا عزیز الله بن سید اسد الله لحسی لحسینی الهندی

Appendix to Theology.

22.

Or. 4738.—Foll. 26; $7\frac{3}{4}$ in. by 6; 9 lines, $3\frac{3}{4}$ in. long; written in fair Nestalik about A.D. 1860.

تحفة الموحدين

Tuḥfat ul-Muvaḥḥidin, a critical review of the principal religions of the world, from the standpoint of pure Deism, by Rājā Rām Mohan Rāi.

Beg. سرت فی اقصاء الارض سهلا و جبلا ووجدت الساکنین فیها متوافقین فی الاعتراف بذات مبدأ الکائنات

The author's position is that belief in one supreme God is common to all men, and therefore rooted in their very nature; whereas belief in the various religious systems rests only on authority and education. As these religions are mutually antagonistic, and as there is no rational ground for adopting any of them in preference to the others, he concludes that they are all equally false. This thesis is first briefly stated in Arabic and afterwards developed in Persian.

On the first page is written: "Tuhfatul Muwahhidin, or a Gift to the Deists; in the original Persian, transcribed from the second edition published in 1859 in Calcutta, by his son Ramaprasad Rai."

Ram Mohan Rai was born in Burdwan in 1780, and died in Paris on the 27th of September, 1833. See notices of his life by Dr. Lant Carpenter, 1835, and by K. S. Macdonald, Calcutta, 1879.

LAW.

23.

Or. 3512.—Foll. 598; $12\frac{1}{4}$ in. by 8; 28 lines, 5 in. long; written in small, neat and close, Neskhi, with ruled margins, probably in the 18th century. [Presented by B. B. Portal.]

لوامع صاحب قرانی

A Persian commentary by Muḥammad

Taki B. 'Ali al-Majlisi, upon the Shi'ah treatise on law of Ibn Bâbawaih, entitled كتاب من لا يحضره الفقيه (Arabic Supplement, no. 330).

Beg. حمدیکه باقلام اشجار و مداد بحار بر صفحه لیل و نهار شرح شطری ازان نتوان نگاشتن ... اما بعد خامه شکسته مستمد فیوض قدسی محمد تقی بن علی الملقب بالمجلسی

Mulla Muhammad Taki B. Maksûd 'Ali Majlisi, a disciple of Bahâ ud-Din 'Âmili, was born A.H. 1003 and died A.H. 1070. See notices of his life in Nujûm us-Samâ, p. 59, and Kisas ul-'Ulamâ, p. 172, where the present work is mentioned and said to have been left unfinished.

In the preface, after a pompous panegyric upon Shâh 'Abbâs II., the author says that, when he had entered upon the seventh decade of his life, he had written a full Arabic commentary [entitled روضة المتقين] upon the work called Kitâb man lâ yahduruhu 'l-Fakîh, and had dedicated it to the Shâh, who ordered him to translate it into Persian. This he did in the present work, which is also dedicated to 'Abbâs II.

The preface is followed by twelve preliminary chapters called فائده, with the following headings: 1. در فضیلت علم و علما, fol. 3b; 2. در وجوب طلب علم, fol. 4a; 3. در بیان علومی که تعلم آن لازم است, fol. 4b; 4. در وجوب اهل بیت سید المرسلین, fol. 6b; 5. رجوع در همه علوم بائمهٔ معصومین, fol. 8b; 6. در اوصاف علمای دینی که از ایشان اخذ علم توان نمود, fol. 9a; 7. اختلاف اخبار وجمع میان آنها, fol. 11a; 8. در تعلیم و تعلم و آداب, fol. 13a; 9. در اجازه, fol. 15a; 10. در مذمت اجتهاد, آن و ثواب آن fol. 16b; 11. در اصطلاحات حدیث, و اراء باطله, fol. 19a; 12. در نیت در طلب علم, fol. 20b.

The commentary proper, which begins with the Basmalah, fol. 24a, extends to the end of the first Juz of the original, treating of purification and prayer. The present volume consists of five sections, each of which has a separate doxology. The second begins with باب غسل الميت, fol. 159b; the third with ابواب الصلوة, fol. 247b; the fourth with باب سجدة الشكر, fol. 411b; and the fifth with باب وجوب الجمعة, fol. 483b. At the end of the second is a colophon, apparently transcribed from the author's original draft, stating that he finished the writing of it in Shavvâl, A.H. 1065. The Arabic text is included in the commentary and distinguished by a red line drawn over it.

A MS. described in the Petersburg Catalogue, no. 253, contains only the first part, كتاب الطهارة, of the same commentary.

HINDUISM.

24.

Or. 4561.—Foll. 161; $9\frac{1}{2}$ in. by 6; about 18 lines, 4 in. long; written in cursive Indian Nestalik; dated 25 Muharram, the second year of the reign of 'Âli Gauhar Pâdishâh (*i.e.* A.H. 1175=A.D. 1761).

Asvamedha Parva, the fourteenth Parva of the Mahâbhârata, translated into Persian.

Beg. آغاز پرب چهاردهم از کتاب مهابهارت که اسمیده پرب گویند در اخر پرب شاشك مذکور شد که راجه جدشتر از بهکهم نپامه پرسید که ما چه کار کنیم

که آن گناهی که ما خویشان و برادران خودرا کشته ایم از ما دور شود

The contents correspond substantially with those of the same section in the version prepared for Akbar, Add. 5640, foll. 160—360 (see Persian Catalogue, p. 57); but the translation is shorter and couched in a plainer style.

The MS. was written for Lālah Bhawāni Parshād.

Copyist: ولی الله متوطن بلده سنبهل

HISTORY.

GENERAL HISTORY.

25.

Or. 2927.—Foll. 256; 13 in. by 9; 27 lines, $6\frac{3}{4}$ in. long; written in small and neat Nestalik, with 'Unvān and gold-ruled margins; dated the 20th of Ābān in the 31st Ilāhi year of Akbar, corresponding with the 29th of Zulka'dah, A.H. 994 (A.D. 1586).

[Nath. Bland.]

جامع التواريخ

The first volume of the great historical work of Rashīd ud-Dīn Faẓl-ullah Ṭabib.

Beg. فهرست کتاب داستانها و فذلك حساب بيانها حمد و ثنا و آفرين حضرت مقدس جهان آفرين

The contents correspond with the latter half, foll. 404—728, of the large folio, Add. 7628, described in the Persian Catalogue, pp. 74—78. They are as follows:

Preface of the Jāmi' ut-Tavārikh (Quatremère's edition, pp. 4—60), fol. 3*b*. Preface of the first volume called Ta'rīkh i Ghāzāni (the latter part of this preface is given in Quatremère's edition, pp. 60—82), fol. 7*b*. Origin of the Turks and history of their tribes, fol. 10*a*. Ancestors of Chingiz Khān, fol. 39*a*. Chingiz Khān, fol. 52*b*. Ukutāi Ḳā'ān, fol. 106*a*. Jūji Khān, fol. 119*b*. Chaghatāi Khān, fol. 125*b*. Tūlui Khān, fol. 130*a*. Kuyuk Khān, fol. 132*b*. Munggā Ḳā'ān, fol. 136*a*. Ḳubilāi Ḳā'ān, fol. 143*b*. Timūr Ḳā'ān, fol. 157*b*. Hūlāgū Khān, fol. 161*a*. Abāḳā Khān, fol. 176*a*. Takūdār, or Aḥmad Khān, fol. 187*a*. Arghūn Khān, fol. 191*b*. Kaikhātū Khān (wanting in Add. 7628), fol. 197*b*. Ghāzān Khān, foll. 199*b*—286.

At the end there is a 'Arz-Dīdah dated in the 49th year of Akbar (A.H. 1013). On the first page is impressed the seal of Mahārāja Tikait Rāi. A full table of chapters, in a modern hand, occupies three pages at the beginning.

To the copies mentioned in the Persian Catalogue may be added one of the same first volume in the Bodleian, Ethé, no. 23. A considerable portion of the second volume is preserved, as shown by Baron Rosen, in two Petersburg MSS. bearing the misleading title Zubdat ut-Tavārīkh. From the analysis given in "Collections Scientifiques de l'Institut," vol. iii., pp. 83—111, it appears that the portion of those MSS. which extends from the beginning of the life of Muḥammad to the end of the history of China, is in verbal agreement with the corresponding part of the complete copy of Rashīd ud-Dīn's work, Add. 7628, foll. 58—336.

26.

Or. 2885.—Foll. 422; 13¼ in. by 7¾; 21 lines, 5½ in. long; written in small and neat Nestalik; dated 28 Rajab, A.H. 1030 (A.D. 1621).
[Sidney Churchill.]

I. Foll. 1—363a. Another copy of the first volume of the Jāmi' ut-Tavārīkh.

Contents: Preface of the Jāmi' ut-Tavārīkh, fol. 1b. Preface of the Ta'rīkh i Ghāzāni, fol. 7b. Turks and their tribes, fol. 12a. Ancestors of Chingiz Khān, fol. 53b. Chingiz Khān, fol. 66a. Ukutāi, fol. 156a. Jūji, fol. 181a. Chaghatāi, fol. 193b. Tūlui, fol. 201b. Kuyuk, fol. 206a. Munggā, fol. 212b. Ḳūbilāi, fol. 225b. Tīmūr, fol. 248b. Hūlāgū, fol. 252a. Abāḳā, fol. 271a. Aḥmad (Takūdār), fol. 283b. Arghūn, fol. 288b. Kaikhātū, fol. 293a. Ghāzān, foll. 296a—363a.

II. Foll. 363b—422a. Continuation of the above history, comprising the reigns of Ul-jā'itu Sulṭān Muḥammad Khudābandah and of his son Sulṭān Abu Sa'īd, A.H. 703—736.

Beg. الحمد لله رب العالمين والعاقبة للمتقين . . . اما بعد بندگی حضرت با رفعت پادشاه اسلام سلطان سلاطين زمان . . . شاهرخ بهادر

It is stated in a short preamble that Shāh-rukh, being fond of history, and having read the great work completed A.H. 704 by Khwājah Rashīd ud-Dīn Fazl-ullah al-Ṭabīb, desired the writer, who does not give his name, to compile a sequel to that work, and to bring it down to the death of Sultan Abu Sa'īd, events subsequent to that date being included in the history of Amir Ṣāḥib Ḳirān (Tīmūr), which was then being written afresh for His Majesty.

The author says at the end that this record had been compiled from several books and trustworthy narrators not further specified: از کتب متفرق و ناقلان معتبر. It is written on the same plan as Rashīd ud-Dīn's work, the Dāstān devoted to each reign being also divided into three Ḳisms. The Dāstān of Abu Sa'īd begins fol. 390b.

A Paris MS. containing the same continuation is mentioned by Quatremère in his preface, p. lxxx.

27.

Or. 2774.—Foll. 369; 13 in. by 9½; 20 lines, 6½ in. long; written in large and neat Neskhi, apparently about the close of the 15th century.
[Comte de Gobineau.]

An imperfect volume of an extensive work on universal history, without title or author's name. It begins abruptly with the following passage of the doxology: هر فرد را از افراد ممکنات بلیاقتی و . . . لایق بیاراست و از امتزاج جواهر سماهی و ارضی حقیقت ادمی زاد را که علی الاطلاق اشرف افریدهاست

It proves to be the first of the four volumes of the Zubdat ut-Tavārīkh, a vast historical work compiled for Prince Bāisunghar Bahādur Khān, son of Sultan Shāhrukh, by Nūr ud-Dīn Luṭf-ullah, known as Ḥāfiẓ i Abru, who died A.H. 834. See the Persian Catalogue, p. 421b, and Quatremère, Histoire des Mongols, p. ciii.

A MS. containing the first two volumes is mentioned by Dorn, Petersburg Catalogue, no. 268. The contents of the same MS., designated by C, and of two others have been fully described by Baron Rosen, Collections Scientifiques de l'Institut, iii., pp. 52—111. That detailed analysis and the accompanying extracts enabled us to ascertain that the present MS. agrees closely, as far as it goes, with Rosen's MS. C. There is, however, a curious discrepancy between the two with regard to the date of composition. While the Petersburg MS. gives A.H. 828, our copy has 830, namely, in the following passage, fol. 3a: درین وقت و زمان که تاریخ بهشتصد و سی رسیده است The latter date is confirmed by another passage, fol. 6b, where the author states that twenty-three years had elapsed from the death of Tīmūr (A.H. 807) to the time of writing: وبعد از انقضاء ایام انار الله برهانه که حالا مدت بیست و سه سال دیگر است

After a long doxology and a wordy panegyric on the reigning sovereign Shāhrukh and upon his son, Pādishāh Zādah Bāisunghar Bahādur Khān, comes the preface proper, fol. 5b, ذکر سبب تالیف کتاب, in which the author states that he had compiled the work by desire of the latter prince, and enumerates his sources, in perfect agreement with the extract given by Rosen from MS. C, pp. 59—66. This is followed by two preliminary chapters on Eras, فصل فی تعریف التاریخ, fol. 8a, and on the science of history, its object, and utility, در بیان حقیقت علم تاریخ و ماهیت ان و موضوع ان و در ذکر غایت و فواید ان, fol. 9a. The history proper begins, fol. 13a, with a chapter on Creation and the history of Adam, without heading. In the subsequent sections there is some evident confusion in the designations of the several chapters and in their ordinal numbers, as stated in the headings. The following is a list of the headings as they appear in the text:

Fol. 22a. جمله اول در ذکر پیغمبران که بعد از ادم صفی صلوات الله علیه بوده اند الی غایة زمان فترت که ما بین روح الله عیسی است وابتدای ظهور مدت محمد الخ

فصل اول از زمان شیث تا باخر ایام نوح علیهما السلم مشتمل بر اخبار سه پیغمبر و حوادث و وقایعی که زمان ایشان واقع شد

This first Faṣl comprises Shīth, fol. 22b; Idris, fol. 24a; Nūḥ, fol. 24b; and the first dynasty of Persia, the Pīshdādis, fol. 28b.

Fol. 66b. فصل اول از باب دوم در بیان ذریت نوح علیه السلم و ذکر حوادثی که بعد از طوفان بود تا زمان ابرهیم خلیل

Fol. 73b. فصل چهارم در قصه ابرهیم پیغمبر

Fol. 89b. فصل سوم از باب دوم در قصهٔ فرزندان ابرهیم و اسحق

Fol. 92a. فصل سیم از مقالت دوم در قصهٔ یوسف ابن یعقوب

Fol. 116b. فصل پنجم از باب دوم در قصهٔ پیغمبران قصهٔ ایوب

After Ayyūb come, without any further distinction of Faṣls, Shu'aib, fol. 118a; Mūsa, fol. 120a; Yūsha', fol. 155b; Kālib and Ḥazkīl, fol. 159a; Alīsa', fol. 160a; the Kings of Bani Isrā'īl, fol. 160b; Dā'ūd, fol. 165a; Sulaimān, fol. 179a; Raj'im [sic] B. Sulaimān, fol. 179a; and Sha'yā the Prophet, fol. 182a.

Fol. 183a. باب دوم از جملهٔ دوم الطبقة الثانیه من ملوك العجم

History of the Kayāni Dynasty, from Kai-kā'ūs to Dārāb.

Fol. 233b. باب دوم از قسم اول و این باب مشتمل است بر پنج فصل فصل اول در ذکر اسکندر

Fol. 244a. فصل دوم در ذکر پیغمبران که بعد از ایام اسکندر بوده اند

Fol. 257a. الطبقة الثالثة من ملوك العجم وهم الاشکانیه

Fol. 261a. فصل چهارم در ذکر حال ملوك روم بعد از اسکندر

Fol. 261*b*. فصل پنجم در ذکر ملکان عرب که بعد از اسکندر بودند تا بوتت اردشیر بابك

This chapter includes the Aṣḥāb i Kahf, fol. 270*a*; Yūnus, fol. 272*b*; Shamshūn ʿĀbid, fol. 276*a*; Jirjīs, fol. 276*b*.

Fol. 279*a*. باب جهارم در ذکر طبقهٔ آخرین از ملوك عجم که ایشانرا ساسانیان خوانند

History of the Sassanides, imperfect at the end. It breaks off shortly after the heading of the reign of Hurmuz, son of Anushirvan.

28.

Or. 2775.—Foll. 228; 9¼ in. by 5; 19 lines, 2¾ in. long; written in elegant Nestalik, with gold-ruled margins; dated Rajab, A.H. 949 (A.D. 1542). [Comte de Gobineau.]

بهجة التواريخ

A compendium of Muslim history, brought down to A.H. 855, by Shukr-ullah B. Shihāb ud-Dīn Aḥmad. See the Persian Catalogue, p. 884.

This copy wants about twelve leaves at the beginning, and has some folios transposed. The folios are to be taken in the following order: 213—220, 5—58, 3, 4 (after which two leaves are lost, corresponding with foll. 114*b*—117*b* of the previous copy, Or. 1627), 59—212, 227, 221—226, 228.

The text begins abruptly with these words, fol. 213: کردم ایشان آن گاو بنجاه هزار سال تمام بخوردند (Or. 1627, fol. 19*b*, line 9). The next page has the heading فصل اول در بیان عقل و نفوس, which belongs to the first of the thirteen Bābs into which the work is divided. The subsequent Bābs begin as follows: II. fol. 29*a*; III. fol. 41*a*; IV. fol. 50*b*; V. fol. 62*b*; VI. fol. 73*b*; VII. fol. 85*b*; VIII. fol. 97*b*; IX. fol. 106*a*; X. fol. 122*b*; XI. fol. 125*b*; XII. fol. 164*b*; XIII. fol. 207*a*.

Copyist: عبد اللطيف بن مولانا علا الدين

For other MSS., see the Leyden Catalogue, no. 907; Aumer, Verzeichniss, 1875, p. 183; Rosen, Institut, iii., no. 9; and Ethé, Bodleian Catalogue, no. 34.

29.

Or. 3643.—Foll. 108; 8½ in. by 5¾; 15 lines, 3½ in. long; written in cursive Nestalik, in the 19th century. [Sidney Churchill.]

مآثر الملوك

A work treating of the institutions, foundations, and wise sayings of kings and ancient sages, by Ghiyāṣ ud-Dīn Khwānd-amīr (Persian Catalogue, p. 96*b*).

Beg. زیب صفحات مآثرات نایضة البرکات سلاطین کامکار . . . . اما بعد بنده فقیر و ذره حقیر غیاث الدین المدعو بخواند الامیر

This work, which is mentioned by Haj. Khal., vol. v., p. 350, is probably the earliest of the celebrated author of Ḥabib us-Siyar. He does not refer in it to any previous composition of his own, and he speaks of his grandfather, the author of Rauẓat uṣ-Ṣafā, as still living. In the preface he states that he had some time contemplated writing a book on the above subject, and was encouraged to carry out that plan by his illustrious patron, Niẓām ud-Daulah wad-Dunyā wad-Dīn Amīr ʿAlīshīr, to whom he devotes a long panegyric.

The first chapter, fol. 4*a*, is entitled ذکر شمه از آثار سخنان ملوك عجم و پادشاهان ما تقدم, and treats of the institutions and maxims of the ancient kings of Persia from Kayūmarṣ to

Anushirvan. The second chapter, fol. 26a, relates to the patriarchs and ancient sages from Adam to Buzurjmihr; the third, fol. 37b, to Muḥammad and the Imams. The remaining chapters follow the usual arrangement of historical works. They treat of the Umayyades, fol. 52a, of the 'Abbasides, fol. 62a, and of the independent dynasties, Ṭāhiris, Sāmānis, Ghaznavis, &c., down to the Kurt dynasty. The last section, which relates to the Khāḳāns of the Turks, breaks off at the second page.

30.

Or. 2928.—Foll. 410; 8¼ in. by 5¼; 15 lines, 3½ in. long; written in small and neat Nestalik; probably about the close of the 18th century. [NATH. BLAND.]

خلاصة الاخبار

The first volume of the well-known historical compendium of the same Khwānd Amir. See the Persian Catalogue, p. 96.

Contents: Preface, fol. 7b. Maḳālah I. Prophets, fol. 16a. II. Philosophers, fol. 125a. III. Kings of Persia, &c., fol. 133a. IV. Muḥammad, fol. 218b. V. Early Khalifs and Imams, fol. 293a. VI. Umayyades, fol. 355b.

31.

Or. 2677.—Foll. 361; 14 in. by 9¼; 35 lines, 6⅛ in. long; written in small and neat Nestalik; apparently in the 16th century. [H. G. KEENE.]

حبيب السير

The third volume of the great historical work of Khwānd Amir. See the Persian Catalogue, p. 98.

Beg. يا رب بثناى خود سخن سازم كن ... اما بعد بر ضمير خورشيد اقتباس هوشمندان سخن شناس در نقاب شبهه و التباس مخفى نخواهد بود

Contents: Juz I. Khāns of Turkistān, Chingiz Khān and his successors, fol. 1b. Juz II. Contemporary dynasties, fol. 73b. Juz III. Tīmūr and his successors, fol. 122b. Juz IV. Shāh Ismā'īl Ṣafavi, fol. 307b.

The following particulars, taken from the present work, may be added to the notice of the author in the Persian Catalogue, p. 96. His father, Humām ud-Dīn Muḥammad B. Khwājah Jalāl ud-Dīn B. Burhān ud-Dīn Shīrāzi, was Vazir to Sultan Maḥmūd Mirza, who succeeded his father Abu Sa'īd in Māvarā-annahr, and died in Samarḳand, A.H. 900. Khwānd Amīr was living in retirement in Busht, a village of Gharjistān, when Muḥammad Zamān, son of Sultan Badi' uz-Zamān, came to that country, A.H. 921, and took him into his service. That prince sent him later on, A.H. 923, to the rebel Amir, Urdūshāh, with the object of inducing him to submit and to surrender Balkh. See Ḥabib us-Siyar, Bombay edition, vol. iii., Juz iii., pp. 194 and 369—71.

32.

Or. 3535.—Foll. 409; 13½ in. by 8; 32 lines, 6¼ in. long; written by several hands in more or less cursive Nestalik; apparently in the 18th century. [SIDNEY CHURCHILL.]

تاريخ ايلچى نظامشاه

The great historical work of Khwurshāh B. Ḳubād al-Ḥusaini, known as Elchi e Nizāmshāh, who died A.H. 972. See the Persian Catalogue, pp. 107—111.

Beg. ديباجهٔ نسخهٔ آفرينش موجودات وخلق نوع گرامى انسان

This volume contains the first five of the

seven Maḳālahs into which the work is divided, with the main part of the sixth, and corresponds with foll. 2—477 of the previously described copy, Add. 23,513. It supplies the name, wanting in the latter MS., of the sovereign to whom the work was dedicated. It is Ibrāhīm Ḳuṭubshāh, who reigned in Golconda A.H. 957—988 (see Briggs' Ferishtah, vol. iii., pp. 395—446). The list of authorities, fol. 2*b*, contains, in addition to those mentioned in the former copy, the Ḥabib us-Siyar, Ta'rīkh i Guzidah, Tafsīr i Shihābi va Kāshifi va Tha'labi, and Ẓafar Nāmah. In the latter part of the MS. the rubrics have not been entered.

Contents: Muḳaddimah, fol. 4*a*; Maḳālah I. Ancient kings, in five Guftārs, beginning foll. 11*a*, 40*b*, 54*b*, 64*b*, 75*a*. Maḳālah II. Muḥammad and Khalifs, in five Guftārs, beginning foll. 79*a*, 101*b*, 105*a*, 127*b*, 132*b*. Maḳālah III. Dynasties contemporary with the Abbasides, in thirteen Guftārs, beginning as follows: Ṭāhiris, fol. 138*b*; Ṣaffāris, fol. 139*a*; Sāmānis, fol. 142*a*; Āl i Buwaih, fol. 147*a*; Ghaznavis, fol. 152*b*; Ghūris, fol. 160*b*; Ismā'ilis, fol. 163*b*; Saljūḳis, fol. 173*a*; Mulūk i Nīmrūz, fol. 186*b*; Kurts, fol. 187*a*; Atābeks, fol. 190*b*; Khwārazmshāhis, fol. 194*a*; Ḳarakhitāis, fol. 203*a*. Maḳālah IV. Moghols, in four Guftārs, viz. 1. Turkish tribes, fol. 204*a*; 2. Chingiz and successors, fol. 207*b*; 3. Hulāgu and successors, fol. 227*a*; 4. Āl i Muẓaffar, fol. 250*a*. Maḳālah V. Tīmūr and successors, in three Guftārs, viz. 1. Tīmūr, fol. 264*b*; 2. Shāhrukh and successors, fol. 310*a*; 3. Bābar and successors, fol. 353. (The latter part of Guftār 2 and the beginning of Guftār 3 are lost; the lacuna corresponds with foll. 406*b*—408*b* of Add. 23,513.) Maḳālah VI. in five Guftārs, the first three of which only are extant, viz. 1. Ḳara-Ḳuyunlus, fol. 372*a*; 2. Aḳ-Ḳuyunlus, fol. 377*a*; 3. Shah Ismā'īl and Ṭahmāsp, fol. 384*b*.

The MS. breaks off in the latter part of Guftār 3, in a passage relating to the events of A.H. 943, at the very point where in the former copy, fol. 477*b*, extracts from Nusakh i Jahānārā are substituted for the original text of Khwurshāh. The corresponding passage occurs at fol. 55*b* of Or. 153.

33.

Or. 4508.—Foll. 355; 13¾ in. by 8¼; 35 lines, 5⅛ in. long; written in minute and close Neskhi in Isfahan, A.H. 1272 (A.D. 1855).

[Sidney Churchill.]

A volume of an extensive work on general history, without title or author's name.

Beg. باب دويم ذكرملوك عجم و سلطنت كيامرث

پوشيده نماند كه موبدان عجم را كمان ان است كه

مدتى مديد و عهدى بعيد عالم از فرمان فرماى خالى بود

On the fly-leaf is a Persian note in a cursive and ill-shaped character, in which the writer, Muḥammad Vali, states that the present MS. of Majma' ut-Tavārīkh was transcribed for him from a copy belonging to his late son, Naṣr-ullah Mirzā Vāni, in Iṣfahan, under the care of his other son, 'Abbās Ḳuli Mirzā, and that he received it from Isfahan on the first of Ṣafar, A.H. 1272. He adds that the history had been written under Shāh 'Abbās I., A.H. 1028. In the body of the MS., fol. 255*b*, A.H. 1026 is incidentally referred to as the present year. The above dates rendered it probable that we had here a portion of the vast historical compilation of Ḥaidar B. 'Ali Ḥusaini Rāzi, which was completed A.H. 1028, and a comparison of the contents has fully confirmed that conjecture.

The hitherto only known copy of Rāzi's work consists of two volumes in the Berlin Library, described by Pertsch, nos. 418-19.

A detailed account of it, with extracts, written by Dr. Gosche for Sir H. Elliot, is preserved among the latter's MSS., now in the Museum, and has been noticed in the Persian Catalogue, p. 887*b*.

In his Historia Ghaznevidarum, Fr. Wilken gives a Latin version of Ḥaidar's preface, pp. xii.—xvi., and in the notes, pp. 139, 153, &c., several extracts from his history. Those passages are found verbatim in our MS., foll. 56*a*, 56*b*, &c.

The work is mentioned in Elliot's History of India, vol. ii., p. 491, and vol. vi., p. 574.

The History of Ḥaidar Rāzi does not contain any original matter, but it is a comprehensive and useful compilation of standard historical works. It consists of five Bābs, subdivided into Fuṣūl, a full table of which has been transcribed from the preface by Dr. Gosche, pp. 33—38. The author gave no title to the work. The title Zubdeh i Tavārīkh rests only on an endorsement of the Berlin MS.

The first half of the present MS., foll. 2—209, contains the main part of Bāb II., namely, Fuṣūl 1—28 of Gosche's table, or nos. 1—26 of Pertsch's Catalogue. The chapters are not numbered. The following table shows the main headings as they appear in the MS., omitting the word ذکر, with which they invariably begin.

Fol. 6*b*.	سلطنت کیان و حکومت کیقباد
Fol. 11*a*.	اسکندر ذو القرنین
Fol. 12*b*.	ملوك طوایف و حکومت اشکانیان
Fol. 13*a*.	بدایة ظهور ساسانیان
Fol. 22*a*.	ملوك ولایت طبرستان
Fol. 23*b*.	حکومت حسام الدوله و اولادش در مازندران
Ib.	خروج سید قوام الدین و رسیدن او بسلطنت
Fol. 24*b*.	حکام کیلان
Fol. 25*a*.	بعضی ملوك مازندران حسام الدوله
Fol. 25*b*.	مرداویج بن زیاد دیلمی و اولادش و اتباعش
Fol. 27*b*.	سلطنة اولاد بویه دیلمی
Fol. 52*b*.	سلطنة طاهریان در خراسان
Fol. 53*a*.	حکومت آل لیث صفار
Fol. 56*a*.	حکومت سبکتکین و اولادش
Fol. 76*a*.	حکومت آل سلجوق
Fol. 158*b*.	خروج حسن صباح و حکومت او در الموت
Fol. 171*b*.	بعضی از حکام خوارزم
Fol. 193*b*.	حکومت امیر موید الدین و اولادش در خراسان
Fol. 197*b*.	حکومت ملوك غور
Fol. 209*b*.	جمعی از غوریان که در بلخ و طخارستان حکومت کرده اند

The MS. breaks off, seven lines after the last heading, with the rubric: حکومت هلاکو خان و اولادش در ایران

The latter half of the MS., foll. 210—355, contains the last portion of Bāb I., namely, Fuṣūl 18—37 of Gosche, nos. 15—34 of Pertsch. It begins abruptly in the middle of the history of al-Muwaḥḥidīn, with an account of the revolt of the Ghumārah tribe after the death of ʻAbd al-Mūmin, and of its suppression, A.H. 561. The succeeding headings are as follows:

Fol. 212*a*.	حکومت طولونیه در مصر
Fol. 213*a*.	سلطنت اخشیده و اولادش
Ib.	آل حمدان

Fol. 216b. حکومت تاج الدوله تتش بن الب ارسلان سلجوقی در شام

Fol. 224a. حکومت ظهیر الدین طغتکین و اولادش

Fol. 231b. حکومت دانشمندیه

Ib. حکام ارتقیه

Fol. 236b. خلافت اسمعیلیه در مغرب و مصر

Fol. 255a. شرفای مکه معظمه

Fol. 255b. حکام بطیحیه

Fol. 256a. حکام بنی کلاب که ایشانرا آل مرداش کویند

Fol. 257a. حکومت بنی عقیل در موصل و غیره

Fol. 259b. حکام بنی اسد که ایشانرا بعضی مزید نیز کویند

Fol. 262b. مشعشعی اول ایشان سید محمد بن سید فلاحست

Ib. حکومت امیر عماد الدین زنکی و اولادش

Fol. 281a. استیلای اسد الدین شیرکوه بر مصر و بعد از او رسیدن حکومت آن دیار بآل ایوب

Fol. 318a. چراکسه الملك المعز عز الدین ایبك

The history of the Circassians, or Mamluk, sultans of Egypt is brought down to the Turkish conquest, and concludes Bāb I.

34.

Or. 4132.—Foll. 290; 11¾ in. by 7¾; 17 lines, 4½ in. long; written in fair Nestalik; dated Muḥarram, A.H. 1247 (A.D. 1831).

[Sidney Churchill.]

خلد برین

A work on general history. The present volume is the last and most valuable portion of what must have been a very voluminous compilation. It consists of two parts respectively designated as the sixth and seventh Ḥadīḳah of the eighth Rauẓah. They contain a full and contemporary record, drawn up in the pompous style of a court chronicle, of the reigns of Shāh Ṣafī and Shāh 'Abbās II. The history of the latter is brought down to A.H. 1071, apparently the year in which the work was finished.

The author does not give his name; but it appears from several passages that he was a brother of the well-known historian of Shāh 'Abbās II., Mirza Muḥammad Ṭāhir Vaḥīd (see the Persian Catalogue, p. 189). Under A.H. 1056, for instance, fol. 182a, he records the appointment of the latter, whom he calls his "excellent brother" (کرامی برادر), to the office of Majlis-navis, and adds that, owing to his protection, he (the author) obtained the post of writer of the royal letters, خدمت تحریر ارقام. In the next following lines it is stated that Mirza Ṭāhir was subsequently raised to the Vazirate, and that at the time of writing, viz. A.H. 1103, he was still holding that office. This, however, must have been inserted after the author's time; for, in another place, fol. 191b, the latter states that in A.H. 1058, when he accompanied Shāh 'Abbās in the campaign which resulted in the taking of Kandahar, he was already upwards of seventy years of age.

The sixth Ḥadīḳah begins as follows:

غرض از چهره پردازی عرایس این اخبار آنکه چون شاهد جلالت از پرده تقدیر پروردکار جلیل رخ نمود

It commences with an account of the accession of Shāh Ṣafī, which took place in Isfahan on the 4th of Jumāda II., A.H. 1038. The events of his reign are recorded year by year, on the same plan as in the 'Ālam-ārāi 'Abbāsi, that is to say, according to the Turkish cycle of twelve solar years. Each year begins with the Naurūz, or festival of the vernal equinox, and the corresponding day of the Hijrah year is given in the preamble. In the following table of the years included in this Ḥadīḳah, the figures in parenthesis refer to the corresponding folios in the next following MS., Or. 3481.

Fol. 4*b*. Yilan-yil, beginning 25 Rajab, 1038 (fol. 4*a*).

Fol. 26*b*. Yunt-yil, 6 Sha'bān, 1040 [read 1039] (fol. 23*a*).

Fol. 41*b*. Ḳui-yil, 17 Sha'bān, 1041 [1040] (fol. 36*a*).

Fol. 50*b*. Bichin-yil, 20 [27] Sha'bān, 1042 [1041] (fol. 44*a*).

Fol. 69*a*. Takhaḳu-yil, 9 Ramazān, 1043 [1042] (fol. 60*a*).

Fol. 82*a*. It-yil, 21 Ramazān, 1044 [1043] (fol. 71*b*).

Fol. 91*b*. Tunguz-yil, 2 Shavvāl, 1044 (fol. 80*b*).

Fol. 103*a*. Sichḳan-yil, 12 Shavvāl, 1045 (fol. 89*b*).

Fol. 109*a*. Ud-yil, 23 Shavvāl, 1046 (fol. 94*a*).

Fol. 113*b*. Pars-yil, 5 Zulḳa'dah, 1047 (fol. 98*a*).

Fol. 124*b*. Tushḳan-yil, 14 Zulḳa'dah, 1048 (fol. 107*a*).

Fol. 129*b*. Lui-yil, 27 Zulḳa'dah, 1049 (fol. 111*a*).

Fol. 132*b*. Yilan-yil, 8 Zulḥijjah, 1050 (fol. 114*a*).

Fol. 136*a*. Yunt-yil, 28 Zulḥijjah, 1051 (fol. 117*a*).

Besides the headings denoting the above years, there are also rubrics for the principal events recorded.

The narrative concludes, fol. 137*a*, with the death of Shah Ṣafī on Monday, 12 Ṣafar, A.H. 1052.

Ten additional chapters, termed Manẓar, contain biographical notices of the prominent men of the reign, classed under the following heads: 1. Ḳurji-bashis, fol. 137*b*; 2. Vazirs, fol. 138*b*; 3. Ṣudūr or Shaikh ul-Islām, fol. 141*a*; 4. Ishik-aḳasi-bāshis, fol. 141*b*; 5. Other officials, including physicians and astrologers, fol. 142*b*; 6. Artisans, fol. 146*b*; 7. Secretaries and accountants, fol. 149*a*; 8. Emirs and Khans, fol. 150*a*; 9. Vazirs of provinces, fol. 155*a*; 10. Holy Sayyids and 'Ulamā, fol. 156*a*.

The seventh Ḥadīḳah begins, fol. 158*b*, as follows: از حدایق پر کل وشقایق روضه هشتم از روضات جنات خلد برین در طراحی کلزار همیشه بهار زمان دولت پایدار خاقان والاتبار

It commences with a record of the accession of Shāh 'Abbās II., on the eve of Friday, 16 Safar, A.H. 1052, and of the events of the first year of his reign. The subsequent years are as follows:

Fol. 171*a*. Ḳui-yil, 9 Muḥarram, 1053 (fol. 147*a*).

Fol. 174*b*. Bichin-yil, 20 Muḥarram, 1054 (fol. 150*a*).

Fol. 177*a*. Takhaḳu-yil, 1 Safar, 1055 (fol. 152*a*).

Fol. 181*b*. It-yil, 11 Safar, 1056 (fol. 156*a*).

Fol. 189*a*. Tunguz-yil, 24 Safar, 1057 (fol. 162*a*).

Fol. 190*a*. Sichḳan-yil, 25 Safar, 1058 (fol. 163*a*).

Fol. 206*b*. Ud-yil, 6 Rabī' I., 1059 (fol. 176*b*).

Fol. 211*b*. Pars-yil, 18 Rabi' I., 1060 (fol. 180*b*).

Fol. 215*a*. Tushḳan-yil, 28 Rabī' I., 1061 (fol. 184*a*). (Lui-yil is not entered.)

Fol. 217*a*. Yilan-yil, 20 Rabī' II., 1063 (fol. 185*b*).

Fol. 221*a*. Yunt-yil, 1 Jumāda I., 1064 (fol. 189*a*).

Fol. 233*b*. Ḳui-yil, 12 Jumāda I., 1065 (fol. 199*b*).

Fol. 241*a*. Bichin-yil, 23 Jumāda I., 1066 (fol. 206*b*).

Fol. 254*b*. Takhaḳu-yil, 4 Jumāda II., 1067 (fol. 217*a*.)

Fol. 263*a*. It-yil, 15 Jumāda II., 1068 (fol. 224*a*).

Fol. 269*b*. Tunguz-yil, 27 Jumada II., 1069 (fol. 229*b*).

Fol. 283*a*. Sichḳan-yil, 8 Rajab, 1070 (fol. 240*b*).

Fol. 289*a*. Ud-yil, 18 Rajab, 1071 (fol. 245*a*).

The last incidents recorded are a complaint made to the Shah by the Hindu merchants of Ispahan of exactions committed by the governor of Bender Abbasi, and the sending by the Shah of stores of corn to relieve a famine raging in the capital.

The history of the reigns of Safi and ʿAbbās II. in the Favāʾid Ṣafaviyyah (Persian Catalogue, p. 133) is avowedly abridged from the present work, and is brought down to the same year.

Copyist: نصرالله بن مرتضی قلی

35.

Or. 3481.—Foll. 246; 10¾ in. by 6¾; 19 lines, 4½ in. long; written in small and close Neskhi; dated Shavvāl, A.H. 1278 (A.D. 1862). [Sidney Churchill.]

Another copy of the same portion of the Khuld i Barīn. The contents are identical with those of the preceding MS.

Copyist: محمد حسن ابن صفر علی الکرمانشهانی

36.

Or. 3498.—Foll. 254; 13 in. by 8; about 25 lines, 4½ in. long; written in small, cursive, and not easily readable Shikesteh, partly in two columns, and in the tabellated form called Siyāḳ; apparently about the middle of the 18th century. [Sidney Churchill.]

زبدة التواریخ

A work on general history, by Muḥammad Muḥsin, Mustaufi of Nādir Shāh, محمد محسن مستوفی سرکار فیض آثار

Beg. زبدة التواریخ انساب و احوال انبیا و اوصیا و پادشاهان و سلاطین زمان از حضرت خیربشر آدم علیه السلام الی یومنا هذا آنکه بعد از حمد و سپاس بیقیاس خداوندی که ضبط قبض و بسط جزو وکل دفترخانه ایجاد عالم علوی و سفلی الخ

In the preface, which contains a pompous panegyric on Nādir Shah, and on his son Riẓa Ḳuli Mirza, the author states that the work was compiled by order of the former for the use of the latter. It was written, as incidentally mentioned, fol. 215*b*, A.H. 1154 (*i.e.* two years before that unfortunate prince was blinded by his father).

The contents are as follows: Adam and the Prophets, fol. 8. Muḥammad, fol. 30. Khulafā i Rāshidīn, fol. 33. Ḥasan and the Imams, fol. 81. Ancient kings of Persia, fol. 100. Bani Umayyah, fol. 110. Dynasties contemporary with the Abbasides, from the Ṭāhiris to the Ḳarakhitāi's of Kirman, fol. 112. The Abbasides, fol. 125. The Moghols, fol. 129. Five subsequent dynasties, viz. Chaupānis, Ilkānis, Abu Isḥāḳ Inju and Muẓaffaris, Kurts, and Sarbadārs, fol. 134. Tīmūr and his descendants in Iran and India, fol. 140. Ḳara Ḳuyunlus and Aḳ-Ḳuyunlus, fol. 140. Ṣafavis, fol. 151.

(The latter portion of this last chapter is of special importance, as being a contemporary record of the decline of the Safavi dynasty and of the rise of Nādir Shāh down to the time of his assumption of the regal title. It includes the following reigns: Sulṭān Ḥusain, fol. 175; Ṭahmāsp II., fol. 182, and the puppet-king 'Abbās III., fol. 188.) The Afghans Mīr Vais, Maḥmūd and Ashraf, fol. 196. Christian kings, foll. 196—205 and 208. Seljūḳs of Rūm, fol. 206. Ancient kings of India, foll. 207, 209—211, 215-216. Kings of Israel, fol. 212.

The contents of the latter part of the volume are very miscellaneous. They relate to the seven climes, fol. 217; to the Pharaohs and the 'Adites, fol. 218; to Lokman, fol. 222; Barṣīṣā, fol. 224; Hārūt and Mārūt, fol. 225; and to the wonders and curiosities of the world, fol. 250. They include a version of the story of Yūdāsaf and Bilauhar, قصه یوداسف و بلوهر, foll. 226—249, extracted from the Kamāl ud-Dīn of Ibn Bābavaih (see Or. 3529).

The MS. is probably due to the pen of the Mustaufi himself, or of one of his secretaries. The headings are written throughout like entries in an account-book, in an almost illegible hand, and a perusal of the text requires a fair practice in Shikesteh.

37.

Or. 3288; 11½ in. by 7¾; 15 lines, 4¾ in. long; written in fair Nestalik, with two 'Unvāns and gold-ruled margins, apparently in the 18th century.

تاریخ محمد شاهی نادر الزمانی

A work on general history, with special reference to India, by Khushḥālchand, son of Jīvanrām Kāyath, secretary to the Divan of the Province of Delhi.

Beg. بهترین بیان و خوشترین ذکر انسان حمد حمیدیست قادر ذو الجلال بیهمال

For the division and contents of the work see the Persian Catalogue, pp. 128, 894, and Elliot's History of India, vol. viii., p. 70.

The present volume begins with a preface relating to the decline of the empire, its causes and remedies, and concluding with a notice of the author's father, fol. 6b. It contains, besides, two detached portions of of the work, namely, the first Kaifiyyat of Maḳālah I., and the latter portion of the first Maṭla' of Maḳālah II.

The contents of Kaifiyyat I. are as follows: Prophets from Adam to Muḥammad, fol. 13b. Ancient kings of Persia, fol. 46a. Descendants of Japhet down to 'Umar Shaikh, father of Bābar, fol. 76b. Early Khalifs, fol. 120a. Umayyades, fol. 126b. Abbasides and contemporary dynasties, fol. 12a. Safavis, fol. 147b. Descendants of Ham in India, fol. 155a.

The Maṭla' begins with a new 'Unvān, fol. 159b, as follows: در زمان سعادت ان پادشاه دریا نوال بتاریخ بیست وششم دی ماه الهی سنه سی ر هفتم از جلوس. It comprises the following chapters: Reign of Shāhjahān. Reign of 'Ālamgīr, fol. 260b. His death, his sons, his officials, and contemporary kings, fol. 344a. Contemporary Shaikhs, fol. 351a. 'Ulamā, who flourished from the time of Akbar to the reign of 'Ālamgīr, fol. 353b. Calligraphers, fol. 358b. History of the period extending from the death of 'Ālamgīr to the defeat of A'ẓam Shāh, fol. 364b. Reign of Shāh 'Ālam, fol. 374a. Contest of his sons, fol. 381a. Reign of Jahāndār Shāh, fol. 387a. Reign of Farrukhsiyar, fol. 396a. Reign of Rafi' ud-Daulah, fol. 416a. Reign of Muḥammad Shāh, foll. 418a—426b.

This last chapter, which has been supplied by another hand, does not appear to belong to the original work. It contains a very brief account of the reign of Muḥammad Shāh down to his death on the 27th of Rabī' II., A.H. 1161.

The contents of foll. 159—341 agree substantially, in spite of many variations, with those of Add. 24,027, foll. 418—601, and the contents of foll. 304—417 correspond with Or. 1654, foll. 7—139. A few extracts from the present work have been given, but under the title of Ta'rīkh Bahādur Shāhi, and without author's name, in Elliot's History of India, vol. vii., pp. 565—67.

A MS. described by Pertsch, Berlin Catalogue, no. 495, contains the latter part of Maṭla' I., and the whole of Maṭla' II. of Maḳālah II.

38.

Or. 3400.—Foll. 154; 7½ in. by 4½; 14 lines, 2½ in. long; written in neat minute Nestalik; apparently in the 19th century. Bound in painted and glazed covers.

[Sidney Churchill.]

لب اللباب

A manual of Muslim history, by Ḥājī Muḥammad Ḳulī Ḳājār.

It begins with a versified prologue, the first line of which is:

بنام انکه در تاریخ و تالیف
کسی را نیست بر وی حد توصیف

The author describes himself as a native of Ganjah, there designated as the greatest of the cities of Turkestan, اعظم بلاد ترکستان, and as descended from a family which for several generations had given soldiers to that land. Although his military duties left him little leisure for study, he had brought together some historical works, and was induced to compile from them an easy and comprehensive abridgment, by means of which any reader could without difficulty ascertain the date and length of the reign of any king, from the origin of Islamism to the time of composition. As a matter of fact the history stops somewhat short of the date of composition, which is expressly stated, fol. 96*b*, to be A.H. 1097.

The work is divided into twenty-three Faṣls as follows: I. The fourteen Ma'ṣūms, *i.e.* Muḥammad, 'Ali and the Imams, fol. 4*a*. II. The three accursed usurpers of the Khilāfat (*i.e.* Abu Bakr, 'Omar and 'Osman), fol. 14*b*. III. Banu Umayyah, fol. 16*b*. IV. Banu 'Abbās, fol. 21*a*. V. Banu Laiṣ Ṣaffār, fol. 34*a*. VI. Sāmānis, fol. 35*b*. VII. Ṭāhiris, fol. 38*a*. VIII. Ghaznavis, fol. 39*b*. IX. Ghūris, fol. 42*b*. X. Āl i Buvaih, fol. 43*b*. XI. Saljūḳis, fol. 48*a*. XII. Khwārazmshāhis, fol. 55*b*. XIII. Atābeks, fol. 58*b*. XIV. Isma'īlis, fol. 61*a*. XV. Ḳarākhitā'is of Kirman, fol. 65*a*. XVI. Chingizkhān and his descendants, fol. 66*b*. XVII. Sarbadārs, fol. 72*b*. XVIII. Timūr and his descendants, fol. 75*a*. XIX. Ḳara Ḳuyunlus and Aḳ Ḳuyunlus, fol. 84*a*. XX. Sultans of Rūm, down to Muḥammad IV., fol. 90*b*. XXI. Uzbaks from Shāhī Beg to the death of 'Abd ul-Laṭīf Khān (two leaves added for the continuation of this chapter have been left blank), fol. 94*b*. XXII. Safavis from Shāh Ismā'īl to the death of Shāh 'Abbās I., A.H. 1038, fol. 96*b* (there are five blank pages at the end). XXIII. Persian poets, fol. 130*a*.

This last Faṣl contains notices of 220 poets, divided into three Bābs, viz. 1. Sixty ancient poets from Rūdagi to A.H. 900, in chronological order (the last is Valī Ḳalandar, a poet of the time of Sultan Bāisunḳar). 2. Thirty poets of the time of Sulṭān Ḥusain, beginning with Sulṭān Ḥusain himself, and ending with 'Abd ul-Jalīl Vā'iẓ, fol. 139*a*. 3. One hundred and thirty modern poets, fol. 144*a*. First come six princes from Shāh Ismā'īl to Shāh 'Abbās II. The remaining poets are given in alphabetical order. The notices are short and mostly confined to a verse or two; a few only have dates.

Copyist: سید حسین هندی معروف میر مغل

39.

Or. 3202.—Foll. 293; 12 in. by 8; 25 lines, 5 in. long; written in small and neat Nestalik; dated Dār us-Salṭanah (Tehran), A.H. 1220 (A.D. 1805). [Kremer, no. 56.]

زينة التواريخ

The first volume of Zīnat ut-Tavārīkh, a general history compiled by order of Fatḥ 'Ali Shāh, by Mirza Muḥammad Raẓi Tabrizi.

Beg. بهار رخسار شاهدان بیان نو و کهن حکایت ستایش دارندهٔ آسمان و زمین

The author, poetically called Bandah, was son of Muḥammad Shafī' Tabrīzi, Vazir of Āẕarbāijān. He held the office of Munshi ul-Mamālik, and was one of the favourites of Fatḥ 'Ali Shāh. He was assisted in the compilation of the Zinat ut-Tavārīkh by Mirza Ibrāhīm Ishtihārdī. He died in Teheran A.H. 1223. See Nigāristān i Dārā, fol. 83, Anjuman i Khāḳān, fol. 40*b*, and Majma' ul-Fuṣaḥā, vol. ii., p. 80.

The present volume contains the first half of the work, namely the Preface, the Introduction (Āghāz), and the first of the two Pīrāyahs into which the work is divided. Its contents are identical with those of Add. 23,514, described in the Persian Catalogue, p. 135.

This copy is due to the pen of Amān-ullah, with the takhalluṣ Naẓir, a poet of some note, who died A.H. 1226. See Majma' ul-Fuṣaḥā, vol. ii., p. 527.

40.

Or. 3333.—Foll. 176; 8½ in. by 4½; about 15 lines, 2½ in. long in a page; written in Shikesteh; dated 1st Rajab, A.H. 1260 (A.D. 1844). [H. A. Stern.]

A compendium of general and Persian history from the earliest times to A.H. 1220, drawn up for the most part in tabular form, with the heading: خلاصة تاريخ بادشاهان عجم و غیره که در ملك ایران سلطنت کرده اند از ابتدای سلطنت کیومرث الی انتهای دولت فتحعلی شاه قاجار انار الله برهانه

There is no preface or author's name. After a tabulated index of contents occupying six pages, the text begins, fol. 5*a*, as follows: کیومرث بن قینان بن انوش بن شیث بن ادم نخستین عدالت جهان و اولین ملوك پیشدادیان است قبل از فرزندان ادم علم کسی بر مسند سلطنت متمکن نشد

The date of composition is given, fol. 169*a*, as A.H. 1250; but the history of the reign of Fatḥ 'Ali Shāh is not brought further down than Ud yil = A.H. 1220. The main divisions are as follows: Ancient kings of Persia from Kayūmarṣ to Yezdegird, fol. 5. Kings of the Arabs, fol. 29*a*. Muḥammad, the first Khalifs and Imams, the Ummayades and Abbasides, fol. 39*a*. Dynasties contemporary with the Abbasides, fol. 69*a*. Moghols, fol. 92*a*. Mulūk ut-Ṭavā'if, fol. 98*a*. Tīmūr and his successors in Īrān, fol. 108*a*. Ḳara Ḳuyunlus and Aḳ Ḳuyunlus, fol. 114*a*. Uzbeks, fol. 119*a*. Safavis, fol. 120*a*. Afghans, fol. 131*a*. Ṣafavi pretenders, fol. 134*a*. Russian invaders, fol. 136*a*. Afshārs, fol. 137*a*. Zends, fol. 150*a*. Ḳājārs, fol. 157*a*.

The last events recorded are the death of Ibrāhīm Khalīl Khān and the expedition of Ḥusain Khān Ḳājār and Ismā'īl Khān Dāmaghāni against Muṣṭafa Khān Shirvāni in

Ḳarābāgh, A.H. 1220 (or A.H. 1221, according to the Ma'āṣir i Sulṭāniyyah, Brydges' translation, pp. 267 and 287).

41.

Or. 2837.—Foll. 204; 12¼ in. by 7¾; 19 lines, 4½ in. long; written in fair Neskhi, apparently about A.H. 1260 (A.D. 1844).

نخبة الاخبار

A compendium of general history, with special reference to Persia, from the earliest time to the date of composition, viz. A.H. 1257, by 'Abd ul-Vahhāb B. 'Ali Ashraf B. 'Ali B. Ismā'īl B. Muḥ. Mahdi Shīrāzi.

Beg. الحمد لله الذی هو الخالق الوهاب وبعباده غفار تواب . . . فبعد چنین گوید جان نثار اصحاب شریعت وخاکسار ارباب طریقت ابن علی اشرف بن علی بن اسمعیل بن محمد مهدی عبد الوهاب شیرازی

The work is divided into a Muḳaddimah, six 'Unvāns, and a Khātimah, as follows:

Muḳaddimah: Creation and Adam, fol. 10*a*. 'Unvān I. Prophets, fol. 13*b*. II. Pre-Islamitic kings, fol. 47*b*. III. Life of Muḥammad, fol. 58*a*. IV. Persian kings in Muḥammad's time, viz. Anushirvān and his successors, fol. 128*b*. V. Lives of Fāṭimah and the twelve Imams, Umayyades, and Abbasides, fol. 131*a*. VI. Dynasties contemporary with the Abbasides and posterior to them, down to the accession of Muhammad Shāh Ḳājār, fol. 142*b*. Khātimah: Reign of Muḥammad Shāh Ḳājār, fol. 199*a*.

The most valuable part of this manual is the latter section, Maḳṣad 2, of 'Unvān VI. It treats of the dynasties which rose in Iran after the Abbasides, under the following ten heads (Ṭā'ifah): I. Moghols, fol. 153*b*. II. Mulūk ut-Ṭavā'if, viz. Chupānis, Ilkānis, Abu Isḥāḳ, Muẓaffaris, Kurts, and Sarbadārs, fol. 156*b*. III. Gurgānis, fol. 162*b*. IV. Turcomans and Uzbeks, fol. 166*b*. V. Safavis, fol. 169*a*. VI. Afghans, fol. 173*a*. VII. Various pretenders who rose after the downfall of the Safavis, fol. 174*b*. VIII. Afshārs, fol. 176*a*. IX. Zauds, fol. 183*b*. X. Ḳājārs, fol. 188*a*.

The Khātimah contains a brief account of the reign of Muḥammad Shāh. The last event recorded is the rising of Aḳa Khan in Kirman, which took place A.H. 1257.

A full table of contents occupies foll. 1—8. At the beginning is a marginal note, dated Rajab, A.H. 1260, in which the author describes the MS. as his autograph draft.

42.

Or. 3378.—Foll. 118; 13¾ in. by 8½; 14 lines, 5 in. long; written in fine large Nestalik, in in the latter half of the 19th century.
[Sidney Churchill.]

نژاد نامه پادشاهان ایرانی نژاد

A history of those dynasties who traced their origin to the ancient kings of Persia, by Riẓa Ḳuli Khān, poetically surnamed Hidāyat, who died A.H. 1288.

Beg. پاك شاهنشاهی را سپاس و ستایش که در کیهان کیائیش همتای و انباز نی و راد خدیوی را نیاز و نیایش

The work was written at the request of the author's Pārsi friend, Mānakji Limji Hūshang Hāturiyā, and after the Majma' ul-Fuṣaḥā, which is often referred to. It is divided into a Muḳaddimah, eighteen Ṭabaḳahs, and a Khātimah.

The Muḳaddimah treats of the five old dynasties mentioned in the Dabistān, and of historical documents bearing upon the ancient kings of Persia. The eighteen Ṭabaḳahs relate to the following dynasties: I. Ṣaffāris, fol. 7*b*. II. Sāmānis, fol. 13*a*. III. Āl i Bāvand, fol. 21*b*. IV. Āl i Buvaih, fol. 25*b*. V. Āl i Kākavaih, fol. 33*a*. VI. Āl i Ziyār, fol. 35*a*. VII. Second Bāvand line, called Gāopārah, fol. 40*a*. VIII. Kings of Nīmrūz or Sīstān, fol. 74*b*. IX. Third Bāvand line, fol. 77*a*. X. Āl i Fazlavaih in Shabānkārah, fol. 79*a*. XI. The Bādūsis of Māzandarān, fol. 82*a*. XII. The Bahmanis of Gujarāt, fol. 83*a*. XIII. Kings of Shīrvān, fol. 84*a*. XIV. Kings of Nūr, fol. 86*a*. XV. Kings of Kajūr, fol. 87*a*. XVI. Kings of Läristān, fol. 88*a*. XVII. Kings of Hurmuz, fol. 89*a*. XVIII. The Jāms of Sind and Multan, fol. 93*a*.

The Khātimah, foll. 93—118, beginning with a sketch of Muḥammad's life, consists of chronological tables extending from the Hijrah to A.H. 1203, where the MS. breaks off. They are written in two columns, and are made up of brief notices of historical events and obituary notices of poets and saints.

For the life and works of the author, see Churchill, Journal of the Royal Asiatic Society, vol. 18, pp. 196—204, vol. 19, p. 163, and Ch. Schefer, Relation de l'Ambassade au Kharezm, p. xvi., and Chrestomathie Persane, vol. ii., p. 79.

Muhammad and the Imams.

43.

Or. 2969.—Foll. 191; 9½ in. by 6⅓; 23 lines, 3⅞ in. long; written in small, neat, and close Neskhi, with 'Unvāns and gold-ruled margins; dated 28 Rajab, A.H. 883 (A.D. 1478).

[SIDNEY CHURCHILL.]

A history of Muḥammad and the Khalifs, brought down to the extinction of the Abbaside Khalifs of Baghdad, by Maḥmūd B. Muḥammad al-Ījī, called Najīb.

Beg. الحمد لله على ما انعم وافضل واعطى واجزل
. . . . اما بعد بدان اعزك الله تعالى فى الدارين كه
بزركترين نعمتى كه الله تعالى بر بندكان كرده است
آنست كه انبيا و رسل را در ميان ايشان مبعوث كردانيد

The author, who was a Sunni, lived apparently about the middle of the ninth century of the Hijrah. One of his latest authorities, quoted fol. 6*a*, is Shaikh ul-Islām 'Imād ud-Dīn B. Kathīr ad-Dimashḳi (d. A.H. 774), of whom he speaks as dead. He gives his own name in the following Isnād, fol. 13*b*: يقول الفقير الى رحمة ربه الحفيظ المجيب
محمود بن محمد الايجى المدعو بنجيب اخبرنا جماعة من
الايمة الاعلام منهم الشيخ الامام ناصر السنة نور الدين
ابو عبد الله محمد بن عبد الله الايجى الحسينى رضى
الله عنه قال اخبرنا الشيخ المسند المعمر ناصر الدين عمر
بن الحسن بن مزيد بن اميله المراغى الحلبي الخ

The last-named traditionist, Ibn Umailah al-Marāghi, from whom the author professes to have received traditions through one intermediate link, died A.H. 778. See al-Durar al-Kāminah, vol. ii., fol. 22.

The first Hadith, quoted in glorification of Muḥammad, is to the following effect: Adam, after his fall, implores forgiveness in the name of Muḥammad, a name which, on first opening his eyes, he had seen inscribed on the Throne.

The contents are as follows: Life of Muḥammad, fol. 3*a*. Khilāfat of Abu Bakr, fol. 15*b*; of 'Omar, fol. 29*a*; of 'Oṣmān, fol. 50*b*; of 'Ali, fol. 57*a*. Ḥasan and Mo'āwiyah, fol. 70*a*. Ḥusain and the Ummayades, whom the author does not call Khalifs, but kings, fol. 72*b*. The 'Abbasides, foll. 116*b*—191*a*.

The work has no specific title. It is endorsed تواريخ خلفا الراشدين, and at the beginning there are the words مولود حضرت پيغمبر صلعم

written in ornamental Kufi within an illuminated border. Both titles are inadequate and misleading.

44.

Or. 3641.—Foll. 304; 10½ in. by 6¼; 17 lines, 3¼ in. long; written in small Neskhi; dated Monday, 16 Ramazan, A.H. 1260 (A.D. 1844).

[Sidney Churchill.]

تذكرة الائمه

Tazkirat ul-A'immah, or Memorial of the Imams, by Muhammad Bākir B. Muhammad Taki (Majlisi), who died A.H. 1110. See the Persian Catalogue, p. 20.

Beg. لحمد لله الذى جعل النبيين لسان صدق فى الاخرين وصير ائمته المعصومين تذكرة للمتقين . . . وبعد چنين كويد خاك راه شيعيان محمد باقر بن محمد تقى

The author says that the chief scope of the work is to establish the divine mission of the Prophet and the holiness of the Imams by evidences drawn from the sacred books of the Jews, Christians, Hindus, and Greeks, and he gives in his preface a rather fanciful enumeration of those books, from which numerous extracts in Hebrew, Chaldee, Armenian, and other tongues, but transliterated in the Arabic character, are given, with interlineary Persian version, in the body of the volume. The author writes in the most unmitigated Shi'ah spirit, and is lavish of curses upon the predecessors of 'Ali and on the antagonists of the Imams.

The work is divided into a Mukaddimah, fourteen Bābs, and a Khātimah, as follows: Mukaddimah: Advent of Muhammad as foretold in the sacred books, fol. 3*a*. Bāb I. Life of Muhammad, fol. 10*a*; events which followed his death, fol. 53*b*; exposition of Muslim sects and of the tenets of Jews, Christians, Brahmins, Magians, and philosophers, fol. 67*a*. Bāb II. Life of Fāṭimah, fol. 98*a*. III. Life of 'Ali, fol. 104*b*; events which followed his death, the Ummayades, fol. 158*b*, and the Abbasides, fol. 186*b*. IV. Ḥasan, fol. 199*b*. V. Ḥusain, fol. 202*b*; events which followed his death, fol. 210*b*. VI. Zain ul-'Ābidin, fol. 216*b*. VII. Bākir, fol. 203*a*. VIII. Ṣādiḳ, fol. 225*b*. IX. Kāẓim, fol. 240*a*. X. Riẓa, fol. 244*a*. XI. Jawād, fol. 247*a*. XII. 'Ali Naki, fol. 249*a*. XIII. Ḥasan 'Askari, fol. 250*a*. XIV. Ṣāḥib ul-Amr, or Mahdi, and his future advent, fol. 251*a*. Khātimah: The Imams in general and evidences in support of their legitimacy, fol. 300*a*.

The sectarian and controversial matter occupies throughout the work more space than the history proper. The Tazkirat ul-A'immah is mentioned among the works of Muhammad Bākir in the Nujūm us-Samā, p. 366, and in the Ḳiṣaṣ al-'Ulamā, p. 158; but with the remark that it is not included in the authentic list of Muhammad Bākir's works drawn up by Muhammad Ṣāliḥ Māzandarāni.

45.

Or. 2881.—Foll. 265; 11⅜ in. by 7; 25 lines, 4¼ in. long; written in small Neskhi; dated A.H. 1228 (A.D. 1813).

[Sidney Churchill.]

رياض الشهاده فى مصايب السادة

A history of the sufferings and martyrdoms of Muhammad and of the holy Imams, by al-Ḥāj Muhammad Ḥasan B. al-Ḥāj Ma'ṣūm al-Ḳazvini. See the Persian Catalogue, p. 155*b*.

Beg. لحمد لله الذى جعل الدنيا جنة لاعدائه وسجنا لاحبائه . . . اما بعد چنين كويد فقير حقير خادم طلبه علوم محمد حسن بن الحاج معصوم القزوينى

The author was a disciple of Aḳā Bāḳir Bahbahāni, who died A.H. 1205 (v. Nujūm us-Samā, p. 342). In the introduction he dwells on the trials and persecutions undergone by the prophets from Adam to Muḥammad, and shows that the sufferings of the latter and of his descendants have far surpassed those of his predecessors. Compassion with these sufferings being a great means of gaining favour with God, and of progressing on the path of piety, he was induced to record them fully in the present work, which is divided into thirty Majlis.

The above introduction is preceded by a preface, the beginning of which is lost. It contains a wordy panegyric upon Fatḥ 'Ali Shāh and upon his son Ḥusain 'Ali Mirzā,[1] whose just rule had restored Fārs to a state of unexampled prosperity, and to whom the work is dedicated. At the end of the preface is a table of chapters, fully stating the contents of the four Majlis contained in the first volume.

The contents of the first volume are as follows: Majlis I. Life of Muḥammad in four Faṣls, viz., 1. From the creation of his "Light" to his mission, fol. 7*b*; 2. From his mission to his flight, fol. 28*b*; 3. From his flight to his last pilgrimage, fol. 41*b*; 4. His death, fol. 66*b*. Majlis II. Life of Fāṭimah in three Faṣls, viz., 1. Her birth and her merits, fol. 76*b*; 2. Her marriage, fol. 84*b*; 3. From the death of Muḥammad to her death, fol. 89*a*. Majlis III. Life of 'Ali in five Faṣls, viz., 1. His birth and supernatural gifts, fol. 99*b*; 2. Hadiths in proof of his Imamship, fol. 108*a*; 3. His virtues and merits, fol. 157*b*; 4. His trials after the death of Muḥammad, fol. 184*a*. 5. His martyrdom, fol. 231*a*. Majlis IV. Life of Ḥasan in four Faṣls, viz., 1. His birth, fol. 246*a*; 2. Proofs of his Imamship and his miracles, fol. 249*a*; 3. His dealings with Mu'āwiyah, fol. 254*a*; 4. His martyrdom, fol. 260*b*.

Copyist: محمد رضا ابن فخر الدين بهبهانى

[1] Ḥusain 'Ali Mirzā had been Farmān-Farmā or governor of Fārs from A.H. 1214 to 1250. He failed in the attempt to seize upon the throne, A.H. 1251, and was put to death by Muḥammad Shāh. See the Persian Catalogue, pp. 727*a* and 1155*b*.

46.

Or. 2882.—Foll. 248; 12 in. by 7¾; 25 lines, 4½ in. long; written in Neskhi, with silver-ruled margins; dated Wednesday, 14 Zul-ḳa'dah, A.H. 1238 (A.D. 1823).

[Sidney Churchill.]

The second volume of the same work, containing eighteen Majlis, the first seventeen of which relate to the lives and martyrdom of Ḥusain, his relatives and companions, and the eighteenth to their avenger, Mukhtār.

The contents are the same as those of Or. 1293, described in the Persian Catalogue, p. 155*b*.

Copyist: ابن ابرهيم اسمعيل الحسينى

47.

Or. 2883.—Foll. 223; 12 in. by 7½; 27 and 28 lines, 5¼ in. long; written in neat Neskhi, early in the 19th century.

[Sidney Churchill.]

The third and last volume of the same work, containing the last eight Majlis, numbered here (in continuation of the twenty-two Majlis comprised in the first two volumes) from 23 to 30. They treat of the later Imams as follows: Majlis XXIII. Zain ul-'Ābidīn, fol. 1*b*. XXIV. Muḥammad Bāḳir, fol. 16*a*. XXV. Ja'far Ṣādiḳ, fol. 36*b*. XXVI. Mūsa Kāẓim, fol. 64*a*. XXVII. 'Ali

Riza, fol. 96*b*. XXVIII. Muḥammad Jawād and 'Ali Naḳi, fol. 127*b*. XXIX. Al-Ḥasan al-'Askari, fol. 151*b*. XXX. Al-Mahdi and his future advent, fol. 167*a*.

In a colophon apparently transcribed from the original MS., the author states that he finished this third volume on Thursday, the 12th of Sha'bān, A.H. 1227.

48.

Or. 2994.—Foll. 243; 12 in. by 8; 21 lines, 4½ in. long; written in small and elegant Shikesteh-āmīz; dated Friday, the last day of Rabī' II., A.H. 1258 (A.D. 1842).

[Sidney Churchill.]

بحر اللآلی

A history of Muḥammad and the Imams, by 'Ali Akbar Shīrāzi, Ṣadr of the province of Fārs.

Beg. الحمد لله رب العالمین والصلوة والسلام علی خیر خلقه . . . اما بعد چنین کوید اقل عباد و کمترین طلاب علی اکبر بن علی بن محمد اسمعیل بن محمد مهدی طاب الله ثراهم

The author, Ḥāji 'Ali Akbar Navvāb, son of Aḳā 'Ali Naḳīb, was the chief of the 'Ulamā of Shīrāz and a great favourite with Ḥusain 'Ali Mirza, Farmān-farmā of Fārs. In his poetical compositions he took the name of Bismil, and his account of contemporary poets entitled Tazkirah i Dilgushā (Berlin Catalogue, no. 667) is one of the sources of Majma' ul-Fuṣaḥā. The author of the latter work, writing A.H. 1283, says that 'Ali Akbar had died a few years previously. See vol. ii., p. 82.

The work was commenced, as stated in the preface, on the 28th of Shavvāl, A.H. 1256. It was planned on a large scale, and was to consist of fourteen volumes containing the lives of as many holy personages, viz. Muḥammad, Fāṭimah, and the twelve Imams, each volume concluding with a sketch of contemporary sovereigns. The only volume extant, perhaps the only one ever written, is the first, namely, the present MS., which contains a very full life of Muḥammad according to Shī'ah tradition. It was finished at the end of Zulḥijjah, A.H. 1257, and the present copy was made from the original draft by the author's son, Abu Ṭālib.

It is divided into thirty-seven Bābs of very unequal extent and a Khātimah. The first five Bābs treat of Muḥammad's birth, fol. 3*a*; his suckling, fol. 8*b*; his marriage with Khadījah, fol. 12*a*; his names and qualities, fol. 13*a*; and his miracles, fol. 14*b*. Bābs 6—15 relate to his mission, to the revelations he received, and to the beginning of his apostolate. The fullest and most important chapters are those which treat of the Hijrah and subsequent events, related year by year as follows: Bāb 16. Muḥammad's flight to Medina, fol. 34*a*. Bāb 17. Events of the first year of the Hijrah, fol. 41*b*. Bāb 18. Second year, fol. 44*a*. 19. Third year, fol. 62*b*. 20. Fourth year, fol. 79*b*. 21. Fifth year, fol. 92*a*. 22. Sixth year, fol. 114*a*. 23. Seventh year, fol. 132*b*. 24. Eighth year, fol. 150*a*. 25. Ninth year, fol. 176*b*. 26. Tenth year, fol. 190*a*. 27. Eleventh year and Muḥammad's death, fol. 200*b*.

Bābs 28—37, foll. 217*a*—234, contain miscellaneous notices, the last Bāb relating to Muḥammad's horses and camels. The Khātimah, foll. 235—243, contains a sketch of the kings of Persia, more especially of those who reigned in Muḥammad's lifetime. The author frequently inserts pieces of Persian verse of his own composition.

On the first page is a Waḳf, or deed of donation, and a verbose eulogy on the work, written by the author's son, Abu Ṭālib, A.H. 1261.

HISTORIES OF SPECIAL DYNASTIES OR REIGNS.

Moghols.

49.

Or. 2970.—Foll. 284; 9 in. by 5; 25 lines, 3⅛ in. long; written in small and distinct Nestalik, with ruled margins, A.H. 1067 (A.D. 1656-7). [Sidney Churchill.]

تاریخ الوصاف

The first three volumes of Ta'rīkh ul-Vaṣṣāf, ending with the first portion of the reign of Ghāzān. The contents have been described in the Persian Catalogue, p. 162. They correspond to pp. 2—391 of the edition lithographed in Bombay, A.H. 1269. The second book begins fol. 96*b*, and the third fol. 179*b*.

Copyist: ابن عبد الله ابو الحسن

For other copies, see Pertsch, Berlin Catalogue, no. 434, and Ethé, Bodleian Catalogue, no. 147.

Muzaffaris.

50.

Or. 2886.—Foll. 187; 9½ in. by 5¾; 21 lines, 3½ in. long; written in small and neat Neskhi, apparently in the 19th century. [Sidney Churchill.]

مواهب آلهی

A history of the Muẓaffari dynasty, by Mu'īn i Yazdi. See the Persian Catalogue, p. 168.

Beg. حمد و ثنای که اشعهٔ لمعاتش جهان [corrected to چون] بارقهٔ نور از چهرهٔ حور تابان باشد

The above beginning differs from that of the previously described copy, Add. 7632, by the omission of five lines after حمد و ثنای که. In other respects the two MSS. are in close agreement. A copy beginning precisely like the present one is described by Ethé, Bodleian Catalogue, no. 286.

Timur.

51.

Or. 4722.—Foll. 145; 8½ in. by 5¼; 13 lines, 2¾ in. long; written in fair Nestalik, with red-ruled margins; dated 9 Sha'ban, A.H. 1161 (A.D. 1748).

[Presented by G. J. Nicholls, Esq.]

تزوك تیموری

Tuzūk i Tīmūri, the pseudo-memoirs of Amīr Tīmūr, by Abu Ṭālib al-Ḥusaini al-'Ariẓi. See the Persian Catalogue, p. 177*b*.

Beg. واقعات السلطان بن السلطان و لخاقان بن لخاقان بادشاه جم جاه خلایق بناه قطب السلاطین عالیجاه امیر تیمور کورکان صاحب قران . . . حمد بلیغ سبحانی را که بمقتضای آیه کریمه انا جعلنا خلیفة فی الارض الخ

Contents: Abu Ṭālib's preface, fol. 3*b*. The Memoirs, beginning with an introductory chapter treating of Tīmūr's rules of conduct and of the presages of his future greatness (pp. 4—20 of Chas. Stewart's translation), fol. 5*b*. The life proper, beginning with Tīmūr's seventh year, A.H. 733, foll. 31*b*—145*a*. The narrative comes to an abrupt termination in a passage relating to the advance of Amīr Mūsa, with ten thousand horse, against Karshi (Stewart's translation, p. 105). This is followed by a detached fragment occupying a page and a half and relating to the mission of Amīr Jāku to Malik Ḥusain (*ib.*, p. 107).

At the beginning and end of the MS. there are several impressions of a large seal bearing the following inscription: بخشی الممالک صمصام الدوله احتشام‌خان خاندوران امیر الامرا بهادر منصور جنگ فدوی عالمگیر پادشاه غازی, with the date 1167. This was a son of the celebrated Khāndaurān who fell in the battle of Karnāl. He received his father's title from Aḥmad Shāh, and was appointed Amir ul-Umarā by 'Ālamgir II., in whose reign he died. See Ma'āṣir ul-Umarā, Add. 6565, fol. 223.

Safavis.

52.

Or. 3248.—Foll. 307; 10 in. by 6½; 16 lines, 4¾ in. long; written in elegant Nestalik, with double-page 'Unvan, gold-ruled margins, and twenty-one whole-page miniatures in fair Persian style, apparently in the 16th century. [Sidney Churchill.]

A history of Shāh Ismā'īl from his rise to his death, without title or author's name.

Beg. جهان آرایی پادشاهان عالم مدار و فرمان روایی خسروان کردون اقتدار از مالک الملکیست .... اما بعد ناشران احوال سلاطین نامدار و راقمان آثار خواقین ذوی الاقتدار صفحات اوراق را که از ارقام شرح انساب خسروان کامیاب تزیین داده اند الخ

The work was written under Shāh Tahmāsp, and probably shortly after his accession, to which the author refers in his conclusion as a recent event. But it must have received subsequent additions, for in the body of the volume there is a mention of A.H. 947. This occurs under A.H. 923, fol. 277*a*, where the author, having spoken of Muḥammad Zamān Mirza, gives a short sketch of that prince's subsequent career in India, stating that, during the retreat of the emperor Humāyūn from Bengal in A.H. 947, the Mirza was drowned in the Ganges.

The history of Shah Ismā'il bears a striking likeness to the corresponding portion of Ḥabib us-Siyar, from which it was evidently copied with some verbal alteration and without any acknowledgment. Matter and arrangement are the same; the headings of chapters and the inserted verses are all but identical. On the other hand, there are here and there in the present work additional details, which point to independent sources of information. The relation between the two works will be fully discussed by Mr. E. D. Ross, who is preparing an edition of our text.

The work begins with a genealogy of Shāh Ismā'īl, carried up to the seventh Imam, and with a rather legendary account of the Shah's forefathers, partly taken from the Ṣafvat us-Ṣafā, in the following order: Firūz Shāh, fol. 2*b*; 'Ivaẓ ul-Khavāṣ and his son Sayyid Muḥ. Ḥāfiẓ, fol. 3*b*; Ṣalāḥ ud-Dīn Rashīd, fol. 4*b*; Ḳuṭb ud-Dīn, *ib.*; Sayyid Ṣāliḥ, fol. 5*a*; Sayyid Jibrīl, fol. 5*b*; Ṣafi ud-Dīn Isḥāḳ, fol. 6*b*; Ṣadr ud-Dīn Mūsa, fol. 11*b*; Sulṭān 'Ali Siyāhpūsh, *ib.*; Shaikh Ibrāhīm, fol. 16*b*; Sulṭān Junaid, fol. 17*a*; Sulṭān Ḥaidar, fol. 20*b*. With this last, the father of Shāh Ismā'īl, the history proper begins under the following headings: Rise of Sulṭān 'Ali, Ismā'il's elder brother, after the death of Sulṭān Ḥaidar, fol. 23*b*. Escape of Sulṭān 'Ali and his brothers from Iṣṭakhar, fol. 25*b*. Death of Sulṭān 'Ali, fol. 27*b*. Ismā'īl's flight to Gilān, fol. 29*a*. His stay in Lāhijān, fol. 32*a*. Death of Rustam Turcoman and accession of Aḥmad Beg, fol. 37*b*. Ismā'īl proceeds to Ardabīl, fol. 41*b*. His march into Shirvān, fol. 53*b*. His victory over Farrukh Yasār Shirvānshāh, fol. 57*a*. Taking of Bādkūyah, fol. 61*a*. The Shah's march to Gulistān and into Āzarbaijān, fol. 64*a*. Contest with Amir Alvand, fol. 66*a*.

Events of A.H. 907, fol. 68*a*. Ismā'īl's entry into Tabrīz and his accession, fol. 72*a*.

The further events of the reign are told year by year as follows: A.H. 908, fol. 79*a*; 909, fol. 91*b*; 910, fol. 106*a*; 911, fol. 114*a*; 912, fol. 120*a*; 913, fol. 122*a*; 914, fol. 134*a*; 915, fol. 151*b*; 916, fol. 177*a*; 917, fol. 197*b*; 918, fol. 208*a*; 919, fol. 218*a*; 920, fol. 243*b*; 921, fol. 256*a*; 922, fol. 262*a*; 923, fol. 273*a*; 924, fol. 277*b*; 925, fol. 279*b*; 926, fol. 282*a*; 927, fol. 286*b*; 928, fol. 297*b*; 929, fol. 300*a*; 930, fol. 302*b*. Accession of Shāh Ṭahmāsp, fol. 305*b*.

No title is given to the work in the preface; but in his conclusion the author designates it as follows: این صحیفه شریفه که مقصود از جهانکشائی خاقان صاحب قران بود. Further on he invokes blessings upon the reigning Shāh, whom he describes as a youthful sovereign who had but recently succeeded to the throne: این تازه نهال چمن شهریاری و نوباوهٔ بوستان کشورکشائی

The last line contains the name of Muḥammad 'Ali B. Nūrā, ذره بیمقدار محمد علی بن نورا, but without any word to explain his connection with the MS. He was probably the copyist or the owner.

The Cambridge University Library possesses a copy of the same work, which will be described in the forthcoming catalogue by Mr. E. G. Browne.

53.

Or. 2939.—Foll. 245; 9½ in. by 5½; 15 lines, 3¼ in. long; written in neat Nestalik; dated Wednesday, 21 Rabī' I., A.H. 1042 (A.D. 1632). [SIDNEY CHURCHILL.]

A history of the reigns of Shāh Ismā'īl and of Shāh Ṭahmāsp, brought down to A.H. 957, by Amīr Maḥmūd B. Amīr Khwāndamīr.

The writer was a son of the well-known author of Ḥabīb us-Siyar, to whom he refers as his father in the present work, fol. 112*a*. He appears to have lived in Herat, and he deals especially with the events that occurred in that city and in the province of Khorasan, especially with the fierce and protracted struggle of the Shahs with the Uzbek invaders. His work is written in the same florid style as the Ḥabīb us-Siyar. It is noticed in the Riyāẓ ush-Shu'arā, fol. 153*a*, and in the Rauẓat uṣ-Ṣafaviyyah, Or. 3388, fol. 3*a*, as the main authority for that period.

The preface, which is imperfect at the beginning, is dated A.H. 955. It contains a wordy panegyric on Shāh Ismā'īl and on the reigning sovereign Shāh Ṭahmāsp, and a dedication to Muḥammad Khān, *i.e.* Sharaf ud-Dīn Ughli Teklu, who was then governor of Khorasan.

The first chapter, fol. 7*a*, treats of the merits and eminent qualities of Shāh Ismā'īl, ذکر بعضی از اوصاف پادشاه جمجاه ابو المظفر نواب کامیاب سپهر رکاب شاه اسمعیل علیه الرحمة, and begins as follows: حکم با منفعت حکیم دانا و عادت مقرون بافادت علیم بی همتا انه تقدس عما تصفه الصافون [الواصفون] تقدسا علیا

This is followed by a chapter on the Shah's genealogy, identical with the corresponding portion of the preceding MS., Or. 3248, fol. 1*b*—2*a*, and beginning: ناشران صحایف اخبار سلاطین و راقمان لطایف آثار ملوك عدالت آئین الخ

Then comes a longer chapter, foll. 9*b*—19*a*, on the merits and supernatural manifestations of the sainted ancestor of the Safavis, Shaikh Ṣafī ud-Dīn of Ardabīl, گفتار در تیمن

بذکر شمه از صفات و خوارق عادات شیخ صفی الدین الاردبیلی علیه الرحمة

After short notices of Ṣadr ud-Dīn Mūsa, Shaikh 'Ali Khwājah, Ibrāhīm, Junaid, and Ḥaidar, comes the history of Shāh Ismā'il, which begins at his birth, fol. 26*b*, and is carried on to his death, fol. 114*a*. The narrative is not divided by years, but by rubrics indicating the chief events recorded. The author observes, fol. 60*b*, that, his main object being the history of Shāh Ṭahmāsp, he confined himself with regard to Ismā'il, both for brevity's sake and from want of sufficient information, to a record of his conquest of Khorasan and a few other events. That portion of the work is avowedly abridged from the Ḥabīb us-Siyar.

The history of Shāh Ṭahmāsp is told in great detail, especially with regard to Khorasan, and occupies foll. 116*b*—229*b*. It concludes with the siege of Herat by the Uzbeks, A.H. 957. The last incidents recorded are the death of their chief, Shāh Muḥammad Sulṭān, and the raising of the siege on the 29th of Jumāda I. of that year.

Foll. 230—244 contain a chronological table of the principal events of Persian history from the birth of Shāh Ismā'il, A.H. 892, to the death of Shāh 'Abbās I.

54.

Or. 2776.—Foll. 164; 9 in. by 6; 17 lines, 3½ in. long; written in fair Nestalik; dated 27 Zulḥijjah, A.H. 983 (A.D. 1576).

[Comte de Gobineau.]

Another copy of the preceding work, wanting the preface and a portion of the introduction. It begins abruptly in the middle of the notice of Shaikh Ṣafi ud-Dīn with a passage corresponding with the third line of fol. 12*b* in the preceding MS.

55.

Or. 4134.—Foll. 193; 10 in. by 6¼; 21 lines, 3¾ in. long; written in small and neat Nestalik; dated Ramazan, A.H. 1024 (A.D. 1615).

[Sidney Churchill.]

احسن التواریخ

History of the reigns of Shāh Ismā'il Ṣafavi, of Shāh Ṭahmāsp, and of Shāh Ismā'il II., by Ḥasan Beg Rūmlū, grandson of Amir Sulṭān Rūmlū.

Beg. حمد و سپاس و شکر بیحد و قیاس سلطانی را سزاست که سرادقات عز و جلالش از سمت حدوث و امکان متبراست

The author states, fol. 115*b*, that he had followed the train of Shāh Ṭahmāsp from the time of the Dizful campaign (A.H. 948) to the year in which he was writing that part of his history, viz. A.H. 980, and that he had witnessed most of the Shah's battles. In A.H. 985, when Muḥammad Khudābandah was proceeding from Shirāz to Ḳazvīn to take possession of the vacant throne, the author paid homage to him in Ḳum, and was taken into his service. See fol. 189*a*.

The author follows a strict chronological order from A.H. 900 to the end of A.H. 985, when the work was completed. Under each year he gives first the political and military transactions in Persia and neighbouring countries, then some miscellaneous occurrences, and lastly obituary notices. The following are the principal dates as stated by Ḥasan Beg: Death of Shāh Ismā'il in the night preceding Monday, 19 Rajab, A.H. 930. Accession of Ṭahmāsp on Monday, 19 Rajab, A.H. 930. Death of Ṭahmāsp in the night before Tuesday, 15 Ṣafar, A.H. 984. Accession of Ismā'il II. on Wednesday, 27 Jumāda I., A.H. 984. Death of Ismā'il II. in the night before Sunday, 13 Ramazān,

A.H. 985. Accession of Muḥammad Khudābandah on Thursday, 5 Zulḥijjah, A.H. 985.

The work concludes with the accession of Muḥ. Khudābandah and the record of a victory gained by Ḳarākhān Beg over a Turkish troop sent by the Pasha of Erzeroum against Shūrah Gil. But the main part of the history was written during the reign of Shāh Ṭahmāsp, and the preface contains a dedication to Ismā'īl II. as prince.

The Aḥsan ut-Tavārīkh is mentioned in the 'Ālam-ārāi 'Abbāsi, Add. 16,684, fol. 22, as the best authority for the reign of Ṭahmāsp. For other copies, see the Petersburg Catalogue, no. 287; Wm. Ouseley's MSS., no. 346; and Ethé, Bodleian Catalogue, no. 287. Extracts have been given by Dorn, Auszüge, pp. 375—421, and by Schefer, Chrestomathie, vol. ii., pp. 81, 87, 108, and 124.

The last two folios of the MS. contain notices of Shaikh Safi ud-Dīn Isḥāḳ and of Shaikh Ṣadr ud-Dīn Mūsa, by a later hand.

56.

Or. 4678.—Foll. 275; 13¼ in. by 7½; 20 lines, 4 in. long; written in large, cursive, and straggling Nestalik; dated Tuesday, 24 Sha'bān, A.H. 1049 (A.D. 1639).

[Sidney Churchill.]

افضل التواريخ

History of the reign of Shāh Ṭahmāsp, from his accession to his death, without author's name.

This is only a portion of a larger history treating of the Ṣafavi dynasty and composed during the reign of Shāh 'Abbās I. Of the preface to the present volume, the last nine lines only are extant. In these the author says that after recording the reign and death of Shāh Ismā'il II. and the reign of Sulṭān Muḥammad Khudābandah, which lasted twelve years, his intention was to chronicle, if life were vouchsafed to him, the events and conquests of the reign of Shāh 'Abbās, that being the main scope and object of his composition:

زیبا بیان را بذکر حال خدیوی بیهمال پادشاه بی شبهه آفاق شاه باستحقاق کلب آستانهٔ خیر البشر.... شاه عباس پادشاه الصفوی الموسوی الحسینی که مطلب ازین مقدمات و غرض از تالیف این تاریخات ذکر حال بی همال آن مظفر خواقین روزکار است .... اکر عمر مستعار امان یافته بسلك تحریر آورد

The first chapter relates to the accession of Ṭahmāsp and to the appointment of Mirza Ḳāsim as Poet Laureate. It begins as follows:

ذکر جلوس بر تخت دولت و تعیین ارکان دولت ملك الشعرای مرزا قاسم آنچه در تاریخ مبسوطه که اسامی مولفان و نام تالیفات ایشان در دیباجه جلد اول افضل التواریخ نوشته شده بنظر رسید و راقم سطور ربط پریشان از مردم صحیح القول که دران عصر بودند تحقیق نمود آنست که

The present volume is designated, fol. 1 kb, and again at the end, fol. 274a, as the first Daftar of the second Jild of Afẓal ut-Tavārīkh, and the second Daftar was to treat, as stated in the latter passage, of the events which followed the death of Ṭahmāsp.

Contents: Accession of Ṭahmāsp, and official appointments, fol. 2a. Attack of 'Ubaid Khān Uzbek upon Herat, and his defeat by Sām Mirza, fol. 4b. Burning of the Vazir I'timād ud-Daulah Jalāl ud-Dīn Maḥmūd Tabrīzi, and appointment of Ḳāzi Jahān to the Vazirate, fol. 8b. Chronological summary of the reign of Ṭahmāsp, fol. 9b. Detailed history of the same reign, in strict chronological order according to the years of the Turkish cycle, from Yunt-yil, corresponding with A.H. 931, to Tunguz-yil = A.H. 984, foll. 15a—274a. There is, however, a lacuna extending from the middle of Bichin-yil = A.H. 969, fol. 243, to the latter part of Sichkan-yil = A.H. 973. The last three pages contain a table of the children and grand-children of Shāh Ṭahmāsp and of the officials of his reign. It is imperfect at the end.

The author appears to have had access to State papers. He frequently quotes royal letters, firmans of investiture, and bulletins *in extenso*. As to previous histories, he refers to Ḥabīb us-Siyar, to Aḥsan ut-Tavārīkh (no. 55), fol. 32*a*, and to Maulānā Nujūmi Haravi, the historian of Khorasan, foll. 17*b*, 50*a*.

57.

Or. 3549.—Foll. 259; 10 in. by 6; 22 lines, 3½ in. long; written in cursive but distinct Nestalik; dated 25 Ramazan, A.H. 1106 (A.D. 1695). [Sidney Churchill.]

History of Shāh 'Abbās I., from his birth to A.H. 1020, including the reigns of Shāh Ismā'īl II. and Sulṭān Muḥammad; by Jalāl ud-Dīn Munajjim Yazdi.

This is the work described in the Persian Catalogue, p. 184. This copy wants about twenty folios at the beginning. It commences in the middle of the account of the siege of Turbat, A.H. 991. The first line, اشتغال نمود و برجی را ازان قلعه از غایت اعتمادی که بوی داشت, corresponds with fol. 32*b*, line 3, of the former copy, Add. 27,241. On the other hand, the defective portion of the latter MS., towards the end, is usefully supplemented by the present copy.

The margins contain extensive extracts from 'Ālam ārāi 'Abbāsi. The MS. is endorsed, "The روز نامه of Molla Jalal Monajjim."

Copyist: محمد همدانی ابن عبد الکریم استاجلو در مقام حیدرآباد

58.

Or. 3388.—Foll. 402; 9½ in. by 6; 23 lines, 3¾ in. long; written in small and neat Nestalik; dated (fol. 385) Zulḥijjah, A.H. 1052 (A.D. 1643). [Sidney Churchill.]

روضة الصفویه

A history of the Ṣafavi dynasty, from its origin to the beginning of the reign of Shāh Ṣafi; by Mirza Beg B. Ḥasan Ḥasani Junābadi.

The first page of the preface has been supplied by Mr. Churchill's care from a copy dated A.H. 1113 in the library of Ṣani' ud-Daulah. It begins as follows: الحمد لله الحکیم الحلیم القدیر الذی تفرد بوجوب الوجود لذاته. After a long doxology, the preface proper begins, fol. 4*b*, with these words: اما بعد بر ضمایر زاکیه فضلای عالم و خواطر صافیه عقلای بنی آدم چهرهٔ شاهد این معنی در تتق اختفا پوشیده نخواهد بود

The author says in the preface that he had first applied himself to philosophy and poetry, but, feeling unequal to composition in either, he turned to history, as not requiring talent of the same order, and it occurred to him to compile a record of the Ṣafavi dynasty, "the crowning glory of the Sultans of the world, and the standard-bearer of the sacred law." The preface concludes with a wordy panegyric on Shāh 'Abbās I., the reigning prince. Further on, fol. 6*a*, we are told that the work was commenced A.H. 1023, while towards the end, fol. 355*b*, A.H. 1028 is incidentally given as the date of composition. It was not finished, however, till a few years later, for it concludes, in its original shape, with a record of the attempt of Ḥāfiẓ Aḥmad Pasha to retake Baghdad, an event of A.H. 1035.

In an appendix written after the death of Shāh 'Abbās, the author gives, fol. 387*a*, the following account of his authorities. For the earliest period and the reign of Shāh Ismā'īl, down to the battle of Chāldirān, he followed the appendix of Ḥabib us-Siyar by Khwāndamīr; for the end of the reign and for that of Shāh Ṭahmāsp down to the war with 'Ubaid Khān Uzbek, the work which Khwājah Maḥmūd, son of Khwāndamīr, wrote for Muḥammad Khān Sharaf ud-Dīn Ughli Taklu (no. 53); for the subsequent period down to the time of Ḳazāḳ Khān B. Muḥammad Khān Taklu (governor of Khorasan, who died A.H. 973), the Nusakh i Jahānārā of Ḳāẓi Aḥmad Ghaffāri Rāzi (Persian Catalogue, p. 111). From that date to the accession of Shāh 'Abbās he relied on information orally received from trustworthy witnesses. Lastly, for the reign of Shāh 'Abbās he depended only upon his own observation, having been, he says, an ocular witness of the most important events, especially of the conquest of Azarbaijan, in which he followed the royal train.

The work is written in a flowery and metaphorical style, not unlike that of the Ḥabib us-Siyar. It is not divided by years, but the principal events are marked by rather prolix headings. It is very sparing of dates, and the few that are given are, with few exceptions, confined to the bare mention of the Hijrah year, without day or month. The first heading is as follows: ذکر بعضی اوصاف شهنشاه مضمار مصاف المستغفر من الکریم الجلیل سلطان شاه اسمعیل بن سلطان حیدر الصفوی که بدان از سایر خواقین ممتاز بود و کوی تفرد از سلاطین ربع مسکون میربود .

Contents: Qualities of Shāh Ismā'īl, fol. 6*a*. His genealogy, fol. 7*a*. Life and miracles of Shaikh Ṣafi ud-Dīn Isḥāḳ, fol. 8*a*; of Ṣadr ud-Dīn Mūsa, fol. 13*b*, and Sulṭān Junaid, fol. 17*a*. Birth of Shāh Ismā'īl and his early life, fol. 19*a*. His accession in Tebriz, A.H. 906, and history of his reign, fol. 41*b*. Accession of Ṭahmāsp and history of his reign, fol. 125*b*. Reign of Shāh Ismā'īl II., fol. 225*a*. Events which followed his death, fol. 230*b*. Reign of Sulṭān Muḥammad, fol. 231*b*. History of Shāh 'Abbās during the reign of Sulṭān Muḥ., fol. 238*a*. His first Julūs and subsequent events, fol. 242*b*. His second Julūs and history of his reign, down to the repulse of Ḥāfiẓ Aḥmad Pasha from Baghdad, foll. 268*a*—385*a*.

This is the conclusion of the original work. At the end the copyist has given the date of transcription, A.H. 1052, in the following verse:

هزار و پنجه و دو بود ماه آخر سال
که راقی بنوشت این کتاب خوب خصال

First Appendix, in which are related the events of the concluding years of the reign and the death of Shāh 'Abbās, which is said to have taken place in Ashraf, on the third of Rabī' I., A.H. 1038, and to have been kept some time secret (strangely at variance with the 'Ālam-ārāi 'Abbāsi, which places the same event on the 24th of Jumāda I. of the same year), foll. 385*a*—387*b*.

Second Appendix.—Enthronement of Shāh Ṣafi on the 4th of Rabī' I., A.H. 1038, and beginning of his reign, foll. 387*b*—402*b*.

This continuation, which is due to the same author, has a preface of its own, beginning: خطبهٔ احوال و اوضاع پادشاه عصر شاه صفی ابن شاه عباس انار الله برهانه .... افتتاح نامهٔ وجود و ابتدای صحیفهٔ مقصود حمد و ثنای واجب الوجوبست که لسان عقل دوربین در بیان شمه ازان بعجز و قصور معترفست

The MS. is imperfect at the end. The last extant chapter relates to the attempt made by the Khan of Bukhara, Imām Ḳuli Khān, to possess himself of Merv, when the Persian general, Murtaẓa Ḳuli Khān was made prisoner by the Uzbeks, and subsequently set free by the Khan of Bukhara (A.H. 1041-42; see Khuld Barin, fol. 55-56). The copy breaks off after the heading of the next following chapter, which relates to the invasion of Khorasan by the troops of Balkh,

کفتار در بیان تاخت و تاراج مجندهٔ بلخ بعضی از ولایت خراسانرا و توجه نمودن نواب خلف بیك ترتیب دفع فساد ایشان الخ

The Rauzat al-Ṣafaviyyah, by Amīr Beg, is one of the authorities quoted in the Majma' ut-Tavārikh of Muḥammad Khalīl (A.H. 1207). See Pertsch, Berlin Catalogue, no. 436.

59.

Or. 3272.—Foll. 355; 13 in. by 7¾; 23 lines, 5¼ in. long; written in neat Nestalik; dated (fol. 279) Friday, 26 Shavvāl, A.H. 1060 (A.D. 1650).

تاریخ عالم آرای عباسی

History of Shāh 'Abbās I., by Iskandar Munshi. See the Persian Catalogue, p. 185.

Beg. عنوان صحیفهٔ سلطنت وعالم آرائی پادشاهان کامکار و دیباچهٔ دیوان خلافت وکشور خدائی شهریاران کردون اقتدار

This fine copy, written only twenty-two years after the completion of the work, wants the Muḳaddimah and the first Ṣaḥīfah. It contains only the history of the reign of Shāh 'Abbās, as follows:

Ṣaḥīfah II. The first thirty years of the reign, namely, from Tunguz-yil = A.H. 996 to the end of Lui-yil = A.H. 1025, fol. 1*b*.

Maḳṣad II. The last twelve years of the reign from Yilan-yil = A.H. 1026 to Lui-yil = A.H. 1037, fol. 280*b*.

In this last section there is a lacuna extending from the middle of Yunt-yil = A.H. 1027 to the middle of Takhāku-yil = A.H. 1030. It corresponds with foll. 365*b*—372*a* of the complete copy, Add. 16,684. There are also about two pages wanting at the end, namely, the last lines of the biographical notices and the Khātimah.

For other copies see Pertsch, Berlin Catalogue, nos. 441—46, and Ethé, Bodleian Catalogue, nos. 289—299.

60.

Or. 2940.—Foll. 247; 11¾ in. by 6; 16 lines, 3¼ in. long; written in elegant Nestalik, with 'Unvān and gold-ruled margins; dated 28 Jumada I., ١٥١, for A.H. 1152 (A.D. 1739).

[Sidney Churchill.]

History of the reign of Shah 'Abbās II., by Mirza Ṭāhir Vaḥīd. See the Persian Catalogue, p. 189*b*.

This copy contains much more than the previously described MS., Add. 11,632. The portion corresponding to the latter occupies foll. 2—156 of the present MS. Foll. 156*b*—247 contain a continuation which extends to Tushkan-yil, the twenty-second year of the reign, corresponding with A.H. 1073-74. The last events recorded are the journey of Shah 'Abbās from Teheran to Isfahan; the arrival at Court of envoys of the king of Abyssinia and of the Imam of Yemen; lastly, the appointments of 'Ivaẓ Beg as Divanbegi, and of Murtaẓa Ḳuli Khan as Beglerbegi of Ḳarabagh.

The author occupied the post of Vezir under Shāh Sulaiman and Shāh Sulṭān Ḥusain. The date of his death is doubtful. Riẓa Ḳuli Khan says in Riyāẓ ul-'Ārifīn, fol. 93*a*, that he died in Isfahan A.H. 1108, while the Zubdat ul-Gharā'ib, fol. 242, refers the same event to A.H. 1110. Both dates are probably too early. Fath 'Ali Khan succeeded him, according to Zīnat ut-Tavārīkh, in A.H. 1120. One of his letters, dated A.H. 1111, in which he takes the title of 'Imād ud-Daulah Muḥ. Ṭāhir, is mentioned in the Turkish Catalogue, p. 89*b*.

In a copy of the same work described by Ethé, Bodleian Catalogue, no. 301, the last date mentioned is A.H. 1064.

61.

Or. 3332.—Foll. 211; 11¼ in. by 6½; 15 lines, 3¾ in. long; written in fair Nestalik, with gold-ruled margins, apparently in the 18th century. [H. A. Stern.]

Another copy of the history of Mirza Ṭāhir Vaḥīd, with the same contents as the preceding, except that it wants about ten folios at the beginning.

62.

Or. 2941.—Foll. 250; 10½ in. by 6¼; 14 lines, 4 in. long; written in fair Nestalik, with 'Unvan and gold-ruled margins, apparently in the 18th century. Partly stained by damp and obliterated. [Sidney Churchill.]

دستور شهریاران

A history of the reign of Shah Sulṭān Ḥusain, by Muḥammad Ibrāhīm B. Zain ul-'Abidīn an-Naṣīrī.

Beg. سبحان الله لك الملك كريم متعال كه بجهت شناخت خويش بمضمون خبر صدق اثر كنت كنزا مخفيا الخ

This is a court chronicle, written in a pompous and turgid style of the most wearisome prolixity. After a doxology which occupies no less than twelve folios comes the preface proper, مقدمه در ذكر سبب نظم كتاب. From this we learn that the author came of a family which had been for several generations devoted to the dynasty, and had been rewarded with high offices, such as the custody of the sanctuaries of Najaf and Mashhad, the Vizārat i Dīvān, Inshā i Mamālik, Istīfā i Mamālik, &c. After having been for a long time out of employment, the author was reinstated in his office of court historiographer. In another passage, under A.H. 1110, fol. 239, he records his appointment as Majlis-navis. There he styles himself Mirza Muḥammad Ibrāhīm Naṣīri, grandson of the late Ṭālib Khān, Vazīr i Dīvān i A'la. In a Persian note written, A.H. 1302, on the first page, it is stated that Naṣīri was the Nisbah of the descendants of Naṣīr ul-Dīn Ṭūsi, several of whom rose to high posts under the Safavis.

The history begins, fol. 14*b*, with an account of the Julūs of Sulṭān Ḥusain, which took place in the Ā'inah Khānah on the eve of Saturday, 14th Zulḥijjah, A.H. 1105, in the Turkish year of It yil. The motto of the new coin is given as follows:

[زد] زتوفیق حق بچهرهٔ زر
سکه سلطان حسین دین پرور

This is followed by a record of the events which took place during the remainder of the above Turkish year. The succeeding years begin as follows:

Fol. 68*a*. Tunguz yil=A.H. 1106, the second year of the reign.

Fol. 78*b*. Sichkan yil=A.H. 1107.

Fol. 146*b*. Ud yil=A.H. 1108.

Fol. 178*b*. Pars yil=A.H. 1109.

Fol. 232*b*. Tushkan yil=A.H. 1110.

The last year is imperfect at the end. The MS. breaks off at the fifth page of a chapter headed ذكر ظهور معظم امور در ممالك سلاطين معاصر وجمل احوال بعضى ازايشان دراين سال سعادت مآثر. The extant portion of that chapter relates to the expedition of Ismā'īl Pasha, governor of Baghdad, against an Arab chief, Shaikh Salmān, in Kerbela.

63.

Or. 4500.—Foll. 97; 8¼ in. by 5; 12 lines, 3 in. long; written in Neskhi, with ruled margins; dated Thursday, 26 Rabī' II., A.H. 1278 (A.D. 1861).

[SIDNEY CHURCHILL.]

A history of the Afghan invasion, translated from Turkish by Ibn Najaf-Ḳuli 'Abd ur-Razzāḳ (see no. 68), with the following heading: بصيرت نامه در كذارش و استيلای افغان بر اصفهان در زمان دولت شاه سلطانحسين

Beg. در زمان شاه سلطانحسين صفوی شخص سياحی از ملت مسيحيه درعالم سياحت باصفهان آمده و در انجا قريب به بيست وشش سال متوقف و ناظر اوضاع بد و نيك جهان بوده

It is stated in the preface that in the time of Shāh Sulṭān-Ḥusain a Christian traveller came to Isfahan, where he resided close on six and twenty years, and, being a keen observer of current events, and especially of the Afghan invasion, wrote in Latin a detailed account of the latter. This was translated into Turkish and printed at Islambol by an Osmanli official, Ibrāhīm by name, who gave to his version the title of بصيرت نامه. A copy, having been brought to Persia, was read by the Heir Apparent (Vali 'Ahd), by whose order the present translation was made by his servant.

It is a faithful, but rather condensed, translation of the well-known history of the Jesuit missionary, Judas Thaddæus Krusinski, originally written in Latin under the title of "Tragica vertentis belli Historia." The Turkish translation, تاريخ سياح در بيان ظهور اغوانيان, was printed by Ibrāhīm Mutafarriḳah at Constantinople, A.H. 1142. It has been subsequently translated into Latin by J. C. Clodius, and from Latin into English by G. N. Mitford, London, 1840. See Flügel, Vienna Catalogue, no. 973, and Krafft, no. 262.

64.

Or. 3602.—Foll. 101; 8½ in. by 5¾; 14 lines, 3½ in. long; written in Shikastah in the 19th century. [SIDNEY CHURCHILL.]

زبور آل داوود

A history of Sayyid Muḥammad Mirza (Shah Sulaimān II.) and his family, by his son Muḥammad Hāshim.

Beg. حمد وثنای بی منتها مبدعی را سزاست كه به نيروی قدرت كامله آبای علوی و امهات سفلی را باهم مربوط نموده الخ

This is the identical work which in another MS. described in the Persian Catalogue, p. 191*b*, bears the title of تذكره آل داود; but the present copy contains the Khātimah, which is wanting in the other. The four parts of which the work consists begin as follows: Muḳaddimah, fol. 2*b*; Maḳālah I., fol. 21*b*; Maḳālah II., fol. 44*b*; Khātimah, fol. 86*b*.

The Khātimah has this heading: خاتمه در بيان و توضيح و ثبت و ضبط سواد قباليجات و وقف ناميجات و ارقام و فتوی و غيره نوشتجات كهنه كه تا حال موجود و از غايت اندراس در شرف تلف و بر طرف شدن است

It contains copies of old title-deeds, donations, legal decisions, &c., relating to estates belonging to the author's family, with dates ranging from A.H. 1021 to 1153.

In Maḳālah II. there are towards the end some additional notices brought down to A.H. 1226; but the account of the author's children, with which the Maḳālah was to conclude, is wanting, and a blank space of three pages has been left for its insertion.

Nādir Shah.

65.

Or. 4775.—Foll. 97; 13 in. by 8; 16 lines, 5¾ in. long; written in fair large Shikastah-āmiz; probably early in the 19th century.

تاریخ جهان کشای نادری

The history of Nādir Shāh, by Mirza Mahdi. See the Persian Catalogue, p. 192.

This MS. contains little more than the first half of the work. It breaks off in the middle of the chapter relating to the siege of Ganjah, A.H. 1147. The last incident mentioned is Nādir's narrow escape from a cannon shot which killed a man by his side and splashed him with brain and blood. See the Tebriz edition of A.H. 1263, p. 520, and Sir William Jones's abridged translation, London, 1773, p. 59.

Zands.

66.

Or. 3592.—Foll. 229; 14 in. by 8½; 22 lines, 5½ in. long; written in close and neat Nestalik, A.D. 1887. [Sidney Churchill.]

گلشن مراد

A detailed history of Karīm Khan and his successors down to the death of Ja'far Khān, A.H. 1203, by Ibn Mu'izz ud-Din Muḥammad Abu 'l-Ḥasan al-Ghaffāri al-Kāshāni al-Mustaufi.

Beg. گلشن مراد سلاطین کامکار را خرمی و طراوت حصول بآبیاری ستایش مالك الملك ذو الجلالی است عظم شانه که تؤتی الملك من تشاء وصف جلال و قادریت اوست ..... اما بعد این کنجینه ایست دل پسند مخزون بلالی آبدار وقایعی چند که کمین غلبه درگاه حضرت سبحانی ابن معز الدین محمد ابو الحسن الغفاری الکاشانی المستوفی بدست کوهرسنجی و جوهر شناسی بعقود جواهر نثر انباشته

The author says in the preface that at the age of seven he had learnt the art of painting, which he cultivated during two years. He then met his father's friend, Mirza Muḥ. Burūjirdi, who advised him to qualify himself for the profession of official writer, in which his father had attained eminence. In obedience to that advice, he applied himself in the first place to arithmetic and account-keeping, علم سیاق, and then to the art of elegant composition, انشا. The project he formed at the time of writing the annals of the reigning sovereign, Karim Khān, was delayed for four years. It was not before A.H. 1198, in the reign of 'Ali Murād Khān, that he was able to put his hand to the work, which, in honour of the then reigning prince, received the title of Gulshan i Murād. A versified chronogram by Ṣabā (Fatḥ 'Ali Khan), inserted in the preface, conveys the same date, A.H. 1198, as that of the composition of the work.

It must, however, be taken as relating to its beginning only, for, further on, fol. 110a, A.H. 1206 is incidentally mentioned as the current year at the time of writing, and it appears from the colophon that it was not finished till A.H. 1210. The author's father, Mirza Mu'izz ud-Dīn Ghaffāri, was governor of Kashan in the time of Karim (see fol. 5a).

The work is divided, according to the preface, into a Mukaddimah treating of the pretenders who rose after the death of Nādir Shah, and three Maḳālahs devoted respectively to the reigns (1) of Karīm Khān, (2) of Abu 'l-Fatḥ Khān and 'Ali Murād Khān, and (3) of the reigning sovereign, whose name is left in blank. This last Maḳālah, however, does not appear in the body of the volume, and there is, moreover, a considerable lacuna, without any apparent break, at the beginning of the work. The Muḳaddimah comes to an abrupt end after the first page and a half, fol. 4a, and Maḳālah I., which was to commence with the genealogy and first rise of Karīm Khān, begins equally abruptly, in the course of the Turkish year It-yil = A.H. 1167-8, the sixth year of the reign, with the march of Karīm Khān from Shiraz to Irak and the taking of Isfahan, ذکر توجه موکب جهان کشا بجانب عراق و تسخیر دار السلطنة اصفهان بعون و عنایت مالك الملك بالاستحقاق

The events of the remainder of the reign are then fully narrated, unfortunately in a very florid and prolix style, under the following Turkish years, each of which begins with a long poetical description of Spring:

Fol. 5b. Tunguz yil, beginning on the 7th of Jumāda II., A.H. 1168.

Fol. 10b. Sichḳan yil, 18 Jumada II., A.H. 1169.

Fol. 13a. Ud yil, 29 Jumada II., A.H. 1170.

Fol. 15a. Bars yil, 11 Rajab, A.H. 1171.

Fol. 16b. Tushḳan yil, 21 Rajab, A.H. 1172.

Fol. 20b. Lui yil, 2 Sha'bān, A.H. 1173.

Fol. 34b. Yilan yil, 13 Sha'bān, A.H. 1174.

Fol. 39b. Yunt yil, 24 Sha'bān, A.H. 1175.

Fol. 53b. Ḳui yil, 5 Ramazan, A.H. 1176.

Fol. 63b. Bichi yil, 16 Ramazan, A.H. 1177.

Fol. 70b. Takhaḳu yil, 27 Ramazan, A.H. 1178.

Fol. 75b. It yil, 9 Shavval, A.H. 1179.

Fol. 78b. Tunguz yil, 20 Shavval, A.H. 1180.

Fol. 81a. Sichḳan yil, 1 Zulḳa'dah, A.H. 1181.

Fol. 84a. Ud yil, 11 Zulḳa'dah, A.H. 1182, Bars yil, Tushḳan yil and Lui yil.

Fol. 86a. Yilan yil, 26 Zulhijjah, A.H. 1186.

Fol. 87b. Yunt yil, 8 Muḥarram, A.H. 1188.

Fol. 92a. Ḳui yil, 18 Muḥarram, A.H. 1189.

Fol. 97b. Bichi yil, 29 Muḥarram, A.H. 1190.

Fol. 102b. Takhaḳu yil, 3 Ṣafar, A.H. 1191.

Fol. 103b. It yil, 13 Ṣafar, A.H. 1192.

The account of the death of Karīm Khān, which took place on Tuesday, the 13th of Ṣafar, A.H. 1193, is followed by an enumeration of his children, fol. 110a, and of the eminent men of his reign, especially of the poets, whose notices, alphabetically arranged under their poetical surnames, occupy foll. 113a—126b.

Maḳālah II., fol. 126b, begins with the installation of Abu 'l-Fatḥ Khān on the throne, and the assumption of sovereign power by Zaki Khān, but it is mainly taken up with the doings of 'Ali Murād Khān. The heading is: مقاله دوم در ذکر سلطنت نواب کامیاب ابو الفتح خان و نواب جهانبان کشور ستان علیمراد خان و باقی سلاطین سلسلهٔ علیهٔ زندیه و ابتدا در شرح جلوس نواب ابو الفتح خان بر سریر خلافت و نشستن زکیخان در دربار پادشاهی بر مسند وکالت دولت و بیان حرکت نواب جهانبان کشور ستان علیمراد خان بامر زکیخان از دار الملك شیراز بجانب عراق و طهران و باقی وقایع آن زمان

It comprises the following years:

Fol. 127*a*. Tunguz yil, beginning 29 Ṣafar, A.H. 1193.

Fol. 145*a*. Sichḳan yil, 13 Rabi' I., A.H. 1194.

Fol. 161*a*. Ud yil, 24 Rabī' I., A.H. 1195.

Fol. 184*b*. Bars yil, 5 Rabī' II., A.H. 1196.

Fol. 196*b*. Tushḳan yil, 17 Rabī' II., A.H. 1197.

Fol. 198*b*. Lui yil, 28 Rabī' II., A.H. 1198.

The death of 'Ali Murād Khān, which happened during his march from Teheran to Isfahan on the 30th of Rabī' I., A.H. 1199, is recorded at fol. 205*a*. Then follows the accession of Istiẓhār ud-Daulah Muḥammad Ja'far Khān, fol. 208*a*. The events of his reign are told under the following years:

Fol. 208*b*. Yilan yil, 8 Jumāda I., A.H. 1199.

Fol. 215*a*. Yunt yil, 19 Jumāda I., A.H. 1200.

Fol. 220*b*. Ḳui yil, 1 Jumāda II., A.H. 1201.

Fol. 225*b*. Bichi yil, 12 Jumāda II., A.H. 1202.

The last events recorded are the march of Ja'far Khān to Isfahan and the flight of 'Ali Ḳuli Khān Ḳājār, fol. 226*b*; the flight of Murtaẓa Ḳuli Khān, son of Muḥammad Ḥasan Khān Ḳājār, to Gilan, fol. 227*a*; lastly, the death of Ja'far Khān, who was assassinated in his palace at Shiraz on the 25th of Jumāda I., A.H. 1203, and the assumption of sovereignty by Sayyid Murād Khan, who maintained himself only seventy days, fol. 228*a*.

In a conclusion, due apparently to the author's son, it is stated that, the author having died soon after the events of the last reign, the work had been completed by Muḥammad 'Ali Khān Shīrāzi, who had been a witness of some of the transactions and campaigns recorded. He finished the work in Kashan on the 6th of Sha'bān, A.H. 1210, in the reign of (Aḳa) Muḥammad Khān, at a time when that sovereign was preparing for his campaign to Khorasan. Then follows a colophon transcribed from the original MS., which had been written for the author of the continuation, Muḥammad 'Ali Khān, and completed on the 5th of Zulḥijjah, A.H. 1210.

Mr. Churchill writes at the end: "This copy was made for me by Molla Aflatun, the Zoroastrian, and completed on the 19th July, 1887, from a copy belonging to the Etimad us-Sultaneh. In January, 1888, Molla Aflatun turned Musselman, and is now known under the name of Mirza Mehdi."

Ḳajars.

67.

Or. 3551.—Foll. 180; 12 in. by $7\frac{1}{2}$; 15 lines, 5 in. long; written in fair Nestalik, with 'Unvān and gold-ruled margins; written about the close of the 18th century.

[SIDNEY CHURCHILL.]

تاریخ محمدی

A history of the rise of the Ḳajars and of the reign of Aḳa Muḥammad, by Muḥammad B. Muḥammad Taḳi as-Sāru'i.

The contents are identical with those of Add. 27,243, described in the Persian Catalogue, p. 199*a*. Like the latter, the present MS. concludes with a poetical eulogy on the work by Fatḥ 'Ali Khān Kāshāni, Malik ush-Shu'arā, takh. Ṣabā, who died A.H. 1238 (Majma' ul-Fuṣaḥā, vol. ii., p. 267).

68-69.

Or. 3278-79.—Two uniform volumes, consisting respectively of foll. 128 and 116; 8 in. by 5½; 15 lines, 3¼ in. long; written by the same hand in cursive Nestalik, and forming a continuous text; dated 9 Zul-ka'dah, A.H. 1236 (A.D. 1821).

مآثر سلطانیه

A History of the rise of the Ḳajars, and especially of the reign of Fatḥ 'Ali Shah from his accession to the end of A.H. 1229, by Ibn Najaf Ḳuli 'Abd ur-Razzāḳ Beg.

سپاس و ستایش فراوان از خاکیان سزای بارگاه کیهان خدائیست که کذارندهٔ پیکر زمین و آسمان الخ

This is the work which has been translated by Sir Harford Jones Brydges under the title of Dynasty of the Ḳajars, London, 1833. An edition of the text published in Tabriz, A.H. 1241, is the first book printed in Persia. It has no pagination. The contents of the work have been described by Hammer in the Jahrbücher, vol. 53, Anz. Blatt, p. 58. A copy consisting of three parts, and ending also with A.H. 1229, is mentioned in Morley's Catalogue, nos. 151—53.

The author, 'Abd ur-Razzāḳ Beg, son of Najaf Ḳuli Khān Dunbuli, Beglerbegi of Tabriz, was a favourite of the Nā'ib us-Salṭanah 'Abbās Mirza. He died A.H. 1243, leaving, besides the present history, a Tazkirah and some poems. His Takhalluṣ was Maftūn. See Tazkirah i Muhammad shāhi, fol. 212b; Majma' ul-Fuṣaḥā, vol. ii., p. 483; and Zinat ul-Madā'iḥ, Or. 2877, fol. 134. The Tazkirah above mentioned, called Nigāristan i Dārā, Or. 3508, concludes with the life and poems of the author.

The first volume of the present copy contains the rise of the Ḳajars and the reign of Agha Muḥammad, foll. 1—15; the accessions of Fatḥ 'Ali Shāh, fol. 16; and the following years of his reign: A.H. 1213, fol. 21b; 1214, fol. 30a; 1215, fol. 42a; 1216, fol. 48b; 1217, fol. 62b; 1218, fol. 66b; 1219, fol. 69b; 1220, fol. 87a; and 1221, fol. 105a.

The second volume comprises the following years: A.H. 1222, fol. 4a; 1223, fol. 15a; 1224, fol. 34b; 1225, fol. 55a; 1226, fol. 70b; 1228, fol. 99a; and 1229, foll. 111a—116.

After fol. 73 there is a lacuna indicated by eight blank pages. It corresponds with 29 pages of the Tabriz edition, consisting of the latter portion of A.H. 1226, and nearly the whole of A.H. 1227. The chapter immediately preceding that lacuna relates to the arrival of Sir Gore Ouseley, whose merits are dwelt upon in glowing terms, a passage omitted in Brydges's version. The concluding part of the latter version falls within the above lacuna.

The Tabriz edition has, in addition to the contents of our MS., the years A.H. 1230—1241, occupying the last seventy-four pages of the volume.

On the fly-leaf at the end of Or. 3279 is written: "Wm. Oliver, Esq., Civil Indian, with Wm. Monteith's compliments."

70.

Or. 2876.—Foll. 153; 11⅝ in. by 7; 15 lines, 4½ in. long; written in fair Nestalik, with gold-ruled margins, A.H. 1248 (A.D. 1832—33).

[Sidney Churchill.]

تاریخ صاحبقرانی

A history of the reign of Fatḥ 'Ali Shah, from his accession to A.H. 1248, with an introduction treating of the rise of the Ḳajar dynasty, by Maḥmūd Mirza Ḳājār.

Beg. حمد پروردگاریرا که بما بندگان قدرت حمد ذات و قوت ادراك اثار صفات عطا فرمود

The author, the fifteenth son of Fatḥ 'Ali Shāh, was born A.H. 1214. He was appointed governor of Nehāvend, and left, besides the present work, a Tazkirah called Safinat ul-Maḥmūd (no. 122), an anthology entitled Bayān i Maḥmūd, and a work called Gulshan i Maḥmūd, treating of the lives and poems of the sons of Fatḥ 'Ali Shāh (no. 121). See Zu 'l-Ḳarnain, Or. 3527, fol. 358*a*; Anjuman i Khāḳān, fol. 33*b*; and Majma' ul-Fuṣaḥā, vol. i., p. 56.

He says, in the preface, that the Shāh, being dissatisfied with the prolixity and abstruse phraseology of the chronicles composed by the court Munshis, selected him among the princes on account of the literary skill displayed in his previous compositions, to entrust him the task of writing the present history, to which the Shāh himself gave the above title. The work was commenced in the last decade of Rabi' II., A.H. 1248, and completed, as stated at the end, on the 14th of Rajab of the same year. The author states in the preface that from his boyhood he had enjoyed the tuition of the Ṣadr i A'ẓam, Mirza Muḥammad Shafi'.

The work begins with the following preliminary chapters: Genealogy of the Ḳajars, fol. 2*a*. History of Fatḥ 'Ali Khān, fol. 2*b*. His expedition in aid of Shāh Sulṭān Ḥusain Ṣafavi, fol. 3*a*. History of Muḥammad Ḥasan Khān, fol. 4*a*. History of Ḥusain Ḳuli Khān, father of Fatḥ 'Ali Shah, fol. 6*a*. History of Muḥammad Shāh, told in great detail, year by year, from A.H. 1193 to his death, foll. 8*b*—57. This concludes what the author calls the first volume (Mujallad).

The second volume, which forms the main part of the MS., foll. 58—153, is devoted to the reign of Fatḥ 'Ali Shāh, from his accession in A.H. 1212 to A.H. 1248. It is divided according to the years of the Hijrah, which form the main headings. The last year included, A.H. 1248, begins at fol. 144*b*. The last event recorded is the coming of the Shahzādah Saif ud-Daulah Sulṭān Muḥammad Mirza from Isfahan to Teheran in the first decade of Rajab.

From notes written on the first page of the volume, it appears that it was presented A.H. 1248 to Bahā ud-Daulah Bahman Mirza, son of Fatḥ 'Ali Shāh, and passed, A.H. 1261, into the possession of 'Ali Ḳuli Mirza, grandson of the Shāh.

71.

Or. 3527.—Foll. 460; 12¼ in. by 8¼; 23 lines, 5 in. long; written in large, but stiff and inelegant, Nestalik, in the latter half of the 19th century. [Sidney Churchill.]

تاریخ ذو القرنین

A history of Fatḥ 'Ali Shāh, from his early life to his death, by Faẓl-ullah al-Munshi, poetically surnamed Khāvari.

Beg. فتح الباب نامهٔ خاقانی و فصل الخطاب رسالهٔ صاحبقرانی سپاس افزون از قیاس شاهنشاهی راست

The author was only fourteen years of age, and still at school, when he first saw Fatḥ 'Ali, then governor of Fārs, and conceived the wish to enter his service. He was employed as secretary under the Ṣadr i A'ẓam, Mirza Muḥ. Shafi', and was afterwards attached during ten years to a Shahzādah whom he does not name.[1] He subsequently became private secretary to the Shāh. Having heard on some occasion His Majesty saying that a historian ought not to make a display of his skill in fine writing, but should use plain language and adhere strictly to truth,

[1] This was Humāyūn Mirza, to whom the author was appointed Vazir, as stated in Majma' ul-Fuṣaḥā.

he resolved to carry out the suggestion. Muḥ. Rāẓī Tabrīzī had chronicled, in his Zīnat ut-Tavārīkh, the first ten years of His Majesty's reign, and Mirzā Muḥ. Ṣādiḳ Marvazī had related, in his Tārīkh i Jahān ārā, thirty-six years of the reign; but the latter had omitted much weighty matter, especially the negotiations and treaties with Turkey and European powers. The author, therefore, who had been nearly thirty years in the service of the Shāh, wishing to leave a record of himself in prose, as he had already done in poetry by his Divan entitled مهر خاوری, wrote the present work, which is divided into two volumes (Jild) and a Khātimah. Each of the two Jilds bears a special title. The first is called نامۀ خاقان, the second رسالۀ صاحبقران.

Contents: Jild I. The realm of Iran, fol. 4a. Genealogy of the Kajars, fol. 6b. History of Fatḥ 'Ali Khān, fol. 7b. Muḥammad Hasan Khān, fol. 8b. His children, fol. 10a. Birth of His Majesty (Fatḥ 'Alī Shāh) on the 6th of Jumāda I., A.H. 1186, fol. 10b. Brief account of the reign of Agha Muḥammad, fol. 12a. Appointment of Fatḥ 'Ali as heir apparent, fol. 19a. Death of Agha Muḥammad and accession of Fatḥ 'Ali Shāh, fol. 19a. Events of Yunt yil, begining in A.H. 1212, fol. 25a, and of the subsequent Turkish years to the end of It yil, A.H. 1241, which completes the first Ḳarn, *i.e.* the first thirty years, of the reign.

Jild II., foll. 242—345, begins with Tunguz yil=A.H. 1242, and contains the history of the last eight years of the reign, down to Yunt yil=A.H. 1249. It concludes with the death of Fath 'Ali Shāh, on Thursday, the 19th of Jumāda II., A.H. 1250, and with the subsequent events down to the accession of Muḥammad Shāh.

The Khātimah, foll. 345b—413, beginning with a chapter on the fair qualities of Fatḥ 'Ali Shah, contains a full account of his children and relatives. It agrees substantially with another MS., Or. 1361, described in the Persian Catalogue, p. 201, which wants only a short epilogue.

The volume concludes with a very copious selection from the Divan of the author, foll. 414—460.

The author, who at the beginning of Jild II., calls himself Faẓl-ullah B. 'Abd un-Nabi Shīrāzi, was a prolific poet. He frequently inserts in the course of his history rhymed chronograms and other extensive pieces of his own composition. Riẓā Ḳuli Khān, who wrote A.H. 1283, mentions the present work and speaks of the author as still living. See Majma' ul-Fuṣaḥā, vol. ii., p. 126. For other notices see Safīnat Maḥmūd, fol. 219; Anjuman i Khāḳān, fol. 52b; Nigāristān i Dārā, fol. 91a; and Tazkirah i Muhammad shāhi, fol. 184a.

The first Jild was written in the life-time of Fatḥ 'Ali Shāh and completed, as stated at the end, on the 6th of Rabi' II., A.H. 1249. The colophon of the original copy in the author's handwriting, transcribed in the same place, is dated Shīrāz, 14 Zulḳa'dah, A.H. 1262.

At the end of the abstract of his Divan the author states that he finished the whole work on the 13th of Rabi' II., A.H. 1263.

72.

Or. 4108.—Foll. 123; 8¼ in. by 5¾; 11 lines, 3½ in. long; written in fair, rather cursive, Nestalik; dated 15 Shavvāl, A.H. 1304 (A.D. 1887). [Sidney Churchill.]

Memoirs of the Court of Fatḥ 'Ali Shāh, by 'Aẓud ud-Daulah Sulṭān Aḥmad.

Beg. فصل ۞ زوجات خاقان خلد مکان چند نمره بودند نمرهٔ اول از خانوادهٔ سلطنت و سایر شعب قاجاریه و بزرگزادگان معتبر ایران بودند

There is no preface. The author's name is found in an epilogue entitled سبب تاليف كتاب. He was the forty-sixth son of Fatḥ 'Ali Shāh, and was, at the time of writing, governor of Hamadān. He composed the present work in obedience to an order of the present Shāh, conveyed to him by the minister of the press, I'timād us-Salṭanah, Mirza Muḥammad Ḥasan, and he completed it in Jumāda I., A.H. 1304. He says that he was only ten years old at the time of Fatḥ 'Ali Shah's death, and that his record is based partly on his own recollection and partly on what he was told by older members of his family.

The work is written in an unpretending gossiping style, and abounds in characteristic anecdotes of the Shah and his entourage. The arrangement is not very methodical. The main contents are as follows:

Notices of the wives and concubines of Fatḥ 'Ali Shāh, and of free women and slave girls attached to the Harem, fol. 1*b*. Etiquette relating to the attendance of the princes at Court, to the rank of the princesses, &c., fol. 25*a*. Principal eunuchs, fol. 31*b*. Wedding festivals of the royal princesses, fol. 33*a*. Anecdotes showing the Shah's regard for the Ḳajar chiefs, fol. 49*b*. Account of the Harem, fol. 51*b*. Notices of the Vazirs of the reign, fol. 63*a*. Reception of Ẓill us-Sulṭān by the Shah; notices and anecdotes relating to the Shah's sons and courtiers, fol. 71*a*. Character and moral qualities of the Shah, fol. 98*a*. Good qualities of Muḥammad Shāh and his treatment of his relatives, fol. 109*b*. Number of the descendants of Fatḥ 'Ali Shāh, fol. 119*b*. Epilogue, fol. 122*b*.

The work has been lithographed in Bombay, A.H. 1306, under the title تاريخ عضدى.

Uzbeks.

73.

Or. 3497.—Foll. 261; 14 in. by 8¾; 31 lines, 5½ in. long; written in fair Neskhi; dated Thursday, 8 Jumāda I., A.H. 1304 (A.D. 1887). [SIDNEY CHURCHILL.]

شرفنامۀ شاهى

A history of 'Abdullah Khān from his birth to A.H. 997, by Ḥāfiẓ Tanish B. Mīr Muḥammad al-Bukhāri, حافظ تنش بن مير محمد البخارى

Beg. زواهر جواهر حمد بيغايت نثار كرپاس والا اساس مالك الملكى را سزاست كه صداى ملكوتش قل اللهم مالك است

'Abdullah Khān, son of Iskandar Khān, is the greatest of the Shaibāni sovereigns. Born A.H. 940, he became the virtual ruler of the Uzbek empire long before he assumed the sovereign title at the death of his father, Iskandar Khān, A.H. 991. He died A.H. 1006. The scantiness of the hitherto available sources on his eventful career is evidenced by the sketchy character of the accounts given of it by Vambéry, History of Bukhara, pp. 282—96, and by Sir Henry Howorth in his History of the Mongols, Part II., Division II., pp. 730—38.

The present work is the only full and authentic history of his life, written by a contemporary witness, who was attached to the Khan's suite; but its undoubted value is to some extent marred by the pompous verbosity of its style and the too frequent absence of precise dates. The work is often called 'Abdullah Nāmah. It has been noticed by Desmaisons in his translation of Abu 'l-Ghāzi Khān, p. 193, note 3. An edition promised by Veliaminof-Zernof has never appeared (v. Zeitschrift der D. Morg.

Gesellsch., Band 38, p. 235). A notice of the work in Schefer's Chrestomathie Persane, vol. ii., p. 216, has been the subject of some observations by S. Churchill, Indian Notices and Queries, vol. iv., no. 41, p. 93.

From a prolix and verbose preface we gather that the author, who from his early youth had been ambitious of distinguishing himself by some historical composition, did not begin to write until 'Abdullah Khān had established his rule over Mavarā-annahr and had made Bukhārā his capital. It was then that the author, now in his thirty-sixth year, undertook the compilation of a full record of the Khān's early life and of his victories. But it was only after he had been admitted to the presence of the great Vazir, Amir Ḳulbābā Kūkaltāsh, and encouraged by that generous patron of letters, that he set about collecting his rough drafts and brought them into their present shape. He then gave the book the title of Sharaf Nāmah i Shāhi, which, as stated in the following lines, forms a chronogram for A.H. 992, the date of composition:

این شرفنامه کش از غایت تشریف قبول
شرف از نام شهنشاه فلك قدر فزود
چه عجب کز پی تاریخ تمام نامش
خامهٔ تحریر شرفنامهٔ شاهی فرمود

It will be seen, however, presently, that the work was brought down to a later date. According to the preface, it was to consist of the following parts: Muḳaddimah treating of the Khan's forefathers from Noah down to his father Iskandar Khān, with a notice of his religious teacher Khwājah Jūibāri. Maḳālah I. History of 'Abdullah Khān from his birth to his accession to the throne. Maḳālah II. His history from his accession to a subsequent date, which is left undefined. Khātimah, on the distinctive qualities of the sovereign, on the holy Shaikhs, 'Ulamā, men of letters, poets, Amīrs, Vazīrs of his reign, on his pious foundations and the public buildings erected by him.

Of the above four parts the present MS. contains only the first two, namely: 1. The Muḳaddimah, foll. 9*a*—31*a*, comprising a genealogical sketch of the descendants of Chingiz Khān, with a fuller account of the Shaibāni branch, and concluding, fol. 27*a*, with a notice of the great saint Khwājah Muḥammad Jūibāri, of the Naḳshabandi order, with his spiritual pedigree, and an account of his son, Khwājah Kalān Khwājim. 2. Maḳālah I., which begins with the following heading: مقالهٔ اولی از ابتدای ولادت با سعادت و زمان ظهور دولت تا ایام جلوس انحضرت بر سریر خاقانی و مسند جهانبانی و تزیین خطبه و سکه بنام نامی و اسم سامی و ذکر صادرات افعال و واردات اقوال و حدوث وقایع و ظهور سوانح دران ایام فرخنده انجام

This Maḳālah, which forms the main bulk of the volume, foll. 31*b* - 259*b*, is brought down to a later date than the above heading indicates; for the death of Iskandar Khān, at the beginning of Jumāda II. (A.H. 991) and the subsequent Julūs of 'Abdullah Khān are recorded in chapters beginning respectively at fol. 203*b* and fol. 205*b*. The rest of the volume is devoted to a record of the next following six years. It concludes with a detailed account of the taking of Herat, which fell after a siege of nearly nine months. The city, we are told, was taken by storm on Monday, the third of Rabi' II., when a scene of general pillage and slaughter ensued. On the fifth the commander, 'Ali Ḳuli Khān, who had retired to the fortress of Ikhtiyār ud-Din, surrendered, and was treacherously massacred with his Ḳizilbāsh followers. The year in which that event took place is not stated in the narrative, but in a long Kasidah composed by the author on that occasion, the date is given in the following chronogram:

خرد کفت ناچار تاریخ سال
مبارك باو باد شهر هری

This would give A.H. 999, which is obviously wrong. According to Jalāl Munajjim, the fall of Herat took place in A.H. 997. In the 'Ālam ārāi 'Abbāsi, the same event is placed in the Sichkan yil, beginning in Jumāda I., A.H. 997, and ending in Jumāda I., A.H. 998.

In his conclusion, fol. 259*b*, the author says: "Here ends Maḳālah I: it will be followed by Maḳālah II." Whether the latter or the Khātimah were ever written is uncertain.

The present copy appears to have been made from a MS. written by Mirza Khush Muḥammad B. Tāsh Muḥammad Bāi Ḳatghan, whose colophon is transcribed at the end. It is dated 19 Jumāda I., A.H. 1239.

Copyist: علی الطالقانی المرجانی

A full table of chapters occupies five pages at the beginning.

Afghans.

74.

Or. 3550.—Foll. 197; 11¼ in. by 6½; 15 lines, 4 in. long; written in neat Nestalik, with 'Unvān and gold-ruled margins; dated 12 Jumāda II., A.H. 1305 (A.D. 1888).

[Sidney Churchill.]

تاریخ احمد شاه درّانی

A history of the Durrāni dynasty of Afghanistan, from the rise of Aḥmad Shāh to the death of Shāh Shujā', A.H. 1257, translated from Hindustani into Persian by Sayyid Ḥusain Shīrāzi Karbalā'i, son of Āḳa Sayyid Riẓāi Shīrāzi, Urdu translator of the Dār ut-Tarjumah, Teheran.

It begins with three Baits, the first of which is:

افغان ز قضا کم کن کر شد یله در آنی
هم سلطنت افغان هم دولت درانی

Then comes the prose doxology, beginning:

حضرت ملك الملكيرا ستایش سزاست که تمام هستی ملك اوست

From a note written on the fly-leaf by the translator, we learn that the Urdu original, entitled واقعات درانی, was the work of Muḥammad 'Abd ur-Raḥmān B. Ḥāji Muḥammad Rūshan Khan, and had been printed in Kānpūr. Some omissions in that work were supplemented and some discrepancies corrected by reference to مطلع الشمس and to تاریخ افغانستان by 'Ali Ḳuli Mirza I'tiẓād us-Salṭanah, son of Fatḥ 'Ali Shāh.

Contents: Genealogy of the Ṣaduzais; disturbed state of Afghanistan and invasion of Nādir, fol. 4*b*. Death of Nādir and reign of Aḥmad Shāh (A.H. 1162—85), fol. 11*b*. Reign of Tīmūr Shāh down to his death on the 7th of Shavvāl, A.H. 1207, fol. 46*b*. Reign of Zamān Shāh down to his deposition, A.H. 1216, fol. 77*a*. Reign of Sultan Maḥmūd till his death, A.H. 1244, fol. 127*b*. History of Shāh Shujā' from his accession to his death, A.H. 1257, fol. 148*a*. Topography of the Duābs and of Afghanistan, foll. 176*a*—197.

India.

75.

Or. 3714.—Foll. 528; 12½ in. by 7½; 12 lines, 4 in. long; written in large and elegant Nestalik, with gold-ruled margins, and profusely ornamented with miniatures and illuminated borders, apparently about the close of the 16th century. Bound in painted and glazed covers.

واقعات بابری

The Memoirs of Bābar, translated from the Turki original by 'Abd ur-Raḥīm Khān. See the Persian Catalogue, p. 244.

Beg. در ماه رمضان سنه هشتصد و نود و نه در ولایت فرغانه در دوازده سالکی پادشاه شدم

The four detached portions of which the Memoirs consist begin respectively as follows:

I. A.H. 899—908 (Erskine, pp. 1—122), foll. 1—156*a*.

II. A.H. 910—914 (Erskine, pp. 127—234), foll. 156*b*—296*b*.

III. A.H. 925—926 (Erskine, pp. 246—284), foll. 297*a*—348*a*.

IV. A.H. 932—936 (Erskine, pp. 290—425), foll. 348*b*—528*b*.

This fine volume contains sixty-eight whole-page miniatures in the most highly finished style of Indian art, and forty-eight pages have coloured drawings of smaller size representing various animals and trees. These miniatures are, with few exceptions, signed by the artists, most of whom bear Hindu names. The following are the names which recur most frequently: Kisu, Sānwlah, Mahis, Jagannāth, Bhūrah, Thirpāl, Nand Gwāliyāri, Bhawāni, Sīvdās, Tulsi, Tiriyā, Pars, Bhagwān, Dhanrāj, Sunkar Gujrāti, Banwāri, Padārat, Rāmdās. The first four are mentioned in Ā'īn i Akbari, translation, vol. i., p. 108, among the masters of the art at the court of Akbar. There are also some Muslim names, such as Ibrāhīm Ḳahhār, Manṣūr Naḳḳāsh (Nādir ul-'Aṣr, see Tuzuk Jahāngīri, p. 235), and Farrukh, the last also mentioned in the Ā'īn i Akbari.

For other copies see Ethé, Bodleian Catalogue, nos. 180—183.

76.

Or. 3271.—Foll. 138; 8½ in. by 5¼; 15 lines, 3 in. long; written in fair Nestalik in the first half of the 18th century; damaged by damp and partly discoloured.

I. Foll. 2—45. تتمه اکبر نامه

A continuation of Akbar Nāmah, comprising the last four years of the reign of Akbar, by 'Ināyat-ullah B. Muḥibb 'Ali.

Beg. بر ضمایر والا شکوه خرد پروران تواریخ پژوه که پرده کشایان اسرار کهن دنیا و دانایان اطوار جهان اعجوبه نما اند پوشیده نماند

The same beginning is found at fol. 12 of another copy, Or. 1854, described in the Persian Catalogue, p. 929*a*. The author's name is given in the following endorsement, apparently in the hand of the copyist: تتمه اکبر نامه از ابتدا چهل و هفتم لغایت سال پنجاهم مولفه عنایت الله محب علی. The same 'Ināyat-ullah B. Muḥibb 'Ali is mentioned as the author of a Takmilah i Akbar Nāmah in Ta'rīkh i Muḥammadi, Or. 1824, fol. 131*b*.

The present work is quite distinct from a similarly entitled history ascribed to Shaikh 'Ināyat-ullah, extracts of which are given in Elliot's History of India, vol. vi., pp. 103—115. While in the latter the murder of Abu 'l-Faẓl is told in a few lines, and without any direct implication of Jahāngīr in the crime, the author of the present work narrates the same event in the most circumstantial manner, and distinctly states that the murderer, Barsingh Dev, acted at the bidding of Jahāngīr. He dwells at length on the courage displayed by Abu 'l-Faẓl in the fatal encounter, on the sad loss entailed by his death, and on the overwhelming grief of Akbar.

II. Foll. 46—138. History of Shāhjahān, from his birth to his accession, ascribed in a contemporary endorsement to Mu'tamad Khān: احوال شاهزادکی شاهجهان مولفه معتمد خان

It begins, without any preface, with the following heading: ذکر سطوع نیر جاه و جلال و طلوع کوکب دولت واقبال یعنی ولادت با سعادت شایسته افسر کیانی زیبنده اورنك کامرانی چراغ افروز دودمان کورکانی شاه جوانبخت بلند اقبال صاحبقران ثانی

The text begins: چون مشیت ایزد عز شانه و اراده حق جل سبحانه بانتظام سلسله صوری و معنوی و ترتیب مصالح دینی و دنیوی الخ

The dates are given throughout with great precision according to the days of the Ilāhi months, with the corresponding dates of the lunar months. The work concludes with the arrival of Shahjahān at Agra, his Julūs on the 8th of Jumāda II., 1037, and an enumeration of the stages of his journey from Junīr to the capital. Some verses inserted after the account of the Julūs end with this line:

شد عهد تو پای مرد ایام آغاز ترا مباد انجام

which shows that the work was written during the reign of Shāhjahān.

Mu'tamad Khān, if such be the author's name, must be a distinct person from his namesake, the author of the Iḳbāl Nāmah. The latter, when referring to himself, uses such a phrase as "the present writer," while in corresponding passages our author mentions Mu'tamad Khān by name.

In a note written on the first page of the volume Mirza Muḥammad B. Mu'tamad Khān states that in Zulḥijjah, A.H. 1157, he received the above two works from 'Ināyat Khān Rāsikh, son of Shams ud-Daulah Luṭf-ullah Khān Bahādur Tahavvur Jang. This same 'Ināyat Khān is mentioned in the Persian Catalogue, p. 876*b*, as the editor of a collection of royal letters.

77.

Or. 3276.—Foll. 314; 10½ in. by 5¾; 15 lines, 3 in. long; written in fair Nestalik, with 'Unvān and gold-ruled margins, apparently in the 17th century.

جهانکیر نامه

The Memoirs of Jahāngīr.

Beg. از عنایات ازلی [ی] غایات الهی یکساعت نجومی از روز پنجشنبه هشتم جمادی الثانی هزار و چهارده هجری کذشته

The contents agree substantially with those of Add. 26,215 described in the Persian Catalogue, p. 253*b*, and with the edition printed at Ally Gurh, 1864, under the title of توزك جهانکیری. The first part of the Memoirs, comprising the first twelve years of the reign, ends at fol. 300*b*, and is followed, without any heading or break in the text, by the second part, beginning with the thirteenth year. The MS. breaks off in the middle of that year at a passage relating to the painter Manṣūr, and corresponding with p. 235, line 32, of the Ally Gurh edition.

On the first page and within an ornamental border is found this misleading title: نامه بهرام از خاقان نزد هرمزد شاه

For other copies see Ethé, Bodleian Catalogue, nos. 219—20.

78.

Or. 3287.—Foll. 134; 10½ in. by 6½; 19 lines, 4¼ in. long; written in fair Nestalik in the 17th century.

لطائف الاخبار

Account of the siege of Kandahār by Dārā Shikūh. See the Persian Catalogue, p. 264b, and Ethé, Bodleian Catalogue, nos. 238-9.

Beg. حمد بیحدی که ابواب فتح را بروی پادشاهان
تواند کشاد

The author, whose name does not appear in the work, was Badi' uz-Zamān Rashīd Khān, who died, as Divan of Shāh 'Ālam, upwards of eighty years old, in Agra, A.H. 1107. See Ta'rīkh i Muḥammadi, Or. 1824, fol. 234b, and Or. 1937, fol. 15b.

This copy wants about a page and a half at the end.

On the first page is a Waḳf, or pious donation, of the book by Mirza Mahdi B. Mirza 'Aṭā-ullah ul-Husaini, dated Muḥarram, A.H. 1109 (A.D. 1697). On the same page is an impression of the seal of General Carnac.

79.

Or. 3610.—Foll. 20; 16 in. by 11; 12 lines, 6¾ in. long; written in fair large Nestalik, with fourteen whole-page and two double-page miniatures, apparently in the 18th century.

Detached fragments of a historical work relating to the reigns of Bahādur Shāh and Jahāndār Shāh. Fol. 1 relates to the death of Bahādur Shāh, and begins as follows:
شهریار کشت و سه ماه در انجاه بغوی و خوربی کذرانیده
چون روز عمر شهریار شب کردید و نقد عمرش بصرف
آمده بود

The work appears to have been composed during the short reign of Jahāndar Shāh. It is written in rather florid prose interspersed with verses, and is very circumstantial, but quite destitute of dates. The subjects of the remaining fragments are as follows:

Foll. 2--3. Kāmbakhsh orders Mir Malang (Aḥsan Khān) and other Amirs to be executed. His defeat and death (A.H. 1120).

Foll. 4—8. Rising of the Sikhs under Banda. Expeditions of Vazir Khān and of Prince Mu'izz ud-Dīn against them (A.H. 1120).

Foll. 9—20. Victory of Mu'izz ud-Dīn Jahāndār Shāh over his brothers. His accession. Poetical description of his mistress La'l Kunwar and of his mad passion for her (A.H. 1124).

Bound up with this volume is a large sheet containing a deed of sale relating to a private house in Lucknow, dated 13 Zulḳa'dah, A.H. 1264 (A.D. 1848).

80.

Or. 3281.—Foll. 86; 8 in. by 4⅞; 15 lines, 3 in. long; written in small and close Nestalik, apparently in the 18th century.

History of the reign of Muḥammad Shāh down to the 14th year.

This is the anonymous work designated in some MSS. as صحیفهٔ اقبال, three copies of which have been described in the Persian Catalogue, viz. Or. 1900, p. 940a; Or. 1656, II., p. 1008a; and Or. 1747, VI., p. 1015b. Compare p. 1055b, VIII.

The present copy has two additional chapters at the beginning. The first begins قال النبی صلی الله علیه وعلی آله وصحبه وسلم ازوا الصالحة جزء من ستة اربعين جزء من النبوة رسمی است قديم وعادق مستديم. It relates to a vision seen by Bīgum Ṣāḥib, mother of Muḥammad Shāh, six days after his birth. The second is a record of that birth, which took place in

Ghaznīn on the eve of the 23rd of Rabī' I., A.H. 1114. The third section, which begins fol. 7b, is identical with the first section of Or. 1900. From that point the contents of both copies are in substantial agreement; but towards the end the present MS. gives in full Muhammad Shah's correspondence with the Persian court, much abridged in the other. It contains, moreover, the appendix (Tazyil) on the Indian seasons mentioned in the Persian Catalogue, p. 1008b.

On the fly-leaf is written: "For Captn. Scott with Mr. Polier's compts."

81-2.

Or. 4609 and 4608.—Two uniform volumes consisting respectively of foll. 140 and 283; 9 lines, 4½ in. long; written in cursive and straggling Indian Nestalik, about A.D. 1796. [G. Cecil Renouard.]

A collection of Akhbār, or news-letters, relating to daily occurrences at the Courts of Dehli, Lucknow, Rāmpur, and the camps of the Mahratta generals from the 18th of Safar, A.H. 1210, to the 23rd of Rajab in the same year (September, 1795—January, 1796).

The news-letters appear to have been received and compiled in Lucknow. Those which relate to the Court of the Vazīr ul-Mamālik Āṣaf ud-Daulah are dated on consecutive days. They are the most circumstantial and the latest in date. The others are from the Court of Dehli, from the camps of the Marattah generals, viz. Daulat Rāo Sindhya, Takoji Holkar, Kāshi Rāo Holkar, from the camp of Navvāb 'Ali Bahādur (the Oude general), and from the seat of Naṣr-ullah Khān of Rāmpūr.

Beg. اخبار دربار معلی واقعه بتاریخ هیجدهم صفر المظفر سنه ۱۲۱۰ هجری مقام شاه جهان آباد دیروز حضرت جهان پناه در مکان تسبیح خانه تشریف اوردند پس سید رضی خان آمده مجرا کرده عرضی میجر پالمر صاحب بهادر برای حضور اقدس و یك قطعه عرضی برای مرزا اکبر شاه بهادر گذرانیده

The first volume ends with the Akhbār of Āṣaf ud-Daulah on the 23rd of Rabī' I. The second volume, Or. 4608, begins with the Akhbār of the Dehli Court on the 26th of Rabī' I., and ends with a news-letter from the camp of Lakhwāji Paṇḍit, dated the 17th of Rajab, and imperfect at the end.

The MS. passed from Renouard's hands into the possession of Dr. John Lee, in whose catalogue it is noticed, p. 57, no. 174.

83.

Or. 4776.—Foll. 345; 12¼ in. by 6¾; 12 lines, 4 in. long; written in cursive Nestalik, apparently in India in the 19th century.

I. Foll. 1—56. مرآت الهند

Revenue tables of the Subahs of Hindostan, written in Siyāḳ, by Muḥammad Laṭīf, son of Muḥammad 'Ali B. Muḥammad Shāh, of Broach in Gujrāt.

Beg. الحمد لله رب العالمین والعاقبة للمتقین .... اما بعد میگوید محمد لطیف ولد محمد علی ابن محمد شاه از اولاد حضرت امیر المومنین ابو بکر ابن ابی قحافه رضی الله عنهما

The preface contains verses in praise of Abu 'l-Faẓl and of Shāh 'Ālam, a celebrated saint who died A.H. 880, and whose tomb in Aḥmadābād is an object of pilgrimage. The author appears to have been a devout worshipper of holy personages. Further on, under Ajmīr, he breaks out again into a panegyric on Mu'in ud-Dīn Chishti, a great saint buried in that city. The date of composition is not given, but a reference to Aurangzib, fol. 3b, shows that the work was written after his time. The tables, which begin, fol. 5a, with Gujrāt, end with Multan.

Another copy is mentioned by Rehatsek, Mulla Firuz Library, p. 102, no. 58.

II. Foll. 57—78. History of the kings of Gujrāt, extracted from the work entitled تاریخ ممالك هند, which was written A.H. 1196 by Ghulām Bāsiṭ. This chapter corresponds with foll. 94b—102a of the MS. Add. 27,250, described in the Persian Catalogue, p. 237. See for another copy Rehatsek, *ib.*, p. 76, no. 15.

III. Foll. 79—345. تذكرة الملوك

A general history of India, treating more especially of the 'Ādilshāhis of Bijapur, by Rafi' ud-Dīn Ibrāhim Shirāzi, who wrote about A.H. 1020. See the Persian Catalogue, p. 316, and Rehatsek, *ib.*, p. 73, no. 11, where the contents are described.

The portion of the work contained in the present MS. corresponds with foll. 46—206 of the complete copy previously described, Add. 23,883. It consists of chapters (Faṣl) 6—9, beginning with the kings of Gujrāt and ending with the Timurides, as described in the Persian Catalogue. But Faṣl 9 is not brought down further than the early part of Akbar's reign. The last section relates to the murder of his Vazir, Atakah Khān, which took place A.H. 970.

On the last leaf is the name of a former owner, John W. Watson.

84.

Or. 2692.—Foll. 393; $12\frac{1}{4}$ in. by $7\frac{3}{4}$; 24 lines, $4\frac{3}{4}$ in. long; written in neat Nestalik; dated (fol. 263b) 12 Sha'bān, A.H. 1258 (A.D. 1842). [E. B. Eastwick.]

I. Foll. 1—263. حديقة العالم

History of the Kuṭubshāhis and of the Niẓāms of Haidarabad, by Mīr Abu 'l-Kāsim, surnamed Mīr 'Ālam. See the Persian Catalogue, pp. 323—25.

Beg. نظام ملك مسخنوری و انتظام قلمرو معنی کستری وقف سالاری حمد شاهنشاهی که الخ

The contents agree with those of the edition lithographed in Haidarabad, A.H. 1266. The second Maḳālah begins at fol. 136a. This copy was written, as stated at the end, by Muhammad Vazir for Mir Muḥammad Ḥusain Mūsavi, whose seal dated 1249 is impressed on the first page.

The MS. was presented A.H. 1285, to whom is not stated, by the latter's daughter, Ḥusaini Begam.

II. Foll. 264—393. تحفة العالم

Account of Shushtar and of the author's travels in India, by 'Abd al-Laṭif B. Abu Ṭālib Shushtari. See the Persian Catalogue, pp. 383-4.

Beg. دلكش صفيرى كه عندليب دشتان سراى خامه پردازی

The work was composed A.H. 1216. An appendix added by the author, A.H. 1219, is written separately, foll. 389—393. At the end is a notice by Aḥmad 'Ali, stating that the author died in Haidarabad on the eve of Monday, the 6th of Zulka'dah, A.H. 1220; but some verses written by the same hand give for the same event the chronogram دريغا آه, *i.e.* 1221.

For other copies see Mulla Firuz Library, p. 69; Pertsch, Berlin Catalogue, no. 98; and Ethé, Bodleian Catalogue, no. 323.

85.

Or. 4688.—Foll. 222; 12 in. by $7\frac{1}{2}$; 17 lines, 5 in. long; written in neat Nestalik, with

'Unvān and ruled margins, apparently in the 19th century.

کوهر عالم تحفة للشاه

A history of Kashmir, by Badī' ud-Dīn Abu 'l-Ḳāsim Muḥammad Aslam, poetically surnamed Mun'imi, son of Maulavi Muḥ. A'ẓam Kūl, with the takhalluṣ Mustaghni.

Beg. فاتحه تواریخ ابدی و اختراع عالم سپاس بیقیاس جناب اقدس خالقی که الخ

The author mentions in his preface the following two works as his principal authorities: 1. The work of Khwājah Muḥ. A'ẓam Dīdahmari, son of Khair uz-Zamān Khān, entitled واقعات کشمیر, and brought down to A.H. 1160 (see the Persian Catalogue, p. 300), the author of which had somewhat curtailed his account of kings so as to devote more space to the lives of Sayyids, saints, and poets. 2. The Nūr Nāmah, a collection of the inspired utterances of the holy Shaikh Nūr ud-Dīn Valī, written down in the language of Kashmīr by one of his disciples, and afterwards translated into Persian, with the title of مرآت الاولیا, by Maulānā Aḥmad 'Allāmah, a panegyrist of Sultan Zain ul-'Ābidīn. In A.H. 1188 the author, having proceeded from Lucknow to Etāwa with the Vazir's army, met there a descendant of the Chak kings of Kashmīr, and obtained from him the autograph MS. of the above-mentioned translation, from which he extracted most of the contents of the first section of his work. For the thirty or forty years which had elapsed since the conclusion of the Vāḳi'āt, he relied on information obtained from trustworthy persons and on his own memory. This would bring the date of composition of the present work to A.H. 1190—1200.

Further on, fol. 6b, there is a full list of sources (given *in extenso* by Ethé, no. 320) which appears to have been bodily taken from the Vāḳi'āt i Kashmir (see the Persian Catalogue, p. 300b). The preface concludes with a dedication in prose and verse to Shāh 'Ālam, and with a table of chapters.

The title, which in the preface, fol. 9a, is given as above, appears in a somewhat different form, namely کوهر نامهٔ عالم, in the dedicatory verses, fol. 7b.

The work is divided into a Muḳaddimah, six Ṭabaḳahs, and a Khātimah, as follows: Muḳaddimah: Peculiarities of Kashmīr, its climate and noteworthy sites, fol. 9a. Ṭabaḳah I. Origins of Kashmīr, conflicting traditions of Muslims and Hindus, and ancient kings, in two Ḳisms, fol. 16b. The second Ḳism, beginning fol. 32a, treats of the Dā'ūdi line and the Pāndus. Ṭabaḳah II. Hindu Rajahs, fol. 54b. Ṭabaḳah III. Muslim kings, fol. 84a. Ṭabaḳah IV. Kings of the Chak line, fol. 132b. Ṭabaḳah V. Timurides, fol. 168.

The fifth Ṭabaḳah, which is the last extant, comes to an abrupt termination with A.H. 1150. The last event recorded is the struggle of the Nāib, Abu 'l-Barakāt Khān, with rebels headed by Mīr Muḥammad Ja'far, resulting in a battle fought by the contending parties on the 14th of Muḥarram, A.H. 1150. See the Vāḳi'āt i Kashmīr, Add. 26,282, fol. 285a, and Newall's abstract in the Journal of the Asiatic Society of Bengal, vol. xxiii., p. 413.

A copy described by Ethé, Bodleian Catalogue, no. 320, breaks off at the same point, which makes it probable that no more was written.

86.

Or. 2699.—Foll. 112; 10 in. by 6¼; 15 lines, 3½ in. long; written in cursive Nestalik; dated 12 Rabi' II., A.H. 1247 (A.D. 1831).

حشمت کشمیر

A history of Kashmir, with an account

of the neighbouring countries, by 'Abd ul-Ḳādir Khān B. Ḳāẓi 'l-Ḳuẓāt Maulavi Vāṣil 'Ali Khān.

Beg. بعد حمد خالق لطيف الخبير که جماعه انبیا و مرسلین را به تنزیل صحایف و کتاب و وحی و الهام خبردار فرموده

For an account of the author and his work see the Persian Catalogue, p. 1016, v. The history was completed, as stated at the end, at Benares, A.H. 1245, A.D. 1830. The main authority followed by the writer for the history of Kashmir is the work of Muḥammad Badi' ud-Din Abu 'l-Ḳāsim Aslam, poetically surnamed Mun'imi, son of Maulavi Muḥ. A'ẓam, surnamed Kūl (see the preceding MS.). It was written, he says, about the beginning of the reign of Āṣaf ud-Daulah under the title گوهر تحفه عالم شاهی.

The work is divided into four Chamans and a Khātimah, as follows: Chaman I. Account of Kashmir, fol. 6*b*, چمن اول در بیان حالت خاص ملك كشمير و جزوى عجايباتش و هندوستان كه جنوبش واقع است. Ancient history and Hindu Rājahs, fol. 6*b*. Muslim kings, fol. 29*a*. Ṣūbadārs under the Timurides down to the conquest by Aḥmad Shāh Durrāni, fol. 55*a*. Curiosities and wonders of Kashmir, fol. 72*b*. Its trade and manufactures, fol. 75*b*.

Chaman II. Description of Tibet and Ḳalmāḳistān, including an account of the religion of the Tibetans and of the painter Māni, fol. 81*a*.

Chaman III. Account of Badakhshān, fol. 90*a*.

Chaman IV. Description of the highlands of Afghanistan, namely, Pagli (?), Ghūr, Ghaznin, and Kūh i Sulaimān; with a brief history of the Afghans, fol. 93*b*.

Khātimah: A short review of the just rulers of India, concluding with a eulogy on the Company's rule, fol. 111*a*.

LOCAL HISTORIES.

87.

Or. 2777.—Foll. 199; 8¼ in. by 4¾; 13 lines, 2½ in. long; written in neat Nestalik, with a highly finished 'Unvān and colour-ruled margins, apparently in the 19th century.

[Comte de Gobineau.]

تاريخ بخارا

History of Bukhara, translated from the Arabic work of Abu Bakr Muḥammad B. Ja'far an-Narshakhi.

Beg. الحمد لله الذى بنعمته تتم الصالحات سپاس و ستايش خداى تعالى را جل جلاله كه آفريننده جهانست

The original author, an-Narshakhi, was born A.H. 286, and died A.H. 348 (see al-Sam'āni, fol. 558*a*). He wrote the history of Bukhara, A.H. 332, for the Sāmānī king, Amīr Ḥamīd Nūḥ B. Naṣr. The work was translated into Persian, A.H. 522, by Abu Naṣr Aḥmad B. Muḥ. B. Naṣr al-Ḳubāvi.

The present MS. contains an abridgment of the latter version made A.H. 574, for the Mufti of Bukhara, Tāj ul-Ma'āli 'Abd ul-'Azīz B. Ḥusām ud-Dīn 'Umar, by Muḥammad B. Zufar B. 'Umar.

This abridged version has been edited by M. Charles Schefer, Paris, 1892. A considerable portion of the work had been previously published by the same scholar in the first volume of his Chrestomathie Persane, pp. 9—55, ٣٥-١٣. A short extract was given by Lerch in the Transactions of the Congress of St. Petersburg, tom. ii., pp. 424—9. The contents have been described by Vambery, History of Bokhara, p. xii. For other copies see Morley's Catalogue, p. 151, and Khanykov, Mélanges Asiatiques, vol. ii., p. 437.

Contents: Preface of Muḥ. B. Zufar, fol. 1*b*. Ḳāẓis of Bukhara, fol. 3*a*. Extract from the

Khazā'in al-'Ulūm of 'Abd ur-Raḥmān B. Muḥ. an-Naishābūri (printed in the Chrestomathie Persane, vol. i., pp. 11—14), fol. 5*a*. The Khātūn, queen of Bukhara, fol. 8*b*. Description of Bukhara, its environs and public buildings (Chrestomathie Persane, pp. ٣٠—١٤), fol. 12*b*. Silver coinage of Bukhara (published by Lerch, *l.c.*, pp. 426—8), fol. 39*b*. Muslim conquest, fol. 42*a*. Division of Bukhara between the Arabs and Persians, fol. 48*b*. Rule of Ḳutaibah B. Muslim, fol. 50*b*. Origins of Āl i Sāmān, fol. 69*a*. Rise of Muḳanna', foll. 77*a*. History of the Sāmānis, fol. 91*b*. This last section is brought down by an-Narshakhi to the accession of Nūḥ B. Naṣr, A.H. 331, fol. 115*b*, and briefly continued by the translator to the death of Manṣūr B. Naṣr, A.H. 365.

The text is in close agreement with M. Schefer's edition, pp. 2—99.

88.

Or. 3391.—Foll. 138; 12½ in. by 7¼; 17 lines, 4 in. long; written in neat Nestalik, with 'Unvān and gold-ruled margins, apparently in the 15th century. [SIDNEY CHURCHILL.]

كتاب قم

A historical and topographical account of the city of Ḳum, written A.H. 378 by Ḥasan B. Muḥammad B. Ḥasan Ḳummi, and translated from Arabic, A.H. 825, by Ḥasan B. al-Ḥasan 'Abd ul-Malik al-Ḳummi.

The translator's preface begins: الحمد لله جاعل العلماء الجما للاهتداء زاهرة واعلاما للاقتداء طاهرة .... چنین کوید مفسر این کتاب ومأول این خطاب اصغر عباد الله جرما و اکثرهم جرما حسن بن الحسن عبد الملك القمی

The translation of the original work begins, fol. 2*b*, as follows: چنین کوید مولف این کتاب حسن بن محمد بن حسن قمی که حق سبحانه و تعالی ایام عمر مولانا صاحب الجلیل کافی الکفاة کشیده کرداناد

The work is dedicated to a mighty Vazīr, Ṣāḥib al-Jalīl Kāfi 'l-Kufāt, whose proper name does not appear. It was apparently Ibrāhīm B. 'Abbād, the famous Vazir of two successive sovereigns of the Buvaihi dynasty, viz. Mu'ayyad ud-Daulah and Fakhr ud-Daulah, who died A.H. 385. The latter prince is named in the preface as the reigning sovereign, and in other passages, foll. 5*b* and 9*a*, mention is made of the Vazīr's father, Shaikh al-Amīn Abu 'l-Ḥasan 'Abbād B. 'Abbās, who is described as the Vazīr of Rukhn ud-Daulah, and is stated to have died A.H. 330. In the preface the author dwells at great length on the merits of his patron, and especially on the benefits conferred by him upon the city of Ḳum, on the magnificence with which he enriched its holy Sharīfs and its 'Ulamā, on the copious water-supply created by him, on the number of books placed by him at the disposal of students, and generally on his just and beneficent administration.

The author was induced to write this book by the fact that his brother, Abu 'l-Ḳāsim 'Ali B. Muḥ. B. al-Ḥasan al-Kātib, then governor of Ḳum, had searched in vain for a history of that city. He compiled it from a number of scattered notices and from oral tradition. Two of the historical chapters are brought down to A.H. 378, evidently the date of composition.

The work is divided into twenty Bābs, subdivided into sections (فصول) amounting altogether to fifty. Of these Bābs only the first five are extant in the MS. The headings of all the twenty Bābs, given at the end of the preface, foll. 9 and 10, are too long to be quoted in full. The heading of Bab I. begins as follows: باب اول در ذکر قم و سبب نام نهادن قم بدین نام بعد از نام نهادن او بفارسی

و ذکر قدیم امر قم و حدیث آن و صورت فتح ناحیت آن و انتهاء حدود آن و مسافت اقطار آن و ذکر طول و عرض و برج طالع ان و عدد راهها و دروازها و میدانها و مساجد و حمامات ان و سبب جدا کردن از اصفهان و وقت شهر ساختن آن و آنچه در بقعه و خطه قم داخل است و بدان تعلق دارد از ضیاعها و نامهاء آن و ذکر باروی کهنه و نو آن و ذکر اول مسجدی که بقم بنا نهادند و منبر دران منصب کردند تا انگاه که مسجد جامع بدان بنا نهادند و منبر بدان نقل کردند الخ

Briefly stated, the contents of the twenty Bābs are as follows: I. Name and origin of Ḳum; its topography and principal buildings, fol. 10*b*. II. Surveys of the land; tribute and taxation, fol. 54*b*. III. Descendants of Abu Ṭālib, fol. 101*b*. IV. Arab settlers of the family of Malik B. 'Āmir Ash'ari, fol. 113*a*. (After fol. 112 there is a lacuna, without any apparent break in the text, so that the end of Bāb III. and the beginning of Bāb IV. are wanting.) V. The Ash'aris after their conversion to Islām, foll. 123—138. (This Bāb concludes in the present MS. with an account of the taking of Sūs by Abu Mūsa al-Ash'ari.) VI. Genealogy of the Arabs of the race of Ḳaḥṭān. VII. Arabs who held sway in Ḳum. VIII. Celebrated battles of the Arabs. IX. Arabs and Persians who ruled in Ḳum, and some renowned secretaries of the Divān. X. Introduction of Islām and notice of some celebrated Persians. XI. Chronicle of the governors of Ḳum from A.H. 89—378. XII. Ḳāẓis of Ḳum. XIII. General chronicle of the Khalifs from the time of Muḥammad to A.H. 378. XIV. Estates belonging to the Sultan. XV. Estates belonging to Ḳum and to private persons. XVI. 'Ulamā. XVII. Men of letters. XVIII. Poets. XIX. Jews and Magians. XX. Peculiarities of Ḳum and miscellaneous historical notices.

The Persian translation was made A.H. 825 by desire of a personage whose name is preceded by a string of almost royal titles, Khājah Fakhr ud-Dīn Ibrāhīm B. 'Imād ud-Dīn Maḥmūd B. Shams ud-Dīn Muḥ. B. 'Ali Ṣafi: الخواجه فخر الحق والدنیا والدولة والدین ابراهیم بن الصاحب الاعظم الخواجه عماد الدولة والدین محمود بن الخواجه شمس الدولة والدین محمد بن علی صفی خلد الله تعالی ظلال عواطفه, who was probably governor of Ḳum or Kashan under Shāhrukh.

On the first page is a circular illuminated border enclosing a title which has been obliterated. Above is written: تاریخ دار المومنین قم الحسین بن علی بن حسن

89.

Or. 3587.—Foll. 179; 8¾ in. by 5; 19 lines, 3 in. long; written in small and neat Nestalik; dated 1 Jumada II., A.H. 835 (A.D. 1432). [Sidney Churchill.]

تاریخ بیهق

A History of the district of Baihaḳ, by Abu 'l-Ḥasan 'Ali B. Shams ul-Islām Abu 'l-Ḳāsim Zaid B. Shaikh ul-Islām Abu Sulaimān Amīrak Muḥammad, &c., al-Baihaḳi.

Beg. سپاس خدایرا که دلایل واضحه و براهین راجحه بر عزت و وحدانیت او امانت کواهی بحق و صدق می کذارند . . . وبعد چنین کوید ابو الحسن علی بن الامام شمس الاسلام ابی القسم زید بن شیخ الاسلام جمال القضاة و الخطبا ابی سلیمان امیرك محمد بن الامام المفتی فخر القضاة ابی علی الحسین الخ

The author belonged to the ancient family of the Ḥākimis, which had given eminent divines and Kadis to Baihaḳ. In the preface he traces up his pedigree to Ḥuzaimah B. Thābit, one of the Companions of the Prophet, and from him upwards to Shem, son of Noah. He completed this work on the fifth of Shavvāl, A.H. 563, in the village of Shashtamad.

He occasionally refers to two works previously written by him in Arabic, namely, لباب الانساب والقاب الاعقاب, treating of the genealogy of the descendants of the Prophet, and مشارب التجارب وغوارب الغرائب, being a continuation of Ta'rikh i Yamīnī. An extract from the latter, relating to Sulṭān Shāh of Khwārazm, and quoted by Ibn ul-Aṣīr in his Kāmil, vol. ix., p. 249, is brought down to A.H. 595. He wrote also a continuation of the Dumyat ul-Ḳaṣr of al-Bākharzi, entitled وشاح الدمية (Ibn Khallikān, De Slane's version, vol. ii., p. 323, and Haj. Khal., vol. iii., p. 238, vi., pp. 442, 510).

The two works which he mentions as his principal authorities are the Ta'rikh Naishābūr, in twelve volumes, by al-Ḥākim Abu 'Abdallah Muḥ. B. 'Abdallah (d. A.H. 405), and Ta'rikh Baihaḳ, by 'Ali B. Abi Ṣāliḥ al-Khuwāri.

In a long preface the author laments the decline of sciences in his day, especially of those which are the special glory of the Arabs, namely, Hadith, genealogy, and proverbs; after which he dilates on the charm and importance of a study of history. The work is rather a collection of biographical notices than a history proper. The contents are as follows:

Preface, fol. 1*b*. Principal countries of the world, fol. 11*a*. Standard works of history, fol. 11*b*. Histories of towns, fol. 13*a*. Eminent peculiarities of Baihaḳ, fol. 13*b*. "Companions" who came to Baihaḳ, fol. 15*a*. Muslim conquest, A.H. 30, fol. 15*a*. Climate, fol. 15*b*. Things in which various countries excel, fol. 17*a*. Plagues peculiar to each country, fol. 17*b*. Capitals of various countries, fol. 18*b*. Dependence of climate on the elements, fol. 19*a*. Etymology of Baihaḳ, its limits, and its division into twelve districts, called ربع, fol. 19*b*. Foundation of Sabzavār, and memorable events which took place there from the time of Bahman B. Isfandiyār to A.H. 455, fol. 22*a*. Ancient families of Baihaḳ, in the following order: Sayyids, fol. 30*b*; Ṭāhiris, fol. 37*a*; Sāmānis, fol. 38*a*; Maḥmūdis, fol. 39*b*; Saljūḳs, fol. 40*a*; Niẓām ul-Mulk and his descendants, fol. 41*a*; Muhallabis, fol. 47*b*; Fūlādvand and his descendants, who were the hereditary Ra'is of Baihaḳ, fol. 52*b*; Ḥākimis, the author's family, fol. 57*b*; the Baihaḳis, fol. 61*b*; Mukhtāris, fol. 65*a*; Mīkālis, fol. 67*b*; and a few more families, the last being that of Muḥ. B. Ibrāhīm Ibn Simjūr, fol. 77*a*. Notices of 'Ulamā, Imāms, and other eminent men who were born in Baihaḳ, or dwelt there, fol. 79*a*. Memorable events in Baihaḳ, from the incursion of Ḥamzah Āẓarak, A.H. 213, to the author's time, fol. 156*a*. Remarkable things peculiar to Baihaḳ, fol. 162*a*. Siege of Sabzavār by Mu'ayyid ud-Daulah Malik ul-Mashriḳ, A.H. 561-2, foll. 166*a*.

This last chapter breaks off, foll. 166*b*, without any visible gap in the text, and is immediately followed by some moral precepts and anecdotes, which conclude the work.

The MS. was apparently transcribed from a copy which was defective at the end.

The latter part of the volume, foll. 171—9, contains three additional pieces written by several hands, namely:

1. Fatḥ Nāmah, or bulletin addressed to Muḥ. Ṣūfi Tarkhān at Herat on a victory gained over Iskandar at Sulṭāniyyah.

2. Notices of Aḥmad B. al-Ḥusain al-Baihaḳi and of al-Farrā, in Arabic, from the Muhimmāt of al-Isnawi.

3. Nasab Nāmah i Mīkāliyyah, or genealogy of the Mīkāli family, by Naṣīr ud-Din Ṭūsi; copy dated A.H. 896.

The Ta'rikh i Baihaḳ is mentioned by Haj. Khal., vol. ii., p. 122. A MS. described by Pertsch, Berlin Catalogue, no. 535, has the same title as ours, but a different beginning.

90.

Or. 2887.—Foll. 93; 9 in. by 5½; 12 lines, 3½ in. long; written in fair large Nestalik, with neat 'Unvān and gold-ruled margins; dated 15 Zulhijjah, A.H. 1286 (A.D. 1870). [Sidney Churchill.]

عقد العلى للموقف الاعلى

A history of the conquest of Kirman by the Ghuzz chieftain, Malik Dīnār, A.H. 581—3; by Afẓal ud-Dīn Aḥmad B. Ḥāmid Kirmāni.

Beg. تعالى الله خالق كل شىٔ وجل الله رازق كل حى قادر خدائى و لطيف رهنمائى كه كلهٔ ازرق و رواق معلق را وراء نواظر بينندكان حجاب عالم غيب كردانيد . . .

چنين كويد مطرز اين اوراق و مبرز اين اعلاق امام عالم تاج الزمان سلطان الافاضل علامة الزمان افضل الملة والدين احمد بن حامد

Afẓal ud-Dīn Kirmâni is chiefly known as the author of the standard history of the Saljūḳs of Kirmān, entitled بدائع الازمان فى وقائع كرمان. See Houtsma, Recueil des textes relatifs à l'histoire des Seljoucides, vol. i., p. xi., pp. ٣٥—١, and Zeitschrift der D. Morg. Ges., Band 39, p. 365. That work is also the main authority of the Simṭ ul-'Ula for the early history of Kirman. See the Persian Catalogue, p. 849*b*.

The present work was composed in Ṣafar, A.H. 584 (see fol. 42*b*), for presentation to Malik Dīnār, as a record of his glorious victories. It is divided into five parts (Ḳism) as follows:

I. Decline of the Saljūḳ dynasty of Kirman, and disturbances which followed the reign of Tughrul Shāh (A.H. 551—565), fol. 6*a*.

II. Invasion and conquest of Kirman by Malik Dīnār, and his eminent qualities (containing a full account of his campaign, from his entering upon the Kirman territory at Arīz, near Kūbinān, on the 22nd of Ramazan, A.H. 581, to the taking of Burdashir in Rajab, A.H. 583, and the complete establishment of his rule), fol. 15*a*.

III. Exhortation to justice and kingly virtues, fol. 44*a*. Early history of Kirman and description of the land and of its principal cities, namely, Jīrāft, Barm, Narmāshīr, Burdashīr, and Sīrjān, fol. 58*b*.

IV. Eulogy on the Vazir Ḳivām ud-Dīn Mas'ūd B. Niẓām ud-Dīn Kaikhusrau, and on his forefathers, fol. 67*b*.

V. Life of the author, fol. 82*b*. Owing to the disturbed state of the country and to a famine which occurred in the Kharāj year 570, the author left Burdashir, intending to repair to the court of Ṭughān Shāh in Khorasan, but did not go further than Kūbinān,[1] where he was induced to stay by the Amīr Mujāhid ud-Dīn, and remained five years. From thence he was taken most unwillingly to Yezd, where the king put him in charge of the hospital, and wished to retain him also as his Munshi. By some artifice, however, he managed to escape from that compulsory service. Having returned to Kūbinān on the 5th of Muḥarram, A.H. 584, he entered at once on the composition of the present work, designed as a suitable offering to the new sovereign of Kirman.

The work is written in florid prose, freely interspersed with Arabic and Persian verses. For an account of the reign of Malik Dīnār, who died A.H. 591, see Houtsma, Zeitschrift, vol. 39, pp. 392—95.

Baron von Rosen gave, in the Zapiski of the Archaeological Society, vol. ii., pp. 182—84, some extracts of the present work, partly

[1] Often written كوبنان in the MS. Yāḳūt, vol. iv., p. 316, spells the name كوبيان.

from a MS., partly from an edition lithographed at Teheran, A.H. 1293.

At the end of our MS. is a colophon transcribed from an earlier copy and dated Rabī' I., A.H. 649.

91.

Or. 3584.—Foll. 97; 6 in. by 3¾; 12 lines, 2¼ in. long; written in small Neskhi, with gold-ruled margins; dated A.H. 1276 (A.D. 1859-60).

[Presented by Sir Fred. Goldsmid.]

The same work. The five Ḳisms begin respectively at foll. *5b*, *15a*, *45b*, *70a*, and *85b*. Like the preceding MS. and the Teheran edition, this copy concludes with a colophon dated Rabī' I., A.H. 649.

In a Persian note written on the first page, the writer states that he had borrowed the MS. from the owner, Col. (now General Sir Fred.) Goldsmid, then passing through Kirman, on his way from Teheran to Karāchi, in Sha'bān, A.H. 1282, and had afterwards returned it to him *viâ* Bombay.

92.

Or. 2778.—Foll. 219; 9 in. by 5½; 15 lines, 3¼ in. long; written in fair Nestalik; dated Sha'bān, A.H. 1273 (A.D. 1857).

[Comte de Gobineau.]

تاریخ طبرستان

History of Tabaristan, written about A.H. 613, by Muḥammad B. Ḥasan B. Isfandiyār, and brought down by an anonymous continuator to A.H. 750.

Beg. حمد و ثنا و مدح بی منتها آفریدگار را سزاست که واهب ارواح و خالق اشباح است .... اما بعد چنین گوید احقر عباد الله محمد بن حسن بن اسفندیار که در سنهٔ ست وستماه الهلالیه

This copy agrees substantially with Add. 7633, the contents of which have been described in the Persian Catalogue, pp. 202—4. Like that MS., it wants Ḳism III., the heading of which as given in the preface is: در نقل ملك طبرستان از آل وشمکیر که آخر ایشان نوشروان بن منوچهر بن قابوس بود با سلاطین محمودیان و سلجوقیان

The other sections begin as follows: Ḳism I., Bāb 1, fol. *6b*. Bāb 2, fol. *32b*. Bāb 3, fol. *45a*. Bāb 4, fol. *53a*. Ḳism II., fol. *83a*. Ḳism IV., fol. *186b*.

For the contents of the Oxford MS. see Ethé, no. 307. The work of Ibn Isfandiyār is frequently quoted by Comte de Gobineau in his Histoire des Perses; see vol. i., p. 263, &c.

93.

Or. 2862.—Foll. 171; 9½ in. by 5½; 21 lines, 3¾ in. long; written in small and neat Nestalik; dated 4 Jumāda II., A.H. 1014 (A.D. 1605).

[Sidney Churchill.]

تاریخ طبرستان

History of Tabaristan, from the earliest time to A.H. 881, by Sayyid Ẓahīr ud-Dīn B. Sayyid Naṣir ud-Dīn Mar'ashi.

Beg. حمد بیحد و قیاس مالك الملکی را که ذات پاکش بصفت دوام و قدم موسوم و موصوفست

This is the work edited by Dorn in the first volume of his "Muhammedanische Quellen zur Geschichte der südlichen Küstenländer des Kaspischen Meeres," St. Petersburg, 1850. A full account of the author's life will be found in the preface, pp. 9—22. For a description of the two MSS., both later than the present one, on which that edition is based, see the preface, pp. 25—28, and the Vienna Catalogue, no. 971. Another work of Ẓahīr ud-

Dīn, a history of Gīlān, is brought down to A.H. 894. See Ethé, Bodleian Catalogue, no. 309.

The present MS. has in its early portion marginal notes in the hand of Riẓa Ḳuli Khān (Lālah Bāshi), and two lost quires of the original MS. have been supplied by the same hand, namely, foll. 2—8, corresponding with the printed text from p. 3, line 4, to p. 21, line 8; and foll. 53—59, corresponding with p. 167, line 13, to p. 186, line 3.

Copyist: محمد رضا بن محمد علی

94.

Or. 4106.—Foll. 399; 9¼ in. by 6¼; 5 lines, 3⅜ in. long; written in fair Nestalik, with 'Unvān and headings alternately red, blue, and gold; dated Rabī' I., A.H. 933 (A.D. 1526). [Sidney Churchill.]

روضات الجنات فی اوصاف الهراة

A history of Herat, from early times to the beginning of the reign of Abu 'l-Ghāzi Sulṭān Ḥusain, with an introduction on the topography of the province, compiled A.H. 897 (fol. 14a) by Mu'īn az-Zamjī al-Asfizārī (fol. 16a). See the Persian Catalogue, p. 206; Ethé, Bodleian Catalogue, no. 310; and Rehatsek, Molla Firuz Library, p. 94.

This important historical work has become chiefly known by copious extracts published by Barbier de Meynard in the Journal Asiatique, 5e Série, vol. xvi., pp. 461—520, xvii., pp. 438—522, and xx., pp. 268—319. The present copy is earlier, more correct, and more complete than the MS. described in the Persian Catalogue. It has only a short lacuna at the end of Rauẓah XXIII. and beginning of Rauẓah XXIV.

The twenty-six Rauẓahs into which the work is divided begin as follows: I. fol. 20b; II. fol. 29a; III. fol. 32b; IV. fol. 39a; V. fol. 59a; VI. fol. 143b; VII. fol. 150a; VIII. fol. 201b; IX. fol. 217a; X. fol. 224a; XI. fol. 225b; XII. fol. 240b; XIII. fol. 250a; XIV. fol. 258b; XV. fol. 272a; XVI. fol. 280b; XVII. fol. 299a; XVIII. fol. 320a; XIX. fol. 326a; XX. fol. 331a; XXI. fol. 358b; XXII. fol. 364b; XXIII. fol. 371a; XXIV. fol. 381b; XXV. fol. 388b; XXVI. fol. 396b. The last two Rauẓahs are wrongly designated in the MS. as the 24th and 25th.

Copyist: زین الدین علی بن شیخ احمد بن قطب الدین

95.

Or. 4836.—Foll. 266; 13½ in. by 8½; 17 lines, 5½ in. long; written by several hands on blue-tinted paper in Nestalik, probably early in the 19th century.

شرف نامه

The well-known history of the Kurds, by Amīr Sharaf ud-Dīn B. Shams ud-Dīn Bitlīsi. See the Persian Catalogue, p. 208b.

This copy has lost the first page and begins, after the last line of the doxology, as follows: اما بعد بر هوشمندان صاحب خبرت پوشیده نماناد که علم تاریخ متضمن فواید بسیار است

This is the shorter recension of the preface. It has been given by Veliaminof-Zernof in the appendix to the second volume of his edition, pp. 2—5.

Contents: Muḳaddimah. Origin of the Kurds, fol. 3a. Ṣaḥīfah I., in five Faṣls, viz.: 1. Jazīrah and Diyārbakr, fol. 5b. 2. Dīnavar and Shahrazūl, ib. 3. Fazlavaihs, or Lūr i Buzurg, fol. 6b. 4. Lūr i Kūchak, fol. 9b. 5. Āl i Ayyūb, fol. 17b. Ṣaḥīfah II., in five Faṣls, viz.: Ardalān, fol. 28b. 2. Hakkāris, fol. 31a. 3. 'Imādiyyah, fol. 32a. 4. Jazīrah, fol. 35b. 5. Ḥiṣn Kaif, fol. 49a.

Ṣaḥīfah III., comprising three Firḳahs, as follows: Firḳah I., in nine Faṣls, viz.: 1. Chimishkazaks, fol. 53a. 2. Mirdāsi, fol. 58a. 3. Ṣāṣūn, fol. 63b. 4. Khizān, fol. 69b. 5. Killīs, fol. 73b. 6. Shīravān, fol. 77a. 7. Zarnḳi, fol. 80a. 8. Suvaidis, fol. 85b. 9. Sulaimānis, fol. 89b. Firḳah II., in ten Faṣls (three of these, numbered 7—9, are wanting in this copy as in all known MSS.), viz.: 1. Suhrān, fol. 94a. 2. Bābāns, fol. 97b. 3. Makri, fol. 101a. 4. Barādūst, fol. 103b. 5. Maḥmūdis, fol. 105a. Dunbulis, fol. 108a. 10. Galhurs, fol. 110b. After this comes an unnumbered section, fol. 111b, relating to the Galbāghi Amīrs, and corresponding with the text given in Veliaminof's Appendix to vol. ii., pp. 36—45. Firḳah III. Kurds of Iran in four Shuʿbahs, fol. 113b.

Ṣaḥīfah IV. Amirs of Bitlis, in a Fātiḥah, fol. 118a, and four Saṭars beginning respectively at foll. 126a, 128a, 130a, and 143a. The fourth Saṭar breaks off, fol. 148a, at a passage corresponding with p. 414, line 15, of the first volume of Veliaminof's edition.

After this, and without any apparent break in the text, comes the latter part of the Khātimah, or history of the Osmanlis, beginning in the middle of A.H. 987, and corresponding with pp. 258—308 of the second volume of Petersburg edition.

The first part of the same Khātimah, imperfect at the beginning and corresponding with pp. 8—258 of the same volume, occupies the remaining portion of the MS., foll. 169a—265b. At the beginning of the MS. there is a table of contents in the Syriac character.

A French translation of the whole work, with a copious introduction and notes, was published in St. Petersburg, 1868—75, by F. B. Charmoy. Two Turkish versions have been described in the Turkish Catalogue, pp. 70—72. For other MSS. of the text see the prefaces of Veliaminof, pp. 16—19; and of Charmoy, p. 4; and Ethé, Bodleian Catalogue, nos. 312—14.

96.

Or. 4900.—Foll. 358; 11¾ in. by 7½; 19 lines, 4 in. long; written in fair Nestalik; dated Rabīʿ I., A.H. 1251 (A.D. 1835).

[Sir Henry Rawlinson.]

Another copy of the preceding work.

This MS. has the longer preface beginning
اما بعد بر ضمیر منیر اکسیر تاثیر ناظمان درر بلاغت
as in the Petersburg edition, and its contents agree closely with Veliaminof's text.

The principal sections begin as follows: Ṣaḥīfah I., fol. 10a. Ṣaḥīfah II., fol. 41a. Ṣaḥīfah III.: Firḳah I., fol. 81a. Firḳah II. comprising eight Faṣls, numbered 1—6 and 10-11, viz., 1. Suhrān, fol. 133a. 2. Bābāns, fol. 136b. 3. Makri, fol. 140b. 4. Barādūst, fol. 144b. 5. Maḥmūdis, fol. 147a. Dunbulis, fol. 151b. 10. Galhurs, fol. 155a. 11. Bānah, fol. 157a. Firḳah III., fol. 158a. Ṣaḥīfah IV., fol. 163b. Fātiḥah, fol. 164a. Saṭar 1, fol. 275a. Saṭar 2, fol. 177a. Saṭar 3, fol. 179b. Saṭar 4, in four Vajhs beginning respectively at foll. 194a, 196b, 199b, and 210a (about a page at the beginning of Vajh 2 is wanting). Ẕail, fol. 215a. Khātimah, foll. 220b—358b.

97.

Or. 2779; 9¾ in. by 5½; 19 lines, 3½ in. long; written in small, close, and cursive Nestalik, apparently in the 17th century.

[Comte de Gobineau.]

احياء الملوك

A history of Sistān from the earliest times to A.H. 1028, by Shāh Ḥusain B. Malik Ghiyūṣ ud-Dīn Muḥammad, of the Ṣaffāri line.

Beg. كلكونهٔ رخساره هنر و زيب عارض نسخ معتبر سپاس خداونديست كه فرع انسانرا در ظاهر بخلعت لقد خلقنا الانسان فى احسن تقويم مخلع فرموده

The author belonged to the princely family of Sīstān, which was represented in his time by Malik Jalāl ud-Dīn Maḥmūd Khān B. Malik Jalāl ud-Dīn Muḥammad. In his account of the genealogy of that prince, which he carries up through sixteen generations to 'Amr B. Laith of the Saffāri dynasty, fol. 9a, the author gives his own pedigree as follows: Shāh Ḥusain B. Malik Ghiyāṣ ud-Dīn Muḥammad B. Shāh Maḥmūd B. Shah Abu Sa'id, this last being the ancestor in the fifth generation of the above reigning prince.

In the preface the author mentions a history of the kings of Sistān, written in Arabic by Abu 'Abdullah in the reign of Shāh Ḳuṭb ud-Dīn B. Shāh 'Ali, and translated into Persian by Abu Muḥammad. A later extensive history, compiled by a maternal grandsire of the author, Amir Muḥammad B. Amir Mubāriz, in the reign of Malik Niẓām ud-Dīn Yaḥya, was no longer extant. The author wrote the greater part of the present work in A.H. 1027, and finished it in 1028. The latest date mentioned is the 25th of Shavvāl of the latter year, when the author was in Isfahan in the suite of Shāh 'Abbās. He refers incidentally to another work of his, a Tazkirah entitled خير البيان (Or. 3397).

The work is divided into a Muḳaddimah, three parts called Faṣl, and a Khātimah, as follows:

Muḳaddimah, treating of the founder of Sīstān (Garshāsf), of its scholars, traditionists and poets, of its peculiarities, of its names, its revenue, and the genealogy of its kings, fol. 2b: مقدمه در بيان آنكه بانى بلدهٔ سيستان و بادى ابادى آنمملكت كيست و اسامى اهل فضل و دانش و راويان حديث و اخبار شعراى نامدار و خصوصيات ولايت نيمروز از عجايب و غرايب و ذكر اسامى ان بلده و وجه تسميه بهر اسم و حاصل آنملك و ذكر نسب ملوك ولايت مذكور

Faṣl I. Rulers of Sīstān from Garshāsf to the introduction of Islām and Arab governors, fol. 10a.

Faṣl II. Descendants of Kisra, who settled in Sistan after the Muslim conquest, down to Ya'ḳūb B. Laiṣ and Khalaf B. Aḥmad. The history is subsequently brought down to Malik Tāj ud-Dīn Abu 'l-Faẓl, the first who assumed the regal title, and, in a further continuation to Malik Ḳuṭb ud-Dīn Muḥammad, fol. 25a. (This Malik Ḳuṭb ud-Dīn was appointed by Timūr, A.H. 805, as successor of his father, Shāhshāhān Shāh 'Ali, in the government of Sīstān.)

Faṣl III. From the time of Malik Ḳuṭb ud-Dīn Muḥammad to the date of composition, fol. 48a.

Khātimah. Career of the author, his travels, and the wars in which he took part, foll. 188b—216b (beginning with the author's presentation to Shāh 'Abbās in Ḳazvīn, A.H. 1027).

The Iḥyā ul-Mulūk is one of the authorities quoted by Riẓā Ḳuli Khān in his Nijād Nāmah, no. 42, foll. 7b, 76b.

A Persian note on the first page states that the MS. was acquired by Comte de Gobineau in Teheran, A.H. 1273 (A.D. 1856-7).

98.

Or. 4901.—Foll. 126; 8¼ in. by 6; 14 lines, 4⅛ in. long; written in fair Nestalik; dated Friday, 16 Sha'bān, A.H. 1255 (A.D. 1839).
[Sir Henry Rawlinson.]

تذكرهٔ شوشتريه

A history of the city and province of Shushtar, by Sayyid 'Abdullah B. Ni'mat-ullah Shūshtari. See the Persian Catalogue, p. 214*b*.

Sir H. Rawlinson wrote on the fly-leaf: "Copied for me at Baghdad from a MS. of Col. Taylor's [Add. 23,534], Oct. 20, 1839."

99.

Or. 3603.—Foll. 200; 8¾ in. by 6¾; 17 lines, 4¼ in. long; written in neat Neskhi; dated Dār ul-Khilāfah (Teheran), Sunday, 9 Rajab, A.H. 1304 (A.D. 1887).
[Sidney Churchill.]

مرآت القاسان

A geographical and historical account of Kashan, by Mirza 'Abd ur-Raḥīm B. Muḥ. Ibrāhīm al-Ḳāsāni, poetically surnamed Suhail.

Beg. بر لوح ضمير ارباب بينش و آلينهٔ صافى
خاطر خداوندان دانش پوشيده و پنهان نباشد

The author belonged to the Ẓarrābi branch of the ancient Dunbuli family, to the history of which he devotes an extensive section of the present work, foll. 131—152. He was a descendant in the fourth generation of Mirza Ḥāji Riẓā'i, a brother of the celebrated Malik ush-Shu'arā Fatḥ 'Ali Khān. He wrote the present work in answer to a questionary drawn up by the Parsee Mānakji, and sent by order of Shāh Nāṣir ud-Dīn to the governors of the various provinces of Iran. Jalāl ud-Dīn Mirza Iḥtishām ul-Mulk, who was then governor of Kashan, entrusted the task of drawing up the answers to Mirza 'Abd ur-Raḥīm on the 9th of Rabi' II., A.H. 1287. The latter spent nine months on the work, which was finished in Muḥarram, A.H. 1288, at the time when the prince was suddenly recalled to Teheran.

The questionary, the arrangement of which is here followed, consisted of six Bābs, each of which contained nine questions. Some of the questions, having no application to Kashan, received only negative answers.

Contents: The author's introduction on the state of the country of Ḳum and Kashan at the time of the Arab conquest, fol. 11*b*.

Bāb I. Ancient and modern names of Kashan and its founder, fol. 13*a*. Its limits, fol. 14*b*. Mountains and rivers, fol. 27*b*. Torrents, springs and aqueducts (ḳanāt), fol. 40*a*. Jungles and deserts, fol. 52*b*. Climate, fol. 54*a*.

Bāb II. Castles, towns, agriculture and population, fol. 56*a*. Gardens, fol. 82*a*. Pasture-grounds, fol. 86*b*. Snow, rain, hail, &c., fol. 87*a*. Plagues and locusts, *ib.* Earthquakes, famines and floods, fol. 90*a*. Wars and revolutions, from the Afghan invasion to the present time, fol. 91*a*. Endemic diseases, fol. 94*a*.

Bāb III. Animals, trees, vegetables, cereals, edible roots, minerals, handicrafts, trade and taxes, fol. 94*b*.

Bāb IV. The principal merchants, fol. 99*a*. Bodily features, stature and longevity of the inhabitants, fol. 101*a*. Their disposition and manners, creed, costume, &c., fol. 101*b*. Marriage laws and condition of women, fol. 105*a*. Wealth, measures and weights, fol. 114*a*. Ancient families and celebrated scholars, divines and officials, fol. 115*a*.

Bāb V. Governors from the time of Nādir to the date of writing, fol. 162*b*. Longitude and latitude, fol. 163*b*. Distances and routes to the frontiers of Persia, fol. 165*a*. Amount of cultivated land, revenue, and police, fol. 166*a*.

Bāb VI. Public buildings and places of pilgrimage, fol. 167*b*. Travellers, and accommodation supplied for them, fol. 168*a*. The author answers this last question in a mystic sense, describing at length the stations of wayfarers on the road to spiritual truth.

Khātimah. Eulogy on the governor Jalāl ud-Dīn Mirza; rewards promised by him to the author; and Kasidah composed by the latter in his praise, foll. 195—200.

Copyist: علی الطالقانی

The following pieces are prefixed to the work:

1. Two notices relating to the present copy, by the author and by Zain ul-'Ābidīn ul-Ghaffāri, in Shikastah, foll. 1, 2.

2. A table of contents in Neskhi, fol. 3.

3. A notice of the work, written at the request of Mr. Churchill, by the author, who here styles himself: عبد الرحیمخان کلانتر مستشار دیوان محاکمات اداره جلیله نظمیه و زمینیه ایران المتخلص بسهیل دنبلی المأخذ کاشانی الوطن طهرانی المسکن

It is written in Shikastah and dated Saturday, 3 Sha'bān, A.H. 1304, foll. 7—10.

BIOGRAPHY.

100.

Or. 4658.—Foll. 284; 9½ in. by 6¼; 21 lines, 4 in. long; written in fair small Nestalik; with ruled margins; dated 12 Rabi' I., A.H. 1088 (A.D. 1677).

I. Foll. 2—128. تاریخ حکماء سلف

History of ancient and modern philosophers, translated from the Arabic work of Shams ud-Din Muḥammad Shahrazūri by Maḳṣūd 'Ali Tabrīzi.

Beg. ای حکیم علی الاطلاق و ای دانای باستحقاق تا از خودی خود بر نیایم چگونه بلبل زبان را بمدح تو سرایم

The proper title of the original work is نزهة الارواح وروضة الافراح فی تواریخ الحکماء المتقدمین والمتاخرین. It was written by Shams ud-Din Muḥammad B. Maḥmūd ash-Shahrazūri about A.H. 600, and consists of two parts treating respectively of the ancient and Muslim philosophers. A MS. of the first part is described in the Leyden Catalogue, no. 1488. A complete copy is noticed by Sachau, Chronologie Orientalischer Völker, p. ل.

The translator says in his preface that, the work having been brought to the notice of the sovereign, only designated as السلطان بن السلطان بن السلطان (evidently Shāh 'Abbās I.), he received his Majesty's commands to translate it into Persian, A.H. 1011.

Contents: Introduction treating of the value of philosophy, of the ancient Greeks (Yūnān), and of their philosophers, fol. 3*a*. Notices of the ancient sages as follows: Adam and Seth, fol. 12*b*; Hermes, fol. 13*a*; Ṭaṭ, fol. 21*a*; Æsculapius, fol. 22*a*; Empedocles, fol. 23*a*; Pythagoras, fol. 24*b*; Socrates, fol. 33*a*; Plato, fol. 50*b*; Aristotle, fol. 56*a*; Theophrastus, fol. 62*b*; Eudemus, fol. 63*a*; Democritus, Hippocrates, Cebes, Aristippus, fol. 63*b*; Plutarchus, Suidas, Alexander Aphrodisiensis, Euthamtius(?) and Ibn Iskandar, Shaikh Yūnāni, fol. 64; Zaradusht, fol. 65*a*; Diogenes Cynicus, fol. 65*b*; Hippocrates, fol. 69*a*; Homerus, fol. 71*b*; Thales, fol. 72*a*; Solon, fol. 74*b*;

Zeno, fol. 76*b*; Iskandar Zulḳarnain, fol. 78*a*; Ptolemæus, fol. 88*a*; Basilius, fol. 90*a*; Luḳmān, fol. 90*b*; Galenus, fol. 98*a*.

The second part devoted to Muslim philosophers begins, fol. 104*a*, with Ḥunain B. Isḥāḳ, Isḥāḳ B. Ḥunain, Ḥunain Ṭabīb, Thābit B. Ḳurrah, Muḥ. B. Zakariyyā Rāzi, &c. The notices are too numerous and too short to be fully enumerated. The last and longest is that of Ibn Sīnā, which begins at fol. 126*b* and breaks off at fol. 128*b*.

II. Foll. 129—278. An extensive collection of anecdotes and historical narratives, imperfect at beginning and end.

It begins with the latter part of an anecdote relating to Abu Naṣr Fārābi as musician. The next paragraph begins: الاعجوبه آورده اند که در سنه خمس و سبعین و ثلثمایه در ایام طالع مرغی از دریای عمان برآمده بزرکتر از فیل

The anecdotes follow a rather loose chronological order. They relate successively to the Ghaznavis, Buvaihis, Saljūḳs, Khwārazmshāhs, Atābeks, Moghols, Īlkānis, Muẓaffaris, Sarbadārs, Timurides down to Sulṭān Ḥusain, and Ḳara-Ḳuyunlus. The extracts begin mostly with such headings as ومن النوادر, or من البدایع, or من الغرایب. Authorities frequently quoted are the following: جامع بی بی صاحب, وصایا نظام الملك, مجمع النوادر, الحکایات, مراة الجنان یافعی, تاریخ کزیده, تاریخ سلاجقه روم ظفرنامه. The latest works quoted are Rauẓat uṣ-Ṣafā and Ḥabīb us-Siyar.

III. Foll. 279—284. A fragment of the Laṭā'if uṭ-Ṭavā'if, by 'Ali B. Ḥusain Kāshifi. See the Persian Catalogue, p. 757*b*.

The fragment consists of the main part of Bāb XIII. and of the whole of Bāb XIV., corresponding with foll. 144—158 of Add. 18,408. For other copies see the Leyden Catalogue, no. 2748; Pertsch, Berlin Catalogue, no. 1013; Ethé, Bodleian Catalogue, no. 454; and Mulla Firuz Library, p. 230.

101.

Or. 4107.—Foll. 157; 9½ in. by 5½; about 21 lines, 3½ in. long; written by several hands in cursive Nestalik, apparently in the 17th century. [SIDNEY CHURCHILL.]

آثار الوزراء

Lives of celebrated Vazirs by Saif ud-Dīn Ḥāji B. Niẓām al-'Aḳīli, dedicated to the Vazir Khwājah Ḳivām ud-Dīn Niẓām ul-Mulk al-Khwāfī. See the Persian Catalogue, p. 969*b*, and Ethé, Bodleian Catalogue, no. 347.

Beg. شرایف تحمیدات حضرت پادشاهی را که در ایجاد کاینات بشریك و وزیر محتاج نکشت

The work is divided into two Maḳālahs, the first of which contains notices of past Vazirs chronologically arranged in twelve Bābs, under the following heads: The first four Khalifs, fol. 5*a*. Ancient kings of Persia (beginning with Pythagoras, Vazir of Gushtāsp, and ending with Buzurjmihr, Vazir of Anushirvan), fol. 5*b*. Umayyades, fol. 10*b*. Abbasides, fol. 14*a*. Āl i Sāmān, fol. 71*a*. Ghaznavis, fol. 72*a*. Āl i Buvaih, fol. 93*a*. Āl i Saljūḳ, fol. 95*b*. Khwārazmshāhs, fol. 121*a*. Chingīzkhān and descendants, fol. 123*a*. Āl i Muẓaffar and Mulūk i Ghūr, fol. 132*b*. Tīmūr and his descendants down to Abu Sa'īd, fol. 134*a*.

Maḳālah II., devoted to the author's patron, is divided into four Bābs, namely, 1. Character and superior merits of Ḳivām ud-Dīn Niẓām ul-Mulk, fol. 141*b*. 2. His career previous to his appointment as Vazir on the 26th of Jumāda II., A.H. 875, fol. 144*b*.

3. His Vazirship (chiefly taken up by his ordinances, which are given *in extenso*), fol. 146*a*.

This third Bāb breaks off at fol. 150*b*. Bāb 4, which was to commemorate the favours bestowed on the Vazir by the sovereign, is wanting.

The date of composition is given, fol. 141*a*, as A.H. 803, سنه ثلث وثمانمايه, evidently by mistake for A.H. 883. The Vazir Ḳivām ud-Dīn was deposed A.H. 892.

Foll. 151—154 contain a portion of a Sufi work on Tauḥīd, the scope of which is stated as follows: غرض ما ذکر کلمهٔ چند است بر توحید بر مشرب صوفیه

The fragment consists of the latter part of the preface and of the first three Faṣls, the last of which is imperfect.

Fol. 156 and two folios at the beginning are detached leaves of a chronicle of the reign of 'Ālamgīr (Aurangzīb), relating to the sixth and seventh years, in Indian Shikastah. Two other leaves at the beginning are a fragment of an Insha.

Lives of Sufis.

102.

Or. 3522.—Foll. 290; 9¾ in. by 5¾; 17 lines, 3½ inches long; written in fair Nestalik, with 'Unvān and gold-ruled margins, after A.H. 1272 (A.D. 1856). [Sidney Churchill.]

ضیاء العارفین

Lives and sayings of the great theosophists ('Urafā) of the first four centuries of Islam, by Faẓl ullah.

Beg. حمد نا محدود و سپاس نا معدود کردگار ودودی را شایسته است که از عین عنایت جمیع موجوداترا از عالم ارواح بواسطهٔ اشباح بجلوهٔ ظهور و شهود رسانید

The author says in the preface that he wrote the present work shortly after his arrival from Irak at Shīrāz, A.H. 1272. He names Nāṣir ud-Dīn Shāh as the present sovereign, and praises as his special patron the governor of Fārs, Mīr Ṭahmāsp B. Daulat Shāh B. Fatḥ 'Ali Shāh. He mentions also his own father, Shaikh ul-Mulūk, حضرت شیخ الملوك که این حقیر را پدر و خداوند والا گهر است, whom he describes as the object of the special favour of Daulat Shāh.

Contents: Preface, with table of chapters, fol. 2*b*. Muḳaddimah treating of Taḳiyyah (concealment of Shi'ah faith from motives of prudence) and of the means of arriving at a fair judgment and discrimination respecting the 'Ulamā and 'Urafā, مقدمه در تقیه و روات و علم تمییز عقلا و تشخیص علما و تحقیق عرفا, fol. 6*a*. Notices of ninety-six 'Urafā, in as many numbered Fuṣūl, alphabetically arranged according to the leading names, fol. 25*a*. The first five are Abu Ẕarr Ghaffāri, banished from Medina by Osman, fol. 25*a*; Uvais Ḳarani, who died A.H. 36, fol. 25*b*; Ibrāhīm B. Dā'ūd Raḳḳi, who died A.H. 326, fol. 31*a*; Aḥmad B. Muḥammad Maghribi, who died A.H. 397, fol. 32*a*; and Abu 'l-'Abbās Muḥammad B. Isḥāḳ, fol. 33*b*.

Khātimah: Discussion of the views of some modern divines for or against Sufis, with extensive extracts from their writings, fol. 228*a*. The writers chiefly quoted are Mulla Aḥmad Ardabili, the alleged author of Ḥadīḳat ush-Shī'ah (d. A.H. 993), Mulla Bāḳir Majlisi (d. A.H. 1110), Muḥammad Ḥasan Kāshāni, and Shahīd i Ṣāni (Zain ud-Dīn B. Nūr ud-Dīn 'Ali al-'Āmili, who was put to death A.H. 966). The Khātimah concludes with an alphabetical list of Sufi writers known to the author, fol. 279, and with a tract of al-Ḥāj Zain ul-'Ābidīn, called Mirza Kūchak Nā'ib uṣ-Ṣadr, on the division of Muslim sciences, and in glorification of 'Ali, foll. 287—290.

On the first page there is a former owner's note, dated A.H. 1296.

Tazkirahs, or Lives of Poets.

103.

Or. 3490.—Foll. 121; 9½ in. by 5¾; 17 lines, 3½ in. long; written in small and neat Nestalik; dated end of Shavvāl, A.H. 976 (A.D. 1569). [Sidney Churchill.]

تحفهٔ سامی

Notices of contemporary poets, by Sām Mirza, son of Shāh Ismā'īl Ṣafavi.

Beg. لله الحمد قبل كل كلام بصفات الجلال والاكرام
. . . سر غزل ديوان فصاحت بيان قافيه سنجان معجز طراز

This valuable copy, written in the author's lifetime, agrees substantially with the MSS. described in the Persian Catalogue, p. 367. The following table shows the beginning of the various divisions of the work and the name of the first poet noticed in each: Ṣaḥīfah I., Shāh Ismā'īl, fol. 3*b*. Ṣaḥīfah II., Ṣafḥah 1, Mīr 'Abd ul-Bāḳi, fol. 13*b*. Ṣafḥah 2, Ḳāẓi Mīr Ḥusain, fol. 28*b*. Ṣaḥīfah III., Mirza Shāh Ḥusain Iṣfahāni, fol. 33*a*. Ṣaḥīfah IV., Khwājah Shihāb ud-Dīn 'Abdullah Bayāni, fol. 37*a*. Ẕail. Maulānā Shāh Maḥmūd, fol. 47*a*. Ṣaḥīfah V., Maṭla' 1, Maulānā Jāmi, fol. 50*a*. Maṭla' 2, Maulānā Sharaf Muḥ. Ṣabri, fol. 84*a*. Ṣaḥīfah VI., Amīr Niẓām ud-Dīn 'Alishir, fol. 106*a*. Ṣaḥīfah VII., Aḥmadi, fol. 115*a*.

The first page has been supplied by a modern hand.

Two copies are described by Pertsch in the Berlin Catalogue, no. 643.

104.

Or. 3396.—Foll. 101; 7½ in. by 4¼; 13 lines, 2⅝ in. long; written in fair Nestalik, apparently in the 17th century. [Sidney Churchill.]

مجالس النفايس

The Taẕkirah of Mīr 'Ali Shīr, translated from Turki into Persian by Shāh 'Ali B. 'Abd ul-'Ali.

Beg. بعد از حمد معبود و درود نبي عاقبت محمود نموده می آيد كه فصيحترين زبانی كه ازان شاعران حكمت شعار بلطايف كفتار آيند

For the original work, see the Turkish Catalogue, p. 273, and, for another translation, the Persian Catalogue, p. 366.

In a short preface the translator says that, Persian being preferred, both in speaking and in writing, by men of letters, the less polished Turki language was generally neglected, especially under the present ruler, Sultan Dīn Muḥammad. Complying, therefore, with the desire of some friends, he had turned into Persian the Taẕkirat ush-Shu'arā of Mīr 'Ali Shīr.

Dīn Muḥammad, son of Jāni Beg and of a sister of 'Abdullah Khān Uzbek, ruled over part of Khorasan during the reigns of 'Abdullah and 'Abd ul-Mūmin Khān. After the death of the latter, A.H. 1006, he was proclaimed Khān in Herat, but soon after he was defeated by Shāh 'Abbās, and died during his flight. See Mir'āt ul-'Ālam, fol. 170*a*, and Howorth, History of the Mongols, part ii., p. 739.

The MS. contains only seven of the eight Majlis into which the work is divided. They begin respectively as follows: I. Ḳāsim i Anvār, &c., fol. 3. II. Sharaf ud-Dīn Yazdi, &c., fol. 15. III. Nūr ud-Dīn Jāmi, &c., fol. 39. IV. Pahlavān Muḥ., &c., fol. 65.

V. Amīr Daulatshāh, &c., fol. 86. VI. Aḥmad Ḥāji Beg, &c., fol. 91. VII. Amīr Tīmūr, &c., fol. 98. This last Majlis breaks off in the middle of the sixth notice, that of Ulugh Beg.

105.

Or. 3506.—Foll. 567; 10¼ in. by 7¼; 26 lines, 4¾ in. long; written in small neat Nestalik, apparently in the 16th century, with the exception of some leaves supplied by a modern hand. [Sidney Cnurchill.]

خلاصة الاشعار و زبدة الافكار

A portion of the extensive Taẕkirah so called by Taḳi ud-Dīn Muḥammad B. Sharaf ud-Dīn 'Ali al-Ḥusaini al-Kāshāni.

The work has been described by Bland, Journal of the Royal Asiatic Society, vol. ix., pp. 126—134, and by Sprenger, Oude Catalogue, pp. 13—46. An abridgment is noticed by Pertsch, Berlin Catalogue, no. 647, and a MS. of the third Rukn is described, without author's name, in the Petersburg Catalogue, no. 321.

The present MS. contains only a small portion of that voluminous anthology, namely, the introductory chapters and the first volume (Mujallad) of the first of the four Rukns, or main divisions of the work.

The first folio, supplied by a modern hand, has the following beginning, differing from that which is given by Sprenger and by Pertsch : حمد و سپاس بار خدائی را جلت عظمته روا و سزاست که عقل را قوة اطلاع بر حقیقت او نیست

The next folio contains, in a fair imitation of the original old writing, a eulogy on the reigning sovereign, Shāh Ṭahmāsp, also noticed by Bland, p. 127, which must have have been written before A.H. 984. It is followed by a later dedication to Shāh 'Abbās, at the end of which the author says that the work was completed at the beginning of A.H. 996 : در اوائل سنهٔ ست وتسعین و تسعمائه که این نسخه فی الجمله صورت اتمام یافته

Fol. 3, the first of the original MS., contains the end of the preface and a full statement of the division and contents of the whole work.

Contents of the present MS.: Muḳaddimah, treating of the need of anthologies and of the reasons for writing this work, fol. 4a. Four chapters (Fuṣūl), beginning respectively at foll. 5a, 7b, 8b, and 16b, treating of Love (see Bland, p. 128), and concluding with Arabic verses by 'Ali B. 'Abi Ṭālib, accompanied by a Persian paraphrase, fol. 19b. Lāḥiḳah, or appendix, on poetry in general, and on the first beginnings of Persian poetry, fol. 28a.

Rukn I., containing in its first part (Mujallad) notices of early poets who lived under Āl i Subuktigin, or Ghaznavis, with very copious extracts from their compositions, occupies the main part of the present volume, foll. 30—559. The notices are arranged in the order indicated in the preface, fol. 3a, differing from that which Sprenger follows. They relate to the following twenty-two poets: 'Unṣuri, fol. 30b. Minuchihri, fol. 53b. Farrukhi, fol. 59a. Asadi, fol. 67b. Nāṣir Khusrau, fol. 73a. Ḳaṭarān, fol. 102b. Abu 'l-Faraj Rūni, fol. 135b. Mas'ūd B. Sa'd B. Salmān, fol. 152b. Azraḳi, fol. 198b. Adīb Ṣābir, fol. 216b. Amir Mu'izzi, fol. 236b. 'Am'aḳ Bukhāri, fol. 279b. Sanā'i, fol. 285b. Mukhtari, fol. 325a. Lāmi' i Jurjāni, fol. 351a. Sūzani, fol. 361a. 'Abd ul-Vāsi' Jabali, fol. 396a. Ḥasan Ghaznavi, fol. 427b. 'Imādi Shahriyāri, fol. 449b. Rashīd Vaṭvāṭ, fol. 468b. Falaki Shirvāni, fol. 500a. Anvari, fol. 512a. The last notice breaks off in the course of the poetical extracts, fol. 559b.

A notice on Khākāni, which, according to the preface, was to begin the second Mujallad of Rukn I., has been appended by a modern hand, foll. 560—564.

The Tazkirah of Mīr Muḥ. Taḳi Kāshāni is one of the authorities mentioned by the author of the Majma' ul-Fuṣaḥā in his preface.

106.

Or. 3389.—Foll. 208; 12 in. by 8¼; 25 lines, 6 in. long; written in Indian Nestalik leaning to Shikastah-āmiz; apparently early in the 17th century. [SIDNEY CHURCHILL.]

بزم آرای

A Tazkirah of ancient and modern Persian poets, by Sayyid 'Ali B. Maḥmūd al-Ḥusaini.

Beg. شکر و سپاس و ستایش بیقیاس و حمد بیحد و ثنای بیعد مر قادر حکیم و صانع قدیم را که لباس هستی در سر موجودات بالا و پستی افکند

The author praises in the preface Jalāl ud-Dīn Akbar as the reigning sovereign, and dedicates the work to his special patron, the Khānkhānān ('Abd ur-Raḥīm B. Bairām Khān; see the Persian Catalogue, p. 244*a*). The date of composition, A.H. 1000, is given at the end, fol. 208*a*, as follows: اتمام و اختتام این مجموعه که مسمی بتذکرة الشعراست وقتی اتفاق افتاد که تاریخ هجری بهزار رسیده بود

It is fully confirmed by internal evidence; for 'Urfi, who died A.H. 999, is spoken of as dead, while Faiẓi, who died A.H. 1004, is referred to as still living. The notices are mere rhetorical displays, almost bare of biographical detail and wholly destitute of dates.

The work is stated in the preface to consist of a Muḳaddimah, seven chapters (Fuṣūl) and a Khātimah; but the Muḳaddimah does not appear in the text. The contents are as follows: Preface, in which the author mentions only two previous Persian Tazkirahs, namely those of Daulatshāh and of Sām Mīrzā, fol. 6*b*. Faṣl I. on the excellence of poetry, fol. 7*b*. Faṣl II. on the meaning of the word شعر, fol. 8*b*. Faṣl III. on the first attempts at metrical speech, *ib*. Faṣl IV. on the first who made Persian verses, fol. 9*a*. Faṣl V., Notices of the kings who composed verses, beginning with the Sāmānis, and ending with Malik Ikhtiyār ud-Dīn Shaibāni, a contemporary of Sultan Sinjar, fol. 9*b*. Faṣl VI., Notices of Vazirs, Ṣudūr, and other great men who indulged in poetry, beginning with Abu 'l-Ḳāsim Aḥmad B. al-Ḥasan Maimandi, and ending with Shaikh Abu Sa'īd Abu 'l-Khair, fol. 16*b*. Faṣl VII., Notices of poets from the time of the Sāmānis and Sultan Maḥmūd, fol. 46*b*. This section, which forms the main bulk of the volume, is arranged in a loose chronological order. It begins with Abu 'l-Ḥasan B. Shahīd al-Balkhi, Abu 'Abdallah B. Muḥ. Rūdagi, Kisā'i Marvazi, 'Unṣuri, Farrukhi, 'Asjadi, Azhari, Abu 'l-Fatḥ Busti, Asadi Ṭūsi, Firdausi, &c., and ends with Ḳāsim Junābadi, who lived under Shāh Ṭahmāsp.

Khātimah. Notices of Sultans, Amirs, men of letters and poets, who lived in the time of Akbar, some of whom were personally known to the author, beginning with Khānkhānān Muḥ. Bairam Khān (father of the author's patron), Sultan Ibrāhīm B. Bahrām Ṣafavi, Khān Aḥmad of Gīlān, &c., and ending with Ramzi Iṣfahāni, Davā'i Sabzavāri, and Rū'i Sāvaji.

A full table of the notices included, in a modern hand, fills seven pages at the beginning.

107.

Or. 3537.—Foll. 380; 15¼ in. by 8½; 31 lines, 5¼ in. long, with additional slanting lines in the margins; written for the most part in four columns in small Nestalik, by Zain ul-'Âbidîn B. 'Ali Hamadâni for the Shâhzâdah Ṭahmâsp Mirza, and dated (fol. 337b) 5 Sha'-bân, A.H. 1227 (A.D. 1812); but embodying some leaves of an earlier MS., written apparently in the 17th century.

[Sidney Churchill.]

میخانه

A Tazkirah of Persian poets, by Hasan B. Luṭf-ullah Ṭihrâni Râzi.

This work is quite distinct from the "Maikhânah u Butkhânah" of Mulla Ṣûfi Mâzandarâni, mentioned by Bland, Journal of the Royal Asiatic Society, vol. ix., p. 165 (see also the Oude Catalogue, p. 88; Ethé, no. 366; and Majma' ul-Fuṣaḥâ, vol. ii., p. 38).

The preface, which has been misplaced, fol. 92b, begins: زیب فهرست صحایف کاینات و زیور عنوان صفایح موجودات ستایش و سپاس بارگاه کبریای خداوندیست

The author states that he wrote this work by desire of his noble patron Ḥasan Beg,[1] who, being fond of poetry, had collected a great number of rare Divans, and that his friend, Sayyid Amîr Muḥ. Ḥusain Tafrishi, prefixed to it a Dîbâjah, or laudatory prologue. He adds that his father, Khwâjah Luṭf-ullah, having been appointed Vazir of Khorasan by Shâh Ṭahmâsp, proceeded to Herat A.H. 968, he being then a boy of tender age, and that after his father's death, A.H. 981, he succeeded to the same office. The preface is imperfect at the end, but the date of composition is found in a passage of the table of contents in which the author says that his account of the Ṣafavi dynasty was to be brought down to the present year, namely A.H. 1040 (fol. 49b, margin). Earlier dates found at the end of some sections—namely, A.H. 1018, fol. 119a; A.H. 1025, fol. 150b; A.H. 1029, fol. 83a; and A.H. 1030, fol. 57a—show that the author had been for many years engaged in his compilation.

According to a first table of contents, fol. 4b, the Maikhânah is divided into a Fâtiḥah, four Maḳâlahs, twenty-eight letters of the alphabet (i.e. notices in alphabetical order), and a Khâtimah. The Fâtiḥah contains Arabic poems classed under four heads, namely: Faṣl 1, 'Ali B. Abi Ṭâlib. Faṣl 2, Saints and Imams. Faṣl 3, Panegyrists of the Prophet and of the holy family. Ḥâshiyah, Other poets.

Of the Persian portion there is a fuller table further on, foll. 47—49. It consists of three Maḳâlahs, of the alphabetical series of notices, and of a Khâtimah, as follows: Maḳâlah I., with this heading: مقالهٔ اول و علم افراشتن بنان بیان سلاطین فصیح زبان عدالت نشان و ملوك نامدار ممالك مدار. It treats of kings endowed with literary talent, beginning with Amîr Falak ud-Dîn Ibrâhîm Sâmâni, and ending with Ḳaidû Khân B. Ḳâshîn B. Okotâi Ḳâ'ân. Maḳâlah II. Saints and great Shaikhs, from Sulṭân Abu Yazîd Basṭâmi to Khwâjah Bahâ ud-Dîn Naḳshaband. Maḳâlah III. Celebrated Vazirs, beginning with Abu 'l-Ḳâsim Aḥmad B. al-Ḥusain and ending with Amîr Abu 'l-Fâtiḥ 'Abd ul-Karîm.

Alphabetically arranged notices, a full list of which is given, beginning with Abu 'Abdallah Muḥ. ar-Rûdagi as-Samarḳandi and ending with Khwâjah Yûsuf Jâmi.

[1] Ḥasan Beg Shâmlu, Beglerbegi of Khorasan, A.H. 1027—1050. See the Persian Catalogue, pp. 682a, 1091a.

The Khātimah, comprising two sections called 'Iḳd, the first of which treats of poetesses, the second of the author's life.

The present copy, however, is very far from fulfilling the expectation raised by the above programme. Several sections are altogether omitted, while others are sadly curtailed, and the original order of the notices, partly owing to misplaced folios, is completely disturbed. The actual contents are as follows:

1. Prologue (the Dībājah above mentioned), fol. 2*b*. It begins with a Rubā'i, the first line of which is:

ای کری مسجد و خرابات از تو

The prose text begins: الهی بنای شنای ذات اقدس و ادای سپاس

The first table of contents, فهرست هذا الکتاب که موسوم است بجنخانه, fol. 4*b*.

2. The Arabic section, without any division, fol. 6*b*. It begins with this line:

الحمد لله العلی الاجلل ثم الصلوة علی محمد الافضل

The poems are written for the most part consecutively, without any break or heading. The following author's names are added in the margins: al-Farazdaḳ, Abu 'l-'Alā, Abu 'ṭ-Ṭayyib (al-Mutanabbi), Abu Tammām. The margins are full of glosses. In the latter part there are a few headings to poems of Ibn al-Fāriḍ, to the Burdah of al-Būṣiri, and to pieces by Abu 'l-Fatḥ al-Busti and by 'Amid ud-Dīn As'ad B. Naṣr ash-Shīrāzi.

3. Table of contents of the Persian section, fol. 47*a*.

4. Maḳālah I. Origins of Persian poetry and notices of kings, namely, Ibrāhīm B. Nūḥ Sāmāni, Abu Manṣūr B. Nūḥ, Maḥmūd B. Subuktigīn, Abu Muḥ. B. Sultan Maḥmūd, Malik Shāh B. Alp Arslān, and Sinjar B. Malik Shāh (breaking off before the end), fol. 49*b*.

5. Notices of Persian poets, foll. 51*b*—380. They fall far short of the number exhibited in the table of contents, foll. 47—49, and the original alphabetical order is frequently inverted. They consist mainly, and in several instances exclusively, of poetical extracts. The latter are often of considerable extent. Those taken from the Divan of Mu'izzi, for instance, fill no fewer than 67 folios, 261—327. The earliest Tazkirahs, those of 'Aufi and of 'Arūẓi Samarḳandi, are occasionally quoted.

The extant notices relate to the following poets: Abu 'Abdallah Muḥ. Rūdagi, fol. 51*b*. Abu Salīk Gurgāni, Abu 'l-Ḥasan Shahīd Balkhi, fol. 53*b*. Abu Sarāḳah 'Abd ur-Raḥmān B. Aḥmad Balkhi, called Amīn Najjār; Abu 'l-Faraj Rūni, panegyrist of Amīr Abu 'Ali Sīmjūr (died A.H. 466), fol. 54*a*. Abu 'l-Faraj Sistāni; Abu Hanīfah Askāni; Abu 'l-Fatḥ Busti; Abu 'l-Muḥaḳḳiḳ Bukhāri, Abu 'l-Muayyad Balkhi, fol. 58*a*. Amīr Abu Muḥ. B. Yamīn ud-Daulah Sulṭān Maḥmūd; Amīr Abu Muẓaffar Ṭāhir B. al-Faẓl al-Jafāni; Saif ud-Daulah Abu 'l-Ḥasan 'Ali B. 'Abdullah Jafāni; Abu 'l-Ḳāsim Aḥmad B. Aḥmad al-Maimandi; Shāh 'Ali Abu Rajā Ghaznavi, fol. 58*b*. Abu 'l-Ḳāsim Firdausi, fol. 59*a*. Abu Yazīd Basṭāmi, fol. 60*a*. Mirza 'l-Mulk Mashriḳi, fol. 60*b*. Ashraf al-Aṣamm Kūshāni, fol. 61*a*. Sharaf ud-Dīn Faẓl-ullah Ḳazvīni, fol. 62*b*. Asadi Ṭūsi (with extracts from the Garshāsp Nāmah), fol. 63*a*. Aṣīr ud-Dīn Akhsikati, fol. 70*a*. Aṣīr ud-Dīn Aumāni, fol. 78*a*. Imāmi Haravi, fol. 84*a*. Azraḳi Haravi, fol. 91*a*. Shaikh Āẕari, fol. 94*a*. Auḥad ud-Dīn Anvari, fol. 96*a*. Auḥad ud-Dīn Māmarghi, fol. 99*a*. Abshār Marghuzi, fol. 106*a*. Ibn Khaṭīb Fūshangi, fol. 107*a*. Badīhi, fol. 107*b*. Sayyid Ḥasan Ashrafi Samarḳandi, fol. 108*a*. Pūr Bahā Jāmi, fol. 110*a*. Auḥad ud-Dīn Gurgānji, fol. 111*a*. Shihāb ud-Dīn Aḥmad Ashrafi, fol. 112*a*.

Bahā ud-Dīn Marghināni, fol. 114*a*. Bahā ud-Dīn Zanjāni, fol. 114*b*. Burhani, fol. 115*a*. Bahā ud-Dīn Muḥ. B. Khwājah Shams ud-Dīn Ṣāḥib Dīvān, fol. 116*b*. Badr ud-Dīn Jājarmi, fol. 117*a*. Jamāl ud-Dīn Samarḳandi; Ja'fari Hamadāni, fol. 119*a*. Nāṣir Ja'fari, fol. 119*b*. Tāj ud-Dīn Ḥasan Ghaznavi, fol. 120*a*. Afẓal ud-Dīn Khāḳāni, fol. 128*b*. Amīr Khusrau Dihlavi, fol. 141*a*. Rafī' ud-Dīn Mas'ūd Lunbāni, fol. 148*a*. Rashīdi Samarḳandi, fol. 151*a*. Rūḥi Shāristāni, fol. 152*a*. Raẓi ud-Dīn al-Khashshāb Samarḳandi, fol. 153*a*. Zain ud-Dīn Sijzi, fol. 155*a*. Amir Zaini 'Alavi, fol. 156*a*. Razi ud-Dīn Naishāpūri, fol. 157*a*. Rashīd ud-Dīn Vaṭvāṭ, fol. 159*a* and fol. 195*a*. Rāfi'i Naishāpūri, fol. 160*a*. Viṣāl Shīrāzi, fol. 160*b*. Sanā'i Ghaznavi, fol. 161*a*. Sa'd ud-Dīn Sa'īd Haravi, fol. 182*a*. Sirāj ud-Dīn Sijistāni, fol. 183*a*. Saif ud-Dīn A'raj Isfarangi, fol. 189*a*. Sharaf ud-Dīn Shufurvah, fol. 190*a*. Shams ud-Dīn Khālid, fol. 192*a*. Shams ud-Dīn Sharafshāh, fol. 193*a*. Ṣā'in ud-Dīn Shīrāzi, fol. 194*a*. Ṣadr ud-Dīn 'Ali Fakhr Shūshtari, fol. 194*b*. Adīb Ṣābir, fol. 198*a*. Farīd ud-Dīn 'Aṭṭār, fol. 202*a*. 'Abd ul-Vāsi' Jabali, fol. 203*a*. 'Am'aḳ Bukhāri, fol. 204*a*. 'Uṣmān Mukhtāri, fol. 205*a*. Ḥamīd ud-Dīn 'Umar B. Maḥmūd Maḥmūdi Balkhi, fol. 213*a*. Ḥamīd ud-Dīn 'Ali B. 'Umar Maḥmūdi, fol. 213*b*. Ḥusām ud-Dīn Muḥ. Nakhshabi, fol. 214*a*. Ḥusām ud-Dīn Bukhāri, fol. 214*b*. Hasan Mutakallim, fol. 215*a*. Ḥasan Dihlavi, fol. 216*a*. Shihāb ud-Dīn Muayyad Nasafi, fol. 217*a*. Abu 'l-Ḳasim Firdausi, fol. 218*a*. Ḥakīm Ḳaṭarān, fol. 223*a*. Naṣir Adīb, fol. 229*a*. Kamāl ud-Dīn Ismā'īl, fol. 230*a*. Ḳādiri, fol. 238*a*. Minuchihri, fol. 239*a*. Mas'ūd i Sa'd i Salmān, fol. 240*a*. Mujīr Bailaḳāni, fol. 241*a*. Nāṣir i Khusrau 'Alavi, fol. 248*a*. Nūr ud-Dīn 'Abd ur-Raḥmān Rāzi, fol. 260*a*. Amīr Mu'izzi Samarḳandi, fol. 261*b*. Mu'īn ud-Dīn Shahristāni, fol. 328*a*. Naṣīr ud-Dīn Ṭūsi, fol. 329*a*. Niẓāmi, fol. 330*a*. Jauhari Zargar, fol. 333*a*. Jamāl ud-Dīn Ashhari, fol. 334*a*. Ibn Jājarmi, fol. 335*a*. Abu 'l-Ma'āli Naḥḥās Rāzi, fol. 335*b*. Pūr Ḥusan Isfarā'ini, fol. 336*b*. Sayyid Ḥasan Iṣfahāni Mijmar, fol. 337*b*. Ẓahīr ud-Dīn Fāriyābi, fol. 364*b*.

A list of the notices in the order in which they appear in the MS. has been written by a modern hand at the beginning, fol. 51*a*.

It may be noticed that in a note appended to a Kasidah of Jamāl ud-Dīn Samarḳandi, fol. 119*a*, and dated Lahore, A.H. 1018, the author designates his anthology by another title, viz. Kharābāt: حررهٔ صاحب این مجموعه که موسومست بخرابات

108.

Or. 3397.—Foll. 407; $10\frac{3}{4}$ in. by $6\frac{1}{2}$; 19 lines, $3\frac{1}{2}$ in. long; written in fair Nestalik; dated 20 Rabi' I., A.H. 1041 (A.D. 1631).

[Sidney Churchill.]

خیر البیان

A Tazkirah of Persian poets, ancient and modern, by Ḥusain B. Ghiyāṣ ud-Dīn Maḥmūd (the author of Iḥyā ul-Mulūk, no. 97).

Beg. شکر توفیق شکرگذاری حمد یکتائیست که تشنگان بادیهٔ اعتقاد را بسر چشمهٔ آب حیات معرفت رسانید

The author, having been often requested by his friends to compose a Tazkirah, determined, at the time of his setting out for Ḥijāz, to comply with their wish. The work was commenced, as stated at the end, A.H. 1017, and completed on his return from that journey in Ramaẓan, A.H. 1019. It was subsequently carefully revised and enlarged, A.H. 1035 (see fol. 304*a*), and received further additions A.H. 1036 (see fol. 130*a*).

In a highly florid and stilted preface the

author says that he was left fatherless in early life, and had attained his twentieth year when Malik ‘Āḳibat Maḥmūd, his protector, fell a victim of his own relatives and of foreign foes. He was himself imprisoned with his brothers, but escaped and joined the son of that prince, Jalāl ul-Islām wa’l-Muslimān, who, with the help of some valiant men of Nimrūz, succeeded in avenging the death of his father, but was compelled by the invasion of the Turkistānis into Khorasan to take refuge in the mountains, and ultimately to repair, accompanied by the author, to Kandahār. When, however, the ruler of Turan died, and Shāh ‘Abbās drove the enemy out of Herat and Khorasan, the author returned to his native land and paid homage to his Majesty, to whom the present work is dedicated. It appears from incidental passages in the Muḳaddimah that the author accompanied Shāh ‘Abbās in his campaign of Khorasan, A.H. 1008, and in other expeditions.

The work is divided into a Muḳaddimah, two Faṣls, and a Khātimah, as follows:—

Muḳaddimah. History of Muḥammad, of the twelve Imams, and of the Safavi dynasty down to A.H. 1033, fol. 9*b*.

Faṣl I. Notices and select poems of the great poets of the past, in loose chronological order; taken from Daulatshāh and Jāmi’s Baharistān, with many additions, fol. 41*b*. The order is nearly the same as in Daulatshāh. After a few Arab poets we find Rūdagi, Ghaḍā’iri, Asadi Ṭūsi, Abu ’l-Faraj Sijzi, Minuchihri Shast Gallah, Pindār Rāzi, ‘Unṣuri, ‘Asjadi, Mas‘ūd B. Sa‘d, Firdausi, Farrukhi, Mu‘izzi, &c. The last notice, which is that of Najib ud-Dīn Jurfādaḳāni, is followed, fol. 127*b*, by the names of a few poets, Kisā’i and others, of whom the author knew nothing but a few verses.

Appendix, added A.H. 1036, consisting of select verses with the bare names of the authors, extracted from two Jangs, or anthologies, sent from India to the prince of Sistan, fol. 130*a*. Additional notices relating to Mas‘ūd B. Sa‘d, Sūzani, Azraḳi, &c., fol. 141*a*. Notices of great Ṣufis, Bāyazid Basṭāmi, Abu Sa‘īd Abu ’l-Khair, ‘Abdullah Anṣāri, Najm ud-Dīn Kubra, and others, fol. 190*b*. Continuation of notices of poets, beginning with ‘Iṣmat Bukhāri and ending with Jāmi, fol. 204*a*. This portion was completed in Jumāda I., A.H. 1018.

Faṣl II. Notices of modern poets, with a preface beginning عقده کشای رشتهٔ سخن و مرسله بند نائره قلم نعت جلال اولیست, and divided into four Aṣls as follows:

Aṣl 1. Poets who lived from the end of the reign of Sulṭān Ḥusain to the end of the reign of Shāh Ismā‘īl Ṣafavi, fol. 216*a*. They are Bābā Fighāni, Ahli Shīrāzi, Naṣibi, Hātifi, Maktabi Shīrāzi, Hilāli, Binā’i, Umīdi, Ḥāli, Lisāni, Shahīdi, Sharīf Tabrīzi, Mushfiḳi Baghdādi, Idrāki Hamadāni, Ahli Khurāsāni, Ẓamīri Hamadāni, Ḳāẓi ‘Īsa, Ḳāẓi Yaḥya Lāhiji.

Aṣl 2. Poets who lived from the accession of Shah Ṭahmāsp to the middle of his reign, fol. 224*b*. They are Ẓamīri Iṣfahāni, Fuẓūli Baghdādi, Sharaf Jahān Ḳazvīni, Ḳāsim Junābadi, Shaikhzādah Lāhiji, Ghazāli Mashhadi, &c.

Aṣl 3. Poets who lived from the middle of the reign of Shah Ṭahmāsp to the rise of Shah ‘Abbās, fol. 236*b*. They are Vali Dashtbayāẓi, Ḥusain Ṣanā’i, Maili Mashhadi, Muḥtasham Kāshi, Nūr ud-Dīn Iṣfahāni, Ḥisābi Naṭanzi, Tīmūr Munshi Farāhi, &c.

Aṣl 4. Poets who lived from the birth of Shāh ‘Abbās to the date of composition, with a preface beginning انعام بردوام و اکرام مالا کلام که از پیشگاه قادر مطلق و کریم بر حق, fol. 279*b*. They are ‘Urfi Shīrāzi, Faiẓi, Naẓiri Naishāpūri, Zuhūri, Shifā'i Iṣfahāni, Rukn ud-Dīn Masīḥ Kāshi, Faṣīḥi Anṣāri, 'Ali Naḳi Kamra'i, Mulhimi Shīrāzi, 'Aṭā'i Jānpūri, Mashriḳi Mashhadi, Shāpūr Firibi, Ṭālib Āmuli, Sāḥiri Tūni, Abu 'l-Ḳāsim Kāzarūni, Malik Ḳummi, Abu Turāb Beg, Kāmi Sabzavāri, Nau'i Khabūshāni, &c. The last is the author, Shāh Ḥusain, poetically surnamed Hādi, who refers for a full account of his life to his historical work Iḥyā ul-Mulūk.

Khātimah. Kings and Amīrs who made verses, beginning with Ṭoghrul Shāh Saljūḳi, Sultan Sinjar, 'Alā ud-Dīn Tukush, Ṭughāu Shāh, Sulṭān Ḥusain, Shāhbeg Khān Uzbek, 'Abdullah Uzbek; and ending with Murshid Ḳuli Sultan Jalā'ir, fol. 410b.

Beg. صد شکر که ساخت خامه ام تذکره
نه تذکره بل نزد خرد تبصره

It was written in Herat and finished in Jumāda I., A.H. 1019.

Khatm i Khātimah. Some great 'Ulamā who were not professed poets, as Bahā ud-Dīn Muḥ. 'Āmili, Mīr Muḥammad Bāḳir (takh. Ishrāḳ), Shaikh 'Abd us-Salām, &c., fol. 431b.

A collection of Ḥadīs, pious sayings, and moral precepts, with the heading در ایراد احادیث خاتمه, foll. 445b—467a.

Khair ul-Bayān is one of the authorities mentioned in the preface of the Majma' ul-Fuṣaḥā.

109.

Or. 4510.—Foll. 324; 10 in. by 5½; 21 lines, 3½ in. long; written in cursive and close Neskhi, apparently in the 18th century. [Sidney Churchill.]

A defective copy of the same work, wanting some of the notices.

Contents: Preface, fol. 1b. Muḳaddimah, fol. 6b. Faṣl I., fol. 31b. Faṣl II., fol. 159a. Aṣl 1, fol. 159b. Aṣl 2, fol. 167b. Aṣl 3, fol. 176a. Aṣl 4, fol. 205a. Khātimah, fol. 299a. Khatm i Khātimah, fol. 312a.

This last section breaks off, fol. 316b, at the end of the notice of Mīr Jalāl ud-Dīn Ḥasan Salā'i (Or. 3397, fol. 439a). Fol. 317 is a misplaced leaf belonging to Aṣl 4. Foll. 318—324 contain miscellaneous poetical extracts. After fol. 175 there is a lacuna corresponding to foll. 234a—237a of Or. 3397.

110.

Or. 4671.—Foll. 285; 9½ in. by 4¾; 21 lines, 2½ in. long; written in small and neat Nestalik; dated 9 Jumāda II., A.H. 1097 (A.D. 1686). [Sidney Churchill.]

تذکرۂ محمد طاهر نصرابادی

A Tazkirah of contemporary Persian poets, compiled A.H. 1083 by Muḥammad Ṭāhir Naṣrābādi. See the Persian Catalogue, p. 368b.

Contents: Muḳaddimah. Kings and Princes, fol. 5b. Ṣaff I. Firḳah 1, Amīrs and Khāns of Iran, fol. 9b. Firḳah 2, Amīrs and Khāns of Hindustan, &c., fol. 30b. Firḳah 3, Vazirs, Mustaufis and Kātibs, fol. 39b. Ṣaff II. Sayyids and noblemen, fol. 54a. Ṣaff III. Firḳah 1, 'Ulamā and litterati, fol. 82b. (This section breaks off in the middle of the notice of Najībā, the last but four, corresponding with fol. 154a of the other copy, Add. 7087. The last two Firḳahs are missing.) Ṣaff IV. Firḳah 1, Poets of Iran, imperfect at the beginning, fol. 104a. (The first extant notice is that of Ḥakīm Ruknāi Kāshi, the second of that section; see Add. 7087, fol. 161a. After fol. 125 there is a lacuna extending from the notice of Mulla Zaki Hamadāni to that of Mirzā Faṣīḥi, corresponding with foll. 178a—186b of Add. 7087.) Firḳah 2, Poets of Mavarā-annahr, fol. 229b. Firḳah 3, Poets of Hindustan, fol. 236b. Ṣaff V. The author's family, fol. 240b. Khātimah. Chronograms and riddles, fol. 250a.

For other copies see Pertsch, Berlin Catalogue, nos. 648-49, and Ethé, Bodleian Catalogue, no. 378.

111.

Or. 4672.—Foll. 229; 12 in. by 7¾; 22 lines, 5 in. long; written in fair Nestalik Shikastah-āmiz, A.H. 1252 (A.D. 1836).

[SIDNEY CHURCHILL.]

سفينهٔ خوشكو

Tazkirah of Persian poets by Khushgu, arranged in alphabetical order by Durri Shushtari.

Khushgu, whose proper name was Bindrāban, received his poetical surname from his master, Muḥammad Afẓal B. Muḥammad Zāhid (born A.H. 1050, died A.H. 1126), as he relates himself in the full notice devoted to his teacher, fol. 69a. The Safīnah, compiled A.H. 1137—1147, consists, according to Sprenger, Oude Catalogue, p. 130, of three volumes, treating respectively of ancient, mediæval and modern poets, in chronological order. The contents of the second volume have been stated in full detail by Ethé, Bodleian Catalogue, no. 376. Copies of the first and second volumes are mentioned by Pertsch, Berlin Catalogue, nos. 652-3. The third is not extant.

In the preface of the present recension, the editor gives the following curious account of the discovery of the original work. (It has been extracted by Mr. Churchill from a copy in the Madrasah i Nāṣiri, at Teheran, the preface being imperfect in the present MS.): In the month of Muḥarram, A.H. 1228, the river flowing by Shushtar was swollen to a torrent by excessive rains. One day, whilst watching the waters, somebody perceived a dark object floating past him, seized it and found that it was a book, which had suffered not a little from immersion, having lost its beginning and end, as well as the back of the binding. He took it home and laid it by him, where it might have remained without further harm, but for his wife and children, who made use of it when wanting paper. A year later, however, it was laid before Sayyid Muḥammad B. Sayyid 'Abd al-Karim al-Mūsavi, who recognized its importance and ordered the editor to read it daily to him.

In a second preface, fol. 5a, the same writer states that Amir 'Aliḳuli Khān Karrūs, who was sent, after A.H. 1236, to restore order in Khūzistān, having been shown at Shushtar the water-carried Safīnah, found it inconveniently arranged for reference, and desired the editor to re-write it in alphabetical order. Hence the present recension, which, in allusion to Safīnah (ship), received the title of Shirā' (sail). It is said to contain 991 notices. These notices range over the whole field of Persian poetry from the earliest time to the period of Khushgu, and are consequently taken from all three volumes of the original work; but they form one alphabetical series, and are distributed under the letters of the alphabet quite promiscuously and without any regard to the chronological arrangement adopted by Khushgu. This will be seen from the following list of the first twenty-one notices under letter Alif.

Mir Jalāl ud-Din *Asīr* Shahrastāni, who died A.H. 1069, fol. 8b. Shaikh *Allahḳuli* Iṣfahāni, fol. 9b. Navvāb Ẓafar Khān *Aḥsan*, who died A.H. 1078, fol. 10*a*. 'Ināyat Khān *Āshnā*, who died A.H. 1077, fol. 10*b*. Mīr 'Abd ur-Rasūl *Istighnā* Kashmīri, who died under 'Ālamgīr, fol. 11*a*. Kāẓi *Asad* Kāshāni, fol. 11*b*. Mīr *Ajri*, one of the Ḥusaini Sayyids of Yazd, *ib*. Mirza 'Abdullah *Ulfat* Khurāsāni. *Azhari* Ḳuhpāyahi. Sayyid *Amīr* Khān 'Ālamgīrshāhi, who died at the beginning of Muḥammad Shāh's reign. Mirza Arjumand *Āzād* (also *Junūn*), son of 'Abd ul-Ghani Beg, who died A.H. 1143, fol. 12*a*. Mīr Luṭf-ullah *Aḥmadi*, of Balgrām, who died A.H. 1143. *Āṣaf* Ḳummi (Muḥ. Ḳuli), who came to India under Shāhjahān, fol. 12*b*. *Ulfati*, son of Ḥusain Sāji, who came to the court of 'Abdullah Ḳutubshāh. Mīr *Afsar*, son of Mīr Sinjar Kāshi. 'Abdullah *Amāni* of Kirman, who entered the service of Mīr Jumlah, fol. 13*a*. Shaikh *Auḥadi*, disciple of Shaikh Auḥad ud-Dīn Kirmāni, who died under Ghāzān Khān, fol. 13*a*. *Abu 'l-Ḥasan* Manjik, of Tirmiḏ. *Ibn Naṣūḥ*, of Fārs. Shaikh Sharaf ud-Dīn *Abu 'Ali* Ḳalandar, under Tughluḳ Shāh. *Imām ud-Dīn* Rāfi'i, who died A.H. 633, fol. 13*b*.

A full alphabetical list of all the notices included in the volume occupies six pages at the end of the preface, foll. 6—8.

The alphabetical series concludes with two notices relating to Yaḥya Khān, son of Aḥmad, Ṭabīb, and to Yamīni Simnāni, after which the above-mentioned Amīr, 'Ali Ḳuli B. Shahvār Karrūs, states that the work was finished on the 12th of Rabī' I., A.H. 1241. This is followed by a few additional notices accidentally omitted, foll. 201*b*—203*a*.

Foll. 203*b*—227*b* form a separate appendix. It consists of Ḳaṣīdahs by Nāṣir B. Khusrau 'Alavi and by Abu 'l-Faraj Rūni, fol. 213*a*, after which come a few pieces by two modern poets, Mirza Abu 'l-Ḳāsim Hamadāni, fol. 214*b*, and Mirza Muḥ. Taḳi 'Ali-ābādi, fol. 218*b*.

112.

Or. 2603.—Foll. 478; 12 in. by 8; 24 lines, 5¼ in. long; written in fair Nestalik, with 'Unvan and gold-ruled margins, for the Sind Amir, Murād 'Ali Khān Tālpur; dated 19 Rabī' II., A.H. 1216 (A.D. 1801).

[E. B. Eastwick.]

رياض الشعرا

The Tazkirah of 'Ali Ḳuli Khān Dāghistāni, poetically called Vālih. See the Persian Catalogue, p. 371 and p. 1086*a*.

Other copies are described by Pertsch, Berlin Catalogue, nos. 656-7, and by Ethé, Bodleian Catalogue, no. 377.

113.

Or. 4709.—Foll. 342; 14 in. by 8½; 24 lines, 6½ in. long; written in cursive Nestalik in the 19th century.

An incomplete copy of the preceding work.

It breaks off in the middle of the third notice under letter ك, that of Karīmi Samarḳandi, which in the complete copy, Add. 16,729, is found at fol. 374*b*.

114.

Or. 2929.—Foll. 251; 11¾ in. by 7¾; 25 lines, 5¼ in. long; written in small and neat Shikastah-āmīz, with 'Unvān and gold-ruled margins; dated Isfahān, Muharram, A.H. 1234 (A.D. 1818). Bound in painted covers, the inner sides of which apparently represent the author seated before a prince.

[Nath. Bland.]

آتشكده

Ātashkadah, the Tazkirah of Ḥāji Luṭf 'Ali Beg, poetically surnamed Āẕur. See the Persian Catalogue, p. 375*a*.

The contents have been fully analysed by Ethé, Bodleian Catalogue, no. 384, coll. 262—293. A notice of the author will be found in the Majma' ul-Fuṣaḥā, vol. ii., p. 73, where he is stated to have died A.H. 1195. The same date is given in Anjuman i Khāḳān, Or. 3390, fol. 108a.

Copyist: ابن مرحوم زين العابدين شيرازى جواد الحسينى

115.

Or. 3386.—Foll. 417; 12¼ in. by 8; 22 lines, 5¾ in. long; written in four columns in legible Neskhi before A.H. 1253 (A.D. 1837).
[Sidney Churchill.]

A Tazkirah of ancient poets, from the earliest times to the ninth century of the Hijrah, with extensive extracts from their works; without preface or author's name.

At the beginning is a table of the poets included, with the following heading: اسامى فحول شعراى متقدمين كه در طبقهٔ اول از سلسلهٔ اول نوشته شده است. From this it appears that the MS. contains only the first Ṭabaḳah of the first Silsilah of a vast compilation. Mr. Churchill states that a MS. belonging to Sipihr, of Teheran, and containing, besides the above Ṭabaḳah, two Silsilahs treating of later and contemporary poets, is endorsed "Tazkirah i Darvish Navā." This Navā is mentioned in Majma' ul-Fuṣaḥā, vol. ii., p. 527, among contemporary poets, as a native of Kāshān, properly called Darvīsh Ḥusain, who took up his abode in Tabrīz, and left at his death a Tazkirah without preface or epilogue. Navā must have died before A.H. 1288, the date of the Majma' ul-Fuṣaḥā. His Tazkirah is also mentioned in the preface of the same work among its sources.

The biographical notices are short, mostly abridged from Daulatshāh, and devoid of dates; but the author appears to have had access to rare Divans, from which he makes considerable extracts. The present MS. seems to be either the autograph of the author or a copy written for him. Some marginal additions, foll. 289a and 383b, are accompanied by directions as to the place at which they were to be inserted.

The following are the poets included; they are arranged in alphabetical order.

Abu 'l-Faraj Rūni, fol. 1b.

Ḥakīm Azraḳi (Zain ud-Dīn Abu Bakr) Haravi, fol. 24a.

Ḥakīm Anvari (Auḥad ud-Dīn), of Abivard, fol. 41a.

Ustād Asadi Ṭūsi, fol. 65a.

Shaikh Auḥadi, of Marāghah, fol. 66b.

Abu 'l-'Alā Ganjavi, fol. 72a.

Sayyid Ḥasan Ashraf al-Ḥusaini Ghaznīni, fol. 72b.

Sayyid Ḥasan Ashrafi (Mu'īn ud-Dīn), of Samarḳand, fol. 78a.

Aṣīr ud-Dīn Akhsīkati, fol. 79b.

Aṣīr ud-Dīn Aumāni ('Abdullah), of Hamadān, fol. 82b.

Imāmi Haravi, fol. 84a.

Binā'i Haravi, fol. 84b.

'Abd ul-Vāsi' Jabali, of Gharjistān, fol. 85b.

Jamāl ud-Dīn 'Abd ur-Razzāḳ, of Isfahan, fol. 92b.

Amīr Ḥusaini Sādāt (Ḥusain B. 'Ali), of Ghūr, fol. 98a.

Ḥāfiẓ Shīrāzi, fol. 103b.

Afẓal ud-Dīn Khāḳāni (Ibrāhīm B. 'Ali) Shirvāni, fol. 108a.

Sayyid Ẕu 'l-faḳār (Ḳivām ud-Dīn Ḥusain) Shirvāni, fol. 119b.

Ustād Rūdagi (Abu 'l-Ḥasan), fol. 121b.

Raẓi ud-Dīn, of Naishāpūr, fol. 126a.

Rashīd Vaṭvāṭ (Rashīd ud-Dīn Muḥ.), of Balkh, fol. 139a.

Ḥakīm Sanā'i Ghaznavi, fol. 158*b*.
Sūzani (Abu 'l-Fazl Shams ud-Din Muḥ.), of Samarkand, fol. 177*b*.
Saif ud-Dīn, of Isfarang, fol. 181*b*.
Shaikh Sa'di Shīrāzi, fol. 184*a*.
Sharaf ud-Dīn Shufurvah (Fazl-ullah), of Iṣfahan, fol. 194*b*.
Shihāb ud-Dīn Adīb Ṣābir, of Bukhara, fol. 197*b*.
Ẓahīr Fāriyābi, fol. 206*a*.
Abu 'l-Ḳāsim Ḥasan B. Aḥmad 'Unṣuri, fol. 214*a*.
'Asjadi ('Abd ul-'Azīz B. Manṣūr), of Marv Shāhijān, fol. 234*b*.
'Imādi Shahriyāri, fol. 235*a*.
'Am'aḳ Bukhārā'i, fol. 241*b*.
Shaikh Farīd ud-Dīn 'Aṭṭār, fol. 247*a*.
Firdausi (Ḥasan B. Isḥāḳ), fol. 253*a*.
Abu Nizām Jalāl ud-Dīn Muḥ. Falaki, of Shamākhi, fol. 283*b*.
Ustād Farrukhi, of Tirmiz, fol. 289*a*.
Farīd ud-Dīn Aḥval, of Isfahan, *ib.*
Ḥakīm Ḳaṭarān B. Manṣūr, of Tirmid, fol. 295*b*.
Kamāl ud-Dīn Ismā'īl, of Isfahan, fol. 309*a*.
Kisā'i (Majd ud-Dīn Abu Isḥāḳ), of Marv Shāhijān, fol. 319*b*.
Lāmi'i, of Jurjān, fol. 321*a*.
Minuchihri Shast Gallah, of Balkh, fol. 327*b*.
Maulānā Jalāl ud-Dīn Rūmi, fol. 331*a*.
Khwājah Majd ud-Dīn Hamgar, fol. 343*a*.
Amir Mu'izzi, fol. 351*a*.
Mukhtāri ('Usmān), of Ghaznīn, fol. 361*a*.
Mas'ūd Sa'd Salmān, of Jurjān, fol. 371*a*.
Mujir Bailaḳāni, fol. 386*b*.
Nāṣir i Khusrau (Ḥujjat), fol. 390*a*.
Shaikh Nizāmi, of Ganjah, foll. 411*a*—417*a*.

Some verses scribbled at the end of the last notice and on the fly-leaf bear dates ranging from A.H. 1253 to 1287.

116.

Or. 3589.—Foll. 409; 14¾ in. by 9; 25 lines, 5½ in. long; written in cursive Indian Nestalik, apparently early in the 19th century.

I. Foll. 3—348. خلاصة الافكار

Khulāṣat ul-Afkār; a Tazkirah of Persian poets, from the earliest period to the author's time, by Abu Ṭālib B. Ḥāji Muḥammad Tabrīzi Iṣfahāni.

Beg. لالی منثور سپاس و ستایش باستحقاق نثار دامن کبریای ناظمی تواند بود .... اما بعد ابجد خوان دبستان هیچمدانی ابو طالب ابن مغفور حاجی محمد تبریزی الاصفهانی بعرض هوش و گوش سالکان مسالک سخندانی میرساند

The work has been described, from a very imperfect copy, in the Persian Catalogue, p. 378*b*. See also Bland, Journal of the Royal Asiatic Society, vol. ix., pp. 153—58; Sprenger, Oude Catalogue, p. 163; and Ethé, Bodleian Catalogue, no. 391, where the contents are fully analyzed. It was commenced in Calcutta, A.H. 1206, when the author was forty years of age, and finished A.H. 1207. It is dedicated to Āṣaf ud-Daulah, and divided into a Muḳaddimah, 28 Ḥadiḳahs, a Zail and a Khātimah. The contents are as follows:

The author's Preface (analyzed by Bland, *l.c.*, p. 154, and partly given in the original text by Sprenger, *l.c.*), fol. 4*b*.

Muḳaddimah. Essay on Persian poetry and on the rules to be observed in the compilation of Tazkirahs (analyzed by Bland, *l.c.*, p. 155), fol. 5*b*. Table of contents, fol. 8*a*.

Notices of 310 poets arranged under the twenty-eight letters of the alphabet, from Abu Sa'īd Abu 'l-Khair to Muḥ. Yūsuf-Jarbādaḳāni (fully stated by Ethé, *l.c.*, coll. 302—312), fol. 10*b*.

Zail. Notices of 159 poets omitted in the preceding section, from Adham Kāshi to Yahya Uzbek (Ethé, coll. 312—14), fol. 291*b*.

Khâtimah. Twenty-three notices relating to the author's friends and to the author himself (Ethé, coll. 314-15), fol. 305*a*.

The author's treatises on ethics, fol. 323*a*; music, fol. 325*a*; prosody and rhyme, fol. 326*b*; and medicine, fol. 331*a*.

II. Foll. 348*a*—404*b*. لب السير و جهان نما

A manual of history, written by the same Abu Ṭālib Khān, A.H. 1208, also dedicated to Âṣaf ud-Daulah. See the Persian Catalogue, p. 895*b*.

Beg. الحمد لله رب العالمين ... اما بعد ابجد خوان دبستان نادانی ابو طالب ابن محمد تبریزی اصفهانی بعرض سالکان مسالك سخندانی میرساند که کتب بسیار از تاریخ و سیر نزد این کمترین جمع شده بود

The work is divided into four Bābs, subdivided into Furū', the contents of which have been described by Bland, *l.c.*, p. 157, and by Elliot, History of India, vol. viii., pp. 298—300. In this copy the work ends with the sketch of the kings of Kashmir.

117.

Or. 4610.—Foll. 530; 14¾ in. by 9¼; 25 lines, 6¾ in. long; written in fair Nestalik, with 'Unvān and ruled margins, in the first half of the 19th century. [Sidney Churchill.]

مخزن الغرايب

Makhzan ul-Gharā'ib, the most comprehensive Tazkirah ever written; compiled by Aḥmad 'Ali Hāshimi Sandīlahi, son of Shaikh Ghulām Muḥammad B. Maulavi Muḥammad Ḥāji.

Beg. کوهر الفاظ فصاحت بنیان و لالی معانی بلاغت توامان شایسته رشته حمد خداوندیست که ....

اما بعد چنین کوید بنده احمد علی هاشمی سندیله ولد شیخ غلام محمد ابن فضیلت ماب مولوی محمد حاجی طاب مضجعه

In the preface the author gives some account of his life. Having left home in his boyhood, he attached himself to the "late" Navvāb 'Izzat ud-Daulah Mirza Ḥasan Suhrāb Jang, son of Mirza Muḥsin, elder brother of Ṣafdar Jang, and with his consent entered the service of Navvāb Ẕu 'l-Faḳār ud-Daulah Mirza Najaf Khān in the imperial Risālah under Shāh 'Âlam. During the troubled period and general dispersion which followed the death of Najaf Khān (A.H. 1196), he associated with natives of Khorasan, Irak and Fārs, and began to eagerly collect poems from every source. These he was subsequently advised by his master, Mirza Muḥ. Ḥasan Ḳatīl, to bring together into a Tazkirah arranged in alphabetical order. The result was the present work, which he compiled at the age of fifty-four and completed, as stated in a chronogram at the end, A.H. 1218.

To the copious list of authorities included in the preface, and given by Sprenger, Oude Catalogue, p. 146, we can add, from the present copy, Nafā'is ul-Ma'āṣir by Mir 'Alā ud-Daulah (Oude Catalogue, p. 46) and the oral communications of Mirza Ḳatīl and others.

The Makhzan ul-Gharā'ib is mentioned in the Persian Catalogue, p. 1015*b*. Its contents, consisting of 3148 notices, have been stated with meritorious fulness and accuracy by Ethé, Bodleian Catalogue, no. 395, coll. 316—396.

An alphabetical index of names, with references to the folios of the present copy, occupies fourteen leaves at the beginning. A note written on the first page shows that the MS. was bought in Haidarabad, A.H. 1247. In A.H. 1275 it was purchased in Kerbela by a Persian prince, Nūr ud-Dīn, son of Badī' uz-Zamān Mirza (see fol. 16*a*).

118.

Or. 2877.—Foll. 180; 11 in. by 6¼; 15 lines, 4 in. long; written in neat Shikastah-āmīz, with 'Unvān and gold-ruled margins. Bound in painted and glazed covers.

[Sidney Churchill.]

زینت المدایح

A collection of poems in praise of Fatḥ 'Ali Shāh, with notices of their authors, by Muḥammad Ṣādiḳ Marvazi, poetically surnamed Humā.

Beg. ای ذکر تو کلفروش بازار سخن
رنکین زتو برك برك کلزار سخن
اوصاف تو دیباچه مجموعه نطق
توحید تو مشاطه رخسار سخن

زینت مدایح و زیب محامد حمد محمودیست جل
ذکره که حمدش زینت زبان و ثنایش زیب بیانست

From the notice of the author's life with which the work concludes, we learn that he was born and educated in Merv Shāhijān. When that place was laid waste by the Uzbeks, he repaired to Kerbela and Najaf, and thence to Kashan, where he studied poetry under Ṣabāḥi (d. A.H. 1206). A history of the Ḳajar Dynasty, which he wrote under the title of Ta'rīkh i Jahān-ārā, brought him to the notice of Fatḥ 'Ali Shāh, who appointed him Court Chronicler, وقایع نکار. When the Shah set out on his campaign against the Goklan in Khorasan, he left the author behind with the task of compiling the present work.

Notices of Humā in Nigāristan i Dārā, Or. 3508, fol. 137; Anjuman i Khāḳān, Or. 3390, fol. 105; and in the Majma' ul-Fuṣaḥā, vol. ii., p. 572, do not give the date of his death. It must have taken place after A.H. 1233, the year to which the Ta'rīkh i Jahān-ārā is brought down (see the Persian Catalogue, p. 200b, and Morley's Catalogue, nos. 154-55). In the Tazkirah i Muhammad Shāhi, written A.H. 1247, he is spoken of as still holding the office of Vaḳā'i' Nigār. Zīnat ul-Madā'iḥ is one of the sources of Majma' ul-Fuṣaḥā; see preface, p. 6.

In the preface, which is chiefly taken up with a wordy panegyric on Fatḥ 'Ali Shāh, the author says that the work comprises poems composed from His Majesty's accession to the seventh year of his reign (A.H. 1218). It was compiled by order of the Shah, who gave it the above title, and consists of four parts, respectively called Ārāyish, Pīrāyah I., Pīrāyah II., and Zīvar.

Contents: Ārāyish. Poems of Fatḥ 'Ali Shāh, fol. 7a. Pīrāyah I. Notices and compositions of the following Court poets, arranged in alphabetical order, with the exception of the Malik ush-Shu'arā, who takes precedence: *Ṣabā* Fatḥ 'Ali Khān, of Kāshān, Malik ush-Shu'arā, fol. 18a. *Razī*, son of Mirza Muḥ. Shafī', Mustaufi of Azarbāijān, fol. 97b. *Saḥāb*, Sayyid Muḥ., son of Hātif, of Isfahan, fol. 106b. *Ṣabūr*, Mirza Aḥmad, nephew of Fatḥ 'Ali Khān, fol. 120b. *Maftūn*, 'Abd ur-Razzāḳ Beg, son of Najaf Ḳuli Khān Dunbuli, fol. 134a. *Nashāt*, 'Abd ul-Vahhāb, Kalāntar of Isfahan, fol. 136a. Pīrāyah II. Compositions of other poets, namely *Bazmi*, Sayyid Ṣādiḳ, of Bidgul, Kashan, fol. 152a. *Khāvari*, Ma'ṣūm, of Kūzah-kunān, Tabriz, fol. 153a. *Sharar*, Ḥusain 'Ali Beg, son of Luṭf 'Ali Beg Āzur, fol. 158a. *Ṣabāḥi*, Sulaiman, of Bidgul, fol. 160a. *Mā'il*, Muḥ. 'Ali, son of Muḥ. Kāẓim, Mustaufi, fol. 162b. *Mijmar*, Sayyid Ḥusain, of Isfahan, fol. 164b.

Zīvar. Life and poems of the author, fol. 166b.

The introductory notices, prefixed to most of the poems, and showing on what occasion they were composed, are of some historical interest.

119.

Or. 3399.—Foll. 221; 11 in. by 7; 15 lines, 4¾ in. long; written in fair Shikastah-āmīz, with silver-ruled margins, in the 19th century. Bound in painted and glazed covers. [Sidney Churchill.]

زينت المدايح

A sequel to the preceding work, by the same author.

Beg. تا نام تو در مديح لايح باشد
دفتر همه عنبرين روايح باشد
سر دفتر زينت المدايح كردم
آن نام كه زينت مدايح باشد
الحمد لمن حمده زين المحامد ومدحه زينت المدايح

It is designated in the preface as the second volume of the work, and contains further pieces of the same poets and compositions of a few new ones. It was compiled, as stated fol. 208*a*, A.H. 1223, and is divided into five parts termed Mīnū, Ghurfah, Rauzah I., Rauzah II., and Ḥadīkah. The contents are as follows:

Mīnū. Poems of Fatḥ 'Ali Shāh, fol. 4*b*. Ghurfah. Poems of Shahzādah Muḥammad 'Ali Mirza, the eldest son of the Shah, poetically surnamed Daulat (died A.H. 1237), fol. 11*b*. Rauzah I., divided into seven Gulbuns. Poems of the following seven Court poets: Ṣabā, fol. 22*b*. Razi, fol. 89*a*. Saḥāb, fol. 92*a*. Ṣabūr, fol. 127*b*. Mijmar, fol. 144*a*. Nashāṭ, fol. 176*a*. Arabic Kasidah by Mirza Muḥ. Ḥusain, son of Mirza Muḥ. Kāẓim Mustaufi, fol. 182*a*.

Rauzah II., in six Gulbuns. Poems of six other poets, viz., *Ḥarīf*, Abu 'l-Ḥasan, of Jandak, fol. 183*b*. *Khāvari*, Ma'ṣūm, fol. 186*a*, *Ṣāḥib*, daughter of Shahbāz Khān Dunbuli, fol. 193*b*. *Farrukh*, Khānlar, son of 'Ali Murād Khān Zand, fol. 195*a*. *Nashāṭi*, 'Abbās, of Hazārjarib, fol. 197*a*. *Nāṭiḳ*, Ṣādiḳ of Isfahan, fol. 201*a*.

Ḥadīḳah. Poems of the author, slightly imperfect at the end, fol. 207*b*.

120.

Or. 3390.—Foll. 204; 11¼ in. by 7¾; 17 lines, 4½ in. long; written in fair Shikastah-āmīz, with gold-ruled margins, A.H. 1234 (A.D. 1819). [Sidney Churchill.]

انجمن خاقان

Tazkirah of the poets who lived in the reign of Fatḥ 'Ali Shāh, by Muḥammad Fāẓil, poetically surnamed Rāvi.

Beg. زيب انجمن خاقان كه زينت بزم زمان باد نام
بديعى است جل شانه

The author tells us in the last chapter that he belonged to the Turcoman tribe called Bāyandari, and was born in Karrūs, a district of Hamadān, A.H. 1198. Having lost his father A.H. 1214, he repaired to Teheran and studied poetry under the Malik ush-Shu'arā Fatḥ 'Ali Khān. His master recommended him to the Shāh, who made him his favourite and reciter of his verses. See Majma' ul-Fuṣaḥā, vol. ii., p. 142, where it is stated that he died A.H. 1252, and Tazkirah i Dārā, Or. 3508, fol. 92*b*.

In the preface the author says that Fatḥ 'Ali Shāh had long desired to see the compositions of the poets of his time collected into one volume, that the task had been undertaken by some scholars, who had failed to carry it out, and was ultimately, A.H. 1234, committed to himself. The Anjuman i Khāḳān is one of the sources of Majma' ul-Fuṣaḥā. The author is mentioned as still alive, A.H. 1247, in Tazkirah i Muḥammad Shāhi, fol. 187*b*.

The work consists of four sections, called Anjuman, and a Khātimah, with the following contents:

Anjuman I. انجمن اول در شمه از احوال و آثار

شهریار کردون اقتدار. An account of the predecessors of Fatḥ 'Ali Shāh, and of his reign, with some specimens of his poetry, fol. 3*b*.

Anjuman II. Notices of the following royal princes and Khāns: Muḥammad 'Ali Mirza *Daulat*, fol. 25*b*. Muḥammad Ḳuli Mirza, *Khusravi*, fol. 29*a*. Ḥusain 'Ali Mirza, Farmān-farmā, fol. 29*b*. Muḥ. Taḳi Mirza *Shaukat*, fol. 30*a*. 'Ali Shāh, fol. 30*b*. Shaikh 'Ali Mirza *Shāpūr*, fol. 31*b*. 'Abdullah Mirza *Dārā*, fol. 32*a*. Imām-virdi Mirza, fol. 33*a*. Maḥmūd Mirza, fol. 33*b*. Muḥ. Riẓa Mirza *Afsar*, fol. 34*b*. Ḥaidar Ḳuli Mirza *Khāvar*, fol. 35*b*. Humāyūn Mirza *Ḥishmat*, fol. 36*a*. Ẓahīr ud-Daulah Ibrāhīm Khān *Ṭughrul*, fol. 36*b*. Muḥ. Ḳāsim Khān, *Shaukat*, fol. 37*a*. Sulaimān Khān *'Izzat*, fol. 37*b*. Allahyār Khān, *Ḥājib*, fol. 38*a*.

Anjuman III. Notices of the following thirty-nine Court poets: *Binavā*, Dā'ūd B. Mahdi aṭ-Ṭūsi, fol. 39*b*. *Baulah*, Mirza Muḥ. Raẓi, fol. 40*b*. *Bismil*, Aḳā 'Ali Akbar, fol. 41*b*. *Bāḳi*, a Sayyid of Isfahan, fol. 42*a*. *Bīdil*, Muḥ. Raḥīm, fol. 42*b*. Mirza *Buzurg* Mu'taman ud-Daulah, fol. 43*b*. *Parvānah*, Mirza Aḥmad, fol. 46*a*. *Ḥasrat*, 'Ali, fol. 47*a*. *Ḥusain*, of Sāri, fol. 47*b*. *Khāvar*, Maḥmūd Khān, fol. 48*a*. *Khāvari*, Sayyid Faẓl-ullah of Shirāz, fol. 52*b*. *Saḥāb*, Sayyid Muḥ., son of Hātif, fol. 55*b*. *Sulṭāni*, Riẓā Ḳuli of Navā, fol. 62*a*. *Sakhā*, Muḥ. Zamān, fol. 62*b*. *Shiḥnah*, Muḥ. Mahdi Khān, fol. 63*a*. *Ṣabā*, Fatḥ 'Ali Khān, fol. 63*a*. *Ṣāḥib* Muḥ. Taḳi Māzandarāni, fol. 78*b*. *Ṣabūr*, Aḥmad, nephew of Fatḥ 'Ali Khān, fol. 79*a*. *Ṭarab*, Mirza Yūsuf Shaikh ul-Islām, fol. 80*a*. *Ṭāhir*, Ḥasan Khān, fol. 80*b*. *Ẓarīf*, Muḥ. Ḥasan, fol. 82*a*. *'Ishrat*, Muḥ. Mahdi al-Ḥusaini, fol. 82*b*. *Farrukh*, Muḥ. Ḥasan Khān, son of 'Ali Murād Khān, fol. 83*a*. *Fikrat*, Sayyid Ni'mat-ullah, fol. 83*b*. *Kaukab*, 'Abd ul-'Ali, fol. 84*a*. *Maftūn*, 'Abd ur-Razzāḳ Beg, fol. 85*a*. *Mijmar*, Sayyid Ḥusain of Ardistān, fol. 85*b*. *Manṣūr*, Muḥ. Riẓā, fol. 89*a*. *Mā'il*, Muḥ. 'Ali, fol. 89*b*. *Mūnis*, Muḥ. Riẓa, fol. 90*a*. *Maḥrūm*, Aḳā Ḥusain 'Ali, fol. 90*a*. *Muḥīṭ*, Ma'ṣūm B. 'Īsa, fol. 90*b*. *Manẓūr*, Muḥ. Ibrāhīm, fol. 91*b*. *Mushīr*, Abu 'l-Ḳāsim Farāhāni, fol. 92*a*. *Nashāṭ*, 'Abd ul-Vahhāb al-Mūsavi, fol. 94*a*. *Nadīm*, Muḥ. of Bārfurūsh, fol. 101*a*. Naṣr-ullah Khān, fol. 101*a*. *Nashāṭi*, 'Abbās of Hazārjarib, fol. 101*b*. *Nuṣrat*, Sulṭān Ḥusain, *ib*. *Vafā*, Ḥusain Farāhāni, fol. 103*b*. *Vafā'i*, 'Abdullah Beg of Tafrish, fol. 104*a*. *Humā*, Muḥ. Ṣādiḳ, fol. 105*a*.

Anjuman IV. Notices of a hundred and twenty other poets, in alphabetical order, from *Āẕur*, Luṭf 'Ali Beg to *Yaghmā* of Jandaḳ, fol. 107*b*. A table of contents is prefixed, fol. 107*a*.

Khātimah. Life and poems of the author, fol. 201*b*.

121.

Or. 3553.—Foll. 66; 11 in. by 7½; 15 lines, 4¾ in. long; written in large Nestalik, with ruled margins; dated 28 Rabī' I., A.H. 1239 (A.D. 1823). [SIDNEY CHURCHILL.]

گلشن محمود

Notices of forty-eight sons of Fatḥ 'Ali Shāh, with specimens of their poetry, by one of them, Maḥmūd Mirza (see above, no. 70).

Beg. صفای گلشن جنان سپاس بیقیاس محمودی است جل جلاله که نزای هشت بهشت غنچه از گلستان رحمت است [اوست]

The work was compiled, as stated in the preface, by order of the Shāh, A.H. 1236. The preface includes a Kasidah in praise of the Shāh, concluding with the following chronogram for the date of composition, which gives only 1235.

پی تاریخ او محمود با صد خرمی کفتا
بیامد گلشن محمود زیب گلشن دوران

Contents: Preface, fol. 1*b*. Glories of the Shah's reign and number of his children, fol. 6*a*. His poems, fol. 8*a*. Notices of the following 47 sons of Fatḥ 'Ali Shāh, with specimens of their verses: Muḥ. 'Ali, fol. 10*b*; Muḥ. Ḳuli, fol. 13*b*. Muḥ. Vali, fol. 15*a*; 'Abbās, fol. 16*b*; Ḥusain 'Ali, fol. 18*b*; Ḥasan 'Ali, fol. 19*b*; Muḥ. Taḳi, fol. 20*b*; 'Ali Ḳuli, fol. 22*b*; Shaikh 'Ali, fol. 23*b*; 'Ali Khān, fol. 24*b*; 'Abdullah, fol. 26*b*; Imām-virdi, fol. 30*a*; Muḥ. Riẓā, fol. 31*a*; Ḥaidar Ḳuli, fol. 32*b*; Humāyūn, fol. 34*a*; Allah-virdi, fol. 36*a*; Ismā'īl, fol. 37*a*; Aḥmad 'Ali, fol. 37*b*; 'Ali Riẓa, Kaiḳubād, fol. 39*b*; Bahrām, fol. 40*b*; Shāhpūr, fol. 41*a*; Malik Ḳāsim, fol. 41*b*; Minuchihr, Hurmuz, fol. 42; Īraj, Kaikā'us, fol. 43; Shāhḳuli, Muḥ. Mahdi, fol. 44; Kaikhusrau, Kayūmarṣ, fol. 45; Jahānshāh, fol. 46; Sulaimān, fol. 47; Fatḥ-ullah, Malik Manṣūr, fol. 48; Bahman, fol. 49; Sulṭān Muḥ., Sulṭān Salīm, fol. 50; Sulṭān Muṣṭafa, Sulṭān Ibrāhīm, fol. 51; Saif-ullah, fol. 52; Yaḥya, Zakariyyā, Muḥ. Amin, fol. 53; Sulṭān Ḥamzah, Sulṭān Aḥmad, Ṭahmūraṣ, fol. 54. Six sons of Ḥusain Ḳuli Khān, brother of Fatḥ 'Ali Shāh, fol. 55. Memoir of the author and his poems, foll. 57*a*—64.

122.

Or. 3545.—Foll. 299; 10¾ in. by 6¼; 21 lines, 3½ in. long; written in fair Nestalik, with an 'Unvan and gold-ruled margins, probably about the middle of the 19th century. Bound in painted covers. [Sidney Churchill.]

سفينة المحمود

A Tazkirah containing notices and select compositions of the poets of Fatḥ 'Ali Shāh's reign, by Maḥmūd Mirza, author of the preceding work.

Beg. اول دفتر بنام ایزد دانا
صانع و پروردکار حی توانا

The author, who mentions in the preface his proficiency in various sciences and in the art of calligraphy, gives the following list of his works:

Safīnat ul-Maḥmūd (the present work);

منتخب المحمود, on the life and miracles of the Prophet;

کلشن محمود, a biographical account of the sons of Fatḥ 'Ali Shāh (no. 121);

مخزن المحمود, on the lives and miracles of saints;

محمود نامه, containing anecdotes and moral precepts; a Risālah on the true dreams and prognostics of Fatḥ 'Ali Shāh;

نصايح المحمود, advice to his son Mas'ūd Mirza;

درر المحمود, his poetical compositions; and

بيان المحمود (see Or. 3552).

The preface concludes with a piece of verse at the end of which is a chronogram for the date of composition, A.H. 1235:

کفت این مجمع محمود پریشان نشود

Majma' i Maḥmūd is the specific title given by the author to his Safīnah, fol. 3*b*: این سفینه که مسمی بمجمع محمود است

A second and later preface begins, fol. 4*b*, as follows: سفینهٔ وجود موجودات بامر ناخدائی در بحرامکان جاریست. There the author states that in A.H. 1240 he received the sovereign's commands to compile an account of contemporary poets, several works previously written on that subject having failed to satisfy the fastidious taste of the Shāh; and that the latter gave to the book, even before its completion, the name of Safīnat ul-Maḥmūd.

The work is divided into four parts called Majlis, viz.:

I. Lives and poems of the Shāh and of the royal princes, fol. 6*b*.

II. The Vazirs and great office-holders,

namely, Nashāt, fol. 24b; Mirza Buzurg, fol. 33a; Ṣabā, fol. 33b; and Farrukh, fol. 47b.

III. Poets of Iran, in the following five sections, termed Martabah, in each of which the notices are arranged according to the Abjad: 1. Irak, about two hundred notices, fol. 49b. 2. Fārs, 33 notices, fol. 198a. 3. Khorasan, 36 notices, fol. 223b. 4. Gilan and Tabaristan, 32 notices, fol. 243a. 5. Azarbaijan, 18 notices, fol. 257a. At the beginning of each Martabah is a table of the poets it includes.

IV. Life and select compositions of the author, fol. 274a.

Safinat ul-Maḥmūd is one of the sources of the Majma' ul-Fuṣaḥā, as mentioned in the preface.

123.

Or. 3508.—Foll. 212; 12 in. by 7; 23 lines, 4½ in. long; written in minute and elegant Nestalik, with 'Unvan and gold-ruled margins, in the 19th century. Bound in painted and glazed covers. [Sidney Churchill.]

نگارستان دارا

A Tazkirah of the poets who lived in the time of Fatḥ 'Ali Shāh, by 'Abd ur-Razzāḳ B. Najafḳuli.

Beg. طراز نگارستان دارا و طراوت بهارستان دلارا
حمد صانعی است جل شانه

The author's historical work, Ma'āṣir i Sulṭāniyyah, nos. 68-69, has been mentioned above. The present work was written A.H. 1241. The preface gives an account of a meeting which took place in that year in Sulṭāniyyah, between Fatḥ 'Ali Shāh and his son, the Nā'ib us-Salṭanah 'Abbās Mirza. The former having expressed a desire for the compilation of a Tazkirah comprising the poets of the period, the prince pointed out the author as a competent person for the task. Hence the present work, which is divided into five parts called Nigārkhānah, or Aivān, as follows:

I. History of Fatḥ 'Ali Shāh and specimens of his poetry, fol. 2b.

II. Royal princes and noble Amirs, arranged according to the date of their birth, fol. 5a. These are the sons, grandsons and nephews, of Fatḥ 'Ali Shāh, as follows: *Daulat*, Muḥ. 'Ali Mirza. *Khusravi*, Muḥ. Ḳuli Mirza. *Shaukat*, Muḥ. Taḳi Mirza. *'Ādil*, 'Ali Shāh. *Vālā*, 'Aliḳuli Mirza. *Shāpūr*, Shaikh 'Ali Mirza. *Dārā*, 'Abdullah Mirza. Imām-virdi Mirza. Maḥmūd Mirza. Humāyūn Mirza. *Khāvar*, Ḥaidar Ḳuli Mirza. *Baizā*, Allah-virdi Mirza. *Jahān*, Jahānshāh Mirza. *Aḥmad*, Aḥmad 'Ali Mirza. *Hishmat*, Muḥ. Husain Mirza. *Surūr*, Ṭahmāsp Mirza. *Ẓiyā*, Naẓar 'Ali Mirza. *Ṭughrul*, Ẓahir ud-Daulah Ibrāhim Khān. *Shaukat*, Muḥ. Ḳāsim Khān. *'Izzat*, Sulaimān Khān. *Ḥājib*, Allahyār Khān.

III. Favourites of the Shah and of the princes, men of letters, Vazirs and other officials, fol. 8b. *Ṣabā*, Fath 'Ali Khān, heads the list as Malik ush-Shu'arā, with extensive extracts from his poems, fol. 9b. The others are arranged in the alphabetical order of their names or takhalluṣ, as follows:

Abu 'l-Ḳāsim, Sayyid ul-Vuzarā, fol. 71a.
Abu 'l-Ḳāsim Hamadāni, fol. 80b.
Ibrāhim Munshi, of Tabriz, fol. 81a.
Ashraf, 'Ali Ashraf of Azarbā'ijān, fol. 81b.
Ishrāḳ, Mirza Muh., of Burūjird, fol. 82b.
Ummīd, Abu 'l-Ḥasan Khān, of Nuhāvand, *ib.*
Bandah, Muḥ. Razi B. Muḥ. Shafi', fol. 83a.
Bīdil, Muḥ. Raḥim, fol. 84a.
Bismil, 'Ali Akbar, fol. 86b.
Chākar, Ḥasan 'Ali Khān, *ib.*
Ḥāli, Fatḥ 'Ali Beg, fol. 87a.
Ḥasrat, Muḥ. Taḳi, fol. 88a.
Mulla Ḥasan, master of Maḥmūd Mirza, fol. 88b.

Mirza Husain B. Mirza Kāzim Mustaufī, fol. 89a.
Mulla Husain Sāravi Kāẓi 'Askar, ib.
Mirza Husain, of Kūzahkunān, ib.
Khāvar, Maḥmūd Khān Dunbuli, fol. 89b.
Khāvari, Fażl-ullah Shīrāzi, fol. 91a.
Rāvi, Muḥ. Fāẓil, fol. 92b.
Sarshār, Najafḳuli Khān, fol. 93b.
Sipihr, Aḳa Muḥ. Taḳi, of Kashan, fol. 95a.
Saḥāb, Sayyid Muḥ., of Isfahan, fol. 95b.
Sakhā, Muḥ. Zamān Khān, fol. 100b.
Shiḥnah, Muḥ. Mahdi Khān, ib.
Shifā, Mulla Riẓā, of Tabriz, ib.
Ṣāḥib, Muḥ. Taḳi B. Mirza Zaki, 'Aliyābūdi, fol. 105a.
Ṣabūr, Aḥmad, nephew of Fatḥ 'Ali Khān, fol. 106a.
Ṣafā'i, Aḥmad B. Mulla Mahdi Narūḳi, fol. 108a.
Ṣadrā, Ṣadr ud-Dīn Muḥ. Tabrīzi, fol. 108b.
Ṭūṭi, Abu 'l-Fatḥ Khān, ib.
Ṭā'ir, Ḥasan Khān, fol. 109a.
Ṭarab, Muḥ. Yūsuf, brother of Abu 'l-Ḳāsim of Karmānshāhān, ib.
'Ishrat, Mahdi Farāhāni, ib.
Mirza Buzurg, 'Isa B. Ḥasan Farāhāni, fol. 110a.
'Azīz, Yūsuf Beg, of Lāhījān, fol. 110b.
Farrukh, Muḥ. Ḥasan Khān, fol. 111b.
Fikrat, Sayyid Ni'mat-ullah, of Lārījān, ib.
Ḳābil, Ḥusain 'Ali Khān, ib.
Kauṣar, Mulla Riẓā, ib.
Kaukab, 'Abd ul-'Ali B. Muḥsin Yazdi, fol. 112a.
Mā'il, Muḥ. 'Ali, of Shiraz, ib.
Mijmar, Sayyid Ḥusain, of Ardistan, fol. 120a.
Manṣūr, Muḥ. Riẓā, of Isfahan, fol. 123a.
Manẓūr, Ibrāhīm, of Shiraz, fol. 123b.
Maḥram, Aḳa Ḥusain 'Ali Afshār, fol. 124a.
Mūnis, Muḥ. Riẓā, of Bārfurūsh, ib.
Nashāṭ, 'Abd ul-Vahhāb, of Isfahan, fol. 124b.
Nadīm, Muḥ., of Bārfurūsh, fol. 128b.
Nashāṭi, 'Abbās, of Hazārjarīb, ib.
Nuṣrat, Sulṭān Ḥusain Beg, of Ṭālish, fol. 129a.
Navā'i, Muḥ. Taḳi B. Riẓā Ḳuli, ib.
Vafā, Muḥ. Ḥusain Ḥusaini, ib.
Vafā'i, 'Abdullah Beg, of Tafrish, fol. 137a.
Humā, Muḥ. Ṣādiḳ, of Merv, fol. 187b.

IV. Notices of about 120 other poets, also in alphabetical order, beginning with Āzād, Mirza Muḥ. 'Ali, of Kashmīr, and ending with Yaghmā, Abu 'l-Ḥasan, of Jandaḳ, fol. 140a.

V. Life and poems of the author, fol. 180b.

Appendix. Notice of 'Andalīb, Muḥ. Ḥusain Kāshi, son and successor of the Malik ush-Shu'arā, fol. 209a.

The work is mentioned in the preface of Majma' ul-Fuṣaḥā, p. 6, as تذكرهٔ عبد الرزاق
بيك دنبلى

124.

Or. 3250.—Foll. 224; 14 in. by 8¼; 21 lines, 5¼ in. long; written in fair Nestalik with 'Unvan and gold-ruled margins for Aḳā 'Ali, Maḥram i Ḥarīm i Shāhinshāhi, A.H. 1257 (A.D. 1841). [SIDNEY CHURCHILL.]

تذكرهٔ محمد شاهى

A Tazkirah of Persian poets, by Bahman Mirza, son of Nā'ib us-Salṭanah 'Abbās Mirza.

الحمد لله رب العالمين ... زينت هر كتاب
ثناى حضرت رب الاربابيست كه ذكر محامد ذاتش
در تذكره و بيان نكهد

After a panegyric on the reigning sovereign, Fatḥ 'Ali Shāh, and on the Nā'ib us-Salṭanah, the author says that he was residing in Ardabil, to the government of which he had been appointed by his father, when he was invited by his elder brother, Muḥammad Shāh, to join him, and, at his request, compiled the present work. The date of composition, A.H. 1247, is conveyed by this chronogram :

پی سال تاریخ پیر خرد
بدریای فکرت بسی غوطه زد
بکفتا بود کوهر آبدار
باسم محمد شه نامدار

It is stated at the end that the work was completed A.H. 1249. Mr. Churchill states in a letter that Bahman Mirza subsequently fled to the Caucasus and died there a few years ago.

The work is divided into three parts called **Rishtah**, and a table of all the poets noticed is found at the end of the preface, foll. 3-4. The contents are as follows:

Rishtah I. Notices of about 150 poets of the past, *i.e.* from the earliest times to the end of the twelfth century of the Hijrah, arranged in alphabetical order, fol. 4*a*. A few Arabic verses by 'Ali B. Abi Ṭālib are prefixed. The alphabetical series begins with Asadi and ends with Yamini, a Sayyid of Kāshān. The notices are short, and too much space is taken up by extensive extracts from such well-known poets as Ḥāfiẓ, Sa'di, Maulānā Rūmi, Firdausi and Niẓāmi.

Rishtah II. History of the Ḳājārs and of Fatḥ 'Ali Shāh, with specimens of his poetry, fol. 173*a*. Notices of the following royal princes: *Daulat*, Muḥ. 'Ali Mirza; *Khusravi*, Muḥ. Ḳuli Mirza; *Shaukat*, Muḥ. Taḳi Mirza; *'Ādil*, Ẓill i Sulṭān; *Dārā*, 'Ali Naḳi Mirza; *Shāpūr*, Shaikh 'Ali Mirza; *Vālā*, 'Abdullah Mirza; Imām-virdi Mirza; Maḥmūd Mirza; Malik Ḳāsim Mirza; *Tughrul*, Ẓahīr ud-Daulah Ibrāhīm Khān; *Ḥājib*, Āṣaf ud-Daulah Allahyār Khān, fol. 176*b*.

Rishtah III. Contemporary poets, also in alphabetical order, as follows:

Abu'l-Ḳāsim B. 'Isa Farāhāni, Ḳā'im Maḳām, fol. 179*a*.
Ashraf, of Ṭabūḥ, Azarbaijan, fol. 182*a*.
Asad-ullah Khān B. Ḥāji Ibrāhīm Khān.
Efendi, Ḥusain Ḳuli Khān, fol. 182*b*.
Āzād, Mirza Muḥ. 'Ali, of Kashmir.
Akbar, Mirza 'Ali Akbar, of Isfahan.
Akhtar, Aḥmad Beg, of Gurjistan.
Asīr, Muḥ. Ḥusain, of Tabrīz, fol. 183*a*.
Bīnavā, Mirza Dā'ūd, of Khorasan.
Bandah, Muḥ. Raẓī, of Tabrīz.
Bīdil, Muḥ. Raḥīm Ṭabib.
Bāḳi, Sayyid 'Abd ul-Bāḳi, of Isfahan.
Bīdil, Muḥ. Amin Khān, fol. 183*b*.
Mirza Taḳi, Ṭabīb.
Mirza Ḥusain B. Mirza Kāẓim Mustaufi.
Mirza Ḥusain, of Kūzahkunān.
Ḥasrat, Muḥ. Taḳi, of Hamadān.
Ḥarif, Sayyid Abu 'l-Ḥasan, of Jandaḳ.
Mulla Ḥusain 'Ali, of Ḳazvin, fol. 184*a*.
Mulla Ḥasan, of Nuhāvand.
Khāvari, Sayyid Faẓl-ullah, of Shiraz.
Khurram, of Azarbaijan.
Ẓarrah, 'Abd ul-Ghani, of Tafrish, fol. 184*b*.
Rāvi, Fāẓil Khān, fol. 187*b*.
Riẓā, son of Mirza Raẓi Tabrizi, fol. 188*a*.
Sarshār, Najaf Ḳuli Khān.
Saḥāb, Ḥāji Sayyid Muḥ., of Isfahan.
Sāghar, Shaikh Muḥ., of Shīrāz, fol. 188*b*.
Shiḥnah, Muḥ. Mahdi Khān, of Mazandaran.
Shā'iḳ, Hādi Beg, of Luristan.
Ṣabā, Fatḥ 'Ali Khān Malik ush-Shu'arā.
Ṣāfi, Ḥāji Mulla Aḥmad, of Narāḳ, fol. 208*b*.
Ṣabūr, Mirza Aḥmad, brother of Fatḥ 'Ali Khān.
Ṭūṭi, Abu 'l-Fatḥ Khān B. Ibrāhīm Khalīl Khān.

Ṭā'ir, Ḥasan Khān, nephew of Ḥāji Ibrāhim Khān.

Ṭabīb, Mirza Muḥ., of Burujird.

'Isa, Mirza Buzurg, Ḳā'im Maḳām, fol. 209*a*.

'Andalīb, Muḥ. Ḥusain Khān, son of Fatḥ 'Ali Khan, fol. 209*b*.

'Āli, Muḥ. Ḥusain, Kalāntar of Shiraz.

'Ājiz, Khalifah Muḥ., of Garmrūd.

Fikrat, Sayyid Ni'mat-ullah, fol. 211*a*.

Fardi, Ṣafar 'Ali Beg Zand.

Ḳābil, Ḥusain Ḳuli Khan.

Kauṣar, Mulla Riẓā, of Hamadan.

Kaukab, Mirza Bāḳir, of Khorasan.

Mā'il, Muḥ. 'Ali Mustaufi, fol. 211*b*.

Maftūn, 'Abd ur-Razzāḳ Beg Dunbuli, fol. 212*b*.

Mijmar, Sayyid Ḥusain Muẕahhib, of Ardistan, fol. 213*a*.

Muẕnib, Shaikh Raḥīm, fol. 215*b*.

Manṣūr, Muḥ. Riẓa, of Isfahan.

Nashāṭ, Sayyid 'Abd ul-Vahhāb, of Isfahan.

Naṣr-ullah, of Ardabil, fol. 220*b*.

Naẓar 'Ali, Ḥakīm Bāshi, of Ḳazvin.

Navā, Darvīsh Ḥusain, of Kashan, fol. 221*a*.

Naṣīb, Aḳā Muḥammad.

Humā, Mirza Muḥ. Ṣādiḳ.

Vālih, Aḳā Muḥ. Kāẓim, of Isfahan, fol. 221*b*.

The Taẕkirah i Muḥammadshāhi is the last of the sources enumerated in the preface of Majma' ul-Fuṣaḥā, p. 6.

125.

Or. 3524.—Foll. 268; 11¾ in. by 8; 24 lines, 5½ in. long; written in fair Nestalik in four columns, about A.H. 1250 (A.D. 1835).

[Sidney Churchill.]

مجمع الفصحا

An extensive Taẕkirah of Persian poets, by Riẓā Ḳuli Khān, poetically surnamed Hidāyat.

Beg. سپاس شکرف مر خالق را شاید وستایش ژرف مر صانعی را باید

This MS. contains an early recension of the work which was completed by the author A.H. 1284, and has been lithographed at Teheran, A.H. 1295. The preface differs from the printed text, and contains a dedication to Muḥammad Shāh, whose accession is described as a recent event. It concludes with a table of the ancient poets included in the work, beginning with Abu 'Abdullah Farālāvi and ending with Yūsuf Ghaznavi. The work proper begins, fol. 7*a*, with the notice of the former, and breaks off in the middle of the extracts from Niẓāmi Ganjavi, the contents corresponding with pp. 65—639 of the first volume of the Teheran edition.

Foll. 191—212 are in a Shikastah character, which is, according to Mr. Churchill, the handwriting of the author.

On the first page is a note by Prince 'Abd ul-Ḥusain Ḳājār, stating that in A.H. 1294 he received this volume as a gift from حضرت اشرف والد, apparently the Shah his father.

126.

Or. 3536.—Foll. 146; 14 in. by 8¾; 25 lines, 6 in. long; written in fair close Neskhi in the latter half of the 19th century.

[Sidney Churchill.]

رياض العارفين

Notices of Sufi poets, with copious extracts from their compositions, by Riẓa Ḳuli B. Muḥammad Hādi, poetically surnamed Hidāyat.

It begins with a Rubā'i, the first line of which is .این باغ که هر کش دلی بفریبد The prose begins as follows: رياض قلوب عارفين محقق و بساتين ارواح سالكين مدقق را خضرت و نظرت از تطرات مطرات فيوضات متكثره

The author remarks in the preface that previous writers on the lives of saints, such as 'Aṭṭār in his Tazkirat ul-Auliyā, Jāmi in his Nafaḥāt ul-Uns, and Nūr-ullah Shushtari in his Majālis ul-Mu'minin, had confined their selections to utterances in prose. This induced him to compile the present collection of the holy men's poetical effusions. The work is dedicated to the reigning sovereign Abu 'l-Muẓaffar Sultan Muḥammad Shāh. It was written, as appears from the concluding section, fol. 140*b*, A.H. 1260, when the author was forty-five years old.

It is divided into one Ḥadīḳah, two Rauẓahs, a Firdaus, and a Khuld, as follows:

Ḥadīḳah. An introduction treating in six chapters, termed Gulbun, of Sufism, of the mode of life adopted by Sufis, and of the conventional terms they use, fol. 4*b*.

Rauẓah I. در ذكر عرفا و مشايخ بترتيب تهجى. Notices of theosophists and holy Shaikhs who composed verses, arranged in alphabetical order, fol. 9*a*. The notices, a table of which is prefixed, are about 170 in number. They begin with Abū Yazīd Basṭāmi, and end with Yūsuf Baṭini Hindi.

Rauẓah II. در ذكر فضلا و محققين. Notices of eminent poets and philosophers who were at times under mystical inspiration, fol. 62*a* (about 100 notices, alphabetically arranged, beginning with Abu 'Ali Sinā, and ending with Yaḥya Lāhiji).

Firdaus. در شرح حال متاخرين و معاصرين. Notices of modern and contemporary Sufi poets, also alphabetically arranged, about 70 in number, beginning with Āgah Shirāzi, and ending with Hamdam Shirāzi, fol. 93*a*.

Khuld, or conclusion, being a notice of the author's life, with ample extracts from his poetical works, fol. 140*b*.

The author states that he was born in Teheran on the 15th of Muḥarram, A.H. 1215, and that his father, Muḥ. Ḥādi, who was treasurer to Aḳa Muḥammad Shāh Ḳājār, died in Shiraz, A.H. 1218. He gives a full list of his numerous works in prose and verse, including the three volumes added to Rauẓat uṣ-Ṣafā and the Majma' ul-Fuṣaḥā (which was not completed until A.H. 1284; see the preface).

At the end is a Masnavi by Mirza Ibrāhīm Kāzarūni, takh. Nādiri, in praise of the present work.

127.

Or. 4511.—Foll. 355; 12 in. by 7; 23 lines, $4\frac{1}{4}$ in. long; written in neat Nestalik, with 'Unvan and gold-ruled margins, A.H. 1259 (A.D. 1843). [SIDNEY CHURCHILL.]

مدايح المعتمديه

A collection of poems in praise of Mu'tamad ud-Daulah Minuchihr Khān, with notices of their authors, compiled by Muḥammad 'Ali, poetically surnamed Bahār.

Beg. تذكره ستايش بى منتهى و نادره نيايش لا يحصى حضرت واجب الوجودى را سزاست جلت الائه و عمت نعمائه

The work was compiled, as stated in the introduction, by desire of Minuchihr Khān (see fol. 37*b*). The author gives at the end a short account of his life, from which it appears that he was a son of the late Aḳā Abu Ṭālib Muẕahhib (or illuminator), of Isfahan, and that, having no taste for study, he took to his father's trade and to poetry.

To the present work he prefixed a memoir of Minuchihr Khān, composed by "the late"

Aḳā 'Ali Rashti, who appears to have written it in the lifetime of Fatḥ 'Ali Shāh and of the Nā'ib us-Salṭanah 'Abbās Mirza. That celebrated general was originally brought to Persia as one of the captives taken by Fatḥ 'Ali Shāh in his Georgian campaign, A.H. 1219. Having won the favour of the Shāh, he was placed, as Ich-Aḳasi Bāshi, in command of the royal Harem, and subsequently sent, with one of the royal princes, to rule over Gilān. As a reward for distinguished services in the Russian war, A.H. 1240, he received the title of Mu'tamad ud-Daulah, and was afterwards actively engaged in military operations in Fārs, Kirmanshahan, Arabistan, and other parts. The memoir, which is written in a wordy and stilted style, is brought down by the compiler, fol. 36b, to the 20th Rajab, A.H. 1259, when Minuchihr Khān, returning from Court, entered Isfahan, the seat of his government.

The notices, which are mostly rhetorical exercises with a minimum of fact, are accompanied by considerable poetical specimens. They relate to the following poets:

Aḳā 'Ali Rashti, fol. 38a.
Adib, Muḥ. 'Ali, of Teheran, fol. 39a.
Adab, Muḥ. Taḳi, of Kirmanshahan, fol. 43b.
Ummid, 'Abbās, of Mazandaran, fol. 45a.
Akhgar, 'Abd ur-Rashīd Khān, fol. 47b.
Anjuman, Mirza Isḥāḳ, of Shiraz, fol. 49a.
Afshān, Mirza 'Abdullah, of Furūshān, fol. 51a.
A'ma, fol. 53a.
Bidil, Ḥāji Muḥ., of Kirmanshahan, fol. 53b.
Baṣir, Aḳa Muḥ. Ibrāhīm, of Isfahan, fol. 55a.
Bismil, Mirza 'Ali Akbar, fol. 57a.
Bahjat, Aḳa Muḥ. Bāḳir, of Isfahan, fol. 57b.
Partav, 'Ali Riẓā, of Lanjān, fol. 58b.
Parvānah, Muḥ. Ṣādiḳ, of Ḳum, fol. 60b.
Parvānah, Muḥ. Ḥusain, of Lanjān, fol. 61a.
Tishnah, Muḥ. Taḳi Khān, fol. 62a.
Tārāj, Aḳa Muḥ. Ḥusain, of Isfahan, fol. 69b.
Tārāj, of Shiraz, fol. 70a.
Ṣāḳib, Muḥ. Ḥusain, fol. 70b.
Chākar, Sayyid Muḥ. Hādi, of Kashan, fol. 73a.
Chākar, Muḥ. Ḳāsim Khān, of Mazandaran, fol. 74a.
Chākar, Naṣr-ullah, of Burujird, fol. 74b.
Ḥakīm, Muḥ. Yūsuf B. Muḥ. Ḥusain Nūri, fol. 78a.
Khurram, son of Pasha Ḳāsim Khān, of Kajūr, fol. 79a.
Khāvar, Maḥmūd Khān, of Azarbaijan, fol. 80a.
Khāvari, Muḥ. Bāḳir, of Herat, fol. 82b.
Khāvari, Fazl-ullah, of Shiraz, fol. 87b.
Khādim, Sayyid Ismā'īl, of Ḳum.
Daryā, Luṭf-ullah B. Mirza Ḳaṭrah, fol. 88b.
Ẕauḳi, Fatḥ-ullah, of Khorasan, fol. 89b.
Ẕabīḥi, Ismā'īl Mirza Afshār, fol. 99a.
Riẓā'i, Muḥ. Riẓā, of Mazandaran, fol. 102a.
Rif'at, Fatḥ-ullah Mirza, son of Muḥ. 'Ali Mirza, fol. 104a.
Rūshan, Aḳa Muḥ. Ṣādiḳ, fol. 108a.
Raunaḳ, Muḥ. Hāshim, fol. 109a.
Zargar, Aka Muḥ. Ḥasan, fol. 110a.
Sīmā, 'Abd ul-Karīm, of Ṭālikhūni, fol. 110b.
Sāghar, Muḥ. Ibrāhīm, of Isfahan, fol. 117a.
Shihāb, Naṣr-ullah, fol. 118a.
Shāhīn, of Kāshān, fol. 147a.
Shihāb, Aḳa Muḥ. Ṭāhir, of Isfahan, fol. 148a.
Shūrish, fol. 157a.
Ṣāḥib Dīvān, Mirza Muḥ. Taḳi, of 'Aliyābād, fol. 157b.
Ṣabā, Malik ush-Shu'arā Fatḥ 'Ali Khān, fol. 159a.
Ṣafā'i, Mulla Muḥ., of Isfahan, fol. 160a.
Ṣafā, 'Abd ul-Vāsi' B. Muḥ. 'Alī Vafā, fol. 161a.

Ziyâ, Mulla Muḥ. Ḥusain, of Isfahan, fol. 162*b*.

Ṭâhir, Muḥ. Ṭâhir, of Hamadan, fol. 168*b*.

'Andalîb, Muḥ. Ḥusain Khân Malik ush-Shu'arâ, fol. 169*b*.

'Ankâ, Muḥ. Raḥîm, of Khorasan, fol. 172*b*.

'Ali, Ḥâji 'Abd ul-Ghafûr, of Isfahan, fol. 174*a*.

Ghazâl, Muḥ. Muḥsin, of Kirman, fol. 175*a*.

Ghâ'ib, Aḳa 'Abbâs, of Burujird, fol. 180*b*.

Ghaughâ, 'Abdullah, of Mazandaran, fol. 181*b*.

Fidâ, Muḥ. Sa'îd, of Ardistan, fol. 184*a*.

Furûgh, Muḥ. Munajjim Bâshi, fol. 190*a*.

Fidâ, Muḥ. Ḥusain, of Isfahan, fol. 202*a*.

Fanâ, Mulla 'Ali Lûr, of Lanjân, fol. 203*b*.

Faizi, Mirza Aḥmad, of Luristan, fol. 225*a*.

Fili, fol. 226*a*.

Ḳa'âni, Ḥabîb B. Mirza Gulshan, fol. 226*b*.

Ḳaṭrah, 'Abd ul-Vahhâb, of Isfahan, fol. 231*a*.

Kaukab, Muḥ. Bâḳir, of Khorasan, fol. 242*a*.

Muḥ. Ḳâsim Khân, son of Ṣabâ, fol. 249*a*.

Miskîn, Muḥ. 'Ali, of Isfahan, fol. 261*b*.

Manẓar, 'Ali Aṣghar, fol. 270*a*.

Maḥjûb, Aḳa Haidar 'Ali, of Shiraz, fol. 282*a*.

Muṭî', of Mazandaran, fol. 296*b*.

Mahjûr, Ḥusain Ḳuli Khân, fol. 304*b*.

Mirza Muḥammad Khân, brother of Muḥ. Yûsuf Ḥakîm, fol. 309*a*.

Aḳa Sayyid Muḥ., of Lanjân, fol. 310*b*.

Munshi, Muḥ. Ḥasan B. Muḥ. Naṣir, fol. 314*a*.

Mirza Muḥ. Khân, son of Malik ush-Shu'arâ, fol. 317*a*.

Majnûn, of Teheran, fol. 319*a*.

Mashrab, Muḥ. 'Ali, of Nâ'în, fol. 322*a*.

Maẓlûm, Ḥâji Muh. Hâshim, fol. 322*b*.

Maḥram, Muḥ. 'Ali, of Shiraz, fol. 323*b*.

Mirza Riẓâ Ḳuli, of Hamadan, fol. 324*a*.

Naghmah, Riẓâ Ḳuli, of Mazandaran, fol. 325*a*.

Nadîm, 'Ali Akbar, brother of Ḳâ'âni, fol. 329*b*.

Nâṭiḳ, Muḥ. Ḥasan, of the family of Ṣabâ, fol. 332*b*.

Nashâṭi Khân, fol. 335*b*.

Viṣâl, Muḥ. Shafi', of Shiraz, fol. 336*a*.

Vafâ, Muḥ. 'Ali, of Ardistan, fol. 336*b*.

Hilâl, Sayyid Abu Ṭâlib, of Kashan, fol. 337*b*.

Humâ, of Shiraz, fol. 339*b*.

Memoirs and poems of the author, foll. 346*b*—355. A tabulated index of the lives occupies two pages at the beginning, foll. 1-2.

This MS. was apparently the copy presented to Minuchihr Khan, whose portrait is found inside the original painted cover.

128.

Or. 4512.—Foll. 357; 13¼ in. by 8; 23 lines, 4½ in. long; written in small and neat Nestalik; dated Isfahan, the last day of Shavvâl, A.H. 1263 (A.D. 1847).

[Sidney Churchill.]

A later enlarged edition of the same work.

The historical introduction is brought down from A.H. 1259 to the death of Minuchihr Khan, which took place on the fifth of Rabî' I., A.H. 1263, foll. 31—35. It concludes with a Kasidah in the Khan's praise, ending with a chronogram for his death.

There are nineteen additional notices relating to the following poets:

Âshuftah, Ḥâji Muh. Ḳâẓim of Shiraz, fol. 44*b*.

Âṣafi, Muḥ. Ja'far, son of Ṣûfi, fol. 54*b*.

Anjum, 'Ali Akbar Khân, fol. 55*b*.

Taẓarv, Faraj-ullah of Azarbaijan, fol. 78*b*.

Ḥayât, Muḥ. Mahdi Ḳâ'ini, fol. 87*b*.

Khâdim, of Isfahan, fol. 101*b*.

Rakhshân, Yûsuf, son of Knyaz Melikof, fol. 117*a*.

Zūri', Aḳa Rajab 'Ali of Isfahan, fol. 122*b*.
Shā'iḳ, Mulla Ḥasan of Isfahan, fol. 159*b*.
Ṭūba, Sayyid Ḥasan of Kashan, fol. 180*a*.
Ghazāli, fol. 193*b*.
Ḳudrat, Sayyid Muḥ. 'Ali of Kashan, fol. 250*a*.
Kāmi, Sulaimān, son of Knyaz Melikof, fol. 252*a*.
Malik, Muḥ. Mahdi of Farahan, fol. 259*b*.
Maẓhar, Murtaẓa Ḳuli Mirza, fol. 260*b*.
Maktūm, Ḥakīm, fol. 274*a*.
Mirza Muḥ. Mahdi of Khui, fol. 281*b*.
Hijrān, Aḳa Fatḥ 'Ali B. Muḥ. Karīm Khān, fol. 344*a*.

129.

Or. 2943.—Foll. 272; 9¼ in. by 5¾; 14 lines, 3 in. long; written in cursive Nestalik; dated 4 Rajab, A.H. 1266 (A.D. 1850).
[Sidney Churchill.]

حديقۀ امام اللهی

A Tazkirah of the poets of Sinandij, the chief town of Persian Kurdistan,[1] by Mirza 'Abdullah B. Muḥammad Aḳā, poetically surnamed Raunaḳ.

Beg. ازهار اشجار حديقه بيان انفس و آفاق و اثمار
نهال آبـال زبان ماسوى للخلاق

The author says in his preface that he had from his childhood devoted himself to the study of poets, ancient and modern, and that, having perused three or four Tazkirahs, he was indignant at finding in them no record of the poets of Sinandij. From a desire to supply that deficiency, he spent ten years, from the twentieth to the thirtieth of his age, during the governorship of the late Governor, Khusrau Khān, in collecting their select compositions. But the work was not completed until A.H. 1265, after the accession of the latter's son, Amān-ullah Khān II., in whose honour he gave it the above title.

Khusrau Khān, son and successor of Amān-ullah Khān I.,[2] held the Vāli-ship of Kurdistan, as we learn from the present work, from A.H. 1240 to his death, A.H. 1250. His son, Amān-ullah Khan II. was appointed to the same government by Muḥammad Shāh Ḳājār, A.H. 1262, at the age of three and twenty; was deposed after a year's tenure, and reinstated by Nāṣir ud-Din Shāh, A.H. 1265.

From the autobiography which concludes the present work we learn that the author was born in Sinandij, where his grandsire, coming from his native city, Hamadān, had settled, A.H. 1120 (read 1220); that his father, left an orphan at the age of nine, was raised to rank and wealth by the Vālī Khusrau Khān; and that he (the author) was appointed Munshi Bāshi, or Head Secretary, by Amān-ullah Khān II. Compare Majma' ul-Fuṣaḥā, vol. ii., p. 150.

The work is divided into the following sections:—

Khiyābān. A short account of Sinandij, fol. 9*b*.

Gulban I. Life and poems of Amān-ullah Khān II., with the poetical surname Vāli, fol. 11*a*.

Gulban II. Notices of poets, thirty-nine in number, in alphabetical order, fol. 29*b*.

Juibār. Notices of two female poets, fol. 221*a*.

Guldastah, or Khātimah. Life and poems of the author, fol. 239*b*.

[1] The place commonly called Sinna, and described by Rich in his Narrative of a Residence in Kurdistan, pp. 199 and 208, where its proper name is said to be Sinendrij.

[2] Amān-ullah Khān I. was forty-seven years of age when Rich visited Sinna in 1820 (A.H. 1235). See *ib.*, p. 211.

The present copy was written by Naṣr-ullah B. Ākā Ibrāhīm Sinandijī for his paternal uncle Mīrzā 'Abdullah Munshi Bāshī (the author) one year after the date of composition.

Memoirs and Travels.

130.

Or. 3203.—Foll. 79; $8\frac{1}{4}$ in. by 6; from 13 to 18 lines, $4\frac{3}{4}$ in. long; written in cursive Nestalik, early in the 19th century.

[Kremer, no. 57.]

نسخهٔ احوال شاهی

Life and teachings of the Indian saint Mulla Shāh, by his disciple Tavakkul Beg Kūlālī.

Beg. بنامش کنم حمد را ابتدا
بحمد الله او هست محمود ما

.... حمد بیغایت و ثناء بی نهایت آن ذات کل را
که قلوب عارفانه از نور جمال خود منور کرده

The author says in the preface that he had become in his sixteenth year a disciple of Mulla Shāh in Kashmir, and had for forty years, with some interruptions, availed himself of his teaching. He adds that he had recorded in the present memoir only what he had himself witnessed or heard from his master's lips. The date of composition, A.H. 1077, is expressed by the above title; but, by some accidental slip in the text, Shāhjahān appears in the preface (instead of 'Ālamgīr) as the reigning sovereign.

Mulla Shāh was born, as stated at the end, A.H. 992, and died in Lahore on the eve of the 15th of Ṣafar, A.H. 1072. See also the Persian Catalogue, p. 690*b*.

An abstract of the present work was published by A. von Kremer in the Journal Asiatique, 1869, i., pp. 105—159.

The MS. belonged originally to Capt. Wm. Deuce, whose name is written in the Persian character on the fly-leaf. In 1834 it passed into the hands of G. C. Renouard, and in 1868 it was purchased for Kremer in London.

131.

Or. 4733.—Foll. 357; $8\frac{1}{2}$ in. by $5\frac{3}{4}$; 15 lines, $3\frac{1}{2}$ in. long; written in fair Nestalik; dated A.H. 1281 (A.D. 1864).

[Sidney Churchill.]

مرآت الاحوال

Mir'āt ul-Aḥvāl, or Memoirs of Aḥmad B. Muḥammad 'Ali B. Muḥammad Bāḳir al-Bahbahānī.

This copy agrees with a former MS., Add. 24,052, the contents of which have been fully described in the Persian Catalogue, pp. 385-6. Its various sections begin respectively as follows: Summary of the whole work, by the author, fol. 2*b*. Preface, fol. 17*a*. Maṭlab I., fol. 19*a*. Maṭlab II., fol. 26*b*. Maṭlab III., fol. 36*a*. Maṭlab IV., fol. 48*a*. Maṭlab V., Maḳṣad 1, fol. 69*b*; Maḳṣad 2, fol. 96*a*; Maḳṣad 3, fol. 234*a*. Khātimah, fol. 327*a*.

The author's colophon, transcribed at the end, is dated 'Azīmābād (Patna) in the third month of the fifth year of the third decade of the third century of the second thousand of the Hijrah, *i.e.* Rabī' I., A.H. 1225.

Foll. 69—79 contain in the margins additional notices by Muḥ. Ṣādiḳ B. al-Sayyid Muḥ. Mahdi B. Amīr Sayyid 'Ali, written in small Neskhi in the reign of Nāṣir ud-Dīn Shāh.

132.

Or. 3523.—Foll. 220; 11¾ in. by 7¾; 21 lines, 4 in. long; written in fair Neskhi leaning to Nestalik, in the 19th century. [Sidney Churchill.]

تجربة الاحرار و تسلية الابرار

Memoirs of 'Abd ur-Razzāk B. Najaf Kuli Dunbuli, with notices of his contemporaries.

Beg. سر شوریده درین بازار پر سودا سامان کجا پذیرد تا طوق عبودیت آفرینندهٔ جهان بر گردن جان نیفکند

The author, three of whose works, Ma'āṣir Sulṭāniyyah, a translation of Krusinski, and a Tazkirah, have been already mentioned (nos. 68, 63, 123), was born, as he states here, fol. 31*b*, in Khui, A.H. 1176, and was taken as a boy to Tabriz, where his father resided as Beglerbegi. After the latter's death in A.H. 1199, he repaired to Shiraz and afterwards to Isfahan.

The present work was written, as stated fol. 215*a*, A.H. 1228, and in another passage, fol. 131*b*, the author says that he was then fifty and some years old. The style is extremely diffuse and artificial, being half Persian and half Arabic, and largely made up of poetical pieces.

Contents: Preface, including a panegyric on Fatḥ 'Ali Shāh, fol. 3*b*. Account of the author's clan, the Dunbulis, and of its eminent men, especially of the author's father, who served with distinction under Nādir and under Muḥammad Ḥasan Khan Kajar, and was confirmed by Karim Khan in the governorship of Tabriz, fol. 15*a*. Birth of the author, and his early life, fol. 31*b*. His arrival at Shiraz; notices of eminent 'Ulamā in Shiraz and Isfahan, fol. 41*b*. Notices of the following contemporary poets, with extensive extracts: Mushtāḳ Isfahāni, fol. 69*a*; 'Āshiḳ, Aḳa Muḥ. Isfahāni, fol. 76*a*; Āzur Begdili Shāmlu (Luṭf 'Ali Beg), fol. 83*a*; 'Uzri Begdili Shāmlu (Isḥāḳ Beg), fol. 96*b*; Hātif (Sayyid Aḥmad Iṣfahāni), fol. 97*b*; Ṣabāḥi (Ḥāji Sulaimān), fol. 111*a*; Ṣahbā (Aḳa Muḥ. Taḳi), fol. 125*b*; with shorter notices of Ṭabīb, fol. 126*a*; Asīri, Ḥājat, Rafīḳ, Ṣāfi, Ṭūfān, fol. 128; Ghālib, Firībi, Darvīsh 'Abd ul-Majīd, Nashāṭ, fol. 129; Naṣīb, Niyāzi, Hijri. Continuation of the author's life, fol. 130*a*. Extract from Mahdi Khān Simnāni's history of the reign of Nādir, fol. 132*b*. Events after Nādir's death; Zand and Lūr dynasties, fol. 143*b*. War between Āzād Khān and Fatḥ 'Ali Khān Afshār, fol. 151*b*. Shiraz under Karīm Khān, fol. 154*b*. Continuation of the author's life, fol. 160*a*. His conversation with friends in a garden at Shiraz, and conclusion of the memoirs, foll. 163*a*—219*b*.

133.

Or. 2769.—Foll. 200; 10¾ in. by 6¾; 11 lines, 4½ in. long; written in fair Nestalik, partly in tabulated form; dated 11 Rabī' II., A.H. 1249 (A.D. 1833).

[Presented by Wm. Wright.]

Itinerary of Sayyid 'Izzat-ullah through Tibet and Turkistan, A.H. 1227-8. See the Persian Catalogue, p. 982.

Beg. احوال سفر بخارا و تفصیل منازل از اتک تا کشمیر

134.

Or. 4908.—Foll. 10; 9 in. by 7; 12 lines, 4½ in. long; written in fair Nestalik about A.D. 1860. [Sir Henry Rawlinson.]

A personal statement addressed by the Raja of Rewari to the Indian Government, with the object of proving his loyal attitude during the Mutiny, in the hope of being restored to his former position.

Beg. از قديم الايام بزرگان ابجانب در هندوستان دارای ملك و فرمان روا بوده اند و ملك بسيار در قبضه ماها بوده است

COSMOGRAPHY AND GEOGRAPHY.

135.

Or. 4383.—Foll. 183; 13¼ in. by 8; 25 lines, 5 in. long; written on blue-tinted paper in cursive Nestalik, with gold-ruled margins and miniatures; dated 17 Shavvāl, A.H. ١٢٠٥, apparently for 1205 (A.D. 1791). Bound in painted covers. [Wallis Budge.]

عجائب المخلوقات

"The Wonders of Creation;" translated from the Arabic of Zakariyyā B. Muḥammad al-Ḳazvini. See the Persian Catalogue, p. 462.

Beg. الحمد لله مبدع العقول والارواح ومنشى النفوس والاشباح

After an Arabic doxology, different from that of the original work, the author's name is given at the bottom of the first page as follows: اما بعد چنين گويد زكريا ابن محمد القزوينى تولاه بفضله وتوسله بلطفه. After this there is an extensive lacuna involving the loss of the preliminary chapters. The next three pages contain the Arabic table of chapters (p. 13, line 21—p. 15 of Wüstenfeld's edition). The text begins, fol. 3*a*, as follows: الاول فى حقيقة الافلاك فى اشكالها واوضاعها وحركتها بطريق الاجمال حكماء گويند كه فلك جسمست بسيط كرى مشتمل بر وسط متحرك بران نه خفيف و نه ثقيل نه حار و نه بارد و نه رطب و نه يابس

The translation, which keeps close to the text, differs from that which has been lithographed at Teheran, A.H. 1264. It breaks off about three pages before the real end of the work, namely, after the first line of the article on 'Ūj B. 'Anāḳ (Wüstenfeld's edition, p. 449, line 24).

The volume is copiously illustrated with miniatures, a few of which are whole-page.

For other Persian translations see Pertsch, Berlin Catalogue, no. 345, and Ethé, Bodleian Catalogue, no. 397.

136.

Or. 4903.—Foll. 78; 11½ in. by 8; 21 lines, 5½ in. long; written in small and cursive Nestalik; dated A.H. 1250 (A.D. 1834-35). [Sir Henry Rawlinson.]

نزهة القلوب

Nuzhat ul-Ḳulūb, a cosmographical work by Ḥamd-ullah Mustaufi; the latter half of the work, from the beginning of Ḳism II., which treats of the geography of Iran, to the author's epilogue.

The contents correspond with foll. 142—241 of the complete copy, Add. 16,736, described in the Persian Catalogue, p. 418. For other copies see Pertsch, Berlin Catalogue, nos. 347—52, and Ethé, Bodleian Catalogue, nos. 406—412.

137.

Or. 4904.—Foll. 84; 11 in. by 7½; 19 lines, 5¼ in. long; written in distinct Nestalik; dated the last day of Rabi' II., A.H. 1256 (A.D. 1840). [Sir Henry Rawlinson.]

The same part of Nuzhat ul-Ḳulūb, transcribed from the preceding MS., as shown by the following note on the first page: "Edward Conolly. Copied at Caubul from a MS. of Major Rawlinson. August 7, 1840."

138.

Or. 4902.—Foll. 392; 11¾ in. by 7½; 23 lines, 4½ in. long; written in distinct Nestalik, with ʻUnvān and red-ruled margins, apparently in the 17th century.

[Sir Henry Rawlinson.]

هفت اقليم

"The Seven Climes;" a geographical work by Amīn Aḥmad Rāzi, chiefly valuable on account of the copious biographical notices which it includes. See the Persian Catalogue, p. 335*b*.

This copy wants about twelve lines at the end. For other copies see Ethé, Bodleian Catalogue, nos. 416—20.

139.

Or. 4617.—Foll. 329; 15½ in. by 10; 26 lines, 6½ in. long; written in clear large Neskhi, with ʻUnvān and gold-ruled margins, before A.H. 1246 (A.D. 1830).

[Sidney Churchill.]

رياض السياحت

A geographical work with copious historical and biographical notices, by Ibn Iskandar Zain ul-ʻĀbidīn Shīrvāni Niʻmatullāhi.

Beg. بوستان حمد و سپاس و گلستان ثناء بى
قياس مر خداونديرا سزاست جل جلاله وعم نواله

The author was a great traveller. All the countries here described, from Morocco to Bengal and from Rumili to Yemen, he had personally visited, and his biographical notices relate mostly to contemporary persons, men in power or religious characters, with whom he had met and conversed. He often indulges in more or less extensive digressions on extraneous subjects, such as the doctrines and observances of Sufis, the secret virtues of letters and of the names of God, the interpretation of dreams (foll. 59—82), traditions relating to the prophets of old, and Shiʻah polemics. The work is mentioned as one of the sources of Majmaʻ ul-Fuṣaḥā (Preface, p. 6). A notice of Jalāl ud-Dīn Rūmi, prefixed to the Bombay edition of the Masnavi, A.H. 1300, is ascribed to the author.

The present volume is the second and last of the work. The first volume, which treats of Persia, had been finished, as the author states here, in Ḳūmshah (district of Isfahan), A.H. 1237. The continuation had been delayed by a period of troubles and by untoward circumstances until the month of Rabiʻ II., A.H. 1242, when the author was induced to write it as a suitable offering to the Shahzādah, Muḥammad Riẓā Mirza.[1] It was completed, as stated at the end, on Monday, the 27th of Ẕulḥijjah, of the same year, and A.H. 1242 is frequently mentioned in the body of the work as the date of composition.

The present volume contains seven sections called Rauẓah, and numbered from two to eight, as follows:

Rauẓah II., comprising a "Siyāḥat" and four "Būstāns," as follows: Siyāḥat; a general description of Tūrān, or Māvarā-annahr, fol. 3*a*. Būstān 1. Principal towns of Tūrān (including Badakhshan) with historical accounts, and notices of poets and saints, fol. 3*b*. Būstān 2. Turkistān, with an account of the Turkish race, fol. 12*b*. Būstān 3. Kābul and dependencies, fol. 15*a*. Būstān 4. Kashmir, fol. 27*a*.

Rauẓah III., comprising a "Sair" and four "Gulistāns," viz., Sair; general account

[1] A son of Fatḥ ʻAli Shāh, born A.H. 1211, and appointed A.H. 1234 to the government of Gilan. See Majmaʻ ul-Fuṣaḥā, vol. i., p. 11, where the prince is spoken of as still living.

of Turkey (Rūm), fol. 44*a*. Gulistān 1. Towns of Anatoli, fol. 44*b*. Gulistān 2. Lesser Armenia, fol. 106*a*. Gulistān 3. Diyārbekr, fol. 111*b*. Gulistān 4. Rumili, fol. 114*b*.

Rauẓah IV., "Tafarruj;" general account of Syria, fol. 121*b*. Firdaus 1. Jund i Urdunn, fol. 123*b*. Firdaus 2. Jund i Dimashḳ, fol. 128*a*. Firdaus 3. Jund i Filisṭīn, fol. 153*a*. Firdaus 4. Jund i Ḳinnisrīn, fol. 195*a*.

Rauẓah V., "Naẓar;" general account of Arabia, fol. 214*b*. Jinān 1. Ḥijāz, including an account of Muḥammad and the Companions, fol. 215*a*. Jinān 2. 'Omān, including Ḥaḍramaut, fol. 226*a*. Jinān 3. Yemen, fol. 228*b*. Jinān 4. Diyār Yathrib, or Tihāmah, including Medina, with an account of the Imams and first Khalifs, fol. 232*b*.

Rauẓah VI., "Kisht"; historical account of Egypt, fol. 245*a*. Gulshan 1. Cairo and Lower Egypt, including a history of Moses and the Jews, of the Fatimides and Ayyubides, fol. 249*a*. Gulshan 2. Ṣa'īd, or Upper Egypt, fol. 266*b*. Gulshan 3. Maghrib, chiefly Morocco, fol. 268*b*. Gulshan 4. Islands of the Mediterranean, fol. 290*a*.

Rauẓah VII., "Gardish;" general account of India, fol. 270*b*. Jannat 1. Bengal, fol. 273*b*. Jannat 2. Deccan, fol. 278*b*. Jannat 3. Sind and Gujrat, fol. 282*b*. Jannat 4. Hindustan, including an account of the Hindu creed and of the kings of Delhi, fol. 286*b*.

Rauẓah VIII., "Gulzār" 1. Countries not visited by the author, but respecting which he had obtained some information, viz., Russia, Bosnia, China, Ḥabash, Khitā, Crimea, Namsah (Austria), Venice, Nepal, and America, fol. 315*a*. Gulzār 2. Seas, lakes, and rivers, fol. 319*b*. Gulzār 3. Islands of India, including a history of Adam and his descendants, fol. 321*b*. Gulzār 4. Springs and wells, fol. 327*a*. Bahar; epilogue in praise of Muḥ. Riẓā Mirza.

On the first page of the volume is a note stating that it was deposited in the library of Muḥ. Riza Mirza, A.H. 1248. On a fly-leaf at the end are entered birth-dates of some of the Prince's sons.

140.

Or. 3677.—Foll. 347; 12 in. by 7½; 23 lines, 5¾ in. long; written in small and elegant Nestalik, with a neat 'Unvān and gold-ruled margins, apparently A.H. 1248 (A.D. 1832).

[SIDNEY CHURCHILL.]

بستان السياحه

A work on geography, alphabetically arranged, with copious historical and biographical notices, by the same author.

Beg. بستان حمد و سپاس و گلشن ثناء بیقیاس مخصوص بارگاه احدی و مختص درگاه صمدیست عز اسمه و جل ذکره ... اما بعد اما محرر این اوراق ... کمترین بندگان نعمة الله الفقیر الجانی ابن اسکندر زین العابدین شیروانی

The author seems to have been a man of liberal views, vast experience, and large sympathies. He shows a predilection for strange religions and heretical sects, of whose tenets he gives a fair presentment, as, for instance, in his notices on the Iblīsis, fol. 19*a*; Yazīdis, fol. 51; Nānakshāhis (or Sikhs), fol. 53*b*; on the followers of Zardusht, fol. 72*a*; on the Christian sects, fol. 143*b*, &c. He was himself a Sufi of the Ni'mat-ullahi order, in which he was initiated by Muḥ. Ja'far Ḳarāgūzli, known as Majẕūb 'Ali Shāh, and he gives, foll. 151—59, a full account of the Sufi system and of the various branches of the sect. His biographical notices relate mostly to great saints and gnostics ('Urafā).

From a rather diffuse preface we gather that the author was transferred in early childhood from his native land to the holy places (Kerbela), where he studied for twelve years under his father and others. At the age of seventeen he started on his travels, visiting the learned, and associating with high and low in every land. At the time of writing he had reached his fifty-fourth year, and he says that the chronogram, مرغوب = 1248, indicates the year of both the commencement and the completion of the present work. At the end, however, it is stated that it was finished in Shiraz on Thursday, the 27th of Shavvāl, A.H. 1247.

The work is divided into an introduction called "Sair," twenty-eight "Gulshans," corresponding with the letters of the Arabic alphabet, and a conclusion called "Bahār."

Contents: "Sair;" introductory remarks bearing chiefly on the ignorance, the spirit of intolerance, and the narrow-mindedness prevailing among Muḥammadan writers, fol. 4*a*.

The twenty-eight Gulshans form a geographical dictionary, occupying the main part of the volume, foll. 5—322. The leading words are mostly names of countries or towns, sometimes names of races or sects, as Tātār, Tājik, fol. 87*b*; Rûs, fol. 129*b*; Yûnān, Yûsufzāi, fol. 321; Shī'ah, fol. 143; and even, in a few instances, words expressing abstract notions, as فضائل انسانی, fol. 181*a*, وحدت وجود, fol. 303*b*. In the case of names of places, the author is always careful to distinguish those he had visited from those which he only knew from hearsay. Gulshan I. begins, fol. 5*a*, with ذکر اقلیم, a description of the seven climes. Then come the following articles: Āẕarbāijān, fol. 15*b*; Alamūt (with an account of the Ismā'ilis), fol. 16*a*; Albustān, fol. 19*a*; Āchi (Achin), fol. 21*a*, &c.

In the absence of conspicuous headings, the following list will not be superfluous. It gives the folio at which each of the remaining Gulshans begin and the first article in each.

II. ب Bāb ul-Abvāb, or Darband, fol. 59*b*. پ Pānipat, fol. 85*a*. III. ت Tāshkand, fol. 87*b*. IV. ث Thalj, fol. 93*b*. V. ج Jābalsā and Jābalḳā, fol. 94*a*; چ Chāch, fol. 100*b*. VI. ح Ḥāji Tarkhān (Astrachan), fol. 102*b*. VII. خ Khandes, fol. 109*a*. VIII. د Dārābjird, fol. 115*a*. IX. ذ Ẕahāb, fol. 125*b*. X. ر Rāz, fol. 126*a*. XI. ز Zābul, fol. 130*a*. XII. س Sāmirah, fol. 132*a*. XIII. ش Shām, fol. 139*b*. XIV. ص Ṣāliḥ-ābād, fol. 148*a*. XV. ض Ẓila', fol. 160*a*. XVI. ط Ṭā'if, fol. 160*a*. XVII. ظ Ẓafir, fol. 162*a*. XVIII. ع 'Ānah, fol. 162*b*. XIX. غ Ghāzīpūr, fol. 173*b*. XX. ف Fās, fol. 176*a*. XXI. ق Ḳāhirah, fol. 190*a*. XXII. ك Kābul, fol. 217*b*; گ Gāgri, fol. 228*a*. XXIII. ل Lār, fol. 249*a*. XXIV. م Māhān, fol. 259*a*; (under Medina is found an account of Muḥammad, the Imams, and the early Khalifs, foll. 264—275). XXV. ن Nābulus, fol. 287*b*. XXVI. و Vāsiṭ, fol. 302*b*. XXVII. ه Hāshimah, fol. 308*a*. XXVIII. ى Yāfā, fol. 316*b*.

"Bahār," the concluding section, is divided into four Gulzārs, viz., I. Interpretation of dreams, fol. 323*a*. II. Stages traversed by the author on his journeys and their distances, fol. 337*a*. This section concludes with an اعتذار or apology. The author excuses any deficiency in the work on the following ground: while passing through Ḳumshah on his way from Shiraz to Kerbela, A.H. 1241, he had been shamefully robbed of all his belongings, including his travelling notes, by Muḥ. Ḳāsim Khān Ḳājār, governor of that place. III. Miscellaneous traditions and narratives, fol. 340*b*. IV. The author's epilogue in praise of the work, fol. 346*b*.

For other MSS. see Mélanges Asiatiques, vol. i., p. 556, and vol. vi., p. 403.

141.

Or. 3666.—Foll. 443; $13\frac{3}{4}$ in. by $8\frac{1}{2}$; 17 lines, $6\frac{1}{4}$ in. long; written in Neskhi on blue-tinted paper; dated 5 Ramazan, A.H. 1273 (A.D. 1857). [SIDNEY CHURCHILL.]

حدائق السياحة

An earlier and shorter edition of the preceding geographical dictionary.

Beg. حدايق حمد و ثنا و رياض سپاس بى منتها مختص واجب الوجوديست

The work is stated at the end to have been completed in Shiraz on Saturday the 18th of Zulhijjah, A.H. 1242, that is to say in the same year as the second volume of the Riyāẓ us-Siyāḥat (no. 139) by the same author, and the preface contains the same dedication as the latter work, although the name of the prince has been left out in the present MS. This first edition is considerably shorter than the later one, and the arrangement is different. The alphabetical order of entries under the same letter which obtains in the latter is not observed in the present one.

The work is divided into a Būstān, twenty-eight Ḥadiḳahs, and a Gulistān. The Būstān, fol. 4b, is identical with the Sair of the preceding MS., and the Ḥadiḳahs correspond with its Gulshans. The first eight begin as follows: I. ا اقليم, fol. 6a. II. ب بحار seas, fol. 87b. III. ت Tiling, fol. 126a. IV. ث Thalj, fol. 134b. V. ج Jābalsā, fol. 135a. VI. ح Ḥabash, fol. 148a. VII. خ Khitā, fol. 156b. VIII. د Dimashḳ. The last two are XXVII. و Venice, fol. 426b. XXVIII. ى Yūnān, fol. 434b. At the end are found the same اعتذار, or apology, as in the preceding MS., fol. 442a, and the Gulistān, a short epilogue, fol. 442b.

SCIENCES AND ARTS.

Encyclopaedias.

142.

Or. 2972.—Foll. 188; $9\frac{1}{2}$ in. by 6; 17 lines, $3\frac{3}{4}$ in. long; written in clear Neskhi, with 'Unvān and gold-ruled margins; dated Shavvāl, A.H. 977 (A.D. 1570). [SIDNEY CHURCHILL.]

جامع العلوم

An encyclopaedia of Muslim sciences, by Fakhr ud-Din Muḥammad B. 'Umar ar-Rāẓi, who died A.H. 606.

Beg. الحمد لله الذى انشانا بتصريفه واثرنا بتشريفه .... اما بعد چنين گويد مولف اين كتاب افضل المتاخرين .... محمد بن عمر الرازى

The author says in his preface that, attracted by the renown of 'Alā ud-Dunya wa'd Din Abu 'l-Muẓaffar Tukush B. Khwārazmshāh, he proceeded to that prince's residence. After spending three years in Khwārazm, he obtained access to His Majesty's presence, and wrote for him the present work, treating of various sciences. It was so planned as to comprise nine propositions out of each science, three of which are easy, three difficult, and three examinatory, *i.e.* designed to test the reader's proficiency.

In other copies the title of the work is جوامع العلوم. In a later edition described by Ethé, Bodleian Catalogue, no. 1481, and comprising sixty sciences, A.H. 574 is given as the date of composition.

The present recension comprised only fifty-seven sciences (one of which is lost in the MS.), namely: الكلام fol. 4a; اصول الفقه fol. 8b; الجدل fol. 10a; الخلافيات fol. 14b; المذهب fol. 19a; الفرايض fol. 24a; الوصايا fol. 27a; التفسير fol. 30a; دلائل الاعجاز fol. 33b;

علل القرات fol. 38b; علم الاحاديث fol. 41a; اسماء الرجال fol. 47a; التواريخ fol. 49b; المغازى fol. 62b; النحو fol. 64b; الصرف fol. 67a; الاشتقاق fol. 70b; الامثال fol. 71a; العروض fol. 74b; القوافى fol. 80a; بدائع الشعر والنثر fol. 83a; مشكلات الشعر fol. 85a; المنطق fol. 88a; الطبيعيات fol. 92a; التعبير fol. 95b; الفراسة fol. 100b; الطب fol. 102a; التشريح fol. 114a; الصيدنة fol. 117b; الخواص fol. 120b; الاكسير fol. 121b; الجواهر fol. 124b; الطلسمات fol. 127b; الفلاحة fol. 132a; قلع الآثار fol. 133a; البيطرة fol. 134a; علم البزاة fol. 136b; الهندسة fol. 138b (المساحة, mentioned in the table, is here missing, owing to the loss of some leaves); جر الاثقال fol. 141a; حساب الهند fol. 143b; حساب الهوائى fol. 146a; علم الوفق والاعداد fol. 147a; علم المعاينة fol. 149b; الموسيقى fol. 151b; الهياة fol. 155a; الاحكام fol. 158b; الرمل fol. 161a; العزايم fol. 163b; الالهيات fol. 168b; مقالات اهل العالم fol. 171a; الاخلاق fol. 173a; السياسات fol. 175b; تدبير المنزل fol. 178a; علم الاخرة fol. 180b; علم الدعوات fol. 183a; اداب الملوك fol. 185a.

For other copies see the Leyden Catalogue, vol. i., no. 16; Ethé, *l.c.*; and Pertsch, Berlin Catalogue, no. 92, where the work is mentioned under the same title as in the next MS., viz. حدائق الانوار فى حقائق الاسرار

143.

Or. 3308.—Foll. 132; 7 in. by 4¾; from 18 to 23 lines, about 3½ in. long; written in small and cursive Nestalik; dated Tuesday, 20 Ramazan, A.H. 893 (A.D. 1488).

[Sidney Churchill.]

حدائق الانوار فى حقائق الاسرار

Another enlarged edition of the same work.

With the exception of the new title, the preface is identical with that of the preceding MS. In the body of the work there is also complete agreement, with the exception of the following three additional chapters: 1. علم آلات الحرب fol. 105a, coming after علم الاثقال; 2. علم الجبر و المقابله, fol. 108a; and 3. علم الارثماطيقى, fol. 109b, both placed after الحساب الهوائى. There are also a few variations in the headings. The chapter headed علم المعانى (fol. 66b) is identical with the علم بدايع الشعر of the preceding MS.; the chapter here called علم بدايع الشعر (fol. 67a) corresponds with the مشكلات الشعر of the latter; and instead of علم المعاينة, we have, fol. 112a, علم المناظر

144.

Or. 3648.—Foll. 406; 9¾ in. by 6; 25 lines, 3¾ in. long; written in small and neat Nestalik, apparently about the close of the 16th century.

[Sidney Churchill.]

رياض الابرار

An encyclopaedia of Muslim sciences, by Ḥusain 'Aḳīli Rustamdāri (see foll. 17b, 68b).

Beg. زينت مجموعهٔ علوم ربانى و زيب ديباچهٔ كتاب كامرانى حمد و ثناى واجب الاداى علامى

In a preface of inordinate length, written in prose copiously interspersed with verses, the author says that he had been twenty years travelling through Iran and other parts of the world in quest of knowledge, and gives a full list of all the standard scientific works which he had studied. In A.H. 978 he left Shiraz, stayed a short time in Isfahan, and repaired to Ḳazvin, then the royal residence, where he expected to find a gathering of masters of science. In this hope, however, he was sadly disappointed. The greater part of the preface is taken up by a violent diatribe against the 'Ulamā of Ḳazvin, who are taxed with crass ignorance, greed, envy, and every kind of wickedness. At last the author, having been prevailed upon by some faithful friends to display to the world his stores of learning, undertook the present work, which he commenced in Muḥarram, A.H. 979, and finished in Rabi' II. of the same year. In the introduction he refers to the preceding work of Fakhr ud-Din Rāzi, which he designates as كتاب ستين on account of the sixty sciences with which it deals, while he calls his own كتاب تسعين as including ninety sciences. It must be confessed, however, that the arrangement is unmethodical. Many sections are jumbles of heterogeneous subjects. There is ample evidence of the author's having held extreme Shī'ah views.

The work is divided into a Fātiḥah, twelve Rauẓahs, and a Khātimah.

The Fātiḥah comprises three Ḥadīkahs, viz.: 1. Criticism on the work of Rāzi, enumeration of the sciences with which it deals, and a full table of contents of the present work, fol. 20*b*. 2. Showing that Amir ul-Mūminīn ('Ali) was the originator of sciences, fol. 22*a*. Commentary on a Khuṭbah of 'Ali called Khuṭbah i Shiḳshiḳiyyah, fol. 26*a*.

Rauẓah I., in sixteen Maḳāls, treating of the Prophet's traditional saying about seventy-three Muslim sects, showing that the one saving sect is the Imāmiyyah, and containing an exposition and refutation of other sects and religions, fol. 39*b*.

Rauẓah II., in three Maḳṣads. A summary of history from Adam to the time of composition, fol. 108*b*.

Rauẓah III., in fourteen Bayāns, fol. 146*a*, the subjects of which are stated as follows: در بیان علم تفسیر و علم معانی و بیان ... و علم بدیع و علم نحو و صرف و علم لغت و علم اشتقاق و علم اصول و منطق و علم رجال و حدیث و فقه که مشتمل بر فرایض و وصایا و احکام عباد است ضمنا و بیانا و مذاهب خمسه شیعه و شافعی و مالکی و حنفی و حنبلی و احکام عبادات

Rauẓah IV., in twelve Rukns, fol. 174*a*, dealing with the following matters: The Muslim creed; the ninety-nine names of God and their virtues; properties of the Surahs and verses of the Coran and of the letters of the alphabet; alchemy (اکسیر); pronunciation and various readings of the Coran; writing and orthography; strange characters; writing implements and coloured inks; the art of removing stains; proverbs and Inshā.

Rauẓah V., in three Aṣls, treating of ethics and politics, of medicine, and of the interpretation of dreams, fol. 197*a*.

Rauẓah VI., in eight Shajarahs, treating of astronomy, astrology, prophecies, and divination, fol. 236*a*. در بیان علم زیجات و تقویمات و احکام نجومی مفصلا و طالع مولود و طالع مسئله و در بیان اصطلاحات اسطرلاب و بیان مقالات جاماسب نامه که متعلق بحالات حضرت رسالت پناه و شاه حقایق آگاه و جناب صاحب الزمان ... است و کیفیت ظهور آن حضرت و دجال بیکبار و خرابی جهان و دلایل نجومی و در بیان علم رمل و علم اکتاف

Rauẓah VII., in twelve Lā'iḥahs, treating of the properties of precious stones, agriculture, and various practical arts, fol. 272*b*. در بیان خواص جواهر و علم فلاحت و علم فراست و علم جر ثقیل و علم نقل میاه و علم ارغنون و علم اقوس و سهام و علم تفرس و علم بیطره و علم بزاءت و علم صیدله و معرفت فراسخ بین اکثر بلاد معموره

Rauẓah VIII., in eight Dauḥahs, treating of riddles, music, prosody, &c. در بیان علم لغز و معما و موسیقی و عروض و قافیه و علم محاورات و علم قرض الشعر

Rauẓah IX., in ten Thamarahs, treating of meteorology, charms and incantations, alchemy, magic, implements of war, &c., fol. 311a. در بیان کاینات جو و علم جفر جامع و خاییه و علم تسخیرات و علم عزایم و علم طلسمات و علم نیرنجات و علم دم و دهم و علم تصرف نفس و علم معیبات و علم کیمیا و علم سیمیا و علم ریمیا و علم آلات حروب و علم اعداد

Rauẓah X., in eight Manẓars, treating of geometry, arithmetic, optics, and terrestrial astronomy, fol. 338a. در بیان علم هندسه و ارثماطیقی و علم جمع و تفریق و ضرب و قسمت و علم جبر و مقابله و علم مساحت و علم مناظر و مرایا و علم هیئه

Rauẓah XI., in three Aṣls, treating of abstruse questions of physics and metaphysics, fol. 359a. در بیان مسایل دقیقه و مباحث مشکلهٔ طبیعیات و تحقیق ان مثل مبحث حرکت و زمان و ذکر شبهات مخالف شرایع الخ

Rauẓah XII., in three Ḥikmats, treating of the existence of God and his attributes, fol. 371a. در اثبات واجب ببراهین دقیقه غیر مستوره و اثبات صفات سلبیه تعالا شانه الخ

Khātimah, divided into a Muḳaddimah, a a Ḳalb, and three Maḳāmahs, treating of the technical terms and the system of the Sufis, foll. 385a—406b.

At the end is a notice of the death of Shāhzādah 'Abd ul-'Aẓīm, son of Shāh Sulaimān, in Teheran, A.H. 1084.

Ethics and Politics.

145.

Or. 3252.—Foll. 146; $8\frac{1}{4}$ in. by $5\frac{1}{4}$; 15 lines, $2\frac{3}{4}$ in. long; written in elegant Nestalik, with neat 'Unvān and gold-ruled margins; dated Rabī' II., A.H. 861 (A.D. 1457).

[SIDNEY CHURCHILL.]

قابوس نامه

Moral precepts and rules of conduct, written by 'Unṣur ul-Ma'āli Kaikā'ūs B. Iskandar B. Ḳābūs for his son Gīlānshāh.

Beg. الحمد لله رب العالمین والعاقبة للمتقین ولا عدوان الا علی الظالمین وصلی الله علی محمد وآله الطیبین . . . اما بعد جنین کوید جمع کننده این کتاب الامیر عنصر المعالی کیکاوس بن اسکندر بن قابوس بن وشمکیر مولی امیر المومنین با فرزند خویش کیلانشاه

The author states at the end that he commenced this work A.H. 475, and that he had then been living up to the age of sixty-three, according to its precepts. The above date, found in all known copies, shows that the statement of Ḥabīb us-Siyar, vol. ii., Juz 4, p. 59, and of Jahān-ārā, fol. 61b, that Kaikā'ūs died A.H. 462 and Gīlānshāh A.H. 470, is incorrect.

The text has been edited by Riẓa Ḳuli Khān, in one volume with the Tuzuk i Timūri, Teheran, A.H. 1285. A French translation by A. Querry, based on an edition dated A.H. 1275, was published in Paris, 1886. For other MSS. see the Leyden Catalogue, vol. iv., p. 207, and Pertsch, Berlin Catalogue, no. 266. For Turkish translations see the Turkish Catalogue of the Museum, p. 116.

146.

Or. 3632.—Foll. 269; $9\frac{1}{2}$ in. by 6; 21 lines, 4 in. long; written in small and archaic Neskhi, with gold-ruled margins; dated 3 Zulka'dah, A.H. 835 (A.D. 1432).

[JOHN LEE.]

A translation of an Arabic treatise on ethics, entitled الذریعه الی مکارم الشریعه, by

Abu 'l-Ḳasim ar-Rāghib al-Iṣfahāni. See Haj. Khal., vol. iii., p. 334, and Flügel, Vienna Catalogue, no. 1839.

The author, whose full name is Abu 'l-Ḳāsim al-Ḥusain B. Muḥ. B. al-Mufaḍḍal al-Iṣfahāni, is chiefly known by another work entitled محاضرات الادبا, and is stated to have died about A.H. 500. See the Arabic Catalogue, p. 333; the Vienna Catalogue, no. 369; Ahlwardt, Verzeichniss, no. 1116; and the Berlin Catalogue, vol. v., p. 6. The present work was, according to Haj. Khal., held in great esteem by al-Ghazzāli.

The Persian translation is designated in the colophon by this title: كنوز الوديعه من رموز الذريعه الى مكارم الشريعه. In his conclusion the translator, who does not give his name, says that he had written it by command of the reigning sovereign, whose name does not occur in this copy, and that he had been previously encouraged to undertake that work by his late father, the great doctor of the age, Shams ud-Dīn Ḥasan Ẓāfir, fol. 267b, بذرم علامه عصره وبحرير دهره شمس الدين حسن ظافر عليه الرحمة. From another copy described by Ethé, Bodleian Catalogue, no. 1430, we learn that the translation was written under Shah Shujā' Muẓaffari (A.H. 760—786).

The MS. is defective at the beginning, and a spurious exordium has been prefixed, fol. 3. The first folio of the original MS., fol. 4, contains a eulogy on Muḥammad and the Khalifs, and ends with a mention of Chingiz Khan and the heathen Tartar dynasty, which is referred to as a thing of the past. The initial words of the original text are: مغربين و مشرقين داير شد فرخنده فال پيغمبرى سايه شهپر دولت بر مفارق اهل خطهٔ عجم انداخت

The next-following folios, 5—8, contain the last four lines of the preface and a full table of contents, occupying eight pages.

The work is divided into seven sections (Fuṣūl), in full agreement with the headings given by Haj. Khal., namely:

I. Treating of man, his faculties, his pre-eminence and moral dispositions, in thirty-five Bābs, fol. 8b: در احوال انسان و قوى و فضيلت و اخلاق او

II. Treating of intellect and speech, in fourty-four Bābs, fol. 102b: در عقل ونطق و متعلقات و اضداد ان

III. Treating of sensual appetites, in fifteen Bābs, fol. 167a: در انچه متعلق بقواى شهوى باشد

IV. Treating of angry passions, in twelve Bābs, fol. 190a: در انچه منوط و متعلق بقواى غضبى است

V. Treating of justice and injustice, love and hate, in ten Bābs, fol. 206a: در عدالت و ظلم و محبة و بغض

VI. Treating of crafts and trades, of expenditure, liberality and avarice, in twenty-two Bābs, fol. 216a: در انچه تعلق بصناعات و مكاسب و انفاق و جود و بخل دارد

VII. Treating of human actions, in six Bābs, fol. 231b: در ذكر افعال

Appendix by the translator, fol. 235a, with this heading: هذا فصل احلحق به الكتاب و اوضح العذر عما تعذر ايراده فى متون الفصول و الابواب

It is divided into three sections (Namaṭ), containing respectively maxims and moral precepts handed down by Arabs, Greeks (fol. 246a), and Persians (fol. 252b).

The translator's conclusion, foll. 267a—269a.

Copyist: محمود بن محمد بن محمود

Sultan Muḥammad Ḳuṭubshāh states, in an autograph note on the fly-leaf, that he purchased the MS. in Ḥaidarabad, A.H. 1027.

147.

Or. 4119.—Foll. 160; 9½ in. by 6¼; 17 lines, 4¾ in. long; written in fine bold and archaic Persian Neskhi; dated Monday, 5 Jumāda II., A.H. 680 (A.D. 1281). [Tho. F. Hughes.]

اخلاق ناصری

The celebrated ethics of Naṣīr ud-Dīn Ṭūsi, who died A.H. 672. See the Persian Catalogue, pp. 441*b*, 1088*a*.

Beg. حمد بی حد و مدح بی عد لایق حضرت عزت مالك الملکی باشد که همچنانك در بدو فطرت اولی الخ

This valuable copy, written within eight years of the author's death, has, like most MSS., the second preface.

For other copies see Pertsch, Berlin Catalogue, no. 268, and Ethé, Bodleian Catalogue, no. 1435.

Colophon: تمام شد کتاب اخلاق ناصری بفرخی وبهروزی وبهجت وپیروزی روز یکشنبه پنجم ماه جمادی الآخر سال بر ششصد هشتاذ هجری بر دست ضعیفترین خلایق و عاجزترین ایشان صدیق بن الخضر بن عبد الله بن شفا المنجم المراغی ابوه در شهر دوقات خذایش بیامرزاد کی این بیچاره را بخیر یاذ دارذ

148.

Or. 2863.—Foll. 187; 8¼ in. by 5¾; 15 lines, 3½ in. long; written in fair Neskhi, apparently in the 15th century. [Sidney Churchill.]

Another copy of the preceding work, wanting the last page.

149.

Or. 4109.—Foll. 156; 10 in. by 6¼; 21 lines, 4 in. long; written in small and elegant Nestalik, with gold-ruled margins, A.H. 947 (A.D. 1540.) [Sidney Churchill.]

نصیحت نامهٔ شاهی

A work on ethics, by Ḥusain B. Ḥasan.

The MS. is imperfect at the beginning. The first page contains the last eleven lines of the doxology, followed by this passage: بعد از حمد حضرت پروردکار و درود نبی مختار میکوید بنده ضعیف ممتحن بانواع زرایا و محن حسین بن حسن احسن الله الیه وغفر له ولوالدیه که بر ضمیر منیر ارباب الباب و خاطر مستنیر اصحاب اداب هرآیینه چون افتاب جهانتاب روشن و بیدا و ظاهر و هویداست که مراد اصلی و مرام کلی از جمله افرینش وجود انسان است

The author, who designates himself by his proper name and patronymic as above, is better known as Kamāl ud-Dīn Ḥusain Khwārazmi. A later work of his, المقصد الاقصی, was dedicated to Ibrāhīm Sulṭān, son and successor of Amīr Shāh Malik, viceroy of Khwārazm (see the Persian Catalogue, p. 144). He died during the invasion of that country by the Uzbeks, A.H. 833.

In the preface, after some remarks on the necessity of a teacher and the requisite qualities of teacher and pupil, the author passes on to a eulogy upon the above-mentioned Amir Shāh Malik. On Friday, the eighth of Rabī' I., A.H. 829, two days before that prince's death, the author was sent for by the princess, and wrote in the Amīr's name two letters to the reigning sovereign, Shāhrukh, and to his son, prince Ulugh Beg. He subsequently took down in writing the dying injunctions and admonitions addressed by the Amīr to his son Ibrahim Sultan and to his own wife, who was then forty-four years of age. After the Amīr's death, and in compliance with the prince's desire, he expanded those precepts into the present work.

It is divided into two books, مقاله, containing jointly twenty Bābs. Maḳālah I., with this heading: در فضایل امتثال اوامر الهی, و اجتناب از زواجر و مناهی, contains eleven Bābs treating of the following subjects: 1. Knowledge of God, fol. 6b. 2. Science and Intellect, fol. 30a. 3. Exhortation to associate with the virtuous, fol. 46b. 4. Justice, fol. 54b. 5. Piety, fol. 63a. 6. Account kept of men's actions, fol. 66b. 7. Humility, fol. 70b. 8. Meekness and forgiveness, fol. 75a. 9. High-mindedness, fol. 79b. 10. Placing God's law above human lust, fol. 85a. 11. Vigilance, fol. 91a.

Makālah II., در آیین خدمت حضرت خاقانی, و رعایت رسوم جهانبانی, comprises nine Bābs, on the following subjects: 1. Faithfulness and loyalty, fol. 104a. 2. Obedience to kings, fol. 110a. 3. Gratitude and fair service, fol. 114b. 4. Deference to parents, fol. 122b. 5. Discrimination of men's worth, fol. 128a. 6. Resignation to fate, fol. 134a. 7. Advantage of religious guidance, fol. 141a. 8. Trust in God, fol. 146b. 9. Khātimah, fol. 152a.

The moral precepts are copiously illustrated by Arabic texts, verses and anecdotes. In the conclusion, fol. 154b, the author refers to a previous work of his, entitled كنوز الحقایق فی رموز الدقایق

150.

Or. 2996.—Foll. 67; 7¼ in. by 4¾; 13 lines, 2½ in. long; written in elegant Nestalik, with 'Unvan and gold-ruled margins, A.H. 956 (A.D. 1549). [Sidney Churchill.]

اخلاق منصوری

A treatise on ethics by Ghiyās, commonly known as Manṣūr.

Beg. حمد بحد ز ازل تا ابد
احدیرا که جز او نیست احد

منشی که هر حرف از مداد انشا بواسطهٔ قلم اعلی بر سر لوح نمایش و هستی آمده رقم اسمی است از اسماء حسناء او .... اما بعد باعث فقیر حقیر غیاث مشهور بمنصور

Mīr Ghiyās ud-Dīn Manṣūr, son of Mīr Ṣadr ud-Dīn Muḥammad Shīrāzī, died A.H. 948. See the Persian Catalogue, p. 826a, and the obituary notice in Aḥsan ut-Tavārīkh, Or. 4134, fol. 116b, where the present work is noticed.

This work was, as stated at the beginning, the first treatise of the third part (وجه) of the Jām i Jahān-numā, a philosophical encyclopædia, which apparently was not completed, and is not mentioned in the notices of the author among his works. Haj. Khal., who gives the title, vol. ii., p. 499, does not appear to have seen the work.

The present treatise is divided into two Majallahs, subdivided into a number of Tajliyahs, the headings of which are given by Flügel, Vienna Catalogue, no. 1860.

151.

Or. 3546.—Foll. 121; 8 in. by 5½; 15 lines, 2¾ in. long; written in fair Neskhi; dated Shushtar, Muḥarram, A.H. 1287 (A.D. 1870). [Sidney Churchill.]

اخلاق شفائی

A treatise on ethics, by Muẓaffar al-Ḥusaini aṭ-Ṭabib al-Kāshānī, poetically surnamed Shifā'ī, who died A.H. 963. See the Persian Catalogue, p. 474a.

Beg. الحمد لله رب العالمین ....
شاهی که بر بسیط زمین عدل شاملش
گسترده فرش امن وامان مرتضی علی است
.... وبعد حقیر کثیر التقصیر مظفر الحسینی الطبیب

الکاشانی المتخلص بشفائی با وجود قلة بضاعت و عدم استطاعت الخ

The author wrote this work by desire of an eminent religious teacher, پیر روشن ضمیر, whom he does not name, and dedicated it to Shah Ṭahmāsp. It is divided into two Maḳālahs, treating respectively of virtues and of vices. The first, fol. 6b, contains the following twenty-one Bābs: 1. عفت; 2. شجاعت; 3. عدالت (in ten Khaṣlats); 4. سخاوت; 5. توکل; 6. اخلاص; 7. رضا; 8. صبر; 9. شکر; 10. قناعت; 11. صدق; 12. تواضع; 13. حیاء; 14. وفا و حسن عهد; 15. حسن خلق; 16. رفق و مدارا; 17. علو همت; 18. آداب; 19. امانت و دیانت; 20. کتمان اسرار; 21. نطق و سکوت.

The second Maḳālah, در اخلاق ذمیمه, fol. 74a, comprises the following seventeen Bābs: 1. جهل; 2. شهوت; 3. غضب; 4. حقد و حسد; 5. بخل; 6. کبر و عجب; 7. نفاق; 8. غیبت و کذب; 9. حب دنیا; 10. مکر و حیله; 11. ریا; 12. نمیمت; 13. طمع; 14. حرص; 15. ظلم; 16. تعجیل; 17. کاهلی; کفران نعمت.

Copyist: ابن حسین الواعظ الشوشتری حاجی محمد

152.

Or. 2739.—Foll. 220; $11\frac{1}{2}$ in. by $6\frac{3}{4}$; 25 lines, 5 in. long; written in fair Neskhi, with ruled margins; dated Thursday, the last day of Rabī' II., A.H. 1106 (A.D. 1694).

ابواب الجنان

A work containing moral and religious precepts, by Muḥammad Rafī' Vā'iẓ.

Beg. بهترین مقال که سرخیل کاروان فنون محاورات تواند بود .... و بعد بر مرات ضمائر اولی البصائر ظاهر و روشن و نزد ارباب اولو الالباب ثابت و مبرهن است که بحکم کریمهٔ وما خلقت الجن والانس الا لیعبدون تخم وجود آدمی الخ

The author, a native of Kazvin and celebrated preacher, poetically surnamed Vā'iẓ, wrote the present work under Shāh 'Abbās II., who is praised in the preface as the reigning sovereign, and died at the beginning of the reign of Sulṭān Ḥusain Safavi, *i.e.* A.H. 1105 or shortly after. See the Persian Catalogue, p. 826a; Nujūm us-Samā, pp. 148—50; and Riyāẓ ul-'Ārifīn, fol. 92b.

The present volume is only the first of eight, of which the whole work was to consist. A MS. containing the first two volumes is described by Ethé, Bodleian Catalogue, no. 1472, and the third was seen by the author of Nujūm us-Samā, *l.c.* Whether the remaining five volumes were ever written is doubtful. The first volume is popular and frequently to be met with. It was one of the first books issued by the Tabriz press about A.H. 1240, and a lithographed edition appeared in Teheran A.H. 1274. It has also been lithographed at Lucknow, 1868.

The headings of the first volume have been given in full by Ethé, *l.c.*; by Flügel, Vienna Catalogue, no. 1861; and by Pertsch, Berlin Catalogue, no. 282. The contents of the present copy are as follows:

Preface, fol. 1b; Muḳaddimah, treating of religious admonition, in three Maṭlabs, fol. 5a. Bāb I., on the transitory world and its pernicious influences, in three Faṣls, viz., 1. Definition of the love of the world, fol. 10a. 2. On the fickleness of the world, fol. 12b. 3. On love of the world in its various aspects and ramifications, fol. 19b. This third Faṣl, which forms the main bulk of the volume, is divided into the following fourteen Majlis: I. Love of rank and power, fol. 20a. II. Love of wealth, fol. 27a. III. Desire of sumptuous dwellings, fol. 34a. IV. Sexual lust, fol. 38b. V. Desire for dainty viands and drinks, fol. 53a. VI. Desire for costly apparel, fol. 61a. VII. Frivolous society, fol. 65a. VIII. Pride and conceit, fol. 83*b*. IX. Hypocrisy, fol. 98*b*. X. Hate and envy, fol. 113*a*. XI. Covetousness, fol. 127*a*. XII. Avarice, fol. 142*a*. XIII. Injustice and tyranny, fol. 173*b*. XIV. Ill-temper and harshness, fol. 198*a*.

153.

Or. 3510.—Foll. 419; 8 in. by 4½; 15 lines, 2¾ in. long; written in fair Neskhi, about A.H. 1152 (A.D. 1739).

[Presented by B. B. PORTAL.]

حلية المتقين

A treatise on rules of conduct and on daily observances, by Muḥammad Bāḳir B. Muḥammad Taḳi, who died A.H. 1110. See the Persian Catalogue, p. 20*a*, and Pertsch, Berlin Catalogue, no. 284, where the headings of chapters are given. For lives of the author see Nujūm us-Samā, p. 100, and Kiṣaṣ ul-'Ulamā, p. 152; and, for a list of his works, Pertsch, Berlin Catalogue, no. 17.

A full table of contents prefixed to the MS., foll. 1—8, is dated Sha'bān, A.H. 1152.

Astronomy.

154.

Or. 3315.—Foll. 83; 7½ in. by 5¾; 20 lines, 4½ in. long; written in small cursive Neskhi, A.H. 855 (A.D. 1451).

[SIDNEY CHURCHILL.]

جهان دانش

A treatise on astronomy, by Sharaf ud-Din Muḥammad B. Mas'ūd al-Mas'ūdi, with this title prefixed in the hand of the copyist: كتاب جهان دانش در علم هيئة تاليف شرف الدين محمد بن مسعود المسعودى

Beg. سپاس خدايرا كه افريدكار جهانست و بديد آرندهٔ زمين و زمانست ... اما بعد چنين ميكويد مولف اين كتاب محمد بن مسعود المسعودى كه چون از تاليف كتاب الكفايت فى علم الهيئة فارغ شدم

This is a Persian translation, by the author, of his own Arabic work al-Kifāyat fi 'ilm al-Hai'at (see Haj. Khal., vol. v., p. 223). It is stated at the end of this copy that the work was finished on Thursday, the 14th of Sha'bān, A.H. 643. A MS. described by Pertsch, Berlin Catalogue, no. 328, is dated A.H. 669; but a later date of composition, A.H. 672, appears in a MS. mentioned in the Bodleian Catalogue, no. 1497. The author wrote also a treatise on Ḥanafi law, الهادى فى الفروع (Haj. Khal., vol. vi., p. 470).

The work is divided into two Maḳālahs, the subdivisions of which are fully enumerated in the preface. The first comprises twenty-three and the second fourteen Bābs. They begin respectively on foll. 4*a* and 55*a*. The original headings are given by Pertsch and Ethé, *l.c.* The Jahān Dānish is one of the authorities quoted by Ḥāfiẓ i Abru. See the Persian Catalogue, p. 423*b*.

The latter part of the MS. contains the following two articles: 1. A table of the 360 Juz into which the Coran is divided, fol. 78*b*. 2. A treatise of Najm ud-Dīn Kubra on the rules of religious life, in seven Babs, foll. 80*b*—83*b*.

Beg. صنف الامام هذه الاداب .... على سبعة ابواب ... باب الاول فى لبس الخرقه هركه را ارادت اين راه بديد ايد

The tract is known as صفة الآداب. See the Persian Catalogue, p. 836*a*.

155.

Or. 2818.—Foll. 118; 7¾ in. by 4; 22 lines, 2½ in. long; written in minute Shikastah-āmiz; dated Isfahan, Friday, 14 Ramazān, A.H. 123 (*i.e.* 1123, A.D. 1711).

[Sidney Churchill.]

I. Foll. 1—4. لباب القول فى الاشارة الى كيفية علم الله. A short Arabic treatise on the nature of God's knowledge, by Muḥammad B. Murtaza, called Muḥsin, محمد بن مرتضى المدعو بمحسن. See the Persian Catalogue, p. 830*a*. The author died A.H. 1091, as stated in Mir'āt ul-Kāshān, Or. 3603, fol. 115*b*.

Beg. الحمد لله الحكيم الذى لا يعزب عن علمه مثقال ذرة

It was composed, according to the preamble, for the author's son Muḥammad, surnamed 'Alam ul-Huda, and is divided into short sections called اصل.

II. Foll. 4*b*—17. The treatise of Naṣir ud-Dīn Ṭūsi on the construction and use of the astrolabe, known as Bist Bāb. See the Persian Catalogue, p. 453*a*.

III. Foll. 18—25. Astrological fragments, in prose and verse, on the influence of the planets, signs of the zodiac, and first days of the year.

IV. Foll. 26—30. Another treatise on the astrolabe, divided, like the first, into twenty Bābs, but distinct from it; without author's name.

Beg. الحمد لله [الذى] جعل لنا وسيلة الى قربه وافضل علينا بارسال خاتم انبيائه .... اما بعد اين رساله ايست در معرفت اسطرلاب مشتمل بر بيست باب و خاتمه باب اول در نام آلات اسطرلاب و خطها و دايرها

V. Foll. 30*b*—108*a*. The commentary of 'Abd ul-'Alī Birjindī on the Bist Bāb of Naṣir ud-Din Ṭūsī. See the Persian Catalogue, p. 453*b*.

The latter part of the MS., foll. 108*b*—118, contains astrological notes relating chiefly to the influences of the signs of the zodiac. At the end is a table of the latitude and longitude of the principal cities of the East, fol. 116*a*, followed by elaborate tables of the Ikhtilājāt, or omens to be drawn from throbbings in various parts of the body, foll. 116*b*—118*a*.

Copyist: حسين ولد مير سيد على لخوسفى القائينى الخراسانى

156.

Or. 2841.—Foll. 220; 10 in. by 6¾; 19 lines, 4½ in. long; written in elegant Nestalik, apparently in the 15th century.

[Sidney Churchill.]

A commentary on the Zīj of Ulugh Beg (see the Persian Catalogue, p. 455*b*), without preface or author's name, endorsed in an old hand, كتاب شرح زيج الغبيكى.

The original text is given in rather long sections preceded by the word متن in red ink, while the commentary is introduced by the word شرح also in red ink. The first two pages are taken up by the beginning of Maḳālah I. down to the heading of Bāb I. The commentary begins at the bottom of fol. 2 as follows: شرح دوازده دور ماه سيصد و پنجاه و چهار روزست و كسرى و يك دور انتاب سيصد و شصت و پنج روز است و كسرى چنانچه تفاوت يازده روز باشد تقريبا و دور ماه يعنى مدت ما بين مفارقت ماه از وضعى معين با انتاب تا معاودت او بهمين وضع بيست و نه روزست و كسرى

The four Maḳālahs begin respectively at foll. 1*b*, 30*a*, 119*b*, and 210*a*. The last words of the commentary are: مضمون اين فصول بسطى احتياج ندارد و نه ببرهانى چه اكثر اين اوضاع ماخوذ است از اصحاب احكام و مستندان تجربه و امتحانست بل وحى و الهام و كيفيت وضع جداول نيز ظاهرست

A Bodleian MS. described by Ethé, no. 1519, which has, we are informed, the same beginning and end as the present, contains a note ascribing the commentary to Maulānā 'Ali Kūshji, and assigning to it the title of سلّم السما.

— — —

Mineralogy.

157.

Or. 2864.—Foll. 45; 8¾ in. by 5¾; 15 lines, 3½ in. long; written in fair Nestalik, apparently in the 17th century.

[Sidney Churchill.]

تنسوقنامه ايلخانى

A treatise on minerals, by Naṣīr ud-Dīn Ṭūsī.

Beg. الحمد لله فاطر الصنايع ومبدع البدايع و ملهم الخلايق و موضع الطرايق .... اما بعد چنين گويد محرر و مولف اين كتاب نصير الدين محمد بن محمد بن الحسين الطوسى

The author states in a short preamble that he had written the work by desire of Hulagu Khān, and had given it the above title because it was customary to offer rarities as presents to sovereigns: و اين را تنسوقنامهٔ ايلخانى نام نهادم چه بخدمت پادشاهان تنسوق آورند. (Tansūḳ is Turkish for a rare and valuable object suitable for a present. It corresponds with the Arabic تحفة.)

The Tansūḳ Nāmah, which was known to Haj. Khal., is mentioned in the Ḥabīb us-Siyar, vol. iii., Juz 1, p. 61, as one of the works of Naṣīr ud-Dīn Ṭūsī. It is divided into four Maḳālahs, namely:

I. On the elements of which minerals are composed and on the causes of the formation of mines, fol. 2*b*: در كيفيت مفرداتى كه جمله معدنيات و غير آن از مركبات عالم سفلى ازان متركب شوند و علل معادن بطريق كلى

II. On precious stones, their origin, properties, value, &c., fol. 6*a*: در جواهر كه از جمله حجر باشد و غير آن و علل حدوث هر يك و كيفيت وجود آن و شرح معادن و خواص و منفعت و مضرت و شبه آن بطريق صناعت و قيمت هر يك و حلا دادن و آنچه مناسب اين نوع باشد

III. On metals, their origin and uses: در انواع فلزات سبعه و علت حدوث هر يك و كيفيت و چون آن و خاصيت و شرح معادن و منفعت و مضرت ان

IV. On perfumes: در عطرها و امثال ان

The MS. was evidently transcribed from a copy which was defective and in a state of confusion. The copyist himself writes in the margin of fol. 25 that some leaves were missing in the original. The beginning of Maḳālah II. is wanting, and most of the contents of Maḳālah III., the heading of which is found at fol. 25*b*, have been transferred to fol. 41*b*.

158.

Or. 3277.—Foll. 73; 8¼ in. by 4¾; 15 lines, 2½ in. long; written in elegant Nestalik, with 'Unvān and gold-ruled margins, apparently in the 16th century.

جواهر نامه

A treatise on precious stones and other minerals, by Muḥammad B. Manṣūr.

Beg. ستايش و سپاس بى اندازه و قياس صانعى را كه جوهرى صنعش بازار كاينات .... اما بعد چون اقل الخليقه بل لا شى فى الحقيقه محمد بن منصور مامور شد

See the Persian Catalogue, p. 464*b*, and Ethé, Bodleian Catalogue, no. 1877.

The MS. wants three or four leaves at the end. It breaks off at the end of the article on Iron, corresponding with fol. 75*a* of the previously described copy, Add. 23,565.

The work has been wrongly assigned to the seventh century of the Hijrah. Abu 'n-Naṣr Ḥasan, mentioned in the preface as the reigning sovereign, was the first ruler of the Aḳ-Ḳuyunlu dynasty, whose original seat was Diyārbekr. He reigned over Persia A.H. 873—882. His son Sulṭān Khalīl, for whom the work was written, was in his father's lifetime viceroy of Fārs. He succeeded to the throne after his father's death, but reigned only six months. See Ta'rīkh i Jahān-ārā, foll. 190—92, and Riẓa Ḳuli's continuation of Rauẓat uṣ-Ṣafā, vol. viii.

Medicine.

159.

Or. 4691.—Foll. 35; 6 in. by 3; 18 lines, 1¾ in. long; written in minute and neat Nestalik, with 'Unvān and gold-ruled margins, apparently in the 16th century.

A treatise on the composition and use of the antidote called Tiryāḳ i Fārūḳ, by Kamāl ud-Dīn Ḥusain Ṭabīb.

Beg. حمد و سپاس سزاوار حکیمیست که ترکیب بدن انسانرا از اجزاء لطیفه و جواهر شریفه ترتیب نموده ... اما بعد چنین گوید کمال الدین حسین طبیب

The author was physician to Shāh Ni'mat-ullah Yazdi (grandson of the famous saint Shāh Ni'mat ullah Valī). After the death of his patron he went to Court, where he became celebrated for his wonderful cures. But Shāh Ṭahmāsp held him in scant esteem, because he was addicted to wine. After the accession of Muḥ. Khudābandah (A.H. 985), he entered the service of Khān Aḥmad in Gīlān, where he spent the last years of his life. See 'Ālam-ārāi 'Abbāsi, fol. 43*a*.

The treatise is dedicated to the author's first patron, Shāh Nūr ud-Dīn Ni'mat-ullah, and is described in the preface as follows: رسالهٔ جامع کامل در بیان اصول ترکیب حاوی بر قانون ترتیب شامل بر زبدهٔ اغراض حکما در اختیارات اجزا و وجوه تاثیر تریاق کبیر که اجل تریاقات و اشرف مرکباتست

It is divided into a Muḳaddimah, three chapters called Rukn, and a Khātimah.

160.

Or. 2865.—Foll. 166; 10¾ in. by 7; 17 lines, 4¾ in. long; written in a cursive Indian character, probably in the 18th century.

[SIDNEY CHURCHILL.]

دستور الاطبا

An exposition of the Indian system of medicine, by Muḥammad Ḳāsim Hindūshāh, commonly known as Firishtah. See the Persian Catalogue, p. 225.

Beg. حمد مر خدائیرا که بر حکم ما ارسلناك الا رحمة للعالمین رایات شوکت محمدی .... ازینجهت مسود اوراق محمد قاسم الملقب بهندوشاه المشهور بفرشته

The author is the well-known historian of India, who died after A.H. 1033. He says in the preface that, after reading the medical works current in Iran, Turan and Arabistan, he was desirous of studying the writings of the physicians of Hindustan, and, finding them extremely trustworthy and accurate, he was induced to write, for the benefit of his Muslim brethren residing in India, the present summary of their teaching.

The work is divided into the following parts: Muḳaddimah, treating of the constituent parts of the body and its humours, in nine Fā'idahs, fol. 2*a*. Maḳālah I. Properties of simple drugs and aliments, in alphabetical order, fol. 10*a*. Maḳālah II. Compound medicaments, in fifteen Bābs, fol. 59*a*. Maḳālah III. Treatment of diseases, in 160 Faṣls, fol. 99*a*. Khātimah, treating of the six tastes or savours, and of the Indian classification of land with regard to the supply of water, fol. 164*b*.

For the Persian headings see Mehren, Copenhagen Catalogue, p. 11; Ethé, Bodleian Catalogue, no. 1601; and Pertsch, Berlin Catalogue, no. 611. In the last-named MS. the work is entitled اختيارات قاسمى بدستور الاطبا

Farriery.

161.

Or. 3483.—Foll. 185; 12¼ in. by 7½; 24 lines, 4½ in. long; written in fair Nestalik; dated A.H. 1263 (A.D. 1847).

[SIDNEY CHURCHILL.]

كنز الهدايه

Translation by Fakhr ud-Dīn B. Aḥmad B. al-Maula Khizr ar-Rūdbāri of an Arabic work on the horse, its diseases and their treatment, entitled الاقوال الكافيه والفصول الشافيه

Beg. حمد بيحد و ثناى لا يعد حكيمى را رواست
كه ابلق كرم رفتار فلك دوار را در عرصه ليل و نهار
دائر فرمود .... اما بعد راوى غمكده كهسارى ... فخر
الدين بن احمد بن المولى خضر الرودبارى

The Arabic original is the work of al-Malik al-Mujāhid 'Ali B. al-Malik al-Mu'ayyad Dā'ūd, of the Rasūli dynasty, who reigned A.H. 721—764. It has been described in the Arabic Supplement, no. 816.

The translator says that in A.H. 1253, when Riẓa Ḳuli Khān, son of Khusrau Khān, took his seat as governor of Kurdistan, his Vazir, Mirza Hidāyat-ullah, son of the late Mirza Aḥmad (noticed in Ḥadiḳat Amān-ullāhi, no. 129, fol. 213*a*), sent for the writer and requested him to translate the above work, to which some additions were made by the translator.

The translation begins fol. 5*a*, and the five discourses (قول), of which the work consists, begin respectively at foll. 8*b*, 19*a*, 63*b*, 100*a*, and 139*b*.

Music.

162.

Or. 2361.—Foll. 269; 9¾ in. by 5¼; 25 lines, 3½ in. long; written in small and neat Nestalik, with 'Unvāns and gold-ruled margins; dated Shāhjahānābād (Delhi), A.H. 1073—75 (A.D. 1662—64).

[SAYYID 'ALI, OF HAIDARABAD.]

A collection of treatises on music, written for Diyānat Khān, an Amīr of Aurangzīb's reign. The contents are mostly Arabic, and have been described in the Arabic Supplement, no. 823. The following are Persian:

I. Foll. 2*b*—15*a*. A treatise on the lawfulness of music, by Muḥammad B. Jalāl Riẓavi, who wrote it A.H. 1028.

Beg. نغمهٔ سپاس بى قياس مخصوص خداوند
بنده نوازيست كه ارباب عشق را حالات عليه موهبت
نمود ... اما بعد اين رساله ايست در جمع مقالات
فقها در باب شنيدن الحان واختلاف و مقاله ايست در
تفصيل اقوال اوليا در سماع آن و تنوع مشارب درويشان
كه بالتماس بعضى از اعاظم امرا اياز حضرت محمودى

فقير محمد بن جلال رضوی در سنه ثمان و عشرين والف ... فراهم آورده

The author expounds very fully the opinions pro and contra of the great Sunni legists and of the most celebrated Sufis. He concludes with a Khātimah, fol. 13*b*, on the proper rules to be observed in the practice of sacred music, در آداب سماع

II. Foll. 15*a*—17*b*. A tract on the lawfulness of sacred music and on terms used by Sufis, by 'Abd ul-Jalil B. 'Abd ur-Raḥmān.

Beg. سپاسی که غبار عقول عقلا وتحرير يذيل نهايه ان نشيند

The work is dedicated to Navvāb Masīḥ uz-Zamān (d. A.H. 1061; see Persian Catalogue, p. 779, no. 30), in whose honour it was entitled Masīḥi مسيحى. It is divided into two books كتاب, the first of which treats, in four Faṣls, of the lawfulness of music, the second of the terms used by Sufis and of the verses sung by them.

The present copy contains only the first three chapters of Book I.

III. Foll. 157*a*—161*b*. A chapter on music, extracted from the Dānish Nāmah i 'Alā'i. See the Arabic Supplement, p. 559*b*, VII.

Beg. خواجه رئيس شيخ على الحسين ابن عبد الله ابن سينا رحمة الله عليه ميكويد كه صناعت علم موسيقى دو جزو است

IV. Foll. 240*b*—246*a*. A treatise on the divisions of the strings in musical instruments, by Ḳāsim B. Dūst 'Ali al-Bukhāri, entitled كشف الاوتار, and dedicated to the emperor Jalāl ud-Din Akbar.

Beg. نغمات حمد كامله حكيم كارسازى را اعظم شانه ... اما بعد عرض ميدارد نقير حقير شهير بقاسم ابن دوست على البخارى هداه الله سواء الطريق

It is an exposition of the sixth Maḳām of the work entitled دوازده مقام, which Darvīsh Ḥaidar Tūniyāni dedicated to Humāyūn Pādishāh.

V. Foll. 247*b*—269*b*. كنز التحف

A treatise on music, without author's name. See the Arabic Supplement, p. 561, XIV.

Beg. شكر وسپاس بى حد وقياس سزاوار حضرت آن پادشاهى كه از سراپرده عظمتش الخ

The introduction, with the heading سبب تاليف اين رساله, contains an allegory on the travels of Fikr and Khayāl, and concludes with a panegyric in prose and verse on the author's patron, Ghiyāṣ ud-Dunyā wa'd-Dīn, whose titles show him to have been a Husaini Sayyid of princely rank.

The date of composition is indicated at the end by the following Rubā'i:

آن روز كز احداث جهان مهمل بود
در آخر اين رساله ام مدخل بود
اندر سنه لى ذ و نو
بيست و دوم جمادى الاول بود

According to this, the treatise was finished on the 22nd of Jumāda II.; but the year, as indicated in the third hemistich, is doubtful, because the last letter but one has no diacritical point. It may be A.H. 741, 749, or 789, according as the unpointed letter is read *bā*, *yā*, or *nūn*.

The work is divided into a Muḳaddimah on the pre-eminence of music, fol. 252*a*, and the following four Maḳālahs, each of which is subdivided into two Ḳisms:

I. Fol. 252*b*. در علمی موسيقى, on the theory of music and on the causes of high and low pitch.

II. Fol. 256*b*. در عملى موسيقى, on the practical side of music.

III. Fol. 261*b*. در تصنیع سازات وتعدیل آن, on the composition of melodies.

IV. Fol. 256*b*. در وصیتی که طالبان این فن را بکار آید الخ, useful advice to students of the art, and appropriate verses.

The last section contains several pieces by Sa'di, whose name is written throughout, شرف الدین سعدی

PHILOLOGY.

Persian Lexicography.

163.

Or. 3299.—Foll. 306; 12 in. by $7\frac{1}{2}$; 10 lines, $4\frac{3}{4}$ in. long; written in large and elegant Nestalik, with 'Unvān and gold-ruled margins, apparently in the 16th century.

[Sidney Churchill.]

مفتاح الفضلا

A glossary of the rare words and proper names occurring in ancient Persian poets, by Muḥammad B. Dā'ūd B. Muḥ. B. Maḥmūd Shādiyābādi.

Beg. حمد متوافر و ثناء متکاثر مر حضرت مصوری قدیم را ... اما بعد چنین میکوید بندهٔ درگاه کردکار امیدوار برحمت پروردکار ... محمد بن داود بن محمد بن محمود شادیابادی

The author has been mentioned in the Persian Catalogue, pp. 556*a*, 561*b*, as a commentator of Anvari and Khāḳāni. He had applied himself from his youth, as he says in the preface, to the study of the old poets, such as Khāḳāni, Mu'izzi, Anvari, Niẓāmi, Ẓahir, Iṣfahāni and Sa'di. In A.H. 873 he compiled the present glossary from the following works: فرهنك نامه فخر قواس و رسالة النصیر و اسدی و مفاتیح الفضایل و سلالة الفضایل و دستور الافاضل و لسان الشعرا

The work is divided, according to the initial letters, into twenty-two Bābs, and each Bāb is subdivided according to the final letters. The words are briefly explained in Persian, sometimes with poetical quotations; and in several instances Hindu equivalents are added. Some articles are illustrated by coloured drawings, which according to a Persian note on the fly-leaf, are 187 in number.

The first three of the author's sources are mentioned by Salemann in his Beilage V., Mélanges Asiatiques, vol. ix., pp. 505—577, under nos. 7, 3 and 11, and the last two under nos. 10 and 13; but of the Mafātīḥ ul-Faẓā'il and the Sulālat ul-Afāẓil no notice has been found.

The first lines under باب الالف, fol. 5*a*, are as follows: آسا آسایش و مانند و نازه آوا آواز را کویند آژا آراینده و این لفظ را جز مرکب استعمال نکرده اند آشنا ضد بیکانه و بر روی آب اشنا کردن

The work has been noticed by Churchill, Journal of the Royal Asiatic Society, vol. xviii., p. 203, note, and, after him, by Salemann, Mélanges Asiatiques, tom. ix., p. 517.

164.

Or. 3398.—Foll. 185; $8\frac{1}{2}$ in. by $5\frac{3}{4}$; 15 lines, $3\frac{3}{4}$ in. long; written in small Turkish Neskhi, A.H. 982 (A.D. 1594).

[Sidney Churchill.]

لغات حلیمی

A Persian-Turkish dictionary, often designated as قائمه by Luṭf-ullah B. Abi Yūsuf al-Ḥalimi, who died after A.H. 886. See the Turkish Catalogue, p. 137*b*. Compare Pertsch, Berlin Catalogue, nos. 141-2; Ethé, Bodleian Catalogue, nos. 1688—90; and Salemann, Mélanges Asiatiques, tom. xix., p. 515, no. 22.

At the end, foll. 157—185, is a fragment of a Persian-Turkish vocabulary.

165.

Or. 3653.—Foll. 147; 8¾ in. by 6¼; 21 lines, 4½ in. long; written in Turkish Neskhi; dated Amasia, Sha'bān, A.H. 948 (A.D. 1541).

Another copy of Lughāt i Ḥalīmi, with marginal additions.

Copyist: فرهاد بن عبد الله

166.

Or. 3216.—Foll. 105; 6½ in. by 4¼; about 15 lines, written in Neskhi, apparently in the 18th century. [Kremer, no. 90.]

تحفهٔ شاهدی

The Persian-Turkish vocabulary of Shāhidi, in tabulated form, with the addition of Arabic equivalents. See the Turkish Catalogue, p. 140*b*.

167.

Or. 3521.—Foll. 75; 8½ in. by 6½; 12 lines, 3¼ in. long, with about 25 slanting lines in the margin; written in fair Nestalik; dated Wednesday, 2 Rabī' II., A.H. 1288 (A.D. 1871). [Sidney Churchill.]

Glossary of the Persian poets, by Ḥusain al-Vafā'i, endorsed رسالهٔ حسین وفائی در لغت

Beg. حمد و ثنای فراوان و شکر و سپاس بیپایان مر آفریدگار بیچون .... اما بعد این رساله ایست در تصحیح لغات فرس

It was written, as stated in the preamble in the reign of Shāh Ṭahmāsp, A.H. 933, and was compiled from the following works: 1. A treatise by Muḥ. B. Hindūshāh Munshi, dedicated to Khwājah Ghiyāṣ ud-Dīn [B.] Rashīd (see the Persian Catalogue, p. 499*a*). 2. The Mukhtaṣar composed by Shams i Fakhri for Shaikh Abu Isḥāḳ B. Amīr Maḥmūd Shāh Injū (*i.e.* معیار جمالی edited by Salemann). 3. The rough draft of a glossary by Shams ud-Dīn Muḥ. Kashmīri. The first of the above works is the authority chiefly followed. The last is also quoted by Surūri. See Salemann, Mélanges Asiatiques, tom. ix., p. 534, no. 35.

The glossary is divided into twenty-eight Bābs, in which the words are classed according to their final letters. The Bābs are subdivided into Faṣls according to the initial letters.

The Risālah, or Farhang, of Ḥusain Vafā'i is one of the sources of the Farhang i Jahāngiri and of the Majma' ul-Furs of Surūri. The work has been described, with extensive extracts, by Salemann, Mélanges Asiatiques, tom. ix., pp. 454—493, and p. 522, no. 46. A copy is mentioned by Pertsch, Berlin Catalogue, no. 119.

Foll. 68*b*—75 contain a letter of Navvāb Muḥsin Mirza and miscellaneous notes.

168.

Or. 2937.—Foll. 429; 10 in. by 6½; 24 lines, 3⅞ in. long; written in small and neat Nestalik, with 'Unvān and gold-ruled margins; dated Sunday, 12 Safar, A.H. 1111 (A.D. 1699). [Nath. Bland.]

فرهنك جهانكيرى

The great Persian dictionary of Jamāl ud-Dīn Ḥusain Injū, who completed it A.H. 1017. See the Persian Catalogue, p. 496*b*.

Contents: Muḳaddimah, fol. 4*b*. Dictionary proper, fol. 17*b*. Khātimah, fol. 362*b*.

Compare Lagarde, Persische Studien, pp. 45—49; Salemann, Mélanges Asiatiques, tom. ix., pp. 537—41; Pertsch, Berlin Catalogue, no. 123; and Ethé, Bodleian Catalogue, no. 1734.

Copyist: ابن علی اکبر الحسینی نصر الله

169.

Or. 3517.—Foll. 109; $10\frac{1}{4}$ in. by $7\frac{1}{2}$; 17 lines, $3\frac{3}{4}$ in. long; written in Nestalik, apparently in India, in the 18th century.

[Presented by B. B. Portal.]

I. Foll. 1—48. A treatise on Persian grammar and on the language of Persian and Indian poets, by Shaikh 'Abd ul-Bāsiṭ.

Beg. عشق ها مجذون حسن اوصاف لیلی افزونست که داغ دلهای تمنا نیازان . . . . بعد هذا از بنده عبد الباسط که بالحاق لفظ شیخ و یای تصغیر مخبر سال تولد خویش است

In the above passage the date of the author's birth is fixed by a chronogram for A.H. 1099. He evidently lived in India: his poetical quotations are mostly taken from an Indian poet, Nāṣir 'Ali, who died A.H. 1108. The work consists of seventeen Bābs, enumerated in the preface; but the present copy contains only the first seven, which treat of the following subjects: I. Meanings of letters and their permutations, fol. 3*a*. II. Grammatical forms of Persian, fol. 14*b*. III. Persian syntax, fol. 19*b*. Compound words, fol. 24*a*. V. Letters elided by poets, fol. 30*a*. VI. Words used as last members of compounds, fol. 32*a*. VII. Differences in style and phrases between ancient and modern poets, fol. 34*a*. VIII. A glossary of words and phrases used by modern poets, in alphabetical order, foll. 37*a*—48*b*. The remaining Bābs treated chiefly of various kinds of poetical compositions.

II. Foll. 49—61. A glossary to the letters of Abu 'l-Faẓl, with the heading فرهنك ثانی مکاتبات علامی فهامی شیخ ابو الفضل بن مبارك اکبرشاهی

Beg. باب الالف القای ربانی بالکسر تلقین خدای که بآواز غیب حاصل شود

The words, chiefly Arabic, are arranged in Bābs under the initial letters; but within the Bābs no further alphabetical order is observed. The explanations are mostly confined to a single equivalent.

III. Foll. 62—68. Commentary on Surah xlviii., from the third Duftar of the Mukātabāt of Abu 'l-Ful , with an interlinear Persian gloss, اغاز دیباجه کجکول یعنی دفتر سیوم مکاتبات ابو الفضل که بر تفسیر سوره انا فتحنا آغاز شده است

IV. Foll. 69—109. A glossary of Arabic words occurring in the letters of Abu 'l-Faẓl, فرهنك مکاتبات ابو الفضل.

Beg. باب الالف مع الالف ارتضا با اول مکسور بثانی زده و سیوم مفتوح بمعنی پسندیدن کذا فی الکنز

The words are arranged in numerous Bābs according to the initial letters, and, in the second place, according to the final letters. The authorities mostly quoted are الکنز, *i.e.* Kanz ul-Lughāt, and Madār ul-Afāẓil.

170.

Or. 3300.—Foll. 317; $11\frac{3}{4}$ in. by 8; 23 lines, $4\frac{5}{8}$ in. long; written in fair Nestalik, with gold-ruled margins, in the 19th century, before A.H. 1281 (A.D. 1864).

[Sidney Churchill.]

فرهنك عباسى

A Persian dictionary, by Ibn Muḥammad Riẓa Ṣadr ud-Din Tabrizi.

Beg. آرايش كفتار دانشوران و بيرايش كردار سخن كستران ستايش خداوند جهان آفرين ... اما بعد بر پيشكاه ارباب دانش وزكا و اصحاب بينش و دها مخفى و پوشيده نماناد

After praising the reigning sovereign, Fatḥ 'Ali Shāh, and his son 'Abbās Mirza, who had been sent as governor to Azarbaijan, and had shown himself a wise ruler and a liberal patron of letters, the author says that the latter prince, finding that existing Persian dictionaries were ill arranged, redundant in some respects and defective in others, had desired him to compile a new one, which would bear his name. In obedience to that command, the author wrote the Farhang i 'Abbāsi, which was commenced A.H. 1225. He extracted the definitions of words from the Burhān i Ḳāṭi', omitting, however, the poetical quotations, and relegated the metaphors and words containing the eight exclusively Arabic letters to a Khātimah, which does not appear in the present MS.

The words are arranged according to the final letters, for the convenience, the author says, of poets looking for rhymes. To each letter a main section, or Bâb, is devoted, and each Bāb is subdivided, according to the initial letters, into sub-sections called Faṣl. A Muḳaddimah comprises six preliminary chapters, termed Numāyish, treating of the following subjects: 1. Superiority of the Persian language and its dialects, fol. 3*b*. 2. Character of the language, distinction between د and ذ, and grammatical forms, fol. 4*a*. 3. Pronouns, fol. 4*b*. 4. Servile letters, fol. 5*a*. 5. Suffixes, fol. 6*a*. 6. Permutations of letters, fol. 6*b*.

171.

Or. 4680.—Foll. 188; 14 in. by 8¾; 21 lines, 5 in. long; written in fair cursive Nestalik; dated 8 Rabi' II., A.H. 1257 (A.D. 1841).

[Sidney Churchill.]

فرهنك محمد شاهى

A Persian dictionary, by Muḥammad Karim B. Mahdi Ḳuli.

Beg. ... الحمد لله الذى خلق الورى و علمه البيان و بعد در هنكامى كه حضرت آسمان رفعت كيوان رتبت اميرزاده

The author was, as appears from the preface, preceptor to Prince Bahman Mirza, son of the Vali 'Ahd 'Abbās Mirza. While the Prince was engaged in composing his Tazkirah i Muḥammadshāhi for his brother Muḥammad Shah (*i.e.* A.H. 1247—49; see no. 124), he desired the author to write also a book as a suitable offering to the same prince. In compliance with that command, the author compiled the present work, which he describes as an abridgment of the Farhang i Jahāngiri, with some additions from the Burhān i Ḳāṭi', and presented it to Muḥammad Shāh, who desired him to add poetical examples in the margins.

The work is divided into a Muḳaddimah, consisting of ten preliminary chapters termed Ṭirāz, fol. 2*a*, and twenty-four Bābs forming the bulk of the dictionary and following the arrangement of the Farhang i Jahāngiri, foll. 6*b*—188.

A later edition, with an enlarged preface, and a new title برهان جامع, was lithographed in Tabriz, A.H. 1260. It is stated at the end to have been collated by the author and written by his brother, Riẓā Ḳuli. It is mentioned by Salemann, Mélanges Asiatiques, tom. ix., p. 563, and by E. G. Browne, "A Year amongst the Persians," p. 554.

Arabic Lexicography and Grammar.

172.

Or. 3273.—Foll. 257; 8¼ in. by 5¼; 17 lines, 3¾ in. long; written in cursive Indian Nestalik, apparently in the 16th century.

دستور الاخوان

An Arabic dictionary explained in Persian, by Ḳāẓi Khān Badr Muḥammad, of Dhār. See the Arabic Supplement, no. 877.

173.

Or. 4195.—Foll. 362; 9½ in. by 7; written in fair Nestalik; dated A.H. 994 (A.D. 1586). [Lane.]

كنز اللغة

An Arabic-Persian dictionary, by Muḥammad B. 'Abd ul-Khāliḳ. See the Supplement to the Arabic Catalogue, no. 878.

174.

Or. 3520.—Foll. 599; 12 in. by 7; 25 lines, 4 in. long; written in small Nestalik, apparently in the 18th century. [Sidney Churchill.]

محمود اللغة

An anonymous Arabic-Persian dictionary, with a preface by Maḥmūd Mirza. See the Arabic Supplement, no. 881.

175.

Or. 3515.—Foll. 142; 9 in. by 6; about 20 lines, 4½ in. long; written in cursive Nestalik; dated 2 Ramazan, A.H. 1186 (A.D. 1772.]

[Presented by B. B. Portal.]

A Persian paraphrase of, and commentary upon, the Shāfiyah, a treatise on Arabic accidence, by Ibn ul-Ḥājib. See the Arabic Catalogue, p. 234*b*.

Beg. ستايش و نيايش بسيار سزاوار حضرت كردگاريرا كه قوانين و قواعد علم تصريف ... بعد هذا محرر اين اجزا محمد سعد

The commentator is Muḥammad [B.] Sa'd, who in the colophon, adds to his name the takhalluṣ Ghālib. The commentary includes the text in short passages distinguished by a black line drawn above them.

After a eulogy in prose and verse on Ibn ul-Hājib and his work, the author begins with the explanation of الحمد لله رب العالمين, as follows: حمد بفتح حاء مهمله و سكون ميم ستودن و سپاس و ستايش در اصطلاح فعلى است كه دال باشد بر تعظيم منعم

The MS. is endorsed شرح فارسى بر شافيه

Various Lexicographical Works.

176.

Or. 2892.—Foll. 369; 15¼ in. by 10; 27 lines, 6¾ in. long; written in cursive Nestalik and Shikastah-āmīz, in the 19th century. [Sidney Churchill.]

سنكلاخ

A dictionary of Oriental Turkish explained in Persian, by Mirza Mahdi Khan, completed A.H. 1173. See the Turkish Catalogue, pp. 264—66, and Ethé, Bodleian Catalogue, no. 1760.

177-86.

Or. 2959—68.—Ten large folio volumes of the Thesaurus of Arabic, Persian and Turkish, by James William Redhouse, in the handwriting of the author. See the Turkish Catalogue, pp. 147—9.

187.

Or. 4905.—Foll. 61; 8½ in. by 6½; 14 lines, 4¾ in. long; written in fair, partly vocalized Nestalik; dated 12 Zulḥijjah, A.H. 1276 (A.D. 1860). [Sir Henry Rawlinson.]

نصاب انکلیسی

A versified English-Persian vocabulary, composed on the same plan as Niṣāb uṣ-Ṣubyān, Tuḥfah i Shāhidi, and similar works, to facilitate the acquisition of English by Persian students; by Shāhzādah Nā'ib ul-Iyālah Farhād Mirza, with the following heading: نصاب انکلیسی که از نتایج خاطر نواب مستطاب شاهزاده اشرف ارفع اعظم نایب الایاله فرهاد میرزا دام اقباله العالی است

A short prose preamble explaining the disposition of the work begins: بدانکه اکثر لغات انکلیسی در تلفظ با صورت کتابت اختلاف دارد و انچه برشته نظم درآمده است موافق تلفظ فصحای ایشان است

The vocabulary begins with the following lines:

در مه دی جام می ده ای نکار ماهرو
کر شمیم آن دماغ عقل کردد مشکبو
فاعلاتن فاعلاتن فاعلاتن فاعلات
از لغات انکلیسی در رمل این قطعه جو
هِدْ سراست و نُوزْ بینی لِپْ لبست و آی چه چشم
تُوِثْ دندان نُوتْ پا و هَنْدْ دست و فِیسْ رو

The words included in the text are again written in three columns beneath each verse, namely, the English in the Roman character on the left, the Persian in the middle, and the Arabic equivalents on the right.

The work was completed on Saturday, the 26th of Sha'bān, A.H. 1269, corresponding with the 4th of June, A.D. 1853, as stated in the concluding lines:

بسال شصت و نه از بعد یکهزار و دویست
بروز شنبه بیست و شش از مه شعبان
بروز چارم از ماه جون که سال حساب
ثلث و خمسین بیش از هزار و هشتصد دان
. . . .
تمام کردید این شعرهای نغز روان

Farhād Mirza was a son of Nā'ib us-Sulṭanah 'Abbās Mirza, consequently a brother of Muḥammad Shāh and an uncle of the present Shah. He showed himself an able, but stern ruler in his government of Fars and Irak, and had the title of Mu'tamad ud-Daulah conferred upon him. He wrote, besides the present work, a Persian commentary on the Khulāṣat ul-Ḥisāb of Bahā ud-Din al-'Āmili, and a Geography entitled Jām i Jam, and dedicated to the present Shah. See Majma' ul-Fuṣaḥā, vol. i., pp. 46—52, and Browne, "A Year amongst the Persians," pp. 105—8, where the Niṣāb i Ingilisi is described, and the author is stated to have died A.D. 1888.

The present copy was written, by order of Farhād Mirza, by Muḥ. Ismā'il 'Ali-ābādi Māzandarāni.

Rhetoric and Insha.

188.

Or. 2944.—Foll. 124; 8½ in. by 5½; from 9 to 12 lines, 2¾ and 3 in. long; written in fair Nestalik, with 'Unvâns and ruled margins; dated (fol. 77) A.H. 1264 (A.D. 1848).

[Sidney Churchill.]

I. Foll. 2—77. حدائق السحر فی دقائق الشعر

A treatise on figures of speech, by Muḥammad B. 'Abd ul-Jalīl al-'Umari, called ar-Rashīd.

Beg. الحمد لله على ما افاض علينا من نعمه المترعة الحياض ومننه المرعة الرياض ... اما بعد چنين كويد مولف ابن كتاب سعد الاسلام ملك الكتاب والبيانيين محمد بن عبد الجليل العمرى المعروف بالرشيد

The author, a well-known poet, surnamed Vaṭvāṭ, died A.H. 578. See the Persian Catalogue, p. 553a. He wrote the present work, as stated in the preface, for his sovereign, 'Alā ud-Dunya wa'd-Dīn Abu 'l-Muẓaffar Atsiz (A.H. 535—551), in order to supersede an earlier work on poetical figures entitled Tarjumān ul-Balāghah, which had been shown to him by that king, and which he found to contain ill-chosen artificial verses, and not to be free from errors.

See Ḥaj. Khal., vol. iii., p. 21, and, for other copies, the Vienna Catalogue, vol. i., p. 205, and Pertsch, Berlin Catalogue, no. 9, art. 6, no. 22, art. 3, and no. 39, art. 1. The work has been lithographed in Teheran, A.H. 1302, in one volume with Divān i Ḳā'āni.

II. Foll. 78—124. Prefaces of Nashāṭ to the Divan of Fatḥ 'Ali Shāh and to the Shāhinshāh Namah of Ṣabā, with some other prose compositions by the same writer.

Beg. ناظم العوالم بديع المناظم احتبس الهواء واحترس العباء

The preface of the Shāhinshāh Nāmah, fol. 91b, begins: نخست چون بنكرى جهانى بينى براز چون وچند

The last piece is the marriage contract of Navvāb Ḥusain 'Ali Mirza, fol. 119a, which is imperfect at the end.

The author, Mirza 'Abd ul-Vahhāb, poetically surnamed Nashāṭ, belonged to the family of the Mūsavi Sayyids of Iṣfahan, and was first Kalāntar of that city. He subsequently became the favourite secretary of Fatḥ 'Ali Shah, who conferred upon him the title of Mu'tamad ud-Daulah. He died A.H. 1244. See Majma' ul-Fuṣaḥā, vol. ii., p. 509; Zinat ul-Madā'iḥ, fol. 136a; Anjuman i Khāḳān, fol. 94a; Safinat ul-Maḥmūd, fol. 24b; Nigāristān i Dārā, fol. 124b; Tazkirah i Muḥammadshāhi, fol. 215b; and the Persian Catalogue, p. 722a. Nashāṭ was a friend of Sir Gore Ouseley, who devotes to him a very flattering notice, quoted in full in Ethé's Bodleian Catalogue, no. 1200.

The above prefaces are probably unequalled examples of the turgid, stilted, and desperately prolix style which may be called Persian Euphuism, and which still finds admirers in the East.

189.

Or. 3344.—Foll. 392; 9¾ in. by 5¾; 19 lines, 4 in. long; written in small Neskhi; dated Wednesday, 9 Ṣafar, A.H. 816 (A.D. 1413).

[Sidney Churchill.]

دستور الكاتب فی تعيين المراتب

The secretary's manual, or rules and models of epistolary composition, by Muhammad B. Hindūshāh, called Shams, al-Munshi al-Nakhjuvāni.

Beg. تحميدى كه سيار فهم دوربين بمراحل و منازل ان راه نيابد ... اما بعد ببايد دانست كه چون حضرت كبريا احدى وجناب جلال لا حدى جل شانه وعظم سلطانه ميخواست الخ

The author mentions in the preface the following great masters of the art: Rashīd ud-Dīn Vaṭvāṭ, Bahā ud-Dīn Muḥ. Baghdādi, Nūr ud-Dīn Munshi, and Raẓī ud-Dīn Khashshāb, but adds that their style had become antiquated. After a panegyric on the reigning prince, Shaikh Uvais Bahādur Khān (the second prince of the Ilkāni dynasty, who reigned A.H. 757—776), he says that he had not had the honour of kissing the royal threshold, but was, from his distant home, invoking blessings upon His Majesty, and had written the present work, in his old age, as a tribute of homage to his sovereign. He adds that he had formerly been invited by Khwājah Ghiyāṣ ud-Dīn Muḥ., in the reign of Abu Sa'īd, to write a similar work, but had not been able to accomplish that task.

Ibn Hindūshāh is also known as the author of a Persian glossary entitled صحاح العجم, and dedicated to the above-mentioned Vazir, Khwājah Ghiyāṣ ud-Dīn. See Pertsch, Gotha Catalogue, p. 36, and Mélanges Asiatiques, tom ix., p. 36.

Contents of the present work: Preface, fol. 1b, concluding with a full table of chapters, foll. 9a—16b. Mukaddimah, fol. 16b, Kism I., comprising four Martabahs, viz., 1. Letters to Sultans, royal ladies (Khātūns) and princes, fol. 19a. 2. Letters to Amirs, Vazirs, Sayyids, Shaikhs, &c., fol. 131a. 3. Letters to 'Ulamā, physicians, professors, &c., fol. 209a. 4. Letters written by Sultans, Amirs, Vazirs, &c., to each other, fol. 247b. Kism II. Edicts, diplomas of investiture, and other official documents, in two Bābs, beginning respectively at fol. 280b and 357a. Khātimah, fol. 383a.

The contents have been described in full by Hammer, Handschriften, no. 185, pp. 171—177. Two copies noticed in the Leyden Catalogue, no. 290, and in the Vienna Catalogue, no. 244 (Hammer's MS.), are later than the present.

Copyist: يسين بن مظفر بن فخر الواعظ

Prosody.

190.

Or. 2814.—Foll. 191; $9\frac{3}{4}$ in. by $6\frac{1}{2}$; 21 lines, 4 in. long; written in Neskhi, apparently in the 14th century. [Sidney Churchill.]

المعجم فی معاییر اشعار العجم

A treatise on Persian metre, rhyme, and poetical figures, with copious quotations from old poets, by Shams i Kais.

The preface, the beginning of which is lost, contains a panegyric on a king, whose name does not appear. He is spoken of as a young sovereign پادشاه جوان, whose seat was Shiraz, and who had lately added to his empire Kish with its dependencies, parts of the Hijaz, Baḥrain, 'Oman, the harbours of the Persian Gulf, and the littoral from Baṣrah to the borders of India. This evidently applies to the Atabek Abu Bakr B. Sa'd B. Zingi, who reigned A.H. 623—658, and whose conquest of Kish, Kaṭīf, Baḥrain and 'Oman took place, as stated in the Jahān-ārā, fol. 104b, A.H. 628. The present work must have been written shortly after the latter date.

Other passages confirm that inference and throw some light on the career of the author, who appears to have spent the early part of his life in Bukhārā. He speaks in the Khātimah of a Faḳih and would-be poet, who came to him in that city, A.H. 601, where he stayed with him five or six years, and whom he subsequently met again in Rai, A.H. 617.

In the preface, when stating the origin of the present work, the author relates how a treatise, which he had formerly written on the same subject, had been lost with other precious books, at the time of the invasion of the infidels (the Moghols), in the rout of the army of the Sultan (Muḥammad Khwārazm-shāh) and of his sons before the fortress of Farzin قلعه فرزین, in the month of Jumāda of the year 17 (A.H. 617). Some quires of that book were subsequently recovered and shown by him to the learned men of Shiraz, who, while pleased with it, objected to the use of the Arabic language in treating of Persian poetry. In compliance with their urgent request, he extracted from it and turned into Persian those parts which treated of that subject.

The work is divided, fol. 6a, into two parts (Ḳism), treating respectively of metre and of rhyme, قسم اول در فن عروض قسم دوم در معرفت قوافی و علم شعر

The first Ḳism is subdivided into four Bābs, with the following headings:

1. در معنی عروض و شرح ارکان و ذکر اسامی و القابی که درین فن مصطلح اهل این علمست fol. 6b.

2. در ذکر اجزا و اوزانی که از ترکیب ارکان عروضی حاصل شود fol. 14a.

3. در ذکر تغییراتی کی باصول افاعیل عروض در اید تا فروع مذکور از ان منشعب شوذ fol. 17a.

4. در ذکر بحور قدیم و حدیث و نقش دوایر و تقطیع ابیات سالم و مزاحف ان fol. 20a.

The second Ḳism, treating of rhymes and of poetical criticism, contains six Bābs, as follows:

1. در ذکر معنی شعر و قافیت و حد و حقیقت ان fol. 84a.

2. در ذکر حروف قافیت و اسامی ان fol. 87b

3. در ذکر حرکات حروف قافیت و اسامی و اشتقاق هریك fol. 113a.

4. در ذکر حدود قوافی و اصناف ان و ذکر حروف و حرکاتی کی لابد هر قافیت باشد fol. 114b.

5. در ذکر عیوب قوافی و اصناف نا پسندیذه کی در کلام منظوم افتذ fol. 118b.

6. در ذکر محاسن شعر و طرفی از صناعات مستحسن کی در نظم و نثر بکار دارند fol. 135b.

There is, besides, a Khātimah, foll. 179—191, containing the author's advice to intended poets.

The work is copiously illustrated with poetical quotations. The most frequently quoted poet is Anvari, and one of the latest is Kamāl Ismā'īl (d. A.H. 635), a contemporary of the author. There are also verses of 'Unṣuri, Daḳīḳī, Farrukhi, Minuchihri, Ghaẓā'irī, Azraḳi, Abulfaraj Rūni, Mas'ūd i Sa'd, Sanā'i, Mu'izzi, Mukhtāri, Sayyid Ḥasan Ghaznavi, Rashīd, 'Imādī (Shahriyārī), Khāḳāni, Mujīr Bailaḳāni, Ẓahīr, Sharaf ud-Din i Shufurvah, and others.

The حدائق المعجم, by Shams i Ḳais, apparently an abridgment of the present work, is quoted in a later treatise on rhyme, noticed in the Persian Catalogue, p. 814b, xii. Two other works of Shams i Ḳais are quoted by Fakhri; see Ethé, Bodleian Catalogue, no. 1371. An anonymous work معیار الاشعار, treating also of metre and rhyme, and composed A.H. 649, is much shorter than the present work, from which it is quite distinct. See the Leyden Catalogue, vol. i., p. 119, and the Persian Catalogue, p. 525a.

The word معجم in the above title is probably to be read Mu'ajjam, in the sense of "turned into Persian." The author refers, fol. 114b, to his previous work as کتاب معرب, "the book written in Arabic." The usual meaning of Mu'jam, "alphabetically arranged," does not apply to this work.

The margins are covered throughout the volume with glosses explanatory of Arabic words, written by a later hand and without any connection with the text.

191.

Or. 2980.—Foll. 115; 9¾ in. by 7¼; from 15 to 18 lines, 4⅜ in. long; written in small and fair Nestalik; dated 25 Rajab, A.H. 1123 (A.D. 1711). [H. A. Stern.]

I. Foll. 1—23. عروض سيفى

A treatise on prosody, by Saifi. See the Persian Catalogue, p. 525*b*, and Pertsch, Berlin Catalogue, nos. 56, 5, 115, 5.

II. Foll. 24, 25. A short tract ascribed to Rashīd ud-Dīn Vaṭvāṭ, giving examples and scansion of sixteen favourite Persian metres.

Beg. الحمد لله رب العالمين والصلوه والسلام على خير خالقه اما بعد اين كتاب عروض اشعار است كه مولاناء عالم فاضل استاد الشعرا رشيد الدين محمد بن على الوطواط ... نوشته ونظم كرده

The first example, در بحر هزج سالم, begins as follows:

هزج را کر تمام ارکان همی خواهی ازو مکذر
بکیر این قطعه را یاد و بکن این وزن را ازبر

III. Foll. 26-35. A treatise on rhyme رساله قافيه, by 'Aṭā-ullah B. Maḥmūd al-Ḥusaini.

Beg. سپاس بی قیاس صانعی را که تاسیس بدایع مصنوعات .... اما بعد این رساله ایست که در علم قوافی بعرف شعرای عجم منتخب از مقطع کتاب تکمیل الصناعه که آن کتاب را این حقیر فقیر عطاء الله بن محمود الحسینی در فن شعر مسوده نموده

Amīr Burhān ud-Dīn 'Aṭā-ullah, born in Naishapur, studied in Herat, and became an accomplished master of prosody and poetical figures. He was for many years engaged in teaching in the Sulṭāniyah and Ikhlāṣiyyah Madrasahs, and his treatises on rhyme and on poetical ornaments are popular. Towards the end of his life he lost his sight and retired to Mashhad, where he died A.H. 929. See Ḥabīb us-Siyar, vol. iii., Juz 3, p. 345; Majālis ul-Mu'minin, fol. 76; and Baber, Pavet de Courteille's translation, vol. i., p. 404.

The present treatise is extracted, as stated in the preamble, from the Maḳṭa', or final section, of a comprehensive work on the art of poetry, entitled تكميل الصناعة, which the author had written by desire of Mīr 'Alī Shīr. (See Ḥaj. Khal., ii., 399, and iii., 425.) It is divided into nine sections called حرف, with the following headings:

1. Fol. 27*a*. در تعریف قافیه
2. *Ib.* در تعداد حروف قافیه و بیان حروف روی و حروفی که پیش ازانست
3. Fol. 29*a*. در بیان حروف که بعد از رویست
4. Fol. 30*a*. در بیان حرکات قافیه
5. Fol. 31*b*. در بیان انواع روی و اوصاف این انواع و القاب قافیه باعتبار این اوصاف
6. Fol. 32*a*. در بیان انواع قافیه باعتبار تقطیع
7. Fol. 32*b*. در عیوب ملقبهٔ قافیه
8. Fol. 34*a*. در بیان عیوب غیر ملقب قافیت
9. Fol. 34*b*. در تحقیق حاجب و ردیف

The author quotes the anonymous معيار الاشعار, noticed in the Persian Catalogue, p. 525*a*. Compare Fleischer, Dresden Catalogue, no. 333.

IV. Foll. 36—38. Jāmi's treatise on rhyme.

See the Persian Catalogue, p. 526*b*, vi.; Ethé, Bodleian Catalogue, no. 894, 33; and Pertsch, Berlin Catalogue, no. 115, 3.

V. Foll. 42—108. A treatise on riddles رسالۀ معما, by Mīr Husain B. Muhammad al-Husaini (see the Persian Catalogue, p. 649*b*), with a commentary. It is stated at the end that the author, Mir Husain Naishapuri, died on the 9th of Zulka'dah, A.H. 904.

The commentary is mixed up with the text, without any distinction. The commentator calls the author his master, and gives at the end chronograms of his own composition for A.H. 912 and 914. He does not explicitly state his name; but he designates himself in the following chronogram by the takhallus Rukni:

ای دوست کتاب شرح رکنی بنویس
ای لب لباب شرح رکنی بنویس
تاریخ کتاب شرح اگر میطلبی
بنویس حساب شرح رکنی بنویس

The above chronogram gives A.H. 916 as the date of composition of the commentary.

VI. Foll. 109—111. Tables of divination کتاب غالب مغلوب, alleged to have been written by Aristotle for Sultan Sikandar.

VII. Foll. 112—115. An anonymous treatise on the twelve musical moods, on their relation to the twelve signs of the zodiac, and on their subdivisions. It is endorsed رسالۀ علوم موسیقی, and begins with a quatrain containing the names of the twelve musical moods, the first line of which is:

عشاق مرا قد حسینی است چو راست

The treatise is divided into short unnumbered sections, with the heading فصل.

192.

Or. 3249.—Foll. 26; 8 in. by 4½; 12 lines, 2¾ in. long; written in fair Nestalik, with 'Unvān and gold-ruled margins; dated Shavvāl, A.H. 1245 (A.D. 1830). [Sidney Churchill.]

A treatise on rhyme, by 'Atā-ullah B. Mahmūd al-Husaini. See the preceding MS., art. iii.

Beg. شکر و سپاس بی قیاس صانعی را که تاسیس بدایع مصنوعات

Riddles.

193.

Or. 3509.—Foll. 200; 7 in. by 4; 15 lines, 2½ in. long; written in Neskhi, apparently in the 15th century. [Sidney Churchill.]

A treatise on Mu'amma (معمی), by Sharaf ud-Dīn 'Ali Yazdi, author of the Zafar Nāmah, who died A.H. 858 (see the Persian Catalogue, p. 173).

Beg. بعد از تیمن و اعتصام بنام خجسته فرجام علامی که نو آموز مکتب تمیلش جون در محفل ملاء اعلی حل معمی کرده .... نموده میشود که باعث بر تحریر این سطور و تسطیر این زبور داعیهٔ تدوین فن معماست

The MS. is endorsed, رساله معما و لغز مولانا شرف الدین علی یزدی.

This is evidently the work entitled Hulal i Mutarraz, حلل مطرز, on which Jāmi based his own treatise on the same subject, inscribed حلیۀ حلل. See Haj. Khal., vol. iii., p. 108, vol. v., p. 638; Pertsch, Berlin Catalogue, no. 32, art. 2; and Ethé, Bodleian Catalogue, no. 894, art. 32. An abstract of the same work, subsequently made by the author, is designated as منتخب حلل مطرز. See the Bodleian Catalogue, no. 1345. Although the title حلل مطرز is not actually found in the text, it undoubtedly applies to the present work, and is easily accounted for by the fact that its main sections are called حلل, while their subdivisions are designated by the word طراز.

The preface begins with some considerations on human speech in general and on the literal and the hidden meanings of the Coran. After these the author states that in A.H. 832 his royal patron, Abu 'l-Fatḥ Ibrāhīm Sulṭān (son of Shāhrukh and Viceroy of Fārs) marched at the head of an army from Shiraz to Azarbaijan, and displayed the most brilliant generalship and prowess, especially in a battle fought before Salmās, in which the rebel Iskandar Turcoman[1] was defeated. A portion of Ibrāhīm Sulṭān's troops were then dismissed to Shiraz, and the author, who had accompanied the prince on that campaign, returned with them, and, pining at his master's absence, he sought solace in the composition of this work. It treats of the art of composing verses which enclose words, mostly proper names, disguised in some ingenious fashion.

Contents: Preface, fol. 2*b*. Two preliminary chapters called Aṣl, fol. 10*a*, viz., 1. در بیان صور حروف و مجالی بروز و ظهور آن, and 2. در تبیین معنی دلالت و اشارت ببعضی از وجوه و طرق ان. Muḳaddimah, fol. 56*b*. Five main sections called Ḥullah (حله), subdivided into chapters termed Ṭirāz. The headings of the Ḥullahs are given in the Muḳaddimah, fol. 57*b*, as follows:

I. حلهٔ اول در شرح ماهیت معمی و لغز

II. حلهٔ دوم در نمایش و آرایش وجوهی که تعلق به تکمیل صورت اسم داشته باشد

III. حله سوم در بیان تحصیل مادهٔ حرفی بحسب صورت کلامی که اشهر و اظهر صور حرفست

IV. حله چهارم در همان مقصد بحسب صورت کتابی

V. حله بنجم در تبیین قواعدی که مبتنیست بر صورت معنوی عددی حرف

The first four Ḥullahs begin respectively at foll. 58*b*, 94*a*, 117*b*, and 181*a*. The early part of the second is wanting, owing to the loss of one or more leaves after fol. 93. The fourth Ḥullah is slightly imperfect at the end, and the fifth is missing.

[1] Amīr Iskandar B. Ḳara Yūsuf was routed by the united forces of Shāhrukh on the 17th of Zulḥijjah, before Salmās (Maṭla' us-Sa'dain, Or. 1291, foll. 158—63).

194.

Or. 3241.—Foll. 60; $9\frac{1}{2}$ in. by $6\frac{1}{4}$; 13 lines, $2\frac{3}{4}$ in. long; written in small and neat Nestalik, with an illuminated border enclosing the first two pages, and gold designs on tinted paper margins; dated A.H. 925 (A.D. 1519). [Sidney Churchill.]

رساله معما

A treatise on the same subject, by Mīr Ḥusain B. Muḥammad al-Ḥusaini, who died A.H. 904. See no. 192, art. v.

Beg. بنام آنکه از تالیف و ترکیب
معمای جهانرا داد ترتیب

Copyist: میر قاسم الهروی

POETRY.

195.

Or. 4906.—Foll. 642; $12\frac{1}{2}$ in. by 8; 25 lines, $4\frac{1}{2}$ in. long; written in fair Nestalik, in four gold-ruled ruled columns, with 'Unvāns and thirty-eight miniatures in rather inferior Persian style, apparently in the 17th century.

[Sir Henry Rawlinson.]

شاهنامه

The Shāhnāmah of Firdausi. See the Persian Catalogue, p. 533.

This copy contains upwards of sixty thousand distichs, or at least ten thousand above the usual number. The excess is accounted for by the following extensive additions to the original text:

I. The Garshāsp Nāmah of Asadi, in two parts, occupying respectively fol. 10*a*, line 24, to fol. 68*b*, line 22, and fol. 73*a*, line 25, to fol. 101*b*, line 20.

The first part begins with this line:

زکردار کرشاسب اندر جهان
یکی نامه بد یادکار از مهان

which in the Gobineau copy, described under no. 201, is found at the end of the prologue, fol. 3*b*, line 6. It is brought down to the death of Atraṭ, father of Garshāsp, and the latter's accession, ending with this verse:

جو بنهادی از جرخ بر کینه تیر
به پیکان درآوردی از جرخ بیر

which occurs at fol. 35*a*, line 27, of the above-mentioned MS.

This first part is separated from the second by a portion of Firdausi's text relating to the history of Faridūn, and corresponding with pp. 31—48 of Macan's edition.

The second part of the Garshāsp Nāmah begins with the line which in the Gobineau MS. follows immediately the last quoted verse, namely:

همان سال ضحاك را روزكار
دژم کشت و شد سال عمرش هزار

It differs in contents and arrangement from the text of the Gobineau MS., and has some additional matter at the end. The death of Garshāsp, with which the latter copy concludes, is recorded here in the first lines of fol. 100*a*. This passage is followed by three sections relating to the mourning of Narīmān, to a letter of condolence written to him by Farīdūn, and to the festive banquet given in his honour by the latter. The epilogue which follows, contains the date of composition, A.H. 458:

ز هجرت بدور سپهری که کشت
شده چار صد سال و پنجاه و هشت

the name of the poet, Asadi,

درین نامه پیشم کر آیدت رای
بدال اسد حرف ده بر فزای

and the statement that the poem consists of nine thousand Baits, and had been composed in the space of two years:

بر آمد همی بیتها نه هزار
دو سال اندرو برده شد روزکار

At the end is a versified colophon dated A.H. 748, evidently transcribed from an earlier MS. The next two pages, fol. 102*a* and *b*, are occupied by a prologue to a collection of select verses from the Shāhnāmah, classed, according to subjects, in thirteen Bābs. It was compiled by one 'Ali B. Aḥmad, and dedicated to Malik Shāh.

II. The Barzū Nāmah, inserted after the episode of Bizhan, and occupying foll. 261*a*—303*a*.

Beg. کنون بشنو از من تو ای زاد مرد
یکی داستانی پر از آز و درد

This poem, the author of which is not known, has been described by Mohl in his preface to the Shāhnāmah, p. xliv., and by Macan in his introductory remarks, pp. xxv.—xxx. The present text agrees with that printed by Macan in the fourth volume of his edition of the Shāhnāmah, pp. 2160—2296. The history of Barzū is briefly told in Iḥyā ul-Mulūk, Or. 2779, foll. 13—15.

The poem is found inserted in another copy of the Shāhnāmah, Add. 27,258, foll. 252b, 261a—301b, and a fragment is noticed by Ethé, Bodleian Catalogue, no. 511. The Barzū Nāmah is ascribed in one of Anquetil's MSS. to a poet Atai. See Macan, p. xxix.

In the epilogue of the Shāhnāmah, fol. 641b, the early date of composition, A.H. 384, noticed in the Persian Catalogue, p. 534b, is given in these words:

بسر شد دکر قصه یزدکرد
بماه سپند ماه بد [sic] روز ارد
زهجرت سه صد سال و هشتاد و چار
بنام جهانداور کردکار

The ordinary conclusion of the epilogue is followed here by about thirty distichs not noticed in other copies. They begin with a reference to the well-known incident of the sum given away by the poet to the beer-seller. The following line and a few more are evidently taken from the famous satire upon Sultan Maḥmūd:

فقاعی نیرزیدم از کنج شاه
وزین پس فقاعی خریدم براه

See Macan, p. 65, and Mohl, Preface, p. xci.

From a somewhat mutilated note on a partly torn fly-leaf, it appears that the MS. once belonged to Timur Mirza, and was purchased by Sir Henry Rawlinson in Baghdad, A.D. 1839. On fol. 446b there is a Rubā'i written by a former owner, A.H. 1157.

196.

Or. 2926.—Foll. 349; $16\frac{1}{4}$ in. by $11\frac{1}{4}$; 25 lines, $7\frac{3}{8}$ in. long; written in cursive Nestalik, in six gold-ruled columns, with nine miniatures; dated A.H. 1246—49 (A.D. 1830—33). [H. A. STERN.]

The first half of the Shāhnāmah, brought down to the accession of Luhrāsp, with the preface of Mirza Baisunghar. (See the Persian Catalogue, p. 536a.)

This copy contains a considerable amount of extraneous matter, amounting in the aggregate to about twenty thousand distichs. It consists of various poems and episodes of later date, inserted at suitable places of the Shāhnāmah, without any break or special heading, so as to form in appearance a continuous text with the genuine poem of Firdausi. These additions are as follows:

I. Foll. 15a, line 23 to fol. 54, line 6. Garshāsp Nāmah کرشاسب نامه, with this beginning:

سراینده دهقان موبد نژاد
ز کفت دکر موبدان کرد یاد

See the Gobineau MS., no. 201, fol. 3b, line 20.

It concludes with the death of the hero and a brief mention of the letter written to his son by Farīdūn. The last lines are:

اکر شد جهان پهلوان از جهان
ترا بر کزیدم میان مهان
سپردم جهان پهلوانی تورا
که هستی بجای برادر مرا

See Or. 2878, fol. 110a.

II. Foll. 63a, line 16, to fol. 93a, line 25. Sām Nāmah سام نامه, beginning, in continuation of Firdausi's text (Macan, p. 96, line 23), with these lines:

تو بنشین بآرام رامش کزین
که من زاهرمن پاك سازم زمین
ز دیو و زجادو به پردازمش
بکام تو ای شاه بآزارمش

The last line is:

خرامید شد سوی آرامگاه
همی گشت گیتی بآئین وراه

The Sām Nāmah is a very late composition ascribed, probably falsely, to Khwājū Kirmānī. See the Persian Catalogue, p. 543*b*, and Rehatsek, Molla Firuz Library, p. 152. Compare Spiegel, Eran, vol. i., p. 559, and Ethé, Litteraturzeitung, 1881, no. 45, col. 1736.

III. Fol. 107*b*, line 23, to fol. 112*b*, line 19. The episode of Rustam's fight with Kuk Kūhzād, beginning:

کنون داستان کک کوه‌زاد
بگویم سراسر چو آمد بیاد

It is printed in the fourth volume of Macan's edition, pp. 2133—2158. It is also found in Add. 27,258, foll. 59*b*—67*b*, and an abstract of the story is given in Iḥyā ul-Mulūk, fol. 11*b*.

IV. Fol. 112*b*, line 19, to fol. 123*a*, line 4. Episodes of the Indian tiger slain by Rustam, of the birth of Farāmurz, and of the sea-monster Batyārah بتیاره, also destroyed by Rustam; beginning:

یکی روز ایام فصل بهار
منوچهر بر تخت بد شهریار

V. Fol. 146*a*, line 6, to fol. 167*b*, line 2. Episode of Shahrang, son of Div i Sapid, and of the encounters of Rustam and Farāmurz with him and other Divs in Māzandarān, beginning:

کنون بشنو از گفته زاد سرو
چراغ صف صدر ماهان بمرو
که چون شد بمازندران پور زال
همه دیو را کرد او پای مال

Serv Āzād, of Merv, is one of the authorities of Firdausi. See Mohl's edition, preface, p. xix., vol. iv., p. 701.

VI. Fol. 167*b*, line 3 to fol. 179*b*, line 25. Farāmurz Nāmah فرامرز نامه, in substantial agreement with a separate copy, no. 199, II.; beginning:

یکی روز بارامش می گسار
نشسته دلیران بر شهریار

See Mohl's preface, p. lxiii. The two preceding articles may be fragments of the same poem. The last line is:

فرامرز از هند پس باز گشت
همه گیتی از وی پر آواز گشت

VII. Fol. 191*a*, line 2 to fol. 192*b*, line 17. A sequel to the episode of Suhrāb, in continuation of this line of Macan's text, p. 376, line :

به پرورده بودم تنش را بناز
برخشنده روز و شبان دراز

The next lines in our text are:

که بینم بجای تو بر پیش خویش
کرا گویم این درد و تیمار خویش
بشب پادشاهی چو افراسیاب
اگر تیغ اورا به بیند بخواب

Suhrāb's mother, Tahmīnah, resolves to avenge his death, but becomes reconciled with Rustam, and gives birth to Farāmurz.

VIII. Fol. 193*a*, line 1, to fol. 221*b*, line 20. Barzū Nāmah برزو نامه, agreeing with no. 195, art. II.

IX. Fol. 249*b*, line 7, to fol. 251*a*, line 10. An episode relating to the warlike daughter of Rustam, Bānū Gushasp, beginning:

چنین خواندم این دفتر دلنواز
ز گفتار فرزانه سر فراز
ز کین خواهی شهریار گزین
سیاوخش فرخنده پاک دین

The last line is:

سه دایه بنازش همی داد شیر
ز شیر سه دایه نمی گشت سیر

This short episode is probably a fragment of the poem entitled Bānū Gushasp Nāmah, described by Mohl in his preface, p. lxiii. A copy mentioned by Ethé, no. 509, has a different beginning from the above.

The preface of Baisunghar, which occupies foll. 1—10, and is in the same handwriting as the bulk of the volume, is dated Rabī‘ I., A.H. 1249. The last leaf of the volume, written by another hand, is dated Ṣafar, A.H. 1246. Half-page miniatures in late Persian style are found at foll. 106, 129, 130, 133—35, 137, 153 and 214. Many blank spaces reserved for miniatures have not been filled in.

197.

Or. 2976.—Foll 275; uniform with the preceding and written by the same hand; dated Shiraz, 1st Jumāda I., A.H. 1252 (A.D. 1836). [H. A. Stern.]

The latter half of the Shāhnāmah, written in continuation of the preceding volume, and containing the following additions:

I. Foll. 59*b*—62*a*. Part of the Āẕarbarzīn Nāmah, a history of Āẕarbarzīn, son of Zāl [*sic*], and of the daughter of Ṣūr, king of Kashmir, with this heading: اغاز داستان آذربرزین پور زال زر که از دختر شاه صور کشمیربست واین یك قسم آذربرزین نامه است

Beg. بزال ستمدیده رفت آکهی
که کشت از فرامرز کیتی تهی

As the story begins with the birth of Āẕarbarzin and ends with his death, the text here given cannot fall much short of the whole poem. It appears to be an abridged version of the history of that hero, whose career is related at much greater length in the next-following poem.

II. Foll. 62*a*—133*a*. Bahman-Nāmah, a poem treating of the wars of Bahman with the heroes of Sistān, and especially with Āẕarbarzīn, son of Farāmurz. The contents have been described by Mohl in his preface to the Shāhnāmah, p. lxvii. The heading is: در ستایش کردن باریتعالی و آغاز داستان بهمن نامه و آذربرزین نامه و ستایش کردن سلطان محمود و چکونکی ایشان

Beg. نخستین سخن نام دادار داد
که بی یاد او نامها هست باد
خداوند دانای پروردکار
رساننده روزی مور و مار

The poet, whose name does not appear, says in his prologue that ten years had elapsed since the death of Malik Shāh:

کنون کشت ده سال تا روزکار
بر آشفت بر نامور شهریار
سر نامداران ملکشاه شاه
کنون کشت شد سوی مینو براه

He was writing, therefore, A.H. 495. He describes the troubles which followed the death of Malik Shāh, and the prowess with which his son succeeded in putting down rebels and establishing his rule. The author approached the royal throne, he says, in Isfahan, and invoked blessings on the sovereign. The prince here referred to can hardly be any other than the son and successor of Malik Shāh, Barkyāruḳ, who reigned A.H. 486—98. The name of Maḥmūd, which appears in the above heading and at the end, fol. 133*a*, would seem to have been introduced by some confusion with Sultan Maḥmūd, the patron of Firdausi. There was, indeed, a son of Malik Shāh called Maḥmūd, but he was only four years of age when raised upon the throne after his father's death, and he died himself about a year later.

The same poem is found in another MS., Or. 2780, no. 201, III., with a different prologue, addressed to Muhammad Shāh, brother and successor of Barkyāruḳ, about A.H. 502.

The narrative begins, fol. 62*b*, line 12, with these verses (corresponding with Or. 2780, fol. 136, line 9):

چنین گفت دهقان موبد نژاد
که بر ما در داستان بر کشاد
که تاج از کیومرث فرخنده پی
بکایك بیامد بکاووس کی

The two texts are in close agreement down to the fight of Bahman with the dragon and to his death, fol. 132*b*, line 6 (Or. 2780, fol. 187*b*, line 5). The concluding lines in the present copy relate to the return of Āẕarbarzīn to Sīstān, and to the death of Zāl, while the concluding portion of Or. 2780 describes the reception by Humāi of the tidings of Bahman's death and her installation on the throne.

An abstract of the contents of Bahman Nāmah will be found in Iḥyā ul-Mulūk, Or. 2779, foll. 19—21.

Foll. 133*a*—275 contain the latter part of the Shāhnāmah, from the accession of Humāi to the death of Yazdagird (Macan, pp. 1248—2089), wanting the last two sections and the epilogue.

This volume contains nine half-page miniatures on foll. 66, 69, 72, 74, 80, 127, 128, 132, 136, and several blank spaces left unfilled.

198.

Or. 4384.—Foll. 307; 13½ in. by 10; 27 lines, 7½ in. long; written in small and neat Nestalik, in six gold-ruled columns, with 'Unvāns, apparently about the close of the 15th century. [Wallis Budge.]

The Shāhnāmah, with the old preface. See the Persian Catalogue, p. 534*a*; Pertsch, Berlin Catalogue, no. 702; and Ethé, Bodleian Catalogue, no. 497.

The MS. is somewhat imperfect at the beginning. The first folios, which must be taken in this order, 2, 3, 1, 5, contain the main part of the old preface, corresponding with pp. 54—68 of Wallenbourg's translation, and the summary of the four Persian dynasties (*ib.* pp. 70—75). Fol. 4, which should come after fol. 219, belongs to the history of Bahrām Gūr, and corresponds with pp. 1517—23 of Macan's edition.

The last six folios should be taken in this order: foll. 302, 306*b*, 306*a*, 303, 304, 305, 307. In the epilogue, the early date of composition, A.H. 384, noticed in the Persian Catalogue, p. 534*b*, is also found, but somewhat differently expressed, in the following line:

زهجرت سه صد سال هشتاد چار

The number of Baits in the MS. is about 48,500. There are nine half-page miniatures, of inferior Persian style, at foll. 31, 51, 85, 93, 120, 158, 192, 239, and 276. The poem is divided into two equal parts, the second of which begins, fol. 141*b*, with the accession of Luhrāsp.

199.

Or. 2946.—Foll. 109; 9¼ in. by 4¾; 19 and 13 lines; written in cursive Nestalik, apparently in India, in the 18th century. [Sidney Churchill.]

I. Foll. 2—49. بیژن نامه Bizhan Nāmah, an episode of the Shahnāmah, with the heading, آغاز داستان بیژن نامه

Beg. کنون کار بیژن بگویم ترا
بدان آب حکمت بشویم ترا

The text corresponds in substance with

Macan's edition, pp. 755—805; but it is swelled by interpolated verses from about 1400 Baits to 1900. The last section, however, relating to the return of Rustam to the Court of Kaikhusrau, is shorter than the original text, and differs from it considerably.

An appendix of 50 Baits, written in a smaller character, treats of the reception of Manīzhah and Bīzhan by Farangīs, and concludes with this line:

چو زین داستان دل بپرداختیم
سوی رزم برزو همی تافتیم

This copy, as well as that of the following poem, was probably written by a Parsee, as appears from this substitute for the usual Bismillah: بنام یزد بخشاینده بخشایشگر مهربان

II. Foll. 50—109. فرامرز نامه Farāmurz Nāmah, a history of the expedition of Farāmurz, son of Rustam, to India, one of the episodes grafted upon the Shāhnāmah.

Beg. بنام خداوند روزی دهان
یکی قصدارم برون از نهان

The fourth line,

یکی روز با رامش و میکسار
نشستند دلیران بر شهریار

is identical with the beginning of another copy above mentioned, no. 196, art. vi., and the two texts are in close agreement. The last line common to both,

صلیب و سکیبا بکیتی نماند
چو بشکسته شد هم بدریا فشاند

is followed in the present copy by four Baits, in which Farāmurz is said to return to Jaipāl:

وزانجا فرامرز یل شد روان
سوی شهر جیپال بنهاد روی
ابا نامداران پرخاشجوی

Two separate MSS. of the above episodes are noticed by Ethé, Bodleian Catalogue, nos. 1078-9.

200.

Or. 2930.—Foll. 240; $9\frac{1}{4}$ in. by $5\frac{3}{4}$; 15 lines, 4 in. long; written in fair Nestalik in two columns; dated Friday, 7 Rabī' II., A.H. 1244 (A.D. 1828). [NATH. BLAND.]

یوسف و زلیخا

Yūsuf u Zulaikhā, by Firdausi. See the Persian Catalogue, p. 545, and Ethé, Bodleian Catalogue, nos. 505—6.

Beg. بنام خداوند هر دو سرای
که جاوید باشد همیشه بجای

This copy is the only one known which contains the full prologue of Firdausi, especially the important account given by the poet, foll. 7*a*—9*b*, of his two predecessors, Abu 'l-Muayyad and Bakhtiyāri. That prologue has been edited by Ethé, mainly from the present MS., in his "Firdausi's Yusuf und Zalikha," 1887, pp. 20—23. The verses in praise of the Pādishāh i Islām, *ib.*, p. 24, are not found in the present MS., but it contains, with some variations, the other two extracts given by Ethé under no. iii., namely, the first from fol. 3*b*, line 11, to fol. 4*a*, line 14; and the second from fol. 2*b*, line 10, to fol. 3*a*, line 6.

For MSS. and printed editions, see Ethé, *ib.*, pp. 7 and 12. An elegant translation of the poem in German verse was published by Freiherr von Schlechta-Wssehrd, Vienna, 1889.

201.

Or. 2780.—Foll. 243; 10 in. by $6\frac{1}{2}$; 23 lines, $4\frac{5}{8}$ in. long; written in minute and neat Persian Neskhi, in six gold-ruled columns, with four rich double-page 'Unvāns of the most highly finished style, gold headings, and miniatures; dated Ṣafar, A.H. 800 (A.D. 1397). [Comte de Gobineau.]

I. Foll. 1—40. كرشاسب نامه

Garshāsp Nāmah, the history of Garshāsp, the hero of Sīstān, written in imitation of the Shāhnāmah of Firdausi; by Asadi (see no. 196, art. i.).

Beg. سپاس از خدا ایزد رهنمای
که از کاف و نون کرد گیتی بپای

The author's name is not found in the text; but in the endorsement, کرشاسب نامه از منظومات حکیم اسدی طوسی, the poem is ascribed, in conformity with Eastern tradition, to Ḥakīm Asadi Ṭūsi. As the latter was the senior contemporary and master of Firdausi, and died, at an advanced age, about A.H. 421—32, the authentic date of the present poem, A.H. 458, noticed under no. 195, and found in the Paris and Oxford MSS. (see Ethé's Catalogue, no. 507, and Mohl's Preface, p. lv.), renders that attribution untenable, and makes it evident that the Garshāsp Nāmah is the work of a later poet who had adopted the same poetical surname as his predecessor. It would be rash, however, to infer from this identity of names a close relationship between the two poets (see Ethé, Verhandlungen des fünften Orientalisten Congresses, 2ter Theil, p. 64). It is well known that names of that class are strictly personal, and do not pass from father to son. Abu Naṣr (or Abu Manṣūr) 'Ali B. Aḥmad al-Asadi al-Ṭūsi, author of the earliest poetical glossary, is probably identical with the later Asadi. See Majālis ul-Mu'minīn, Add. 16,716, fol. 579, and Salemann, Mélanges Asiatiques, vol. ix., p. 507. The same name, with another Kunyah, is found in a MS. of the Garshāsp Nāmah described by Pertsch, Gotha Catalogue, no. 40, art. 2.

What we learn from internal evidence, in addition to the above-mentioned date, is that the author composed this poem for Abu Dulaf, prince of Arrān (to whose name the Majma' ul-Fuṣaḥā, i., p. 107, adds the Nisbah ککری, from Karkar, a town of Arrān):

[1] ملك بو دلف شهريار زمين
جهاندار ارّانی پاك دين

and that before writing it he was not known as a poet. This appears from the following verse in the epilogue:

دل من سوی شعر نشناخته راه
مرا کرد شاعر سخنهای شاه

The contents of the poem are described by Mohl, Preface of the Shāhnāmah, pp. lv.—lviii.; they are briefly stated in the Iḥyā ul-Mulūk, Or. 2779, foll. 10—11, and by Rehatsek, Molla Firuz Library, p. 164. Extensive extracts are given in Majma' ul-Fuṣaḥā, vol. i., pp. 110—139.

After a prologue, which occupies four pages and a half, the narrative begins, fol. 3b, as follows:

سراینده دهقان موبد نژاد
ز گفت دگر موبدان کرد یاد
که برشاه جم جون برآشفت بخت
بناکام ضحاك را داد تخت

In the present copy the poem concludes with the death of Garshāsp (Majma' ul-Fuṣaḥā, p. 135, line 23). The subsequent sections and the epilogue are wanting.

The first portion of the poem, from fol. 3b, line 21, to fol. 6a, line 20, corresponds with the text printed in the fourth volume of Macan's edition of the Shāhnāmah, from p. 2109, line 23, to p. 2133, line 9.

---

[1] The above is the reading of the Majma' ul-Fuṣaḥā, p. 113. In the present MS. the second hemistich is: جهاندار دیرانی پاك دين

II. Foll. 41—132. شهنشاه نامه

Shahanshāh Nāmah, a rhymed history of Chingīz Khān and his successors down to A.H. 738, by Aḥmad of Tabrīz.

Beg. بنام خداوند جان آفرین
نگارندهٔ آسمان و زمین

The title of the poem and its dedication to Abu Sa'īd are found in the following lines of the prologue, fol. 42*b*:

شهنشاه نامه نهم نام این
بنام شهنشاه روی زمین
خداوند گیتی و دیهیم وگاه
جهان جهان آفرین را پناه
جوانبخت و فرمان روا بو سعید
جهان آفرینش زجان آفرید

The narrative begins with Japhet, son of Noah, and a sketch of his descendants in the Moghol line down to Timujin, afterwards Chingīz Khān. The headings of this introduction are as follows:

Fol. 42*b*. داستان یافث بن نوح علیه السلام
Fol. 44*a*. نشاندن غلامی بپادشاهی بر جائ آی
Ib. داستان قیان و نکوز
Ib. بیرون آمدن مغول از کوه و گرفتن بادشاهی
Fol. 45*a*. داستان آلان قوا
Ib. گرفتار شدن همنای خان بدست لشکر التان
Fol. 46*a*. نشستن قوتله بر پادشاهی
Ib. داستان بسوکا بهادر
Fol. 46*a*. رزم کردن بسوکا با تموجین تاتاری
Fol. 46*b*. اندر زادن تموجین از مادر و جگونگی ان
Fol. 47*a*. داستان تموجین و خاتون او

The history of Chingīz Khān is told at great length down to fol. 69*a*. The subjects of the next-following sections are Okotai, Tuli Khan, fol. 70*a*; Jalāl ud-Dīn Khwārazm Shāh, fol. 73*a*; Jaghatai, fol. 79*b*; Kuyuk Khān, fol. 81*b*; Mūng Ḳā'ān, fol. 82*b*; and Hulāgu Khān, fol. 84*a*.

The rest of the poem is taken up with the wars of Hulagu and the reigns of his successors in Persia down to the author's time.

It appears from the epilogue that the author commenced the work by order of Abu Sa'īd, spent eight years upon its composition, and completed it A.H. 738, two years after the death of his royal patron, when Shaikh Ḥasan Buzurg had raised Muḥammad Khān to the throne. The date of composition and the poet's name are found at the end:

درین گفت وگو شد مرا هشت سال
گر احمد بنالد کی گوید منال
. . . .
جو از سال شد هفصد و سی و هشت
ستم دیده این نامه را در نوشت

The copy is dated the 14th of Rajab, A.H. 800. It is endorsed: چنگیز نامه منظومات احمدی.

III. Foll. 134—187. بهمن نامه

Bahman Nāmah, the poem above mentioned, no. 197, II., with a different beginning.

Beg. سپاس از خدا ایزد رهنمای
کی از کاف و نون کرد گیتی بپای
یکی کش نه یار و نه انباز بود
نش آغاز باشد نه انجام بود

The prologue is much longer than in the preceding copy, and contains a panegyric on the reigning sovereign, Muḥammad Shāh, brother and successor of Sultan Barkyāruḳ. The poet describes at length two events which took place in the early part of his reign. The first is the capture of Shahdiz, a stronghold held by the Ismā'īlis, close to

Isfahan. It was taken by storm after a year's siege, and the chief was flayed alive (A.H. 500; see Kāmil, vol. x., p. 299). The second is the great battle in which Muḥammad Shāh routed and slew Malik ul-'Arab, *i.e.* Amir ul-'Arab Saif ud-Daulah Ṣadaḳah B. Mazyad (A.H. 501; see Kāmil, *ib.*, p. 306). Here the poet describes a huge dragon which came down from the sky before the battle, and was taken as an omen of victory. The same incident is mentioned in Ta'rīkh i Guzīdah.

The beginning and conclusion of the narrative have been given above under no. 197, II.

This copy is dated in the last decade of Rabi' I., A.H. 800. The poem is ascribed in the endorsement, بهمن نامه منظومات حکیم آذری, to Ḥakīm Āẕari. This is, apparently, owing to a confusion with a later Bahman Nāmah, a history of the Bahmanis of Deccan, by Shaikh Āẕari, who died A.H. 866 (see the Persian Catalogue, pp. 43*a*, 642*a*).

The Mujmil ut-Tavārīkh, translated by Mohl, Journal Asiatique for 1843, i., pp. 395 to 418, mentions a Bahman Nameh written in verse, by Ḥakīm Īrānshāh (ایرانشاه) B. Abi 'l-Khair; but the line there quoted is not found in our MS. In Majma' ul-Fuṣaḥā, vol. i., p. 110, it is stated that the Bahman Nāmah was attributed by some to Jamāli Mihrijirdi. In another place, p. 494, the latter poet is explicitly called author of Bahman Nāmah, and is mentioned as one of the contemporaries of Lāmi'i, who lived about A.H. 500.

IV. Foll. 188—243. کوش نامه

Kūsh Nāmah, by the author of the preceding poem.

Beg. ترا ای خردمند روشن روان
زبان کرد یزدان ازین سان روان
خرد داد و جان داد و پاکیزه هوش
دل روشن و چشم بینای و گوش

In the prologue the author, whose name does not appear, gives again a poetical description of the great battle in which his sovereign defeated and slew the king of the Arabs. He refers to the preceding poem and to the princely reward he had received for it, and in token of gratitude dedicates the present one to his royal patron. He then passes on to the subject-matter of his poem in the following lines, fol. 190*a*:

درین داستان ژرف بنگر کنون
چو بر خوانند از پیش تو رهنمون
چنین تا بگیتی چه کردست کوش
سر مرزبانان فولاد هوش
دو چشم آسمان گون و چهره چو خون
ببالا و بیکر زپیلی فزون

The hero of the poem, Kūsh, surnamed Pīldandān, "the elephant-tusked," is represented as a contemporary of Zohak and Farīdun, and his warlike exploits range over all the known world from China to Maghrib. According to the Mujmil ut-Tavārīkh, Kūsh Pīldandān B. Kūsh was a brother's son of Garshāsp. See Mohl, Journal Asiatique, 1843, i., pp. 391, 414. Some episodes of the Kūsh Nāmah have been described by Comte de Gobineau, Histoire des Perses, vol. i., pp. 139—144. In the endorsement the poem is ascribed, like the preceding, to Āẕari.

Copyist (foll. 132, 243): محمد بن سعید بن سعد الحافظ القاری

The MS. is ornamented with eleven miniatures in good Persian style. They occupy two-thirds of the page or more, and are found at foll. 14, 18, 29, 44, 49, 61, 89, 169, 171, 202, 213.

The contents of this MS. have been briefly

noticed by Comte de Gobineau in the Mélanges Asiatiques, vol. vi., p. 404. They were more fully described in the Athenæum, 31 May, 1884.

202.

Or. 2878.—Foll. 119; $12\frac{1}{2}$ in. by 8; 17 lines, $4\frac{1}{2}$ in. long; written in four columns in elegant Nestalik, with 'Unvān, gold-ruled margins, gilt headings and miniatures, apparently in the 16th century. Bound in stamped leather covers.

[Sidney Churchill.]

Another copy of the Garshāsp Nāmah (see no. 201, i.). The prologue is abridged to fifty-two Baits, and does not contain the name of Abu Dulaf. The narrative begins at the top of the third page, fol. 3*b*, and the record of the death of Garshāsp, with which the former copy concludes, is found at fol. 112*a*. It is followed by several sections relating to Narīmān and to his conflict with Ra'd i Ghammāz, Lord of Sipand Kūh (partly printed in the Majma' ul-Fuṣaḥā, pp. 135—138). The epilogue, foll. 118-19, consists only of reflections on the transitory nature of worldly greatness and of prayers, without any mention of the poet's patron.

In the colophon is found the curious notice that the author, Maulānā Asadi, was the sister's son of Firdausi: تمام شد کتاب کرشاسب از کفته مولانا اسدی خواهر زادهٔ مولانا فردوسی علیه الرحمت

The MS. contains two whole-page miniatures in Persian style at the beginning, and six half-page miniatures at foll. 13, 40, 52, 82, 96 and 108.

Copyist: پیر محمد بن قاسم الکاتب

203.

Or. 2945.—Foll. 94; $10\frac{3}{4}$ in. by 6; 16 lines, $3\frac{1}{2}$ in. long; written in cursive Nestalik in two ruled columns; dated Jumāda II., A.H. 1275 (A.D. 1859). Bound in painted and glazed covers.

[Sidney Churchill.]

Selection from the Divan of Farrukhi, with this heading: زبده و نخبه دیوان قصاید افصح الفصحا المتقدمین حکیم ابو الحسن فرخی رهٔ

Beg. بر آمد نیلکون ابری ز روی نیلکون دریا
چو رای عاشقان کردان چو طبع بیدلان شیدا

Farrukhi, whose original name was Abu 'l-Ḥasan 'Ali B. Ḳulū', was a native of Sistan, distinguished alike by musical skill and poetical genius, and a dependant of the local ruler, Amir Khalaf B. Aḥmad (deposed A.H. 393 by Sultan Maḥmūd; see Kāmil, vol. ix., p. 122). Leaving his native country in search of fortune, he repaired to Balkh and won the favour of Amīr Abu 'l-Muẓaffar Ṭāhir Chaghāni, by whose liberality he was enabled to appear in state at the Court of Ghaznah. There he became one of the favorite poets of Sultan Maḥmūd, and died A.H. 429, leaving, besides numerous poems, a treatise on rhetorics entitled Tarjumān ul-Balāghah. See Majma' ul-Fuṣaḥā, vol. i., pp. 439—65, where extensive extracts from his Divan are given, and Khair ul-Bayān, Or. 3397, fol. 51*b*. The date 470, assigned by Taḳi Kāshi, Oude Catalogue, p. 15, to Farrukhi's death, is evidently much too late.

The contents of the present MS. are an alphabetical series of Kasidahs with headings indicating to whom they were addressed, fol. 2*b*, three Tarjī'-bands, fol. 86*b*, Ḳiṭ'ahs and Rubā'is, fol. 91*a*, and an appendix containing some Ghazals and additional Rubā'is, foll. 92*b*—94*a*. Most of the Kasidahs are in praise of Sultan Maḥmūd, of his son Muḥammad and of his brother, Amīr Yūsuf. A notice of the poet is prefixed, foll. 1*b*—2*a*.

The MS. was written by a student called Abu 'l-Ḳāsim, for Muḥ. Mahdi B. Muṣṭafa al-Ḥusaini al-Tafrishi, surnamed Badā'i'-Nigār.

The same Selection was subsequently edited by the same Muḥ. Mahdi B. Muṣṭafa, poetically surnamed Mukhliṣ, Teheran, A.H. 1301, with a preface which includes the biographical notice above-mentioned. The contents of that lithographed edition are identical with those of the present MS., with the exception that the additional pieces of the appendix have been inserted into the body of the work.

Another edition of Farrukhi's Divan was lithographed in Teheran, A.H. 1302. It contains Kasidahs, in alphabetical order, more numerous than in the first edition, but without headings, and two short Ghazals at the end. Some pieces have been edited by M. Schefer in the second volume of his Chrestomathie persane, pp. 247—52. A translation of Riza Ḳuli Khān's notice of Farrukhi will be found in the same volume, p. 242.

204.

Or. 3246.—Foll. 286; 11 in. by 6¾; about 19 lines, 3¾ in. long; written in two red-ruled columns in cursive Nestalik; dated (fol. 262) Tuesday, Ramazan, A.H. 1248 (A.D. 1833). Bound in painted and glazed covers. [Sidney Churchill.]

I. Foll. 1—212. دیوان فرخی

The Divan of Farrukhi; see the preceding MS.

Beg. بر آمد نیلگون ابری ز روی نیلگون دریا

Contents: Kasidahs in alphabetical order, partly agreeing with the Teheran edition of A.H. 1302, but much more numerous. Tarji'-bands, fol. 202*a*, beginning:

همی گفتم که کی باشد که خرم روزگار آید

Ghazals, fol. 207*a*, beginning:

بحق انکه مرا هیچکس بجای تو نیست
جفا مکن که مرا طاقت جفای تو نیست

Rubā'is, fol. 210*b*, beginning:

ای دوست مرا دیده همی نتوانی
بیهوده زمن روی چرا گردانی

II. Foll. 213—262. دیوان عنصری

The Divan of 'Unṣuri.

Contents: Kasidahs in alphabetical order, fol. 213*b*, with the same beginning as in no. 205. Additional Kasidahs not alphabetically arranged, fol. 250*b*. Rubā'is, fol. 261*a*, beginning:

ور نه رخ تو بزلف پنهان بودی
عنبر ببها همیشه ارزان بودی

III. Foll. 263—286. A collection of Kasidahs alphabetically arranged, designated in the colophon as the Divan of Rūdagi: تمت الدیوان للاستاد ابو الحسن رودکی

Beg. تا دل من درهوای نیکوان کشت آشنا
در سرشك دیده ام کردون نماید آشنا

It is stated, however, in a note at the beginning, that the poems are by Ḳaṭarān, and have been wrongly ascribed to Rūdagi, as they are found in the Divan of the former. In fact most pieces are found in the Divan of Ḳaṭarān, no. 207.

The same writer, who signs himself Bahman B. 'Abdullah Mirza B. Fatḥ 'Ali Shāh, makes an exception in favour of two pieces which he says are really by Rūdagi. The first is a Kasidah beginning, fol. 277*a*, as follows:

مادر می را بکرد باید قربان
بچه اورا گرفت و کرد بزندان

(In Majma' ul-Fuṣaḥā it is given under Rūdagi, vol. i., p. 238, but said to be really by Ḳaṭarān).

The second is the well-known piece beginning:

یاد جوی مولیان آید همی بوی یار مهربان آید همی

Copyist: ابو طالب

205.

Or. 2843.—Foll. 111; 8¼ in. by 5¼; 12 lines, 3½ in. long; written on blue-tinted paper in neat Shikastah-āmiz, with 'Unvān and gold-ruled margins; dated Teheran, 28 Zulhijjah, A.H. 1278 (A.D. 1862).

[Sidney Churchill.]

دیوان عنصری

The Divan of 'Unṣuri, Malik ush-Shu'arā at the Court of Sultan Maḥmūd, who died A.H. 431. See the Persian Catalogue, p. 1031*b*, II.

It is alphabetically arranged, and begins with a Kasidah in praise of Sultan Maḥmūd, the opening line of which is:

دل مرا عجب آید همی ز کار هوا
که مشکبوی ساب گشت و مشکبوی صبا

The alphabetical series of Kasidahs is followed, fol. 102*a*, by three Ḳiṭ'ahs and Ghazals, and, fol. 104*a*, by an alphabetical series of Rubā'is, beginning:

شاها ادبی کن فلك بدخورا
کاکفت رسانید رخ نیکورا

The Divan includes a Kasidah of Abu Zaid Ghaẓā'iri (who died A.H. 426; Majma' ul-Fuṣaḥā, vol. i., p. 368) and a "replica" by 'Unṣuri, foll. 59—65.

A similarly arranged Divan with nearly the same contents was lithographed in Persia without date. A later and fuller edition, probably lithographed in Teheran, is dated A.H. 1298. Copious extracts are given in Majma' ul-Fuṣaḥā, vol. i., pp. 355—67.

MSS. noticed by Sprenger, Oude Catalogue, p. 528, and by Ethé, Bodleian Catalogue, no. 521, are not in alphabetical order. They begin with a Kasidah in ان, which is found in the present MS., fol. 70.

Copyist: میرزا علی خان مازندرانی المتخلص به بدیهی

206.

Or. 2844.—Foll. 81; 8¼ in. by 6¼; 15 lines, about 4 in. long; written in cursive Shikastah-āmiz, A.H. 1274 (A.D. 1857-8).

[Sidney Churchill.]

دیوان منوچهری

The Divan of Minuchihri, with the heading دیوان قصاید افصح المتقدمین حکیم ابو النجم احمد المعروف بشصت کله المتخلص بمنوچهری دامغانی الشهیر به بلخی

Beg. همی ریزد میان باغ لولوها بزبورها
همی سوزد میان راغ عنبرها بجمرها

Abu 'n-Najm Aḥmad of Dāmaghān, surnamed Shaṣt Gallah, took the poetical name Minuchihri from his first patron, Amir Minuchihr of Gurgan, who succeeded his father Amir Ḳābūs, A.H. 386. After that prince's death in A.H. 411, he repaired to Ghaznah, paid his court to the Malik ush-Shu'arā 'Unṣuri, and became one of the panegyrists of Sultan Maḥmūd and of his son and successor, Sultan Mas'ūd. He died A.H. 432 (see Majma' ul-Fuṣaḥā, vol. i., p. 542) or A.H. 439, as stated in the Teheran edition of the Divan.

The first edition of his Divan was published in Teheran by the learned Riẓa Ḳuli Khān, who prefixed to it a biographical notice of the poet. A second edition was lithographed in Teheran, A.H. 1297. M. A. de Biberstein Kazimirski, who had published in 1876 a specimen of the Divan, drawn from a MS. in his possession, has since edited the whole text, enlarged from the Teheran edition, with translation and notes, Paris, 1886. This edition contains an extensive historical introduction on the reign of Sultan Mas'ūd, pp. 17—142, and Riẓa Ḳuli's biographical notice in text and translation, pp. ۲-۴ and 143—147.

The contents of the present copy differ by some additions and changes in the arrangement from those of the Teheran edition of 1297, and agree on the whole better with that of Kazimirski. The Musammaṭāt begin, fol. 64*b*, with this line,

خیزید و خز آرید که هنگام خزان است
باد خنك از جانب خوارزم وزان است

(Kazimirski, no. 58), and are followed, fol. 79*b*, by a few Ḳiṭ'ahs and Ghazals.

207.

Or. 3317.—Foll. 254; 8 in. by 4¾; 18 lines, 2¾ in. long; written in small and neat Nestalik in two gold-ruled columns, with 'Unvān, apparently early in the 19th century. Bound in painted and glazed covers.

[Sidney Churchill.]

دیوان حکیم قطران

The Divan of Ḥakīm Ḳaṭarān.

Beg. تا دل من در هوای نیکوان کرد اشنا
در سرشك دیدهٔ کردانم چو مرد اشنا

Ḳaṭarān was a native of Jabal, or the Dailami Highlands, and lived in Tabriz, where Nāṣir i Khusrau met him A.H. 434 (see Schefer's translation of Sefer-Nâmeh, p. 18). He addressed most of his poems to the Sultans and Amirs, who held sway in Azarbaijan under Sultan Toghrul I., especially to Amir Faẓlūn and Shāh Abu Naṣr Mamlān (appointed governor of a district of Azarbaijan, A.H. 450; see Kamil, vol ix., p. 448). Ḳaṭarān is called Tabrizi in the earliest Tazkirah, that of 'Aufi. See Riyāẓ ush-Shu'arā, fol. 368*b*, Haft Iḳlīm, fol. 509*b*, and Majma' ul-Fuṣaḥā, vol. i., p. 466. A.H. 465 is given in the last work as the date of his death. Some pieces of the Divan will be found in Schefer's Chrestomathie Persane, vol. ii., pp. 240—47.

The Divan consists for the most part of Kasidahs in alphabetical order, without headings. These are followed, fol. 202*a*, by Tarjī' bands and Ḳiṭ'ahs, beginning:

سپاه نو بهار آمد درو گیتی دگرگون شد
که هامون همچو گردون گشت گردون همچو هامون شد

At the end, fol. 245*b*, is a series of Rubā'is without alphabetical order, beginning:

چون مار بود میان زبن میر اجل
چون شیر بود بگاه کین میر اجل

The MS. is endorsed دیوان حکیم رودکی, but this has been corrected in a note showing that the mistake arose from a confusion between Abu Naṣr Mamlān, patron of Ḳaṭarān, and Naṣr B. Aḥmad Sāmāni, patron of Rūdagi.

208.

Or. 2879.—Foll. 81; 8¼ in. by 5; 17 lines, 2¾ in. long, with additional slanting lines in the margin; written in neat Nestalik, apparently in the 19th century.

[Sidney Churchill.]

A smaller collection of the poems of Ḳaṭarān.

Beg. فغان من همه از زلف تابدار سیاه
که گاه پردهٔ لاله است و گاه معجر ماه

The first Kasidah is found at fol. 173 of the preceding MS. The Divan concludes with another Kasidah, which occurs at fol. 94 of the latter copy, and begins thus:

گشت کوه و باغ در زیر گل بیجاده رنك
شاخ وسم از گل چریدن کرد چون بیجاده رنك

An appendix, foll. 72*b*—81*b*, contains some additional pieces beginning:

در جویبارها که نوشت این نگارها
گایدون پر از نگار شد این جویبارها

On the first page is a note of a former owner with the date A.H. 1278.

209.

Or. 2845.—Foll. 160; 8¼ in. by 4¾; 23 lines, 2⅝ in. long; written in minute and very neat Nestalik, apparently early in the 19th century. [Sidney Churchill.]

دیوان ناصر خسرو

The Divan of Nāṣir i Khusrau 'Alavi.

Beg. در بند مدارا کن و در بند میانرا
در بند مکن خیره طلب ملکت دارا

Nāṣir i Khusrau was born in Ḳubādiyān, near Balkh, A.H. 394, and died in Yumgān, in the province of Badakhshān, A.H. 481. For notices of his life, see the Persian Catalogue, p. 1086*b*; Ethé, Actes du sixième Congrès, Leide, 1885, Part 2, pp. 171—237; and Majma' ul-Fuṣaḥā, vol. i., pp. 607—633, where copious extracts from the Divan are given.

A lithographed edition of the Divan, alphabetically arranged, with an abridgment of the alleged autobiography of the author, was printed in Tabriz, A.H. 1280.

The contents of the present MS. are not in alphabetical order, although they begin with the first Kasidah of the Tabriz edition. The second Kasidah of the MS., beginning

تا کی خوری دریغ ز برنائی
زین چاه آرزو چه بر نائی

is found at p. 230 of the Tabriz edition.

The last complete Kasidah in the MS., beginning

تمیز و هوش و فکرت و پنداری

occurs at p. 272 of the same edition. The MS. breaks off at the tenth Bait of the next piece, which is not found in the lithographed edition, and begins:

ای شده مفتون بقولهای فلاطون
حال جهان بازشده است دگرگون

210.

Or. 3323.—Foll. 333; 8¼ in. by 6¼; 14 lines, 3¼ in. long; written in fair Nestalik; dated 9 Jumāda I., A.H. 1296 (A.D. 1879). [Sidney Churchill.]

The Divan of the same poet alphabetically arranged.

Beg.

خداوندی که در وحدت قدیمست از همه اشیا
نه اندر وحدتش کثرت نه محدث را ازو انها

Two prose pieces are prefixed, viz., 1. A notice of the poet, by Taḳi ud-Din Muḥ. al-Ḥusaini (no. 105), fol. 1*b*. 2. The autobiography of Nāṣir i Khusrau, foll. 4*b*—20*b*.

The contents of the Divan are much fuller than those of the Tabriz edition. The alphabetical series of Kasidahs, which ends fol. 317*a*, is followed by two longer pieces, the beginnings of which are as follows:

Fol. 317*a*.

ای گنبد زنگارگون ای پر جنون و پرفنون

Fol. 321*a*.

خدایا عرض و طول عالمی را توانی در دل مور آفریدن

At the end, fol. 326*a*, are some Ḳiṭ'ahs beginning:

آن کیست یکی دختر دوشیزه زیبا
از بوی و مزه چون شکر و عنبر و سارا

211.

Or. 3713.—Foll. 179; 11¼ in. by 7¾; 31 lines, 6 in. long; written in distinct Persian Neskhi, in four red-ruled columns, with gilt 'Unvāns; dated Tabriz, from Tuesday, 6 Rabī' II., A.H. 692, to Friday, 5 Ṣafar, A.H. 697 (A.D. 1293—98). [SIDNEY CHURCHILL.]

I. Foll. 2*b*—17*a*. دیوان ابو الفرج

The Divan of Abu 'l-Faraj Rūni, who died about the close of the fifth century of the Hijrah. See the Persian Catalogue, p. 547; Ethé, Bodleian Catalogue, no. 523; and Majma' ul-Fuṣaḥā, vol. i., pp. 70—78.

Beg. سپهر دولت ودین افتاب هفت اقلیم
ابو المظفر شاه مظفر ابرهیم

The Divan is not in alphabetical order. The Kasidahs are followed, fol. 16*a*, by Mukaṭṭa'āt beginning:

مسلمان وار بندت داد خواهم
تو خود پند مسلمان کی بذیری

and, fol. 16*b*, by Rubā'is beginning:

ای مطلع دولت ای سر افراز عمید
ای صاحب روزگار منصور سعید

II. Foll. 17*b*—18*a*. Rubā'is by Majd ud-Dīn Hamgar, الرباعیات من کلام خواجه مجد الدین همکر رحمه الله

Beg. در غلام اشکره دار کوید حرف الالف
دیدمش جو سرو سهی ان سبز قبا
دست کرفته باشهٔ صید ربا

Hamgar was a native of Shiraz, who traced his origin to Anushirvan. He was a panegyrist of the Atabek of Fars, Sa'd B. Abu Bakr B. Zingi, and of the great Ṣāḥib Divān, Shams ud-Din Muḥammad. He died A.H. 686. See Sprenger, Oude Catalogue, p. 478; Ethé, Bodleian Catalogue, no. 678; and Majma' ul-Fuṣaḥā, vol. i., pp. 594—8.

The Rubā'is are in alphabetical order, and break off in letter ت. For the continuation see below, artt. IV. and VII.

III. Foll. 18*b*—35*b*. دیوان ازرقی

The Divan of Azraḳi.

Beg. ز نور قبهٔ زرین آینه تمثال
زمین تفته فرو بوشد آتشین سربال

Zain ud-Dīn Abu Bakr Azraḳi lived at the Court of Ṭughān Shāh, the Saljūḳ prince of Nishapur, and died in Herat, A.H. 526 or 527. See Sprenger, Oude Catalogue, p. 366; Pertsch, Berlin Catalogue, no. 711; and Majma' ul-Fuṣaḥā, vol. i., pp. 139—52.

The Divan consists almost entirely of Kasidahs, many of which are addressed to Ṭughān Shāh B. Muḥ., to Mīrānshāh B. Ḳāvurd, who reigned in Kirmān A.H. 487—494, and to several Vazirs of the same period. They are not in alphabetical order. At the end, fol. 34*b*, are Rubā'is beginning:

ای رای تو با صحت کردون شده جفت
بیذا بر تو هرچه فلک راست نهفت

IV. Fol. 35*b*—36*a*. Rubā'is of Majd ud-Din Hamgar, continued from fol. 18, with the heading: این رباعی در زندان کفته است در حبس سلطان سید ابو بکر بن سعد

با حکم خدائی که قضایش اینست
می ساز دلا مکر رضایش اینست

V. Foll. 36*b*—125*a*. دیوان انوری

The Divan of Anvari. See no. 215, v.

Beg. کر دل و دست بحر و کان باشد
دل و دست خدایکان باشد

Contents: Kasidahs not alphabetically arranged, but grouped under the persons to whom they are addressed.

Mukaṭṭa'āt, fol. 83*a*, beginning:

کسی که مدت سی سال شعر باطل کفت
خدای بر همه کامیش داد بیروزی

Rubā'is, fol. 118*a*, beginning:

از مشرق دست گوهر آل نظام
ده ماه تمام را طلوعست مدام

VI. Foll. 125*b*—173*b*. دیوان مختاری

The Divan of Mukhtāri. See no. 215, VII.

Beg. ترا بشارت باد ای ولایت کرمان
بفتح نامهٔ شاه از دیار هندستان

Kasidahs arranged under the persons in whose praise they are written. Hazaliyyāt and Ghazaliyyāt, fol. 165*b*, the latter of which begin as follows:

آن چه آغاز خطست ای بسر از بهر خدای
زلف بر گوش نه و غالیه بر مشك مسای

Masnavis, fol. 166*a*, the first of which is entitled مهر نامهٔ یحیی, and begins:

گنبد لاجورد دایره کرد
سال خورده سبهر سال نورد

Rubā'is, fol. 170*a*, beginning:

ملکت ملك (corrected to حکمت ملکا) نفس بقارا
جان شد
عدلت سبب دم زدن حیوان شد

VII. Foll. 173*b*—179*b*. Rubā'is of Majd ud-Dīn Hamgar, continued from fol. 36, and extending from د to ی.

In some verses at the end the transcriber, Isḥāḳ B. Ḳivām Muḥ. Hamgar, states that this copy of the Rubā'is of his grandfather was finished on Friday, the 5th of Ṣafar, A.H. 697 in obedience to the commands of Fakhr i Millat u Dīn Khwājah i Jahān, son of Naṣīr ud-Dīn Aḥmad, in Tabrīz.

The Divan of Mukhtāri was transcribed, as well as the preceding Divans, by Muḥammad Shāh B. 'Ali B. Maḥmūd Iṣfahāni, ساکن بمحلت کران, who finished the last on Tuesday, 6 Rabī' II., A.H. 693.

212.

Or. 2889.—Foll. 119; 8 in. by 5; about 22 lines of varying length; written in small and cursive Nestalik Shikastah-āmīz; dated Teheran, from 22 Jumāda II., A.H. 1289, to Wednesday, 28 Jumāda I., A.H. 1293 (A.D. 1872—76). [Sidney Churchill.]

I. Foll. 2—8. An Arabic Kasidah, composed in prison, by Sa'īd B. As'ad, with this heading: قصيدة الحبسيه لسعيد بن اسعد امير اتابك ابو بكران احبسه فى قلعة الاشكنوان وقال

Beg. من يبلغن حمامات ببطحاء
مثعات بسلسال وخضراء

II. Foll. 10—24*a*. دیوان لامعی

The Divan of Abu 'l-Ḥasan Lāmi'i.

Beg. مانوی نقش است رویت ای نگار آذری
کز تو در دلها چنین مهراست و چندین داوری

Lāmi'i, a native of Jurjān, was a disciple of Ghazzāli, and a panegyrist of Malik Shāh and of the great Vazir of the Saljūks, Niẓām ul-Mulk. His rich fancy obtained for him the surname of Baḥr ul-Ma'āni. He died in Samarḳand in the reign of Sultan Sinjar (A.H. 511—552). See Ātashkadah, Riyāẓ ush-Shu'arā, fol. 396*a*, and Majma' ul-Fuṣaḥā, vol. i., pp. 494—501, where copious specimens of his compositions are given. A very small collection of his Kasidahs, in alphabetical order, was lithographed in Teheran, A.H. 1295, under the title of Divān i Ḥakīm Lāmi'i.

The present Divan is not alphabetically arranged. It consists of Kasidahs and of a few short poems without any headings. It contains many pieces not found in the Teheran edition.

III. Foll. 24*b*—43*b*. دیوان عنصری

The Divan of 'Unṣuri; see no. 205. It is

not in alphabetical order, and begins like the Oude and Bodleian MSS. with this line:

توانگری و بزرگی و کام دل بجهان
نکرد حاصل کس جز بخدمت سلطان

It consists entirely of Kasidahs, the last of which begins as follows:

شه مشرق و شاه زابلستانی   خداوندا قران صاحبقرانی

IV. Foll. 44*b*—75*a*. دیوان رشید الدین وطواط

The Divan of Rashīd ud-Dīn Vaṭvāṭ; see the Persian Catalogue, p. 553*a*, and Majma' ul-Fuṣaḥā, vol. i., p. 222.

Beg. بهار جانفزا آمد جهان خرم زیبا
بباغ و راغ گستردند فرش حله و زیبا

It consists of two series of Kasidahs, the first of which is in alphabetical order. The second, which is not so arranged, begins, fol. 57*a*, as follows:

ساقیا شاهد رعنای گل انداخت نقاب
زلف سنبل شد از آسیب صبا پرخم و تاب

V. Foll. 75*b*—119*a*. دیوان منوچهری

The Divan of Minuchihri; see above, no. 206. This is the text edited by Riẓa Ḳuli Khān, with his notice of the poet at the beginning, foll. 75*b*-76*b*, revised and enlarged by Muḥ. Ḥusain B. Aḳa Muḥ. Mahdi Arbāb Isfahāni, poetically surnamed Adīb. The contents are the same as those of the Teheran edition of A.H. 1297.

213.

Or. 2995.—Foll. 179; 8¾ in. by 5; 14 lines, 3½ in. long; written in fair Nestalik; dated Friday, 10 Ramazan, A.H. 1264 (A.D. 1848).
[Sidney Churchill.]

I. Foll. 2*b*—87*a*. دیوان ازرقی

The Divan of Azraḳi, with the same beginning, and generally the same arrangement, as in a preceding copy, no. 211, III. The Rubā'is begin, fol. 81*b*, as follows:

مرجاه ترا بلندی جوزا باد
درگاه ترا سیاست دریا باد

II. Foll. 87*b*—148*a*. دیوان امامی

The Divan of Imāmi Harawi, who lived in Kirman and Isfahan, and died in the latter place, according to Taḳi Kāshi, A.H. 686. See Sprenger, Oude Catalogue, p. 17, no. 46, and p. 439; Daulatshāh, III., 10; Haft Iḳlīm, fol. 194*b*; Riyāẓ ush-Shu'arā, fol. 15*b*; Atashkadah, fol. 76*a*; Ethé, Bodleian Catalogue, no. 676; and Majma' ul-Fuṣaḥā, vol. i., pp. 98—101.

Contents: Kasidahs, not alphabetically arranged, beginning:

سحرگه در جهان جان بعون مبدع اشیا
مسافت قطع میکردم زلا تا حضرت الا

Muḳaṭṭa'āt, fol. 132*b*, beginning:

تاج دین و دولت ایصدریکه گرد موکبت
دیده افلاک و انجم را مکحل میکند

III. Foll. 148*b*—175*b*. دیوان فرید الدین احول

The Divan of Farid ud-Dīn Aḥval, a contemporary of Imāmi and of Majd ud-Dīn Hamgar, and panegyrist of Atabek Sa'd B. Zingi. See Daulatshāh, II., 13; Riyāẓ ush-Shu'arā, fol. 332*b*; Haft Iḳlīm, fol. 355; Oude Catalogue, p. 397; and Majma' ul-Fuṣaḥā, vol. i., pp. 377—80.

It consists exclusively of Kasidahs, without alphabetical order or headings, and begins as follows:

آب زلال نوشید از دست ساقی دل
مایل بمل بود نه زانکو بمال مایل

IV. Foll. 176*a*—179*b*. Three additional Kasidahs ascribed in the heading to Imāmi امامی راست

Beg. همچو مهر خاور و باد از ختن
دیشب آنسنگین دل سیمین ذقن

The MS. was written for Malik ush-Shu'arā Mirza Sarkhush, by Ja'far Ḳuli B. Muḥ. Taḳi Jājarmi.

214.

Or. 3302.—Foll. 227; 7½ in. by 4¾; 15 lines, 3¼ in. long; written in distinct Neskhi, before A.H. 1280 (A.D. 1863).

[Sidney Churchill.]

دیوان حکیم سنائی

The Divan of Ḥakīm Sanā'i, with a preface by the author. See the Persian Catalogue, pp. 549—551.

Beg. of the Preface: سپاس و ستایش مبدعیست که شخص پاك سخن دان سخن کوی را ابداع کرد

Beg. of the Divan:

ای در دل مشتاقان از یاد تو بستانها
بر حجت بیچونی از صنع تو برهانها

Among the conflicting statements regarding the date of Sanā'i's death, the most generally accepted is that he died in the very year in which he completed the Ḥadiḳah, *i.e.* A.H. 525. That date is decidedly wrong. It has been pointed out by Ethé, Bodleian Catalogue, no. 528, that Sanā'i gives A.H. 528 as the date of composition of his Ṭarīḳ at-Taḥḳīḳ. A further proof is afforded by the present Divan, for it contains no fewer than three pieces on the death of Amir Mu'izzi, who was killed by a stray shot of Sultan Sinjar, A.H. 542. The third of these, which contains an allusion to the cause of his death, fol. 137*b*, is as follows:

تا چند معزای معزی که خدایش
زنجا بفلك برد وقبای ملکی داد
جون تیر فلك بود قرینش سره آورد
پیکان ملك برد و به تیر فلکی داد

The most probable date is that given by Taḳi Kāshi, Or. 3506, fol. 286, viz., A.H. 545. It has been adopted in the Atashkadah and in Riyāẓ ul-'Ārifīn, fol. 75*b*.

The preface, foll. 2—12, agrees substantially with that which in other MSS. (Persian Catalogue, p. 550*b*, and Bodleian Catalogue, no. 530) is prefixed to the Ḥadiḳah. The author, who calls himself Majdūd Sanā'i, describes the state of despondency from which he was roused by his spiritual guide, Aḥmad, son of Mas'ūd, and, after some reflections on the vanity of all science, shows that real charity consists in imparting to the sad and weary such spiritual knowledge as will make their hearts glad.

The preface concludes with a table of the ten Bābs into which the Divan is divided, viz.:

I. اندر توحید و حکمت و امثال و آن سی و شش قصیده است

II. در مدایح جمله هفتاد و نه قصیده است بیست و یك قصیده مدح سلطان و باقی پراکنده در هر کسی

III. سیر العباد الی المعاد مثنوی که در قاضی محمد منصور سرخسی کوید به سرخس

IV. اندر مراثی و آن هفده قصیده است

V. در حکم و امثال و آن سی و سه مقطع است

VI. در اهاجی در هر انواع و آن جهار پنج قصیده است

VII. مطایبه نامه مثنوی که به بلخ کفتست

VIII. اندر غزل و آن دویست و شصت قصیده است

IX. اندر رباعیات از هر نوع و آن جهار صد و جهل و سه رباعیست

X. حدیقه فی الحقیقه

The actual contents of the MS. fall far short of the above programme. The division into Bābs is not observed, the matter is considerably curtailed, the seventh Bāb and the tenth (the Ḥadīḳah) are omitted, and the order of others is inverted.

Contents: Religious and moral Kasidahs, fol. 13*b*. Kasidahs in praise of Bahrāmshāh, of his father and predecessor, Sultan 'Alā ud-Daulah Abu Sa'd Mas'ūd (A.H. 492—508) and others, fol. 36*b*. A Sufi poem, entitled كنوز الحكمة و رموز المتصوفه, fol. 62*b*, beginning:

طلب ای عاشقان خوش رفتار
طرب ای نیکوان شیرین کار

(mentioned in Nafaḥāt ul-Uns, p. 697, under the title رموز الانبیا و کنوز الاولیا).

Other Sufi poems in Kasidah form, fol. 76*a*. Ghazals, fol. 75*a*, beginning:

تا شیفتهٔ عارض گل رنگ فلانم
با پشت خمیده چو سر چنگ فلانم

and some laudatory and miscellaneous pieces. Elegies مراثی fol. 137*a*. Satires, fol. 146*a*. Ghazals, fol. 146*b*. Rubā'is and Ḳiṭ'ahs, fol. 174*b*, beginning:

در مرگ حیوة اهل داد و دینست
وز مرگ روان پاك را تمکینست

The Masnavi entitled سیر العباد الی المعاد (designated in the table as Bāb III.), foll. 186*b*—221*a*, beginning:

مرحبا ای برید سلطان وش
تحفت از آب و تاحت از آتش

An appendix, foll. 221*a*—227*a*, contains anecdotes and letters of Sanā'i.

Copyist: عبد الباقی بن رجبعلی جرپادقانی

215.

Or. 4514.—Foll. 153; $9\frac{3}{4}$ in. by $6\frac{1}{2}$; 35 lines, $4\frac{1}{2}$ in. long, with additional lines round the margins; written in a very minute Nestalik in six columns; dated from Jumāda I., A.H. 1009 (fol. 116*b*) to 14 Rabi' II., A.H. 1023 (fol. 76*b*) (A.D. 1600—1614).

[Sidney Churchill.]

I. Foll. 3*a*—40*b*. The Ḥadīḳah of Sanā'i, to which is prefixed the preface of Muḥammad B. 'Ali al-Raffā, imperfect at the beginning, followed by that of Sanā'i, fol. 4*a* (see the Persian Catalogue, p. 550; Ethé, Bodleian Catalogue, no. 528; and Pertsch, Berlin Catalogue, no. 717).

II. Foll. 40*b*—42*a*. Another Masnavi by Sanā'i, with the heading كتاب سیر العباد الی المعاد المسمی بکنوز الرموز. See above, no. 214, fol. 186.

III. Foll. 42*b*—76*a*. The Divan of Sanā'i; see no. 214.

Beg. ای منزه ذات تو عما یقولون الظالمون
کفت علمت جمله را ما لم تکونوا تعلمون

The Kasidahs, which are not in alphabetical order, are followed, fol. 66*a*, by Ghazals beginning:

مرد دنیا باز باید تا که درد دین کشد
سرمهٔ تسلیم را در چشم دنیابین کشد

and, fol. 74*a*, by Muḳaṭṭa'āt beginning:

هر که چون کاغذ و قلم باشد
دو زبان و دو روی گاه سخن

In the colophon the preceding articles are designated as كلیات قدوة المحققین . . . ابو المجد مجدود بن آدم سنائی الغزنوی

IV. Foll. 76*b*-77*b*. An extract from the Persian translation of Yamini entitled محمود الآثار, by Abu 'l-Sharaf Nāṣiḥ B. Ẓafar B. Sa'd al-Munshi al-Churpādaḳāni (Persian Catalogue, p. 157), or rather from the translator's continuation. It relates to the events of A.H. 582, and, first, to the great cataclysm which had been foretold for that year.

V. Foll. 78*b*—116*b*. دیوان انوری

The Divan of Anvari, alphabetically arranged, with the usual beginning. See further on, no. 218. The Muḳaṭṭa'āt begin on fol. 96*a*, and the Ghazals on fol. 108*a*.

VI. Foll. 117*b*—134*b*. دیوان سید حسن غزنوی

The Divan of Sayyid Ḥasan Ghaznavi, who died A.H. 565. See the Persian Catalogue, pp. 999*b*, 979*a*, Or. 3506, fol. 427, and Majma' ul-Fuṣaḥā, pp. 192—6.

Beg. یا رب این ماٸیم واین صدر رفع مصطفاست

یا رب این ماٸیم این فرق عزیز مجتباست

A biographical notice of the poet, by Taḳi ud-Dīn Kāshi, is prefixed to the Divan. The latter begins with an alphabetical series of Kasidahs without headings. These are followed, fol. 127*a*, by Tarkib-bands and Tarjī's beginning:

جانا ز مشك سلسله بر گل فکندهٔ

بر گوش لاله حلقه ز سنبل فکندهٔ

and, fol. 129*b*, by Muḳaṭṭa'āt beginning:

کشت روشن ندا که ایزد فرد

بهر شاه ایلجهان بدید آورد

Further on, fol. 131*a*, are found Ghazals beginning:

ای مونس جان من کجائی   از دیدهٔ من جدا چرائی

and, fol. 133*a*, Rubā'is beginning:

ای جان دل ریش بر جهان بیش منه

ای کاه ضعیف کوه بر خویش منه

VII. Foll. 135*b*—153*b*. دیوان عثمان مختاری

The Divan of 'Uṣmān Mukhtāri, who died A.H. 544 or 554. See the Persian Catalogue, p. 543*a*, Or. 3506, fol. 325, and Majma' ul-Fuṣaḥā, vol. i., pp. 598—607.

Beg. روزگاری خوشترست از شکر و عنبر ترا

تا سمن در عنبرست لاله در شکر ترا

The Divan consists chiefly of Kasidahs in alphabetical order, with headings indicating in whose praise they were composed. Most of them were addressed to Arslān Shāh B. Kirmānshāh, the Saljūḳi prince of Kirman (A.H. 494—536). There are also some in praise of the Ghaznavi Sultans, Arslān Shāh B. Mas'ūd and his brother and successor Bahrāmshāh, and others addressed to 'Aẓud ud-Daulah Dailami, to Ṭamghāj Khān, and to some contemporary Vazirs. The Kasidahs are followed, fol. 150*b*, by Muḳaṭṭa'āt beginning:

خرکهٔ خاقان ترکستان شه مالك رقاب

آسمانست و جمال ارسلان خان آفتاب

At the ends are some Ghazals and Rubā'is, fol. 151*b*, and a few Masnavis, fol. 152*a*.

216.

Or. 3374.—Foll. 127; 9¼ in. by 6; 12 lines, 3¾ in. long; written in fair Nestalik in two columns; dated A.H. 1287 (A.D. 1870). [SIDNEY CHURCHILL.]

دیوان مختاری

The Divan of Mukhtāri, see no. 215, VII.

Beg. بر اختیار بندگی مالك الرقاب

نصر من الله آمد فال من از کتاب

This first Kasidah is in praise of Arslānshāh Saljūḳi of Kirman. It is given in Majma' ul-Fuṣaḥā, vol. i., p. 599. The Kasidahs are not in alphabetical order, and have no headings. The Ghazals begin, fol. 118*b*, as follows:

چون مهر باوج خویش بر شد

احوال جهان همه دگر شد

At the end are a few Ḳiṭ'ahs and Rubā'is.

217.

Or. 3320.—Foll. 149; 9½ in. by 4¾; 20 lines, 2¾ in. long; written in elegant Nestalik in two gold-ruled columns, with 'Unvān; dated 23 Rabī' I., A.H. 1016 (A.D. 1607). [Sidney Churchill.]

دیوان عبد الواسع جبلی

Beg.

بطبع خوش بصدق دل بطوع تن بمهر جان
بزرك وخرد وخاص وعام ووحش وطیر وانس وجان

The poet, a native of Gharjistan, lived mostly in Herat and Ghaznin, and was a panegyrist of Bahrāmshāh Ghaznavi and of Sultan Sinjar Saljūḳi. He died, according to Taḳi Kāshi, Or. 3506, fol. 397, A.H. 555. See Sprenger, Oude Catalogue, pp. 16 and 444; Daulatshāh, ii., 2; Haft Iḳlīm, fol. 260a; Riyāẓ ush-Shu'arā, fol. 96a; and Majma' ul-Fuṣaḥā, vol. i., pp. 185—192. A MS. of the Divan with the above beginning, is fully described in Ethé's Bodleian Catalogue, no. 538.

Contents: Kasidahs, not alphabetically arranged, mixed with some Kiṭ'ahs, fol. 1b. Ghazals, fol. 127a, beginning:

ایا ساقی المدام مرا باده ده تمام
سمن بوی ولاله فام که تا من درین مقام

Rubā'is, fol. 140a, beginning:

آنکه که تهی نبود پیرایهٔ ما
از خاك دریغت آمدی سایهٔ ما

Copyist: صالح بن میرزا علی خاتوناباذی

218.

Or. 3233.—Foll. 422; 9½ in. by 5½; 18 lines, 3 in. long; written in very neat Nestalik in two gold-ruled columns, with four rich 'Unvāns; dated Thursday, 20 Rajab, A.H. 1154 (A.D. 1741). [Sidney Churchill.]

دیوان انوری

The Divan of Anvari. See above, no. 215, v.; the Persian Catalogue, p. 554; Pertsch, Berlin Catalogue, no. 713; Ethé, Bodleian Catalogue, no. 543; Majma' ul-Fuṣaḥā, vol. i., pp. 152—167; M. Ferté, Journal Asiatique, 1895, i.; and Zhukovski's Essay on Anvari's life and poetry, published in Russian, St. Petersburg, 1883, and reviewed by Pertsch, Literatur Blatt für Orientalische Philologie, Band II., pp. 10—18.

In this MS. the Divan is divided into four parts, marked by separate 'Unvans, containing respectively the Kasidahs, the Muḳaṭṭa'āt, the Ghazals, and the Rubā'is. In each part the contents are arranged in alphabetical order. The initial verses of the four parts are as follows:

I. Fol. 1b.

ای قاعده تازه زدست تو کرم را
وی مرتبه نو ز بنان تو قلم را

II. Fol. 207b.

ای خصم تو پست و قدر والا
وی عقل تو پیر و بخت برنا

III. Fol. 319b.

از دور بدیدم آن پری را
آن رشك بتان آذری را

IV. Fol. 391b.

نه صبر بکوشهٔ نشاند مارا
نه عقل بکام دل رساند مارا

In the first two parts the poems have headings indicating their subject and metre. At the end of the third part are found a satire, fol. 386b, and a Masnavi, entitled حدیث عمزاد و دخترش, fol. 387b.

Copyist: محمد مومن شیرازی

219.

Or. 3312.—Foll. 149; 6 in. by 4; 18 lines, 2 in. long; written in small and cursive Nestalik; dated Zulhijjah, A.H. 132 (probably for 1132, A.D. 1720).

[Sidney Churchill.]

A commentary upon the Mukaṭṭaʻāt of the Divan of Anvari, by Abu 'l-Ḥasan al-Ḥusaini Farāhāni. See the Persian Catalogue, p. 556b, where the same author's commentary on the Kasidahs is described. Both commentaries are mentioned by Ethé, Bodleian Catalogue, no. 557.

Beg. ای نام تو قالب عبارت را روح

.... تعالی الله چه قادریست متعال که بستون خامه

... شیرازه بند دفتر حیرانی ابو الحسن الحسینی فراهانی را قرار داد

The author refers in the preface to his previous commentary on the Kasidahs, and prefixes to the present work an introduction on the six kinds of Persian poetry. The commentary follows the alphabetical order of the Mukaṭṭaʻāt. The first line quoted is:

ای صدری که از روی بزرگی
فلك را نیست با قدر تو بالا

(see Or. 3233, fol. 209a). Only such passages are cited as require explanation. In conclusion the author claims the indulgence of the readers on account of his youth.

For other copies see the Oude Catalogue, p. 332, no. 100, and Mélanges Asiatiques, vol. iv., p. 54.

Copyist: محمد هاشم الهمدانی

220.

Or. 3486.—Foll. 540; 13½ in. by 9¼; 15 lines, 3¾ in. long in the centre of the pages, and about 31 oblique lines round the margins; written in large and elegant Nestalik, with gold-ruled margins, a rich double-page ʻUnvān and gold headings; dated A.H. 841 (A.D. 1437-8). [Sidney Churchill.]

I. Foll. 1b—327b. دیوان انوری

The Divan of Anvari, to which is prefixed, foll. 1b—3a, a prose preface by an anonymous editor.

Beg. of the preface: مهم تر شغلی که اصحاب نطق و دراست بدان نازند و ارباب فهم و فراست دستور سازند حمد خداوندیست که وهم از ادراك وصف او حیرانست

After a pompous eulogy on the poet, whom he calls اوحد الملة والدین عماد الاسلام والمسلمین .... تاج الشعرا علی بن محمد اسحق الانوری the editor says that, having found Anvari's poems, especially those of his latter days, scattered and exposed to loss, he deemed it incumbent upon himself to collect and arrange them, and to compile a table in order to render the search for them easy. There is, however, no such table in the MS.

The Divan begins, fol. 3b, with a Kasidah in praise of Sultan Sinjar, with the heading: فی مدح سلطان الاعظم سلطان سنجر نور مرقده, the opening line of which is:

گردل و دست بحر و کان باشد
دل و دست خدایگان باشد

The arrangement is not alphabetical. Some Kasidahs at the beginning have headings indicating their subject. The Mukaṭṭaʻāt begin, fol. 203b, as follows:

نکرتا حلقهٔ اقبال نا ممکن نجنبانی
سلیما ابلها لا بل که محروما و مسکینا

Then follow six Ghazals, fol. 321b, beginning:

ای کرده در جهان غم عشقت سمر مرا
وی کرده دست عشق تو زیر و زبر مرا

and Rubā'is, fol. 323*a*, beginning:

ای کوهر تو خلاصه عالم کل
باذ از تو دو قوم را دو مستی (؟) حاصل

II. Foll. 328*b*—540*b*. دیوان مولانا سیف الدین اسفرنجانی

The Divan of Saif Isfarangi, who died according to Taḳi Kāshi, A.H. 666, or, as stated in Majma' ul-Fuṣaḥā, vol. i., p. 252, A.H. 672, at the age of eighty-five. See the Persian Catalogue, p. 581*b*.

Beg. شب جو بردارد حجاب از هودج اسرار من
خفته کیرد صبح را جشم دل بیدار من

The first section contains Kasidahs and Tarji'-bands, many of which have headings indicating their subjects. They are generally arranged under the names of the persons in whose praise they were composed. The remaining sections are two Muḳaṭṭa'āt and one Ghazal, fol. 536, beginning:

جیست آن صورت دلکیر که کر نقش ورا
بر در خانه کنی دیو نیاید در وی

Rubā'is, fol. 537*b*, beginning:

پیوسته بر آنم که بمانم از خود
خود را بحیل باز رهانم از خود

The margins throughout the volume form a continuous text, consisting of the following works:

III. Foll. 1*b*—343*a*. دیوان مولانا سلمان

The Divan of Salmān Sāvaji, who died A.H. 779. See the Persian Catalogue, p. 624*b*; Pertsch, Berlin Catalogue, no. 837; Ethé, Bodleian Catalogue, no. 807; and Majma' ul-Fuṣaḥā, vol. ii., p. 19.

Beg. هر دل که در هوای هویّت مجال یافت
عنقای همتش دو جهان زیر بال یافت

Contents: Kasidahs or Tarji'-bands, partly provided with headings indicating the persons to whom they are addressed, without alphabetical arrangement.

Marṣiyahs, fol. 195*a*, beginning:

ای سپهر آهسته رو کاری نه آسان کردهٔ
ملك ایرانرا بمرك شاه ویران کردهٔ

Muḳaṭṭa'āt, fol. 205*a*, beginning:

حبذا صدر صفه که بهست
بهمه حال از بهشت برین

Another series of Ḳiṭ'ahs فی القطعه, fol. 329*b*, beginning:

زهی آصف صفاتی کز کفایت
ترا ملك سلیمان در نکینست

Ghazals in alphabetical order, fol. 243*a*, beginning:

اکر حسن تو بکشاید نقاب از جهره دعوی را
بکل رضوان بر انداید در فردوس اعلی را

Rubā'is, fol. 334*a*, beginning:

ای آنك تو طالب خدائی بخودا
در خود بطلب کز تو جدا نیست خدا

IV. Foll. 343*b*—540*b*. غزلیات خسرو

Ghazals of Amir Khusrau Dihlavi (Persian Catalogue, p. 609), alphabetically arranged.

Beg. حمد رانم بر زبان لله رب العالمین
انك جان بخشید از قران هدی للمتقین

This first piece is the opening of the Divan entitled وسط الحیوة (see Oude Catalogue, p. 468, and Ethé, no. 753), from which most of the contents of the present collection are taken. The first three pieces, which are in praise of God فی التوحید, are followed by a piece beginning:

ای بدرماندکی پناه همه
کرم تست عذر خواه همه

which is at the head of the Ghazals in the same Divan.

The alphabetical series of Ghazals begins, fol. 345*a*, as follows:

آورده ام شفیع دل زار خویش را
پندی بده دو نرگس خونخوار خویش را

At the end are a few Muḳaṭṭaʻāt, fol. 538*a*, and some Rubāʻis, fol. 539*a*. The latter begin:

پاك است خداوند کریم اکبر
بیرون زخیال و دانش و عقل بشر

This fine and well-preserved MS. is the work of two skilled penmen, who wrote very similar hands. The main text in the centre was written by ʻAli B. Shaʻbān B. Ḥaidar al-Ushturjāni, while the marginal text is signed Zain al-Kātib al-Iṣfahāni.

221.

Or. 3401.—Foll. 180; 9 in. by 5¼; 12 and 15 lines; written in cursive Nestalik Shikastah-āmīz; dated Jumāda II., A.H. 1259 (A.D. 1843). [Sidney Churchill.]

I. Foll. 3—105. تحفة العراقین

Tuḥfat ul-ʻIrāḳain by Khāḳāni (Persian Catalogue, p. 560*a*), with the prose preface, foll. 3—7. The poem is imperfect at the end.

II. Foll. 106—180. مفتاح الکنوز

A commentary upon the Divan of Khāḳāni by Riẓa Ḳuli, poetically surnamed Hidāyat (see no. 42).

Beg. مفتاح ابواب کمال و کلام و مصباح ضلال و ظلام... اما بعد چون این فقیر راجی بعنایت رضا قلی مخلص بهدایت

The author says in the preface that, although he was aware that commentaries had been written on Khāḳāni's Divan, he had not seen any. He therefore thought it expedient to give his own explanations of rare words and phrases occurring in the Kasidahs, Tarkībs, Marṡiyahs and Muḳaṭṭaʻāt. He wrote the present commentary in the days of the Fast, and in the midst of engrossing occupations. He concludes by stating his intention of writing later on a commentary upon Tuḥfat ul-ʻIrāḳain.

For other commentaries on the Kasidahs of Khāḳāni, see the Persian Catalogue, pp. 561-62; Oude Catalogue, p. 462; Pertsch, Berlin Catalogue, no. 742; and Ethé, Bodleian Catalogue, nos. 572-3.

Copyist: زین العابدین

222.

Or. 3325.—Foll. 106; 6¾ in. by 5; 17 lines, 2¾ in. long; written in small and fair Nestalik; dated beginning of Ramaẓan, A.H. 873 (A.D. 1469). [Sidney Churchill.]

دیوان ظهیر فاریابی

The Divan of Ẓahīr Fāriyābi, with a preface.

Beg. of the Preface: سپاس بی غایت و افرین بی نهایت قادری را که دو شمع در حجرهٔ دماغ بر افروخت

Beg. of the Divan:

چو زهره وقت صبوح از افق بساز چنك
زمانه نیز کند نالهٔ مرا آهنك

After some considerations on the noble gift of speech and on the relative merits of prose and poetry, the unknown author of the preface says that untoward circumstances had torn him away from his native place and from his parents, and that his great desire was to meet Ẓahir ud-Din Ṭāhir B. Muḥ. al-Fāriyābi, and to gather from converse with him knowledge and wisdom, but he was balked in his purpose by adverse fate, and, ere he could reach him, the poet had departed for the abode of bliss. The writer was fain to collect the scattered poems of Ẓahīr in a Divan, which he dedicated to the Vazir Majd ud-Daulah wa'd-Din Aḥmad B. Muḥammad.

The same preface is noticed by Sprenger, Oude Catalogue, p. 579, and by Ethé, Bodleian Catalogue, no. 582.

Contents of the Divan: Kasidahs not alphabetically arranged, with a few Tarkib-bands, some of which have rubrics indicating to whom they were addressed, fol. 66. Mukaṭṭa'at, fol. 68*b*, beginning:

صر ملوك جهان شهريار روى زمين
بدست ودل حسد بحر وغيرت كانى

Ghazals, fol. 97*b*, beginning:

اى بعيدى دام بروى تو شاد
عيد را روى تو مبارك باد

Rubā'is, fol. 996*b*, beginning:

اى خيل ستاركان سپاه و حشمت
دوران فلك مطيع تيغ و قلمت

For notices of Ẓahīr, who died A.H. 598, and of MSS. of his Divan, see the Persian Catalogue, p. 562*b*; Schefer's Chrestomathie, vol. i., p. 112; Majma' ul-Fusaḥā, vol. i., pp. 330—36; Rosen, Institut, p. 205; Pertsch, Berlin Catalogue, nos. 691, 747-8; and Ethé, Bodleian Catalogue, nos. 582—4. The Divan was lithographed at Lucknow, A.H. 1295.

This copy was written by Yūsuf B. 'Abd ul-'Aziz for the library of Amīr Bakāri Beg B. Iskander Beg.

223.

Or. 3301.—Foll. 124; 7½ in. by 4; 15 lines, 2 in. long; written in neat Nestalik, with two 'Unvāns and gold-ruled margins, apparently in the 16th century. Bound in stamped and gilt covers.

[Sidney Churchill.]

Another copy of the Divan of Ẓahīr Fāriyābi, with the same preface.

The contents of the Divan agree to some extent with those of the preceding copy. The Mukaṭṭa'āt begin with the same piece, fol. 59*a*; but there are further on, fol. 92*a*, a few Ghazals, and some additional Kasidahs. The Rubā'is, foll. 117*b*—124*a*, have the same beginning.

224.

Or. 2880.—Foll. 370; 11¾ in. by 8; from 13 to 22 lines, about 4½ in. long; written in fair Nestalik; dated from Muharram to Jumāda I., A.H. 1245 (A.D. 1829).

[Sidney Churchill.]

I. Foll. 1*b*—117*a*. ديوان ظهير فاريابى

The Divan of Ẓahīr Fāriyābi (see no. 222), with the usual beginning:

سپيده دم كه شدم تا حرم سراى سرور
شنيدم آيه توبوا الى الله از دم حور

The same beginning is found in many copies. See Add. 7733, Persian Catalogue, p. 563; Oude Catalogue, no. 542; Ethé, no. 584; and Pertsch, Berlin Catalogue, no. 747. The Kasidahs are followed by Mukaṭṭa'āt, fol. 114*b*, beginning:

اى ز آثار كرد موكب تو
غصها خورده مشك تاتارى

The Ghazals begin on fol. 80*b*, which should immediately precede fol. 114*b*, as follows:

اى بعيد دلم بروى تو شاد
عيد را روى تو مبارك باد

Rubā'is begin, fol. 114b:

دوش این خردم نصیحتی نهان گفت
در گوش دلم گفت دلم با جان گفت

II. Foll. 118b—140a. دیوان منوچهری شصت کله

The Divan of Minuchihri. See no. 206.

Beg. همی ریزد میان باغ لولوها بزنبرها
همی سوزد میان راغ عنبرها بجمرها

It consists only of select Kasidahs without alphabetical arrangement.

III. Foll. 140b—197b. دیوان ازرقی

The Divan of Azraḳi. See no. 211, III.

Beg. بنور قبه زرین آینه تمثال
زمین تقته فرو پوشد آتشین سربال

Kasidahs, not in alphabetical order, followed by a few Ḳiṭ'ahs, and, fol. 191b, by Rubā'is beginning:

ای رای تو با ضمیر گردون جفت
پیدا بر تو هرچه فلک راست نهفت

IV. Foll. 198b—341b. دیوان جمال الدین عبد الرزاق

The Divan of Jamāl ud-Din Iṣfahāni, whose proper name was 'Abd ur-Razzāḳ. He was a contemporary of Khāḳāni and Mujir Bailaḳāni, and father of a better known poet, Kamāl ud-Dīn Iṣfahāni. He died, according to Taḳi Kāshi, A.H. 588. See the Persian Catalogue, p. 581a, and Majma' ul-Fuṣaḥā, vol. i., pp. 177—183.

Beg. هر نفس کان برمن وما بی جلال ذو الجلال
در جهان جان بر آری آن وبالست آن وبال

The beginning given by Sprenger, Oude Catalogue, p. 446, occurs here at fol. 207b.

Contents: Kasidahs and Tarjī's without alphabetical order or headings; Muḳaṭṭa'āt, fol. 305b, beginning:

آیا صدری که چرخ پیر چون تو
جوانی در همه معنی نیارد

Ghazals, fol. 323a, beginning:

ای بر میان چرخ کمر از وفری تو
وی بر زبان خلق دعاو ثنای تو

Rubā'is, fol. 333a, beginning:

دلدار کمان دلبری کرد بزه
وافکند بکرد مه بر از مشک کره

V. Foll. 342b—370a. دیوان قاضی نور الدین اصفهانی

The Divan of Nūr ud-Dīn Iṣfahāni, poetically surnamed Nūri, who died A.H. 1000. See the Persian Catalogue, p. 669a.

Beg. کهی که چشم تو در خانهٔ کمان آید
شکست در صف چندین هزار جان آید

Contents: Kasidahs without alphabetical order. Ghazals, fol. 354a, beginning:

تو هیچگونه محابا نمیتوانی کرد
حذر زآتش دلها نمیتوانی کرد

Mufradāt, fol. 362b, and Rubā'is, fol. 364a, with some other short pieces. The Rubā'is begin:

خوش وقت دلی که سبحه را تار گسیخت
بگذاشت کلیسای و زنار گسیخت

Copyist: محمد علی بن محمد باقر الکاشانی

225.

Or. 2834.—Foll. 374; 10¾ in. by 6¾; 19 lines, 4 in. long; written in elegant Nestalik in four gold-ruled columns, with a double-page 'Unvān and five single-page ones, ornamental headings blue and gold, and twenty-six miniatures, half-page or more, in fair Persian style; dated Sunday, mid-Shavvāl, A.H. 895 (A.D. 1490). Bound in painted and glazed covers.

خمسهٔ نظامی

The five poems of Niẓāmi. See the Persian Catalogue, p. 564; Pertsch, Berlin Catalogue, no. 719; Rosen, Institut, p. 171; Ethé, Bodleian Catalogue, nos. 585, &c., and 1981; and Majma' ul-Fuṣaḥā, vol. i., pp. 637—654.

I. Foll. 1*b*—31*a*. Makhzan ul-Asrār, مخزن الاسرار

II. Foll. 31*b*—105*a*. Khusrau u Shīrīn, خسرو و شیرین

The prologue is in praise of Atabek Muḥammad, and the date of composition, A.H. 571, is given, fol. 102*a*, as follows:

گذشت از پانصد و هفتاد و یکسال
نزد بر خط خوبان کس چنین خال

III. Foll. 105*b*—165*a*. Laili u Majnūn, لیلی و مجنون

The name of the king of Shīrvān, to whom the poem is dedicated, is written, fol. 111*a*, احتشان

IV. Foll. 165*b*—233*a*. Haft Paikar, هفت پیکر

In this, as in most early copies, the prince for whom the poem was written, is called, fol. 169*b*, 'Alā ud-Dīn کرب ارسلان

شاه کرب ارسلان کشور گیر
به از ارب ارسلان بکنج و سریر

This 'Alā ud-Dīn was Lord of Marāghah, where he was besieged by Aitughmish, A.H. 602 (see the Kāmil, vol. xii., p. 156). He was a descendant of Aḳsunḳur Aḥmadīlī, who was murdered by the Bāṭinis, A.H. 527 (*ib.* vol. x., p. 483), and whose son joined Atabek Ildughuz in his Georgian war, A.H. 558 (*ib.* vol. xi., pp. 189, 218, 280).

V. Foll. 233*b*—325*a*. Iskandar Nāmah, اسکندر نامه, Part I.

The prologue contains a dedication to the Atabek Nuṣrat ud-Dīn; but the epilogue, fol. 324*b*, is addressed to Malik 'Izz ud-Dīn.

ملك عز الدین انکه از داد او
خورد هر کسی باده بر یاد او

VI. Foll. 325*b*—374*a*. The second part of the Iskandar Nāmah, with the heading: کتاب اقبال نامه

It contains in the prologue, fol. 329*a*, that dedication to Malik Ḳāhir 'Izz ud-Dīn Mas'ūd B. Nūr ud-Dīn, of Mosul, which has been noticed in the Persian Catalogue, p. 569*a*, and begins طرف دار موصل بمردانگی. Al-Malik al-Ḳāhir succeeded his father at the end of Rajab, A.H. 607 (Kāmil, vol. xii., p. 193).

This dedication, if really written by Niẓāmi, would show that the poet was still alive some time after that date. The epilogue is also addressed to Malik 'Izz ud-Dīn Mas'ūd.

An English translation of the first part of the Iskandar Nāmah was published by H. Wilberforce Clarke, London, 1881.

Copyist: جلال الدین محمد

226.

Or. 2931.—Foll. 504; 9 in. by 6; 21 lines, 2½ in. long, with 16 slanting lines in the margin; written in elegant Nestalik in two gold-ruled columns, with five highly finished double-page 'Unvāns, ornamental gold headings, and twenty-one half-page miniatures in fair Persian style; dated (fol. 499) 3 Zul-ka'dah, A.H. 878 (A.D. 1474).

[Nath. Bland.]

The same five poems in the following order: Makhzan ul-Asrār, fol. 2*b*. Khusrau u Shīrīn, fol. 48*b*. Laili u Majnūn, fol. 145*b*. Haft Paikar, fol. 229*b*. Iskandar Nāmah,

Part I., designated in the colophon as شرف نامهٔ اسکندری, fol. 321*b*. Part II., with the heading اقبال نامه, fol. 439*b*.

The date of Khusrau u Shirin, fol. 144*b*, is A.H. 579 instead of A.H. 576 as in the Persian Catalogue, p. 566*a*:

گذشت از پانصد و هفتاد و نه سال

The name of the king of Shirvan, fol. 153*b*, is written اخستان, and that of the king for whom Haft Paikar was composed appears, fol. 235*a*, in this line:

شاه کرب ارسلان کشور کیر

به از الب ارسلان بتاج و سریر

The date of the same poem, fol. 321*a*, is A.H. 593, as in the Persian Catalogue, p. 567*a*: از پس پانصد و نود سه قران

The second part of Iskandar Nāmah has, fol. 444*a*, the same dedication to Malik Ḳāhir 'Izz ud-Din Mas'ūd, of Mosul, as in the preceding MS., beginning:

طرف دار موصل بمردانکی

The epilogue is also addressed to the same 'Izz ud-Din Mas'ūd.

227.

Or. 2932.—Foll. 380; 11¼ in. by 7; 19 lines, 3¾ in. long; written in small and fair Nestalik in four gold-ruled columns, with a rich double-page 'Unvān and five single-page ones, with ornamental headings white on gold, and miniatures, apparently in the 16th century. Bound in painted and glazed covers. [Nath. Bland.]

The same five poems, viz., Makhzan ul-Asrār, fol. 1*b*; Khusrau u Shirin, fol. 33*b*; Laili u Majnūn, fol. 116*b*; Haft Paikar, fol. 176*b*. Iskandar Nāmah, with the heading شرف نامه اسکندری, fol. 242*b*; Part II., also called شرف نامه, fol. 332*b*.

The last poem has, fol. 336*a*, the dedication to Malik Ḳāhir 'Izz ud-Din Mas'ūd B. Nūr ud-Din, as noticed in the preceding copies.

This volume contains twenty whole-page miniatures in fair Persian style, fifteen of which belong to the original MS., while five, foll. 199, 210, 214, 225, 229, have been inserted at a later date.

228.

Or. 4385.—Foll. 314; 11 in. by 6¾; 23 lines, 4 in. long; written in small Nestalik in four gold-ruled columns, with four 'Unvāns and gilt headings; dated (foll. 147, 314) A.H. 1005, and Sha'bān, A.H. 1006 (A.D. 1597-8). [Wallis Budge.]

The same five poems in the following order: Makhzan ul-Asrār, wanting the first page, fol. 1*a*. Khusrau u Shirin, fol. 26*b*. Haft Paikar, fol. 93*b*. Laili u Majnūn, fol. 148*b*. Iskandar Nāmah, Part I., fol. 198*b*. Part II., with the heading خرد نامه

In the dedication of the Haft Paikar, fol. 96*a*, the prince is designated as follows:

شاه کربه ارسلان کشور کیر

به از الب ارسلان بتاج و سریر

Copyist: ابن ابرهیم محمد الدین الاصطهباناتی

229.

Or. 4386.—Foll. 381; 12 in. by 8; 19 lines, 5¼ in. long; written in fair Nestalik in four ruled columns, with six 'Unvāns; dated Wednesday, 1 Sha'bān, A.H. 1237 (A.D. 1822). [Wallis Budge.]

The five poems of Niẓāmi in the following order: Makhzan ul-Asrār, fol. 3*b*; Khusrau u Shīrīn, fol. 34b; Laili u Majnūn, fol. 123b; Haft Paikar, fol. 181b; Iskandar Nāmah, Part I., fol. 246b; Part II., fol. 334b.

Written for Muḥammad Sulṭān B. Muṣṭafa Ḳuli Khān by Muṣṭafa B. Aḥmad Siyāhkūhi.

230.

Or. 4730.—Foll. 141; $8\frac{3}{4}$ in. by $5\frac{1}{2}$; 15 lines, $3\frac{1}{2}$ in. long; written in the Hebrew character, apparently in the 18th century, with miniatures. [Sidney Churchill.]

The Haft Paikar of Niẓāmi, imperfect at beginning and end. Fol. 1, the lowest third of which is alone extant, begins with the following verse, which belongs to the latter part of the prologue (Lucknow edition of A.H. 1290, p. 12, line 19):

באלנאני כה בלגה כארנד
סר בגדר אצם פרו נארנד

[بالغانی که بلغه کارند سر بجدر اصم فرو نارند]

The same leaf has been patched with the upper two-thirds of a folio, the contents of which belong to the latter part of the poem, and begin with the heading:

שכאית כרדן מטלום אול

[شکایت کردن مظلوم اول]

See the Lucknow edition, p. 101.

The first extant heading of the original text, fol. 5b, is that of the last section of the prologue (Lucknow edition, p. 16), viz.:

דר פצילת סכן ונציחת פרזנדאן גויד

[در فضیلت سخن و نصیحت فرزندان کوید]

The latter part of the poem is lost. The last heading of the MS., fol. 140a, corresponds with the first heading of p. 98 of the Lucknow edition. It is as follows:

גשן סאכתן בהראם וכבר יאפתן אז שורש לשכר

[جشن ساختن بهرام و خبر یافتن از شورش لشکر]

The MS. contains twelve rather rude and faintly painted miniatures, some of which are more or less rubbed and obliterated.

231.

Or. 2933.—Foll. 99; $12\frac{1}{4}$ in. by $8\frac{1}{4}$; 12 lines, 3 in. long; written in fair Nestalik in two gold-ruled columns, with an 'Unvān, rich gold designs covering the margins throughout the volume, and sixty-three miniatures, mostly whole-page, in the best style of Indian art; dated 25 Muḥarram, in the 8th year of Muhammad Shāh, corresponding with A.H. 1139 (A.D. 1726). Bound in painted and glazed covers. [Nath. Bland.]

An abridgment of Khusrau u Shīrīn, a poem of Niẓāmi.

It is stated at the end that the original poem, as read by Ḳābil-rām, had 6500 Baits, while this selection consists only of 1522 Baits.

A table of the miniatures occupies three pages at the beginning.

232.

Or. 3513.—Foll. 365; $8\frac{1}{2}$ in. by 6; 15 lines, $3\frac{3}{4}$ in. long; written in fair Nestalik, apparently in India at the close of the 18th century. [Presented by B. B. Portal.]

شرح اسکندر نامه

A commentary upon the first part of the Iskandar Nāmah, by Sirāj ud-Din 'Ali Khān, poetically surnamed Ārzū, who died A.H. 1169 (Persian Catalogue, p. 501b).

Beg. الحمد لله تعالی حمدا متکاثرا ... اما بعد این نسخه ایست شرح ابیات اسکندر نامه ملك الکلام استاد الانام ... خواجه نظام الدین کنجوی

Although many commentaries had been written by learned men, ancient and modern, upon this poem, none of them was found sufficient to explain the difficult verses and phrases of the text. This induced the author, as he states in a short preamble, to write the present commentary.

The text is not given in full. The verses commented on are only indicated by the initial words.

Ārzū's commentary has been given in extenso, with a few additions, in the margins of the Iskandar Nāmah lithographed at Bombay A.H. 1277. It forms the basis of the glosses in the Calcutta and Lucknow editions, as stated by Sprenger, Oude Catalogue, no. 426. For another MS. see Pertsch, Berlin Catalogue, no. 736.

Copyist: محمد مفاخر ساکن قصبه بهکیه

233.

Or. 2934.—Foll. 134; 10 in. by 5½; 21 lines, 3¾ in. long; written in small and neat Nestalik, apparently in the 17th century.

[Nath. Bland.]

A commentary upon Makhzan ul-Asrār, by Muḥammad B. Ḳivām B. Rustam al-Balkhi. See the Persian Catalogue, p. 573*b*.

This copy has lost the first page of the preface. It begins with a passage corresponding with Add. 26,149, fol. 3*a*, first line. At the end, fol. 134*b*, is a note of purchase dated A.H. 1091. In the margins and on the fly-leaves are a few notes in the handwriting of Sir William Jones.

234.

Or. 3376.—Foll. 129; 9 in. by 5¾; 15 lines, 2 in. long, with about 30 sloping lines round the margins; written in fair Nestalik on green-tinted paper; dated Thursday, 2 Zul-ka'dah, A.H. 1002 (A.D. 1594).

[Sidney Churchill.]

I. Foll. 1*b*—27*a*. دیوان نجیب جرپادقانی

Divan of Najīb Jurpādaḳāni.

Beg. بکو که رنك چرا کردهٔ بدستان دست

بخون کیست که آلودهٔ ازین سان دست

Sprenger states in the Oude Catalogue, p. 513, that Najib ud-Din Churbádgány lived towards the end of the Seljûk dynasty and under the Khwārazmshāhis, and that he died probably A.H. 625 or 635, the date 665 found in Taḳi Kāshi's Tazkirah being evidently due to a clerical error. This is fully confirmed by the present Divan. It contains a Kasidah, fol. 3*a*, in praise of Uzbak, the last Atabek of Azarbaijan (A.H. 607—612):

شه جهان ملك ازبك که از سیاست او

رسوم حادثه از کردش زمن بر خاست

and other poems addressed to 'Alā i Daulat u Dīn, *i.e.* 'Alā ud-Dīn Tukush Khwārazmshāh and to 'Imād ul-Mulk, general of the Khwārazmshāh (see Kāmil, A.H. 614, vol. xii., p. 206).

Najib witnessed the Moghul invasion to which he alludes in this line, fol. 4*b*:

درین زمانه که یاجوج فتنه را دستست

که جمله عالم ازان با نفیر و فریادست

But he cannot have survived it long, for in the same piece he refers to his age as being over seventy:

خرد بخندد بر من که آن هوس که نبود

مرا بعهد جوانی ز بعد هفتاد است

Contents: Kasidahs and a few Ḳiṭ'ahs in alphabetical order, breaking off at fol. 21*b*, before the end of letter ی. (The initial verses quoted by Sprenger and by Ethé, Bodleian Catalogue, no. 637, occur in our

MS. respectively at fol. 21*a* and fol. 21*b*.) Ghazals, fol. 22*a*, beginning:

چشم مست که چنان می زده و دلتنگست
راستی هرچه فراخست درو نیرنگست

Rubā'is in alphabetical order, fol. 23*a*, beginning:

جز غم که ندیم دل سودای ماست
کس نیست که او مونس تنهای ماست

For notices of Najib see also Haft Iḳlīm, fol. 394*a*; Riyāẓ ush-Shu'arā, fol. 440*a*; and Majma' ul-Fuṣaḥā, vol. i., p. 634.

II. Foll. 23*b*—108*b*. An anonymous Divan, which proves to be that of Rashid Vaṭvāṭ. See above, no. 212, iv.

Beg. ای طلعت تو نیکو وی قاست تو زیبا
زلفین تو چون عنبر رخسار تو چو دیبا

The initial line quoted above, no. 212, iv., in the Oude Catalogue, p. 542, and in the Majma' ul-Fuṣaḥā, p. 223, is found in the present MS. at fol. 28*b* in the margin. Some Tarji'-bands begin, fol. 90*b*, as follows:

جانا دلم بعشق گرفتار میکنی
جان مرا نشانهٔ تیمار میکنی

Muḳaṭṭa'āt, fol. 104*a*, beginning:

ای مرتضی نیابت سلطان شرق را
منسوخ کرده صدق تو آیات زرق را

The Divan is imperfect at the end.

III. Foll. 109*a*—129*a*. A Divan imperfect at the beginning, which is found to be that of Azraḳi. See no. 211, iii. It begins with the latter part of an alphabetical series of Kasidahs, extending from the end of letter ل to ی. The first Kasidah, the beginning of which is wanting, ends with this line:

فالهای زده ام خوب و حکیمان گویند
کز قضای ازلی خیر و مهین آید فال

The same Kasidah is to be found in Or. 3713, fol. 22*a*. At the end, fol. 125*a*, there are some Rubā'is beginning as in the above named copy.

Throughout this last fragment the leaves are torn at the top, and part of the writing is lost.

235.

Or. 4131.—Foll. 293; 9¾ in. by 6; 23 lines, 3½ in. long; written in minute and neat Nestalik in four gold-ruled columns, with two full-page miniatures and two highly finished double-page 'Unvāns at the beginning, five smaller ones in the body of the volume, and gold headings; dated 22 Rajab, A.H. 877 (A.D. 1472).

[Ẓuhūr ud-Dīn Aḥmad Khān.]

Six poems by Farid ud-Din 'Aṭṭār (who died A.H. 627; see the Persian Catalogue, pp. 344 and 576), designated in the colophon as کتاب سته افضل المتکلمین .... شیخ فرید الدین عطار, namely:

I. Fol. 3*b*. Ilāhi Nāmah, الهی نامه

Beg. بنام انکه ملکش بی زوالست
بوصفش عقل صاحب نطق لالست

This first line is in most copies the second of the poem. See the Persian Catalogue, p. 576*a*, ii.; Ethé, Bodleian Catalogue, nos. 622, art. 11, 623, art. 5; and the Kulliyyāt lithographed at Lucknow, 1872, pp. 771—943.

II. Fol. 80*b*. Manṭiḳ uṭ-Ṭair, منطق الطیر

Beg. آفرین جان آفرین پاك را
انکه جان بخشید مشتی خاك را

In the epilogue the author says that he finished the poem A.H. 583:

بانصد و هشتاد و سه کذشت سال
هم بتاریخ رسول ذو الجلال

The Manṭiḳ uṭ-ṭair includes, foll. 93—98, the story of Shaikh Ṣan'ān mentioned in the Turkish Catalogue, p. 302. For other copies see the Persian Catalogue, p. 576*a*, I.; Pertsch, Berlin Catalogue, no. 753; Ethé, Bodleian Catalogue, no. 622, art. 13; and the Lucknow edition, pp. 1049—1165.

III. Fol. 136*b*. Asrār Nāmah, اسرار نامه

Beg. بنام انکه جانرا نور دین داد
خرد را در خدادانی یقین داد

This work was lithographed in Teheran, A.H. 1298. For MSS. see the Persian Catalogue, p. 576*a*, III.; Pertsch, Gotha, no. 52; and Ethé, no. 622, art. 14.

IV. Fol. 170*b*. Muṣībat Nāmah, مصیبت نامه

Beg. حمد پاك از جان پاك ان پاك را
که خلافت داد مشتی خاك را

See the Persian Catalogue, p. 576*b*, IV.; Pertsch, Berlin Catalogue, no. 761; Ethé, no. 622, art. 12; and an extract by Rückert, Zeitschrift der D. M. G., vol. xiv., pp. 280—288.

V. Fol. 258*b*. Kanz ul-Ḥaḳā'iḳ, كنز الحقائق

This poem begins with the same verse as the Asrār Nāmah. See Sprenger, Oude Catalogue, no. 137, where the initial line is different, and Ethé, nos. 622, art. 18, and 623, art. 9.

VI. Fol. 274*b*. Miftāḥ ul-Futūḥ, مفتاح الفتوح

Beg. پناه من بحق کو نمیرد
بآهی عذر صد عصیان پذیرد

This is one of the esoteric works of 'Aṭṭār, who enjoins that it be withheld from the unfit:

وصیت کردم ای یار یگانه
که از ناساز پوشی این ترانه

See Ethé, nos. 622, art. 19, 623, art. 10, 627, art. 3.

In the body of the volume there are nine miniatures in Persian style, at foll. 13, 34, 50, 92, 96, 125, 145, 192 and 264. Foll. 59—74 and 248—256 have been damaged by fire and are in part illegible.

236.

Or. 2747.—Foll. 309; 9½ in. by 6¼; 21 lines, 4¼ in. long; written in fair Nestalik in four gold-ruled columns, with five 'Unvāns and gold headings; dated 22 Zulhijjah, A.H. 889 (A.D. 1485).

Six poems by the same author, viz.:

I. Fol. 2*b*. Mukhtār Nāmah, مختار نامه, with a prose preface beginning: حمد و سپاس بی
قیاس خداوندی را که اشراق آفتاب الوهیت او

Beg. of the verses:

ای پاکی تو منزه از هر پاکی
قدوسی تو مقدس از ادراکی

See the Persian Catalogue, p. 576*b*, VI., and p. 577*b*, III.; Ethé, Bodleian Catalogue, no. 622, art. 21; and Molla Firuz Library, p. 167. The Mukhtār Nāmah, with the same preface, occupies pp. 946—1047 of the Lucknow edition of the Kulliyāt. This copy breaks off in the middle of Bāb XI. (Lucknow edition, p. 974).

II. Fol. 17*a*. Ilāhi Nāmah, الهی نامه (see no. 235, I.), imperfect at the beginning. It commences abruptly in the middle of Maḳālah III. (Lucknow edition, p. 801), and has some lacunae in the body of the work.

III. Fol. 84*b*. Manṭiḳ uṭ-Ṭair. See no. 235, II.

IV. Fol. 145*b*. Muṣībat Nāmah. See *ib.*, IV.

V. Fol. 238*b*. Asrār Nāmah. See *ib.*, III.

VI. Fol. 281*b*. Vaṣlat Nāmah, وصلت نامه

Beg. ابتدا کردم بنام کردگار
خالق هفت وشش وپنج وچهار

See the Persian Catalogue, p. 579*a*, II., and Ethé, Bodleian Catalogue, nos. 622, art. 7, 623, art. 2, and 624, art. 17.

237.

Or. 2888.—Foll. 273; $9\frac{1}{4}$ in. by $6\frac{1}{4}$; 19 lines, $4\frac{1}{4}$ in. long; written in small and neat Nestalik in four gold-ruled columns, with two tasteful 'Unvāns; dated Rabī' II., A.H. 893 (A.D. 1488). [Sidney Churchill.]

Two poems by Farīd ud-Dīn 'Aṭṭār, viz.:

I. Foll. 1—162. The first part of Jauhar uz-Zāt, جوهر الذات, corresponding with pp. 2—298 of the Lucknow edition of the Kulliyāt.

Beg. بنام انکه نور جسم و جانست
حدای اشکارا و نهانست

There are some transpositions. The text corresponds with the pages of the above edition taken in this order: 2—43, 129—174, 100—129, 43—100, 174—298. In the latter portion there are two lacunae corresponding with pp. 250—252 and 276—282 of the Lucknow edition. For other copies see the Persian Catalogue, p. 576*b*, I.; Pertsch, Berlin Catalogue, nos. 759-60; and Ethé, Bodleian Catalogue, nos. 622, art. 3, 623, art. 7.

II. Foll. 163—273. Khusrau u Gul, خسرو وگل

Beg. بنام انکه نور جسم و جان ساخت
طلسم کنج جان هر دو جهان ساخت

The story of the loves of Khusrau and Gul was abridged by 'Aṭṭār from his own Khusrau Nāmah. From the prologue it appears that the latter was founded upon a prose narrative which a friend of the poet had asked him to turn into verse.

In a further passage, fol. 173*a*, 'Aṭṭār mentions several of his previous poems, namely, Musibat Nāmah, Ilāhī Nāmah, Asrār Nāmah, and Maḳāmāt uṭ-Ṭuyūr (*i.e.* Manṭiḳ uṭ-Ṭair), and says of the first two that he had commenced them in the druggist's shop, where five hundred people came to him every day to have their pulses felt:

مصیبت نامه ام کاندر جهانست
الهی نامه کاسرار نهانست
بدارو خانه کردم هردو آغاز
چکویم رو درستم زین وزان باز
بدارو خانه پانصد شخص بودند
که در هر روز نبضم می نمودند
میان ان همه کفت و شنیدم
سخن را به ازین روی ندیدم

The epilogue concludes with an elegy upon the poet's mother lately deceased.

For other copies, see the Persian Catalogue, p. 576*b*, V., and Ethé, Bodleian Catalogue, no. 622, art. 6.

This MS. once belonged to Sultan Muḥammad Ḳuṭubshāh (A.H. 1025—35), whose seal impressed on fol. 163 reads سلطانمحمد قطبشاه بنده شاه نجف

238.

Or. 3238.—Foll. 100; $7\frac{1}{4}$ in. by $4\frac{3}{4}$; about 15 lines, $3\frac{1}{4}$ in. long; very incorrectly written in a rude and ill-shaped character, probably in India in the 18th century. [Sidney Churchill.]

A collection of Sufi poems, by Ḳuṭb ud-Dīn.

Beg. ای لال در صفت ثنایت زبان ما
او کیست کو بجورد تو کوید ترا ثنا

It consists of short pieces in the form of Ghazals, in which the poet uses mostly قطب دین, sometimes قطب alone, for his takhalluṣ. They are alphabetically arranged in the early part of the collection, foll. 1—34. In the remaining portion there is no apparent order. At the end are some Rubā'is.

Most of the contents are found in a similar, but larger, collection lithographed in Lucknow, A.H. 1296, under the title, دیوان خواجه قطب الدین بختیار کاکی. Ḳuṭb ud-Dīn Bakhtiyār Kāki, the famous Indian saint, to whom the Divan is ascribed, died in Delhi, A.H. 633. See the Persian Catalogue, pp. 432*b* and 973*b*. He is mentioned as poet in Riyāẓ ush-Shu'arā, fol. 319*a*; Sham' i Anjuman, p. 387; Makhzan ul-Gharā'ib, fol. 351*b*; and Riyāẓ ul-'Ārifīn, fol. 146*b*. A copy of the same Divan is mentioned in the Oude Catalogue, p. 537.

The latter part of the MS., foll. 63—87, contains Sufi comments, perhaps by the same author, on some sayings of Muḥammad, and further on, foll. 88—100, miscellaneous extracts and notes.

239.

Or. 2846.—Foll. 191; 8 in. by 4¾; 17 lines, 2⅝ in. long; written in fair Nestalik, with two 'Unvāns and gold-ruled columns; dated in the second decade of Rabi' I., A.H. 1019 (A.D. 1610). [Sidney Churchill.]

I. Foll. 2*b*—86*b*. دیوان اثیر اومانی

The Divan of Aṣīr Aumāni.

Beg. دمید بوی حیات از نسیم باد صبا
چمن زبلبل و گل باز شد بیرك و نوا

Aṣīr ud-Dīn 'Abdullah, called Aumāni, from Aumān, a village of the district of Hamadān, is said to have been a disciple of Naṣīr ud-Dīn Ṭūsi. He was a contemporary of Kamāl Iṣfahāni and a panegyrist of Sulaimān Shāh, prince of Kurdistan. He died, according to Taḳi Kāshi, Oude Catalogue, p. 17, no. 51, A.H. 665. See also Daulatshāh, III., ١٢; Ātashkadah, fol. 114*b*; Riyāẓ ush-Shu'arā, fol. 8*b*; Maikhānah, fol. 78*a*; Tazkirah i Navā, fol. 82*b*; and Majma' ul-Fuṣaḥā, vol. i., p. 105.

The Divan contains Kasidahs in alphabetical order, Ghazals (fol. 43*b*) beginning:

در دلم چون آتش عشق تو تابان میشود
شمع کردارم تن از سر تا بپایان میشود

Tarji'-bands, and Muḳaṭṭa'āt imperfect at the end.

II. Foll. 87*a*—103*a*. A Divan, imperfect at the beginning, which is found to be by Adib Ṣābir, who died A.H. 540. See the Persian Catalogue, p. 552*a*, and Majma' ul-Fuṣaḥā, vol. i., pp. 314—25, where copious extracts are given.

The contents of this fragment are mostly found in the complete copy, Or. 327.

It begins with the latter part of an alphabetical series of Kasidahs. The first complete poem, which begins

دلم عاشق شدن فرمود و من در حکم فرمانش
در افتادم بآن دردی که پیدا نیست درمانش

is found in Or. 327, fol. 27.

At the end, fol. 99*b*, are Muḳaṭṭa'āt and Ghazals beginning as follows:

بهیچ وقتی اگر نام کهتری شنوی
مرا و نام مرا اندران شمار شمر

III. Foll. 104*b*—156*b*. دیوان شرف الدین

The Divan of Sharaf ud-Dīn i Shufurvah, so called from Shufurvah, a village near Isfahan. See Majma' ul-Fuṣaḥā, vol. i., p. 302. His proper name was 'Abd ul-Mu'min. He was a panegyrist of Sultan Toghrul Saljūḳi, and died about A.H. 600. See Taḳi Kāshi, Oude Catalogue, p. 17, no. 35; Pertsch, Berlin Catalogue, no. 681, art. 2, ٢; and Ethé, Bodleian Catalogue, col. 201, no. 47;

Daulatshāh, III., 6; Riyāẓ ush-Shu'arā, fol. 227; Maikhānah, fol. 190*a*; and Tazkirah i Navā, fol. 194*b*.

Beg. حمد و ثنا خالق زمین و زمانرا
صانع بی آلتی همین و همانرا

The Kasidahs, which are in alphabetical order, are followed, fol. 144*b*, by a Tarkīb-band in praise of Sultan Toghrul, beginning:

پیش سلطانند در فرمان بری
آدمی و وحش و هم دیو و پری

and by some Muḳaṭṭa'āt without alphabetical arrangement.

IV. Foll. 157*a*—191*b*. دیوان رفیع الدین مسعود لنبانی

The Divan of Rafī' ud-Dīn Mas'ūd Lunbāni, who was a native of Lunbān, near Isfahan, and a contemporary of the preceding. According to Taḳi Kāshi, he died young, A.H. 603. See the Oude Catalogue, p. 17, no. 38; Daulatshāh, III., 7; Riyāẓ ush-Shu'arā, fol. 180*a*; Haft Iḳlīm, fol. 361*a*; Maikhānah, fol. 148*a*; and Majma' ul-Fuṣaḥā, vol. i., p. 234.

The Divan wants the first page. It consists of Kasidahs and Muḳaṭṭa'āt mixed together and without any apparent order.

The first complete piece is one of five Baits beginning:

نظام حال بدیدست دین و دنیی را
هزار شکر کنم لطف حق تعالی را

This series includes a few short poems in Arabic. At the end are some Ghazals, the first of which, fol. 186*b*, begins:

فروغ عارض خوب از قمر دریغ مدار
حلاوت لب لعل از شکر دریغ مدار

and Rubā'is, fol. 189*a*, beginning:

جانا بجهان مصطبه رندی نیست
کانجا بجمالت ارزومندی نیست

Copyists: (fol. 156) روحی رستمداری and (fol. 191) محمد طالقانی

240.

Or. 3253.—Foll. 375; $6\frac{3}{4}$ in. by 5; 21 lines, $2\frac{1}{4}$ in. long, with about 35 oblique lines round the margin; written in minute but distinct Nestalik, apparently A.H. 811 (A.D. 1409).

[Sidney Churchill.]

مثنوی معنوی

The Masnavi of Maulānā Jalāl ud-Dīn Rūmi, who died A.H. 672. See the Persian Catalogue, p. 584*b*; Pertsch, Berlin Catalogue, no. 763; and Ethé, Bodleian Catalogue, no. 616.

All six volumes (Mujallad) have the usual prefaces, except the first. They begin respectively as follows: I., fol. 1*a*; II., fol. 59*b*; III., fol. 114*b*; IV., fol. 183*b*; V., fol. 239*b*; VI., fol. 301*b*. The date at the end, fol. 371*a*, reads: سنه احدی و عشرین سبعمایه, *i.e.* A.H. 721; but it has evidently been tampered with. The original writing appears to have been احدی عشر و ثمانمایه, A.H. 811.

The following references may be added to those given in the Persian Catalogue. The contents of the Masnavi have been fully described by Hammer in the Sitzungsberichte der K. K. Akademie, Phil. Hist. Classe, vol. vii., pp. 626, 693, 728, 762, 785, 818. The first book was translated by J. W. Redhouse, London, 1881, and an abridged translation of the poem was published by E. H. Whinfield, London, 1887.

Copyist: شمس الدین محمد ناطقی طبسی

Five pages at the end, foll. 371*b*—373*b*, contain Rubā'is ascribed to Jalāl ud-Dīn and to Shaikh Auḥad ud-Dīn Kirmāni.

241.

Or. 2816.—Foll. 157; 8 in. by 6; 19 lines, 4¼ in. long; written in fair Shikastah-āmīz; dated end of Shavvāl, A.H. 1200 (A.D. 1786).
[Sidney Churchill.]

لب لباب معنوى

A selection from the preceding poem, by Ḥusain B. 'Ali al-Baihaḳi, called al-Kāshifi, who died A.H. 910.

Beg. بعد از تقديم وظايف حمد و ثناى حضرت واجب الوجود

In the preface the author describes the work as abridged from a larger selection previously made by himself and entitled لباب المعنوى فى انتخاب المثنوى. It is one of the earliest works of Ḥusain Kāshifi. The date of composition, A.H. 875, appears in the epilogue, fol. 152*b*:

روز شنبه اخر ماه صيام
كشت اين نو باوهٔ غيبى تمام
سال هجرت هشتصد و هفتاد و پنج
مرتفع شد اين طلسم از روى كنج

For other copies, see Sprenger, Oude Catalogue, p. 491; Pertsch, Berlin Catalogue, no. 777; Ethé, Bodleian Catalogue, no. 661.

Foll. 152*b*—156*a* contain extracts from the Divan of Shams i Tabriz.

Copyist: محمد رضاى موسوى ولد مرحوم مير محمد فاضل

242.

Or. 3514.—Foll. 300; 9½ in. by 6; 15 lines, 3¾ in. long; written in large Nestalik with ruled margins, probably in the 18th century.
[Presented by B. B. Portal.]

Another copy of the preceding work.

243.

Or. 2866.—Foll. 330; 9 in. by 6; 21 lines, 3¼ in. long; written in neat archaic Neskhi, with 'Unvān and gold-ruled columns; dated 1 Jumāda II., A.H. 774 (A.D. 1372).
[Sidney Churchill.]

ديوان جلال الدين رومى

The Divan of Jalāl ud-Din Rūmi.

Beg. اى دل جه بوى اشنيدهٔ در عذران تقصيرها
زان سوى او جندين وفا زين سوى تو جندين جفا

A copy described in the Vienna Catalogue, no. 527, has the same beginning.

Contents: Ghazals in alphabetical order, fol. 2*b*. Tarjī'āt, fol. 294*b*, beginning:

بلبل سرمست آ زبراى خدا
مجلس كل بين و بمنبر برآ

Rubā'is, fol. 314*b*, beginning:

عيد آمد و عيدانه جمال سلطان
عيد انه كى ديدست جنين در دو جهان

An edition lithographed at Lucknow, 1878, with the title ديوان حضرت شمس تبريز, is not so full as the present MS. It begins with this line: اى طائران قدس را عشقت فزوده بالها, which is found at fol. 21*a* of our copy. For other MSS. see the Persian Catalogue, p. 593; Pertsch, Berlin Catalogue, no. 778; and Ethé, Bodleian Catalogue, no. 673. Majma' ul-Fuṣaḥā, vol. i., pp. 286—302, contains copious extracts.

244.

Or. 4689.—Foll. 36; 13¾ in. by 7¾; 17 lines, 4¼ in. long; written in fine Nestalik on brown-tinted paper, with a rich 'Unvān and illuminated borders throughout, apparently in the 17th century.

A shorter Divan of the same poet, endorsed دیوان حضرت شمس تبریزی

Beg. الحمد لله الذی توّا نه [به] نعت الازل
الماجد الفرد الذی غفرانه یمحو الذلل [sic]

After three pieces in praise of God, the alphabetical series of Ghazals begins, fol. 3b, as follows:

ای عاشق دیوانه بکدم بخرابات آ
جام ازلی بستان آنکه بمناجات آ

The Ghazals rhyming in ا extend to fol. 34a. They are followed by five Ghazals in ب and one in ت.

The MS. once belonged to the library of Muḥammad Shâh, of Delhi. On the fly-leaf are some 'Arz-dîdahs dated in his reign, and a seal of A.H. 1132.

245.

Or. 2847.—Foll. 130; 8 in. by 5½; 12 lines, 3½ in. long; written in Shikastah-âmîz; dated Teheran, Saturday, 26 Rajab, A.H. 1279 (A.D. 1863). [Sidney Churchill.]

I. Foll. 2—93. دیوان امامی

The Divan of Imâmi Haravi. See above, no. 213, II.

Beg. سحرکه در جهان جان بعون مبدع اشیا
مسافت قطع می کردم زلا تا حضرت الا

Contents: Kasidahs in alphabetical order, fol. 2b. Muḳaṭṭa'ât, fol. 63b, beginning:

زهی بهای تفکر بسیط عالم غیب
هزار بار بهر یك نفس نه[به] پیموده

Ghazals, fol. 80a, beginning:

زلفت اندر تاب چینی دیگر است
کفرت اندر زلف دینی دیگر است

Rubâ'is, fol. 88a, beginning:

ای از کل دولت تو شاهی بوئی
در بند جهان برغم هر بد کوئی

II. Foll. 94—130. A short Divan, without author's name.

Beg. تا دل من بهوای نیکوان کشت آشنا
در سرشك دیده کردانم شد چه مرد آشنا

It is a selection from the Divan of Ḳaṭarân (see no. 207), and consists of Kasidahs in alphabetical order, with three Ḳiṭ'ahs and two Rubâ'is at the end.

Copyist: میرزا علی خان مازندرانی المتخلص به بدیهی

246.

Or. 2948.—Foll. 289; 6¾ in. by 4½; 12 lines, 2 in. long in the centre, and 25 oblique lines round the margins; written in neat Nestalik, with 'Unvân and illuminated headings; dated (fol. 287b) Wednesday, 10 Rabi' I., A.H. 844 (A.D. 1440). [Sidney Churchill.]

کلیات سعدی

The complete works of Sa'di. See the Persian Catalogue, p. 595.

Contents: Preface of Bîsutûn, wanting a few lines at the beginning, fol. 2a. Sa'di's preface, fol. 6a. The five Majlis, fol. 13b. Risâlah i Ṣâḥib Dîvân, fol. 47a. Reason and Love, fol. 50a. Advice to kings, fol. 53b. Risâlah i Sulṭân Abaḳâ, fol. 66b. Risâlah i Ankiyânu, fol. 68a. Risâlah i Malik Shams ud-Din, fol. 69b. Arabic Kasidahs, fol. 71b. Persian Kasidahs, fol. 85a. Marâṣi, fol. 114a. Ghazals in one alphabetical series, including the Ṭayyibât and the Badâ'i', fol. 137b. Khawâtîm, foll. 271b—288b, breaking off in the course of letter م (Harington's edition, fol. 425a).

The margins form a continuous text, consisting of the following works: Gulistân, fol. 1b, breaking off before the end (Harington, fol. 91b): Bustan, fol. 97a, slightly imperfect at the beginning. Ghazaliyyât i

Kadim, fol. 227*b*. Ṣāḥibiyyah (wrongly headed كتاب بدايع) fol. 238*b*. Muḳaṭṭaʻāt, fol. 264*a*. Rubāʻiyyāt, fol. 267*b*. Mufradāt, fol. 274*b*. Hazaliyyāt (Harington, fol. 475*a*), fol. 276*b*. Khabiṣāt (Harington, fol. 479*a*), foll. 283*b*—287*b*.

For other MSS. see the Persian Catalogue, p. 595; Rosen, Institut, pp. 175—199; Ethé, Bodleian Catalogue, no. 681; and Pertsch, Berlin Catalogue, no. 781.

247.

Or. 2743.—Foll. 350; 10½ in. by 6¼; 18 lines, 2½, with 12 oblique lines in the margin; written in neat Nestalik, with gold-ruled margins and illuminated borders, a rich double-page ʻUnvān at the beginning, and twelve single-page ones in the body of the volume, apparently in the 16th century.

Another copy of the Kulliyyāt i Saʻdi, containing: Preface of Bisutūn, fol. 3*b*. The five Majlis, fol. 7*a*. Risālah i Ṣaḥib Divān, fol. 25*a*. Risālah dar ʻAḳl u ʻIshḳ, fol. 27*a*. Naṣiḥat i Mulūk, fol. 29*a*. Naṣiḥat i Sulṭān Abaḳā, fol. 37*b*. Ḥikāyat i Malik Shams ud-Din, fol. 41*a*. Gulistan, fol. 42*b*. Bustan, fol. 126*b*. Ṭayyibāt, fol. 211*b*. Muḳaṭṭaʻāt, fol. 218*b*. Badāʼiʻ, fol. 221*b*. Khavātīm, fol. 251*b*. Ghazaliyyāt i Ḳadim, fol. 261*b*. Arabic Kasidahs, fol. 268*b*. Persian Kasidahs, fol. 276*b*. Marāṣi, fol. 302*b*. Mulammaʻāt, fol. 306*b*. Tarjiʻāt, fol. 311*a*. Ṣāḥibiyyah, fol. 317*b*. Fardiyyāt, fol. 330*b*. Muṭāyibāt, fol. 332*b*. Muẓḥikāt, fol. 338*a*. Rubāʻiyyāt, foll. 345*a*—349*b*.

There are two whole-page miniatures at the beginning, two at the end, and ten rather smaller in the body of the volume at foll. 18, 49, 74, 95, 134, 157, 189, 201, 216, and 343. They are in fair Persian style.

On the first page is the seal of Muḥammad Ḳuli Ḳuṭubshāh, and a note stating that the MS. had been presented by Khwājah Muẓaffar ʻAli Dabīr, A.H. 1016. On the same page is the name of a subsequent owner, J. H. Harington, editor of the Kulliyyāt.

248.

Or. 4779.—Foll. 522; 10½ in. by 6¼; 18 lines, 3½ in. long; written in fair Nestalik, with three ʻUnvāns and gold-ruled columns, probably in the 17th century.

Another copy of the Kulliyāt.

Contents: Preface of Bisutūn, fol. 1*b*. The first Risālah, fol. 5*a*, imperfect at the end. The second Risālah, fol. 8*a*, imperfect at the beginning and wanting the fifth Majlis. Gulistan, fol. 18*a*. Bustan, fol. 85*b*. Arabic Kasidahs, fol. 201*a*. Persian Kasidahs, fol. 217*b*. Marāṣi, fol. 252*b*. Mulammaʻāt, fol. 258*a*. Tarjiʻ, fol. 262*b*. Ṭayyibāt, fol. 266*b*. Badāʼiʻ, fol. 382*b*. Khavātīm, fol. 435*b*. Ghazaliyyāt i Ḳadim, fol. 454*b*. Ḳitʻahs and Masnavis (Ṣāḥibiyyah), fol. 464*a*. Muṭāʼibāt, fol. 485*a*. Muḳaṭṭaʻāt, fol. 494*b*. Muṭāʼibāt in prose, fol. 500*b*. Rubāʻis and Fardiyyāt, fol. 507*a*.

249.

Or. 4120.—Foll. 118; 9 in. by 5½; 14 lines, 2¾ in. long; written in elegant Nestalik, with two richly illuminated pages at the beginning, a tasteful and highly finished ʻUnvān, gold-ruled margins, and illuminated headings; dated A.H. 886 (A.D. 1481). Bound in fine stamped leather covers.

[Tho. Fiott Hughes.]

گلستان سعدى

The Gulistan of Saʻdi. See the Persian Catalogue, p. 597*a*.

This fine copy was written at Shamākhi by Sharaf ud-Din Ḥusain for Sultan Nāṣir ush-Shariʻah wa'd-Din Shirvānshāh.

250.

Or. 4387.—Foll. 105; $6\frac{3}{4}$ in. by $4\frac{1}{4}$; 14 lines, $2\frac{1}{2}$ in. long; written in fair Nestalik, with 'Unvān and gold-ruled margins; dated Constantinople, Muḥarram, A.H. 933 (A.D. 1526). [Wallis Budge.]

Another copy of the Gulistan.

Copyist: شفیعی

251.

Or. 4121.—Foll. 147; $9\frac{1}{2}$ in. by $5\frac{3}{4}$; 15 lines, $2\frac{3}{4}$ in. long; written in fair Nestalik, with a highly finished double-page 'Unvān and gold-ruled columns, apparently early in the 16th century. Bound in stamped and gilt leather covers. [Tho. Fiott Hughes.]

بوستان سعدی

The Bustan of Sa'di. See the Persian Catalogue, p. 597*b*.

Copyist: محمد قاسم بن شادیشاه

To the translations mentioned in the Persian Catalogue may be added those of M. Barbier de Meynard, Paris, 1880, and of G. S. Davie, London, 1883.

252.

Or. 3261.—Foll. 35; 20 in. by $11\frac{1}{2}$; 7 lines, 6 in. long; written in very large and elegant Nestalik in gold on illuminated ground, with a rich 'Unvān, ornamental heading, and miniatures, apparently in the 18th century. Bound in stamped and gilt covers.

پند نامه

The Pand-Nāmah, called from its initial word Karimā, and ascribed to Sa'di.

Beg. کریما به بخشای بر حال ما
که هستم اسیری کمندی هوا

There are two whole-page miniatures in fair Indian style at the beginning and two at the end, besides four smaller ones at foll. 3, 9, 13, and 22.

For other copies, see the Persian Catalogue, p. 865*b*, III.; Pertsch, Berlin Catalogue, no. 781, art. 24; and Ethé, Bodleian Catalogue, no. 688, art. 12.

Copyist: فضل الدین لاهوری

253.

Or. 3262.—Foll. 11; $9\frac{3}{4}$ in. by $5\frac{3}{4}$; 11 lines, $3\frac{1}{2}$ in. long; written in Nestalik, with gold-ruled margins and three miniatures of very second-rate Indian style, apparently in the 19th century.

Another copy of the same poem.

254.

Or. 3647.—Foll. 211; $8\frac{1}{4}$ in. by $5\frac{1}{4}$; 13 lines, $3\frac{1}{4}$ in. long; written in fair Nestalik, with 'Unvān and gold-ruled margins, apparently in the 17th century; containing twenty-four miniatures in a rather grotesque and inferior Persian style, much defaced. [Sidney Churchill.]

دیوان هارون

The Divan of Hārūn.

Beg. صبر بخشای آلهی دل نالان را
آشکارا نکند تا غم پنهانی را

Hārūn was a son of the great Ṣāḥib Divān Shams ud-Din Muḥammad, and a friend of Sa'di. See Riyāẓ ush-Shu'arā, fol. 500*b*; Majma' ul-Fuṣaḥā, vol. i., p. 656; and Ethé, Bodleian Catalogue, col. 394, no. 3048.

The Divan consists for the most part of

Ghazals in alphabetical order. At the end are two Tarji'S, fol. 205*b*, beginning:

ای با تو حیات جاودانی
وی بیتو بری ز زندگانی

and Rubā'is alphabetically arranged, fol. 209*a*, beginning:

یا رب ز غم جهان کن آزاد مرا
غمگینم و از کرم بکن شاد مرا

Slightly imperfect at the end.

255.

Or. 2949.—Foll. 338; 7¾ in. by 4; 19 lines, 2⅜ in. long; written in neat Nestalik, with four 'Unvāns and gold-ruled columns; dated (fol. 182*b*) 1 Ramazan, A.H. 896 (A.D. 1491).
[Sidney Churchill.]

خمسهٔ امیر خسرو

The first four poems of the Khamsah of Amīr Khusrau Dihlavi. See the Persian Catalogue, p. 615*b*; Pertsch, Berlin Catalogue, no. 629; and Ethé, Bodleian Catalogue, no. 766.

The first, مطلع الانوار, is imperfect at the beginning. The original writing begins with this line, fol. 2*a*:

کلک من از گنج خدایی خم است
چیست که در گنج خدایی کم است

This is the fortieth Bait of the section در ترتیب کتاب. Seven Baits have been prefixed by a later hand.

The other three poems begin respectively as follows: Shīrīn u Khusrau, fol. 73*b*; Majnūn u Laili, fol. 183*b*; and Haft Bihisht, fol. 250*b*.

Copyist (fol. 249): احمد مسیحی

256.

Stowe, Or. 14.—Foll. 174; 7¼ in. by 4; 12 lines, 2 in. long; written in small and elegant Nestalik, with a rich 'Unvān, gold-ruled columns, blue and gold headings, and miniatures, apparently early in the 16th century. Bound in neatly stamped and gilt covers.

قران السعدین

Ķirān us-Sa'dain, a Masnavi poem by Amīr Khusrau Dihlavi. See the Persian Catalogue, p. 611*b*, xii.; the Berlin Catalogue, no. 833; and the Bodleian Catalogue, no. 773.

There are two whole-page miniatures at the beginning, and four at foll. 33, 78, 95, and 159. They are in highly finished Persian style, and remarkable for the diminutive size of the figures introduced.

On the fly-leaf: "Presented by Sir Richd. Worsley, Bart., who procur'd it at Aleppo from a Persian who bro't it from Ispahan."

The following Rubā'i in praise of the binding is stamped in relief on both sides of the cover:

این جلد چو نقش روی خوبان طراز
آراسته پیکرست و بیننده نواز
یاخود در جنتست کز عالم فیض
بر ناظر این کتاب میکردد باز

257.

Or. 3322.—Foll. 123; 8¾ in. by 6; from 20 to 25 lines, 4½ in. long; written in bold archaic Neskhi, apparently in the 14th century. [Sidney Churchill.]

Collected works in prose and verse of Sharaf ud-Dīn Fazl-ullah al-Ķazvīnī.

The author is chiefly known by his history

of the ancient kings of Persia, كتاب المعجم, which is not included in the present volume. See the Persian Catalogue, p. 811*b*; Pertsch, Berlin Catalogue, no. 428; and Ethé, no. 285. His name appears in the following heading, fol. 82*a*: هذه القصيده الموسومه بمرآة الهجاء من مخترعات الامام العالم العارف الفاضل واضح الدقايق والحقايق محبوب الخالق والخلايق شرف الملة والحق والدين فضل الله القزوينى رحمة الله عليه

The MS. is imperfect at beginning and end. It has also some internal lacunae, so that the following three works which it contains are more or less defective.

I. Foll. 1*a*—21*b*. A work, the main subject of which is a contest between the candle and the lamp, محاضره شمع و قنديل, which the author professes to have overheard in a mosque. It begins abruptly with the following lines:

اكرموا عمتكم النخل از مايه نباتى بمرتبت حيوانى ترقى كنند

بتدريج و قرار و انتظار و تربيت كردن
مه نو بدر و باران در و خون مشك و حجر كوهر

The work is written in very ornate prose, freely interspersed with Arabic sentences written in large character, and with Arabic and Persian verses. In the introduction the author complains of the infirmities of age. He was then over seventy, or, as he poetically puts it, "the eagle of old age had made its nest on the summit of seventy and odd years," اكنون كه عقاب كبر سن بر قله هفتاد و اند اشيانه ساخت. He then describes the hesitations he went through before starting on a journey, which brought him, A.H. 732, to the royal camp of Abu Sa'id Bahādur at Ujān, اوجان, and the gracious reception he met with at the hands of that sovereign's Vazir, Ghiyāṣ ud-Din Muḥammad B. Rashid, whom he followed to Tabriz, and for whom he wrote this work.

This copy is imperfect; it breaks off at this line, fol. 21*b*: بارها دعوى نوران اشك و هملان سرشك و سيلان دمع كردى

II. Foll. 22*a*—57*a*. A treatise on the art of epistolary composition, designated in the colophon as الترسل النصرية, and probably so called from its being dedicated to the author's royal patron, Atabek Nuṣrat ud-Dīn, who reigned A.H. 695—733.

It begins in the course of a section relating to the formulas of prayer or blessings which are to follow the names of kings and men of rank in letters addressed to them. The next-following chapter has this heading: در بيان مقادير سخن و شناختن اسلوب و طرز هر كس از ارباب سخن The remaining contents may be briefly described as follows: Dates of month and year, fol. 24*a*. Titles and honorific epithets used in addressing the following persons: the Pādishāh, the Amir ul-Umarā, the Atabek, kings of Shabānkārah, the Ṣāḥib Divān, kings of Fārs, Amīrs, and various classes of men of lower degree, concluding with the eunuchs and ladies of the Harem, fol. 25*a*. Models of letters suitable for various occasions, including appointments to the offices of Kazi, Mudarris, Shiḥnah, and Mustaufi, fol. 32*a* (two of the letters are dated, A.H. 727 and 730). Arabic and Persian verses suitable for quotation in correspondence, fol. 51*a*—57.

III. Foll. 57*b*—83*b*. The Divan, beginning with a Kasidah in praise of the Atabek Nuṣrat ud-Din, the heading of which is: يمدحه [يمدح for] الملك الاعظم نصرة الحق والدين طاب مثواه

Beg. سايه لطف خدا مطلع خورشيد ظفر
شاه كاوس نسب خسرو جمشيد سير

The contents are not systematically arranged, partly owing, perhaps, to lacunae and transpositions in the MS. They are largely made up of short pieces (Ḳiṭ'ahs) of two lines or more, expressing religious thoughts or moral sentiments, with such headings as در مرتبه, در توکل و اعتماد, در دلاوری, صبر, &c. Besides the initial Kasidah, the Divan includes the following longer poems: 1. A Kasidah entitled Mir'āt un-Najāt, being a religious poem on the resurrection and the duty of preparing for death, fol. 82*a*, beginning:

یا خالق البریه یا واهب العطا

2. A Tarji', fol. 107*b*, with the following burden:

که همه هرچه است یك سراوست
جان و جانان و دلبر و دل و دوست

3. A Kasidah in praise of the Vazir Ghiyās ud-Din Muḥ., illustrating various poetical figures, with explanatory glosses, fol. 112*b*:
قصیدة المصنوعه من کلامه یمدح الصاحب الاعظم مالك رقاب الامم غیاث الدنیا والدین محمد اعلی الله شانه

Beg. اکنون که شد ز سنبل و گل باغ چون نگار

There is also a Kit'ah addressed to the Vazir 'Aṭā Malik, fol. 120.

258.

Or. 4482.—Foll. 342; 7¾ in. by 3½; 19 lines, 1⅞ in. long, with 26 diagonal lines in the margin; written in fair Nestalik with gold-ruled columns; dated (fol. 166*a*) 12 Rabi' I., A.H. 1010 (A.D. 1601).

I. Foll. 1—166. دیوان شیخ اوحدی

The Divan of Auḥadi, who died A.H. 738. See the Persian Catalogue, p. 618*b*.

Beg. سر پیوند ما ندارد یار
چون توان شد ز وصل برخوردار

Contents: Kasidahs and Tarji'-bands, some of which are in praise of the Imams, fol. 1*b*. The Tarji' beginning هوس کعبه و آن منزل و آن جاست مرا, noticed in the Persian Catalogue, is found on fol. 4*a*. Ghazals in alphabetical order, fol. 11*b*, beginning:

راه کم کردم چه باشد گر براه آری مرا
رحمتی بر من کنی واندر پناه آری مرا

A Marṣiyah, fol. 27*a*. Another alphabetical series of Ghazals, fol. 27*b*, beginning:

ای غم عشق تو یار غار ما
جز غمت خود کس نزیبد یار ما

Rubā'is, fol. 158*a*, beginning:

یا رب جبروت و پادشاهیت که دید
کنه کرم نا متناهیت که دید

II. Foll. 166*b*—239*a*. جام جم, Jām i Jam, a Masnavi by the same poet. The date of composition in the epilogue is A.H. 733, as in the copy described in the Persian Catalogue, p. 619*b*. For other MSS. see Pertsch, Berlin Catalogue, no. 834; the Strassburg Catalogue, no. 3; and Ethé, Bodleian Catalogue, no. 785.

III. Fol. 239*b*—248*b*. ده نامه, Dah Nāmah, another Masnavi by the same poet.

Beg. بنام انکه مارا نام بخشید
زبان را در فصاحت کام بخشید

This Masnavi contains ten letters addressed by an imaginary lover to his mistress. It was composed, as stated in the prologue, at the request of the Vazir Vajih ud-Din Shāh Yūsuf, a grandson of Naṣir ud-Din Ṭūsi, who was tired of the old Dah Nāmahs, and wanted one which had the charm of novelty. Compare Ḥaj. Khal., vol. iii., p. 239. A copy is mentioned in Molla Firūz Library, p. 128.

The poem was written A.H. 706, as stated in this line at the end:

بسال ذال و واو از سال هجرت
بپایان بردم این در حال هجرت

IV. Foll. 249b—342b. دیوان فغانی

The Divan of Fighāni, who died A.H. 925. See the Persian Catalogue, p. 651a.

Beg. خطی که یکرتمش آب روی نه چمنست
نشان خاتم سلطان دین ابو الحسنست

Contents: Kasidahs, fol. 249b. Ghazals, fol. 268a, beginning:

ای سر نامه نام تو عقل گره کشای ما
ذکر تو مطلع غزل عشق سخن سرای ما

Ḳiṭ'ahs, fol. 339b, beginning:

فغانی فی المثل در عالم خاك
اگر نانرا نمی یابی و گر آب

Rubā'is and Fardiyyāt, fol. 340a, beginning:

تا هستی ما فنای مطلق نشود
جانرا صفت بقا محقق نشود

For other copies see Ethé, no. 992, and Pertsch, Berlin Catalogue, no. 900.

259.

Or. 4932.—Foll. 142; 7¼ in. by 4; 15 lines, 2½ in. long; written in small and neat Nestalik, with 'Unvān and gold-ruled margins; dated Herat, 1 Jumāda II., A.H. 1036 (A.D. 1627). Bound in stamped and gilt leather.

[Tho. Fiott Hughes.]

جام جم

"Jām i Jam;" a poem by Auḥadi. See the preceding MS., art. II.

The date of composition, A.H. 733, is given in the following line, fol. 140b:

چون ز تاریخ بر کشادم فال
هفتصد رفته بود و سی و سه سال

Copyist: فخر الدین احمد المشهور بملا خورد الکاتب

260.

Or. 3387.—Foll. 325; 10 in. by 5; about 19 lines, 3 in. long; written in fair Nestalik; dated 22 Muḥarram, A.H. 841 (A.D. 1437).

[Sidney Churchill.]

دیوان عتیقی

The Divan of Jalāl ud-Dīn 'Atīḳi, of Tabriz, who died A.H. 744. See Taḳi Kāshi, Oude Catalogue, p. 18, no. 72.

Beg. ای صبا داری نسیم آشنائی مرحبا
زنده‌ام کردی جزاك الله خیرا یا صبا

In the Haft Iḳlīm, fol. 512, the poet is called Jamāl ud-Din 'Atīḳi. He was a son of Ḳuṭb ud-Dīn 'Atīḳi, who was also a native of Tabriz and a poet. Jamāl ud-Din was a favourite with the Vazir Khwājah Rashīd ud-Din. The father, Ḳuṭb ud-Din, and the son, Jalal ud-Din, are noticed together in Majma' ul-Fuṣaḥā, vol. i., p. 338.

This very extensive Divan consists exclusively of Ghazals and of Rubā'is, both arranged in alphabetical order. The latter begin, fol. 310a, as follows:

نتوان گفتن ز نامسلمانیها
کان زلف کند بدل ز ویرانیها

261.

Or. 4910.—Foll. 140; 8 in. by 4¾; 12 lines, 2¾ in. long; written in fair Nestalik; dated Jumāda I., A.H. 1237 (A.D. 1822).

I. Foll. 1—95. Laili Majnūn, a Turkish poem by Fuẓūli. See the Turkish Catalogue, p. 206b.

Beg. دهقان حدیقهٔ حکایت صرّافجواهر روایت

This copy wants the prologue and the epilogue. Its contents correspond with foll. 16a—92b of Or. 405.

II. Foll. 96—140. A selection from the Divan of Ibn Yamin, designated in the colophon as منتخبات من ديوان ابن يمين جار الله قدس الله روحه

The author, whose proper name was Fakhr ud-Din Maḥmūd Faryūmadi, died A.H. 745. See the Persian Catalogue, p. 825*b*, III., and the Oude Catalogue, p. 433.

The first piece is a short Kasidah addressed to a king not named, and beginning:

ای پیك پی خجسته نسیم سحرکهی
لطفی کن از برای دل خستهٔ رهی

The second is a short moral poem in the shape of a Ghazal, beginning:

اکر ز ابر بلای سپهر زنکاری
فشاند بر کل زردم سرشك کلناری

Most of the contents consist of Ḳiṭ'ahs without any systematic arrangement. For MSS. of the Divan see the Petersburg Catalogue, no. 403, and the Bodleian Catalogue, no. 790. Two copies of the Muḳaṭṭa'āt are noticed in the Vienna Catalogue, nos. 563-4. A German translation by Schlechta-Vssehrd was published in Vienna, 1852.

Copyist: محمد حسن بن اسد بيك ساكن الارومى من طائفة الكاور

262.

Or. 3375.—Foll. 234; 9 in. by 5¾; 19 lines, 4 in. long; written in fair Nestalik, apparently in the 15th century.

[SIDNEY CHURCHILL.]

ديوان خواجو

The Divan of Khājūi Kirmāni, who died about A.H. 750. See the Persian Catalogue, p. 620.

Contents: 1. Kasidahs and Tarji's, being mostly laudatory poems arranged under the personages in whose praise they were composed, with headings giving their names in full.

This section begins with a Kasidah rhyming in ار, the first sixteen Baits of which have been supplied by a later hand. It begins with this line:

همه را کل بدست و مارا خار
همه را بهره کنج و مارا مار

This Kasidah is quoted in Majma' ul-Fuṣaḥā, vol. ii., p. 16, and said to be an imitation of a poem by Sanā'i. The first section includes Kasidahs addressed to the last Moghul sovereign, Abu Sa'id Bahādur Khān, to his Vazir, Ghiyāṣ ud-Dīn Muḥammad, to Amir Mubāriz ud-Dīn Muḥammad, founder of the Muẓaffari dynasty, to Ḳāẓi Shams ud-Dīn Maḥmūd B. Ṣā'in (v. Persian Catalogue, p. 621*a*), and to other princes, officials, and saints of the period.

2. A second series, consisting mostly of Muḳaṭṭa'āt, fol. 57*b*, beginning:

شك مريم ريختم چون شمع و انكه چون مسيح
پيش اين محراب مينا تا سحر كردم قيام

3. Ghazals in alphabetical order, fol. 80*b*, beginning:

سبحان من يسبحه الرمل فى القفار
سبحان من تقدسه للحوت فى البحار

The same beginning is noticed by Ethé, Bodleian Catalogue, no. 794, art. 8. The sixth piece, which is really the first of the alphabetical series, begins:

ميرود آب رخ از بادهٔ كلرنك مرا
ميزند راه خرد زمزمهٔ جنك مرا

4. Another and larger series of Ghazals not alphabetically arranged, foll. 129*a*—234*a*, imperfect at the beginning.

The first complete Ghazal begins:

خوشا خراب محبت ز ساغر ازلى
قدح بروى صبوحى كنان لم يزلى

The Divan of Khwājū is included in his Kulliyāt, described by Ethé, Bodleian Catalogue, no. 794.

263.

Or. 2833.—Foll. 779; 13 in. by $9\frac{3}{4}$; 27 lines, $6\frac{1}{2}$ in. long, with about 58 oblique lines round the margins; written in neat Persian Neskhi in four gold-ruled columns, with a rich and highly finished double-page 'Unvān, gold headings, and illuminated marginal ornaments; dated Shiraz, last decade of Ramazan, A.H. 807 (A.D. 1405).

[Sidney Churchill.]

ظفر نامه

The Zafar Nāmah, a Muslim chronicle in verse by Ḥamd-ullah Mustaufi, with the Shahnāmah of Firdausi in the margins.

Beg. بنام خدائی کی هست و یکیست
جزاو دردو کیتی خداوند نیست

In the preface of his Ta'rikh i Guzidah, written A.H. 730, the author states that he was then engaged on an extensive versified chronicle, which he intended to complete in 75,000 Baits. See the Persian Catalogue, p. 81*a*. That plan was carried out, and the result was the present work, which is stated in the prologue, fol. 5*a*, to comprise exactly the above number of Baits, or about 10,000 Baits for each century:

درین نامه از هفصد و جند سال
بکفتم حکایت ز هر کونه حال
سخن شد بهر صذ ده اندر هزار
بهفتاد و بنج آمذ آنرا شمار

After dwelling in the prologue on the excellency of poetry, the author bestows a glowing eulogy on the Shahnamah of Firdausi, but deplores the corrupt and defective condition of the copies of the poem current in his day. Although he knew on good authority that it originally consisted of 60,000 lines, he hardly ever found in any copy more than about 50,000. He therefore brought together the best MSS. he could find, and spent six years in compiling from them a standard text brought up to the legitimate number of 60,000 lines. This is the text found in the present copy. It occupies the margins from the beginning to fol. 736*a*, where the Ẓafar Nāmah ends, and from that point to the end of the volume it fills the centre of the page as well as the margins.

The author relates further how he had been urged by his friends to compose a rhymed history, as a sequel to the Shahnamah and in the same form, and how, after some pleas of inability, he had yielded to their instances and had set to work, but not before invoking Firdausi's blessing on his book, in the hope that a single verse in it might win for him God's mercy, as had been the case with his predecessor. On that occasion he tells the well-known anecdote of the holy Shaikh, Abu 'l-Ḳāsim Gurgāni, who had at first refused to perform the prayer over the corpse of Firdausi.

At the suggestion of the author's friends, the chronicle was called Ẓafar Nāmah:

ظفر نامه کن نام این نامه را
بذین تازه کن رسم شهنامه را

It is divided into three parts designated by the terms Kitāb or Ḳism, treating respectively of the Arabs, the Persians, and the Moghols, as stated in the following lines, fol. 5*a*:

کتاب نخستین ز کار عرب
بدیذ آمذه نکتهای عجب
باسلامی انرا لقب آمذه
جو اسلام از اهل عرب آمذه

کتاب دوم شرح حال عجم
در او کشته پیدا ز بیش و زکم
باحکام آنرا نهادم بنام
جو بر حکم دین آن دول شذ تمام
کتاب سیوم آمذه از مغول
فروزنده جون از جمن برك کل
بسلطانی آمذ مر آنرا خطاب
جو دارذ بسلطان دین انتساب

From the epilogue, fol. 736*a*, we learn that the author, who was forty years when he began the work, spent fifteen years upon its composition; and that out of the 75,000 lines of which it consists, 25,000 are devoted to the Arabs, 20,000 to the Persians, and 30,000 to the Moghols:

کشیذم درین پانزده سال رنج
بگفتم سخن پانزده بار بنج
عرب بیست و بنج وعجم بیست هزار
مغول سی هزار آمذ اندر شمار

About his sources the author is reticent. He says vaguely that he drew his information from Arabs and from Moghol chiefs:

ز تازیك و از سروران مغول
بجستم حکایت ز جزو و کل

He concludes with the date of completion, which he gives according to three eras, namely, A.H. 735, the year 1644 of Alexander, and the year 702 of Yezdegird:

ز هجرت شذه هفصد و سی و بنج
بر از رنج این نامه ام بوذ کنج
ز اسکندری از هزار این زمان
جل و جار وسیصد [ششصد] فزون سالیان
ز شه یزدکردی دو بر هفتصد
فزون کشته شذ رهنمایم خرذ

کتاب ظفر نامه کردم تمام
ز ما بر بیمبر دروذ و سلام

In spite of the poetical form which he adopted, the author is very precise as to facts and dates, and his third book will be found valuable for the history of the Moghol period. He gives, for instance, fol. 512*a*, a very vivid description of the wholesale slaughter wrought by the Moghols in his native place, Kazvin. His information was partly derived from his great-grandsire, Amin Naṣr Mustaufi, who was ninety-three years old at the time.

The contents of the Ẕafar Nāmah are the following:

Book I., with the heading قسم الاسلامیه من کتاب ظفر نامه. Life of Muḥammad, fol. 5*b*. Khilāfat of Abu Bakr, fol. 99*b*. 'Umar, fol. 113*b*. 'Osman, fol. 134*a*. 'Ali, fol. 140*b*. Ḥasan, fol. 153*a*. Banu Umayyah, fol. 154*a*. Banu 'Abbās, fol. 200.

Book II. Persian dynasties, with the title قسم الاحکامیه من ظفر نامه فی ذکر العجم. Ṣaffāris, fol. 255*a*. Sāmānis, fol. 261*b*. Ghaznavis, fol. 276*a*. Ghūris, fol. 297*b*. Dailamān, fol. 304*b*. Saljūḳs, fol. 320*a*. Saljūḳs of Rūm, fol. 376*a*. Khwārazmis, down to the death of Sultan Jalāl ud-Din, fol. 380*a*. Ismā'īlis of Iran, fol. 409*a*. Salghari Atābaks of Fārs, fol. 435*b*. Ḳarakhitā'is of Kirmān, fol. 440*b*.

Book III. Moghols, قسم السلطانیه من کتاب ظفر نامه فی ذکر المغول. Origin of the Turks and Moghols, fol. 447*b*. Oghūz Khan, first ruler of the Turks, fol. 448*a*. His son Gurkhān, fol. 450*b*. History of the Moghols after Oghūz Khan, fol. 451*a*. Alānḳuwā, ancestress of Chingīz Khan, fol. 452*a*. Būdunjar, ninth forefather of Chingiz Khan and his descendants down to Basūgāi, fol. 454*a*. Chingīz Khan, fol. 459*b*. Okotai Ḳā'ān, fol. 529*b*. Tūshi Khan and his descendants in Dasht Kipchak, fol. 551*a*. Jaghatai Khan and his successors in Turan, fol. 552*a*. Tūli Khan, fol. 553*a*. Barkatāi Khātūn, fol. 553*b*. Kuyuk Khan, fol. 554*b*. Mangu Ḳā'ān, fol. 557*b*. Timūr Ḳā'ān and his successors, fol. 580*a*. Hulagu Khan, fol. 581*b*. Abaḳa Khan, fol. 632*b*. Aḥmad Khan, fol. 645*a*. Arghun Khan, fol. 655*a*. Kaikhatu Khan, fol. 662*a*. Bā'idu Khan, fol. 666*a*. Ghazan Khan, fol. 674*b*. Uljaitu Sultan Muḥammad, fol. 708*a*. Abu Sa'id Bahādur Khan, foll. 722*a*—735*b*.

The last events recorded in the reign of Abu Sa'id are the deposition and banishment of Amir Shaikh Ḥasan, A.H. 732, and the arrest of some rebellious Amirs who had besieged the Sultan in his palace, A.H. 734. In the section relating to Hulagu, a full list of his descendants, tabulated in Siyāḳ form, occupies foll. 627—31. Further on, foll. 684—92, the author gives a poetical version of the Pand Nāmah of his master Rashid ud-Din in twelve Majlis.

The transcriber's name at the end of the Shah Nāmah is Maḥmūd al-Ḥusaini. The same name, with the addition of بن سعيد بن عبد الله, is found in the colophon of the Ẓafar Nāmah, fol. 736*a*; but there it has evidently been substituted for another name which had been erased.

This MS. was noticed in the Athenæum for 1885, p. 314.

264.

Or. 2947.—Foll. 146; 7½ in. by 4½; 16 lines, 2½ in. long; written in Neskhi, apparently early in the 19th century.

[Sidney Churchill.]

The collected works of 'Ubaid Zākāni, who died A.H. 772. See the Persian Catalogue, p. 809*b*, and the Oude Catalogue, p. 527.

This copy is imperfect at beginning and end. The contents are as follows:

I. Foll. 1*a*—47*b*. The Divan, comprising: 1. Kasidahs and occasional pieces, many of which are in praise of the reigning sovereign of Fārs, Jamāl ud-Din Shaikh Abu Isḥāḳ (A.H. 742—754; see the Persian Catalogue, p. 435*b*). The first complete Kasidah begins:

خوش آن نسیم که بوی ززلف یار آرد
بعاشقی خبر بار غم کسار آید

2. Fol. 25*b*. Ghazals, in which the poet calls himself عبید, and sometimes عبید زاکانی; beginning:

خوشا کسی که ز عشق و میش رهائی نیست
غمش ز رندی و میلش بپارسائی نیست

3. Fol. 32*a*. Rubā'is, beginning:

ای در سر هرکس از تو سودای دکر
در راه تو هر طایفه را رای دکر

4. Fol. 35*b*. Tarjī'-bands, beginning:

وقت انشد که کار درپایم [دریابم]
در شتابست عمر بشتابم

5. Fol. 39*b*. Masnavis, beginning:

جهان پهلوان رستم زورمند
که بر چرخ کردان فکندی کمند

6. Fol. 42*a*. Ḳiṭ'ahs and short pieces of two Baits, of a licentious nature, designated at the end as التضمینات. Imperfect at the beginning.

II. Fol. 48*a*. A Masnavi, the poet's own love-story, beginning:

خدایا [تا] ازین فیروزه ایوان
فروزد ماه و مهر و تیر و کیوان

The prologue contains a dedication to Shaikh Abu Isḥāḳ, and in the epilogue is found the date of composition, A.H. 751:

به بهتر طالع فرخنده تر فال
زهجرت نهصد [هفصد] و پنجاه و یکسال

بنظم آوردم این درد دل ریش
بهر کس باز گفتم قصه خویش

The poem is mentioned as عشاق نامه by Sprenger, Oude Catalogue, p. 527, and by Flügel, Vienna Catalogue, no. 567, art. 2.

III. Fol. 69*b*. نوادر الامثال, rare proverbs, or maxims of prophets and sages, in prose and verse; Arabic.

Beg. الحمد لله المنزه عن الانداد والامثال

See the Vienna Catalogue, no. 567, art. 4.

IV. Fol. 85*b*. ده فصل, humouristic definitions of current words, in ten chapters, also called تعریفات.

Beg. شکر و ثنا حضرت خالق را جل ذکره

See Fleischer, Leipzig Catalogue, no. 306, fol. 67; the Vienna Catalogue, no. 567, art. 7; and Pertsch, Berlin Catalogue, no. 9, art. 9.

V. Fol. 89*b*. اخلاق الاشراف, a satire on contemporary manners.

Beg. شکر نا محصور و حمد نا محدود حضرت واجب الوجودی را

See Fleischer, *ib.*, fol. 59; Vienna Catalogue, *ib.*, art. 3; and Pertsch, Berlin Catalogue, no. 14, art. 69.

VI. Fol. 106*b*. رساله دلگشا, a collection of witty sayings and comic anecdotes in Arabic and Persian.

Beg. الحمد لله علی نعمه و نواله ومنه

See Fleischer, *ib.*, fol. 72, and the Vienna Catalogue, no. 567, art. 5.

VII. Foll. 140*b*—146*b*. رساله ریش, a humouristic treatise on beard.

Beg. شکر و سپاس پادشاهی را که بدست مشاطه قدرت

It ends abruptly with this first line of a Rubā'i:

آن نوع بلا که ریش میخوانندش

See the Vienna Catalogue, *ib.*, art. 6.

Some of the above writings have been edited in a volume printed at Constantinople, A.H. 1303, under the title منتخب لطائف نظام الدین مولانا عبید زاکانی. That edition contains a notice of the poet and the following treatises: Akhlāḳ ul-Ashrāf (above, art. v.), Rīsh Nāmah (art. vii.), Ta'rīfāt (art. iv.), Masnavi i Jalḳ (fol. 37*b* of this MS.), Taẓmīnāt u Ḳiṭa'āt (art. i., 6), and Risālah i Dilgushā (art. vi.).

265.

Or. 2815.—Foll. 317; 8 in. by 4½; 17 lines, 2¾ in. long; written in elegant Nestalik, with three 'Unvāns, gold-ruled columns, and gilt headings; dated A.H. 883 (A.D. 1478).

[Sidney Churchill.]

دیوان سلمان الساوجی

Collected poems of Salmān Sāvaji, who died A.H. 779 (see the Persian Catalogue, p. 624*b*), as follows:

I. Fol. 2*a*. Kasidahs and Tarjī'-bands, wanting the first page, beginning with the 14th Bait of the opening Kasidah in praise of God, the first line of which is, هر دل که در هوای هویت مجال یافت. See the Oude Catalogue, p. 555; Pertsch, Berlin Catalogue, no. 837; and Ethé, Bodleian Catalogue, no. 807.

The contents, which are not alphabetically arranged, consist mostly of Kasidahs in praise of Amir Shaikh Ḥasan, of his wife Dilshād Khātūn, and of his son Sultan Uvais. The section breaks off with the tenth Bait of a

Kasidah in praise of the latter prince, which begins:

ذرهٔ از پی خورشید بجان میکردید
لله الحمد که آن ذره بخورشید رسید

II. Foll. 106b. کتاب ترجیع, Book of the Tarji's. Of this section the first page is alone extant. It contains the beginning of a Tarji' which is found entire in Add. 27,314, foll. 326b—328. It begins:

ما مریدان کوی خماریم
سر بسجد فرو نمی آریم

III. Fol. 117a. Ghazals, in alphabetical order, slightly imperfect at the beginning. The first extant Ghazal begins:

نظری نیست بحال منت ای ماه چرا
سایه برداشت زمن پیرو تو ناگاه چرا

IV. Fol. 219b. Rubā'is, beginning:

دست جو بکارد کلك را بتراشید
دانی که سرانکشت تو جون بخراشید

V. Fol. 223b. خورشید و جمشید, Khwurshid u Jamshid, a Masnavi. See Pertsch, Berlin Catalogue, no. 837, art. 2, and the Persian Catalogue, p. 625a, i.

VI. Fol. 284b. فراق نامه, the book of absence, a Masnavi. See the Persian Catalogue, p. 625b, ii.

Copyist: عبد الوهاب بن سلیمان خاکی

266.

Or. 4909.—Foll. 376; 6¾ in. by 5; 15 lines, 2½ in. long, with ten additional lines in the margin; written in small and neat Nestalik, with gold-ruled columns and with illuminated titles and gold headings; apparently in the 15th century.

The Divan of the same poet, with the usual beginning: هر دل که در هوای جلالت مجال یافت

Contents: Kasidahs and Tarkibs, fol. 1b. Marāṣi, fol. 138a, beginning:

ای صبحدم جه شد که کریبان دریدهٔ

Muḳaṭṭa'āt, fol. 146a, beginning:

حبذا صدر صفهٔ که بهشت [بهست]
بهمه پایه از بهشت برین

Tarji'āt, fol. 171b, beginning:

ما مریدان کوی خماریم

Ghazals, in alphabetical order, fol. 176a, beginning:

اکر حسن تو بکشاید نقاب از چهره دعوی را

Rubā'is, fol. 269a, beginning:

نقشیست درین خانه اکر وا خواند

Khurshīd u Jamshīd, fol. 275b. Firāḳ Nāmah, fol. 349a.

The last poem is imperfect at the end. At the bottom of the last page is written در هجرهٔ نبوی ۷۹۵, *i.e.* A.H. 795; but whether this was the original date of the MS. is uncertain.

267.

Or. 2710.—Foll. 207; 4⅞ in. by 2¾; 12 lines, 1¾ in. long; written in small and neat Nestalik, with two double-page 'Unvāns, gold-ruled columns, and miniatures; dated Wednesday, 14 Jumāda I., A.H. 1025 (A.D. 1616). Bound in painted and glazed covers.

دیوان حافظ

The Divan of Ḥāfiẓ, who died A.H. 791. See the Persian Catalogue, p. 627b.

Contents: Preface of Gulandām, fol. 3b (see the Persian Catalogue, p. 628b). It may be added that Ḳivām ud-Din 'Abdullah, whose lecture-room, according to Gulandām, Ḥāfiẓ used to attend, was the greatest doctor of Shīrāz in his day. He died, as stated in the Shadd ul-Izār, Or. 3395, fol. 45*b*, A.H. 772). Kasidahs, fol. 9*b*, beginning:

ثنا کریم خداوندی که بی مثل است و بی همتا
پس ازو نعت پیغمبر ز جان و دل کنم انشا

This section ends with a Tarji' in praise of the Imām Shāh i Khurāsān, and with a Masnavi beginning:

ایا نسیم سحر جانم فدای تو باد

Ghazals in alphabetical order, fol. 25*b*, with the usual beginning: الا یا ایها الساقی

Masnavis, fol. 198*b*, beginning:

ساقیا سایه ابر است و بهار و لب جوی

(This section includes the Sāķi Nāmah, fol. 200*a*, and the Mughanni Nāmah, fol. 201*a*, both abridged.)

Ķiṭ'ahs, fol. 202*b*, beginning as in the Calcutta edition of 1791, fol. 134*b*:

خسروا دادگرا بحردلا شیر کفا
ای جلال تو به انواع هنر ارزانی

Rubā'is, fol. 204*b*, beginning, as in the Calcutta edition of 1791, fol. 150:

جز نقش تو در نظر نیاید مارا
جز کوی تو رهگذر نیاید مارا

Copyist: محمد رحیم

The MS. contains five miniatures, nearly whole-page, in modern Persian style, at foll. 57, 73, 106, 129, and 160.

To the editions of the Divan mentioned in the Persian Catalogue may be added that of Major H. S. Jarrett, founded upon Brockhaus's text, and printed in Calcutta, 1881. A literal English translation with notes, by H. Wilberforce Clarke, Calcutta, 1891, is based upon Major Jarrett's text. For MSS. see Rosen, Institut, nos. 66—76; Pertsch, Berlin Catalogue, nos. 840—53; and Ethé, Bodleian Catalogue, nos. 815—53.

268.

Or. 3247.—Foll. 75; 13 in. by 8¾; 12 lines, 4¼ in. long; written in large and elegant Nestalik, with a whole-page and a single-page 'Unvān, gold headings, and gold-ruled margins, and with two whole-page miniatures in good Persian style, about A.H. 907 (A.D. 1501-2). The wide margins are covered with coloured designs.

[Sidney Churchill.]

The Divan of Ḥāfiẓ, with a preface by Bayāni.

Beg. of preface:

این کنج معانی که تهی از عیب است
نقشی است که از صحیفهٔ لا ریب است

.... یا کریم حمدا متوالیا لمن نظم بقدرته بیان المتکلمین

The writer's name appears in the following line, fol. 6*a*:

رسید اشارت عالی که نام خویش بکن
بیانی کلک بیانی برین صحیفه رقم

This recension of the Divan was compiled, as stated in the preface, from various MSS., A.H. 907, by the Shāhzadah Abu 'l-Fatḥ, son of Sulṭān Ḥusain Baiķarā. The writer of the preface was the successor of Mir 'Ali Shir, Khwājah 'Abdullah Marvārid, poetically surnamed Bayāni, who died A.H. 922. See the Persian Catalogue, p. 1094*a*.

The Divan contains only Ghazals in alphabetical order, with the usual beginning, and three Rubā'is at the end.

The first page is covered with 'Arzdidahs and seals of the reign of Shāhjahān. The earliest of the latter is dated A.H. 1042.

269.

Or. 4773.—Foll. 203; 7½ in. by 4½; 12 lines, 2½ in. long; written in fair Nestalik, with two 'Unvāns and gold-ruled columns, apparently in the sixteenth century.

The Divan of Ḥāfiẓ, with the preface of Gulandām, foll. 1—7*a*.

Contents: Ghazals, alphabetically arranged, with the usual beginning, fol. 7*b*. A Masnavi, fol. 186*b*, beginning:

سر فتنه دارد دگر روزگار
من و مستی فتنهٔ چشم یار

A Saḳi Nāmah, fol. 189*a*, beginning:

بیا ساقی از من برو پیش شاه
بگو این سخن کین شه جم کلاه

Ḳiṭ'ahs, fol. 191*b*, beginning:

نور خدا نمایدت آئینهٔ مجردی

Mukhammas, fol. 196*b*, beginning:

در عشق تو ای صنم چنانم
کز هستی خویشتن بجانم

Tarkib, fol. 198*b*, beginning:

ماهی جو تو آسمان ندارد
سروی جو تو بوستان ندارد

Rubā'is, fol. 200*b*, beginning:

مردی ز کنندهٔ در خیبر پرس
اسرار کرم ز خواجهٔ قنبر پرس

The original text breaks off at fol. 201*b*. A last folio has been supplied by a modern hand.

270.

Or. 4388.—Foll. 150; 5 in. by 3; 15 lines, $1\frac{1}{2}$ in. long; written in small and neat Nestalik, with a double-page 'Unvân, gold-ruled columns, and gilt borders, apparently in the 17th century. [Wallis Budge.]

The Divan of Ḥāfiẓ, consisting chiefly of Ghazals in alphabetical order, with the usual beginning. They are followed, fol. 139*a*, by a Tarji'-band (Calcutta edition of 1791, fol. 139*b*) beginning:

ای داده بباد دوستداری
این بود وفا و عهد داری

After this come a few Ḳiṭ'ahs, Masnavis, and Rubā'is; but the latter part of the MS., foll. 143—150, as well as foll. 3—7 at the beginning, is disfigured by holes, and more or less of the writing is lost.

271.

Or. 3588.—Foll. 182; $8\frac{1}{2}$ in. by $4\frac{1}{2}$; written in fair Nestalik in three gold-ruled columns, with about 18 oblique lines in each column; dated (foll. 115 and 160) Zulhijjah, A.H. 1086 and A.H. 1088 (A.D. 1676—78). [Sidney Churchill.]

I. Foll. 1—115. The Divan of Ḥāfiẓ.

Contents: Preface of Gulandām, wanting the first leaf, fol. 1*a*. Kasidahs, fol. 3*a*, beginning:

ای در رخ تو پیدا انوار پادشاهی
وز فکرت تو پنهان صد حکمت الهی

The same beginning is noticed by Pertsch, Berlin Catalogue, no. 849.

The third Kasidah, beginning خیر مقدم مرحبا ای طایر میمون قدم, is found in the Calcutta edition of 1791, fol. 6.

Ghazals, in alphabetical order, slightly imperfect at the beginning, fol. 8*a*. The first lines belong to the Ghazal beginning ای فروغ ماه حسن (Brockhaus's edition, no. 2).

Tarji'-bands, fol. 98*a*, beginning as in Or. 4388:

ای داده بباد دوستداری

Masnavis, fol. 99*b*, beginning:

شاهی که پناه ملك و دینست
درخورد هزار آفرینست

Muḳaṭṭa'āt, fol. 106*a*, beginning:

بسمع اشرف فردوسی زمانه رسان
که ای ز روی تو روشن چراغ دیده حور

See Pertsch, Berlin Catalogue, no. 849.

Rubā'is, in alphabetical order, fol. 111*a*, beginning:

جز نقش تو در نظر نیاید ما را

See Pertsch, *ib.*, and supra, no. 267.

II. Foll. 115*b*—160*a*. دیوان شیخ علی دابا کوهی

The Divan of Shaikh 'Ali Bābā Kūhi.

Beg. بنام حضرت بیچون خالق دانا
که در دهان دلم اوست ایفزمان کویا

'Ali Bābā, poetically surnamed Kūhi, was a disciple of Shaikh Abu 'Abdallah Muḥ. Khafīf Shīrāzi, surnamed Shaikh Kabīr, who died in Shiraz on the 23rd of Ramazan, A.H. 371 (Shīrāz Nāmah, Add. 18,185, fol. 109*b*; Shadd ul-Izār, Or. 3395, fol. 26; and Pertsch, Berlin Catalogue, no. 605). Kūhi lived to a great age, and died, according to the Shadd ul-Izār, fol. 155*b*, A.H. 442, in great renown of sanctity, at Shiraz, where his tomb was an object of pilgrimage.

The Divan consists of religious poems in Ghazal form, arranged in alphabetical order. At the end there are some Rubā'is beginning, fol. 158*b*, as follows:

بیواسطهٔ چشم خدارا دیدم
یعنی رخ یار مصطفا را دیدم

III. Foll. 160*b*—166*a*. An anonymous commentary expounding the mystic sense of the Ghazal of Ḥāfiẓ (Brockhaus, no. 525), beginning: درهمه دیرمغان نیست چو من شیدائی

Beg. دربیت تا بحکم وجوب اداء حق اخوت در شرع تنوت

It is followed, fol. 164*b*, by similar comments on this line of Ḥāfiẓ (Brockhaus, no. 237):

پیر ما کفت خطا بر قلم صنع نرفت
آفرین بر نظر پاك خطا پوشش باد

IV. Foll. 169*b*—182*a*. An alphabetical series of Ghazals by a poet who designates himself by the takhalluṣ Fāris.

Beg. ای درکنف ذات تو آسوده زبانها
وی راهروان سر کوی تو روانها

This is the poet mentioned as Faris by Sarkhush, Or. 470, fol. 102*b*. The line quoted there,

عشق آمد و زالابش نن بی اثرم کرد

is found in our MS., fol. 175*b*. The poet is probably the same as Mirza Muḥammad Fāris mentioned in several Tazkirahs without any further notice. See Ṣuḥuf Ibrāhīm, Berlin Catalogue, no. 663, ب, 8; Makhzan ul-Gharā'ib, Bodleian Catalogue, col. 361, no. 1947; and Rūz i Rūshan, p. 499. He must have lived before A.H. 1087, the date of the present copy.

Prefixed to the above, as a separate section, foll. 167*b*—169*a*, are a few Kasidahs probably due to the same poet.

Beg. ای از تو ریاض دل ما طور تمنا
یاد تو جکر سوزتر از آتش موسی

272.

Or. 4745.—Foll. 120; $8\frac{1}{2}$ in. by 6; 16 lines, $5\frac{1}{4}$ in. long; written in the Hebrew character; dated the 8th day of Ailūl, A.M. 5499 (A.D. 1739). [SIDNEY CHURCHILL.]

The Divan of Ḥāfiẓ, with the heading:

דיואן כואנה חאפט שיראזי

[دیوان خواجه حافظ شیرازی]

followed by the usual beginning:

אלא יא אידהא סאקי אדר כאסא ונאוילהא
כה עשק אסאן נמוד אול ולי אופתאד משכלהא

[الا یا ایها الساقی ادر کاسا و ناولها
که عشق آسان نمود اول ولی افتاد مشکلها]

At the end of the alphabetical series of Ghazals are found the following sections: פי אל מקאטעאת [فی المقطعات], fol. 111b; ולהו תאריכאת [وله تاریخات], fol. 113a; the Sāķi Nāmah (סאקי נאמה), fol. 113b; a Masnavi (מסנוי), fol. 116b; and the Rubā'is (רבאעיאת), fol. 115b.

273.

Or. 3206.—Foll. 240; 9 in. by 6; 21 lines, 3¾ in. long; written in Neskhi, A.H. 966 (A.D. 1559). [Kremer, no. 184.]

The latter half of Surūri's commentary upon the Divan of Ḥāfiẓ. See the Turkish Catalogue, p. 157b, and Ethé, Bodleian Catalogue, no. 853.

274.

Or. 3205.—Foll. 518; 8 in. by 5¼; 23 lines, 3¾ in. long; written in Neskhi; 17th century. [Kremer, no. 183.]

Sūdi's commentary upon the Divan of Ḥāfiẓ. See the Turkish Catalogue, p. 158b.

275.

Or. 2950.—Foll. 217; 7¼ in. by 4; 14 lines, 2¼ in. long, with about 27 slanting lines in the margin; written in small and neat Nestalik, with gold-ruled columns and some illuminated headings; dated Tuesday, 4 Sha'bān, A.H. 888 (A.D. 1483). [Sidney Churchill.]

دیوان کمال خجندی

The Divan of Kamāl Khujandi, who died A.H. 803. See the Persian Catalogue, p. 632b.

It begins with a Kasidah in praise of God, the first line of which is:

افتتاح سخن آن به که کند اهل کمال
بثنای ملك الملك خدای متعال

This is immediately followed by Ghazals in alphabetical order, beginning:

ایها العطشان فی وادی الهوی
جوی جویان جانب دریا بیا

Muķaţţa'āt, fol. 203b, beginning:

جو دیوان کمال افتد بدستت
نویس از شعر او چندان که خواهی

Fardiyyāt, fol. 213a; Rubā'is, fol. 213b, beginning:

تا فکرت من بنهاد بنیاد سخن
آباد شد از من طرب آباد سخن

Foll. 216-17 should be taken after fol. 6. For other MSS. see the Strassburg Catalogue, no. 13; the Berlin Catalogue, no. 854; and the Bodleian Catalogue, no. 857.

Copyist: شاهبور بن خداداد شاهبور اصفهانی

The margins form a continuous text. It consists of extracts, mostly Ghazals in alphabetical order, from the Divans of the following ten poets:

Khusrau (Dihlavi), foll. 2—6, 216-7, 7—38.

Beg. باز دل کم گشت در کویش دیوانه را

Ḥāfiẓ Shīrāzi, fol. 38b.

Beg. ساقی بنور باده بر افراز جام را

Ķāsim (ul-Anvār), who died A.H. 837 (Persian Catalogue, p. 635), fol. 63b.

Beg. بسوخت آتش عشق تو زهد و تقوی را

Jāmi, fol. 83*b*.

Beg. ای درهوای مهر تو ذرات کاینات

Suhaili (died A.H. 907; see the Persian Catalogue, p. 756*a*, and Ethé, no. 981), fol. 115*b*.

Beg. خوان نوال تست غذا بخش جان ما

Saifi (Yādgār Beg, d. 870; see Ethé, no. 888), fol. 143*b*.

Beg. تا باو کردم عیان عشق نهان خویش را

Riyāẓi (d. 884; Persian Catalogue, p. 1074*a*, and Ethé, no. 890), fol. 166*b*.

Beg. صنع او آن دم که نقش کنبد افلاک بست

Muḥyi (probably Muḥyi Lāri, who died, however, about 45 years after the date of the MS.; v. Persian Catalogue, p. 655), fol. 184*b*.

Beg. درغم عشق تو زان نکذشت کار دل مرا

Kātibi (d. 838; v. Persian Catalogue, p. 637, Berlin Catalogue, no. 864), fol. 201*b*.

Beg. آفاق بر صداست ز کوه کناه ما

Hātifi (d. 927; v. Persian Catalogue, p. 652*b*), foll. 212*b*—215*b*.

Beg. تا برفت آن سنك دل از دیدهٔ روشن مرا

276.

Or. 3303.—Foll. 202; 8¼ in. by 5; 15 lines, 2¾ in. long; written in elegant Nestalik, with 'Unvān and gold-ruled columns, apparently early in the 16th century.

[Sidney Churchill.]

The Divan of Kamāl, with the same beginning and nearly the same contents as in the preceding copy.

The Muḳaṭṭaʻāt begin, fol. 196*a*, with the same piece as in no. 275. The Rubāʻis begin, fol. 202*a*, also with the same line.

277.

Or. 3313.—Foll. 195; 7 in. by 4¼; two distinct MSS. bound together.

[Sidney Churchill.]

I. Foll. 2—65; 21 lines, 2½ in. long; written in small Turkish Nestalik, with 'Unvān and gold headings, probably about A.D. 1600.

دیوان مغربی

The Divan of Maghribi, of Tabriz, who died A.H. 809. See the Persian Catalogue, p. 633.

At the beginning is a short prose preamble of four lines, the initial words of which are: الحمد لله الذی انشا عروض الکون بسبب الجسم الثقیل والروح الخفیف

Contents:. Ghazals in alphabetical order, beginning:

خورشید رخت جو کشت پیدا
ذرات دو کون شد هویدا

Tarjiʻāt, fol. 51*b*, beginning:

آفتاب وجود کرد اشراق
نور او بنکر بسر [*sic*] کرفت آفاق

Rubāʻis, fol. 62*b* (with a few Ḳiṭʻahs at the end), beginning:

ای کشته عیان روی تو از جام جهان
پیدا شده از نام خوشت نام جهان

A copy with the same beginnings is described by Ethé, Bodleian Catalogue, no. 859. See also Pertsch, Berlin Catalogue, no. 855, and Majmaʻ ul-Fuṣaḥā, vol. ii., p. 30.

II. Foll. 66—195; 13 lines, 2¾ in. long: written in fair Nestalik with gold heading and ruled margins; dated Bagdad, 15 Jumāda II., A.H. 953 (A.D. 1546).

دیوان الشیخ شمس المشرقی

The Divan of Shams Mashriḳi.

The author was a holy personage and a Sufi poet; but he cannot be identified with the great mystic, Shams i Tabriz, who is not known by the name of Mashriḳi. In the inscription prefixed to the Divan he is designated by the following titles: دیوان شیخ المحققین حبر المدققین قدوة المشایخ والعارفین مولانا شمس الملة والدین المشرقی التبریزی قدس سره

He must have lived before A.H. 855; for that year is stated at the end to have been the date of an early copy, from which the present MS. was transcribed.

At the beginning of the Divan are two Kasidahs, respectively in praise of God and of the Prophet. The former begins:

یا ناظم الجواهر یا عاقد اللآل
سل ناظم المناظم نظما بل انفصال [*sic*]

The further contents are as follows:

Ghazals in alphabetical order, fol. 68*a*, beginning:

انکس که نهان بود پس پردهٔ اشیا
شد دررخ هرذره چو خورشید هویدا

A Tarkib and two Tarji'-bands, fol. 170*a*, beginning:

ساقی بیار بادهٔ که هشیار مانده ایم
با ما تو یار باش که بی یار مانده ایم

Muḳaṭṭa'āt, fol. 183*a*, beginning:

ز توحیدم شبی پرسید درویشی سخن دانی
خمش گشتم بر آشفت او ز الحاحش بر آشفتم

Rubā'is, fol. 187*a*, beginning:

الشمس لشمس ذاتکم مرآت
الشمس المصباحکم مشکات

In the Ghazals the author uses three forms of takhalluṣ, namely, شمس مشرق ,مشرقی, and شمس مشرقی. In the colophon he is designated as follows: مولانا شمس الملة والدین المشرقی التبریزی الشهیر بالقطابی. He is not to be confounded with Mirza Malik Mashriḳi, of Mashhad, who lived in the time of Shāh 'Abbās I. See Maikhānah, fol. 60*b*, and Khair ul-Bayān, fol. 311*b*.

278.

Or. 2997.—Foll. 46; 9 in. by 5¼; 13 lines, 2¾ in. long; written in neat Nestalik, with 'Unvān and gold-ruled margins, mounted on tinted paper; dated A.H. 992 (A.D. 1584).

[Sidney Churchill.]

روضة العاشقین

A poem of the class known as Dah Nāmah. It is a collection of letters in verse addressed by an imaginary lover to his mistress, with a prose preface; by 'Aziz-ullah, called Zāhidi, who uses 'Aziz as his poetical surname.

Beg. of the Preface: سپاس بیقیاس صانعی را که از صنعة تجنیس و ترصیع در احسن کلام وجود تحسین نهاد

The poem begins, fol. 4*a*, as follows:

چون بر آورد دل نواز آغاز
نامهٔ کرد دل نواز آغاز
خاك ره جست و آبحیوان یافت
خواند فصلی ز باب حیوان یافت

We learn from the preface that the author had repaired to Herat, A.H. 810, and had spent there about ten years, engaged in study. Having found a patron in Sultan Bāisunghar Bahādur Khān, he composed for him the present poem, A.H. 820. It consists of a thousand Baits, in which Tajnis and other rhetorical figures, enumerated in the preface, are illustrated by examples.

The epilogue contains the above date of composition and a panegyric on Sultan Baisunghar.

279.

Or. 4135.—Foll. 404; 9¾ in. by 6½; 17 lines, 3¾ in. long; written in neat Nestalik, with tasteful 'Unvān and gold-ruled columns, apparently in the 15th century.

[Sidney Churchill.]

دیوان سید نعمت الله ولی

The Divan of Ni'mat-ullah Vali, who died A.H. 834. See the Persian Catalogue, p. 634b.

After a short doxology in prose, beginning الحمد لله الذی عین عین الاعیان بفیضه الاقدس, comes a short Masnavi, with this initial line:

خوش بکو ای یار بسم الله بکو
هرچه میجوی ز بسم الله بجو

The first section consists of a mixture of pieces of various forms, Masnavis, Ghazals, Dubaitis, and Rubā'is. The alphabetical series of Ghazals which form the main bulk of the volume begins, fol. 32b, with this verse:

جام کیتی نماست سید ما
جان و جانان ماست سید ما

The remainder of the Divan comprises—

Pious precepts in Masnavi verse, fol. 342b, with other Masnavis, beginning:

باطن و ظاهر ارکنی طاهر
پاك باشی بباطن و ظاهر

Dubaitis in alphabetical order, fol. 349a, beginning:

سر محبوب خود مکن پیدا
کر چه پیداست در همه اشیا

Rubā'is, alphabetically arranged, fol. 376b, beginning:

بنواخت مرا لطف آلهی به خدا
هر درد که بود از کرم کرد دوا

Fardiyyāt, also in alphabetical order, fol. 394b, beginning:

در آینه تمام اشیا
بنمود جمال جمله اسما

Very similar contents will be found in an edition lithographed at Teheran, A.H. 1276. For MSS. see Sprenger, Oude Catalogue, no. 419, and Pertsch, Berlin Catalogue, nos. 856—58. Copious extracts, with a biographical notice, are to be found in Majma' ul-Fuṣaḥā, vol. ii., p. 42.

280.

Or. 3304.—Foll. 261; 8½ in. by 5¾; 15 lines, 3 in. long; written in elegant Nestalik, with 'Unvān and gold-ruled columns; dated Jumāda II., A.H. 857 (A.D. 1453).

[Sidney Churchill.]

I. Foll. 1—221. دیوان قاسم الانوار

The Divan of Ḳāsim ul-Anvār, who died A.H. 837. See the Persian Catalogue, p. 635b.

Beg. من بیچارهٔ سودا زده سرکردانم
که باوصاف خداوند سخن حون رانم

Contents: Ghazals in alphabetical order, fol. 2a, beginning:

ای صبح سعادت ز جبین تو هویدا
این حسن چه حسنست تقدس و تعالی

Tarjī'-band, fol. 199b, beginning:

بیا ای عشق عالم سوز بی غم
قدم بر چشم من نه خیر مقدم

(See Aumer, no. 85.)

Muḳaṭṭa'āt, fol. 204a, beginning:

قبله جان من توئی کیل فرشته رنك و بو

This section includes several pieces written entirely or partly in Turki.

Rubā'is, fol. 211*a*, beginning:

مستدعیم از حضرت سلطان قدم
یك جرعه شراب را که سر تا بقدم

A Masnavi relating to Tīmūr's death, beginning:

الا ای شاهباز ملك لاهوت

(see Add. 18,874, fol. 219, and Ethé, no. 862, fol. 231), and other Masnavis.

II. Foll. 221*b*—243. A Sufi tract in Masnavi verse, known as Anīs ul-'Ārifīn, انیس العارفین, by the same author, with a prose preface beginning: منت خدایرا جلت عظمته وعلت کلمته که بشعشعهٔ انوار اسرار. See the Persian Catalogue, p. 636*b*, II.; Aumer, no. 85, fol. 185; and Ethé, no. 862, fol. 233.

III. Foll. 244—261. Another Sufi tract in prose, diversely called رساله الامانه or انیس العاشقین, by the same author.

Beg. شکر و سپاس و حمد بی قیاس سزاوار حضرتیست

(See the Persian Catalogue, p. 636*b*, III.; Ethé, no. 862, fol. 257; and Aumer, no. 85, fol. 205.) It concludes with a separate chapter designated as نصیحت درویشان, "Advice to Dervishes," fol. 255*b*, beginning: اول نصیحتی که سلامت دین

Copyist: سلطان علی بن محمد مشهدی

For other copies of the Divan, see Pertsch, Berlin Catalogue, nos. 859—63; the Leyden Catalogue, vol. v., no. 2587; Ethé, Bodleian Catalogue, nos. 862—66; and, for the author's life and poetical extracts, Majma' ul-Fuṣaḥā, vol. ii., p. 27.

281.

Or. 2951.—Foll. 235; 9½ in. by 6¼; 17 lines, 4⅜ in. long; written in fair large Nestalik, with three 'Unvāns and gold-ruled margins; dated 10 Zulka'dah, A.H. 877 (A.D. 1472).

[Sidney Churchill.]

Another copy of the Divan of Ḳāsim ul-Anvār, with the same beginning and nearly the same contents as the preceding, namely:

Ghazals (wanting a leaf at the beginning), fol. 21. Tarji', fol. 170*a*. Muḳaṭṭa'āt, fol. 180*b*. Rubā'is, fol. 186*b*. Masnavis, fol. 191*b*. Anis ul-'Ārifīn, fol. 195*b*. Anis ul-'Āshiḳīn, with the heading رساله حوریه, fol. 215*b*. The Masnavi relating to Tīmūr's death, with a preface beginning: برادر عزیز را سعادت ابدی مساعد باد, fol. 232*b*. (The Masnavi is also included in the Divan, fol. 191*b*.)

Copyist: عبد الله بن جعفر

282.

Or. 3500.—Foll. 326; 8¾ in. by 5¼; 17 lines, 3¼ in. long; written in elegant Nestalik, with a neat 'Unvān and gold-ruled columns; dated Jumāda I., A.H. 864 (A.D. 1460).

[Presented by Amīn us-Sulṭān 'Ali Asghar Khān.]

دیوان عصمت بخارائی

The Divan of 'Iṣmat of Bukhārā. See the Persian Catalogue, p. 736*b*.

Beg. تعالی الله زهی قیوم دانا
تعالی الله زهی حی توانا

The date A.H. 829 assigned by Daulatshāh to the death of 'Iṣmat, and generally adopted, is too early. He died A.H. 840, as testified by chronograms quoted by Rāḳim, Rosen, Institut, p. 121, and by Ethé, Bodleian Catalogue, no. 861.

Contents: 1. Kasidahs and Tarkibs arranged under the names of the persons praised. These are mostly princes of the house of Timūr, principally Sultan Khalil, son of Mīrānshāh, foll. 61—101; Ulugh Beg, foll. 27—53; Baisunghar and Ibrahim Sulṭān. This section includes a piece of Turki prose, foll. 123-4, with the heading قيس اولكان لاركا روح الله اثر كوركوزدى احيا دين

2. Marāṣi, or elegies on the death of Sultan Khalil, Shaikh Saif ud-Dīn, Khwājah 'Abd ul-Avval, Muḥ. Pārsā, and Khwājah 'Iṣām ud-Dīn, fol. 125b, beginning:

ای فلك خرگاه ویران کن که سلطان غایبست
بخت گو بر خاك بنشین جون سلیمان غایبست

3. Muḳaṭṭa'āt, without alphabetical arrangement, fol. 146a, beginning:

با خرد گفتم ای مدبر کار
که بدانش جو تو نشان ندهند

4. Ghazals, also without alphabetical order, fol. 183b, beginning:

ای ز عشق آوازه در کون و مکان انداخته
آفریده حسن دانش در جهان انداخته

5. Rubā'is, fol. 306b, beginning:

ای سایه رحمتت پناه همه کس
وی خاك درت گریزگاه همه کس

6. Mu'ammas or logogriphs in verse, fol. 311a.

7. Ornate compositions in mixed prose and Masnavi verse, addressed to Baisunghar and others, foll. 316b—326b.

A MS. with similar contents is described by Sprenger, Oude Catalogue, no. 275.

283.

Or. 3306.—Foll. 23; 6½ in. by 4; 12 lines, 2¼ in. long; written in neat Nestalik, with gold-ruled columns; dated Herat, A.H. 875 (A.D. 1470-71). [Sidney Churchill.]

حال نامه

Ḥāl Nāmah, also called Gūy u Chaugān, a Masnavi by 'Ārifi, who died A.H. 853. See the Persian Catalogue, p. 639b, and Ethé, Bodleian Catalogue, no. 872.

Beg. زان بیش که حسب حال گویم
از صانع ذو الجلال گویم

This copy does not contain any date of composition; but the poet says in the epilogue, fol. 21b, that fifty years of his life had elapsed at the time of writing:

پنجاه گذشت سال عمرم
یکنیمه شکست بال عمرم

Copyist: محمد بن اظهر الخطاط

284.

Or. 3233.—Foll. 86; 6 in. by 3; 11 lines, 1¾ in. long; written in neat Nestalik, with 'Unvān and gold-ruled columns; dated Muḥarram, A.H. 882 (A.D. 1477).

دیوان امیر شاهی

The Divan of Amīr Shāhi, who died A.H. 857. See the Persian Catalogue, p. 640a, and Taḳi Kāshi, St. Petersburg Catalogue, p. 311.

Beg. یا رب بسوز سینه زندان باك باز
یا رب بآب دیدهٔ مستان ما بناز

The third piece in the MS. is the first of the alphabetical series of Ghazals, and that with which most copies begin. Its first line is: ای نقش بسته نام خطت بر سرشت ما

At the end, fol. 80a, are a few Muḳaṭṭa'āt, beginning:

دران کوش من بعد شاهی بدهر
که روزی بانصاف ازین خوان خوری

An edition lithographed in Constantinople, A.H. 1288, has nearly the same contents, but differently arranged. It begins with this line:

بیا ای از خط سبزت هزاران داغ بر دلها

which is found at fol. 10*b* of the present copy. For other MSS., see Pertsch, Berlin Catalogue, no. 866; Ethé, nos. 875—81; and Rosen, Institut, nos. 65, 2, 77-8.

Copyist: ابو اسحاق محمد بن محمد کواری

285.

Or. 3334.—Foll. 79; 6 in. by 3½; 12 lines, 1⅝ in. long; written in neat Nestalik, with three 'Unvāns and gold-ruled columns; dated (fol. 42) 1 Rajab, A.H. 924 (A.D. 1518).

[H. A. Stern.]

I. Foll. 1—42. دیوان شاهی

The Divan of Shāhi (see the preceding MS.), consisting of Ghazals in alphabetical order, with some Rubā'is at the end.

Beg. ای نقش بسته نام خطت با سرشت ما
وین حرف شد ز روز ازل سرنوشت ما

Ḳiṭ'ahs and Rubā'is, fol. 38*b*, beginning:

شبی با صراحی همی گفت شمع
کای هر شبی مجلس آرای دوست

II. Foll. 44—71. دیوان ریاضی

The Divan of Riyāẓi Samarkandi, who died A.H. 884. See the Persian Catalogue, p. 1074*a*, and Ethé, no. 890.

Beg. صنع او آندم که نقش گنبد افلاك بست
نامهٔ حیرت ببال طایر ادراك بست

The Divan consists of Ghazals in alphabetical order, with three Rubā'is at the end. The Ghazal the first line of which is given in the Persian Catalogue and by Ethé is the second in the present MS.

III. Foll. 71*b*—79. دیوان موالی

The Divan of Muvāli, beginning:

آثار صنع بیچون در تست آشکارا
بگذار تا ببینم در روی تو خدارا

Muvāli was a native of Tūn, and a skilled physician. He lived in Yazd, and was often in the society of Shāh Nūr ud-Dīn Ni'matullah (who died A.H. 834). See Haft Iḳlīm, fol. 334. He is also mentioned under Tūn in the Atashkadah, p. 73, but the date of his death is uncertain.

The Divan consists of Ghazals in alphabetical order, but it breaks off with the second of the Ghazals rhyming in د.

286.

Or. 3305.—Foll. 113; 7¾ in. by 4¾; 12 lines, 2¾ in. long; written in elegant Nestalik, with five 'Unvāns and gold-ruled columns, apparently about the close of the 15th century.

[Sidney Churchill.]

Select Ghazals by the following poets, alphabetically arranged under each poet:

1. Ṭūsi, who died A.H. 869 (Persian Catalogue, p. 735*a*, no. 11), fol. 1*b*.

Beg. موییست یا خیال میانت بچشم ما
ای سرو راست کوی میان تو و خدا

This is the seventh Ghazal in Ṭūsi's Divan, Add. 16,561, fol. 81*b*. There are six Ḳiṭ'ahs of two Baits each at the end.

2. Jāmi, fol. 28*b*, beginning:

ای مه خرگه نشین از رخ برافکن پرده را

3. Ashraf, who died A.H. 854 (see the Persian Catalogue, p. 735*a*, and Ethé, no. 874), fol. 43*b*.

Beg. گر بحکایت آورم این غم عاشقانه را
آتش دل برون کند از دهنم زبانه را

4. Amir Hasan, who died A.H. 727 (Persian Catalogue, p. 618*a*, and Ethé, no. 780), fol. 56*b*.

Beg. ای کمر بسته بی وفائی را
یك طرف کرده آشنائی را

This is the twelfth Ghazal in the poet's Divan, Add. 24,952, fol. 38*b*.

5. Kamāl Khujandi, who died A.H. 803 (see above, no. 275), fol. 62*b*.

Beg. بگذار دران کوی من اشك فشانرا
تا دیده دهد آب گل و سرو روانرا

There are fifteen Kiṭ'ahs at the end.

6. Ṭāli'i, who died A.H. 858 (Persian Catalogue, p. 735*b*), fol. 89.

Beg. از خدا خواهم که تیر او کند در سینه جا
پی بمقصد می برم کر راست می آرد خدا

There are three Kiṭ'ahs at the end.

7. 'Ārifi, who died A.H. 853 (see above, no. 283), foll. 108*b*—113*b*.

Beg. ای بر سریر مملکت حسن پادشا
بنشین بشه‌نشین رواق دو چشم ما

On every page of this last section there are two Ghazals, the first of which is by 'Ārifi and the second, composed in the same metre and with the same rhyme, by Shauki. The first Ghazal of the latter poet begins:

از آه دل نشد قدت از دیده ام جدا
آن سرو نیست این که ببادی رود زجا

Judging from the apparent date of the MS., this last poet cannot be much later than the ninth century of the Hijrah. He cannot be identified with the later Shaukis mentioned in the Tazkirahs.

287.

Or. 4123.—Foll. 284; 9¼ in. by 5¼; 15 lines, 2¾ in. long; written in choice Nestalik, with four highly-finished 'Unvāns, the first of which consists of a rich border enclosing two pages, with gold-ruled columns and gilt headings; dated Monday, 7 Rabi' II., A.H. 894 (A.D. 1489). Bound in fine stamped and gilt leather covers.

[Tho. Fiott Hughes.]

دیوان جامی

The Divan of Jāmi, with a prose preface beginning: موزون ترین کلامی که غزل سرایان انجمن انس و محبت

This is the earliest collection of Jāmi's poems, dedicated to Sultan Abu Sa'id, about A.H. 867. The same preface is found in two previously described MSS., Persian Catalogue, p. 644*a*, as well as in the Vienna Catalogue, no. 595; the Petersburg Catalogue, no. 439; and the Bodleian Catalogue, nos. 947—954. It is also found in the edition lithographed in Lucknow, 1876, under the title کلیات جامی, the contents of which are nearly the same as those of the present MS., but somewhat differently arranged. Compare Rosen, Institut, p. 257.

Contents: Preface, fol. 2*b*. Kasidahs, with the heading فی التوحید, mostly of a religious character, fol. 5*b*, beginning:

بسم الله الرحمن الرحیم
اعظم اسماء حکیم علیم

Ghazals, alphabetically arranged, fol. 10*b*, beginning:

یا من بدا جمالك فی کل ما بدا
بادا هزار جان مقدس ترا فدا

A Masnavi in praise of 'Ali, فی مناقب حضرت امیر المومنین علی کرم الله وجهه, fol. 249*a*, beginning:

سلام علی صاحب الدلدلی
امام الوری مرتضی کاملی

Four Tarjī'āt, fol. 251*a*, beginning:

ماه معین جیست خاك بای محمد
حبل متین ربقه ولاء محمد

Marṣiyahs, fol. 263*b*, beginning:

صاحب دلان که بیشتر از مرك مرده اند
اب حیات از قدح مرك خورده اند

Muḳaṭṭa'āt, fol. 267*b*, beginning:

دلا منشین دربن ویرانه جون جغد
سوی مرغان قدسی اشیان بر

(the same as with Rosen, Institut, p. 238).

Rubā'is, fol. 270*a*, beginning:

با زلف تو نافه را سر مسکینیست
با روی تو ماه رسته از خود بینیست

Mu'ammayāt, fol. 279*a*, beginning:

در شهر دو جا کرفته ارباب مقر
یك جای یکی و دیکران جای دکر

It will be seen that most of the contents of this early Divan have found their way into the first of the three later Divans of Jāmi, as described by Baron Rosen, Institut, pp. 234—39.

This precious copy was written in the life-time of the poet.

288.

Or. 4681.—Foll. 168; 7¼ in. by 4; 17 lines, 2¾ in. long; written in small and neat Nestalik, with gold-ruled columns; dated Rabī' I., A.H. 868 (A.D. 1463).

[Sidney Churchill.]

This precious MS., written thirty years before Jāmi's death, contains another early collection of his poems, without preface.

Beg. بسم الله الرحمن الرحیم
اعظم اسماء علیم حکیم

The contents agree in a great measure with those of the first Divan, or فاتحة الشباب, as described by Baron Rosen, Institut, pp. 234—38, especially in the alphabetical series of Ghazals, where the initial lines under most letters are the same as those given in the above work.

Contents: Poems in praise of God and Muḥammad, with the heading فی التوحید (including the Tarji' in praise of the latter, which begins with ماه معین, and has been noticed in the preceding MS., fol. 251), fol. 1*a*.

Alphabetical series of Ghazals, fol. 8*a*, beginning as in the preceding MS.

Three Tarjī'āt, fol. 151*a*, beginning:

ای بروی تو جشم جان روشن
وز فروغ رخت جهان روشن

Two Tarkīb-bands, fol. 158*b*, the first of which occurs in the preceding MS. under the heading of Marṣiyahs, and begins thus:

صاحب دلان که پیشتر از مرك مرده اند

Muḳaṭṭa'āt, fol. 162*a*, beginning:

رخ زرد دارم زدوری آن در
زده داغ ودردم درون دل آذر

Rubā'is, fol. 164*b*, beginning:

یا من ملکوت کل شیء بیده
طوبی لمن ارتضاك ذخرا لغده

Mu'ammayāt, fol. 165*b*, the first of which is headed سلطان عبد اللطیف, and begins:

یکی در سلطنت تابنده بین خورشیدفر ماهی

The following colophon is found at the end of this last section, fol. 166*b*: تمت الکتاب بعون الملك الوهاب حرره العبد الفقیر عبد الرحیم تفرجی الحسینی فی ربیع الاول بالسنه ثمان وستین وثمانمایه

Fol. 167, containing Rubā'is, is misplaced; it should come after fol. 164.

Fol. 168 contains the latter part of the poet's epilogue, namely, the end of a Masnavi in praise of the reigning Sultan (Abu Sa'īd) and a few lines of prose, with two Rubā'is, partly obliterated, at the end, in the first of which Jāmi alludes to his age as being fifty:

در پنجهٔ پنجهم کنون افتاده

289.

Or. 4513.—Foll. 275; 9½ in. by 6; 23 lines, 4¾ in. long; written in Neskhi in four ruled columns, with seven rude 'Unvāns; dated from Rabi' I., A.H. 907, to Jumāda I., A.H. 908 (A.D. 1501-2).

[Sidney Churchill.]

هفت اورنك جامى

The Haft Aurang, or seven Masnavi poems, of Jāmi. See the Persian Catalogue, p. 644*b*.

The MS. wants the first leaf, and begins with the second page of Jāmi's preface. The seven poems are placed in the order in which they are enumerated in that preface, viz., 1. Silsilat uz-Zahab, fol. 1*b* (the second Daftar begins at fol. 45*b*, the third at fol. 64*b*). 2. Salāmān u Absāl, fol. 78*b*. 3. Tuḥfat ul-Aḥrār, with preface, fol. 92*b*. 4. Subḥat ul-Abrār, fol. 113*b*. 5. Yúsuf u Zulaikhā, fol. 148*b*. 6. Laili u Majnūn, fol. 204*b*. 7. Khirad Nāmah i Iskandari, fol. 249*b*.

Copyist: درويش على بن مولانا درويش محمد كاتب

Two of the above poems, Yūsuf u Zulaikhā and Laili u Majnūn, are in a later and more cursive hand.

The Haft Aurang forms the first part of the Kulliyāt i Jāmi, an early MS. of which, supposed to be the poet's autograph, has been minutely described by Baron Rosen, Institut, pp. 215—259. For other copies see Pertsch, Berlin Catalogue, no. 876, and Ethé, Bodleian Catalogue, nos. 897—902.

290.

Or. 2935.—Foll. 284; 9¼ in. by 6; 21 lines, 4 in. long; written in small and fair Nestalik in four gold-ruled columns, with nine 'Unvāns; dated Herat, A.H. 934 (A.D. 1528).

[Nath. Bland.]

Another copy of the Haft Aurang, containing the seven poems in the same order, viz., 1. Silsilat uz-Zahab, with Jāmi's preface, fol. 2*b* (Daftar II., fol. 52*b*, Daftar III., fol. 73*b*). 2. Salāmān u Absāl, fol. 87*b*. 3. Tuḥfat ul-Aḥrār, fol. 103*b*. 4. Subḥat ul-Abrār, fol. 126*b*. 5. Yūsuf u Zulaikhā, fol. 164*b*. 6. Laili u Majnūn, fol. 215*b*. 7. Khirad Nāmah i Iskandari, fol. 255*b*.

Copyist: على هجرانى

The first part of the MS., foll. 2—102, is by a later hand, that of 'Abd ur-Raḥīm B. Maḥmūd, and is dated 1 Rabi' I., A.H. 1009 (A.D. 1600).

291.

Or. 4122.—Foll. 178; 16 in. by 10¼; 12 lines, 4⅔ in. long; written in fine large Nestalik, with a gorgeous double-page 'Unvān, illuminated borders and headings, and whole-page miniatures, apparently in the 17th century. Bound in rich stamped and gilt leather covers.

[Tho. Fiott Hughes.]

يوسف و زليخا

Yūsuf u Zulaikhā, by Jāmi. See the Persian Catalogue, p. 645*a*, III.

The miniatures are in fair Persian style and cover the entire page. There are two on opposite pages at the beginning, two similarly placed at the end, and ten in the body of the volume, viz., at foll. 33, 51, 69, 73, 76, 87, 98, 101, 140 and 155.

An English translation by R. T. H. Griffith was published in London, 1882.

Copyist: شاه محمد الکاتب

292.

Or. 4535.—Foll. 156; 11 in. by 6½; 14 lines, 3¾ in. long; written in neat Nestalik with a richly illuminated double-page 'Unvān, gold-ruled columns, and twenty-six miniatures, mostly whole-page or nearly so, in fair Persian style, apparently in the 16th century. Bound in gilt leather covers. [Ẓuhūr ud-Dīn Aḥmad Khān.]

Another copy of Yūsuf u Zulaikhā.

The first page is covered with notes of former owners. The earliest of these states that the MS. was bought at the price of six thousand rupees for the library of Sultan 'Alā ud-Dīn Sikandar Shāh, A.H. 913. But the handwriting betrays a suspicious likeness to that of a much later note, written by the last owner, Maulavi Ḥāji Ẓuhūr ud-Dīn Aḥmad Khān.

Appended to the volume are descriptions of the subjects of the miniatures in Persian and English by the same Ẓuhūr ud-Dīn, foll. 157—183.

293.

Or. 4389.—Foll. 139; 10¾ in. by 6½; 15 lines, 2⅜ in. long; written in small and elegant Nestalik, with a rich double-page 'Unvān, gold-ruled columns, gilt headings, illuminated marginal ornaments on every page, and two whole-page paintings, foll. 58-9, in fair Persian style; dated Bukhara, Sha'bān, A.H. 975 (A.D. 1568). [Wallis Budge.]

A third copy of Yūsuf and Zulaikhā.

It wants a folio in the epilogue, the last lines of which are misplaced at fol. 34.

294.

Or. 4390.—Foll. 129; 7¼ in. by 4; 15 lines, 2½ in. long; written by several hands in a cursive character, probably in the 18th century. [Wallis Budge.]

A fourth copy of the same poem.

295.

Or. 2867.—Foll. 135; 10 in. by 6¾; 20 lines, 4 in. long; written in fine small Nestalik in four gold-ruled columns, with two tasteful 'Unvāns and gold headings, about A.D. 1500. [Sidney Churchill.]

Four poems by Hātifī, who died A.H. 927, viz.:

I. Fol. 2a. هفت منظر, Haft Manẓar, a Masnavi in imitation of the Haft Paikar of Niẓāmi. See the Persian Catalogue, p. 653b, and Ethé, Bodleian Catalogue, no. 1016.

This copy wants the first page. It begins with this verse:

پادشاهی کی بتو نسپرده
کز تواش دیگری تواند بره

II. Fol. 24b. شیرین خسرو, Shirīn Khusrau, the second poem of the Khamsah of Hātifī.

Beg. خداوندا بعشقم زندگی ده
بفرقم تاج عز بندگی نه

See the Oude Catalogue, p. 422; the Vienna Catalogue, vol. i., p. 581; Pertsch, Berlin, nos. 906-7; and Ethé, Bodleian Catalogue, nos. 1013—15.

III. Fol. 50a. لیلی مجنون, Laili Majnūn, the first poem of the Khamsah. See the Persian Catalogue, p. 652b; Pertsch, Berlin Catalogue, nos. 903—5; and Ethé, Bodleian Catalogue, nos. 996—1005.

This copy wants the first page. It begins with this verse:

مایم و ندامت و تحسر
سر کشتهٔ وادی تحیر

IV. Fol. 74*b*. تمر نامه, Timur Nāmah, a poetical history of Timūr, the fourth poem of the Khamsah. See the Persian Catalogue, p. 653*b*; Pertsch, Berlin Catalogue, nos. 908-9; Ethé, Bodleian, nos. 1006—12; and Rehatsek, Mulla Firuz Library, p. 69.

This fine MS. was written by Sulṭān Muḥammad Nūr, a pupil of Sulṭān 'Ali, and one of the penmen employed by Mir 'Alishir.

296.

Or. 3316.—Foll. 97; 7 in. by 4½; 11 lines, 2¼ in. long; written in choice Nestalik, with a neat 'Unvān and gold-ruled columns; dated Herat, 5 Ramazan, A.H. 892 (A.D. 1487).

[Sidney Churchill.]

لیلی مجنون

Laili Majnūn, by Hātifi. See the preceding MS., art. III.

Copyist: علی بن نور

297.

Or. 2838.—Foll. 140; 9 in. by 5¼; 15 lines, 2½ in. long; written in elegant Nestalik, with a neat 'Unvān, gold-ruled columns, gold headings, and three whole-page miniatures in good Persian style (foll. 20, 76, and 121); dated A.H. 945 (A.D. 1538).

[Zuhūr ud-Dīn Aḥmad Khān.]

تمور نامه

Timūr Nāmah, by Hātifi. See no. 295, IV.

Copyist: کمال نشابوری

298.

Or. 3280.—Foll. 109; 5¾ in. by 3½; 10 lines, 1⅞ in. long; written in Neskhi; dated 27 Shavvāl, A.H. 1240 (A.D. 1825).

لیلی و مجنون

Laili u Majnūn, a Masnavi by Maktabi.

Beg. ای بر احدیتت ز آغاز
خلق ازل و ابد هم آواز

Maktabi took his takhalluṣ from his profession, that of a schoolmaster. He lived in Shiraz at the same time as Ahli Shirāzi (d. A.H. 942), and composed the present poem A.H. 895. That date, conveyed by the chronogram کتاب مکتبی, and the number of distichs, amounting to 2160, are given in the following lines of the epilogue (fol. 109*a*):

جون مکتبی این کتاب بکشود
تاریخ کتاب مکتبی بود
ابیات که در حساب پیوست
آمد دو هزار و ششصد و شست

The correct reading of the last line is, according to the next and other copies, یکصد instead of ششصد.

For notices of Maktabi see Taḳi, Oude Catalogue, p. 38, no. 56; Riyāẓ ush-Shu'arā, fol. 414*a*; Ātashkadah, p. 309; and Majma' ul-Fuṣaḥā, vol. ii., p. 40. For other MSS. see the Leyden Catalogue, vol. ii., p. 121; Oude Catalogue, no. 344; Aumer, no. 101; and Ethé, Bodleian Catalogue, no. 892.

Copyist: محمد رضا

299.

Or. 2985.—Foll. 90; 5¾ in. by 3¾; 12 lines, 2 in. long; written in Nestalik; dated 24 Shavvāl, A.H. 1261 (A.D. 1845).

[Henry A. Stern.]

Another copy of the Laili u Majnūn, of Maktabi.

300.

Or. 3379.—Foll. 75; 11¾ in. by 8; 15 lines, 4½ in. long; written in fine Nestalik in the 18th century. [SIDNEY CHURCHILL.]

The Turki Divan of Sulṭān-Ḥusain Baiḳarā, with a Persian paraphrase by Muḥammad Rafi'. See the Turkish Catalogue, p. 299.

301.

Or. 3633.—Foll. 50; 8¼ in. by 5¼; 15 lines, 2¾ in. long; written in Neskhi, with two 'Unvāns and gold-ruled columns; dated Mecca, Sunday, 14 Ramazan, A.H. 951 (A.D. 1544). [J. LEE.]

فتوح الحرمين

A poetical description of the rites of the pilgrimage to Mecca and Medina, by Muḥyi. See the Persian Catalogue, p. 655.

Beg. ای دو جهان غرقهٔ الای تو
کون و مکان قطرهٔ دریای تو

The text agrees closely with the edition lithographed in Lucknow, 1875. The above beginning, which is also that of the Berlin MS. described by Pertsch, no. 214, is the twenty-second Bait of the MS. noticed in the Persian Catalogue, while the latter has the beginning given by Ḥaj. Khal., vol. iv., p. 385. The first line of the Vienna copy, no. 893, 2, is the fifteenth Bait of the present MS.

The second part of the poem, treating of Medina, has a distinct frontispiece, and begins:

باد صبا دان گل بر نشاند
نکهت یثرب بمشام رساند

There are numerous coloured drawings representing the Haram and the various places visited by pilgrims at Mecca and Medina. They correspond closely with the drawings of the Lucknow edition.

At the end, and by another hand, is a certificate of pilgrimage delivered to Ḥāji Ḥaidar Maḥmūd Shāh Zamaki, A.H. 951.

This MS. is noticed in the catalogue of Dr. John Lee, no. 176.

302.

Or. 4124.—Foll. 114; 7¾ in. by 4¾; 12 lines, 2½ in. long; written in small and elegant Nestalik, with a rich and highly-finished double-page 'Unvān at the beginning, and a single-page one further on, gold designs in the margins, and gold-ruled columns; dated A.H. 957 (A.D. 1550). Bound in tastefully painted covers.

[THO. FIOTT HUGHES.]

Two Masnavis by Hilāli, who died A.H. 935 or 936. He was put to death, as stated in Aḥsan ut-Tavārikh, fol. 86*b*, on account of some obnoxious verses, by 'Ubaid Khān Uzbek. The later date, 936, is given by Rāḳim; see Rosen, Institut, p. 126. Sām Mirza assigns a still later date, A.H. 939, to Hilāli's death. See the Persian Catalogue, p. 656.

I. Foll. 1—59. صفات العاشقين, Ṣifāt ul-'Āshiḳin, or "Qualities of Lovers," a mystic poem.

Beg. خداوندا دری از غیب بکشای
جمال شاهد لا ریب بنمای

For other MSS., see the Oude Catalogue, no. 263; Pertsch, Berlin Catalogue, no. 913; and Ethé, no. 1026.

II. Foll. 60—114. شاه و درویش, King and Dervish. See the Persian Catalogue, pp. 656 and 1090*b*; Pertsch, no. 914; and Ethé, no. 1022.

The poem has been translated into German verse by Ethé, Morgenländische Studien, 1870, p. 197.

This copy is due to the well-known calligrapher, Sulṭān Muḥammad Nūr.

303.

Or. 2848.—Foll. 275; 10¼ in. by 7½; 19 lines, 5 in. long; written in fair Nestalik in four gold-ruled columns; dated Zulka'dah, A.H. 965 (A.D. 1558).

[Sidney Churchill.]

کتاب معجزات

A Masnavi poem treating of the lives and miracles of Muḥammad, of 'Ali and of the Imams, by Ḥairati, who died A.H. 961. See the Persian Catalogue, p. 874*b*.

The MS. is somewhat imperfect at the beginning. The first extant chapter has the heading سبب نظم کتاب و تذییل بمدح نواب کامیاب شاه عالم پناه, and begins as follows:

مرا عمری هوای شاعری بود
درین رنگم خیال ساحری بود

After speaking boastfully of the fame he had achieved in various kinds of poetry, such as Ghazals and Kasidahs, the author says that he had not yet tried his hand at Masnavi. On one occasion, when he was present at Court, a book entitled Bahjat, and treating of Muḥammad, 'Ali, and the holy family, having been brought from Shiraz to the Shah, he obtained his Majesty's leave to turn it into Masnavi verse. Hence the present work, which was completed, as stated at the end, A.H. 953. The date is expressed by the title, slightly altered by 'Imālah,' as stated in the following lines, fol. 275*a*:

چو دانایان پی تاریخ اتمام
کمال سعی را دادند انجام
هم از اعجاز این ابیات فاخر
کتیب معجزات آمد بخاطر
ازین معنی دل من فیض یابست
که هم تاریخ و هم نام کتابست

The prologue concludes with a panegyric on Shāh Ṭahmāsp. The work, it is hardly necessary to say, displays the most extravagant 'Ali-worship and the usual Shi'ah perversion of history. The names of the three predecessors of 'Ali in the Khilāfat are duly accompanied by the customary imprecation علیه اللعنة

The work is divided into forty-four sections, فصول, the first of which, fol. 2*b*, has this heading: الفصل الاول در بعضی از علامات نبی علیه الصلوة والسلم. The contents may be briefly described as follows: Faṣl 1—16. Life and miracles of Muḥammad. Faṣl 17. در معجزات امیر المومنین علیه السلام, Prodigies of 'Ali, thirty-nine of which are enumerated, fol. 87*b*. Faṣl 18. Incidents of his life, در بعضی قضایای امیر المومنین, forty in number, fol. 106*a*. Faṣl 19. His merits and eminent parts, fol. 123*a*. Faṣl 20. Election of Abu Bakr, fol. 127*b*. Faṣl 21. Opposition to Abu Bakr, fol. 130*a*. Faṣl 22. History of Fadak, fol. 134*a*. Faṣl 23. Election of 'Umar, fol. 136*a*. Faṣl 24. Proclamation of 'Osman, fol. 139*a*. Faṣl 25. Succession of 'Ali, fol. 143*a*. Faṣl 26. Battle of the Camel, fol. 145*a*. Faṣls 27—29. Battle of Ṣiffīn, fol. 152*b*. Faṣls 30—31. War with the Khawārij, fol. 182*b*. Faṣl 32. Ḥasan and Ḥusain, fol. 188*a*. Faṣl 33. Zain ul-'Ābidīn, fol. 195*a*. Faṣl 34. Muḥammad Bāḳir, fol. 202*b*. Faṣl 35. Ja'far Ṣādiḳ, fol. 211*a*. Faṣl 36. Mūsa Kāẓim, fol. 226*a*. Faṣl 37. 'Ali Riẓa, fol. 233*a*. Faṣl 38. Muḥ. Javād, fol. 246*a*. Faṣl 39. 'Ali Naḳi, fol. 251*b*. Faṣl 40. Ḥasan 'Askari, fol. 260*a*. Faṣls 41—44. Ḥujjat-ullah Ḳā'im biḳusṭās (the Mahdi) and his future advent, foll. 266*a*—274.

304.

Or. 2870.—Foll. 36; 6¾ in. by 4½; 11 lines, 2¾ in. long; written in Shikastah, with gold-ruled margins; dated A.H. 1140 (A.D. 1727-8). [Sidney Churchill.]

رند و زاهد

"The Rake and the Ascete," in prose and verse, by Fuzūli, who died A.H. 963. See the Turkish Catalogue, p. 39b.

Beg. ای برتو سجود زاهدان وقت نماز
وی رغبت رندان بتو هنگام نیاز

The text agrees with the edition lithographed in Teheran, A.H. 1275. The MS. contains seven miniatures in late Persian style, corresponding exactly in their disposition and the attitude of the two personages with the drawings of the Teheran edition. It was written for Muḥammad Mu'min Khān Shīrāzi by his father. A copy is noticed by Pertsch, Berlin Catalogue, no. 683, art. 4.

305.

Or. 4911.—Foll. 244; 7¾ in. by 4¾; 14 lines, 2¾ in. long; written in plain Nestalik; dated Constantinople, 2 Zulka'dah, A.H. 1036 (A.D. 1627).

1. Foll. 2—167. دیوان فضولی

The Divan of Fuzūli, with a preface by the poet, beginning: الله الله چه خزانه ایست
معانی که از ابتدای خلقت اشیا اصحاب شرایع و اهوا
باختلاف مذاهب و آرا

A part of the preface is lost. From the remaining portion it appears that the poet collected these erotic poems, written in an easy Persian style, to comply with the desire of a fair youth who had no taste for his Turkish and Arabic compositions. The collection is far richer than the Divan noticed in the Persian Catalogue, p. 659b. It has no fewer than fifty Ghazals rhyming in Alif against twelve in the latter.

Contents: Ghazals in alphabetical order, fol. 4b, beginning:

باسمك اللهم یا فتاح ابواب المنا
یا غنی الذات یا من فیه برهان الغنا

Tarkīb, fol. 103b, beginning:

خیز ساقی بساط می بر چین
می بمستان بده زیاده ازین

Muḳaṭṭa'āt, fol. 107b, beginning:

در صدف صدق جناب متولی
کز رای منیرش عتباتیست منور

Sāḳi Nāmah, a Masnavi, fol. 118b, beginning:

سر از خواب غفلت چو برداشتم
لوای فراست بر افراشتم

Rubā'is, fol. 130b, beginning:

ای کرده بلطف خرد مکرم مارا

Rind u Zāhid, a Masnavi (see the preceding MS.), foll. 141b—167b. Imperfect at the end. The lost portion corresponds with the last fifteen pages of the Teheran edition.

II. Foll. 168—238. هفت منظر

Haft Manẓar, a Masnavi by Hātifi. See no. 295, I.

This copy wants the prologue and the introductory part of the story. It begins with this line:

چون بهجران اوفتادش کار

which is found at fol. 12b of the complete copy, Add. 26,166.

306.

Or. 4616.—Foll. 283; 8¼ in. by 5; 15 lines, 3 in. long; written in small Nestalik, apparently in India in the 18th century.

دیوان اشکی

The Divan of Ashki, imperfect at the beginning.

Mīr Ashki, a native of Ḳum, went to India and died at Agra, or Delhi, A.H. 972. See the Oude Catalogue, p. 30, no. 349, pp. 56 and 118. The Divan consists almost exclusively of Ghazals in alphabetical order. The first extant begins as follows:

ویران جهان زدیدهٔ تر میکنم بیا
عالم ز کریه زیر و زبر میکنم بیا

The Ghazals rhyming in ب begin, fol. 26*b*, with this line:

دوش وقت صبح دیدم روی آن مه را بخواب
چون شدم بیدار دیدم در مقابل آفتاب

At the end are a few Rubā'is, fol. 281*b*, beginning:

ای آنکه مه از شرم رخت کاشته است
با سبزه لب لعل تو آراسته است

and, fol. 283*a*, some Ḳiṭ'ahs, the first line of which is:

مطلب مال در جهان اشکی
تا نکردی اسیر محنت و غم

The MS. is dated in the twenty-fifth regnal year, probably of Muḥammad Shāh (A.H. 1155): تمت تمام شد بتاریخ دهم ماه محرم سنه ۲۵

307.

Or. 3504.—Foll. 164; 8½ in. by 6¼; 21 lines, 4¼ in. long; written in small and rather cursive Nestalik in four columns; dated Wednesday, 13 Rabi' II., A.H. 973 (A.D. 1565). [Sidney Churchill.]

I. Foll. 1—64. A poem in Masnavi verse, written in imitation of Sa'di's Bustan, and designated in the epilogue by the title بوستان خیال, by 'Abdi.

Beg. بنام بزرك جهان آفرین
که کوید ز جانش جهان آفرین

After the usual sections in praise of God and the Prophet, and a description of the Mi'rāj, the prologue contains a eulogy on the reigning sovereign, Shāh Ṭahmāsp, whose name the poet says he will raise to the sky, as Sa'di immortalised that of Abu Bakr B. Sa'd, fol. 9*b*:

اکر سعدی از نام ابو بکر سعد
خط شاهد نظم را کرد جعد
کنون عبدی از نام طهماسب شاه
سخن را زند بر فلك بارکاه

In a subsequent chapter, fol. 10*a*, سبب نظم کتاب, 'Abdi gives some account of his life and works. Finding that poetry enjoyed but scant favour in his day, he turned to an official career, and obtained a high post in the royal Divan. But, remaining true to his poetical vein, he composed, under the surname of Nuvīdi, Kasidahs, Ghazals, and a Masnavi on the subject of Salāmān and Absāl. He subsequently adopted the above takhalluṣ, 'Abdi, and wrote a Masnavi entitled جوهر فرد, in imitation of the Ḳirān i Sa'dain of Khusrau, and another Masnavi in imitation of Khiẓr Khān u Duval Rāni, by the same poet. These formed the first two poems of a contemplated Khamsah, the present poem being the third. It is divided like its prototype, the Bustan, into ten Bābs, enumerated at the end of the prologue, fol. 11*a*. The author says that his anecdotes are drawn from genuine records, and especially from the recent work of an eminent historian, whose name was Aḥmad (meaning, no doubt, Ḳāẓi Aḥmad Ghaffāri, author of the Nigāristān ; see the Persian Catalogue, p. 106).

The headings of the ten Bābs are as follows:

I. Fol. 12*a*. در شرح حال پادشاهان

II. Fol. 20*a*. در شرح حال وزرا

III. Fol. 24*b*. در شرح حال مستوفیان و کتاب

IV. Fol. 28*b*. در شرح حال علما

V. Fol. 32*a*. در شرح غازیان ظفر فرجام و سپاهیان مریخ انتقام که بمردی و مردانکی بدرجات عالی رسیده اند

This section concludes with a poem, in the style of Firdausi, on the story of Bizhan, بیژن نامه, foll. 35—42.

VI. Fol. 43*a*. در باب شعرا

VII. Fol. 49*b*. در شرح حال اغنیا و ترغیب بجود و سخا

VIII. Fol. 53*a*. در شرح حال فقرا

IX. Fol. 56*b*. در شرح حال عاشقان

X. Fol. 61*a*. در شرح حال جوانان

The work was completed on the second day of Rabī' I., A.H. 961, as stated in the following lines, fol. 64*b*:

بروزی که فردوس من شد درست
دوم روز بود از ربیع نخست
نوشتم بامداد مشکین مداد
مرین خاتمه بر ورق با مراد
چو کسترد کلکم ظلال جلال
فلك یافت تاریخ نظمم ظلال

We learn from Taḳi Kāshi, Oude Catalogue, p. 37, no. 499, that the poet, whose real name was Khwājah Zain ul-'Ābidīn 'Ali, of Shīrāz, filled for many years the office of Mustaufi, that he wrote two Khamsahs in imitation of Niẓāmi, a poem entitled جام جمشید, and three Divans, and that he died in Ardabīl, A.H. 988.

II. Foll. 65—164. خزاین الملکوت

Khazā'in ul-Malakūt, a religious poem by the same 'Abdi.

Beg. ان اولی الشروع بسم الله
ابتدی بسمه و احمد له

The poem deals chiefly in praises of Muḥammad, of the Imams, of the Shāh, and in anecdotes of saints and Sufis. In a short prose-preamble the author enumerates the seven sections, termed Khizānah, into which it is divided. They have the following headings:

I. Fol. 65*b*. خزانهٔ اول موسوم بصحیفهٔ لا ریب مشتمل بر بسمله و حمدله وما یتعلق بهذا الباب

II. Fol. 77*b*. خزانهٔ دوم منعوت بلوح مسطور در نعت خاتم الانبیا

III. Fol. 93*b*. خزانهٔ سیوم مشهور ببحر مسجور محتوی بر مناقب ائمهٔ معصومین

IV. Fol. 114*b*. خزانهٔ چهارم معروف بمنثور شاهی در حسن سیر شاه دین پرور

V. Fol. 129*b*. خزانهٔ پنجم مسمی بمروّج الاسواق در خیرخواهی خواص و عوام

VI. Fol. 146*b*. خزانهٔ ششم مکنی بمهیّج الاشواق در حقیقت عشق و محبت

VII. Fol. 158*b*. خزانهٔ هفتم مدعو بنهایت الاعجاز در خاتمهٔ کتاب

The date of composition, A.H. 968, is conveyed in the following lines, fol. 164*a*:

. . . . . . فراغ ازین فکرت
نهصد و شصت و هشت از هجرت
حظ جانهاست این خجسته کتاب
سال ختمش از حظ جانها یاب

308.

Or. 2986.—Foll. 92; $6\frac{3}{4}$ in. by 4; 13 lines, $2\frac{3}{4}$ in. long; written in fair Nestalik, with 'Unvān and gold-ruled margins, about the middle of the 19th century, with eleven miniatures in modern Persian style.

[H. A. Stern.]

فرهاد و شیرین

Farhād u Shirīn, a Masnavi by Vaḥshi, who died A.H. 991 (Persian Catalogue, p. 663*b*), with a continuation by Viṣāl Shirāzi, who died A.H. 1263 (v. Majma' ul-Fuṣaḥā, vol. ii., p. 528).

Beg. الهی سینهٔ ده آتش افروز
دران سینه دلی وان دل همه سوز

For other MSS. see the Persian Catalogue, p. 663*b*, III.; the Berlin Catalogue, no. 918; Ethé, Bodleian Catalogue, nos. 1039—42; and Rosen, Institut, p. 262.

The continuation by Viṣāl begins, fol. 43*a*, as follows:

هزاران پرده بر قانون عشقست
بهر یك نغمها ز افسون عشقست

Vaḥshi's original poem with the continuation of Viṣāl has been lithographed in Teheran, A.H. 1263. Both are included in the Divan of Viṣāl, lithographed in Teheran, A.H. 1275.

309.

Or. 4913.—Foll. 175; 8 in. by $4\frac{1}{2}$; 14 lines, $2\frac{3}{4}$ in. long; written in fair Nestalik; dated 1 Muḥarram, A.H. 1048 (A.D. 1638).

I. Foll. 1—90. دیوان ثنائی

The Divan of Ṣanāi's Mashhadi.

Beg. در روش حسن نازهست بسی خوش نما
عشوه بطرز ستم غمزه برنك جفا

The poet, whose proper name was Mir Ḥusain B. Ghiyāṣ ud-Dīn, lived in Khorasan in the reign of Shah Ṭahmāsp, and visited India under Akbar. There he associated with Faiẓi and 'Urfi. He died A.H. 996. See the Oude Catalogue, pp. 43, 120; Sham' i Anjuman, p. 102; and Khair ul-Bayān fol. 244*b*.

Contents: Kasidahs in alphabetical order, fol. 1*b*. Muḳaṭṭa'āt, fol. 65*a*, beginning:

شهریارا بجاك درکه تو
که خدایش نیافرید سما

A Masnavi, fol. 68*b*, beginning:

بیا دل بمیخانهٔ اهل راز
بکش جام معنی صورت کداز

Ghazals alphabetically arranged, fol. 74*a*, beginning:

راندی بخشم از بر خود ای پسر مرا
صد خار حسرتست ازین در جکر مرا

Rubā'is, fol. 85*a*, beginning:

فریاد که دیده غرق خون کرد مرا
دل از ره عقل و دین برون کرد مرا

For other copies see the Oude Catalogue, p. 578; Ethé, Bodleian Catalogue, no. 1045; and Pertsch, Berlin Catalogue, no. 919.

II. Foll. 93—175. Kasidahs of 'Urfi without alphabetical arrangement. They begin, as in the Divan noticed by Sprenger, p. 528, with this line:

اقبال کرم میکزد ارباب همم را
همت نخورد نیشتر لا و نعم را

The MS. breaks off in the middle of a Kasidah beginning:

سری در عهد سامانی ندارد
کسی کر آب دارد نان ندارد

310.

Or. 2079.—Foll. 217; 9 in. by 5; 17 lines, 2¾ in. long; written in cursive Nestalik; dated Tuesday, 22 Rabī' II., A.H. 1033 (A.D. 1624). [H. A. STERN.]

دیوان عرفی شیرازی

The Divan of 'Urfi Shīrāzi.

Beg. دادم بچشم او دل اندیشه پیشه را
غافل که زود میشکند مست شیشه را

Contents: 1. An alphabetical series of Ghazals, the first of which, beginning as above, is found in the Cawnpore edition of the Kulliyyāt, A.H. 1297, p. 5, margin. The series ends with the first Ghazal in ه (*ib.* p. 108, margin), beginning:

ساغر لبریز وصل بر کف مشتاق نه

2. Another alphabetical series of Ghazals, extending from ا to ش, beginning, fol. 19*b*:

روشن شد آفتاب چراغش زداغ ما

The last Ghazal (Cawnpore edition, p. 77, margin), begins:

کجاست نشتر مژکان دوست تا دل ریش

3. Kasidahs, without alphabetical arrangement, fol. 57*b*, with the usual beginning:

ای متاع درد در بازار جان انداخته

4. The latter part of an alphabetical series of Ghazals from ن to ی, fol. 94*a*, beginning with the first Ghazal in ن (Cawnpore edition, p. 103), the first line of which is:

پیش بردم در قمار عشق جانان باختن

5. Another series of Kasidahs, fol. 99*b*, beginning (Cawnpore edition, i., p. 15):

جهان بکشتم و دردا که هیچ شهر و دیار

This is the Kasidah known as ترجمة الاشواق. See no. 419, XII.

6. Muḳaṭṭa'āt, fol. 136*b*, beginning (*ib.*, p. 120):

منم عرفی امروز کز کشت طبعم
بود خرمن افشان کف خوشه چینان

7. Majma' ul-Abkār, a Masnavi in imitation of the Makhzan ul-Asrār of Niẓāmi, followed by some other Masnavis, and beginning, fol. 144*b*:

بسم الله الرحمن الرحیم
موج نخستست ز بحر قدیم

See the Persian Catalogue, p. 667*b*, III.; the Berlin Catalogue, no. 920, art. 2; the Bodleian Catalogue, no. 1051, no. 114*b*; and the Cawnpore edition, p. 138.

8. Fragments of a Masnavi on Farhād and Shirin, the same as in the following MS., art. II., and in the same order, fol. 186*b*:

9. Rubā'is, fol. 199*b*. The same as in the following MS., art. I.

10. Twenty-one additional Rubā'is, foll. 215*b*—217*a*. Compare the کلیات عرفی, described by Rosen, Institut, no. 84.

311.

Or. 3204.—Foll. 28; 9½ in. by 4⅛; 19 lines, 2⅓ in. long; written in Nestalik, apparently in the 18th century. [KREMER, no. 182.]

I. Foll. 1*b*—17*a*. Rubā'is by 'Urfi, about

two hundred in number, without alphabetical arrangement.

Beg. یا رب نفسی ده که ثنا پردازم
وین نغمه باهنك نوا پردازم

The same Rubā'i, with سزا instead of نوا, is found in the Cawnpore edition of the Kulliyāt, A.H. 1297, p. 134. The last Rubā'i contains in its last hemistich,

اول دیوان عرفی شیرازی

a chronogram for A.H. 996, the year in which the Divan of 'Urfi was completed.

II. Foll. 17*b*—28*a*. Some Masnavis, also by 'Urfi.

Beg. صباحی دلکشا جون خنده حور
که شادی مست بود اندوه مخمور

The first and longest relates to a meeting of Shirin and Farhād. Some of the next-following pieces also relate to Farhād. The name of 'Urfi appears in the following line, fol. 25*b*:

کرامت کن بعرفی جند جامی
من آرام سوزی درد نامی

These are evidently detached fragments of the Masnavi Farhād u Shīrīn, mentioned in the Persian Catalogue, p. 667*b*, iv. The opening line quoted there, خداوندا دلم بی نور تنکست, is found among the present fragments, fol. 24*b*. The same beginning is noticed in the Oude Catalogue, p. 527; in the Berlin Catalogue, no. 920, art. 3; and by Rosen, Institut, p. 262.

312.

Or. 2872.—Foll. 245; 9½ in. by 5¾; 15 lines, about 3 in. long; written in fair Nestalik in two gold-ruled columns, with an 'Unvān, apparently in the 17th century.

[Sidney Churchill.]

دیوان امانی

The Turkish and Persian Divans of Amāni, an Amīr of Turkish race, who lived under Shāh Ṭahmāsp and Shāh 'Abbās I., and died probably shortly after A.H. 1016. See the Turkish Catalogue, p. 301.

The Persian Divan occupies foll. 90—245. It begins with an alphabetical series of Ghazals, wanting the first page or two. The first complete Ghazal begins as follows:

بود یا رب دمد صبح وصال این شام هجرانرا
صبا آرد بوی ما شمیم جعد جانانرا

The last Ghazal, which breaks off before the end, fol. 175*b*, begins:

تشریف بویرانه ام اوردی و رفتی
افزوده بدرد دل و جان دردی و رفتی

The remainder of the Divan is not in its original order. Some folios are lost and others are transposed. It contains: 1. Masnavis, the first of which, fol. 176, is imperfect at the beginning. The second, fol. 177*a*, begins as follows:

آفرید آفریدکار غفور
پیش از هر دو کون آن یکنور

2. Rubā'is, in alphabetical order, fol. 190*b*, with the exception of the first, which begins:

آنانکه بدرکهت پناه آوردند
عفوی عجبی پی کناه آوردند

3. Muḳaṭṭa'āt, fol. 204*a*, beginning:

بکاشان یکی اهرمن کشته آصف
که از خلق او خلق را دل دو نیست

4. Tarjī'āt, fol. 212*a*. The first piece wants the beginning. The next is in praise of Shāh Ṭahmāsp and has the following burden:

پادشاه عادل و ظل اله
سید عالی نسب طهماسب شاه

5. Kasidahs, fol. 225*b*, beginning:

يا شفيع الذنوب شد پيدا
بطفيلت دو كون وما فيها

313.

Or. 2839.—Foll. 23; 8½ in. by 4¾; 15 lines, 2½ in. long; written in fair Nestalik on gold-sprinkled paper, with 'Unvān, gold-ruled margins, and three whole-page miniatures, in highly finished Indian style, 17th century. [Ḥaji Zuhūr ud-Dīn.]

سوز و كداز

"Sūz u Gudāz," a poem by Nau'ī. See the Persian Catalogue, p. 674*a*; the Bodleian Catalogue, no. 1064; and the Berlin Catalogue, no. 928.

At the beginning are two seals, one with the name Sulaimān and the date A.H. 1146, the other bearing the name of Archibald Swinton Rustam Jang Bahādur, in the Persian character, and the date 1174 (A.H.).

314.

Or. 3274.—Foll. 102; 7¼ in. by 3½; 15 lines, 2¼ in. long; written in fair Nestalik in two gold-ruled columns, on gold-sprinkled paper, apparently in the 17th century. [S. de Sacy.]

I. Foll. 1—79. خسرو و شيرين

"Khusrau u Shīrīn," a Masnavi by Ja'far.

Beg. خداوندا رهى از غيب بنماى
زغيبم جشم دل برعيب بكشاى

The author is Ja'far Beg Ḳazvīnī, afterwards Āṣaf Khān, who died under Jahāngīr, A.H. 1021. See the Persian Catalogue, p. 118*a*. It is stated in Ma'āṣir ul-Umarā, fol. 20*b*, that, in the opinion of many judges, no one after Niẓāmī had told the story of Khusrau and Shīrīn better than Ja'far Beg.

In the prologue the poet says that he had been from an early age addicted to poetry, and that, having been compelled by adverse fortune to seek employment by the pen and the sword, he had repaired from Iran to Hindustan, and had found a generous patron in the person of the sovereign Jahāngīr, to whom a long panegyric is devoted. The narrative begins on fol. 11*b*, and the last section, fol. 78*b*, has the heading كابين كردن شيرين خسرورا. The last line is:

ز زر چندانكه كان زان بيش و كم داشت
ز كوهر انچه دريا در شكم داشت

The poem has apparently been left unfinished. For another copy see Ethé, Bodleian Catalogue, no. 1069.

II. Foll. 80—101. Kasidahs, Ḳiṭ'ahs, Ghazals, &c., by the same Ja'far, without any systematic arrangement.

Beg. زهى سلاسل زلفت كمند كردن جان
شكست خورده زچشم تو لشكر ايمان

Some of the Kasidahs are addressed to Akbar, others to Jahāngīr. Among the Ḳiṭ'ahs are chronograms for the death of the former and the accession of the latter. Towards the end, fol. 98*b*, is a Tarjī' of some length, beginning:

افسوس كه روزكار بركشت
غم آمد و غمكسار بركشت

The MS. is described in S. de Sacy's Catalogue, Paris, 1842, "Manuscrits," p. 45, no. 262.

315.

Or. 3275.—Foll. 62; 7 in. by 3½; 15 lines, 2 in. long; written in neat Nestalik with gold-ruled columns, apparently in the 17th century.

فرهاد و شيرين

An earlier recension of the poem noticed under the preceding no., art. I., endorsed نسخهٔ فرهاد و شيرين

Beg. خداوندا دلی ده شاد از اندوه
درو گنجایش غم کوه تا کوه

It is substantially the same work as the Khusrau u Shirin, in a somewhat shorter form. The second line,

دلی از خارخار عشق پر نیش
ز هر نیشی دو صد جا بیشتر ریش

is identical with the sixth in the preceding text.

The present MS. ends with this line:

که حال جوی شیرین باز داند
باستقبالش ارد کسر تواند

The same line, slightly altered, is found in the preceding copy, fol. 66*b*. It is the thirteenth Bait of the section inscribed رفتن خسرو بقصر شيرين و شكار را بهانه ساختن

A MS. with the same beginning, and dated as early as A.H. 995, is described by Ethé, Bodleian Catalogue, no. 1068. The present MS., however, contains a text of later date; for the prologue includes a panegyric on Jahāngir, who is explicitly named in this line, fol. 9*a*:

جوان شد بار دیگر عالم پیر
بعهد شاه نور الدین جهانگیر

The above beginning is given by Haj. Khal., vol. iii., p. 138, as that of the Khusrau u Shirin of Āṣaf Khān.

316.

Or. 3255.—Foll. 231; 8½ in. by 4½; 17 lines, 2½ in. long; written in fair Nestalik; dated Rabi' I., A.H. 1070 (A.D. 1659).

[Sidney Churchill.]

ديوان نظيرى

The Divan of Naẓiri, of Nishapur, who died in India, A.H. 1022. See the Persian Catalogue, p. 817*b*.

Contents: Ghazals in alphabetical order, beginning:

اذاما شيت ان تحيى حيوة حلوه المحيا

Rubā'is, fol. 150*b*, beginning:

ای از تو صور نگار هر جا کوری

Kasidahs, fol. 159*b*, beginning:

ای جلالت خلوت از اغیار تنها ساخته

For other copies see the Oude Catalogue, p. 515; Ethé, no. 1074; and Pertsch, Berlin Catalogue, no. 929.

317.

Or. 2952.—Foll. 145; 8¼ in. by 5; 12 lines, 2 in. long; written in fair Nestalik with a rich double-page 'Unvān, gold-ruled columns and gilt headings; dated Monday, 14 Rabi' II., A.H. 1058 (A.D. 1648). Bound in painted and glazed covers. [Sidney Churchill.]

محمود و آياز

"Maḥmūd u Āyāz," a Masnavi by Zulāli, who died about A.H. 1025. See the Persian Catalogue, p. 677*a*.

Copyist: محمد سعيد

There are two whole-page miniatures in Persian style, foll. 65 and 71.

For other copies see Pertsch, Berlin Catalogue, no. 933, and Ethé, Bodleian Catalogue, no. 1081, art. 7.

318.

Or. 3667.—Foll. 96; 7¼ in. by 4¼; 12 lines, 2¼ in. long; written in small and neat Nestalik, with four 'Unvāns and gold-ruled columns, A.H. 1049 (A.D. 1639).

[Sidney Churchill.]

I. Foll. 1—49. دیوان ابو تراب بیك

The Divan of Abu Turāb Beg.

Beg. دگر ز لاله نو رسته کوه فصل بهار
چو مادریست که فرزند پرورد بکنار

The author was a native of Jūshḳān, who lived in Kashan in the reign of Shāh 'Abbās I. He asked Ṣādiḳi Beg, a poet of Isfahan, to bestow upon him a takhalluṣ, but before he had time to use it, he took to opium and left off writing verses. He died A.H. 1026 (Ṣubḥi Gulshan, p. 10). Taḳi Kāshi, Oude Catalogue, p. 24, no. 258, speaks of him as one of his contemporaries. In Khair ul-Bayān, fol. 320b, he is mentioned as the favourite poet of Shāh 'Abbās I., and as being still alive (A.H. 1019).

Contents: Kasidahs, &c., fol. 1b. A Sāḳi Nāmah in Tarjī' form, fol. 5b, beginning:

ساقی بده آن جام که ماه شب تارست
آن باده که گلگونه رخسار بهارست

A Narrative in Masnavi verse, fol. 16b, beginning:

راوی افسانه ارباب جود
پردهٔ رخسار معانی کشود

Chronograms relating to contemporary events in Kashan, with dates ranging from A.H. 1005 to 1012, fol. 22b.

Ghazals alphabetically arranged, fol. 23a, beginning:

ای ز تو بند بر زبان نطق سخن سرای را
فکر تو باعث جنون عقل گره کشای را

Rubā'is, fol. 48a, beginning:

روزی که لبت را بشراب اندازد
یاقوت لبت بمشك ناب اندازد

II. Foll. 50—73. دیوان نصیر

The Divan of Naṣīr i Hamadāni, with a short preface by the author, beginning: یگانهٔ که هزار و یك نام مبارکش هزار و یك شمع برافروخت

Khwājah Naṣīr ud-Dīn B. Khwājah Maḥmūd, also called Naṣīrā, of an ancient and noble family of Hamadān, went to India to the court of Akbar, and thence to that of Ḳuṭubshāh (Riyāẓ ush-Shu'arā, fol. 456a). He died A.H. 1030 (Nigāristān i Sukhan, p. 122).

Contents: Kasidahs, fol. 52b, beginning:

زهی نقاب تو فانوس چشم بزم حضور
بملك حسن تو صحرا نشین تجلی طور

Sāḳi Nāmah in Tarjī' form, fol. 65b, beginning:

ساقی بده آن می که جگر گوشه جامست
زان شیشه که در بزم طرب پیش سلامست

Muḳaṭṭa'āt, fol. 69a, beginning:

ایکه از تاب شعلهٔ طبعت
خشك شد نخل وادی ایمن

At the end is a chronogram for the taking of Ganjah, by Shah 'Abbās, A.H. 1015.

Ghazals beginning, fol. 73b, with a separate 'Unvān:

خدا ز شهر بگرداند آفت مارا
که داده گریه ما سر بکوه و صحرا را

Rubā'is, fol. 88b, beginning:

وقتست که دهقان فلك گردد سست
در سنبله اش حبه نماند چو نخست

319.

Or. 2998.—Foll. 126; 7 in. by 4; 10 lines, 2 in. long; written in elegant Nestalik, with three double-page 'Unvāns and gold-ruled columns, apparently early in the 17th century. [Sidney Churchill.]

دیوان نظام دست غیب

The Divan of Nizām Dast i Ghaib.

The author, whose full name is Mirza Nizām ul-Mulk, son of Amir Amin ud-Din

Husain, belonged to an illustrious family of Sayyids of Shiraz, called Sādāt i Dast i Ghaib. The author of Khair ul-Bayān speaks of him, fol. 347, as a highly talented young man, whom he met on his way to Mecca (A.H. 1017), and gives copious specimens of his poetry.

In a preface occupying the first eighteen pages of the MS., Abu Ḥayyān Māli, an intimate friend of the poet, dwells on his remarkable genius and poetical taste, and deplores his premature death, which took place on Sunday the 25th of Zulḥijjah, A.H. 1029, adding that he was buried opposite the tomb of Ḥāfiẓ. The above date was embodied by the poet's uncle in the following chronogram:

پرسیدم از ارباب خرد تاریخش
کفتند نماند پادشاه شعرا

The Divan, which spread rapidly in the author's lifetime, is described as consisting of about 2500 Baits and being chiefly devoted to praises of the Prophet and the Imams. The preface was written in the last decade of Ramazan, A.H. 1030. Ṭāhir Naṣrābādi gives also A.H. 1029 as the date of Niẓām's death, adding that he was then only thirty years of age (Add. 7087, fol. 204).

Contents of the Divan: Kasidahs, fol. 10*b*, beginning:

ز دیده بیرخ او دل نمیشود روشن
چو آفتاب نباشد چه سود از روزن

Ghazals, fol. 30*b*, beginning:

ذوق محبتی کو تا سر کنم فغانرا
ویران کنم بآهی بنیاد آسمانرا

Rubā'is, fol. 83*b*, beginning:

آن رفت که دل وصل نکاری میخواست
در بزم پریرخان قراری میخواست

Masnavis, fol. 96*b*, beginning:

دلا چند بینی شکست از خمار
شکستی کرت هست در توبه آر

Tarji'āt and Tarkibs, the first of which is a Sāḳi Nāmah, fol. 105*a*, beginning:

ساقی بده آن می که برنك لب یارست
آن می که رخ ساقی ازو رشك بهارست

Copyist: محمد قاسم کاتب

320.

Or. 3505.—Foll. 211; 10 in. by 6½; 11 lines, 4¼ in. long; written in large Nestalik, apparently in the 17th century. [Sidney Churchill.]

دیوان علی نقی کمرهٔ

The Divan of 'Ali Naḳi Kamara'i, who died, according to Ṭāhir Naṣrābādi (Oude Catalogue, p. 91), A.H. 1030. See the Persian Catalogue, p. 818*a*, iv., and Or. 2975, v. Mir Ḥusain mentions him in Khair ul-Bayān, fol. 310, as still alive.

To the Divan is prefixed a prose preface by the author, containing a dedication to Imām Ḳuli Khān (see the Persian Catalogue, p. 681*a*), whom he begs to excuse him for not attending his court. It begins as follows, fol. 1*b*: حمدی که شاه بیت قصیدهٔ کمال را شاید درخور خداوندیست

Contents of the Divan: Kasidahs in praise of Shāh 'Abbās, Ḥātim Beg, Murshid Ḳuli Khān, Imām Ḳuli Khān and others, beginning:

چو خفتکان لحد را صباح روز نشور
ز خواب مرك جهاند نهیب نفخه صور

Chronograms, fol. 66*a*, beginning:

اعتماد الدوله حاتم بیك کامد
اسمانش بندهٔ کیوان غلامی

This section contains two chronograms for A.H. 1018. This shows that the date A.H. 1013, assigned in Riyāẓ ush-Shu'arā to the author's death, is too early.

Ghazals in alphabetical order, fol. 82*b*, beginning:

ای نام همایونت طغراچه فرمانها
خورشید صفت طالع از مطلع دیوانها

Rubā'is, fol. 200*b*, beginning:

کم حوصلگیست اینکه سالك بیگاه
خواهد شود از حقیقت عشق آگاه

321.

Or. 3324.—Foll. 160; 9 in. by 6; 5 lines, 2¾ in. long; written in fair Nestalik, with 'Unvāns and gold-ruled columns, in the 17th century. Bound in stamped leather covers.

[Sidney Churchill.]

دیوان شاپور

The Divan of Shāpūr, of Teheran, who died about A.H. 1030. See the Persian Catalogue, p. 674*b*, and Ethé, Bodleian Catalogue, no. 1072.

Contents: Kasidahs, mostly in praise of 'Ali and the Imams, beginning:

چه مژده دارد ازان شاخ گل نسیم بهار
که رقص میکند از شوق بر سرم دستار

Two Tarjī's, fol. 21*b*, beginning:

عشق از سر زلف صید بندی
تاییده بعشق من کمندی

Masnavis, fol. 29*b*, beginning:

صباحی زاب کوثر روی شسته
گلی از چشمهٔ خورشید رسته

Ghazals in alphabetical order, fol. 38, beginning with the same line as the Divan described in the Persian Catalogue.

Rubā'is, fol. 152*b*, beginning:

بر خیز چه خفتی ای ندیم سحری
کاورد سفیده دم شمیم سحری

This last section appears to be imperfect at the end.

Shāpūr went twice to India, A.H. 996, and again A.H. 1019, and was treated there with great distinction. He returned thence to Persia, where he was still living when Mir Ḥusain wrote his Khair ul-Bayān (see fol. 314), *i.e.* A.H. 1019—1035.

322.

Or. 4912.—Foll. 191; 11 in. by 7; 12 lines, 4 in. long; written in fair large Nestalik, with 'Unvāns, illuminated headings, and ornamental borders throughout, dated A.H. 1054 (A.D. 1644).

دیوان میرك

The Divan of Mīrak, composed in close imitation of the Divan of Ḥāfiẓ, with a prose preface by the author, beginning: تمجید و تحمید خالقی که قایل کلام معجز نظام انا افصح العرب والعجم الخ

Mīrak Naḳḳāsh, or Mīrak the painter, says in the preface that he was at heart a Dervish and a worshipper of the great mystic Ḥāfiẓ. His Divan includes, fol. 182*b*, a Masnavi in praise of Shah 'Abbās II., and a chronogram for his accession, A.H. 1052. It appears from a short epilogue that the Divan was composed in the next following year in the space of four months. The date is expressed by this chronogram:

جستی تاریخش از خرد گفت
بی جهد بگو جواب حافظ

Contents: A long Tarjī'-band, fol. 4*a*, beginning:

تا مهر رخ تو شد دل آرا
شد دیده عقل و عشق بینا

A Sāḳi Nāmah, fol. 13*a*, with this burden:

ساقی بده آن باده که در ظل سحابیم
لب تشنه رخساره آن آتش و آبیم

Ghazals in alphabetical order, fol. 14*b*, beginning:

بده ساقی می گلرنك تا شوید غم از دلها
که از ملك دل هر یك بر آرد کام حاصلها

Masnavis with the heading مناجات نامه, fol. 177*b*. Chronogram on the accession of 'Abbās, and Rubā'is alphabetically arranged, fol. 183*b*. A Masnavi entitled حکایت قضا و قدر, fol. 187*b*.

Copyist: طاهر ابن محمد جان نقاش کاشی

323.

Or. 3319.—Foll. 315; $11\frac{3}{4}$ in. by $6\frac{1}{4}$; 15 lines, 3 in. long; written in fair Nestalik, with two 'Unvāns and gold-ruled columns; dated Zul-ḥijjah, A.H. 1071 (A.D. 1661).

[Sidney Churchill.]

دیوان قدسی

The Divan of Ḳudsi, who died in India A.H. 1056. See the Persian Catalogue, p. 684*b*.

Contents: Preface by Mulla Ṭughrā, fol. 1*b*. See the Persian Catalogue, p. 685, v., and Ethé, no. 1102, art. I.

Kasidahs in alphabetical order, fol. 8*b*, beginning:

من آن نیم که کنم سرکشی ز تیغ جفا

The same beginning in the Oude Catalogue, p. 536; Berlin, no. 941; and Bodleian, no. 1102, art. 6.

Tarkībs, fol. 93*a*, beginning as in the Persian Catalogue, p. 685, II.:

سنك زیر سر ز سرکردانیم سنك اسیاست

Ghazals alphabetically arranged, fol. 119*a*, beginning:

داده عشقم باده نابی که میسوزد مرا

See the Oude Catalogue, *l.c.*, and Berlin, no. 940, art. 3.

Rubā'is in alphabetical order, fol. 190*a*, beginning:

سر حلقه مباش بزم روزردانرا

A long Masnavi called ظفر نامه, on the victories of Shāhjahān, fol. 199*b*, beginning:

بنام خدائی که داد از شهان
جهان پادشاهی بشاه جهان

and other Masnavis. See the Persian Catalogue, p. 685, VIII.; Ethé, no. 1106; and Berlin Catalogue, no. 940, art. 1.

Copyist: محمد جعفر بن محمد طاهر الحسینی قدم کاهی

324.

Or. 3234.—Foll. 257; 9 in. by 5; 21 lines, $2\frac{3}{4}$ in. long; written in fair Nestalik with gold-ruled columns; dated Muḥarram, A.H. 1029 (A.D. 1619). Bound in gilt and stamped leather covers.

[Sidney Churchill.]

دیوان فیاض

The Divan of Fayyāẓ Lāhiji.

Beg. چو زهرۀ صبوح از افق بسازد جنك
زمانه نیز کند ناله مرا آهنك

Fayyāẓ is the takhalluṣ of the celebrated philosopher, Mullā 'Abd ur-Razzāḳ B. 'Ali Lāhiji, who died under Shāh 'Abbās II., about A.H. 1060. See above, no. 9, and Ḳiṣaṣ ul-Khāḳāni, fol. 157. His Divan contains poems in praise of his master Mullā Ṣadrā, of Mir Bāḳir Dāmād, and of Shāh Ṣafi.

Contents: Kasidahs, fol. 1*b*. Muḳaṭṭa'āt, fol. 79*a*, beginning:

صدر جهان و عالم جان و سپهر فضل

Tarkībs, fol. 85*b*, beginning:

السلام ای کوهرت در پای عدل و داد و دین

Ghazals, in alphabetical order, fol. 105*b*, beginning:

الهی فیض مشرب ده که دلگیرم ز مذهبها
نمیدانم چه میخوانند این طفلان بمکتبها

Rubā'is, fol. 235*b*, beginning:

فیاض ازل که بزم هستی آراست
جام صحن از می معانی پیراست

A Sāki Nāmah and other Masnavis, fol. 244*a*, beginning:

بیا ساقی اسباب می ساز کن
سر خم بنام خدا باز کن

325.

Or. 4391.—Foll. 347; 10 in. by 5¾; 12 lines, 4½ in. long; written in large and cursive Nestalik, apparently in the 17th century. [Wallis Budge.]

دیوان حاذق

The Divan of Ḥāẕiḳ, beginning:

حاذق ز کجا ترا چه سان آوردند
زآرامکه عدم دوان آوردند

From several passages of the Divan (foll. 33*b*, 31*b*, 35*b*) it appears that the author lived in India under Shāhjahān, and was over seventy years of age at the time of writing. This is sufficient to establish his identity with Ḥakīm Ḥāẕiḳ B. Humām B. Maulānā 'Abd ur-Razzāḳ Gīlāni, who was born at Fatḥpūr Sikri, near Agra, in the reign of Akbar, was sent by Shāhjahān on a mission to the Uzbek prince Imām Ḳuli Khān, and was afterwards appointed, in the fourth year of the reign, to the confidential post of عرض مکرر. In his old age he retired to Agra, where he died A.H. 1068. See Ma'āṣir ul-Umarā, Add. 6565, fol. 154; Riyāẓ ush-Shu'arā, fol. 122; Makhzan ul-Gharā'ib, fol. 116*b*; and Sham' i Anjuman, p. 127. Verses quoted in the Makhzan are found in the present MS.

The Divan has a marked religious and Shī'ah character. It is divided into two sections, the first of which, foll. 1—39, contains Rubā'is, and the second, foll. 40—347, Ghazals in alphabetical order. The latter is imperfect at the beginning. The first complete Ghazal begins:

آنکه می نوشد زلعلت بشکند پیمانه را
آنکه در کوی تو ره یابد بسوزد خانه را

There is a lacuna extending from the beginning of letter ش to that of letter م, and in the latter part the original order has been disturbed in the binding.

The original colophon has been erased, and a spurious one, with the date سنة ستة مایه عشرین, has been substituted for it.

326.

Or. 2849.—Foll. 43; 6½ in. by 3½; 15 lines, 1¾ in. long; written in small and neat Nestalik, with gold-ruled columns, probably in the 17th century. [Sidney Churchill.]

دیوان شیدا

The Divan of Shaidā, imperfect at beginning and end.

Shaidā was born in Fatḥpūr, a town near Agra, where his father, a native of Mashhad, had settled. He served under Jahāngīr and Shāhjahān, and died in Kashmīr about A.H. 1080. See the Persian Catalogue, p. 1083*a*; Riyāẓ ush-Shu'arā, fol. 246*b*; Sham'i Anjuman, p. 220; and Hamishah Bahār, Oude Catalogue, p. 124.

The MS. contains only Ghazals in alphabetical order. The first extant begins as follows:

نه موج آب نکارد نکار زلف ترا
نه دست باد زند شانه مار زلف ترا

The Ghazals come to an end on the last page, at the bottom of which the Rubā'is begin as follows:

ای همچو سرشك از مژه برجسته زمن
ای بوده ترا کریز چون بسته زمن

327.

Stowe, Or. 15.—Foll. 196; 9 in. by 5½; 12 lines, 2½ in. long; written in fair Nestalik, probably about the close of the 17th century.

دیوان فرج

The Divan of Faraj-ullah Shūshtari, who uses Faraj as his poetical name.

Beg. اذا ناولتنی الصهباء ذقتها ثم ناولها
کزان لب نشاه کوثر رساند باده در دلها

Faraj-ullah, a native of Shūshtar, went over to India, and was seen by Taḳi Auḥadi in Kambāyat (Riyāẓ ush-Shu'arā, fol. 333b). He settled in Haiderabad, and was raised to rank and wealth by the Ḳuṭubshāh, namely 'Abdullah Ḳuṭubshāh, who reigned A.H. 1035—83, and is mentioned in the following line of the Divan, fol. 58b:

رشك ایران شد دکن در عهد عبد الله شاه
هر چه خواهی است اما بادهٔ شیراز نیست

See Sham'i Anjuman, p. 374. His Arabic verses are praised by Sayyid 'Ali Ma'ṣūm (Arabic Supplement, p. 625), who saw him in his father's house in Haiderabad, and says that the poet was then (about A.H. 1080) seventy years old. See Sulāfat al-'Aṣr, Or. 120, fol. 440b. Faraj-ullah is also mentioned by Ṭāhir Naṣrābādi among contemporary poets. See the Oude Catalogue, p. 98.

The Divan consists mainly of Ghazals in alphabetical order. These are followed, fol. 183b, by a few Ḳiṭ'ahs, and, foll. 184b—194a, by Rubā'is beginning:

ای رازق وحش و طیر و بی نطق و فصیح
قسمت بحسن رسان و روزی بقبیح

On the first page is a note of a former owner, Aḥmad B. Mūsa Ruhāvi, dated A.H. 1122.

328.

Or. 3282.—Foll. 512; 10¼ in. by 5¾; 17 lines, 3¾ in. long; written in Nestalik, with four 'Unvāns and gold-ruled columns; dated A.H. 1104 (A.D. 1692-3). [S. de Sacy.]

دیوان صائب

The Divan of Ṣā'ib, of Tabrīz, who died A.H. 1088. See the Persian Catalogue, p. 693a.

Contents: Kasidahs, fol. 1b, beginning:

بادها مشکین نفس شد ابرها کوهر نثار
خوش بآیین تمام امسال آید نو بهار

Ghazals, in alphabetical order, fol. 18b, beginning, as in the Lucknow edition of A.H. 1292, and several MSS.:

اکر نه مد بسم الله بودی تاج عنوانها

Fardiyyāt, also alphabetically arranged, fol. 421b, beginning:

نیست سوی حق بجز تسلیم راه بنده را

Short pieces of two or three Baits, in alphabetical order, foll. 430b—512b, beginning:

ای خار و خس بجز ثنای تو صحنها

Copyist: عبد الجلیل ولد شاه خلیل خراسانی

The MS. is mentioned in the Catalogue of S. de Sacy's Library, Manuscrits, p. 49, no. 288. For other copies see Rosen, Institut, p. 264; Pertsch, Berlin Catalogue, no. 956; and Ethé, no. 1131.

329.

Or. 2694.—Foll. 779; 10¼ in. by 5¾; 16 lines, 3¼ in. long; written in cursive Nestalik, with 'Unvān and ruled columns; dated 15 Zul-ka'dah in the 26th regnal year of Muḥammad Shāh=A.H. 1156 (A.D. 1743).

[E. B. Eastwick.]

The second volume of a most extensive collection of Ṣā'ib's poems.

It contains the latter half of the Ghazals in their alphabetical arrangement from letter ذ to letter ی.

The first Ghazal, which is found at p. 484 of the Lucknow edition of A.H. 1202, begins:

ای بیاد لعل میکون تو کام جان لذیذ
در فراقت در دل شبهای تار افغان لذیذ

The latter part of the volume contains the following sections:

1. Initial verses of the Ghazals in د, fol. 709*a*.

2. Fardiyyāt, fol. 738*b*, beginning:

حسرت اوقات غفلت چون ز دل بیرون رود

3. Pieces of two or three Baits, in alphabetical order, fol. 746*b*, beginning:

خدایا در بدر این نعرهٔ مستانهٔ مارا
مکن نومید از حسن قبول افسانهٔ مارا

4. Turkish Ghazals, foll. 773*b*—777*b*, beginning:

نه احتیاج که ساقی ویره شراب سنکا
که اوز پیالهسی وردی آفتاب سنکا

The MS. was written for Rustam 'Ali Khān by Hidāyat-ullah, dwelling in Kāshān.

330.

Or. 3541.—Foll. 263; 10¼ in. by 4¾; 17 lines, 2¾ in. long; written in neat Shikastah-āmīz, with 'Unvān and ruled columns, apparently about the close of the 17th century.

[Sidney Churchill.]

دیوان ارشد

The Divan of Arshad.

Beg. ای که هرسو سر زلفی پریشان کرده
از گلی رخسار عالم را گلستان کرده

Mirza Muḥammad Arshad, son of Mirza 'Ali Akbar, born at Barnābād, lived mostly in Herat in the time of Shah 'Abbās II., and excelled especially in Masnavi. The author of Ḳiṣaṣ ul-Khāḳāni, who wrote A.H. 1076, Add. 7656, fol. 179, describes him as being then past forty years of age. Arshad himself states his age very precisely, fol. 77*b*, in a chronogram relating to a son who was born to him, A.H. 1084, when he had reached his fifty-ninth year:

ز امید فرزند بودم ملول
که عمرم به پنجاه و نه در رسید

He must therefore have been born A.H. 1025. The Divan includes chronograms ranging from A.H. 1048 to 1089. Most of the Kasidahs are in praise of the Imams and of the successive viceroys of Khorasan, Ḥasan Khān Shāmlu and his son and successor 'Abbās Ḳuli Khān. The latter, who ruled over Khorasan A.H. 1050—90, appears to have been the special patron of the poet.

Contents: Kasidahs, fol. 1*b*. Tarkibs and Tarji's, fol. 48*b*. Muḳaṭṭa'āt, fol. 54*a*. Masnavis and chronograms, fol. 77*a*. Ghazals, in alphabetical order, fol. 82*b*, beginning:

ای در ره تحقیق تو سرگشته خبرها
در شعشعهٔ حسن تو آشفته نظرها

Rubā'is, fol. 231*b*, beginning:

آندل که ز اسرار ازل آگاه است
دست طلبش ز غیر حق کوتاه است

Prose preface to a Masnavi entitled ابر گهر بار which the poet completed by desire of his patron in Herat, fol. 261*b*.

Beg. لله الحمد که نسیم نو بهار نفسم تا از چمن دل و مرغزار جگر وزیدن آغاز کرده

331.

Or. 3634.—Foll. 126; 8¾ in. by 4½; 17 lines, 2½ in. long; written in small cursive Nestalik, partly on tinted paper with flowery designs, in Kābul and Ḳandahār; dated Monday, 21 Zulhijjah, in the 42nd year of the reign (of Aurangzīb), *i.e.* A.H. 1109 (A.D. 1698). [Sir Gore Ouseley.]

دیوان مجذوب

The Divan of Majẕūb, whose proper name was Mir Muḥammad, of Tabrīz, and who died A.H. 1093. See the Persian Catalogue, p. 696*b*, and the Oude Catalogue, p. 479.

Contents: Kasidahs, fol. 4*b*, beginning as in the previously described MS., Or. 309.

Ghazals, alphabetically arranged, fol. 14*a*, beginning:

الهی عبدك العاصی اتاکا
مقرا بالذنوب فقد دعاکا

Mukhammas, Tarjīʻ, Masnavis, and chronograms, fol. 110*b*, beginning:

حسن را آینه در کار بود
جوهر دل قابل دیدار بود

Rubāʻis, foll. 120*a*—125*b*.

The MS. is noticed in Dr. John Lee's Catalogue, no. 182.

332.

Or. 3487.—Foll. 206; 8¾ in. by 4½; 14 lines, 2¾ in. long; written in fair Nestalik, with two ʻUnvāns and gold-ruled columns, apparently in the 17th century.

[Sidney Churchill.]

دیوان راقم

The Divan of Rāḳim, with a preface in prose.

Beg. of the preface:

ای برون از احاطهٔ ادراك
قدست از نسبت تقدس پاك

تعظیم دربار کبریائی که کرسی نشینان عرش المعراج معرفت

Beg. of the Divan, fol. 8*b*:

ای ذکر تو سر رشته تسبیح صحفها
بی حمد تو پیمانه خالیست دهنها

Rāḳim is the takhalluṣ of Mirza Saʻd ud-Din Muḥammad, son of Khwājah ʻInāyat, a merchant of Mashhad. He went with his father to India in the time of Shāhjahān. After his return to Persia he was appointed by Shāh Sulaimān (A.H. 1078—1105) Vazir of Herat, and, afterwards, of the province of Khorasan, and became known as a liberal patron of poets. See Riyāẓ ush-Shuʻarā, fol. 191*b*, and Shamʻ i Anjuman, p. 167. A copy of his Divan, described by Sprenger, Oude Catalogue, p. 540, contains a chronogram for A.H. 1084.

In the preface Muḥ. Ṣādiḳ Mashhadi, who appears to have been a dependant of the poet, enlarges on the praises of his patron, and states that, although he had received from the Shāh the office of Dastūr, with the title of Āṣafi, and was fully engrossed by the affairs of state, he yielded at times to poetical inspiration.

The Divan consists exclusively of short pieces in the form of Ghazals arranged in alphabetical order.

333.

Or. 3644.—Foll. 173; 8¾ in. by 5¼; 11 lines, about 3 in. long; written in neat Nestalik, with two 'Unvāns and gold-ruled columns, about the close of the 17th century.

[Sidney Churchill.]

دیوان نورس

The Divan of Nauras.

Beg. چمن شکفت و گل آراست بزم روحانی
رساند باغ بساغر شراب ریحانی

Nauras is the takhalluṣ of Muḥammad Ḥusain Dumāvandi, who came as a young man from his native place, Dumāvand, to Isfahan, and was recommended by the famous poet Ṣā'ib to Muḥammad Zamān Khān. Ṭāhir Naṣrābādi mentions him among his living contemporaries, and Ḥazīn says that he died in Isfahan. See Add. 7087, fol. 300*b*; the Oude Catalogue, pp. 103, 139; and Riyāẓ ush-Shu'arā, fol. 472*a*. The Divan contains several Kasidahs in praise of the reigning sovereign, Shāh Sulaimān, an occasional poem on a Ḥammām built in the town of Dumāvand, and chronograms for dates ranging from A.H. 1084 to 1105 (the last is an addition to the original text, fol. 170*a*).

The contents are: 1. Kasidahs in praise of Imam 'Ali Riza, the first of which is entitled فخر المناقب. 2. A second series of Kasidahs, with an 'Unvān, fol. 10*b*, beginning:

بسته ام تا در رهش بر بادپا نعل شتاب
چون فلك بوسد رکاب سایه ام را آفتاب

The first Kasidah is again in praise of the same Imam, but the others are addressed to Shāh Sulaimān, to Zamān Khān, Ṣafī Ḳuli Khān, and Shaikh 'Ali Khān I'timād ud-Daulah. 3. Ghazals, in alphabetical order, fol. 35*b*, beginning:

طراز از اسم اعظم داشت چون خاتم سلیمانرا
ز بسم الله داد اکلیل کلکم فرق دیوانرا

4. Opening verses and various pieces, مطالع و متفرقات, fol. 124*a*, including chronograms. 5. Masnavis, fol. 138*b*, two of which are of some extent, and are respectively entitled حاتمیه and قضا و قدر. 6. Mu'ammas, or riddles, fol. 153*a*. 7. Prose pieces, foll. 160*b*—169*a*, the first of which is a letter relating to the Mir'āt ul-Jamāl of Ṣā'ib.

The margins of a great part of the volume, and foll. 170—173 at the end, contain additional verses by the same hand as the text, but in a smaller character.

334.

Or. 4774.—Foll. 212; 10 in. by 6; 15 lines, 3¼ in. long; written in fair Nestalik, with gold-ruled columns, apparently early in the 18th century.

دیوان واعظ

The Divan of Rafī' ud-Dīn Vā'iẓ Ḳazvīni, who died about A.H. 1105. See above, no. 152, and Ethé, Bodleian Catalogue, no. 1144.

This copy wants the first page, and begins with the second Ghazal of the complete MS., Add. 7812, the first line of which is:

ای بار داده کعبه کویت براهها
کستاخ بارگاه قبول تو آهها

Contents: Ghazals, in alphabetical order, fol. 1*a*. Ḳiṭ'ahs, fol. 117*b*. Fardiyyāt, fol. 121*b*. Kasidahs, fol. 130*b*, beginning:

فصل دی شد آتش سوزی هوا را در سر است
سرد مهریهای دورانرا ظهور دیگر است

(See Add. 7812, fol. 181*b*.) A Tarkīb, fol. 160*b*. Rubā'is, fol. 162*b*, beginning:

از بهر خلافت پیمبر بی کفت
طاقت انکس که بود زهرا را جفت

Chronograms, fol. 172a. Masnavis, fol. 184b. The longest of these, foll. 191b—204a, relates to the famous battle of Shāh Ismā'il and Shaibak Khān. It begins as follows:

فرازنده دست و تیغ زبان
چنین کرده تسخیر ملك بیان

335.

Or. 3285.—Foll. 242; 9 in. by 5; 15 lines, 3 in. long; written in cursive Nestalik, apparently in India, in the 18th century.

دیوان سروری

The Divan of Surūri, with a preface in prose, beginning: الحمد لله علی نواله والصلوة علی محمد وآله سرور دلهای دانش آمای بلاغت سنجان

Beg. of the Divan:

الهی در طریق عشق آسان ساز مشکلها
بیابانها خطرناك و بسی دورست منزلها

The preface was written, at the request of the poet, by Sāḳi, who is better known by the title of Musta'idd Khān, ساقی مشهور به مستعد خان, conferred upon him A.H. 1119, and died A.H. 1136 (see the Persian Catalogue, pp. 936b, 1083b). He praises the author of the Divan, whom he calls Sikandar Surūri, as the great mystic poet of the period:

فی زماننا هذا تبسم آموز غنچهٔ سخن چهره افروز شاهد این فن ناشناس غمکدهٔ دوری سکندر سروری

The Divan consists chiefly of Ghazals of a religious or mystic character, in alphabetical order. One of these, fol. 202b, is in praise of 'Ālamgir. The Rubā'is which follow, fol. 208a, contain many eulogies on Muḥyi ud-Din Jilāni, to whose order, the Ḳādiri, the author evidently belonged.

The Muḳaṭṭa'āt, fol. 233b, begin with this verse:

بیاد حق سروری زنده کن دل
اگر خواهی حیات جاودانی

They include some chronograms. The last of these gives A.H. 1114 for the compilation of the Divan, which is here designated as گلدستهٔ اسرار:

بحمد الله که دیوان سروری
شده گلزار از گلهای اسرار
. . . .
رقم زد خامه ام سال بهارش
ببین گلدستهٔ گلهای اسرار

At the end is a Kasidah entitled قصیدهٔ عیان المعانی, foll. 237—242, beginning:

کار دین کن ار سری اندر سر تو کر سراست

336.

Or. 2936.—Foll. 357; 12 in. by 7½; 25 lines, 4¼ in. long; written in neat Nestalik, in four columns divided by illuminated borders, ornamented with three rich 'Unvāns and seventy-nine miniatures of Indian style, and gilt between the lines throughout, apparently about the beginning of the 19th century.

[Nath. Bland.]

حملهٔ حیدری

Ḥamlah i Ḥaidari, a poetical account of 'Ali's life, by Bāẕil, who died A.H. 1124 (see the Persian Catalogue, p. 704), with the continuation of Mir Ghulām 'Ali Āzād, which is noticed in the Persian Catalogue, p. 705, Add. 25,806.

The poem of Bāẕil is divided into two parts, the second of which is marked by an 'Unvān, fol. 227b, and begins with the Khuṭbah of Muḥammad, corresponding with p. 175

of the Lucknow edition. The continuation of Āzād begins, also with an 'Unvān, fol. 310*b*. For other MSS., see Ethé, Bodleian Catalogue, nos. 518-19.

337.

Or. 3668.—Foll. 16; 7¾ in. by 5; 9 lines, 2⅞ in. long; written in neat Nestalik, with gold-ruled margins, in the 19th century.

[Sidney Churchill.]

گل کشتی

Gul i Kushti, a Masnavi, by Mīr Najāt, who died about A.H. 1126. See the Persian Catalogue, p. 821*b*, v.

The date of composition, as given in the following line of the epilogue, is somewhat ambiguous:

غنچه گل که بود بر سر دل تاریخ است

This means, according to the Indian commentators, that the numerical value of غنچه گل, namely 1108, is to be added to that of دل, viz. 34. Accordingly, the date would be A.H. 1142. This, however, is inadmissible; for Najāt died before that date, and there exists a copy of the poem dated A.H. 1128 (see Rosen, Institut, p. 209). The true interpretation of بر سر دل is that only the head, *i.e.* the initial letter, of دل is to be taken into account, which gives 1108+4, or A.H. 1112.

The poem has been lithographed, with a commentary by Ratan Singh, in Lucknow, 1881, and with another by Gobind Rām in Murādābād, 1884. For MSS., included in the Divan of Najāt or separate, see Pertsch, Berlin Catalogue, no. 674, ١٥, and Ethé, Bodleian Catalogue, nos. 1162, 1164-5.

338.

Or. 3542.—Foll. 135; 10⅜ in. by 5¼; 20 lines, 2⅞ in. long, with oblique lines round the margins; written in a cursive Indian character; dated 9 Rabi' I., A.H. 1133 (A.D. 1720).

[Sidney Churchill.]

رباعیات بیدل

The Rubā'is of Bīdil (Persian Catalogue, p. 706*b*), in alphabetical order.

Beg. آنکس که منزه است از آب و گل ما
بی او عدم است خلوت و محفل ما

At the end of the alphabetical series, fol. 126, is a colophon, in which the copyist states that, while he was engaged in transcribing these verses, the poet, Mirza 'Abd ul-Kādir Bīdil, died on Thursday the fourth of Ṣafar, A.H. 1133.

The latter part of the MS., foll. 126*b*—135, is occupied by a section of mixed contents, consisting of satires in Kasidah form, Mukhammasāt, and Rubā'is, by the same poet, and imperfect at the end.

Beg. این دور دور خیر است وضع متین که دارد
باد بروت مردی غیر از سرین که دارد

A similar collection of Rubā'is is noticed in the Berlin Catalogue, no. 969. The first piece there mentioned is the seventh of the present MS. See also the Oude Catalogue, no. 175.

339.

Or. 3286.—Foll. 87; 6½ in. by 4; 14 lines, 2½ in. long; written in neat Nestalik, with two 'Unvāns and gold-ruled margins; dated 21 Shavvāl, A.H. ١٢٠٥ (for 1205, A.D. 1791).

دیوان طبیب

The Divan of Ṭabīb, with a prose preface by the author.

Beg. of the preface: هر چند تمهید بساط عریضه
نکاری بعنوانی که شایسته نظر الهوت

Beg. of the Divan, fol. 10*b*:

حاشا که کشم بهر طرب ساغر خم را
از غم چه شکایت من خو کرده بغم را

The author, Mīrzā 'Abd ul-Bāķī, of the Mūsavi Sayyids, was the son of Mīrzā Muh. Rahīm, who had been Hakim Bāshī, or head physician, to Shāh Sulṭān Husain Ṣafavī. He served in the same capacity under Nādir Shāh. After that sovereign's death, he became Kalāntar of Isfahan, but resigned that charge in favour of his younger brother Mīrzā 'Abd ul-Vahhāb, and died A.H. 1168. See Atashkadah, p. 412, and Majma' ul-Fuṣaḥā, vol. ii., p. 340, where it is said that Ṭabīb's Divan amounted to two or three thousand Baits. The verses quoted there are found in the present MS.

In the preface the author refers, in extremely prolix and involved style, to his retirement from worldly pursuits after the death of Nādir Shāh, and to his pilgrimage to the holy places.

The Divan consists of Ghazals in alphabetical order. At the end, fol. 79*b*, are some Rubā'is, beginning:

رفتی تو و رفت زندگانی افسوس
آمد پیری و شد جوانی افسوس

and a Masnavi on Maḥmūd and Ayāz, قطعه محمود و ایاز, fol. 83*b*, beginning:

شنیدم من که محمود جوانبخت
که بودش در جهان هم تاج وهم تخت

Copyist: علی اصغر الهمدانی

340.

Or. 3236.—Foll. 349; 9½ in. by 5¾; 17 lines, 3½ in. long; written in neat Nestalik Shikastah-āmīz, with two 'Unvāns and gold-ruled columns; dated A.H. 1200 (A.D. 1786).

[Sidney Churchill.]

دیوان عاشق

The Divan of 'Āshiķ.

Beg. درین خرابه پر غم که نیست جای سرور
خوش آنکه پیش نگیرد بجز طریق عبور

Aķa Muḥammad 'Āshiķ, of Isfahan, was a poor man, earning his livelihood as a tailor; but he had poetical genius, and excelled especially in amatory poems. Āzur, who mentions him among his contemporaries (Ātashkadah, p. 414), says that he died A.H. 1181. See also Makhzan ul-Gharā'ib, fol. 304; Bodleian Catalogue, col. 356, no. 1755; Majma' ul-Fuṣaḥā, vol. ii., p. 346; and Sham' i Anjuman, p. 293. This poet must not be confounded with an earlier 'Āshiķ, who wrote a Masnavi entitled عیش و طرب, A.H. 1079 (Oude Catalogue, p. 339).

Contents: Kasidahs, fol. 1*b*. Ghazals in alphabetical order, fol. 42*b*, beginning:

زهی مثالی که چون جمالت نبسته نقشی زمانه زیبا
بخنده شیرین بزله شکر بغمزه لیلی بعشوه سلمی

(The same beginning is found in a Berlin MS., Pertsch, no. 948, which contains only the Ghazals.) A Mukhammas, fol. 302*b*. Rubā'is, fol. 303*a*, beginning:

زاهد بهوس که خلد در بکشاید
عابد کوید که قرب حق میباید

Chronograms, with dates ranging from A.H. 1154 to 1181, fol. 326*b*. The first relates to the accession of Shāh Sulaimān II., A.H. 1163, and begins:

افراخت بتسخیر جهانی علم فتح
دارای فلک مرتبه همچون شه انجم

341.

Or. 2869.—Foll. 130; 8 in. by 5¾; 16 lines, 3½ in. long; written in cursive Nestalik, apparently about the close of the 18th century. [SIDNEY CHURCHILL.]

Another copy of the Divan of 'Āshiḳ, containing only Ghazals in alphabetical order, beginning as the corresponding section of the preceding MS.

The colophon states that this Divan of Aḳa Muḥammad Iṣfahāni, poetically called 'Āshik, was completed on Thursday in Tafrish, no more precise date being added.

342.

Or. 2850.—Foll. 152; 6½ in. by 3¾; 14 lines, 2½ in. long; written in small and neat Shikastah; dated Ṣafar, A.H. 1195 (A.D. 1781). [SIDNEY CHURCHILL.]

دیوان طوفان

The Divan of Ṭūfān.

Beg. قاصد بباد وعده وصل آورد ز یار
هجرم هزار مرتبه بهتر ز انتظار

Mirza Ṭayyib, of Hazār Jarib, Māzandarān, poetically styled Ṭūfān, lived in Isfahan, and was dreaded for the pungency of his satires. At last he repented of his wicked ways, and retired to Najaf, where he died A.H. 1190. See the Persian Catalogue, p. 808*a*, iii.; Ātashkadah, p. 413; and Majma' ul-Fuṣaḥā, vol. ii., p. 341.

Contents: Kasidahs, fol. 2*b*. Masnavis, fol. 61*b*, beginning:

آنکه پر آواز دارد در زمن
بحر دانش را ز طوفان سخن

Ghazals, in alphabetical order, fol. 104*b*, beginning:

باشك سرخ كردم چارهٔ رخساركاهى را
ولى درمان ندانم چيست درد رو سياهى را

Rubā'is, fol. 150*b*, beginning:

ای زآتش عشقت بدلم سوز امروز
وی سوز تو در جان غم اندوز امروز

At the end are written verses composed by Āẕur on the poet's death, the last hemistich of which is a chronogram for A.H. 1190:

آسود چو در خاك نجف آذر گفت
طوفان در دریای نجف شد ز صفا

343.

Or. 2868.—Foll. 137; 10¾ in. by 6¼; 12 lines, 2¾ in. long; written in elegant Nestalik on gold-sprinkled paper, with an 'Unvān, gold-ruled columns, and gilt headings; dated in the thirty-first year of Muḥammad Shāh, A.H. 1161 (A.D. 1748). [SIDNEY CHURCHILL.]

واله و سلطان

"Vālih u Sulṭān," a romantic poem in Masnavi rhyme, by Faḳir.

Beg. ای واله حسن دلکشت جان
عشق تو بهر دو کون سلطان

Mīr Shams ud-Dīn Faḳīr 'Abbāsi, an eminent poet and scholar, was born at Delhi, A.H. 1115, of an ancient and noble family. He wrote two able treatises on prosody and on poetical figures, a Divan, and several Masnavis. He composed the present one at the request of its hero, 'Ali Ḳuli Khān Vālih (Persian Catalogue, p. 372*a*), with whom he was intimate. It treats of the love-story of Vālih and his affianced bride Khadījah Bigam, poetically surnamed Sulṭān, who had been seized by force and married to one of the Afghan officers of Ashraf. The author of 'Iḳd i Ṣurayyā (Add. 16,727, fol. 68*b*), writing A.H. 1199, says that he had been lately informed that Faḳīr had perished in a shipwreck near Baṣrah on his return from a pilgrimage to Najaf. For other notices, see Sham' i Anjuman, p. 378, and Makhzan ul-Gharā'ib, Or. 4610, fol. 344, Bodleian Catalogue, col. 362, no. 1993.

In the section entitled در سبب نظم کتاب, fol. 10*b*, the poet relates in the following verses how he had been sent for by Vālih, who suggested to him the subject of the present poem:

لزکی صنمی است قبلهٔ من
عشقش زده آتشم بخرمن
آن لحظه مرا بلب رسد جان
کارم بر لب خدیجه سلطان
آواره چو کرد باد ازویم
که غمگین کاه شاد ازویم

The date of composition, A.H. 1160, is fixed by two chronograms in the following lines of the epilogue, fol. 132*b*:

آمد چو بدل خیال تاریخ
شد نظم منیع سال تاریخ
تاریخ دکر ز شخص معنی
ظاهر شودت اکر بجوئی

Further on, fol. 133*b*, the poet says that he had embodied in his poem the contents of letters written by Khadījah Sultan to her lover, as well as the passionate outpourings of the latter.

This fine copy has been revised by the author, who writes at the end: بنظر تصحیح شمس الدین نقیر عباسی دهلوی عفی الله عنه در آمد

Copyist: محمد رفیع

344.

Or. 3239.—Foll. 167; 7 in. by 4; 11 lines, $2\frac{3}{4}$ in. long; written in fair Nestalik, with three 'Unvāns and gold-ruled columns; dated (fol. 131*b*) A.H. 1174 (A.D. 1760).

[Sidney Churchill.]

دیوان وفا

The Divan of Vafā.

Beg. مبادا همچو من بیجا کسی از خان و مان خیزد
که زینسان هر که خیزد آتشش از مغز جان خیزد

Mirza Sharaf ud-Din 'Ali Ḥusaini Ḳummi, called Aḳāsi Beg, and poetically surnamed Vafā, was born A.H. 1137 in Ḳum, where his father was in charge of the sanctuary of the Imāmzādah Fāṭimah. Having reasons to fear Nādir Shāh, he escaped, with great difficulty, from Persia, and reached Delhi A.H. 1162. There he was warmly received by 'Ali Ḳuli Khān Vālih, who devotes to him a long and sympathetic notice in the Riyāẓ ush-Shu'arā, Or. 2693, fol. 452, and quotes a Kasidah which the young poet had composed in his (Vālih's) praise, and which is found in the present MS., fol. 21*b*. It is stated in Sham' i Anjuman, p. 520, that Vafā stayed thirty years in India and died A.H. 1200. The same date is given in Rūz i Rūshan, p. 760. A copy of the Divan is described in the Oude Catalogue, p. 584.

Contents: 1. Kasidahs in praise of the Imams, of Vazir Āṣafjāh, of Vazir Ṣafdar Jang, and of 'Ali Ḳuli Khān Ẓafar Jang. At the end are two chronograms, Turkish and Persian, for the accession of 'Ālamgir II., A.H. 1167, and additional Kasidahs in a smaller and closer character.

2. Ghazals in alphabetical order, fol. 31*b*. The first, which has been completely obliterated, was apparently the same as in the Oude Catalogue. The end of the first hemistich, زبانم را, is still visible. The second Ghazal begins:

شد بلند از بس بوصف قامتت افغان ما
دم زدیوان قیامت میزند دیوان ما

3. Rubā'is, fol. 132*a*, beginning:

فی باغ طلب دارم وفی ساغری
فی نغمهٔ ارغنون و فی نالهٔ فی

4. Tarkibs, Mukhammasāt and Tarji's, fol. 142*a*.

5. A Masnavi, fol. 163*a*, beginning:

الهی شور عشقم در سر انداز
فروزان اخگرم در مجمر انداز

It breaks off at fol. 164*b*. The next three folios, which contain Ghazals, are misplaced; they should come after foll. 59 and 100.

345.

Or. 2851.—Foll. 207; 8 in. by 5; 14 lines, 3 in. long; written in cursive Nestalik, with ruled margins; dated A.H. 1241 (A.D. 1826).
[Sidney Churchill.]

دیوان سید کوچك

The Divan of Sayyid Kūchak.

Beg. بیا ساقی بده جامی ازان خمخانه دلها
که تا فانی شوم از خود بگیرم راه واصلها

The author, who uses mostly کوچك alone, but sometimes سید کوچك as his takhallus, is not mentioned in the Tazkirahs. He is designated in the colophon as a great mystic and religious guide, تحفه الرضویه مولانا قدوة العارفین ومرشد الفقراء والمساکین مولانا اقا سید کوچك رفع الله مراجعه

From the contents of the Divan, which is designated in the colophon as Tuḥfat ur-Riẓaviyyah, he appears to have been a Sufi Faḳīr living in Mashhad and a devout worshipper of the great Imam known as Shāh i Khurāsān, to whom several of his odes are addressed. No precise date is found in the Divan, but the author refers to Shāh 'Abbās II. and to Shaikh Bahā'i (Bahā ud-Dīn 'Āmili) as men of a remote past (see foll. 193*a*, 206*a*). He probably did not live much earlier than the date of the present MS.

The Divan consists of mystic and religious poems in Ghazal form, arranged in alphabetical order. At the end, fol. 205*b*, is a Masnavi beginning:

شنیدستم ز شاه عباس ثانی
که از دل کرده ترك دار فانی

It relates how Shāh 'Abbās brought to shame and confusion the strict rigorists who passed a severe judgment on his conduct.

346.

Or. 2999.—Foll. 161; 7½ in. by 4¼; 14 lines, 2½ in. long; written in Shikastah; dated 27 Rabi' I., A.H. 1199 (A.D. 1785).
[Sidney Churchill.]

خسرو شیرین

"Khusrau Shīrīn;" a Masnavi by Nāmi.

Beg. بنام آنکه در عنوان نامه
بود نامش نخستین نقش خامه

Nāmi is the poetical surname of Mirza Muḥammad Ṣādiḳ Mūsavi, the historian of the Zand dynasty, who died A.H. 1204. See the Persian Catalogue, p. 196*a*; Ātashkadah, p. 439; and Majma' ul-Fuṣaḥā, vol. ii., p. 523.

This poem is designated in the prologue as the first composition of the author. It was written at the time when the poet came to Shiraz in the suite of Karim Khān, who is praised as the reigning sovereign:

مرا در موکب سالار کشور
خدیو ظلم سوز عدل پرور

وکیل قایم آل محمد
که دور دولتش بادا مخلد
گذار افتاد سوی ملك شیراز
چه شیراز آنکه بر جنت کند ناز

The prologue concludes, fol. 11*b*, with a laudatory address to Āẕur, author of the Atashkadah.

For another copy see Ethé, Bodleian Catalogue, no. 1191.

347.

Or. 3321.—Foll. 182; 6 in. by 3¾; 12 lines, 2¼ in. long; written in neat Shikastah, with 'Unvān, gold-ruled columns, and eight miniatures, apparently early in the 19th century. Bound in painted and glazed covers.

[Sidney Churchill.]

Another copy of the preceding poem.

It wants the last section, مناجات بدرگاه آلهی, which occupies foll. 159—61 in the preceding MS.

At the beginning is a note showing that the MS. was given, A.H. 1260, by Nāṣir ud-Din Shāh to his servant Ḥusain 'Ali.

348.

Or. 4515.—Foll. 82; 8¼ in. by 5½; 12 lines, 2¾ in. long, with oblique lines round the margins; written in Shikastah-āmīz; dated Friday, 22 Jumāda II., A.H. 1240 (A.D. 1825).

I. Foll. 3—57. وامق و عذرا

Vāmiḳ u 'Aẕrā, a Masnavi by the same poet, Nāmi. See the Persian Catalogue, p. 813*a*, iv., and Ethé, Bodleian Catalogue, nos. 1192-3.

Beg. ای بنامت افتتاح هر کلام
ای ز نامت نامهٔ نامی تمام

The narrative begins, fol. 7*a*, with these verses:

قصه پردازان این نیکو سیر
می دهند از داستان زینسان خبر
کز ملوك پیش شاهی نیك خواه
در یمن بودش سریر عز و جاه

II. Foll. 57*b*—72*b*. ده نامه

Dah Nāmah, or ten love-letters, by Ibn 'Imād.

Beg. الحمد لخالق البرایا والشکر لواهب العطایا
ای نام تو صدر هر کتابی
آرایش فضل هر خطابی

Ibn 'Imād is placed by Daulatshāh, who quotes the above beginning of his Dah Nāmah, among the contemporaries of Ḥāfiẓ, v., 15. He was a native of Khorasan, but lived in Shiraz, where he died, according to Rūz i Rūshan, p. 17, A.H. 800. A copy is mentioned by Pertsch, Berlin Catalogue, no. 687, 3.

III. Foll. 72*b*—74*a*. A Masnavi by Mulla Ḥasan.

Beg. ز تنهائی دلم خون شد خدارا
بمن کن مهربان باد صبارا

It is a love-letter written by a prisoner to his beloved.

IV. Foll. 75*b*—82. An alphabetical glossary to the poems of Ḳā'āni, لغات مشکله کتاب حکیم قاآنی

It does not proceed beyond letter ش.

349.

Or. 2953.—Foll. 58; 7 in. by 4; 20 lines, 2 in. long; written in small and neat Shikastah-āmiz; dated Saturday, 28 Sha'bān, A.H. 1262 (A.D. 1848).

[SIDNEY CHURCHILL.]

Another copy of the Vāmiķ u 'Azrā of Nāmi, wanting the prologue.

Beg. [sic]قصه پردازان این پیکر سهر
میدهند از داستان زینسان خبر

Copyist: محمد وکیل ابن مرحوم فضل الله تبریزی

350.

Or. 3488.—Foll. 162; 8¼ in. by 5½; 17 lines, 3¼ in. long; written in Shikastah-āmiz, with two 'Unvāns, silver-ruled columns, and gold headings, about the beginning of the 19th century. [SIDNEY CHURCHILL.]

دیوان رفیق

The Divan of Rafiķ, or, as he is called in the colophon, Maulānā Ḥusain Iṣfahāni, دیوان املح المتاخرین مولانا حسین متخلص برفیق اصفهانی

Beg. زامد و رفت روز و شب بجهان
باز آمد بهار و رفت خزان

Mulla Ḥusain was the son of a greengrocer in Isfahan, and he carried on his father's trade; but he cultivated the society of the men of letters, who appreciated his poetical talent. He reached an old age, and died A.H. 1212. See Safinat ul-Maḥmūd, fol. 184a; Anjuman i Khāķān, fol. 132b; Atash-kadah, p. 300; and Majma' ul-Fuṣaḥā, vol. ii., p. 142.

Contents: Kasidahs, fol. 1b. Chronograms, with dates ranging from A.H. 1187 to 1202, fol. 19a. Ghazals, alphabetically arranged, fol. 43b, beginning:

بود که در گذرند از گناهکاری ما
که بیش از گنه ماست شرمساری ما

Masnavis, fol. 131b, beginning:

بشنوید ای دوستان احوال من
بنگرید ای دوستداران حال من

Muķaṭṭa'āt, fol. 139b, beginning:

ای برده رشح جام تو جمشید را زهوش
وی داده نور روی تو خورشید را ضیا

Rubā'is, in alphabetical order, fol. 152b, beginning:

یاران که وفادار شنیدم همه را
عمری بوفا ز پی دویدم همه را

On the first page are some notes of former owners, the earliest of which is dated A.H. 1239.

351.

Or. 4238.—Foll. 105; 13¼ in. by 8; 17 lines 6 in. long; written in Nestalik; dated Bombay, in the year 1256 of Yazdagird (A.D. 1886). [JAMES DARMESTETER.]

جنگنامه نواب غلام محمد خان

A poetical account of the life of Ghulām Muḥammad Khān, by Maulavi Ghulām Jilāni Rāmpūri, with the following heading: لشکر آرای جنود مجنده مضامین حمد حضرت رحمن و هزیمت نمای افواج دریای امواج خیالات فاسده نفس شیطان

Beg. بنام شهنشاه بی تخت و تاج
که بخشد زر مهر و مهرا رواج

Ghulām Muḥammad was the second son of the famous Rohilla chief Faiẓ-ullah, of Rāmpūr. His political career was a very brief one. Shortly after the death of his father, on the 18th of Zulḥijjah, A.H. 1208 (A.D. 1794), he put his elder brother Muḥammad 'Ali to death, and, after various encounters with the British troops and those of Âṣaf ud-Daulah, he was obliged to surrender, and was sent a prisoner to Benares. See the history of the Rohillas, Or. 1639, foll. 76—78; Mill's History of India, vol. vi., p. 46; and the "Ruhela Afghans," Calcutta Review, vol. 61, p. 224.

The poem begins with a long prologue, foll. 2—20. The historical portion starts from the death of Faiẓ-ullah and the ensuing conflict among his sons, fol. 21*a*, with this heading: شروع داستان عبرت بیان وفات نواب فیض الله خان مغفور و وقوع منازعت و مشاجرت در میان اخلاف آن امیر مبرور

The sending of Ghulām Muḥammad to Benares is recorded on fol. 53*a*. The rest of the volume is taken up by a narrative of his wanderings to Mecca and Medina and his journeys to Rāmpūr, fol. 59*b*, to Kābul, fol. 72*a*, and to Kashmīr, fol. 78*a*, on all of which the author appears to have accompanied him; and by an account of his dealings with the Vazirs of Oude and the English authorities.

In one of the concluding chapters the author speaks of the Indian campaign of Zamān Shāh (A.H. 1213) and of the offers of service made to him by Ghulām Muḥammad, fol. 96.

In the next chapter, fol. 100, he relates, with great exultation, the murder of Mr. Cherry by Vazīr 'Ali at Benares (in the same year). In the last, fol. 101, the death of his hero is rather hinted at under cover of mystic phrases than explicitely told.

In the epilogue, fol. 104*b*, the date of composition is indicated by the following chronogram:

زنظمی در در یکتا برآر
که تاریخش سالش بود آبدار

But the text is evidently corrupt and the date uncertain.

The title of the poem and the author's name are found in the following colophon transcribed from the original MS.: الحمد لله والمنة که کتاب فیضی نصاب مسمی به جنگنامه نواب غلام محمد خان صاحب بهادر المعروف بجنگ ذوخواه از تصنیف مجمع فضایل و کمالات ومنبع فواضل نکات جناب مولوی غلام جیلانی صاحب مرحوم مغفور رامپوری در شهر رجب المرجب سنه ۱۲۹۱ بتاریخ یکم روز هفته صورت اتمام پذیرفت

Copyist: موبد خداداد اردشیر ایرانی

On the fly-leaf is a note by Prof. James Darmesteter ascribing the poem to "the well-known Derwish Monshee Jumal eddeen." Lower down: "J'ai fait copier ce manuscrit à Bombay sur un MS. prêté par Gal Azímeddin Khan, général en chef du Nabab de Rampor et son Vakil. Il m'a dit qu'il n'y avait que deux copies de ce MS. dans le Rohilkand, l'original (dans la Bibl. du Nabáb?) et sa copie."

352.

Or. 2817.—Foll. 59; 13½ in. by 9; 17 lines, 4¾ in. long; written in elegant Nestalik in four gold-ruled columns, with two highly finished 'Unvāns and illuminated headings; dated Muḥarram, A.H. 1194 (A.D. 1780).

[SIDNEY CHURCHILL.]

I. Foll. 1—52. خسرو شیرین

"Khusrau and Shīrīn," a Masnavi imitated from the poem of Niẓāmi, by Shihāb.

Beg. درة التاج نامه نام خدای
کاسمان و زمین از اوست بپای

The poet designates himself only by his

takhallus, which occurs twice in the prologue, foll. 2*a*, 10*b*:

درسخن بیش ازین مپیچ شهاب
بر کران دار زورق از گرداب
زگناهان غمین مباش شهاب
دل قوی دار و روز عیش متاب

His proper name, as found in the following MS., was Mirza 'Abdullah B. Ḥabib-ullah Turshizi. He was successively the panegyrist of Shahzādah Maḥmūd, the Afghan, in Herat, and of Agha Muḥammad Ḳājār, in Persia, and died A.H. 1215. See Safinat ul-Maḥmūd, fol. 238*b*, and Majma' ul-Fuṣaḥā, vol. ii., p. 253.

The prologue contains a panegyric on 'Ali Murād Khān, who is addressed as the reigning sovereign, fol. 4*b*:

افتاب سپهر سلطانی
تاجدار سریر کیوانی
خان خانان علیمراد که هست
آسمان پیش قصر جاهش پست

'Ali Murād Khān, son of Allah Murād Khān, and step-son of Ja'far Khān Zand, is stated in the Ta'rikh i Giti-Gushā'i, Add. 23,524, fol. 91*a*, to have assumed sovereignty in Isfahan shortly after the death of Karim Khan, A.H. 1193. He made himself afterwards master of Shiraz, and remained the virtual head of the Zand empire until his death, which took place A.H. 1198.

As to his own life, the author only says (fol. 5*b*), that he had been for five years wandering through every land in great distress, lavishing praises on the great without obtaining any reward. The narrative, which begins fol. 6*a*, follows the main incidents of the poem of Niẓāmi, but on a much reduced scale.

The poem was completed on the 15th of Rabi' I., A.H. 1194, as stated in the following lines of the epilogue, fol. 51*b*:

پانزده روز از ربیع نخست
چون بر آمد شد این سواد درست
سال تاریخ آن ز روی شمار
از هزار و نود فزون صد و چار

The date of transcription, "Muḥarram, 1194," is apparently a mistake for "Muḥarram, 1195."

In a Persian note written on the first page, درة التاج, the first words of the poem, are given as its title: کتاب درة التاج احوالات خسرو شیرین از مصنفات شهاب واحوالات علیمراد خان

II. Foll. 53—59. An unfinished poem by the same Shihāb on the career of 'Ali Murād Khān, to whom it is dedicated.

Beg. سر نامه حمد جهان آفرین
کز او شد پدید آسمان و زمین

The poet's name is found in this line, fol. 54*b*:

بوصف تو بادا زبان شهاب
شناور چو ماهی بدریای آب

The narrative begins on fol. 56*b*. The author relates how his hero marched from Shiraz to Isfahan, crushed the rebellion of Zulfaḳār Khān (Afshār), and ordered that chief to be beheaded. The last leaf, which is disconnected from the preceding, treats of the same prince's victorious encounter near Hamadān with 'Ali Naḳi Khān (son of Ja'far Khān Zand), and of the latter's defeat and flight to Shiraz.

353.

Or. 3318.—Foll. 289; $10\frac{1}{2}$ in. by $5\frac{3}{4}$; 18 lines, $3\frac{3}{4}$ in. long; written in fair large Neskhi;

dated Friday, 18 Ramazan, A.H. 1232 (A.D. 1817). [Sidney Churchill.]

I. Foll. 1—221. دیوان شهاب

The Divan of Shihāb (see the preceding MS.), with a preface by the author, which begins as follows: مطلع دیباچه دیوان سخن و مقطع دفتر معانی نو و کهن حمد و سپاس فردیست

Beg. of the Divan, fol. 4b:

ای بسته بزنجیر فلك پای زمانرا
وز پرده تقدیر بر اورده جهانرا

In the preface the author gives his proper name in full: Ibn Habib-ullah Turshizi 'Abd-ullah, with the takhalluṣ Shihāb, and states that he compiled this Divan by desire of his patron, Shāhzādah Maḥmūd, A.H. 1206, and divided it into four parts (Ḳism), viz., 1. Kasidahs in praise of the Imams and of royal persons. 2. Kasidahs in praise of Amirs and Vazirs. 3. Muḳaṭṭa'āt. 4. Hazliyyāt u Ahāji, *i.e.*, humoristic pieces and satires. The Rubā'is are included partly in the third, and partly in the fourth part. The preface concludes with an enumeration of the other works of the author, namely Khusrau Shīrīn, Yūsuf Zulaikhā, Bahrām Nāmah, Tazkirat ush-Shu'arā, 'Iḳd i Guhar on astrology, Murād Nāmah, a history of 'Ali Mardān Khān Zand, all of which are in verse. The Tazkirat ush-Shu'arā and the Murād Nāmah were not yet completed. Two prose works, Tazkirat ul-Vuzarā and Ta'rīkh i Mujadval, were also still unfinished.

The contents of the Divan are as follows: 1. Kasidahs in praise of the Prophet, the Imams, and of royal personages. The latter are Timūr Shāh, Shāhzādah Maḥmūd, to whom most pieces are addressed, Shāhzādah Kāmrān and Abu 'l-Fatḥ Khān.

2. Kasidahs in praise of Amirs and Vazirs, fol. 35*a*.

3. Ghazals, fol. 60*b*, beginning:

ایز کارستان صنعت شد کلنارها
در گلستان جمالت غنچه رخسارها

4. Muḳaṭṭa'āt, fol. 63*a*.

5. Hazliyyāt, fol. 104*a*, beginning:

منت خدای را که مرا بر جمیع خلق
داد ان تسلطی که بشاهنشهان نداد

6. A supplement to the Divan, consisting of pieces composed subsequently to the date of its compilation, foll. 142*a*—241. It contains Kasidahs in praise of Shahzādah Maḥmūd, a Marsiyah on the death of Timūr Shāh (A.H. 1207), Muḳaṭṭa'āt, including chronograms for A.H. 1207-1208, a long Masnavi, foll. 172—193, being a satirical biography of Muṣṭafa Ḳuli Khān, governor of Turshiz and the sworn enemy of the poet, and numerous satirical pieces.

II. Foll. 222*b*—289. دیوان میرم

The Divan of Mīram, with a preface in prose and verse by the author, beginning with a Tarji', the first line of which is:

عشق سلطان بینشان آمد
مالك الملك لا مكان آمد

and the burden:

غیر یکذات در دو عالم کو
لیس فی الکاینات الا هو

The prose part of the preface begins, fol. 224*a*, as follows: حمد بیحد دانای را که صورت نظم بدیع کاینات رقم زده کلك تصویر اوست

The author says that, having composed a few jocular Ghazals, he had collected them at the request of some friends. He had followed, he says, the example of Shaikh Sa'di, and had, like him, conveyed spiritual thoughts under the veil of sensual images.

The poet, who calls himself, fol. 283*a*, Mīram Siyāh, was a native of Ḳazvīn, but lived chiefly in Herat from the time of Sulṭān Ḥusain Baiḳarā to that of Humāyūn. Sām Mirza, who mentions him in Tuḥfah i Sāmi (written about A.H. 957), fol. 118*b*, as still living, says that he led a dissolute life and that his verses reflected his character. He is mentioned in Khair ul-Bayān, fol. 262*b*, as an imitator of 'Ubaid Zākāni. It is stated in Ṣubḥ i Gulshan that he composed two Divans, the second of which was of a jocular character and had been written by desire of Khwājah 'Abd ul-Ḥayy. A Divan of his composition, but with a different beginning, is mentioned by Ethé, Bodleian Catalogue, no. 1029.

Contents: Ghazals in alphabetical order, fol. 225*b*, beginning:

ای لطف تو ره نمای هر گمراهی
وز سر تو آگه دل هر آگاهی

Muḳaṭṭa'āt, fol. 276*b*, beginning:

شبی گفت میرم بمه پاره
که بود از رخش مهر تابان خجل

Rubā'is, fol. 279*b*, beginning:

ای قادر قیوم رفیع الدرجات
وای آئینه ذات تو اسمای صفات

Another collection of Rubā'is of an extremely coarse and licentious nature, with a short preface, beginning: اما بعد چنین گوید عرق دریای گناه ابلیس با تلبیس گمراه میرم سیاه که درین زمان لطیف, from which it appears that it was compiled at the instance of Khwājah 'Abd ul-Ḥayy, fol. 283*a*.

Beg. دوشینه سر کیر من شعبدارا
بر باد چو ساخت گفتم آن رعنارا

354.

Or. 3543.—Foll. 137; 9½ in. by 5¾; 17 lines, 3¼ in. long; written in fair Shikastah-āmīz, with three 'Unvāns and gold-ruled columns, in the 19th century. Bound in handsome painted and glazed covers.

[Sidney Churchill.]

کلیات مجمر

The collected works of Mijmar.

Mijmar was the poetical surname of Aḳa Sayyid Ḥusain, of the family of Ṭabāṭabā'i Sayyids in Ardistān. He lived at first in Isfahan under Fatḥ 'Ali Shāh. Having repaired to Teheran, he received through the protection of Mirza 'Abd ul-Vahhāb, Munshi ul-Mamālik, the title of Mujtahid ush-Shu'arā. He died still young, A.H. 1225. See Safinat ul-Maḥmūd, fol. 107*b*; Anjuman i Khāḳān, fol. 85*b*; Zinat ul-Madā'iḥ, fol. 164*b*; Nigāristān i Dārā, fol. 120*a*; and Majma' ul-Fuṣaḥā, vol. ii., p. 465.

Contents: Some anecdotes in prose and verse, in the style of the Gulistan, بعضی از حکایات بسیاق گلستان شیخ علیه الرحمة

Beg. خواجهٔ کاینات فرماید الظلم ظلمات یوم القیامه

A Masnavi, fol. 9*b*, commenting on Ḥadiths relating to Creation, and beginning:

ای سوز درون سینه ریشان
سوزان ز تو سینهای ایشان

Kasidahs and Tarkībs, fol. 20*b*, beginning:

که کرد بی مدد غیر باز کونه بنا
براز اساس جهان سقف گنبد مینا

Most Kasidahs are in praise of Fatḥ 'Ali Shāh and relate to events of his reign and occurrences at Court. They have headings indicating their subjects. Some are addressed to the Vazir i A'ẓam Mirza Muḥammad Shafi' and other officials. Another series of short Kasidahs, fol. 74*b*.

Ghazals, alphabetically arranged, fol. 90*b*, beginning:

ای نام تو زیب داستانها
عنوان صحیفهٔ بیانها

Mukaṭṭa'āt in three distinct series, beginning respectively foll. 107*b*, 112*a*, and 120*b*.

Rubā'is, fol. 134*b*, beginning:

یا رب بسبوکشان مستم بخشای
بر مغبچگان می‌پرستم بخشای

Fardiyyāt, fol. 136*b*.

355.

Or. 3544.—Foll. 81; 8¾ in. by 5¼; 16 lines, 3⅝ in. long; written in fair Nestalik, about A.H. 1232 (A.D. 1817).

[Sidney Churchill.]

دیوان فرخ

The Divan of Farrukh.

Beg. تا آن نگار کرده ز خونم نگار دست
بیرون بقتلم آمده از هرکنار دست

Muḥammad Ḥasan Khān, commonly called Khānlar Khān, and poetically styled Farrukh, was the son of 'Ali Mardān Khān Zand, and, on his mother's side, a grandson of Muḥammad Ḥasan Khān Ḳajar. He was therefore a near relative of Fatḥ 'Ali Shāh, with whom he was a great favourite. He died, according to Riẓa Ḳuli Khān, in Kirman, A.H. 1237. See Majma' ul-Fuṣaḥā, vol. ii., p. 383, and, for other notices, Safinat ul-Maḥmūd, fol. 47*b*; Zinat ul-Madā'iḥ, fol. 195*a*; Anjuman i Khāḳān, fol. 83*a*; and Nigāristān i Dārā, fol. 111*b*.

Contents: Kasidahs, fol. 2*b*. Ghazals, in alphabetical order, fol. 40*a*, beginning:

روزم بفغان شب شد شب روز بیا ربها
یا رب بود آن روزی کاخر شود این شبها

Mukhammas, &c., fol. 73*a*. Rubā'is, fol. 76*b*, beginning:

ای داد ز آتش جگرسوز فراق
فریاد ز محنت غم اندوز فراق

The Rubā'is are followed, fol. 79*a*, by a few Ḳiṭ'ahs and Kasidahs.

From notes written on the first page and at the end, it appears that this copy was presented by the author to Prince Iraj Mirza, A.H. 1232. It afterwards passed into the hands of Shahzādah Sulṭān Muṣṭafa, who substituted his name for that of the first owner.

356.

Or. 2984.—Foll. 277; 8¾ in. by 6; 11 lines, 3½ in. long; written in Nestalik Shikastah-āmiz, about A.H. 1237 (A.D. 1822).

[H. A. Stern.]

درة التاج

A miscellaneous volume in prose and verse, designated in the following heading as the fourth volume of Khamsah i Dā'ūd-shāhi by Ḥasan Chelebi, poetically surnamed Shaidā,

جلد چهارم از خمسهٔ داودشاهی دام اقباله العالی کتاب
درة التاج وغرة الابتهاج کلیات وقایع مطابق شهر رجب
سنه ۱۲۳۶ تا رمضان سنه ۱۲۳۷ زادهٔ طبع حسن چلبی

The author was evidently a dependant of Dā'ūd Pasha, governor of Baghdad; and the main part of the volume, foll. 56—212, is occupied by a rhymed chronicle, in which the movements of the Pasha and the daily occurrences at the residence, from Rajab A.H. 1236 to Ramazan A.H. 1237, are minutely recorded. It begins as follows:

بنام انکه نام او عظیم است
خداوندی کریمی کان قدیم است

It is divided into short sections, the subjects of which are indicated by rubrics.

The first part of the volume, foll. 5—55, contains the author's prose compositions, namely, 1. Panegyrics upon Dā'ūd Pasha and upon his son Yūsuf Beg, beginning: بهترین فصل که طوطی ناطقه در بوستان آفرینش و شکرستان دانش و بینش. 2. Precepts of Buzurjmihr to Anushirvān, fol. 14a. 3. A tract on divine power as manifested in human souls, در صفات و آثار نفوس از قدرت ربانی, fol. 21a. 4. Story of the Vazir and the thought-reader, حکایت وزیر و مرد رداف سخن, and other moral anecdotes, fol. 28a. 5. On the faculties of man, fol. 45a. 6. Sayings of great Sufis, گفتار مشایخ, fol. 51b.

The latter part of the volume contains the Divan of the author, namely, 1. Kasidahs, mostly in praise of Dā'ūd Pasha and of Yūsuf Beg, beginning, fol. 213b:

ای درخشان آفتاب شاهی از سیمای تو
شاهراه شرع روشن خسروا از رای تو

2. An astrological treatise in Masnavi, رساله منظومیه نجومیه, fol. 241b, beginning:

مرد دانا سخن ادا نکند
تا بنام حق ابتدا نکند

3. Ghazals, in alphabetical order, fol. 261b, beginning:

به بین بر عارضش ای شیخ زلف عنبر افشانرا
ز حق مکذر نکهدارم چسان ناموس ایمانرا

4. Rubā'is, fol. 271b. 5. Khātimah, fol. 276b.

A full tabulated index of the contents of the volume occupies two pages at the beginning. From a note written on the outer edge of the MS., it appears to have belonged to Yūsuf Beg.

'Unvān and ruled margins, about the middle of the 19th century. [Sidney Churchill.]

دیوان قطره

The Divan of Ḳaṭrah, beginning:

سپاس نیست سزا جز بخالق بر حق
قدیم و عالم و قادر خدای بر مطلق

Mirza 'Abd ul-Vahhāb Ḳaṭrah, of Chahār Maḥāll, Isfahan, was a panegyrist of Fatḥ 'Ali Shāh. He attached himself to the Shah's son, Maḥmūd Mirza, then governor of Nuhavend. Besides a Divan of great extent, he composed a Masnavi on the expeditions of Muḥammad and 'Ali, and another, entitled Fatḥ Nāmah, on the campaign of Mukhtār. Riẓā Ḳuli Khan, writing A.H. 1284, speaks of him as still living. See Majma' ul-Fuṣaḥā, vol. ii., p. 422, and, for earlier notices, Anjuman i Khāḳān, fol. 175a; Safīnat ul-Maḥmūd, fol. 176; Nigāristān i Dārā, fol. 167a; and Madā'iḥ ul-Mu'tamadiyyah, fol. 231.

Contents: Kasidahs, alphabetically arranged, in praise of Muḥammad, 'Ali, and the Imams, fol. 1b. Kasidahs in praise of Fatḥ 'Ali Shāh and his son Muḥammad Taḳi Mirza, fol. 70b. Chronograms relating to buildings, weddings, births, and other occurrences at Court, with dates ranging from A.H. 1230 to 1235, fol. 142a. Tarji's in praise of Muḥammad and of 'Ali, fol. 165a. Satirical pieces, fol. 171a. Ghazals, in alphabetical order, with blank spaces left for additions, fol. 179b, beginning:

ای قاصر از کمال تو اوهام کاینات
معدوم با وجود جناب تو ممکنات

357.

Or. 3489.—Foll. 198; 8 in. by 5½; 12 lines, 3 in. long; written in fair Nestalik, with

358.

Or. 3235.—Foll. 211; 8½ in. by 5¼; 12 lines, 3¾ in. long; written in fair Nestalik, with gold-ruled columns, about the middle of the 19th century. [Sidney Churchill.]

دیوان خاوری

The Divan of Khāvari, whose proper name was Mirza Fazl-ullah Shīrāzi, and who has been already mentioned as author of Ta'rīkh Zu'l-karnain, no. 71.

Beg. زهی رزاق انس و جان حی خلاق جان بخشا
خداوند خداوندان جهان بان جهان آرا

A notice of the poet, extracted from Anjuman i Khākān (no. 120), occupies two pages at the beginning.

Contents: Kasidahs, in alphabetical order, mostly in praise of Fath 'Ali Shāh, of Humāyūn Mirza, and of the Sadr i A'zam Mirza Shafī', fol. 2b. A Tarkīb-band and a Tarjī', fol. 78b. Ghazals, alphabetically arranged, fol. 84b, beginning:

دمی از پرده بیرون کن خدارا روی زیبارا
که تا مجنون خود سازی هزاران همچو لیلارا

Masnavis, fol. 168b, with the heading درصفت گرمای عرض راه خراسان, beginning:

بجوزا چو شد مهر زرین کلاه
ز مغرب بمشرق سفر کرد شاه

Mukatta'āt, including many chronograms, with dates ranging from A.H. 1216 to 1237, fol. 177b. Rubā'is, fol. 201b, beginning:

با لطف تو بخت همنشین است مرا
بی بهر تو ادبار قرین است مرا

The date A.H. 1237 written at the end of the Kasidahs appears to relate to the compilation of the Divan.

359.

Or. 3484.—Foll. 121; 11¼ in. by 7; 17 lines, 3¾ in. long; written in fair Nestalik, with 'Unvān and gold-ruled margins, in the first half of the 19th century. Bound in painted covers. [Sidney Churchill.]

دیوان خاور

The Divan of Khāvar, with a prose preface beginning: ترصیع هر سخن از سپاس خداوندی است که بی واسطه دخیلی نظم موجوداترا تاسیس ازوست

Beg. of the Divan, fol. 4b:

دلم از سوز عشق پر شرر است
وین عجب دامنم زدیده تراست

Haidar Kuli Mirza, poetically surnamed Khāvar, was the fourteenth son of Fath 'Ali Shāh, who appointed him governor of Gulpāigān. After his father's death, he took up his abode in Teheran, where he died in the reign of Muhammad Shāh. See Majma' ul-Fusahā, vol. i., p. 25; Safīnat ul-Mahmūd, fol. 18b; Anjuman i Khākān, fol. 35b; Nigāristān i Dārā, fol. 8a; and Gulshan i Mahmūd, fol. 32b.

The preface, written in florid style, evidently by a dependant of the prince, contains a panegyric on Fath 'Ali Shāh and an encomium on the Shāhzādah and on his Divan, which was compiled A.H. 1238. The contents of the latter are Kasidahs, a Tarkīb on the death of Husain (fol. 6a), Ghazals in alphabetical order (fol. 9b) beginning:

توئی در طور و در سینا توئی پنهان توئی پیدا
تورا جویم بجان و دل چه در سرّا چه در ضرّا

Masnavis beginning with a Sāki Nāmah, and a few Kit'ahs, fol. 93a; Rubā'is in alphabetical order, fol. 114b, beginning:

در میکده دوش با بت بی پروا
گفتم دو سه جام باده ام می پیما

The last Rubā'i is Turkish.

360.

Or. 3245.—Foll. 55; 8¼ in. by 5¾; 6 lines, 2¾ in. long; written in large and elegant Nestalik, with marginal additions in a smaller character in red ink, about A.H. 1240 (A.D. 1824). [SIDNEY CHURCHILL.]

اخلاق الاولياء

Moral precepts in Masnavi verse, by Abu 'l-Ḥasan B. Muḥammad Ḳāẓim Jājarmi, with a prose preface, beginning: الحمد لله رب العالمين . . . اما بعد چنين كويد بندهٔ حقير كثير التقصير ابو الحسن ابن محمد كاظم جاجرمى عفى الله عن جرائمهما

The first line of the poem is:

وقاك الله اى فرزند مسعود
زهرچت نيست دروى راحت و سود

Being prevented by his occupations from writing, for the benefit of his son Naṣr-ullah, a full treatise on ethics, the author was induced, A.H. 1239, to confine himself to these few precepts in verse, namely, 280 maxims in about 400 distichs, adding to each as a confirmation, a verse of the Coran, a Hadith, or some saying of the sages.

361.

Or. 3284.—Foll. 277; 10½ in. by 6; 15 lines, about 3¾ in. long; written in cursive Nestalik in Lodiana; dated Monday, Rabī' I., A.H. 1241 (October, 1825).

ديوان شاه شجاع

The Divan of Shāh Shujā', or Shujā' ul-Mulk, the Durrāni king of Afghanistan, who died A.H. 1258.

Beg. الهى بلبل توحيد كردان اين زبانم را
بخندان از نسيم صبحكاهى كلستانم را

The main bulk of the Divan consists of Ghazals alphabetically arranged, in which the royal author uses his own name as a takhallus in three forms, viz., Shujā', Shāh Shujā', and Shujā' ul-Mulk. He adopts the last form, fol. 277a, in the following chronogram for A.H. 1240, the year in which the compilation of the Divan was begun and completed:

شاه شجاع الملك اين منظومه را
كرد چون آغاز اول سال مرغ
كشت اتمامش هم اندر بعد سال
سال تاريخش بود اعداد مرغ

This was also the time about which Shāh Shujā' composed his Memoirs (see the Persian Catalogue, p. 905), which have been partly translated by the late Lieut. S. W. Bennett in the Asiatic Journal, vol. 30, Asiatic Intelligence, p. 6. In a letter written by the same gentleman to Mr. Macdonald, dated Lodianah, Oct. 23, 1825, and bound up with the present MS., he says: "The noble author finished his work and presented me with it on the 20th of Sept., 1825. This is a copy of the original." For the history of Shāh Shujā' see Kaye, War in Afghanistan, and Rehatsek, last years of Shāh Shujā', translated from Ta'rikh i Sulṭāni, Indian Antiquary, vol. xv., pp. 162, 261, 289.

Contents: Ghazals, fol. 1b. Sāḳi Nāmah, fol. 233b, beginning:

كجائى بيا ساقى هوشمند
رهان اين دل غم كشان را زبند

Mughanni Nāmah, fol. 237a. Mukhammasāt, fol. 240b. Rubā'is, fol. 251a, beginning:

ابذات ترا وصف ز حد بيرونست
مسكين در تو به زهد قارونست

Fardiyyāt, fol. 259b. Tarjī'āt, fol. 266b.

362.

Or. 4516.—Foll. 95; 6½ in. by 5; 11 lines, 3⅛ in. long; written in Shikastah in the 19th century.

دیوان نشاط

The Divan of Nashāṭ, consisting only of Ghazals in alphabetical order, and beginning:

پیداست سرّ وحدت از اعیان اما تری
العکس من المرایا والنفس فی القوی

The same beginning has been noticed in the Persian Catalogue, p. 722*b*. Nashāṭ is the poetical surname of Mirza 'Abd ul-Vahhāb, of Isfahan. See above, no. 188, II., and Ethé, Bodleian Catalogue, no. 1200.

363.

Or. 4914.—Foll. 75; 8½ in. by 5¼; 15 lines, 2⅞ in. long; written in fair Shikastah-āmīz, with gold-ruled margins; dated Ṣafar, A.H. 1257 (A.D. 1841).

Another MS. of the Divan of Nashāṭ, with the same beginning as the preceding, but with fuller contents.

364.

Or. 3528.—Foll. 146; 12 in. by 8; 23 lines, 3⅞ in. long; written in neat Nestalik, with two 'Unvāns and gold-ruled columns; dated Shiraz, A.H. 1253 (A.D. 1837).

[SIDNEY CHURCHILL.]

Two Masnavi poems by Riẓa Ḳuli Khān, poetically styled Hidāyat (see no. 42), both mentioned by the author in Majma' ul-Fuṣaḥā, vol. ii., p. 582, among his early works, namely:

I. Foll. 1—109. هدایت نامه

"Hidāyat Nāmah," a poem containing moral and religious precepts illustrated by apologues and anecdotes in the style of the Masnavi of Jalāl ud-Dīn Rūmi and in the same metre.

Beg. طوطی جان مست مستان کشته است
زانکه محو شکّرستان کشته است

The poem is divided into sections, with long prose rubrics indicating their subjects.

III. Foll. 110—146. انیس العاشقین

"Anīs ul-'Āshiḳīn," a religious and mystic poem, with anecdotes of saints and Sufis.

Beg. ای عشق تو چون محیط و دل فلک
سبحان الله سالک المسلک

It is divided into twelve Maḳālahs, with long prose rubrics.

The present copy breaks off before the end of the twelfth Maḳālah.

The MS. belonged to the library of Ṣanī' ud-Daulah Muḥammad Ḥasan Khān, whose stamp is pasted on the first leaf.

365.

Or. 3377.—Foll. 238; 13¼ in. by 8; 25 lines, about 4¾ in. long; written in cursive Nestalik; dated Ramazan, A.H. 1283 (A.D. 1866).

[SIDNEY CHURCHILL.]

دیوان هدایت

The Divan of the same poet, Riẓa Ḳuli Khān Hidāyat.

Beg. ای درد تو درمان جان شیدا
وی وصل تو نایاب تر ز عنقا

The greater part of the Divan consists of Ghazals in alphabetical order. At the end are found the following sections:

Mukaṭṭa'āt, alphabetically arranged, fol. 205b, beginning:

ای ملك زاده آزادهٔ والا والی
که ز اشغال ولایات ترا مشغلها

Tazminat, with the heading, تضمینات مصارع مجمر و غیره در غزلیات, fol. 219b. Mukhammasāt, fol. 221b. Tarji'iyyāt, fol. 223a.

A Masnavi, fol. 228a, beginning:

الا ای خرابانیان الست
که از بادهٔ عشق هستید مست

Rubā'is, in alphabetical order, fol. 230b, beginning:

رنج است تمام خواب و بیداری ما
محنت همکی مستی و هشیاری ما

The copyist, 'Abdullah B. Ibrāhīm Tabrīzi, states at the end that the number of Baits in the Divan amounts to about eleven thousand two hundred.

366.

Or. 3237.—Foll. 141; 7¾ in. by 5¼; 12 lines, 3 in. long; written in Neskhi in the latter half of the 19th century.

[Sidney Churchill.]

دیوان غمامی

The Divan of Ghamāmi, beginning:

بنام آنکه بود هرچه هست ازو بر پا
نه منتها بود اورا بذات و نه مبدا

The poet, of whom no record has been found, appears to have lived in Yazd about the middle of the nineteenth century. His Divan contains numerous references to that city, one among others to Mirza Muṭṭalib its governor, and a number of chronograms with dates ranging from A.H. 1252 to 1268. Among those there is a curious one, fol. 125b, fixing by anticipation the poet's own death at A.H. 1295, with the remark that it was composed twenty-six years before the event, that is to say A.H. 1269.

Contents: Kasidahs, mostly in praise of 'Ali, fol. 1b. Ghazals in alphabetical order, fol. 36b, beginning:

الا یا ایها العشاق ای از عشق غافلها
که از جانها نیندیشید هیچ از خواهش دلها

Tarji', Tarkīb-band and Mukhammas, fol. 104b. Mukaṭṭa'āt, including chronograms, fol. 117a, beginning:

بعهد تولیت میرزا ابرهیم ان
که بود بانی تعمیر این قدیم بنا

Rubā'is, fol. 131b. Masnavis, fol. 139b, beginning:

پیری از احوال دل کودکی
کفت ز دردیش رسید اندکی

367.

Or. 3240.—Foll. 124; 8¼ in. by 5; 23 lines, 2½ in. long; written in small and close Nestalik; dated Ispahan, A.H. 1261 (A.D. 1845).

[Sidney Churchill.]

دیوان قاآنی

The Divan of Ḳā'āni, beginning:

دوشم ندا رسید ز درکاه کبریا
کی بنده کبر بهتر ازین عجب بیریا

Ḳā'āni is by common consent the greatest of the modern poets of Persia. His proper name was Mirza Ḥabīb-ullah, and he was born in Shiraz. At the age of seven years he left his father, Mirza Abu 'l-Ḥasan, poetically surnamed Gulshan, and repaired to Mashhad to apply himself to study. In a short time his precocious poetical genius drew public attention to him, and he became a favourite of the governor, Ḥasan 'Ali

Mirza Shujā' us-Salṭanah. The latter recommended the youthful poet to his father, Fatḥ 'Ali Shāh, who conferred upon him the title of Mujtahid ush-Shu'arā. Ḳā'āni remained at the capital during the reigns of Muḥammad Shāh and of the present Shāh, who both treated him with great regard and liberality. He was a great adept in all Muslim sciences and an eminent linguist. French being then in favour, he made himself so perfect a master of it that, according to his biographer, "but for his dress, it might have been doubted whether he was a native of Pārs or of Paris." Ḳā'āni died at Teheran, A.H. 1270, leaving a Divan of considerable extent, which was lithographed at Teheran, A.H. 1277, and a collection of anecdotes in prose and verse, called کتاب پریشان, lithographed in the same place, A.H. 1302. See a full notice of his life in Ganj i Shāigān, pp. 362 to 410 (prefixed in an abridged form to the Teheran edition of the Divan); Majma' ul-Fuṣaḥā, vol. ii., p. 402; Madā'iḥ ul-Mu'tamadiyyah, fol. 226*b*; and E. G. Browne, "A Year amongst the Persians," p. 118.

The present copy of the Divan consists exclusively of Kasidahs arranged in alphabetical order. As it was written nine years before the poet's death, it naturally does not include his later compositions, and its contents fall far short of those of the printed edition.

368.

Or. 3000.—Foll. 56; 9 in. by 5¼; 11 lines, 3¼ in. long; written in elegant Nestalik, with two 'Unvāns and gold-ruled columns; dated A.H. 1263 (A.D. 1847). Bound in painted and glazed covers.

[Sidney Churchill.]

ضياء النور

A poem on mystic love, written in the style and metre of the Masnavi, and illustrated by anecdotes and sayings of Sufis; by Ibn 'Ali Akbar 'Ali Aṣghar, poetically styled Nayyir, with a prose preface by the author, beginning: الحمد لله الذى تجلى لنا بنور جماله وخلى بيننا وكثير من نواله

Beg. of the poem, fol. 3*b*:

يا ضياء النور اى جان جهان
اى سر سردفتر سرّ نهان

In the preface, after a panegyric on the Vazir, Ḥāji Mirza Aḳasi, the author describes the present work as abridged from a longer poem composed in his youth.

According to a note written by Mr. Churchill on the first page, the original Masnavi was lithographed on the margin of Nūr al-Anvār, Teheran, A.H. 1301, and the date of its composition is given in the following chronogram:

طرح نه از غرفه بنما در حساب
که بود تاریخ این زیبا کتاب

This gives A.H. 1285 – 9 = 1276, a date posterior to that of the present copy. The poem which bears that date must therefore be a later work of 'Ali Aṣghar.

Copyist: محمد الخوانساری

369.

Or. 2954.—Foll. 63; 8½ in. by 5½; 12 lines, 3 in. long; written in elegant Nestalik, with a highly finished 'Unvān and gold-ruled columns, in the latter half of the 19th century. [Sidney Churchill.]

بهرام و بهروز

Bahrām u Bihrūz, a tale in Masnavi verse, by Vaḳār.

Beg. بنام انکه دانش داد جان را
بدانش داد آرایش جهان را

Mirza Aḥmad Shirāzi, poetically styled Vaḳār, was the son of the poet Viṣāl, who died in Shiraz, A.H. 1263 (see no. 308). Four years after his father's death he went to India with his brother, Mirza Maḥmūd Ṭabib, takh. Ḥakim. After staying about two years in Bombay, he returned home and proceeded, A.H. 1274, to Teheran, where he was favourably received by Nāṣir ud-Din Shāh. He was then forty-two years of age. See Majma' ul-Fuṣaḥā, vol. ii., p. 548. He wrote, A.H. 1281, a collection of anecdotes in the style of the Gulistān, entitled Anjuman i Dānish, and lithographed in Teheran, A.H. 1289.

The heroes of the tale, Bahrām and Bihrūz, are two brothers, natives of Gilan, the first addicted to pleasure, the other living for wisdom and virtue. The heroine is Gauhar, their uncle's daughter. In the prologue, after a panegyric on Nāṣir ud-Din Shāh, the author describes the work as a poetical version of a tale he had found in India, A.H. 1266. In the epilogue, written eight years after his return, he bestows the highest praise upon Sayyid 'Aṭā, a Persian exile, who had been his benefactor in India, and for whom he claims the Shah's clemency.

On the first page is a Persian note declaring the MS. to be in the handwriting of the author, the 'late' Vaḳār. It is confirmed by the seals of the three great penmen of the period, Mirza Zain ul-'Ābidīn Shirāzi, Mirza Shaikh-'ali, and Mirza Muḥammad Ḥusain.

370.

Or. 3256.—Foll. 12; 8½ in. by 5¼; 10 lines, 3 in. long; written in elegant Nestalik with 'Unvān and gold-ruled margins, about the middle of the 19th century.

[Sidney Churchill.]

Six Kasidahs in praise of Nāṣir ud-Din Shāh, by the six sons of the poet Viṣāl Shirāzi, namely:

1. Aḥmad *Vaḳār* (see the preceding MS.), whose poem begins as follows:

   چند کویند که فردوس چنینست و چنان
   پرده بردار که مشهود شود باغ جنان

2. Maḥmūd *Ḥakīm*, who died A.H. 1268, at the age of thirty-nine. See Majma' ul-Fuṣaḥā, vol. ii., p. 102.
3. Muḥammad *Dāvari*. See *ib.*, p. 130.
4. Abu 'l-Ḳāsim *Farhang*, who died a few years ago. See E. G. Browne, "A Year amongst the Persians," p. 119.
5. Muḥammad Ismā'īl *Tauḥid*, see Majma' ul-Fuṣaḥā, p. 84.
6. 'Abd ul-Vahhāb.

The writing is very similar to that of the preceding MS., and is said to be that of Vaḳār.

371.

Or. 3251.—Foll. 152; 7¾ in. by 4½; 7 lines, 1½ in. long; written in Neskhi, about A.H. 1277 (A.D. 1860-61).

[Sidney Churchill.]

فرهنك خدا پرستی

"Farhang i Khudā-parasti," a poem on the martyrs of Karbalā, by Maḥram.

Beg. · در موسم عاشورا در تکیهٔ دولت
بکرفته عزا بهر دعای شه ملت

Mirza 'Abdullah B. Mirza Muḥammad 'Ali, surnamed Lisān ul-Ḥaḳḳ, was born in Yazd, and adopted the poetical surname of his father, Maḥram. He spent his youth in Kirmanshahan, and afterwards settled in Teheran in the time of Muḥammad Shāh, who conferred upon him the title of Malik ush-Shu'arā'i 'Irāk, and appointed him professor of French in the Dār ul-Funūn. After a time he retired into private life and applied himself to the composition of poems in praise of the Imams. See Majma' ul-Fuṣaḥā, vol. ii., p. 457, and Ganj i Shāigān, p. 412.

The present poem is of the kind called Musammaṭ. It was composed, as stated at the beginning, on the occasion of a Ta'ziyah performed by order of Nāṣir ud-Dīn Shāh, and contains a detailed description of the martyrdom of one hundred and seventy-two men, who fell by the side of Ḥusain on the field of Karbalā, beginning with Ḥurr B. Zaid Riyāḥi, and ending with 'Ali al-Aṣghar. The last two words of the above title form a chronogram for A.H. 1277, the year in which the poem was composed. This is stated in the epilogue, fol. 149*a*, as follows:

اینك بكواه قول محرم
تاریخ شدش خدا پرستی

At the beginning and at the end are found eulogies, in prose and verse, upon the author and his work, by the following writers: Mirza Muḥammad Sāvaji, fol. 1*b*. Mirza Muḥammad Ḥasan Taslim, fol. 4*b*. Mirza Humā (Shīrāzi), fol. 149*b*. Mirza Bidil, fol. 150*b*. Mirza Ṣafā'i Kātib, fol. 151*a*, and the daughter of Ḥakīm Ẕauḳi, fol. 152*b*.

The MS. bears at the beginning the seal of the author, Lisān ul-Ḥaḳḳ.

The poem was lithographed in Teheran, A.H. 1281, with a portrait of the author.

372.

Or. 3243.—Foll. 126; $7\frac{3}{4}$ in. by $5\frac{3}{8}$; 11 lines, 4 in. long; written in a straggling Indian Nestalik, about A.D. 1880.

[SIDNEY CHURCHILL.]

قیصری نامه

"Kaiṣari Nāmah," a poetical account of recent events in India, under the Viceroys Lord Lytton and Lord Ripon, by Munshi Bishan Lal, poetically styled Nāẓir.

Beg. پس از حمد ونعت خدا و رسول
سخن را قوی بسته باید اصول

In the prologue the author dedicates the poem to Her Majesty (from whose Indian title its name is derived) through the medium of his patron, Sayyid Aḥmad Khān, of Delhi. The work is divided into three parts called Daftar. The first, fol. 10*a*, is a succinct history of the growth of the British Empire in India from the first settlement in Calcutta to the assumption by the Queen of the title Ḳaiṣar i Hind. The second and third Daftars, beginning respectively at foll. 68*a* and 86*b*, treat more fully of the events of Afghanistan from the Kabul campaign, under Lord Lytton, to the final establishment of 'Abd ur-Raḥmān Khān on the throne. The work was finished, as stated in the epilogue, on the tenth of Zulhijjah, A.H. 1297 (November, 1880).

At the beginning, fol. 2, is a short statement of the contents, and, fol. 3, an encomium on the work and its author by Maulavi Muḥammad Isḥāḳ, professor of Madrasat ul-'Ulūm, Delhi, who describes the author as a Muslim convert.

373.

Or. 3254.—Foll. 121; $8\frac{1}{4}$ in. by 6; 13 lines, $3\frac{1}{4}$ in. long; written in fair large Nestalik; dated 20 Rabī' I., A.H. 1298 (A.D. 1881).

[SIDNEY CHURCHILL.]

I. Foll. 1—56. قصاید عامل الدین

Kasidahs of 'Āmil ud-Din, with a prose

preface by the author, beginning: حمد مختص ذات حضرت پروردگار است بر بسیار نعمتهای او

The author's full name is 'Āmil ud-Din Muḥammad Ṭāhir B. Mulla Abu Ṭālib, and he uses 'Āmil as his takhalluṣ. In the preface, which is dated the 16th of Ṣafar, A.H. 1298, he says that in the springtide of youth he had composed two volumes of poetry, one containing Ghazals and Rubā'is, the other, the present one, consisting of Kasidahs in praise of 'Ali and Ḥusain.

The Kasidahs, including also some Mukhammasāt, form an alphabetical series, and begin as follows, fol. 3*b*:

سحرم هاتف غیبی ز وفا کرد ندا
گفت رو آر بدرگاه غریب الغربا

II. Foll. 56*b*—118. A Masnavi by the same poet on the fate of 'Ali Akbar, Ḳāsim B. Ḥasan, and other martyrs of Karbalā.

Beg. ستایش کنم داور پاك را
که او داد هر فهم و ادراك را

A long prologue contains the author's view on a fifth soul, described as a privilege of the Imams; further, a number of anecdotes with spiritual or mystic import, and a Sāḳi Nāmah. The narrative begins, fol. 78*a*, with the heading گفتار در ساقی نامه و آغاز داستان حضرت علی اکبر

The poem is slightly imperfect at the end. It breaks off, fol. 118*b*. The next three folios contain additional Kasidahs. The MS. is, according to the following colophon, the author's own draft: تمت الکتاب کاتبه وناظمه محمد طاهر ابن ابو طالب در سنه هزار دویست نود هشت

— —

Anthologies.

374.

Or. 4110.—Foll. 445; 9⅓ in. by 6¼; 25 lines, 4 in. long; written in a rather uncouth Indian Neskhi, with rudely illuminated headings, apparently in the 15th century.

[Sidney Churchill.]

A copious Persian anthology, without title or author's name.

The author lived in India, and wrote this work during the short reign of Sulṭān ush-Shark Mubārak Shāh, who succeeded to the throne of Jaunpūr A.H. 803, and died in the subsequent year (see Elliot, History of India, vol. iv., p. 38; Firishtah, vol. i., p. 289; and Brigg's translation, vol. i., p. 498). This appears from the heading of a long poem (Muwashshaḥ) addressed to that Sultan by Malik 'Azīz-ullah, and dated A.H. 803 (foll. 222*b*—227). In that heading the author speaks of the Sultan as the reigning sovereign, adding to his name خلد ملکه.

The work is divided into sections termed Ḳism, in which the poems are arranged according to their subjects, to the various kinds of poetical composition, or to the poetical figures which they illustrate, the authors of most pieces being named in the heading. The poets quoted range from the time of Firdausi to that of Ḥāfiẓ, and include a number of Indian poets unknown to Persia. The sections must have originally amounted at least to one hundred and one; but the MS. is defective at the beginning and at the end, and has besides some internal lacunæ, so that many of the Ḳisms are lost, while in some instances the headings are wanting or illegible.

The contents may be briefly described as follows: Ḳism I. (the beginning of which is lost). Poems in praise of God, by Firdausi

'Amīd Lūnaki, Mughīs Hānsavi (mentioned in Haft Iklim, fol. 147a, without any date), Khwājū Kirmānī, and Sa'di, fol. 5a. II. Poems in praise of the Prophet, fol. 15b. III. and IV. احكام فقه, a versified treatise on law, composed A.H. 693, fol. 28a. V. Laudatory poems by Anvari, Khākāni, Kamāl Isma'il, Minuchihri, Mu'izzi, Katarān, Nizāmi, Mughīs Hānsavi, &c., fol. 33a (breaking off fol. 111, and followed by a misplaced leaf containing riddles, and by the last five pages of a section on the poems called Muvashshah). VII. Tarjī'āt, by Zahīr Fāriyābi, Khwājū, Kamāl Isfahāni, Falaki, Sa'di, Hamīd Kalandar, Fakhr ud-Din 'Irāki, and Salmān, fol. 115a. VIII.—XI. Mudavvarāt, and other pieces written in fanciful shapes, fol. 152a. XIV.—XVI. Mukhammasāt, Musallas and Murassa', fol. 159a. XXIII. (misplaced). Proverbs ضرب الامثال, fol. 164a. XVII.—XXIX. Verses illustrating various kinds of poetical figures, fol. 165b. LXXIII. ميزان الاوزان, pieces which may be read in several metres, fol. 218b. LXXIV. Ghazals, chiefly by Khākāni, Sa'di, Hāfiz, 'Ubaid Zākāni, and Kamāl, fol. 228b. LXXV. The Masnavi entitled Duzd u Kāzi, followed by a vast number of Ghazals of a religious character, chiefly by Sa'di and Humām, fol. 282a. LXXVI. Mukhammasāt, fol. 379b. LXXIX., and three other Kisms with uncertain headings, containing artificial verses, fol. 384b. XCIII. Prosody, fol. 399b. XCIV. Music, fol. 402a. XCV. Masnavis, viz., extracts from the Shāh Nāmah, Gul u Bulbul, &c., fol. 403b. XCVI. Mukatta'āt and Marāsi, fol. 414a. XCVII. Rubā'is, without poet's names, fol. 427a. XCVIII. Mufradāt, fol. 443b (imperfect at the end).

Foll. 1—4, misplaced at the beginning of the volume, contain Kism CI., treating of riddles, also a Tarkib-band and Marsiyah by Salmān.

In a passage occurring fol. 222b the author calls his book Dastūr ush-Shu'arā, این کتاب من دستور الشعراست. This may be either a mere description of its scope or its specific title.

An addition by a later hand on the margin of fol. 18b is dated Delhi, 15 Zulka'dah, A.H. 935 (A.D. 1529).

375.

Or. 3244.—Foll. 184; 9¼ in. by 6¼; 15 lines, 3⅓ in. long; written in elegant Nestalik, with gold-ruled columns, apparently early in the 16th century. [Sidney Churchill.]

An extensive anthology of select Ghazals by various poets, from the time of Sa'di to the first half of the tenth century of the Hijrah, by Fakhri B. Muhammad Amiri.

The MS. begins abruptly with the latter part of the preface, from which it appears that the work was compiled for the Vazir Habib-ullah. It is evidently the anthology entitled تحفة الحبيب, mentioned in the Oude Catalogue, p. 12, and in the Persian Catalogue, p. 366b.

The Ghazals are arranged in alphabetical order, and have rubrics indicating their authors. The MS. breaks off towards the end of the Ghazals in ی. The latest poets included are Binā'i, Āsafi, Āhi, Hilāli, Ahli, and the compiler himself, Fakhri (fol. 184a).

The first Ghazal is by Sa'di, and begins:

مشتاقی و صبوری از حد گذشت یارا
گر تو شکیب داری طاقت نماند مارا

The second is by Humām, and begins:

با آنکه بر شکستی چون زلف خویش مارا
گفتن ادب نباشد پیمان شکن نگارا

The last is by Navā'i (Mir 'Ali Shir), and begins:

ناوك شوخی که در دل همچو جانی مانده

در تن زارم چو مغز استخوانی مانده

An anthology of princely poets, Rauzat us-Salāṭīn, by the same Fakhri, is described by Pertsch, Berlin Catalogue, no. 644.

376.

Or. 4772.—Foll. 337; 9½ in. by 6; 21 lines, 4¾ in. long; written in small and close Nestalik in four red-ruled columns; dated (fol. 324), Thursday, 23 Rabi' I., A.H. 1170 (A.D. 1756).

A collection of Masnavis by ancient and modern poets, more especially by those who lived in India during the tenth and eleventh centuries of the Hijrah.

Omitting some of the lesser pieces, the main contents are as follows:

Fol. 1*b*. ساقی نامه, by Ẓuhūri (d. 1024). See Ethé, no. 1076, fol. 31.

Fol. 55*a*. قضا و قدر, by Salim (d. 1057). Persian Catalogue, p. 796*b*, VIII.; Berlin Catalogue, no. 674, art. 12; and Ethé, nos. 1113-14.

Fol. 58*a*. سوز و گداز, by Nau'i (d. 1019). Persian Catalogue, p. 674*a*.

Fol. 62*a*. قضا و قدر, by Ṭālib Āmuli, beginning:

شنیدم روزی از طرز آشنائی

Fol. 64*a*. قضا و قدر, by Ḥakīm Ruknā (v. Berlin Catalogue, no. 12, art. 10), beginning:

شنیدم روزی از پاکیزه رائی

Fol. 65*a*. قضا و قدر, by Salim 'Aṭṭār Yazdi, takh. Sālim, beginning:

چمن پیرای گلزار حکایت

Fol. 67*b*. قضا و قدر, by Ẓiyā (Nūr ullah Iṣfahāni, under Shāh 'Abbās I.; see Atashkadah, p. 186), beginning:

شنیدم روزی از بیخورد و خوابی

Fol. 70*b*. Extracts from فرهاد و شیرین, by 'Urfi, and from poems on the same subject by Vaḥshi, fol. 74*a*, and Shāpūr, fol. 80*b*.

Fol. 83*a*. مثنوی ساغر کش لطف ازلی, by Nāṣir 'Ali (Berlin Catalogue, no. 674, art. 15), beginning:

الهی ذره دردی بجان ریز

Fol. 96*a*. گلزار عباسی, by Mirza Ṭāhir Vaḥid, beginning:

خسروی بود در دیار عراق

Fol. 103*b*. مثنوی نرگسدان, by Mulla Ismā'īl Ẓabiḥi Yazdi (Oude Catalogue, p. 122), beginning:

چنین خواندستم از اخبار غیبت

Fol. 111*a*. Extract from محمود و ایاز, by Zulāli.

Fol. 124*b*. Extract from خلد برین, by Vaḥshi.

Fol. 125*a*. Masnavi of Salīm on the visit of a caravan to the tomb of Ḥātim.

Fol. 126*b*. Masnavi on the battle of Shāh Ismā'il with Shaibak Khān, by Vā'iẓ Ḳazvini (no. 334), beginning:

سزاوار شکر آفریننده است

Fol. 133*a*. The story of Shaikh Ṣan'ān, from Manṭiḳ uṭ-Ṭair, by 'Aṭṭār (see the Turkish Catalogue, pp. 185*b*, 302*b*), beginning:

شیخ صنعان پیر عهد خویش بود

Fol. 138*a*. The story of Mālik Dīnār, by Bābā Ḳāsim Khādim (a sister's son of Mir Najāt, v. Rūz Rūshan, p. 193), beginning:

دوستان همدمان هوا داران

Fol. 140*a*. بیمار و طبیب, by Mulla Sharif Iṣfahāni, beginning:

سوی ویرانه ام آمد سحری جلوه کنان

Fol. 141*a*. محمود و ایاز, by Anisi Shāmlu (Persian Catalogue, p. 1032*b*, IV.), beginning:

شبی بر تخت دولت خفته محمود

Fol. 145*a*. ناظر و منظور, by Vaḥshi Yazdi, beginning:

نوا پرداز قانون فصاحت

Fol. 159*a*. هفت پیکر, by Niẓāmi.

Fol. 188*a*. قضا وقدر, by Mir Yaḥya (Persian Catalogue, p. 1002*a*), beginning:

بغفلت ایکه رفته روزگارت

Fol. 190*b*. هشت بهشت, by Amir Khusrau Dihlavi.

Fol. 218*b*. نان و حلوا, by Bahā ud-Din 'Āmili.

Fol. 225*a*. ترجمة الشوق, a Kasidah by 'Urfi Shirāzi, and other Kasidahs by Anvari, Mukhliṣ Kāshi, Bābā Kāsim Khādim, Firdausi, Salim, Shaukat, Ṣā'ib, Naẓiri, Sālik, Mashrab, Aminā, Dā'ūd Mutavalli, Shāh Akbar, and Ghani Kashmiri.

Fol. 238*b*. Masnavi of Salim, describing a meadow at Lāhijān.

Fol. 239*b*. Salāmān u Absāl, by Jāmi.

Fol. 246*b*. ساقی نامه, by Mir Raẓi Artimāni (Oude Catalogue, p. 93, and Berlin Catalogue, no. 674, art. 7), beginning:

آلهی بستان میخانه ات

Fol. 249*a*. سراپا, by Sayyid 'Ali Mihri (Persian Catalogue, p. 796, VIII.), beginning:

ای بت چابك شیرین حرکات

Fol. 250*b*. معراج الخیال, by Mulla 'Ali Riẓa Tajalli (Persian Catalogue, p. 738*a*, and Berlin Catalogue, no. 674, art. 5), beginning:

در سرم دیگر هوای عشق یار

Fol. 253*b*. زبور العاشقین, by Mirza Da'ūd Mutavalli, beginning:

عزیزان دوستان مهر آفرینان

Foll. 255*b*. هدیة الاحباب, by Ẕabiḥi Yazdi, beginning:

دوستان یاران عزیزان های های

Fol. 257*a*. دردوست, by Mirza Ḥasan Yazdi, takh. Vāhib, beginning:

کیم من مستمندی درد پرورد

Fol. 260*a*. پهلو بندی, by Mirza 'Abdullah Ḳummi, takh. Sha'af, beginning:

ز پهلو بندی چرخ جفا جو

Fol. 260*b*. گل کشتی, by Mir Najāt. See Persian Catalogue, p. 821*b*, v.

Fol. 265*a*. Two Masnavis, by Aminā Mudaḳḳiḳ Yazdi, beginning:

ظهوری بانشاء خوان خلیل

Fol. 269*b*. A Masnavi in praise of Kashmir, by Salim, beginning:

سخن هر جا ز صنع کردگارست

Fol. 274*a*. Other Masnavis by Salim, Kalim, and Vaḥshi.

Fol. 285*b*. سد سکندر, a satire by Nāṭiḳ (see Oude Catalogue, p. 108), beginning:

من چه کنم صافدلی درد نوش

Fol. 287*a*. Other satires by Salim, Shafi'ā i Aṣar (d. A.H. 1124; see Oude Catalogue, p. 149), Ẕiyā Isfahāni, Firdausi, and and Najāt.

Fol. 295*a*. فرهاد و شیرین, by Fauḳi, beginning:

کبوتر باز بام خوش بیانی
چنین زد چکه بر مرغ معانی

Fol. 303*b*. Kasidahs, Sāḳi Nāmah, and a musical treatise in prose by the same Fauḳi. The last is dated A.H. 1122.

Fol. 310*b*. Some pieces of ornate prose,

viz., كلشن خيال, by Ṭāhir Nasrābādi, بحر طويل, by Shāhid Ṭihrāni and Mihri, two pieces entitled قورق شراب, by Aḳa Ḥusain Khwānsāri and by Ṣā'ib, and other pieces by Naṣīrā i Hamadāni and Ṭughrā i Hindi.

The transcriber, Badī' Muḥ. B. Muḥsin Yazdi, who may also be the compiler, gives in the following colophon, fol. 324a, his name and his genealogy carried up to Shaikh 'Abd ul-'Āli al-'Āmili: تم الكتاب ... على يد اقل العباد ... اليزدى مولدا الهرندى الاصبهانى محتدا ... المدعو ببديع محمد بن محمد محسن بن محمد شريف ..... بن الشيخ عبد العالى الهاشمى العاملى فى اصيل يوم الخميس الثالث والعشرين من شهر ربيع المولود ... من شهور سنه سبعين ومايه بعد الالف من الهجرة

The remaining folios, 324a–337b, contain miscellaneous poetical pieces, chiefly Ghazals by Maghribi, Sa'di, &c., and fragments of the Masnavi entitled سحر حلال, by Ahli Shīrāzi. See the Persian Catalogue, p. 657b. This last portion of the MS. is dated A.H. 1206.

377.

Or. 3552.—Foll. 191; 11¾ in. by 8; 12 lines, 4 in. long; written in fair large Nestalik about the middle of the 19th century.

[Sidney Churchill.]

بيان المحمود

A copious collection of the initial lines of Ghazals by contemporary poets, compiled by Maḥmūd Mirza (see no. 70).

Beg. بيان محمود در ستايش خداوند معبود سبحانه عن التحديد و الحدود

The author refers in the preface to his previous Tazkirah, Safīnat ul-Maḥmūd (no. 122), and says that he had compiled the present work immediately after completing the latter. The date of composition, A.H. 1240, is fixed by the following line of a Ḳiṭ'ah composed in praise of the work by Aḳa Muḥammad Taḳi, poetically surnamed Sipihr (Majma' ul-Fuṣaḥā, ii., p. 156), and appended at the end:

زد بتاريخش رقم كلك همايون سپهر
كين بيان از هر زبان محمود چون چارم كتاب

The preface concludes with three pieces of the author's composition, a Kasidah in praise of the work and of Fath 'Ali Shāh, a Ḳiṭ'ah and a Rubā'i.

After the preface, foll. 7b—24a, comes a list of all poets included in the work, arranged in alphabetical order under their poetical surnames, with brief notices giving little more than the proper name and birthplace of each. The remainder of the MS. contains the opening Baits of Ghazals. They are arranged in alphabetical order according to the rhyme-letters, and, under each of these, according to the initial letters of the Baits. The name of the poet is written by the side of each verse in the margin.

378.

Or. 3604.—Foll. 178; 12¼ in. by 7¾; 21 lines, 6 in. long; written in four columns in cursive Nestalik on bluish paper, in the 19th century.

[Sidney Churchill.]

بديع الافكار

A Persian anthology with biographical notices, by Sayyid 'Abd ur-Raḥim al-Mūsavi B. Mīr Muḥammad Bāḳir 'Aliyabādi, poetically surnamed Munṣif.

Beg. ثنائى كه از حد حصر افزون و از حيز تعداد بيرون است مخصوص ذات واقف اسرار بيرون و درونيست كه

The author was born, as stated at the end, in Sāri, A.H. 1197. It appears from the preface that he wrote the present work for Muḥ. Kāzim Mirza, eldest son of Muḥ. Ḳuli Mirza, son of Fatḥ 'Ali Shāh, at the young prince's request, in order to save him the trouble of carrying about many volumes of poetry. It was commenced in Sāri, A.H. 1237, when the prince's father assumed the government of Tabaristan, and was finished on the 3rd of Jumāda II., A.H. 1239. The author made use of several Divans and of the following Tazkirahs: Haft Iḳlīm, Daulatshāh, Tuḥfah i Sāmi, Bahāristān, Ātashkadah, and Zīnat ul-Madā'iḥ by Humā (no. 118).

The work is divided into six Ḳisms, containing respectively poems belonging to six kinds of poetical compositions, namely Kasidahs, Ghazals, Masnavis, Muḳaṭṭa'āt, Rubā'is and Tarji'-bands. In each Ḳism the pieces are alphabetically arranged according to the takhallus of the authors, with the exception of those of royal princes, which take precedence. The contents are as follows:

Ḳism I., fol. 5*a*. Kasidahs, beginning with one by Fatḥ 'Ali Shah, and several by the royal prince Muḥ. Ḳuli Mirza (Khusravi, who died A.H. 1260; Majma' ul-Fuṣaḥā, vol. i., p. 25).

The alphabetical series begins with Anvari and ends with Yūsuf Amiri.

Ḳism II., fol. 89*b*. Ghazals, beginning with some by Khusravi and other princes. The alphabetical series begins with Ahli Turshīzi and ends with Yūsuf Beg Istājlu.

Ḳism III., fol. 117*a*. Masnavis of Ahli Shīrāzi and others, ending with Hijri Abu 'l-Ḳāsim.

Ḳism IV., fol. 140*a*. Muḳaṭṭa'āt, from Anvari to Humāyūn of Isfahan.

Ḳism V., fol. 152*b*. Rubā'is, from Ustād Abu 'l-Faraj to Yamīn ud-Dīn Ṭughrā'i.

Ḳism VI., fol. 163*a*. Tarji'-bands, beginning with Jāmi and ending with Hātif.

Life and poems of the author, foll. 174*a*—178*b*.

379.

Or. 4673.—Foll. 343; $11\frac{3}{4}$ in. by 8; 21 lines, $5\frac{3}{4}$ in. long; written in cursive Nestalik, in four gold-ruled columns, with three 'Unvāns, apparently about the middle of the 19th century. Bound in painted and glazed covers. [Sidney Churchill.]

میزان طبایع

A Persian anthology compiled by Ḥaidar Ḳuli Mirza, poetically styled Khāvar (see his Divan, no. 359), with a preface by an anonymous dependant of the prince, beginning: ستایش و سپاس مر معبود بیزوالی را رواست که صحایف طرایف الخ

After a glowing eulogy on the reigning sovereign, Fatḥ 'Ali Shāh, and on the incomparable poets of his time, the writer says that Ḥaidar Ḳuli Mirza in compiling this work had been content to group together poems composed by various poets with the same metre and rhyme, and had refrained from entering upon biographical details or literary criticism. He states in conclusion that the work was completed A.H. 1242.

The anthology comprises Kasidahs, Ghazals, and Rubā'is, by ancient and modern poets, in three separate sections, in each of which the alphabetical order of the rhymes is followed, and the names of the poets form the headings.

The Kasidahs begin, fol. 4*b*, as follows:

عروس عافیت انکه قبول کرد مرا
که عمر بیش بها دادمش بشیز بها

The following are the poets included under the rhyme-letter ا: Anvari, Saḥāb, Mijmar

(Sayyid Ḥusain Iṣfahāni), Khāḳāni, Salmān, Mu'izzi, Madhūsh (Muḥ. Ṣādiḳ Gulpāigāni), Rashid Vaṭvāṭ, Khusravi, Khāvari (Fazl-ullah Shirāzi), Hātif, Sabāḥi (Ḥāji Sulaimān), Ẓahir Fāriyābi, and Ṣabā (Fatḥ 'Ali Khān).

The Ghazals begin, fol. 108*b*, with one by Khāḳān (Fatḥ 'Ali Shāh), the first line of which is:

بیك کرشمه پری پیکری دل مارا
چنان ربود که ترکان متاع یغمارا

The Rubā'is occupy foll. 330*b*—343*a*.

TALES AND FABLES.

380.

Or. 3529.—Foll. 33; 11¼ in. by 7½; 23 lines, 5⅜ in. long; written in fair Nestalik, apparently in the 18th century.

[SIDNEY CHURCHILL.]

[قصۀ بلوهر و یوذاسف]

The story of Bilauhar and Yūẕāsaf, by Ibn Bābavaih.

Beg. ابن بابویه علیه الرحمة والرضوان در کتاب کمال الدین و تمام النعمه بسند خود از محمد بن زکریا روایت کرده است که پادشاهی بود در ممالك هندوستان با لشکر فراوان و مملکت وسیع

This is the work, of Buddhistic origin, which has become known in Europe, through the medium of a Christian version in Greek, as the "Book of Barlaam and Josaph," and which was translated into Arabic verse in the eighth century by Abān Lāḥiḳi. See Zotenberg, Notice sur le Livre de Barlaam et Joasaph, Notices et Extraits, tom. xxviii; and Fihrist, pp. 119, 163, 305.

The present text is taken, as stated at the beginning, from Ibn Bābavaih's work entitled كمال الدين وتمام النعمة. This is one of the numerous Arabic writings of the celebrated Shī'ah theologian, who died in Rai, A.H. 381 (see the Arabic Supplement, no. 330). A copy is described by Ahlwardt in the Berlin Catalogue, no. 2721, and to Dr. Hommel belongs the credit of having discovered in that voluminous MS. the Arabic original of our Persian version. See Weisslovits's "Prinz und Derwisch," 1890, p. 132. Muḥammad Ibn Zakariyyā, quoted as authority at the beginning of the Persian translation, although not in the Arabic text, is, as Dr. Hommel suggests with great probability, no other than the renowned physician and philosopher Rāzi, who was a contemporary of Ibn Bābavaih, and like him lived at Rai.

Full accounts of the present MS. have been published, with extensive extracts, by Baron Rosen and Dr. von Oldenburg in the Zapiski of the Archaeological Society, vol. iii., pp. 273—76, and vol. iv., pp. 229—65. An abridgment of the work in Arabic was published by Dr. Hommel from a Halle MS. in the Verhandlungen des VII. Orientalisten-Congresses, Semitische Section, pp. 138—162. Another and fuller Arabic text was lithographed in Bombay, A.H. 1306.

Another copy of the same Persian version is included in the Zubdat ul-Tavārikh, no. 36, foll. 226—240. In the heading it is described as extracted from the 'Ain ul-Ḥayāt of Aḳā Muḥ. Bāḳir [Majlisi], who gives it on the authority of Ibn Bābavaih, مرحوم اقا محمد باقر در عین الحیوة بسند معتبر از ابن بابویه که در کمال الدین از محمد زکریا نقل کرده است

According to this, it was probably Muḥ. Bāḳir, who translated into Persian the Arabic text of Ibn Bābavaih.

381.

Or. 2799.—Foll. 280; 9 in. by 5½; 23 lines, 3¾ in. long; written in neat Nestalik, with 'Unvān and gold-ruled margins; dated A.H. 908 (A.D. 1502). [Sidney Churchill.]

انوار سهیلی

The well-known version of Kalilah and Dimnah, by Ḥusain Kāshifi. See the Persian Catalogue, p. 756*a*, and, for other MSS., Pertsch, Berlin Catalogue, no. 1000; Rosen, Institut, no. 104; and Ethé, Bodleian Catalogue, no. 431.

382.

Or. 2956.—Foll. 196; 7¾ in. by 5; 15 lines, 5¾ in. long; written in fair Nestalik, with ruled margins, apparently in the 15th century. [Sidney Churchill.]

مرزبان نامه

A book of apologues, written in imitation of Kalilah and Dimnah.

Beg. حمد و ثنای که روائح ذکر آن جون ثنایای صبح بر نکهت دهان گل خنده زند

This is a modern version, in elegant prose, of the old Marzabān Nāmah, written in old Persian and in the dialect of Ṭabaristān by the Ispahbad Marzabān B. Rustam B. Sharvīn in the fourth century of the Hijrah. A full account of the origin and contents of the work will be found in C. Schefer's Chrestomathie Persane, vol. ii., pp. 194—209. The author of the present version, whose name does not appear in our MS., is, according to M. Schefer, Sa'd al-Varāvīnī, so called from Varāvīn, a village of Azarbaijan. He wrote this work in Ispahan, and dedicated it to a Vazir who in the preface is only designated by his Laḳab, Khwājah Zain ud-Dīn, or, as written in the next copy, Khwājah Rabīb ud-Dīn, but whose proper name is given at the end, fol. 194*b*, namely, Rabīb ud-Dīn Abu 'l-Ḳāsim Hārūn. In the same passage the Atabek Uzbek B. Muḥammad B. Ildugnz, who reigned in Azarbaijan A.H. 607—612, is named as the reigning sovereign.

In the preface the author enumerates the standard works of elegant prose which he had taken as his models, beginning with Kalilah, Sindbād Nāmah, Maḳāmāt i Hamīdi, &c. The most recent of these is the Persian translation of the Yamīni, which was written about A.H. 602 (see the Persian Catalogue, p. 158). The preface concludes with a table of the nine Bābs into which the work is divided. They bear the following headings:

Fol. 9*b*.	در تعریف کتاب و ذکر واضع	I.
Fol. 25*b*.	در ذکر ملك و وصایای که فرزندان را فرمود	II.
Fol. 39*b*.	در ذکر ملك اردشیر و داناء مهران به	III.
Fol. 58*a*.	در ذکر دیو کاوپای و داناء دینی	IV.
Fol. 74*b*.	در ذکر دادمه و داستان	V.
Fol. 95*a*.	در ذکر زیرك و زروی	VI.
Fol. 125*b*.	در ذکر پیل و شیر	VII.
Fol. 152*a*.	در ذکر شتر و شیر پارسا	VIII.
Fol. 176*a*.	در ذکر عقاب و ایرا و آزاد چهره	IX.

In an appendix entitled ذیل الکتاب, fol. 194*b*, the author, after dilating on the merits of his book, describes a library founded by his patron in Isfahan and the rich store of works on every science which it contained. The appendix wants about two pages at the end.

For other MSS., see Dorn, Petersburg Catalogue, p. 406; the Leyden Catalogue, vol. i., p. 353; the Paris Catalogue, p. 304, no. 384; Molla Firuz Library, p. 231, no. 49; and Schefer, Chrestomathie, vol. ii., p. 209. The Marzabān Nāmah has been translated into Arabic and lithographed in Cairo, A.H. 1278. See also Sprenger's Library, no. 1248, and Pertsch, Gotha Catalogue, vol. iv., p. 427.

383.

Or. 2973.—Foll. 187; $8\frac{1}{2}$ in. by $5\frac{1}{4}$; 15 lines, 3 in. long; written in elegant Shikastah, A.H. 1277 (A.D. 1860—61).

[Sidney Churchill.]

Another copy of the Marzabān Nāmah.

The nine sections, termed in this copy Faṣl, begin as follows: I. fol. 8*a*; II. fol. 24*a*; III. fol. 47*a*; IV. fol. 55*a*; V. fol. 71*b*; VI. fol. 91*a*; VII. fol. 120*b*; VIII. fol. 146*b*; IX. fol. 166*a*; and the Khātimah, fol. 183*a*.

384.

Or. 2781.—Foll. 363; $9\frac{1}{2}$ in. by 6; 25 lines, $3\frac{3}{4}$ in. long; written in small and neat Nestalik, with 'Unvān and gold-ruled margins, apparently in the 16th century.

[Comte de Gobineau.]

داراب نامه

The Dārāb Nāmah, by Abu Ṭāhir Ṭarasūsi.

The first folio is mutilated, so that about half of the first seven lines is lost, but the missing words are supplied by the next copy. The beginning is as follows: الحمد لله رب العالمين . . . از راویان اخبار و ناقلان آثار و خوانندگان قصص و تواریخ استاد فاضل کامل ابو طاهر بن حسن بن علی بن موسی الطرسوسی اسعده الله فی الدارین چنین روایت میکند که مر زال زر را سه پسر بود یکی رستم دوم زواره سیم شغاد و این شغاد از کنیزك هندی بود

The author, who is called here Abu Ṭāhir B. Ḥasan B. 'Ali B. Mūsa aṭ-Ṭarasūsi, has been mentioned in the Turkish Catalogue, p. 220, as the author of Ḳirān i Ḥabashi and other romances. The present work, although dealing largely with the life and adventures of Iskandar, is generally called Dārāb Nāmah (a title not found in this copy), from Dārāb, the hero of its first portion. Although its framework and leading names are borrowed from the Shāhnāmah, it is a pure romance, in which the original legend is all but lost under a luxuriant growth of the most fanciful fiction. The contents have been briefly, but very aptly, described by J. Mohl in his preface to the Shāhnāmah, p. 74, and by B. Dorn, Mélanges Asiatiques, tom. vii., p. 174-5, and p. 406-7. The short account of the work in Charles Stewart's Catalogue, p. 7, no. xiv., is misleading.

The work is divided into sections of unequal length, the beginning of which is marked by this invariable rubric: اما مولف اخبار و گذارندهٔ اسرار ابو طاهر طرسوسی ازین قصه چنین روایت میکند

The narrative begins with a mention of the three sons of Zāl i Zar, and of the artifice by which Shaghād compassed the death of his brother Rustam. After a brief account of Bahman and Ardashīr, we are told, fol. 2*b*, how Humāi secretly gave birth to the latter's posthumous child, afterwards called Dārāb, and entrusted him, like Moses, enclosed in a coffer, to the stream of Euphrates. The life and adventures of Dārāb occupy the first part of the volume down to fol. 128*b*, where his death and the accession of Dārāb junior (داراب کهین) are briefly recorded. The marvellous career of his son Iskandar, whose clandestine birth had been previously described, fol. 126, fills the remainder of the volume, which is slightly defective at the end. The last pages deal with the wall built by Iskandar against Yājūj and Mājūj, with his journey, under the guidance of Khiẓr, to the land of darkness and to the spring of the water of life, and with his miraculous conveyance from thence to Mount Ḳāf. The last words are: فرشته گفت این سنگ بر مثال تست و این خاك بر مثال خاك گور ترا بازی نماید که از سر تا پای جهان از تری و خشکی

385.

Or. 4615.—Foll. 129; 14 in. by 9¼; 25 lines, 5⅝ in. long; written in fair Nestalik, with 'Unvān, gold-ruled margins, and numerous miniatures, probably about the close of the 16th century.

Another copy of the Dārāb Nāmah, containing only the first part of the work, namely, the story of Dārāb, and closely agreeing, as far as it goes, with the preceding MS. It ends abruptly at the point where Nāhīd, the newly-wedded bride of Dārāb, sent back by him to her father Filḳūs, bewails her hard fate. The last words are: و آن دختر بنشست و سر بزانو نهاد و گریستن گرفت آن بخت بد خویش که از پدرش خراج دو ساله گرفتند و چون چهار ماه گذشت

This passage occurs on fol. 126*b* of the preceding MS., line 13.

This MS. is profusely adorned on almost every folio with miniatures in the best style of Indian art. It is probably one of those which were illuminated for the emperor Akbar. The miniatures are generally signed by the artists, mostly Hindus, and among these are found the following six, mentioned in the Ā'īn i Akbari, Blochmann's translation, p. 108, as painters employed by Akbar: Kesu, Farrukh, Mādhu, Jagan, Mahis, and Sānwlah. Other artists whose names frequently recur in the MS. are Nānhā, Bhagwān, Dhanu, Chaturbhuj, Mithrā, Tiriyyā, and Bhūrah, also two bearing Muslim names, viz. Ibrāhīm Ḳahhār and Mukhliṣ. Several of the above names have been already mentioned as attached to miniatures in the Vāḳi'āt i Bābari, no. 75.

The last page of the MS. bears the vermilion stamps of the kings of Oude.

386.

Or. 3600.—Foll. 2; 2 ft. 8 in. by 2 ft. 2 in.; 19 lines, 21 in. long; written in fine large Nestalik, apparently in the 17th century.

[Presented by Rev. STRATON CAMPBELL.]

Two detached leaves of a huge MS. of the romance of Amir Ḥamzah Ṣāḥibḳirān. Each of them has a portion of the text on one side and a large picture in Indian style on the other.

Fol. 1 begins as follows: راوی این روایت زیبا اینچنین نقش بست بر دیبا که چون دیو شاهزاده نور الدهر را در دریا انداخت

It is related in the first lines how Prince Nūr ud-dahr, having been thrown into the sea by a Div, is rescued by the prophet Elias. This is the subject represented in the picture. The text of the second folio deals with the adventures of Zummurrud Shāh, the giant king of the sun-worshippers. The picture represents him falling head foremost from his castle and being seized by Malik Īraj.

For MSS. of that voluminous tale, see the Persian Catalogue, pp. 760—62, and Ethé, Bodleian Catalogue, no. 473. An Arabic version is noticed by Pertsch, Gotha Catalogue, no. 2420.

387.

Or. 3501.—Foll. 253; 10¼ in. by 5½; 18 lines, 3⅝ in. long; written in small and elegant

Nestalik, with 'Unvān and gold-ruled margins, in the latter half of the 19th century. Bound in painted and glazed covers.

[Sidney Churchill.]

حقيقة الحقائق شاهيه

A work in proof of the superiority of man to all other beings, by Muḥammad 'Ali B. Iskandar ash-Shirvāni.

Beg. رب اشرح لی صدری و يسر لی امری واحلل عقدة من لسانی يفقهوا قولی لك الحمد يا ذا الجود والعلی ... اجناس سپاس خورشيد اقتباس و انجم قياس که از مقياس عقول و حواس جن و ناس خارج است

This is a much expanded version and Sufi adaptation of the famous "Contest between man and animals," which forms part of the twenty-first treatise of the Ikhwān uṣ-Ṣafā (see the Arabic Supplement, p. 481b). It is written in florid prose, freely interspersed with verses, with Arabic texts from Coran and Hadis, and with passages of Sufi writers. It was composed, as stated in the introduction, fol. 24b, in Ardabil in the month of Jumāda II., A.H. 1250, and is dedicated to Muḥammad Shāh B. 'Abbās Shāh B. Fath 'Ali Shāh Ḳājār. The date of completion, A.H. 1252, is given in a versified chronogram at the end:

طبع افسرده گفت تاريخش
هی بيان شرافت الانسان

The scope of the work is set forth in the following line, fol. 29b: كتابی در شرافت انسان بر كل ما فی الكون والامكان كائنا ما كان

Its full title, as given in the same passage is: حقيقة الحقائق شاهيه فی التلويح الی ترجيح المسالك النعمت الهيه

The author was an extensive traveller, who had wandered over most parts of the Muslim world in search of religious teachers and of great mystics. From a full account of those travels, foll. 21—24, the following particulars may be briefly stated. Having left as a boy his native country for the holy shrines of Irak, he spent there close upon twenty years, studying under his father and other holy men. He lost his father and many of his friends, who died as martyrs during the incursion of the Vahhābis. He then repaired to Baghdad and to Irak 'Ajam, where he met his brother al-Ḥāj Zain ul-'Ābidin (author of Riyāẓ us-Siyāḥat, no. 139), and a holy man, Ḥāji Muḥ. Ja'far Hamadāni, called Majzūb 'Ali Shāh. Hence, after a stay in Shiraz, he sailed to India, and visited in succession Karachi, Haidarabad, Shikarpur, Surat, Bombay, Puna, Tiling, Aurangabad, Haidarabad of Deccan, Machli-Bandar, Sikakul, Pegu, Calcutta, Murshidabad, Benares, Lucknow, Agra, Delhi, Lahore, Kashmir, Peshawar, Kabul, and the Kūhistān of the Hazārah, where he fell captive into the hands of the cruel Uzbeks, and was taken to Ḳunduz, seat of Ḳilich Kuli Khān. After his release he reached Kandahar, Herat, and Mashhad, and, finally, Hamadān. There he met again his old master, Majzūb 'Ali Shāh, who sent him on a pilgrimage to Mecca and Medina. From the latter place he went through Syria and Rūm to Istambol, where he stayed three years, and witnessed the revolt of the Janissaries. After some more pilgrimages and a stay of six years at Cairo, he returned by way of Mecca and by sea to Shiraz, and thence to Teheran, Tabaristan and Gilan.

Contents: Introduction treating chiefly of mystic lore. Life of the author, fol. 21b. Eulogy on the Shah, fol. 25a. Preface proper, سبب تاليف, fol. 29a.

The narrative begins at fol. 29b, and deals at first with the legend of Kayūmars, the murder of Siyāmuk, and the hostility of

Jinns and animals towards men, down to the time of Sulaimān. Complaints of the hawk, fish, snake, bee, and other animals against man, fol. 54. Messengers sent by Malik Dādbakhsh and by the animals, fol. 76a. Beginning of the trial before Malik Dādbakhsh. Debate of the camel with the sage of Hijaz, fol. 95b. Debate of the ant with the sage of Shām, fol. 106a. Debate of the fox with the sage of Khiṭā, fol. 119a. Debate of the spider with the sage of Rūm, fol. 127a. Debate of the tortoise with the sage of Irak, fol. 135b. Debate of the sage of Hindustan with the peacock, fol. 146b. Debate of the sage of Shirvan with the Humāi, fol. 153b. (The sage of Shirvan is evidently meant to represent the author himself, who here displays at great length his mystical lore.) Allegorical description of the author's journey to the region of the soul, اقليم نفس, foll. 242b—253a.

388.

Or. 3223.—Foll. 232; 12 in. by 8½; 15 lines, 6 in. long; written in large Nestalik, apparently in India about the close of the 18th century.

قصة الجوهر

The tale of Muḥammad Mas'ūd Shāh, son of 'Azīz Shāh, king of Isfahan, and of his loves with Nīk-Iḳbāl, daughter of the Vazir Farrukhfāl, and with Gītī-ārā.

This is an enlarged version of the tale mentioned in the Persian Catalogue, p. 773a. The above title is found in a versified prologue beginning:

بدان ای مرد عاقلند عاقل
که هستی در جمیع علم کامل

in which the writer puts the tale into the mouth of a young man called Sulṭān 'Ali, whom he had met on the road and invited to his house. The prose narrative begins, fol. 3a, as follows: الحمد لله رب العالمين ... قصه ... اثار و داستان طرازان روزكار ... چنين روايت ميكنند كه در شهر اصفهان پادشاهى بود عزيز شاه نام كه صيت جاه و حشمش چون باد صبا باطراف جهان رسانده

There are miniatures in Indian style on foll. 4, 5, 12, 14 and 33, and, further on, a few unfinished sketches in outline. Spaces reserved for pictures in the remainder of the volume have not been filled in.

In the colophon the work is called قصه محمد مسعودشاه پادشاه

Collections of Anecdotes.

389.

Or. 3590.—Foll. 126; 10¼ in. by 5¾; 20 lines, 4 in. long; written in neat Nestalik, probably in the 17th century.

الفرج بعد الشده

The Persian translation of "al-Faraj ba'd ash-Shiddah," or tales of deliverance from distress or danger. See the Persian Catalogue, p. 751b.

Beg. از ارباب معنى و اصحاب هنر چنان اقتضا كرد كه درين معنى

This is not the real beginning of the work, but the first line of the second chapter of the preface, ذكر تصنيف اين كتاب. See the complete copy, Add. 7673, fol. 3b.

At the end there are some lacunæ, and the MS. breaks off with the verse beginning اى عادت تو چه خور, which is found in the last-named MS. at fol. 341b. There are about seven or eight folios wanting at the end.

The Persian translation was lithographed at Bombay, 1859. For other MSS. see Krafft, p. 54; Asiatisches Museum, pp. 291, 351; Mulla Firuz, p. 228; and Pertsch, Berlin Catalogue, no. 1021.

390.

Or. 3507.—Foll. 37; $9\frac{1}{2}$ in. by $5\frac{1}{2}$; 21 lines, $3\frac{5}{8}$ in. long; written in fair Nestalik; dated Rabi' II., A.H. 1017 (A.D. 1608).

[Sidney Churchill.]

چهار مقاله

Chahār Makālah, or the Four Discourses, by Aḥmad B. 'Umar B. 'Ali an-Niẓāmi al-'Arūẓi as-Samarkandi.

Beg. حمد و شکر و سپاس مر آن پادشاهی را که عالم عود و معادرا بتوسط ملائکه کروبی و روحانی در وجود آورد .... آغاز کتاب بنده مخلص و خادم معتقد احمد بن عمر بن علی النظامی العروضی السمرقندی الخ

The author, who was apparently a native of Samarkand, must have been well advanced in years when he wrote the present work; for he says at the outset that he had then spent forty-five years of his life in the service of the Ghūri dynasty. From various passages of the Chahār Makālah the following particulars of his life may be gathered. While he was still in Samarkand, A.H. 504, he received some information about the poet Rūdagi from the Dihkan Abu Rajā Aḥmad B. 'Abd uṣ-Ṣamad al-'Ābidi (fol. 15a). Two years later, A.H. 506, he was at Balkh conversing with 'Umar Khayyām, whom he revered as his master, and whose tomb he afterwards visited in Nishapur, A.H. 530 (fol. 27a). In A.H. 510 we find him at Nishapur (fol. 5a), and, in the course of the same year, at Herat, from whence he repaired to the court of Sultan Sinjar, near Ṭūs. There he received advice and encouragement from the Malik ush-Shu'arā, Amīr Mu'izzi, and paid a visit to the tomb of Firdausi (foll. 18a, 22b). In A.H. 914 he was again in Nishapur in the company of Mu'izzi (fol. 22a).

Niẓāmi 'Arūẓi is chiefly known by his prose works, viz., the present one and a collection of anecdotes entitled مجمع النوادر, both of which are mentioned by Haj. Khal., vol. ii., p. 656, and vol. v., p. 405. But he ranked also high as a poet. He is noticed by 'Aufi, Oude Catalogue, p. 4, no. 56, among the great poets of Māvarā-unnahr. See also Daulatshāh, i. 13; Haft Iḳlīm, Add. 16,734, fol. 562b; and Majma' ul-Fuṣaḥā, vol. i., p. 635. He calls himself in the present work, fol. 13a, one of the four poets who immortalised the name of the kings of Ghūr.

Chahār Maḳālah was written for a prince of that house, namely, al-Malik Ḥusām ud-Daulah wa'd-Din Abu'l-Ḥasan 'Ali B. Mas'ūd. Although that prince's name is preceded in the preface by the most pompous regal titles, he does not appear to have ever attained sovereign rank. He is mentioned in Ṭabaḳāt i Nāṣiri, Raverty's translation, p. 425, as one of the sons of Malik Fakhr ud-Dīn Mas'ūd, who was installed by his younger brother, the great Sultan of Ghaznīn, 'Alā ud-Dīn Ḥusain Jahān-sūz, on the throne of Ghūr and Tukhāristān (see Ṭabaḳāt i Nāṣiri, pp. 347—365).

After bestowing due praise on the young prince, the author proceeds to eulogize his nearest relatives, namely, his father, Fakhr ud-Daulah wa'd-Din Mas'ūd, the reigning king of Bāmiyān, his brother Shams ud-Dīn Muḥammad (who afterwards succeeded to the throne), and his mighty uncle, the above-mentioned Sultan, 'Alā ud-Dīn Ḥusain, all three being spoken of as still living.

The precise date of composition is not given, but it can be brought within narrow limits. The work must have been written between the death of Sultan Sinjar, who is spoken of as dead, and that of Sultan 'Alā ud-Din Husain, who is described as the reigning sovereign, that is to say between A.H. 552 and 556. For the death of the latter see Kāmil, vol. xi., p. 179, and Jahān-ārā, fol. 117.

The work consists, as its name implies, of four Maḳālahs, treating respectively of four classes of men of whose services kings stand in need, namely, Vazirs, poets, astrologers, and physicians, and of the sciences and qualifications requisite for each, the whole being illustrated by historical anecdotes. Some preliminary chapters, foll. 2*b*—6*a*, treat of cosmology and of the various faculties of minerals, plants, animals and, lastly, man. They include a curious observation on the voluntary motions of some plants, which are thereby raised to the confines of the animal kingdom. The four Maḳālahs begin as follows:

I. در ماهیت دبیری و کیفیت دبیر کامل Fol. 6*a*.

II. در ماهیت شعر و صلاحیت شاعر Fol. 12*a*.

III. در ماهیت علم نجوم و غزارت منجم Fol. 23*b*.

IV. در ماهیت علم طب و هدایت طبیب Fol. 29*a*.

The second Maḳālah is of especial value as containing notices and anecdotes relating to early Persian poets, such as Rūdagi, 'Unṣuri, Farrukhi, Mu'izzi, Badīhi, Firdausi, &c. It is frequently quoted in later Tazkirahs.

The Chahār Maḳālah was lithographed in Teheran, A.H. 1305. For another copy see further on, no. 41*d*.

391.

Or. 2676.—Foll. 290; 13¼ in. by 9; from 29 to 33 lines, about 6¾ in. long; written in fine old Neskhi, with a gilt frontispiece and ruled margins; dated Wednesday, 24 Ramazan, A.H. 732 (A.D. 1332). [H. G. Keene.]

جامع الحکایات

Jāmi' ul-Ḥikāyāt, the celebrated collection of historical anecdotes by Muḥammad 'Aufi. See the Persian Catalogue, p. 749*b*, and Ethé, Bodleian Catalogue, no. 324.

This fine volume has unfortunately been damaged by damp, and some leaves, foll. 48—52, are slightly mutilated. It contains the last three of the four books (Ḳism) into which that extensive work is divided.

The fourth Ḳism, which derives a special interest from its chapters on geography and natural history, is placed first, and has the following inscription written in the Ṣulsi character on two gilt borders at the top and bottom of its first page: قسم چهارم از کتاب جامع الحکایات و لوامع الروایات در فواید خوف و رجا

The first of the twenty-five Bābs which it contains has no special heading, and begins as follows: جوامع [read جامع] این حکایات محمد عوفی می کوید وقتی شهاب الدین عیوقی که وکیل خاص در سلطان سکندر بوذ و بخدمت شیخ الشیوخ مجد الدین بغدادی نامه نوشت و درخواست کرد که بهمت عالی مدد باید فرموذ الخ

In the complete copy, Add. 16,682, this anecdote is the third of the first Bāb, fol. 326*a*; but there are great differences between the two texts. The headings of the remaining Bābs, which also partly differ from those given by Flügel in the Vienna Catalogue, vol. i., pp. 411—12, are in the MS. as follows:

II. در عواید خدمت ملوك و سلاطین Fol. 7a.

III. در فواید خوف و رجا Fol. 9b.

IV. در تاثیر دعا و ذکر کسانی کی ببرکات دعا خلاص یافتند Fol. 12b.

V. در دعوات ماثور یاذ کرد شوذ Fol. 15b.

VI. در عجایب فالهای خوب کی زده اند Fol. 18b.

VII. در حکایه کسانی کی بورطه محنت در ماندند باتفاق جلیس خلاص یافتند Fol. 21b.

VIII. در ذکر جماعتی کی از دست دزدان خلاص یافتند Fol. 25b.

IX. در ذکر جماعتی که از جنك سباع ضاری خلاص یافتند Fol. 28b.

X. در ذکر جماعتی که بمحنت عشق فرو ماندند و بمراد نرسیدند Fol. 34a.

XI. در ذکر جماعتی که در ورطه عشق کرفتار شذند و بعاقبت بمراد رسیدند Fol. 37b.

XII. در ذکر جماعتی که بورطه هلاك افتادند و بعاقبت . . . Fol. 49b.

XIII. در عجایب قضا و قدر و موافقت و مخالفت ان Fol. 54b.

XIV. در بیان غرایب خلقت Fol. 59a.

XV. در اعمار حیوانات و ذکر طول و عرض ان Fol. 61b.

XVI. در بیان ممالك و مسالك صرود و جروم Fol. 64b.

XVII. در ذکر روم و حبشه و هند Fol. 68a.

XVIII. در ذکر بناها عجایب Fol. 71a.

XIX. در ذکر عجایب طلسمات Fol. 74b.

XX. در ذکر اشیا و عجایب Fol. 77b.

XXI. در ذکر خواص سباع و وحوش و عجایب تاثیر ایشان Fol. 80b.

XXII. در ذکر سباع ضاری و وحوش درنده Fol. 85b.

XXIII. در ذکر غرایب حیوانات Fol. 90b.

XXIV. در ذکر غرایب طیور Fol. 93a.

XXV. در طرفی از طرف و ملح و هزل Fol. 96a.

This last chapter breaks off at the second page.

Kism II., which follows next, has lost the first Bāb. The following are the headings of the extant chapters:

II. در ستایش . . . . و تواضع Fol. 97a.

III. در فضیلت عفو کردن Fol. 99b.

IV. (در فواید حلم) Fol. 105a.

V. در فضیلت علو همت Fol. 116a.

VI. در فضیلت ادب Fol. 119a.

VII. در فضیلت رحمت و شفقت Fol. 124a.

VIII. در فضیلت توکل و تسلیم Fol. 126b.

IX. در فضیلت سخا و مروت Fol. 128b.

X. در بیان لطف و کرم Fol. 130b.

XI. در فضیلت ضیافت و ذکر . . . Fol. 134a.

XII. در ذکر شجاعت Fol. 139a.

XIII. در فضیلت صبر و ذکر ان Fol. 142a.

XIV. در فواید مزید شکر و ذکر ان Fol. 145a.

XV. در حزم و اندیشه و ذکر ان Fol. 147b.

XVI. در زهد و ورع و فضیلت ان Fol. 152b.

XVII. در فضیلت جد و جهد Fol. 157a.

XVIII. در فضیلت نطق و سکوت Fol. 161a.

XIX. در فضیلت وفا Fol. 164b.

XX. در اصلاح ذات البین وصلت رحم Fol. 168b.

XXI. در فواید کتمان سر Fol. 171a.

XXII. در فضیلت امانت وفواید ان Fol. 174b.

XXIII. دربیان مکارم اخلاق و محاسن شیم Fol. 179a.

XXIV. در عزیمت و نیت کارها و فواید ان Fol. 185b.

XXV. در فواید عواید استمداد و مشورت کردن با مردمان Fol. 188b.

This last Bāb concludes with some verses in praise of the Vazir Niẓām ul-Mulk Ḳivām ud-Dīn, to whom the work was dedicated.

Ḳism III. is complete, and has the following headings to its twenty-five Bābs:

I. در بیان اختلاف طبایع انسان Fol. 193b.

II. در مذمت حقد و حسد Fol. 196b.

III. در مذمت حرص و بیان احوال حریصان Fol. 199b.

IV. در مذمت طمع Fol. 202b.

V. در ذکر طراران و دزدان و حکایت نوادر ایشان Fol. 205b.

VI. در لطایف حکایات کذابان و کلمات ایشان Fol. 209b.

VII. در مذمت دروغ کفتن و فواید صدق Fol. 213b.

VIII. در ذکر جماعتی که دعوی پیغمبری کردند بدروغ و ذکر مولد ایشان Fol. 218b.

IX. در مذمت بخل و حکایت بخیلان Fol. 224a.

X. در مذمت خلف وعده و نقض عهد Fol. 228b.

XI. در مذمت جهل و حکایة احمقان Fol. 232b.

XII. در مذمت ظلم و ذکر باذشاهان ظالم Fol. 236a.

XIII. در مذمت فظاظت و درشت خویی Fol. 240a.

XIV. در مذمت خساست و دنائت همت و ذکر خسیسان Fol. 243b.

XV. در مذمت اسراف و تبذیر Fol. 247b.

XVI. در مذمت خیانت در مال و ملك و حرم و غیران Fol. 250b.

XVII. در مذمت ناحفاظی Fol. 253a.

XVIII. در مذمت کفران نعمت و جماعتی که ببلای ان ماخوذ شدند Fol. 256b.

XIX. در مذمت نمام و غمز و سعایت Fol. 261a.

XX. در مذمت تعجیل و فواید تانی Fol. 264a.

XXI. در ذکر جماعتی ناحفاظ بی اعتقاد بی اصل Fol. 268b.

XXII. در ذکر زنان زیرك خردمند و لطایف اقوال ایشان Fol. 273a.

XXIII. در ذکر زنان پارسا نیکو سیرت Fol. 276b.

XXIV. در ذکر زنان نا پارسا نا حفاظ Fol. 280b.

XXV. در مکرها زنان و حکایت کیدها ایشان Fol. 285b.

A table of chapters of the three Ḳisms, by a later hand, has been prefixed to the volume.

Notes written on the title-page show that the MS. was bought A.H. 1119 by Burhān ud-Dīn Pārsā, and that it subsequently passed into the possession of a Mr. Gordon Ṣāḥib.

392.

Or. 4392.—Foll. 222; 11 in. by 8; 25 lines, $6\frac{1}{2}$ in. long; written in fair large Neskhi, with a gilt heading; dated 2 Jumāda II., A.H. 741 (A.D. 1340). [Wallis Budge.]

A portion of the first book of the Jāmi' ul-Ḥikāyāt.

It contains the preface and the first ten Bābs of Ḳism I., with some lacunæ and transpositions, as follows:

Preface, fol. 1*b*. Bāb I., در معرفت افریدکار تعالی, fol. 5*a*. A fragment of Bāb IX., fol. 11*a*. The latter part of Bāb III., fol. 15*a*. Bāb IV., در ذکر ملوك عرب و عجم و تواریخ دولت ایشان, fol. 21*b*. Bāb V., در ذکر تواریخ خلفا و بیان مآثر ایشان, fol. 67*a*. Bāb VI., در فضیلت عدل, fol. 128*b*. Bāb VII., در سیر ملوك و مآثر ایشان, در ملك داری و نیکو کاری, fol. 142*b*. Bāb VIII., در لطایف کلمات ملوك و سلاطین, fol. 157*b*. Bāb IX., در سیاست بادشاهان, fol. 164 (breaks off fol. 165). The latter part of Bāb I., fol. 166*a*. Bāb II., در معجزات انبیا علیهم السلام و ذکر احوال و اقوال ان, fol. 171*b*. Bāb III., در ذکر کرامات اولیا و مقامات اصفیا, fol. 197*b*. The latter part of Bāb IX., fol. 204*a*. Bāb X., در توقیعات بادشاهان, fol. 210*b* (breaking off fol. 212). Disjointed fragments, belonging for the most part to Bāb IV., fol. 213—222.

On the first page is an illuminated circular ornament with an inscription showing that the MS. was written for the library of some great Vazir called Ḥusām ud-Dīn Ṣirāf: برسم خزانة ... الصدر المعظم .... حسام الملة و الدین صیراف

Copyist: محمود بن احمد بن محمد التستری

393.

Or. 3207.—Foll. 153; 7 in. by 4¾; 17 lines, 2¾ in. long; written in fair archaic Neskhi, probably in the 13th century.

[Kremer, no. 210.]

A collection of anecdotes relating to saints and Sufis, without author's name.

Beg. الحمد لله رب العالمین والعاقبة للمتقین ... ثنا و ستایش مر خدایرا که افریدکار جهانست و افریدکار همهٔ جانوران است

The author was a Sunni, living apparently in the fifth century of the Hijrah. He reflects in the preface on the depravity of the time. "Holy Pīrs and pious men," he says, "are dead, and have carried away piety with them. Whoever wishes to keep his faith and be saved must not look to the men of his time or follow their example, but he must meditate on the lives of past worthies, and walk in their path, so that he may reach the degree of holiness at which they arrived."

The work is divided into twenty Bābs, enumerated in the preface, and each Bāb contains ten narratives headed حکایت. The headings of the Bābs are as follows:

I.	اندر خوردن حلال و نکاه داشتن قوت خویش	Fol. 4.
II.	در ریاضت و نفس را قهر کردن	Fol. 10.
III.	اندر رنج بردن و جهد کردن بر طاعت حق تعالی	Fol. 15.
IV.	اندر ترسیدن از خدای تعالی	Fol. 19.
V.	اندر نکاه داشتن زبان	Fol. 28.
VI.	اندر حکایات تایبان و سبب توبهٔ ایشان	Fol. 34.
VII.	اندر کرامات اولیا خدای تعالی	Fol. 54.
VIII.	اندر دعاها که کردند و در وقت مستجاب شد	Fol. 61.
IX.	اندر صدق اولیا و خبر دادن بر یکدیکر	Fol. 66.
X.	اندر توکل کردن بر خدای تعالی در همه حال	Fol. 69.
XI.	در سخا	Fol. 75.

XII. در ورع امرا Fol. 83.

XIII. در زهد النسا Fol. 89.

XIV. در کرامات صبیان Fol. 97.

XV. در کرامات اکابر Fol. 112.

XVI. در کرامات فقرا Fol. 121.

XVII. در اعانه خدای تعالی بر متحیران را Fol. 133.

XVIII. اندر اوقات اولیا و کرامات ایشان Fol. 141.

XIX. خوابها که دیده اند بزرگان را از بس مرك Fol. 146.

XX. حکایات براکنده از هر نوع Fol. 150.

The anecdotes relate to holy personages and Sufis of the first three centuries of the Hijrah, such as the early Khalifs, Amīr ul-Mu'minin 'Umar, 'Uṣmān, 'Ali, Mālik B. Dinār, Ibrāhīm Adham, Bāyazid Basṭāmi, Ẕu 'l-Nūn Miṣri, Sahl Tustari, Ibrāhīm B. Shaibān (d. A.H. 307), &c. The latest authority quoted is Abu Sa'īd Khargūshi (fol. 48), who died A.H. 407 (see the Arabic Supplement, no. 509), and whose work entitled Shi'ār uṣ-Ṣāliḥin (fol. 56) is the only one quoted by name.

This copy breaks off towards the end of the second anecdote of Bāb XX. A colophon by a later hand has been added. It is dated Rabī' I., A.H. 786 (A.D. 1384).

394.

Or. 2974.—Foll. 261; 10½ in. by 7; 15 lines, 5¼ in. long; written in large and distinct Neskhi, with ruled margins; dated Monday, the last day of Ṣafar, A.H. 910 (A.D. 1504).

[Sidney Churchill.]

نکارستان معینی

The Nigāristān of Mu'ini Juvaini. See the Persian Catalogue, p. 754b, and Daulatshāh, vi. 2. The seven Bābs begin respectively as follows: I. fol. 15b; II. fol. 47a; III. fol. 75b; IV. fol. 104a; V. fol. 161a; VI. fol. 192b; and VII. fol. 226a.

Copyist: عبد الرحیم بن الیاس بن علی شاه بن نصرالله بن قوام الدین التبریزی

395.

Or. 4907.—Foll. 254; 12 in. by 8; 22 lines, 4¾ in. long; written in cursive Nestalik, probably about the close of the 18th century.

[Sir Henry Rawlinson.]

زینت المجالس

A collection of anecdotes and miscellaneous notices, by Majd ud-Din Muḥammad al-Ḥusaini, surnamed Majdi. See the Persian Catalogue, p. 758, and Pertsch, Berlin Catalogue, no. 1017.

This copy presents lacunæ and transpositions which are not indicated by any break in the text. It begins with the heading: ذکر بعضی از قضایا که در زمان حیات حضرت رسول و بعد از وفات ان سرور از امیر المومنین حیدر صدور یافت, which belongs to the fifth Faṣl of Juz I. The same heading is found at fol. 49b of the complete copy, Or. 239, the contents of which are described in the Persian Catalogue.

The contents of the present MS. are as follows:

Juz I.: Latter part of Faṣl 5, fol. 1b. Faṣl 6, fol. 31b. Faṣl 7, fol. 52a. Faṣl 8, fol. 58b. Faṣl 9, fol. 64a. Faṣl 10, fol. 66b.

Juz II.: Faṣl 1, fol. 69b. Faṣl 2, fol. 72a. Faṣl 3, fol. 83a. Faṣl 4, fol. 92a. Faṣl 5, fol. 103b. Faṣl 6, fol. 109b. Faṣl 7, fol. 112a (breaking off at a passage corresponding with Or. 239, fol. 163a, line 16).

Juz V.: Faṣl 6, fol. 114b.

Juz IV.: Faṣl 8, fol. 117a. Faṣl 9, fol. 117b. Faṣl 10, fol. 120a.

Juz V.: Faṣl 1, fol. 123b. Faṣl 2, fol. 125b. Faṣl 3, fol. 127b. Faṣl 4, fol. 130a. Faṣl 5, fol. 131b. Faṣl 7, fol. 137a. Faṣl 8, fol. 141a. Faṣl 9, fol. 142b. Faṣl 10, fol. 144b.

Juz VI., fol. 146b. Juz VII., fol. 165b. Juz VIII., fol. 189b.

Juz IX.: Faṣl 1, fol. 221a. Faṣl 2, Geography of Iran and other countries, fol. 224a, breaking off in the course of the account of Egypt. Faṣl 9, imperfect at the beginning, fol. 244a—254b.

The extant portion of this last, or historical, section contains accounts of the Aḳ Ḳuyunlus, of the Uzbeks, fol. 246a, and of Shāh Isma'īl Safavi, fol. 247a. The last is brought down to A.H. 928.

On the fly-leaf: "Bought at Teheran. 4 Tomans. Jan. 12, 1838. H. Rawlinson."

396.

Or. 2957.—Foll. 119; 8¼ in. by 6¼; 15 lines, 3⅝ in. long; written in Nestalik; dated 1 Jumada II., A.H. 1291 (A.D. 1874).

[Sidney Churchill.]

خزان و بهار

A collection of moral tales and anecdotes in ornate prose and verse, by Muḥammad Sharīf B. Shams ud-Dīn Muḥammad, poetically styled Kāshif.

Beg. چمن آرای فرج بعد از شدت در خزان و بهار
روزگار لطف شامل حضرت سبحانی است

The author gives an account of his life and writings in a Khātimah, fol. 116b, written, like the whole work, in a florid style overloaded with metaphors. From it the following data may be gathered. His father (commonly called Shamsā i Shīrāzi) was a native of Shiraz settled at Kerbela. Driven from thence by Sunni persecution, A.H. 1006, he repaired to Isfahan, the author being then three years old, and proceeded, two years later, to Mashhad. After seven months spent in the holy city, he returned to Isfahan, where the author stayed twenty-three years, engaged in study and literary pursuits. They subsequently proceeded to Rai (Teheran), where the author lost his father, A.H. 1035, and discharged during fifteen years the office of Ḳāẓi. He wrote the present work at the request of his younger brother, Muḥ. Ismā'īl Munṣif (in the MS., مصنف; see the Oude Catalogue, p. 91, and Atashkadah, p. 312), who had written to him from India to that effect. It was completed, as stated at the end, A.H. 1060; but the following chronogram, occurring in the last line, gives a later date, A.H. 1063:

بتاریخ وی گفت رای رزین
که باید خزان و بهار این چنین

In the same Khātimah the author enumerates his previous works as follows: In verse, Laili Majnūn, Haft Paikar, 'Abbās Nāmah, Ghazals, Kasidahs, Rubā'is, &c.; in prose, Sirāj ul-Munīr (Persian Catalogue, p. 861b), Durr i Maknūn, Ḥawāss i Bāṭin, and miscellaneous compositions. Most of these works are also mentioned in the Tazkirah of Ṭāhir, Oude Catalogue, p. 91, and in Riyāẓ ush-Shu'arā, fol. 394b.

The tales are mostly taken, as stated in the preface, from "Faraj ba'd az Shiddat" (Persian Catalogue, p. 751b), the style of which the author considered too plain and bare of rhetorical ornaments; but some of them relate to later periods down to the author's time.

The Khazān u Bahār is divided into a Muḳaddimah, fourteen chapters termed Asās, and the above-mentioned Khātimah. The Mukaddimah, fol. 5a, is in glorification of 'Ali, whose fourteen virtues are illustrated by incidents of his life. The same virtues form the headings of the chapters called Asās, which are as follows: I. صبر, fol. 10a. II. رحم, fol. 15b. III. ادب, fol. 27a. IV. طهارت, fol. 34a. V. عبادت, fol. 42a. VI. لطف, fol. 49b. VII. يقين, fol. 57a. VIII. حلم, fol. 64b. IX. قناعت, fol. 73a. X. نصرت, fol. 80a. XI. مروت, fol. 86a. XII. سخاوت, fol. 91a. XIII. كرامت, fol. 99b. XIV. هدايت, fol. 106a.

The work was lithographed at Tabriz, A.H. 1294. A MS. has been fully described by Baron v. Rosen, Institut, no. 107.

397.

Or. 3499.—Foll. 236; 14 in. by 8½; 21 lines, 5¼ in. long; written in fair Nestalik, with ruled margins, apparently in the first half of the 19th century. [Sidney Churchill.]

مفرح القلوب

"Mufarriḥ ul-Ḳulūb," a work treating of moral virtues, illustrated by the precepts of Muḥammad and the Imams, and by tales and anecdotes, with an historical appendix, by Muḥammad Nadīm B. Muḥammad Kāẓim.

Beg. مفرح القلوبی که ذکر صنایع کوناکون و تعداد
آلای از حد افزون ابواب فرح بر قلوب عارفان
حقیقت بین کشاید

The author, who is known by his poetical surname Nadīm, was a native of Bārfurūsh in Māzandarān. His father had been Khwān-sālār, or steward, to Agha Muḥammad, and he became himself a great favourite with Fatḥ 'Ali Shāh, who employed him as reader and librarian. He died A.H. 1241. See Nigāristān i Dārā, fol. 129a, and, for other notices, Anjuman i Khāḳān, fol. 101a; Safīnat ul-Maḥmūd, fol. 249; and Majma' ul-Fuṣaḥā, vol. ii., p. 514.

The author says in the preface that he had been brought up at Court, and had had his mind improved by the conversation of the learned men who gathered there. He was encouraged to undertake the present work by the Shāh, who gave to it the above title.

The work is divided into five Bābs, each subdivided into two Faṣls, and a Khātimah. The Faṣls treat of various religious and moral qualities specified in the headings, which are as follows:

Bāb I.: Faṣl 1, fol. 4b. در معرفت الله و حقیقت توحید. Faṣl. 2, fol. 8b. در آداب سخن کفتن و کوهر بیان سفتن و خاصیت خاموشی

Bāb II.: Faṣl 1, fol. 12a. در فضیلت حلم و حیا و شرم و ذکا. Faṣl 2, fol. 15b. در شیوه توکل و رضا بقضا

Bāb III.: Faṣl 1, fol. 16b. در ذکر شجاعت و مردانکی و آثار فتوت و پهلوانی. Faṣl 2, fol. 49b. در فضیلت حسن خلق و آمیزش با خلق و سلوك هر کس

Bāb IV.: Faṣl 1, fol. 51a. در آداب تواضع و فروتنی و فضیلت درانکـار نفس و بردباری. Faṣl 2, fol. 53b. در سخاوت و جوانمردی و طریقه مروت و فرزانکی

Bāb V.: Faṣl 1, fol. 90a. در ذکر قناعت و شکر. Faṣl 2, fol. 93a. در فضیلت صبر و شکیبائی کذاری.

Some of the tales included are of considerable extent, and deserve a special notice. They are as follows: Shahzādah Abu 'l-Manṣūr and Humāi Farrukh-rukh, foll. 27a—49b. Abu 'l-'Alāi Mauṣili, the merchant's son, and princess Ḳamar-sīmā, foll. 58a—90a.

Malik Kamāl ud-Dīn, son of Masīḥā i Zāhid, foll. 94b—113b.

The Khātimah, which occupies more than half the volume, is of some historical importance, as containing a very full account of the reign of Agha Muḥammad and of the first years of Fatḥ 'Ali Shāh. It is divided into the following five sections termed Maḳālah:

I. Lineage of Fatḥ 'Ali Shāh and history of his forefathers, fol. 113b. II. His birth and subsequent events, fol. 120b. This section is chiefly taken up by a detailed account of Agha Muḥammad's career, with separate headings for the following years: A.H. 1205, fol. 134a; A.H. 1206, fol. 138a; A.H. 1207, fol. 141b; A.H. 1208, fol. 147a; A.H. 1209, fol. 154a; A.H. 1210, fol. 158a. III. Accession of Fatḥ 'Ali Shāh and subsequent events, fol. 166a, with a special heading for A.H. 1212, fol. 179b. IV. Provincial governments committed to the Shah's sons, fol. 189a. V. Description of the Shah's person and qualities, of his family, his army, his establishment, palaces, and other buildings, fol. 208a.

The date of composition is not given. It can hardly be much later than A.H. 1220, which is the last date mentioned in Maḳālah IV., fol. 198b.

LETTERS, STATE PAPERS, AND AUTOGRAPHS.

398.

Or. 3482.—Foll. 295; 12 in. by 7; about 30 lines, $4\frac{1}{2}$ in. long; written in neat Nestalik, with 'Unvān and gold-ruled margins, apparently in the 17th century.

[Sidney Churchill.]

مجمع الانشا

A collection of royal letters and state papers of the Persian Court, from the time of the Saljuks to the reign of Shāh 'Abbās II., by Abu 'l-Ḳāsim Beg Aivāghli Ḥaidar.

Beg. اکر چه فاتحه الکتاب خطاب جز لحمد حمد حضرت احدیت نتواند بود

This is a somewhat imperfect copy of the collection described in the Persian Catalogue, pp. 389—91, under the title نسخهٔ جامعه مراسلات اولی الالباب. The above title, مجمع الانشا, is found in the preamble of Juz II., fol. 66b. The contents of the present copy have been described in the Turkish Catalogue, p. 86. Its concluding portion, foll. 278b—295, contains letters and firmans of the emperor Akbar, several of which are addressed to 'Abdullah Khān Uzbek. The last piece is the investiture of Shahbāz Khān as Subadar of Malwa.

From a Persian note on the first page it appears that Muḥsin B. 'Abdullah Mīr-Akhur-Bāshi received this volume as a present from Sayyid Mīr Muḥammad Taḳi Mustaufi, near Teheran, A.H. 1278.

399.

Or. 3402.—Foll. 88; $7\frac{1}{2}$ in. by $5\frac{1}{4}$; 15 lines, $3\frac{1}{4}$ in. long; written in Nestalik; dated 1 Sha'bān, A.H. 1115 (A.D. 1703).

[Sidney Churchill.]

گلدستهٔ اندیشه

A collection of prose compositions, chiefly letters, by Ibn 'Abd ul-Fattāḥ Muḥammad Amin al-Vaḳāri aṭ-Ṭabasi al-Yazdi, with a preface by the author.

Beg. نخستین دیباچه غنچهٔ که از کلبن خامهٔ دبیران

سخن پرداز گلشن راز شگفتن آغاز نماید .... چنین
گوید گوشه نشین کلبهٔ خاکساری ابن عبد الفتاح محمد
امین الوقاری الطبسی ثم الیزدی

The author appears to have lived in the latter half of the eleventh century of the Hijrah. Two of his compositions are respectively dated A.H. 1078 and 1081, and among his letters is one addressed to Malik ush-Shu'arā Ṣā'ib, who died A.H. 1088.

The collection is divided into twelve sections called Barg. The first contains prefaces, including one to the author's Divan. The others consist of official documents and letters. In quoting his own verses the author always designates himself by the Takhalluṣ Vaḳūri.

The last eight leaves, foll. 81—88, contain the latter part of a similar collection by Muḥammad Mu'min, poetically styled Ghairi, Fīrūzābādī: منشیات حضرت ... علامی مولانا
محمد مومن غیری تخلص فیروزهبادی رحمة الله علیه

400.

Or. 4937.—Foll. 290; 8 in. by 4¾; about 20 lines, 3 in. long; written by several hands and in various characters, for the most part, about the close of the 17th century. [Sidney Churchill.]

جنك میرزا عبد الكریم

A Jung, or album of autographs and miscellaneous extracts, compiled by Ḥāji Mirza 'Abd ul-Karīm B. Yaḥya Khān al-Ḳazvīni.

Mirza 'Abd ul-Karīm, who lived in Ḳazvīn, and occasionally in Isfahan, towards the close of the eleventh century of the Hijrah, appears to have been on intimate terms with the great scholars of the period, who obliged him by entering in his album with their own hands original compositions, or extracts from their own or other men's works. These entries, which bear dates ranging from A.H. 1080 to 1126, are for the most part in prose and relate to Shī'ah tradition and theology, also to philosophy, medicine and mathematics. The most noteworthy writers included, with the dates of their entries, are as follows:

Mulla Khalīl B. Ghāzi Ḳazvīni, who died in Ḳazvīn, A.H. 1089, pp. 26-27.

Rafī' ud-Dīn Muḥ. B. Fatḥ-ullah Ḳazvīni, takh. Vā'iẓ, A.H. 1089, pp. 38—48.

Muḥammad Bāḳir, brother and disciple of Mulla Khalīl, A.H. 1080, p. 51.

Muḥ. Ṣāliḥ B. Muḥ. Bāḳir Ḳazvīni, called Raughani (v. Amal ul-Āmil, p. 64), pp. 56—68.

Aḳa Raẓī ud-Dīn Muḥ. B. al-Ḥasan (d. A.H. 1096), A.H. 1080, p. 72.

Mīr Muḥ. Ma'ṣūm Ḳazvīni (d. A.H. 1091), A.H. 1080, pp. 73—75.

Mīr Ṣadr ud-Dīn Muḥ. B. Muḥ. Ṣādiḳ Ḳazvīni, A.H. 1080, pp. 78—80.

Muḥ. Muḥsin B. Shāh Murtaẓa, called Faiẓ (d. 1091), pp. 81—84.

'Ali B. Muḥ. al-'Āmili, great-grandson of Shahīd aṣ-ṣāni (d. A.H. 1103), p. 87.

Murtaẓa B. Muḥ. Mu'min, great-nephew of Muḥsin Kāshi, pp. 93-4.

Muḥ. B. Murtaẓa Hādi, nephew of Muḥsin Kāshi, A.H. 1096, pp. 95-6.

Muḥ. B. Murtaẓa, Nūr ud-Dīn, brother of Muḥsin, A.H. 1095, p. 97.

Muḥ. Bāḳir B. Muḥ. Taḳi Majlisi, A.H. 1088, pp. 105—7.

Muḥ. B. 'Abd ul-Fattāḥ Tanakābuni (d. A.H. 1124), pp. 112—133.

Muḥ. Hādi B. Mulla Ṣāliḥ Māzandarāni (Ḳiṣaṣ ul-'Ulamā, p. 171), A.H. 1088, pp. 142—148.

Muḥ. Muḥsin B. Niẓâm ud-Dîn Muḥ. Sâvi, A.H. 1080, pp. 197—204.

'Ali B. Muḥ. aṭ-Ṭabâṭabâ'i, Abu 'l-Ma'âli (Amal i Âmil, p. 224), pp. 229—231.

Ḳa Jamâl ud-Dîn Muḥ. B. Ḳa Ḥusain Khwânsâri (d. A.H. 1125), pp. 278-9.

Muḥ. Ḥusain B. Mulla Ṣâliḥ Mâzandarâni, A.H. 1088, pp. 406—12.

'Ali Aṣghar B. Yûsuf Ḳazvîni, A.H. 1109, pp. 446-7.

The latter part of the album was reserved for poetical autographs. It contains those of Ṣâ'ib, pp. 472—5; Murtaẓa Ḳuli Khân B. Ḥasan Khân Shâmlu, takh. Bâlâ, pp. 477-8; Dâ'ûd (Muḥ. Dâ'ûd Mustaufi, d. A.H. 1133; see Sham' i Anjuman, p. 155), pp. 485—500; Îmâ (Mirza Ismâ'îl, d. A.H. 1132), pp. 502-3; Ḥâli, 'Abdullah Karbalâ'i, A.H. 1090, pp. 537—43; and Ta'ṣîr, Muḥ. Muḥsin Iṣfahâni, A.H. 1091, pp. 562—5.

In addition to the above-mentioned autographs, the volume comprises a vast number of miscellaneous treatises, extracts and notices, in Arabic and Persian. Some of the most extensive are a tract by Ḳa Jamâl ud-Dîn Khwânsâri, entitled تقويم الاوليا, pp. 374—403, and treatises of Shi'ah law and controversy, by Baha ud-Dîn al-'Âmili, pp. 280—324.

From an entry on p. 9 we learn that the album was given by 'Abd ul-Karîm to his son Taḳi ud-Dîn Muḥammad. After passing through several hands it came into the possession of a grandson of Fatḥ 'Ali Shâh, Shâhzâdah Mu'ayyid ud-Daulah Ṭahmâsp B. Daulatshâh, governor of Fars, who made use of some blank pages, pp. 53, 69, 152, 168, for entries in his own hand, and of some leaves at the end, pp. 571—579, for pieces in prose and verse written for him by others, A.H. 1277—79. He subsequently made the book over to his son, 'Abd ul-Ḥusain Khân, for the sum of 100 Tumans, as stated by the latter, p. 558. There is also an autograph of another grandson of Fatḥ 'Ali Shâh, Farhâd Mirza, dated A.H. 1280, p. 52.

Short biographical notices have been added to some of the entries by 'Abd ul-Ḥayy Munshi Tafrishi, takh. Sarkhwush, A.H. 1131. They contain frequent references to a work entitled روضات الجنات, printed in Teheran, A.H. 1306.

Subjoined to the volume is a quire of 23 pages, containing a detailed list, drawn up in Persian by a modern hand, of the contents of the album.

401.

Or. 4934.—A box containing the following three paper rolls. [Sidney Churchill.]

I. 9 ft. by 10 in.; 45 lines, written in fine large Divani.

Firman of Ya'ḳûb Beg, confirming two descendants of Imam 'Ali B. Mûsa Riẓa, namely, Sayyid Niẓâm ud-Dîn Sulṭân Aḥmad and Sayyid Kamâl ud-Dîn 'Aṭâ-ullah, in the charges which from the time of Shâhrukh had been hereditary in their family, viz., those of Naḳîb of the Sayyids, of administrator of the endowments attached to the sacred tombs of Sitti Fâṭimah and Imam Ṭâhir 'Ali B. Muḥ. Bâḳir in Ḳum, and of Khaṭib and Imam in the Mosque of Imam Ḥasan 'Askari in the same city; dated Ḳum, 15 Ramazan, A.H. 884 (A.D. 1479).

Ya'ḳûb Beg, son of Ḥasan Beg, founder of the Aḳ-ḳuyunlu dynasty, reigned from A.H. 883 to his death, A.H. 896.

At the top of the Firman the name of the sovereign appears as follows: مير ابو المظفر يعقوب بهادر سوزو. His seal, which is impressed at the end, reads : ان الله يامر بالعدل والاحسان يعقوب بن حسن بن على بن عثمان

The text begins : فرزندان کامکار ابقاهم الله تعالى وامراء نامدار و صدور شریعت شعار و وزراء رفیع مقدار و حکام و سادات و قضاة و مشایخ وموالی واشراف و اهالی و اصول و اعیان و عمال و مباشران و کلانتران و کدخدایان و معماران مدینه قم بدانند

II. 7 ft. by 10 in.; 36 lines, written in fair Divani.

Firman of Alvand Beg, confirming the above-named Sayyids in their offices; dated Ḳum, 14 Rajab, A.H. 904 (A.D. 1499).

Alvand Beg, son of Yūsuf Beg, was the last prince of the Aḳ-ḳuyunlu dynasty. He was defeated and expelled by Shāh Ismā'īl Ṣafavi, A.H. 907.

His name appears in the heading ميرابو المظفر الوند بهادر سوزو, and in the seal at the end : الوند بن يوسف بن حسن بن على بن عثمان

III. 2 ft. 4 in. by 11 in.; 8 lines, written in smaller Divani and partly obliterated.

Firman of Shāh Ismā'īl, whose seal is impressed at the top, conferring upon Sayyid Rashīd ul-Islām the custody of the above-named shrines in Ḳum; dated 1st of Jumāda II., A.H. 918 (A.D. 1512).

402.

Or. 4935.—Thirty-five sheets or slips of various sizes, mounted in one volume, forming a further series of royal Firmans, in continuation of the preceding no., and extending from the reign of Shāh Ṭahmāsp to that of Nāṣir ud-Dīn Shāh, as follows :

[Sidney Churchill.]

I. 18 in. by 7¾; 15 lines in Shikastah-āmīz. Copy of a Firman of Shāh Ṭahmāsp, conferring the custody of the Ḳum shrines upon Sayyid Shujā' ud-Dīn Sulṭān Maḥmūd Riẓavi, son of Sayyid Murshid ud-Dīn Rashīd ul-Islām (mentioned in the Firman of Shāh Ismā'īl above described); dated 18 Jumāda I., A.H. 948 (A.D. 1541). At the back are two lines of writing by Mulla Ṣadrā Shīrāzi.

II. 16 in. by 9; 6 lines of writing in Nestalik. Firman of Shāh Ṭahmāsp, conferring the Ṣadārat of the provinces of Shirvān and Shaki upon Amīr 'Abd ur-Razzāḳ; dated Ramazan, A.H. 961 (A.D. 1554).

III. 8¾ in. by 6½; 5 lines. Firman of Shāh Ṭahmāsp appointing six Ḥāfiẓ to recite the Coran at the tomb of his sister in the Ḳum shrine; dated first decade of Jumāda II., A.H. 972 (A.D. 1565).

IV. 21 in. by 10; 11 lines. Firman of Sultan Muḥammad Khudābandah, granting a yearly allowance to Muḥammad Aḳā Mudarris Iṣfahāni and his children; dated Rabi' II., A.H. 986 (A.D. 1578).

V. 18 in. by 9; 13 lines. Firman of Shah 'Abbās I., assigning to Amīr Ẓahīr ud-Dīn Ibrāhīm Riẓavi the revenue of his late brother, Mīr Shams ud-Dīn Yūsuf, custodian of the Ḳum shrine; dated Shavvāl, A.H. 1017 (A.D. 1609).

VI. 14 in. by 8; 5 lines. An autograph of Shāh Ṣafi relating to a gift presented by 'Abd ur-Razzāḳ of Chūbārah; dated Zu 'l-ḥijjah, A.H. 1039 (A.D. 1630).

VII. 14 in. by 8¾; 9 lines. Firman of Shāh 'Abbās II., referring to the ordinances of his father and grandfather in favour of Christian monks, and ensuring full freedom and protection to some bare-footed Carmelite monks who had come to Isfahan; dated Rabi' II., A.H. 1052 (A.D. 1642).

VIII. 10½ in. by 7½; 6 lines. Firman of Shāh 'Abbās II., granting a yearly pension of fifty Tumans to Maulānā Muḥ. Bāḳir

Khurāsāni; dated Sha'bān, A.H. 1068 (A.D. 1658).

IX.A 15½ in. by 8¼; 12 lines. Firman of Shāh 'Abbās II., relating to a tax to be levied on waste land belonging to the shrine of Ḳum and recently reclaimed; dated Zulḳa'dah, A.H. 1071 (A.D. 1661).

IX.B 13 in. by 7½; 3 lines. Firman of Shāh Ṣafī (afterwards Shāh Sulaimān), appointing Ḳurbān 'Ali Ayāghchi as one of the servants of the palace; dated Rabī' I., A.H. 1078 (A.D. 1667).

X.A 2 ft. 6 in. by 11½ in.; 20 lines. Firman of Shāh Sulaimān, appointing Mīr Hidāyat, son of Mīr Muḥ. Taḳi, to the post of Shaikh ul-Islām in Mashhad; dated Zulḳa'dah, A.H. 1079 (A.D. 1669).

X.B 12 in. by 9½; 8 lines. Firman of the same in confirmation of a pension granted to the children of Mirzā Ṣāliḥ Tabrīzi; dated Shavvāl, A.H. 1084 (A.D. 1673).

XI. 14 in. by 8¾; 8 lines. Firman of Shah Sulaimān regarding the taxation of Armenian weavers of Isfahan; dated Ramazan, A.H. 1094 (A.D. 1683).

XII. 16 in. by 10; 6 lines. Firman of Sulṭān Ḥusain, appointing a European moulder in the royal arsenal; dated Ramazan, A.H. 1122 (A.D. 1710).

XIII. 2 ft. 10 in. by 10½ in.; 52 lines. Firman of Sulṭān Ḥusain, relating to the administration of the revenue belonging to the shrine of Imam Zain ul-'Ābidīn; dated Jumāda I., A.H. 1125 (A.D. 1713).

XIV. 18 in. by 11½; 7 lines. Firman of Sulṭān Ḥusain, assigning a house in Isfahan to Captain Francis; dated Rajab, A.H. 1130 (A.D. 1718).

XV. 16 in. by 11¼; 14 lines. Firman of Shāh Ṭahmāsp II., relating to the endowments of the shrine of Imam Zain ul-'Ābidīn; dated Rabī' II., A.H. 1143 (A.D. 1730).

XVI. 18 in. by 9; 11 lines. Petition of Muḥ. Yaḥya, of Isfahan, complaining of extortions, and Firman of Nādir Shāh in answer to the same; dated Rajab, A.H. 1153 (A.D. 1740). The legend of the seal is مظهر لطف الهی نادر است, with the date A.H. 1148.

XVII. 19½ in. by 9½; 17 lines. Firman granted by Nādir Shāh to Sulṭān Muḥammad Beg, Ḳurchi Bāshi, in reward for faithful service, exempting from taxes his estate near Isfahan; dated Rabī' II., A.H. 1156 (A.D. 1743).

XVIII. 16 in. by 9; 7 lines. Firman of Ibrāhīm Shāh (nephew of Nādir) to Muḥibb 'Ali Khān, Ishik Aḳasi Bāshi, regarding the locating of Afshār tribes in Lanjān and neighbouring places; dated Rabī' II., A.H. 1162 (A.D. 1749). The legend of the seal is سلام علی ابراهیم, with the date 1162.

XIX. 19½ in. by 10; 9 lines. Firman of Shāhrukh, confirming Mirza Abu 'l-Ḥasan in his office of Taujīhgari in Isfahan; dated 16 Zulhijjah, A.H. 1169 (A.D. 1756).

XX. 15 in. by 9; 10 lines. Firman of Karim Khān, appointing Mirza Khalīl to the office of Mustaufi of Marāghah; dated Muḥarram, A.H. 1177 (A.D. 1763).

XXI. 17 in. by 8¾; 7 lines. Firman of Karim Khān granting to the same Mirza Khalīl an annual allowance of thirty Tumans; dated Rabī' II., A.H. 1186 (A.D. 1772).

XXII. 10 in. by 9; 5 lines. Firman of Ja'far Khān, conferring upon a son of Mirza Aḥmad the office of his late father; dated Zulḳa'dah, A.H. 1199 (A.D. 1785). Imperfect at the beginning.

XXIII. 17 in. by 9½; 5 lines. Firman of Ja'far Khān, enjoining obedience to a Nā'ib Mutaṣaddi sent to Isfahan; dated Jumāda II., A.H. 1202 (A.D. 1788).

XXIV. 10½ in. by 12½; 9 lines. Firman

addressed to Muḥammad Ḥusain Khān, governor of (?), with instructions to send troops against a band of robbers who had plundered a caravan travelling from Dār ul-'Ibādat to Isfahan; dated Zulka'dah, ١٢٣, probably for A.H. 1230 (A.D. 1815). Some seals at the back are dated A.H. 1227.

XXV. 17 in. by 13; 8 lines. Firman of Fatḥ 'Ali Shāh, relating to arrears of taxes in Fārs; dated Jumāda II., A.H. 1237 (A.D. 1822).

XXVI. 17 in. by 12; 6 lines. Firman of Fatḥ 'Ali Shāh, sending a robe of honour to Muḥammad Khān Ḳājār, Nā'ib; dated Sha'bān, A.H. 1238 (A.D. 1823).

XXVII.A 14 in. by 9; 6 lines. Firman of Sultan Muḥammad Shāh to his brother Bahman Mirza, governor of Azarbaijan, regarding the debts of the late Aḳa Jāni Khān; dated Jumāda I., A.H. 1259 (A.D. 1843).

XXVII.B 17 in. by 13¼; 11 lines. Firman of the same to Aḳa Muḥ. Ṣāliḥ, Mujtahid of Kirmanshahan, assigning to him a yearly allowance of 300 Tumans; dated Jumāda I., A.H. 1259 (A.D. 1843).

XXVII.C 16½ in. by 13; 7 lines. The same to the same, sending him a robe of honour; same date.

XXVIII. 18 in. by 14½; 14 lines. Firman of Nāṣir ud-Dīn Shāh to Ḥishmat ud-Daulah Ḥamzah Mirza, governor of Azarbaijan, announcing the appointment of Sultan Maḥmūd Mirza as Vali-'Ahd; dated Zulḳa'dah, A.H. 1265 (A.D. 1849).

XXIX. 17½ in. by 11; 6 lines. Firman of the same, deposing Mirza Aḳa Khān from the office of Ṣadr i A'ẓam in Tabriz, and confirming the appointment of Rukn ud-Daulah Ardashīr Mirza as governor of Azarbaijan; dated Muḥarram, A.H. 1275 (A.D. 1858).

XXX. 17 in. by 13¼; 7 lines. Firman of Nāṣir ud-Dīn Shāh to his uncle Muḥ. Raḥīm Mirza, governor of Khui and Salmās; dated Rabī' I., A.H. 1275 (A.D. 1858).

XXXI. 14 in. by 8¼; 7 lines. Appointment of Bābā Khān Munshi as secretary for the drawing up of military orders; dated A.H. 1283 (A.D. 1866).

403.

Or. 4936.—A large collection of detached leaves and slips of various sizes, containing autographs of royal personages, statesmen, scholars, and poets of modern Persia, with other documents of historical interest.

[SIDNEY CHURCHILL.]

A full and detailed description of the contents would require more space than we have at our disposal. We must confine ourselves to a brief enumeration of the most important articles, as follows:

1. Autograph of Sulṭān Ḥusain Ṣafavi on a deed of manumission relating to a Georgian slave, A.H. 1111; attested by the Mujtahid Jamāl ud-Dīn Khwānsāri.

2. Autograph letter of 'Abbās Mirza Nā'ib us-Salṭanah, written from Kirman, A.H. 1246; attested by his son, Farhād Mirzā.

3. Autograph of Muḥammad Shāh, dated A.H. 1261; attested by his brother Farhād Mirza.

4. Two more autographs of Muḥammad Shāh.

5. An autograph account of Mazendaran, by Nāṣir ud-Dīn Shāh, written for the "Iran."

6. Three letters of Nāṣir ud-Dīn Shāh to Ḥusām us-Salṭanah, governor of Khorasan, A.H. 1278, 1279, and 1288. The handwriting is that of Dabīr ul-Mulk, whose seal is at the back.

7. Autograph letter of Mahd Auliyā, mother of Nāṣir ud-Dīn Shāh, to her daughter 'Izzat ud-Daulah.

8. Autograph of the Valī 'Ahd, or heir-apparent, on a letter of Dabīr us-Salṭanah, A.H. 1310.

9. Autograph verses by Muḥammad Khān Majd ul-Mulk.

10. Autograph letter of the Ṣadr i A'ẓam, 'Ali Aṣghar Amin us-Sulṭān.

11. Account of the siege of Mashhad by Aḥmad Shāh Durrāni, written by Muḥ. Naṣīr Tabrīzi, A.H. 1168.

12. Undertaking of Sardār Sulṭān Aḥmad, governor of Herat, regarding the admission of Russian traders, A.H. 1276.

13. Autograph letter of Bahā-ullah, the Babi apostle, to Ḥāji Ẓahīr ud-Daulah, written in Arabic in a minute character, and beginning: ان يا محمد بشر فى نفسك بما نزل عليك كتاب قدس كريم وفيه ما ينقطعك عن ملك السموات والارض ويبلغك الى ساحة عز مبين. The seal bears the names حسين و على and the date A.H. 1279. At the top of the page there is a contemptuous reply of Ẓill us-Sulṭān to Ẓahir ud-Daulah, who had sent him the letter of Bahā-ullah.

14. Autograph letter of the famous Abd-elcader to M. Gaulois (?), موسيوا كولوى, recommending the bearer, Ḥāji Muḥyi ud-Dīn, a merchant trading in Tangier and Fez; A.H. 1296.

Autographs of the following scholars and poets:

15. Bahā ud-Dīn al-'Āmili, A.H. 995.

16. Muḥ. Ḳāẓim Vālih, A.H. 1215.

17. Zain ul-'Ābidīn Shīrvāni, Teheran, A.H. 1215. See no. 139.

18. Mirza Ṣādiḳ Marvazi. See no. 118.

19. Yaghmā Jandaḳi. See Majma' ul-Fuṣaḥā, vol. ii., p. 580.

20. Viṣāl Shīrāzi, A.H. 1248. See no. 308.

21. Mulla Hādi Sabzavāri, who died A.H. 1295.

22. Furūghi, A.H. 1302.

The collection includes also calligraphic specimens of celebrated penmen, such as Mīr 'Imād, Maulānā Shafī'ā, Mirza Aḥmad Nairīzi, Khwājah Ikhtiyār, Mirza Ghulām Riẓa, and Mirza Kūchak, pupil of Darvish.

404.

Or. 4679.—Foll. 61; 8¾ in. by 6½; from 15 to 21 lines, about 5 in. long; written in small cursive Shikastah, in Shavvāl, A.H. 1272 (A.D. 1856). [Sidney Churchill.]

Copies of treaties and conventions concluded by the Persian Court with Turkey, England, Russia, Spain and France, of instructions given to Persian envoys, and of official accounts of their interviews in St. Petersburg and in Constantinople, with dates ranging from A.H. 1224 to A.H. 1272.

According to a note written by Mr. Churchill at the beginning, this collection formed part of instructions issued by Mirza Aḳa Khan I'timād ud-Daulah, then Prime Minister of the present Shah, to the Persian Envoy at Constantinople.

The first piece is a treaty between Fatḥ 'Ali Shah and Sultan Maḥmūd, dated 19 Zulḳa'dah, A.H. 1238: صورت عهد نامه منعقده مابين خاقان مغفور فتحعلى شاه و سلطان محمود

Beg. غرض از تحرير اين كتاب مستطاب اينكه درين چند سال بر حدوث بعضى عوارض د ميان دولتين عليتين اسلام روابط صلح و صفوت الخ

The last is a letter containing the official

Persian account of the advance of Dost Muḥammad into Khorasan in A.H. 1272.

The English treaties included, foll. 6—13, bear the names of Sheil, Jones, Gore Ouseley and Ellis. A full table of contents occupies two pages at the beginning.

405.

Add. 29,217.—A box containing 6 rolls, the description of which follows.

[Warren Hastings.]

A.—A paper roll 27 ft. long by $12\frac{1}{2}$ in.

The leading text in this extensive document is drawn up in Persian, and occupies twenty-six lines. It is a declaration by 'Ali Ibrāhīm Khān, respecting the manner in which he had acquitted himself as governor of Benares, his maintenance of public order, his suppression of various abuses, and his impartial administration of justice. He refers especially to the measures he had taken for the relief of a famine which raged there, A.D. 1783, and concludes with an appeal to the inhabitants of Benares for confirmation of his statements.

Beg. خیر خواه خلایق علی ابراهیم خان بسماعت سایر عمدکان و ساکنان بلده بنارس میرساند

The Persian text is followed by a Hindi translation in the Devanagari character. Numerous testimonials in various Indian characters, with signatures and seals, fill the whole space above and below the above document. The latter is not dated. A.H. 1198 (A.D. 1784) is the latest date appearing in the seals affixed.

'Ali Ibrāhīm Khān, author of some historical works and several Tazkirahs, died A.H. 1208. See the Persian Catalogue, pp. 328, 375; the Oude Catalogue, p. 180; Pertsch, Berlin Catalogue, no. 663, &c.

B.—A paper roll 2 ft. 6 in. by $9\frac{1}{2}$ in.

A congratulatory address of the inhabitants of Benares to Warren Hastings on the issue of his trial, dated Phālgun Suklasaptami, Samvat 1852 (February, A.D. 1796).

The text is Sanskrit written in the Devanagari character. It is followed by a number of signatures in various Indian characters, and by a Persian translation occupying fifteen lines, and beginning as follows: جمیع جمهور انام سکنه بلده بنارس برهمنان و غیره هنود و مسلمان بجناب نواب معلی القاب عماد الدوله بهادر جلادت جنگ بعرض میرساند

C.—A paper roll 7 ft. long by $9\frac{1}{2}$ in.

A similar address in Sanskrit, with a Persian translation, accompanied by numerous signatures, and testimonials; dated Baisākh, Sūdi-Sattami, Samvat 1853, and 5 Zulḳa'dah, A.H. 1210 (May 1796).

D.—A paper roll 5 ft. long by $9\frac{1}{2}$ in.

A congratulatory address written by the inhabitants of Benares to Warren Hastings on the same occasion. It is written in Persian in sixteen lines, without date, and is followed by numerous seals and signatures. It begins as follows: عرض جامع رعایا و کافه برایا هنود واسلام کاسب و تاجر و غیره فرایق اختلاف المذاهب بلده بنارس بجناب والا نواب عماد الدوله بهادر

E.—A paper roll 5 ft. long by $6\frac{1}{2}$ in.

A congratulatory address written by the inhabitants of Calcutta to Warren Hastings on the same occasion.

The text is Persian. It occupies 28 lines, and its wording agrees closely with that of the preceding document. It is also undated, and begins as follows: عرض جمهور شرفا و نجبا و تجار و غیره فریق مختلف المذهب سکنه شهر کلکته بجانب نواب اعتماد الدوله بهادر

The Persian text is followed by a Bengali translation and numerous signatures, also in the Bengali character.

F.—A paper roll 2 ft. 6 in. long by 8 in.

Another copy of the preceding address, containing only the Persian text, also undated, with seals and signatures in the Persian character.

406.

Or. 3260.—Foll. 171; 8 in. by 6½; about 9 lines, 5 in. long; written in large Nestalik; dated Monday, 15 Rabī' II., A.H. 1206 (A.D. 1791).

Military rules of Tipu Sultan, drawn up by Zain ul-'Ābidīn, A.H. 1197, endorsed قواعد تیپو سلطان

This is the work described by Ethé, Bodleian Catalogue, no. 1903, under its proper title, فتح المجاهدین, and with the full name of the author, Zain ul-'Ābidīn B. Sayyid Razi, of Shūshtar.

The Persian text is written on the left side, the opposite page being occupied, foll. 2—86 and 114—161, by a partial English translation. The first page of the text is wanting, but the translation shows that the beginning was that given by Ethé, viz.: فتح ملك سخنوری و تسخیر اقلیم معنی بروری بصمصام ثنای سلطانی میسر آید

Contents: Zain ul-'Ābidīn's preface in praise of Tipu Sultan, fol. 2. Introduction treating of the creed and religious duties of Muslims, especially of the obligation of Jihād, and of the treatment of unbelievers, fol. 16. On strategy, تدابیر حرب, fol. 63. Commands and exercises of infantry, fol. 75. Duty of the Sipahdārs, Bakhshis, &c., fol. 113. Rules relating to rounds, guards, sentries, salutes, &c., fol. 124. Rules relating to artillery practice, fol. 140. Urdu songs for soldiers, fol. 161.

On the fly-leaf is a notice of the work by Major Gen. Geo. G. Pearse, who says that the MS. was procured by him in Madras, A.D. 1882.

407.

Or. 4543.—A single sheet, 18 in. by 7½; containing 22 lines, 4½ in. long on the recto, and 25 on the verso, besides additional lines in the margins; written in Shikastah with gilt 'Unvān, dated 7 Ramaḍān, A.H. 1210 (June 1787).

A letter addressed to "Maréchal de Castries, Ministre de la Marine," مرشال دی کاستری مینستر لا مارین, applying for French assistance in order to recover the writer's Jāgīr from the English, and for the settlement of claims upon the French Company. The writer, whose name does not appear, begins by recording the services rendered by his grandfather, Navvāb Ghulām Imām Ḥusain, to the French Company, and says that his own Jāgīr had been originally conferred on his uncle, Ghulām Ḥusain Khān, called Ḥusain 'Ali Khān, by the emperor Muḥammad Shāh. The letter contains frequent references to Tipu Sultan, who had married a sister of the writer.

PAINTINGS.

408.

Stowe, Or. 16.—Foll. 60; 17 in. by 10½; bound in painted and glazed covers.

An album of miniatures and calligraphic specimens, mounted on stout gold-sprinkled paper, with ornamental borders.

On the second folio, in the centre of an

oval illuminated border, is the stamp of Aurangzīb, which reads "Abu 'l-Ẓafar Muḥyi ud-Dīn Muḥammad 'Ālamgīr Pādishāh Ghāzi," with the date A.H. 1079, and with the names of the emperor's forefathers up to Timur, written in a circle round his own. The album, however, is of later date. Its first owner appears to have been the Navvāb of Oude, Āṣaf ud-Daulah, whose seal is impressed at the top of most leaves. The seal contains the following titles: "Vazīr ul-Mamālik Āṣaf ud-Daulah Āṣafjāh Yaḥya Khān Bahādur Hizabr Jang," and is dated A.H. 1190.

The miniatures consist of portraits of the Timuride emperors and their Amirs, of hunting scenes and other subjects of Indian life and fiction. The portraits are mostly without names, but those of Aurangzīb, foll. 3*a*, 5*a*, 9*a*; of Jahāngīr, foll. 2*b*, 4*b*; of Shāhjahān, fol. 13*b*; and Akbar, fol. 26*b*, are easily recognized. Some of the miniatures are evidently imitations of European models, as, for instance, one representing Christ with the crown of thorns, fol. 18*a*.

The dates of the specimens of calligraphy range from A.H. 972 to 1171. Some are signed by well-known penmen, as Mīr 'Ali, Mīr 'Imād, Abd ur-Rashīd, Javāhir Raḳam Sāni (Mīr 'Ali Khān), and Hidāyat-ullah Zarrīn Raḳam.

The covers are ornamented outside with miniature portraits in the Indian style, and with Ghazals of Ḥāfiẓ round the borders; inside, with two identical paintings on a large scale, representing a lady and gentleman in the costume of Louis XIV.'s time.

409.

Stowe, Or. 18.—Eight Hindu drawings of various sizes, apparently of the latter half of the 18th century, bound in one volume, 18 in. by 9.

The first is a portrait of Navvāb Ḳāsim 'Ali Khān, Sūbahdār of Bengal. The others represent scenes of Indian life and Rāginis.

410.

Stowe, Or. 19.—A paper roll, 5 ft. long by 8 in.

A drawing in water-colours representing an Indian prince riding on an elephant, preceded and followed by numerous mounted retainers and ladies carried in sedan chairs and palanquins; apparently about the beginning of the 19th century.

411.

Or. 2787.—Foll. 62; 17¾ in. by 10; with richly gilt margins.

[Ẓuhūr ud-Dīn Aḥmad Khān.]

An album of Indian drawings and specimens of calligraphy, collected by Mu'taḳad ud-Daulah Himmat-yār Khān, an Amir of the Niẓām's Court, and completed on the 29th of Jumāda I., A.H. 1204 (A.D. 1790).

On the first page, within an illuminated circular border, is an impression of the collector's seal, dated A.H. 1200, and reading as follows: همت یار خان بهادر معتمد جنك معتقد الدوله معتمد الملك فدوی آصف جاه نظام الملك

In a versified chronogram at the end it is stated that the collection occupied no fewer than twenty-nine years, having been commenced A.H. 1176 and completed A.H. 1204. From a further note, fol. 62, we learn that the album was got up at a cost of 5780 rupees.

The drawings are partly portraits of Indian princes and Amirs, partly pictures of Hindu mythological subjects, and of scenes of Eastern fiction and Indian life. The portraits bear the following names: Timur, fol. 5*b*. Humāyūn, fol. 6*b*. Akbar, fol. 7*b*. Shāhjahān, fol. 9*b*. 'Ālamgīr, fol. 10*b*. Muḥammad Shāh, fol. 11*b*. Abu 'l-Ḥasan Ḳuṭubshāh, fol. 13*a*. Aḥmad Shāh, fol. 14*a*. 'Ali 'Ādil Shāh, fol. 14*b*. Bahādur Shāh, fol. 15*b*. Barīdi Pādishāh, fol. 16*b*. 'Abd-ullah Khān Uzbek, fol. 18*a*. Dārā Shikūh, fol. 20*a*. Shujā', fol. 21*a*. Bidār-bakht, fol. 22*a*. 'Āli Gauhar (Shāh 'Ālam), fol. 23*a*. Nāṣir Jang Shahid, fol. 24*a*. Āṣafjāh, of Haidarabad, fol. 24*b*. Ḥāmid Khān, fol. 25*a*. Himmat-yār Khān Shahid, fol. 26*a*. The owner of the album in his youth, fol. 27*a*. Mubāriz Khān, fol. 28*a*. Yūsuf Khān, Nāẓim of Haidarabad under Bahādur Shāh, fol. 29*a*. Mir Jumlah, fol. 30*a*. Aṣālat Khān, fol. 31*a*. 'Ali Mardān Khān, fol. 31*b*. 'Umdat ul-Mulk Shāhjahāni, fol. 32*b*. Jānsipār Khān, fol. 33*b*. Rūḥ-ullah Khān, fol. 35*a*. Fatḥ-ullah Khān, fol. 36*a*. Sa'ādat-ullah Khān, fol. 36*b*. Najābat Khān, fol. 37*b*. Sa'd-ullah Khān, fol. 39*a*. Mir Aḥmad Khān, son-in-law of Ḳuṭubshāh, fol. 40*a*. Rājah Bijai Singh, fol. 40*b*. Ranvar Singh, fol. 42*a*. Rājah Jaisingh Savāi, of Jaipūr, fol. 43*a*. Chand Bibi, fol. 55*b*. Nūrjahān Bigam, fol. 58*a*.

Among the other pictures the following may be especially noticed: Sulaimān sitting on his throne and surrounded by a crowd of genii and wild animals, fol. 2*b*. Māni, the painter, with two female figures designated as Firingis, or European ladies, fol. 47*b*. A Chinese lady, drawn by a Chinese artist, fol. 57*a*. Matwāli Bang-sāz, a large picture representing a highly dressed Indian female selling Bang, and a crowd of customers in various stages of intoxication, fol. 58*b*.

The calligraphic specimens are in fine Nestalik and various kinds of Shikastah. They are signed by Mu'jiz Ḳalam, Rūshan Ḳalam, Zarrīn Ḳalam, Mushkīn Ḳalam, 'Abd ur-Rashīd, Maḥmūd Shihābi, Abu 'l-baḳā Mūsavi, and other famous penmen. They bear dates ranging from A.H. 1119 to 1184.

A companion volume of smaller size, Or. 2787B, contains a full, but rather inaccurate, description of the contents of the album, drawn up in very peculiar English, apparently by its late owner, Ẓuhūr ud-Din Aḥmad Khān.

412.

Or. 4938.—A collection of drawings, consisting principally of portraits of royal persons and statesmen of the Persian Court.

[Sidney Churchill.]

The portraits are as follows:

I. A contemporary portrait of Karim Khān Zand.

II. Portrait of Muḥammad Shāh, by Muḥammad Ḥasan Afshār, A.H. 1263.

III. Portrait of Nāṣir ud-Din Shāh, standing with his left hand resting upon a gun, by Mirza Bābā al-Ḥusaini al-Imāmi.

IV. Portrait of the same, sitting on a sofa, by Muḥammad Iṣfahāni, A.H. 1272.

V. Photograph of the same, carte de visite size.

VI. Portrait of the Shāhzādah, I'tiẓād us-Salṭanah 'Ali Ḳuli Mirza, minister of sciences, commerce, and arts, A.H. 1280.

VII. Portrait of 'Imād ud-Daulah, by Ṣani' ul-Mulk (Mirza Abu 'l-Ḥasan Ghaffāri Kāshāni).

VIII. Photograph of a Persian prince, without name.

IX. Portrait of Mirza Agasi, by Ṣani' ul-Mulk.

X. Portrait of the Kisikchi Bāshi, Mirza Muḥammad Khān Ḳājār, by the same, A.H. 1267.

XI. Portrait of Mirza Aḳa Khān, by the same.

XII. Portrait of Khusrau Khān Kirmāni, by the same.

XIII. Portraits in black and white of Aḳā Raḥīm 'Ali Beg, Lalah-bāshi of Amīr Dūst Muḥammad Khān, and of Mirza Bīdil Kirmānshāhi, by Asad-ullah Khān Ghaffāri Kāshāni, A.H. 1283.

XIV. A photographic group of Riẓa Ḳuli Khan Lalah Bāshi, the Vali'ahd Muẓaffar ud-Dīn Mirza, as a boy, and two attendants.

XV. Another photographic group, with Nāṣir ud-Dīn Shāh as a boy.

XVI. Portrait of a Persian lady, by Mirza Maṭlab, A.H. 1304.

Among the other drawings the following may be mentioned:

XVII. Sketches of illustrations for the Arabian Nights, by Ṣanī' ul-Mulk.

XVIII. Miniature in imitation of Renaissance style, by Mirza Bahā Imāmi.

XIX. Views of the Kāẓimaim Mosque, by 'Ali Ḳuli Beg Mūsavi.

XX. Pen and ink drawings of a gazelle and of a wild goat, by Nāṣir ud-Dīn Shāh.

XXI. Drawing of an old man in a sitting posture, warming his hands and feet over a fire, by Malik ush-Shu'arā Mirza Maḥmūd Khān, A.H. 1310.

INSCRIPTIONS.

413.

Stowe, Or. 17a.—Twenty-five large coloured plates, being plans and elevations of Tāj Maḥall, Moti Masjid, and other monuments at Agra, with facsimiles of the detail of their ornamentation and of their inscriptions, drawn by native artists about A.D. 1812, and bound up in a volume 3 ft. 5 in. long by 2 ft. 6 in.

414.

Stowe, Or. 17b.—Foll. 40; 9¾ in. by 7¼ in.; described on the title-page as follows: "This contains a faithful Copy of the Inscriptions on the Outside of and within the Mausoleum, or Taaje, at Agra, in India, taken by a Moonshee who was employed by the Bengal Government to superintend and shew the Place to Visitors, and which were carefully translated under the Inspection of the Adjutant-General of the Bengal Army in the Year 1812-13. G. Nugent."

The text of the Arabic inscriptions is written in clear vocalized Neskhi, with an interlinear English version. It consists of the following extracts from the Coran: On the outside of the great gate of Mumtāz Mahall, Sūrat ul-Fajr, fol. 1*b*. Inside, Sūrahs 93—95, fol. 3*b*. Round the Rauẓah, Sūrah 36, fol. 5*a*. Round the arch of the Rauẓah, Sūrahs 81, 82, 84, 98, fol. 13*a*. Round the interior of the Rauẓah, Sūrahs 67, 48 and 76, fol. 17*a*. On the top of the tomb of Mumtāz Maḥall, Sūrah 41, v. 30, Sūrah 40, v. 7, and other verses, fol. 27*b*. Obituary date of Mumtāz Maḥall, A.H. 1040, fol. 29*a*. On the eastern and western sides of the same tomb, the ninety-nine holy names of God and some verses of the Coran, fol. 29*b*.

Persian inscription on the tomb of Shahjahan, with the date of his death, 26 Rajab, 1076, fol. 32*a*. Persian inscriptions of Moti Masjid and Dīvān i Khāṣṣ, fol. 32*b*. Historical account of the death of Mumtāz Maḥall, fol. 35*b*. Inscriptions on great guns, fol. 39*a*.

On three additional leaves at the end is found an "Extract from a Journal written by Lady Nugent, by whom these Drawings were given to the Marquess of Buckingham." It is followed by "*Lines written on seeing the Taaje by Lady N[ugent].*"

415.

Or. 4595.—Foll. 119; 11 in. by 6¾; 9 lines, 4½ in. long; written in large Nestalik and Neskhi; dated 17 Zulka'dah, A.H. 1232, corresponding with 29 September, A.D. 1817.

Inscriptions of the principal buildings of Shāhjahānābād and old Delhi, transcribed in imitation of the original characters.

Beg. مسجد جامع دار الخلافه شاهجهان آباد یازده
در بیرون دارد و هفت در اندرون

There is neither preface nor title. In the colophon, Ḥafiẓ ud-Dīn Aḥmad is named as the author, and Aṣghar 'Ali Beg, commonly called Sangin Beg, as the transcriber. The latter wrote subsequently under the title سیر المنازل, a more detailed work on the same subject, for which see the Persian Catalogue, p. 431, and Pertsch, Berlin Catalogue, no. 536.

Contents: Masjid Jāmi', Masjid Akbarābādī, and other Masjids of Delhi, fol. 1*b*. Buildings within the fortress, fol. 20*a*. Environs of Delhi, Dargāh i Ḳadam Sharīf, &c., fol. 21*b*. Masjid Jāmi' in the old fort, fol. 32*b*. Masjid of Niẓām ud-Dīn Auliyā and neighbouring tombs, fol. 42*b*. Tomb of Humāyūn, fol. 63*b*. Lāt of Fīrūz Shāh, fol. 65*b*. Shrine of Shāh Mardān, fol. 66*b*. Masjid Mūthah, fol. 68*b*. Shrine of Nāṣir ud-Dīn Chirāgh Dihlavi, fol. 72*b*. Masjid Ḳuvvat i Islām, fol. 78*a*. Tomb of Sultan Shams ud-Dīn, fol. 93*a*. Shrine of Khwājah Ḳuṭb ud-Dīn, fol. 103*a*. Tughluḳābād, fol. 116*b*. Shrine of Imām Nāṣir ud-Dīn in Sonipat, fol. 118*b*.

416.

Or. 4768.—A sheet of thick paper, 16 in. by 10½. [Presented by H. E. M. James, Esq., Commissioner of Sind.]

Paper-cast of a Persian inscription kept in a shrine dedicated to Khwājah Khiẓr on an island situated in the Indus, opposite Rohri, and known as Khwājah Khiẓr Island. The inscription consists of the following versified chronogram, giving A.H. 341 as the date of the erection of the shrine:

جو این درگاه والا شد هویدا
که اب خضر دارد در جوانی
خضر با خط شیرین در نوشته
بیع تاریخش از درگاه عالی

The date is also written in Arabic figures under the last line. The style and character of the inscription point to a much later period, probably not earlier than the 17th century. A second sheet of the same size contains an ink impression of the inscription, a modern transcript of which on a smaller sheet is added.

MSS. OF MIXED CONTENTS.

417.

Or. 2852.—Foll. 103; 8½ in. by 5; 12 lines, 3¼ in. long; written in small and close Shikastah-āmiz; dated Jumāda II., A.H. 1293 (A.D. 1876). [Sidney Churchill.]

I. Foll. 1—49. لطیفهٔ غیبی

A treatise on the mystical meaning to be attached to sensual images in the Divan of Ḥāfiz, and in defence of the poet against the censures of ignorant detractors; by Muḥammad B. Muḥammad ad-Dārābi.

Beg. فصیح ترین کلامی که فصحای بلاغت شعار
و بلغای فصاحت دثار کتابه دیوان خود سازند

The author left his native place, Dārābjird, for Shiraz, where he spent most of his life. He also visited India, for he states incidentally in the present work, fol. 49*a*, that he was in Aḥmadābād, A.H. 1062. The text of our MS. is much fuller than a lithographed edition printed at Teheran, A.H. 1304, under the title لطيفهٔ غيبيه. The latter, however, contains, p. 122, a passage not found in the MS., in which the author states that he wrote the work at Shiraz in the space of two weeks, A.H. 1087. He left also a Sufi work, مقامات العارفين, and a treatise on the lawfulness of singing, entitled شوق العارفين و ذوق العاشقين.

The present work, which is also called, fol. 8*a*, ترجمهٔ لسان الغيب, is divided as follows: Muḳaddimah, on the spiritual meaning of words according to Sufi usage, fol. 8*a*. Bāb I. Sufi interpretation of some obscure lines of the Divan, fol. 9*b*. Bāb II. Spiritual meaning of other verses, fol. 27*b*. Bāb III. On the real meaning of passages which, taken literally, seem to conform with the Ash'ari doctrine, fol. 41*a*. Khātimah, on some instances of omens drawn from the Divan, fol. 47*a*.

II. Foll. 50—103. A collection of royal and private letters, with a short preamble beginning: حمد و ثنائى كه لمعات لمحات صدق و نفحات نفحات اخلاص ان ديده دل را منور و دماغ جانرا معطر دارد

The letters, which are all undated, are as follows: Shāh 'Abbās I. to Jehāngīr on the latter's accession, fol. 51*a*. Akbar to Shāh 'Abbās I., fol. 52*b*, and the latter's answer, fol. 57*a*. Humāyūn to Ṭahmāsp, fol. 64*a*. Akbar to 'Abdullah Khan Uzbek, fol. 65*a*. Akbar to Khānkhānān, son of Bairām Khān, fol. 70*a*. Abu Ṭālib Khān I'timād ud-Daulah to a Sayyid, fol. 73*a*. Akbar to Khānkhānān, fol. 74*a*. Dastūr ul-'Amal, or rules and ordinances addressed by Akbar to officials, fol. 77*a*. Sulṭān Ḥusain Baiḳarā to Shāh Ismā'īl, fol. 81*b*. Private letters by Naṣīrā i Hamadāni, Āṣaf Khān, Ibrāhīm Khān, Ḳāsim Kāhi, Abu Ṭālib Kalīm, Ṣadr ud-Dīn Shīrāzi, and Mirza Ibrāhīm Hamadāni. The last piece is Muḥ. Zamān Khān's preface to a Bāz Nāmah, foll. 83*a*—103*b*.

418.

Or. 2955.—Foll. 190; 6½ in. by 3¾; 15 lines, about 2¼ in. long; written in cursive Nestalik or Shikastah-āmīz; dated from 8 Rabī' I., A.H. 1274, to 25 Rabī' I., A.H. 1275 (A.D. 1857-8). [Sidney Churchill.]

I. Foll. 1—60. Chahār Maḳālah, by Niẓāmi 'Arūẓi; dated Ḳaryat ul-'Arab, Kirman, 25 Rabi' I., A.H. 1275. See no. 390.

II. Foll. 61*b*—131. Farhād u Shīrīn, by Vaḥshi, with the continuation of Viṣāl; see no. 308.

This copy contains, in addition to the former, Viṣāl's prologue to his continuation, foll. 97*b*—99*a*, beginning:

بعهد خسرو بيمثل و مانند
شهنشاه جهان كيتى خداوند

That continuation extends from fol. 99*a* to fol. 131*b*. It is dated Kirman, last day of Rajab, A.H. 1275. At the end is a note stating that the writer, having found, A.H. 1293, in a printed copy, نسخه مطبوعى, at Tafrish, some additional leaves, had transcribed them to complete the present MS.

This addition occupies foll. 132*a*—144*b*. It relates to the death of Farhād, and begins:

از آن پس كرد كلكون را سبكخيز
بكوه بيستون بر رغم پرويز

It ends with a panegyric on Farhād Mirza (son of Nā'ib us-Salṭanah and governor of Fārs) and upon Nāṣir ud-Dīn Shāh. It is said at the end to have been composed twelve hundred seventy and odd years after the Hijrah:

پس از هجرت بسال کارجمند است
هزار و دو صد و هفتاد و اند است

a date posterior to the death of Viṣāl.

This last piece is dated end of Zulhijjah, A.H. 1293 (A.D. 1877).

III. Foll. 145—190. مرآت المحققین

"Mirror of the Gnostics," a Sufi tract by Ḥamīd ud-Dīn.

Beg. العظمة لله العلی العظیم الذی رفع السموات بغیر عمد ووضع المشکوة فیها من النجوم بغیر عدد

The author's name occurs in the following passage, fol. 152*b*: چنین گوید فقیر مسکین المتوصل بحبل المتین وبطریقة المعصومین حمید الدین

The above title was suggested to the author in a vision by his spiritual guide, as stated further on, fol. 154*b*: رساله تالیف کن و مرآت المحققین نام ان تصنیف کن. The same title is repeated at the end, 190*a*: این جام جهان نما را که بمرآت المحققین مسماست

The tract is written in prose interspersed with verses, without any division. It concludes with a Masnavi in glorification of the religious order of Ḳalandars.

The present copy is written in very cursive Shikastah, and dated Wednesday, 8 Rabiʻ I., A.H. 1274.

Another copy, dated A.H. 1248, is mentioned, without author's name, by Pertsch, Berlin Catalogue, no. 8, art. 3.

Copyist: محمد بن نور محمد

419.

Or. 2975.—Foll. 373; 9½ in. by 5; 15 lines, about 2¾ in. long; written in more or less cursive Nestalik, partly in diagonal lines, with various dates ranging from Muḥarram, A.H. 1077 (fol. 183), to Muḥarram, A.H. 1088 (fol. 187) (A.D. 1666—77). The first sixteen leaves are dated Kashan, 1 Muḥarram, A.H. 1115 (A.D. 1703).

[Sidney Churchill.]

I. Foll. 4*b*—16*a*. The Lavā'iḥ of Jāmi, with the heading رساله مسمی بلوائح الابرار. See the Persian Catalogue, p. 44*a*; Rosen, Institut, no. 113; the Berlin Catalogue, no. 238, art. 3; and the Bodleian Catalogue, no. 894, art. 16.

II. Foll. 17*b*—74*a*. سراج المنیر.

A collection of moral anecdotes, by Muḥammad Sharīf B. Shams ud-Dīn Muḥammad, poetically surnamed Kāshif.

Beg. ستایش کریمی را که حلیهٔ خلقش زیوریست زیبنده

The work was finished, as stated at the end, on Friday at the end of Rabiʻ I., A.H. 1030. See the Persian Catalogue, p. 861*b*, and no. 422, I. For the same author's Khazān u Bahār, see no. 396.

III. Foll. 76*b*—114*a*. Farhād u Shīrīn, by Vaḥshi. See no. 308.

IV. Foll. 83*b*—105*b* (margin). فرهاد و شیرین

Farhād u Shīrīn, a Masnavi by Fauḳ ud-Dīn Aḥmad Yazdi, poetically surnamed Fauḳi, with a prose preface by the author, beginning: بعد از حمد خداوند جهان و نعت پیغمبر آخرالزمان و آل و اصحاب آن خلاصه دوران

The preface is in Sufi style, and chiefly in praise of the Malāmiyyah branch of the order, to which the author evidently belonged. The poem begins, fol. 86*b*, as follows:

سخن تر تیزك بستان فکر است
سخن طوطی هندوستان فکر است

It is extremely coarse and obscene.

V. Foll. 116b—183a. دیوان علی نقی کمرهٔ

The Divan of 'Ali Naki Kamra'i. See no. 320.

Beg. ای نام همایونت سر دفتر دیوانها
خورشید صفت طالع از مطلع دیوانها

A similar beginning is noticed in the Oude Catalogue, no. 412.

VI. Foll. 188a—203b. Kasidahs by Vahshi, written in oblique lines, beginning:

یکجهان جان خواهم و چندان امان از روزگار

VII. Foll. 204b—221b. سحر حلال

Sihr i Halāl, by Ahli Shīrāzi. See the Persian Catalogue, p. 657b; Berlin Catalogue, no. 16, art. 2; and the Bodleian Catalogue, no. 1027.

VIII. Foll. 222a—232b. Kasidahs by the same poet, beginning as in the Persian Catalogue, p. 658a, III., and in the Bodleian Catalogue, no. 1027, art. 3.

IX. Foll. 233a—236a. شیر و شکر

Shīr u Shakar, a Masnavi by Shaikh Bahā ud-Dīn Muhammad. See the Persian Catalogue, p. 831a, XXIX., and the Berlin Catalogue, no. 674, art. 21. Lithographed with Nān u Halvā, Teheran, A.H. 1279.

X. Foll. 236b—262a. Select Ghazals, by Mīr Abu 'l-Hasan Farāhāni, Zafar Khān, Zuhūri, fol. 238b; Tālib Kalim, fol. 244b; and Sā'ibāi Tabrīzi, fol. 253b.

XI. Foll. 263b—281b. سوز و گداز

Sūz u Gudāz, a Masnavi by Nau'i. See no. 313.

XII. Foll. 282b—300a. ترجمة الشوق

A Kasidah by 'Urfi entitled Tarjumat ush-Shauk, beginning:

جهان بگشتم و دردا که هیچ شهر و دیار

(see no. 310, art. 5), with a Takhmīs by Sā'ib, beginning:

بسی ز گردش دوران و چرخ کج رفتار

XIII. Foll. 302a—305a. معراج الخيال

A Kasidah by Nizām (no. 319), beginning:

فضای باختر گردید گلگون از می حمرا

XIV. Foll. 305b—314a. Kasidahs of 'Urfi, beginning:

چون دارد از طریق محمد نشان علی

XV. Foll. 314a—317a. Kasidah of Nāsir i Khusrau, beginning:

الا ای زاده گردون الا ای زبدهٔ ارکان

XVI. Foll. 317a—319a. A Masnavi without author's name, beginning:

شنیدم روزی از رعنا جوانی

XVII. Foll. 320a—326b. قضا و قدر

A Masnavi by Muh. 'Ali Taslīm, beginning:

شنیدم روزی از خونابه نوشی

XVIII. Foll. 327b—333b. اعتقادیه مولانا طغرا

A Masnavi on 'Ali's creed, by Maulānā Tughra (Persian Catalogue, p. 742a), beginning:

حکم از زبان خالق اکبر کند علی

XIX. Foll. 334b—347b. An anonymous commentary on 'Ali's speech known as خطبة البيان

Beg. الحمد لله رب العالمين ... در بیان شرح خطبة البيان امیرالمومنین علی بن ابی طالب علیه الصلوة والسلام

XX. Foll. 348a—357b. نان و حلوا

Nān u Halvā, a Masnavi by Bahā ud-Dīn 'Āmili. See the Persian Catalogue, p. 679a.

XXI. Foll. 358a—372b. Kasidahs of Anvari, written in oblique lines, beginning:

باز این چه جوانی جمالست جهانرا

420.

Or. 3307.—Foll. 94; 7¼ in. by 5; 15 lines, 3 in. long; written in fair Nestalik, with red-ruled margins; dated (fol. 48) Friday, 20 Ramazan, A.H. 877 (A.D. 1473).

[Sidney Churchill.]

I. Foll. 2—48. حدائق السحر

A treatise on poetical figures, by Rashid Vaṭvāṭ. See above, no. 188, I.

II. Foll. 48*b*—60. الاحيا فى علم حل المعما

A treatise on riddles, by Minūchihr the merchant, surnamed Badi' at-Tabrizi.

Beg. شكر و سپاس عليمى را جل ثناؤه كه فطرت لوح ادم را نقش پذير كرده ... اما بعد چنين كويد مولف اين تاليف احقر عباد الله الرفيع منوجهر التاجر الملقب ببديع التبريزى

From the preface it appears that the author was engaged in trade, and was travelling in Rūm with his father, when the latter died, A.H. 794. Passing through Ardabil, he met some scholars who had read a former work of his, انيس العارفين. It was at the request of one of these that he wrote the present treatise, which he completed in Yazd.

The author claims to be the first to write a treatise on riddles. He divides them into two species respectively called لغز and معما, and gives as an example of the latter a Mu'ammā composed on his own name, Minūchihr, by his revered master, Shaikh Kamāl Khujandi.

III. Foll. 63—94. انيس العشاق

A treatise on the terms and metaphors used by poets in describing female beauty, by Sharaf Rāmi. See the Persian Catalogue, p. 814*a*; Ethé, Bodleian Catalogue, no. 1339; and Pertsch, Berlin Catalogue, no. 35, art. 2.

421.

Or. 3314.—Foll. 113; 7 in. by 4½; 16 lines, 2¾ in. long; written in Nestalik; dated Rajab, A.H. 1233 (A.D. 1818).

[Sidney Churchill.]

I. Foll. 1*b*. A short treatise on mensuration, كتاب علم مساحت, without author's name.

Beg. اما بعد اين رساله ايست در علم مساحت و آن مشتمل بر چند فصل است فصل اول در ذرعى كه بنى هاشم قرار داده اند مشهور بكز شرع كه معمول خراسانست

II. Fol. 5*b*. A treatise on arithmetic, هذا حساب فارسى, divided into three Maḳālahs, without author's name.

Beg. الحمد لله رب العالمين ... اما بعد اين كتاب مشتمل است بر سه مقاله مقاله اول در حساب اهل هند و ان مشتملست بر مقدمه و دو باب

III. Fol. 32*b*. انيس العشاق

Anis ul-'Ushshāḳ, by Sharaf Rāmi. See the preceding MS., art. III.

IV. Fol. 63*b*. A treatise on rhyme, by 'Aṭā-ullah, رساله در علم قوافى. See no. 191, art. III.

V. Fol. 82*a*. حديقة الحقائق

A treatise on poetical figures, written for Shaikh Uvais by Sharaf Rāmi, and more properly entitled حقائق الحدائق.

Beg. بعد از حمد بيحد وصلواة بيعد چنين كويد اقل الشعراء شرف ابن محمد الرامى احسن الله عواقبه كه مدتى مديد و عهدى بعيد در سخن پردازى

For the division of the work and for other copies, see Rosen, Institut, p. 282, no. 101, art. 4; Krafft, no. 68; the Berlin Catalogue, no. 35, art. 1; and the Bodleian Catalogue, no. 1340.

422.

Or. 3642.—Foll. 202; 9¼ in. by 5¼; 19 lines, 2½ in. long; written in Nestalik and in Shikastah-āmīz, partly in diagonal lines, with gold-ruled margins; dated from Muḥarram A.H. 1073 to 17 Zulḥijjah, A.H. 1088 (A.D. 1662—78). [Sidney Churchill.]

I. Foll. 16b—64a. سراج منیر

Sirāj Munīr, a collection of moral tales by Muḥammad Sharīf B. Shams ud-Dīn Muḥ. See no. 419, II.

II. Foll. 64b—70b. حسن و عشق

A mystic allegory in prose, the hero of which is Rūḥ, the human soul; by Fuẓūli.

Beg. حمد بیحد احدی را سزاست که ریاض بدنرا باب روان پرورده و حسن را مظهر عشق و عشق را زیور حسن کرده

III. Foll. 71a—84b. The three prose compositions of Ẓuhūri, namely Gulzār i Ibrāhim, Khwān i Khalil and Dībājah i Nauras, imperfect and with some leaves transposed. See the Persian Catalogue, p. 741b, and the Berlin Catalogue, no. 1056.

IV. Foll. 84b—95b. رند و زاهد

"The Rake and the Ascete," by Fuẓūli. See no. 304.

V. Foll. 103a—113a. A piece in ornate prose written, like art. III., for Sultan Ibrāhīm 'Ādilshāh, and designated at the end as الرسالة الموسومه بالعرض لشکر (sic). Imperfect at the beginning.

VI. Foll. 121b—143b. The Divan of Nūri, who died A.H. 1000. See no. 224, v., and the Petersburg Catalogue, p. 402.

Beg. شبم سیاه چنان کرده سایهٔ هجران
که طور دل نشود روشن از سیاهی آن

The Kasidahs are followed by an alphabetical series of Ghazals, fol. 130a, beginning:

یاد آن بزم که بودیم طربناك آنجا
زهر خوردیم بصد رغبت تریاك آنجا

There are a few Ḳiṭ'ahs and Rubā'is at the end.

VII. Foll. 144b—178b. The Divan of Ṣaidi, who died A.H. 1069. See the Persian Catalogue, p. 689b, and Rosen, Institut, p. 264.

Beg. گردون نصیب دیده من کرد بیحساب
دردی که چشم آینه ارد در اضطراب

Ghazals, fol. 150a, beginning:

شد بسکه از خرام تو تغییر حالها
از جا در امدند بگلشن نهالها

VIII. Foll. 180b—197a. The Divan of Ummidi, who died A.H. 930. See the Persian Catalogue, p. 1091a; Majma' ul-Fuṣaḥā, vol. ii., p. 7; and Ethé, Bodleian Catalogue, no. 1017.

Beg. زهی طلعتت بر فراز رکایب
فروزان چو بر آسمان نجم ثاقب

The Divan consists only of Kasidahs. It is preceded by a preface, in which the editor, Mas'ūd ul-Ḥasani, states that he had collected the scattered poems of Rukn ud-Dīn Mas'ūd Ummīdi by desire of Shāh Ṣafi. The preface begins ستایشی که زبان بیان از ادای آن عاجز آید متکلمی را درخور است

IX. Foll. 197b—199. A Tarkib-band in praise of Ḥusain, without author's name, beginning:

کشتی شکست خورده طوفان کربلا
در خاك و خون فتاده بمیدان کربلا

It is followed by a Kasidah in praise of the twelve Imams by Birahman.

Besides the above works, the MS. contains

at the beginning some pieces from the Divan of Shams i Tabrizi, and in other places miscellaneous notes and extracts in prose and verse.

LATEST ACCESSIONS.

423.

Or. 4898.—Foll. 302; 10¼ in. by 6¼; 19 lines, 3⅝ in. long; written in small Nestalik, with red-ruled margins, apparently in the 16th century. [Sir Henry Rawlinson.]

تاریخ خیرات

A work on universal history, imperfect at beginning and end, without author's name.

The extant portion of the preface begins in the middle of a passage relating to early chronology and to the uncertainty of Muḥammad's genealogy, as follows: و درین معنی قایل کوید بنجاه و یك زآدم و حواست تا رسول هفده نبی هفتاد ولی اند وهفده شاه. Lower down the author states in the following verses that he entered upon the composition of the work in Rajab, A.H. 831:

خونم از دیده شد روان تا جمع
کردم این نسخه را بدینمنوال
فکر تاریخ ابتدا کردم
بود ماه رجب ولیکن سال
غرضم چون نبی و آلش بود
کشت تاریخ من هم از رخ آل

He must, however, have spent many years over it, for his account of Shāhrukh is brought down, fol. 229*b*, to that prince's death, A.H. 850. The preface contains, fol. 1*b*, a tabulated list of forty-nine authorities. The last is the Majma' ut-tavārikh, which is ascribed to Maulānā Shihāb ud-Dīn 'Abdullah (*sic*), known as Ḥāfiẓ i Abru, and is said to be a summary of all the earlier chronicles. The above title is found in the following passage, fol. 5*b*: بتاریخ خیرات موسوم کردانیده چه مقصد اقصی و مطلب اعلی ازین اذکار تکرار و تذکار حکایات و روایاتست که محاسن اعمال و مکارم افعال ملوك اطراف و حکام اکناف باشد

After some preliminary chapters on the creation of Adam, on his expulsion from Paradise, and on the conflicting accounts of the time elapsed between Adam and Muḥammad, the author states that the work is divided into three Ḳisms and a Makhlaṣ or conclusion. The Ḳisms are subdivided into a number of Ṭabaḳahs, the subjects of which are given, somewhat at variance, in respect of Ḳism III., with the actual contents of the MS., which are as follows:

Ḳism I., treating very fully of the ancient dynasties of Persia in four Ṭabaḳahs, viz., 1. Pishdādis, fol. 8*a*. 2. Kayān, fol. 23*b*. 3. Ashkānis, fol. 47*b*. Sāsānis, fol. 48*b*.

Ḳism II., comprising the five following Ṭabaḳahs: 1. Ancestors of Muḥammad, traced down from Seth, and life of the Prophet, fol. 71*a*. The Khulafā i Rāshidīn, or first three Khalifs, fol. 81*b*. The twelve Imams, fol. 95*b*. The Umayyade Khalifs, fol. 107*a*. The Abbasides, fol. 113*a*.

Ḳism III., comprising, as stated in the preface, thirteen Ṭabaḳahs (but in the body of the work, only twelve), treating of the following dynasties: 1. Ṭāhiris, fol. 127*a*. 2. Ṣaffāris, fol. 130*b*. 3. Sāmānis, fol. 139*a*. 4. Ghaznavis, fol. 145*a*. 5. Dailamān, fol. 151*b*. 6. Saljūḳis of Iran, fol. 161*b*, of Kirman, fol. 183*b*, and of Rūm, fol. 184*b*. 7. Atabeks of Shiraz, fol. 186*a*. 8. Ghūris, fol. 193*b*; Ghūris of Bāmiyān, fol. 193*b*; Khiljis of India, fol. 200*b*. 9. Ismā'ilis, fol. 206*b*, in two Maḳālahs, viz., Ismā'ilis of Maghrib, fol. 207*a*, and Ismā'ilis of Iran, fol. 225*a*. 10. Khwārazmshāhis, fol. 242*a*. 11. Ḳarakhitā'is of Kirman, fol. 248*a*. 12. Turks and Moghols. This Ṭabaḳah comprises a Maṭla' on the genealogy of the Turkish tribes, fol. 262*a*, and a Maḳṣad treating of the Moghols who ruled over Iran from Chingiz Khān to Abu Sa'īd, fol. 262*b*.

The Makhlaṣ, or conclusion, fol. 286*b*, is devoted to the history of Timur. After recording his death, fol. 298*b*, the author enumerates his sons, and dwells especially on the career of the fourth, Mirza Shāhrukh, from his boyhood to his death, A.H. 850. This is followed, fol. 299*b*, by a narrative of the embassy sent by Shāhrukh to China, A.H. 822. This section, which occupies the last seven pages of the MS., is imperfect at the end. It is an extract from the diary of the mission drawn up by Khwājah Ghiyāṣ ud-Dīn Naḳḳāsh, and quoted at greater length in the Maṭla' us-Sa'dain. See Or. 1291, foll. 134—145, and Quatremère, Notices et Extraits, vol. xiv.

In the division of his work the author appears to have followed very closely the plan of a history compiled A.H. 830-31 by Muḥammad B. Amīr Faẓl-ullah al-Mūsavi and entitled اصح التوارخ. See Ethé, Bodleian Catalogue, no. 32.

424.

Or. 4899.—Foll. 435; $11\frac{3}{4}$ in. by $6\frac{3}{4}$; 35 lines, $3\frac{3}{4}$ in. long; written in small and close Neskhi, probably in the 18th century; slightly mutilated at the beginning.

[Sir Henry Rawlinson.]

تاريخ الفى

The second volume of the great chronicle compiled for Akbar and entitled Ta'rīkh i Alfi (see the Persian Catalogue, p. 117), comprising the Riḥlat years 501—791 (A.H. 511—801).

The volume begins with this heading: جلد ثانى تاريخ الفى از سال پانصد و يكم از رحلت خير البشر الى الف اول از رحلت آن سرور عليه صلوات الله الملك الاكبر

The narrative begins as follows: در اوايل اينسال سلطان سنجر بن سلطان ملكشاه از خراسان لشكرها جمع نموده بخاطر بهرام شاه اولاد سلطان محمود غزنوى كه پناه بوى اورده بود الخ

The corresponding passage is found in Or. 142, fol. 310*b*.

The MS. breaks off before the end of A.H. 801 in the course of an account of the clandestine escape of Sultan Aḥmad from Baghdad, and of his taking refuge with Ḳara Yūsuf in Diyārbekr (see Or. 465, fol. 296*b*).

For other copies of the Ta'rīkh i Alfi, see Rehatsek, Molla Firuz Library, pp. 94, 95; Pertsch, Berlin Catalogue, no. 417; and Ethé, Bodleian Catalogue, no. 99.

425.

Or. 4948.—Foll. 248; $10\frac{1}{2}$ in. by 7; 31 lines, $4\frac{3}{4}$ in. long; written in small Neskhi; dated Thursday, the 1st of Muḥarram, A.H. 893 (A.D. 1487).

قانون الادب

An Arabic dictionary explained in Persian, by Abu 'l-Fazl Ḥubaish B. Ibrāhīm B. Muḥammad at-Tiflīsi.

Beg. سپاس خدايرا كه قادر بر كمالست قديم و توانا و بى زوالست ... چنين كويد شيخ اديب ابو الفضل حبيش بن ابرهيم بن محمد التفليسى كه چون از تصنيف كتاب بيان التصريف بپرداختم نكاه كردم بكتبهايى كه در علم ادب بپارسى هركس ساخته بودند كتابى نديدم كه اسما و افعال و جمع و حرف اين

جمله مشروح اندرو موجود بود جنانك معنى هر يكى ازانرا ياد كرده شد بپارسى واضح دران كتاب ديدار كرده باشند كه هر خواننده و آموزنده ان ازو فهم كند و دريابد

The author says in the preface that, having found no book in which the vocables of Arabic were fully and lucidly explained in Persian, he proceeded to compile one from the following sources: كتاب غريب المنصف [المصنف ؟] وكتاب جمهره وكتاب مجمل اللغه وكتاب اصلاح المنطق وكتاب ديوان الادب وكتاب صحاح اللغه وكتاب ابواب الادب وكتاب الفاظ مجموع وكتاب غريب ابو عبيده وكتاب ادب الكاتب وكتاب النهار وكتاب الروضه وكتاب مشكل اللغات وكتاب مجموع لاداب وكتاب مخ... الفاظ وكتاب الفاظ ابن سكيت وكتاب الفاظ عبد الرحمن وكتاب شرح فصيح الكلام وكتاب غريب القران وكتاب غريب الحديث وكتاب اصلاح وكتاب العين وكتاب الداخل وكتاب نسيم السحر وكتاب لب الادب وكتاب الاشتقاق وكتاب مشكل قتيبه وكتاب الواسط وكتاب ابنية الاسما والافعال وكتاب حقايق اللغه وكتاب تسمية الاشياء وكتاب مقامات حريرى وكتاب فقه اللغه وكتاب ترجمان القران وكتاب السامى فى الاسامى وكتاب دستور اللغه وكتاب مصادر قاضى وكتاب المدخل فى اللغه وكتاب الغنيه وكتاب مبادى اللغه وكتاب البذله وكتاب الارشاد فى اللغه وكتاب خلاص نطنزى وكتاب البلغه وكتاب مقدمة الادب وكتاب بيان اللغه وكتاب المقصور والممدود وكتاب مثلث قطرب وكتاب السلامه وكتاب شرح سبع طول وكتاب شرح الحماسه

He adds that he had collected and arranged in alphabetical order the select matter of the above works, and had called his book Ḳānūn ul-Adab, as being a classical norm and standard for Persian readers, especially for poets on account of the rhyme, and for men of letters with regard to difficult words: وزان پس كزين كلام اين كتابهاء نفيس را كه ياد كرده شد بترتيب جمله حروف بنسق درين كتاب ياد كردم و نامش كتاب قانون الادب نهادم زيرا كه اين كتاب در ادب اهل عجم را اصل و قانون بزرك است خاصه شعرارا از بهر قافيه شعر و ادبا را از بهر لغات مشكل

Many of the works included in the above list were unknown to Haji Khalfah, who gives their bare titles on the authority of the present work (see vol. vi., p. 341, no. 13,772). As far as they can be identified in the absence of the names of most authors, one of the latest appears to be the Muḳaddimat ul-Adab by Zamakhshari, who died A.H. 538. This would make it probable that the author, whose precise date is not known, lived in the latter part of the sixth century of the Hijrah. The archaic character of his Persian style points to the same period. In his dictionary of simple medicaments, entitled Naẓm us-Sulūk (Haj. Khal., ii., p. 302, and Uri, p. 129, no. 535), a copy of which has recently been acquired by the Museum, Ḥubaish quotes no more recent authority than Ibn Jazlah, who died A.H. 493. It must be noted, however, that he is not noticed by Ibn Abi Uṣaibi'ah, who wrote his Lives of Physicians about A.H. 650. See Wüstenfeld, Arabische Aertzte, no. 73.

The preface is followed by a preliminary chapter, in which the author shows by numerous examples the multiplicity of meanings of some Arabic words and the various forms they assume in prose and verse. He then proceeds, fol. 6b, to expound the plan of the dictionary, which is peculiar and rather complicated.

The words are arranged under the final letters, each of these forming a Kitāb. Each Kitāb is divided into nine sections called

نوع, according as the vowel preceding the last letter is *a*, *u*, *i*, *ā*, *ū*, *ī*, or *a*, *u*, *i* followed by a quiescent consonant. Each of these sections is again subdivided into subsections containing respectively words of two, three, four, five and six letters.

At the end of the dictionary are found the following two chapters (instead of three announced in the preface): Faṣl I., exhibiting the various forms of broken plurals with the corresponding singulars, fol. 210*b*. Faṣl II., containing a full list of the forms of Maṣdar or infinitive, fol. 220*a*.

An appendix occupying foll. 222—248, with the heading كتاب تصريف افعال, is a full treatise on the conjugation of Arabic verbs, both regular and irregular, with paradigms. It is not due to Ḥubaish, but to one of his disciples, who says that his late master had not fully expounded that subject in his work entitled Ṭaṣrif i Kalām : جون نكاه كردم استاد ما رحمه الله حبيش از سبب اختصار كتاب تصريف كلام نه كفته است ما درميان دو فصل وى نهاديم

Copyist : محمد بن ادريس

For another copy see Uri, no. 1054.

ALPHABETICAL INDEX OF TITLES.

In this and in the following indexes the numerals refer to the numbers under which the MSS. are described. Works which are only incidentally mentioned are distinguished by figures of lighter type in the reference.

ابواب الجنان	152.
آتشکده	114.
آثار الوزرا	101.
احسن التواریخ	55.
احکام فقه	374.
الاحیا فی علم المعما	420 II.
احیاء الملوک	97.
اخبار دهلی	81-2.
اخلاق الاشراف	264 V.
اخلاق الاولیاء	360.
اخلاق شفائی	151.
اخلاق منصوری	150.
اخلاق ناصری	147-8.
آذربرزین نامه	197 I.
اسرار نامه	235 III., 236 V.
اسکندر نامه	225—9, 232.
اصح التواریخ	423.
افضل التواریخ	56.
الاقوال الکافیه	161.
الهی نامه	235 I., 236 II.
انجمن خاقان	120.
انجمن دانش	369.
انوار سهیلی	381.
انیس العارفین	280 II., 281, 420 II.
انیس العاشقین قاسم	280 III., 281.
انیس العاشقین هدایت	364 II.
انیس العشاق	420 III., 421 III.
اوراد فتحیه	20.
ایقان	13.
بانوگشسب نامه	196 IX.
بحر اللآلی	48.
بدائع الازمان فی وقائع کرمان	90.
بدیع الافکار	378.
برزو نامه	195 II., 196 VIII.
برهان جامع	171.
بزم آرای	106.

بستان السياحت	140-41.
بصيرت نامه	63.
بوستان خيال	307 I.
بوستان سعدى	251, 246—8.
بهجة التواريخ	28.
بهرام نامه	353.
بهرام و بهروز	369.
بهمن نامه	197 II., 201 III.
بيان فارسى	12.
بيان المحمود	377, 70, 122.
بيژن نامه	199 I.
بيژن نامهٔ عبدى	307 I.
بست باب	155, II., V.
بيمار و طبيب	376.
پند نامهٔ سعدى	252-3.
پهلو بندى	376.
تاريخ احمد شاه درانى	74.
— افغانستان	74.
— الفى	424.
— بخارا	87.
— بيهق	89.
— جديد	15.
— جلال منجم	57.
— جهان آرا	71, 118.
— جهانكشاى نادرى	65.
— حكماى سلف	100 I.
— خلفاء راشدين	43.
— خيرات	423.
— ذو القرنين	71.
تاريخ سياح	63.
— شاه اسمعيل	52.
— شاه اسمعيل و شاه طهماسب	53, 54.
— شاه عباس ثانى	60, 61.
— صاحبقرانى	70.
— طبرستان لابن اسفنديار	92.
— طبرستان لظهير الدين	93.
— عضدى	72.
— قم	88.
— محمد شاه	80.
— محمد شاه نادر الزمانى	37.
— ممالك هند	83 II.
— نيشابور	89.
— الوصاف	49.
تبصرة العوام	7.
تتمه اكبر نامه	76.
تجربة الاحرار	132.
تحفة الاحرار	289-90.
تحفة الحبيب	375.
تحفة الخاقانى	4.
تحفهٔ سامى	103.
تحفهٔ شاهدى	166.
تحفة العالم	84 II.
تحفة العراقين	221 I.
تحفة الموحدين	22.
تذكرة الابرار	5.
تذكرة الائمه	44.
تذكرة الشعراء	353.
تذكرهٔ شوشتريه	98.

تذکرهٔ طاهر نصرابادی	110.
تذکرهٔ محمد شاهی	124, 171.
تذکرة الملوك	83 III.
تذکرهٔ نوا	115.
ترجمة الاشواق	310 5.
ترجمة الشوق	419 XII.
ترجمهٔ لسان الغيب	417 I.
الترسل النصريه	257 II.
تزوك تيموری	51.
تزوك جهانكيری	77.
تضمينات عبيد زاكانی	264 I.
تعريفات عبيد زاكانی	264 IV.
تقديس الانبيا	10.
تقويم الاوليا	400.
تكملهٔ اكبر نامه	76.
تمور نامهٔ هاتفی	295 IV., 297.
تنسوقنامهٔ ايلخانی	157.
جام جم اوحدی	258 II., 259.
جام جم فرهاد ميرزا	187.
جام جمشيد	307 I.
جامع التواريخ	25-6.
جامع الحكايات	391-2.
جامع العلوم	142.
جنك ميرزا عبد الكريم	399.
جنكنامه غلام محمد خان	351.
جواهر نامه	158.
جوهر الذات	257 I.
جوهر فرد	307 I.
جهان دانش	154.
جهانكير نامه	77.
چهار مقاله	390, 418.
حال نامه	283.
حدائق الانوار	143.
حدائق السحر	188, 420 I.
حدائق السياحة	141.
حدائق المعجم	190.
حديقة امان اللهی	129.
حديقة الحقائق	421 V.
حديقهٔ سنائی	215.
حديقة العالم	84 I.
حسن و عشق	422 II.
حشمت كشمير	86.
حقائق الحدائق	421 V.
حقائق الدقائق	18.
حقيقة الحقائق شاهيه	387.
حلل مطرز	193.
حلية المتقين	153.
حملهٔ حيدری	336.
حواس باطن	396.
خرد نامهٔ اسكندری	289-90.
خزان و بهار	396.
خزائن العلوم	87.
خزائن الملكوت	307 II.
خسرو نامهٔ عطار	237 II.
خسرو و شيرين جعفر	314 I., 315.
——— شهاب	352, 353.
——— نامی	346-7.
——— نظامی	225—9, 231.

خسرو و گل	**237** II.
خطبة البيان	**419.** XIX.
خلاصة الاشعار	**105.**
خلاصة الافكار	**116.**
خلد برین	**34-5.**
خلد برین وحشی	**376.**
خمسهٔ داود شاهی	**356.**
خمسهٔ خسرو دهلوی	**255.**
خمسهٔ نظامی	**225—9.**
خمسهٔ هاتفی	**295.**
خوان خلیل	**422** III.
خورشید و جمشید	**265** V., **266.**
خیر البیان	**108-9.**
داراب نامه	**384-5.**
دانش نامه	**162** III.
در دوست	**376.**
در مکنون	**21**, 396.
درر المحمود	122.
درة التاج	**356.**
دزد و قاضی	**374.**
دستور الاخوان	**176.**
دستور الاطبا	**160.**
دستور الشعراء	**374.**
دستور شهریاران	**62.**
دستور الکاتب	**189.**
دقائق الحقائق	**18.**
دوازده مقام	102 IV.
دول رانی	307 I.
ده فصل عبید زاکانی	**264** IV.
ده نامه ابن عماد	**348** II.
ده نامه اوحدی	**258** III.
دیباجه نورس	**422** III.
دیوان ابن یمین	**261** II.
— ابو تراب بیك	**318** I.
— ابو الفرج رونی	**211** I.
— اثیر اومانی	**239** I.
— ادیب صابر	**239** II.
— ارشد	**330.**
— ازرقی	**211** III., **213**, **224** III., **234** III.
— اشکی	**306.**
— امامی	**213** II., **245** I.
— امانی	**312.**
— امیدی	**422** VIII.
— انوری	**211** V., **215** V., **218—20.**
— اوحدی	**258.**
— ثنائی	**309** I.
— جامی	**287-8.**
— جعفر	**314** II.
— جلال الدین رومی	**243-4.**
— جمال اصفهانی	**224** IV.
— حاذق	**325.**
— حافظ	**267—74**, 417 I.
— حسن غزنوی	**215** VI.
— الخاقانی	**221** II.
— خاور	**350.**
— خاوری	**358.**
— خسرو دهلوی	**220** IV.
— خواجو	**262.**

ديوان راقم	332.
— رشيد وطواط	212 IV., 234 II.
— رفيع لنبانى	239 IV.
— رفيق	350.
— رياضى	285 II.
— سرورى	335.
— سلطان حسين	300.
— سلمان	220 III., 265.
— سنائى	214, 215 III.
— سيد كوچك	345.
— سيف اسفرنكى	220 II.
— شاپور	321.
— شاه شجاع	361.
— شاهى	284-5.
— شرف الدين شفروه	239 III.
— شمس تبريز	243-4.
— شمس مشرقى	277 II.
— شهاب	353 I.
— شيدا	326.
— شيدا حسن چلبى	356.
— صائب	328-9.
— صيدى	422 VII.
— طبيب	339.
— طوفان	342.
— ظهير فاريابى	222—4.
— عاشق	340-1.
— عامل الدين	373.
— عبد الواسع جبلى	217.
— عبيد زاكانى	264 I.
ديوان عتيقى	260.
— عرفى	309 II., 310.
— عصمت	282.
— على نقى كمرۀ	320, 419 V.
— عنصرى	204 II., 205, 212 III.
— غمامى	366.
— فرج	327.
— فرخ	355.
— فرخى	203-4.
— فريد الدين عطار	213 III.
— فضل الله قزوينى	257 III.
— فغانى	258 IV.
— فياض	324.
— قاآنى	367.
— قدسى	323.
— قطب الدين	238.
— قطران	204 III., 207-8, 245 II.
— قطره	357.
— كمال خجندى	275-6.
— كوهى	271 II.
— لامعى	212 II.
— مجذوب	331.
— مجمر	354.
— مختارى	211 VI., 215 VII., 216.
— مغربى	277 I.
— مشرقى	277 II.
— منوچهرى	206, 212 V., 224 II.
— موالى	285 III.
— ميرك	322.

ديوان ميرم سياه 353 II.
— ناصر خسرو 209-10.
— مجيب جربادقانى 234 I.
— نشاط 362-3.
— نصير 318 II.
— نظام دست غيب 319.
— نظيرى 316.
— نعمت الله ولى 279.
— نورس 333.
— نورى 224 V., 422 VI.
— واعظ 334.
— وفا 344.
— هارون 254.
— هدايت 365.
الذريعه الى مكارم الشريعه 146.
رباعيات مجد الدين همكر 211 II., IV., VII.
رسالة الامانه 280 III., 281.
رسالهٔ ترياق فاروق 159.
رسالهٔ حسين وذكى 167.
رسالهٔ دلكشا 264 VI.
رسالهٔ صاحبقران 71.
رساله در قافيه لعطاء الله 191 III., 192, 421 IV.
رساله در قافيه لجامى 191 IV.
الرسالة القشيريه 16.
رساله معما لمير حسين 192 V., 194.
رساله معما لشرف الدين يزدى 193.
رموز الانبيا وكنوز الاوليا 214.
رند وزاهد 304-5, 422 IV.
روضات الجنات 94.—100.
روضة الصفويه 58.
روضة السلاطين 375.
روضة العاشقين 278.
روضة المتقين 23.
رياض الابرار 144.
رياض السياحة 139.
رياض الشعراء 112-3.
رياض الشهادة 45-7.
رياض العارفين 126.
ريش نامه 264 VII.
زاد المعاد 11.
زائده زاد المعاد 11.
زبدة التواريخ لحافظ ابرو 27.
——— لحيدر رازى 33.
——— لمحمد محسن 36.
زينة المجالس 395.
زبور العاشقين 376.
(شرح) زيج الغ بيك 156.
زينة التواريخ 39, 71.
زينة المدائح 118-9.
زبور آل داود 64.
ساغر كش لطف ازلى 376.
ساقى نامه 376.
سام نامه 196 II.
سبحة الابرار 289-90.
سحر حلال 419 VII.
سد سكندر 376.
سراج القلوب 3.
سراج المنير 419 II., 422 I.

سفينهٔ خوشكو 111.
سفينة المحمود 122, 70.
سلالة الافاضل 163.
سلامان و ابسال 289-90.
سلسلة الذهب 289-90.
سلّم السما 156.
سمط العلى 90.
سنكلاخ 176.
سوز و كداز 313, 376, 419 XI.
سير العباد الى المعاد 214, 215 II.
سيرة المنتهى 10.
(شرح) شافيه 175.
شاه و درويش 302 II.
شاهنامه فردوسى 195—9, 263.
شاهنشاه نامه 201 II., 188 II.
شرعة الاسلام 4.
شرف نامه 95-6.
شرف نامهٔ شاهى 73.
شوق العارفين 417 I.
شير و شكر 419 IX.
شيرين و خسرو امير خسرو 255.
شيرين و خسرو هاتفى 295 II.
صحاح العجم 189.
صحيفهٔ اقبال 80.
صفات العاشقين 302 I.
صفة الآداب 154.
ضياء العارفين 102.
ضياء النور 368.
عالم آراى عباسى 59.
عباس نامهٔ كاشف 396.
عجائب المخلوقات 135.
عرض لشكر 422 V.
عروض سيفى 191 I.
العروة لاهل الخلوة 19.
عشاق نامه 264 II.
عقد العلى 90-91.
عقد كهر 333.
عين الحيوة 380.
فتح المجاهدين 406.
فتوح الحرمين 301.
فراق نامه 265 VI., 266.
فرامرز نامه 196 VI., 199 II.
الفرج بعد الشدة 389, 396.
فرهاد و شيرين عرفى 310-11, 376.
فرهاد و شيرين نوقى 419 IV., 376.
فرهاد و شيرين وحشى 308, 376, 418 II., 419 III.
فرهنك جهانكيرى 168.
فرهنك خداپرستى 371.
فرهنك عباسى 170.
فرهنك محمد شاهى 171.
فرهنك مكاتبات ابو الفضل 169 II., IV.
قابوس نامه 145.
قانون الادب 425.
قران السعدين 256, 307.
قصهٔ امير حمزه 386.
قصهٔ بلوهر و يوذاسف 380, 36.
قصة الجوهر 388.
قصهٔ شيخ صنعان 376.

قصهٔ مسعود شاه	388.
قصهٔ یوذاسف و بلوهر	380, 36.
قضا و قدر	419 xvii., 376.
قیصری نامه	372.
کتاب قم	88.
کتاب معجزات	303.
کتاب من لا یحضره فقیه	23.
کرشاسب نامه	195 i., 196 i., 201-2.
کشف الاوتار	162 iv.
الکفایة فی علم الهیئة	154.
کل کشتی	337, 376.
کل و بلبل	374.
کلدستهٔ اسرار	335.
کلدستهٔ اندیشه	399.
کلزار ابراهیم	422 iii.
کلزار عباسی	376.
کلستان سعدی	248-50.
کلشن خیال	376.
کلشن محمود	121, 122, 70.
کلشن مراد	66.
کلیات سعدی	246—8.
کلیات سلمان	265-6.
کلیات عبید زاکانی	264.
کلیات مجمر	354.
کمال الدین وتمام النعمة	380.
کنز التحف	162 v.
کنز الحقائق	235 v.
کنز اللغه	173.
کنز الهدایه	161.
کنوز الحقائق	149.
کنوز الحکمه	214.
کنوز الرموز	215 ii.
کنوز الودیعه	146.
کوش نامه	201 iv.
کوهر عالم	85, 86.
کوهر مراد	9.
کوهر نامهٔ عالم	85, 86.
کوی و چوکان	283.
لب السیر	116 ii.
لب اللباب	38.
لب لباب معنوی	241-2.
لباب الانساب	89.
لباب القول فی الاشارة الی علم الله	155 i.
لباب المعنوی	241.
لطائف الاخبار	78.
لطائف الطوائف	100 iii.
لطیفهٔ غیبی	417 i.
لغات حلیمی	164-5.
لوامع صاحب قرانی	23.
لوائح جامی	419 i.
لیلی و مجنون جامی	289-90.
——— فضولی	261 i.
——— کاشف	396.
——— مکتبی	298-9.
——— نظامی	225-9.
——— هاتفی	295-6.
مآثر سلطانیه	68-9.
مآثر الملوک	29.

مثنوی جلال الدین رومی	240.
مثنوی جلق	264.
مجالس النفائس	104.
مجمع الابکار	310 7.
مجمع الانشا	398.
مجمع التواریخ	33.
مجمع التواریخ حافظ ابرو	423.
مجمع الفصحاء	125.
مجمع محمود	122.
مجمع النوادر	390.
مجنون و لیلی	255.
محاضرات الادباء	146.
محاضره شمع و قندیل	257 I.
محمود الآثار	215 IV.
محمود اللغه	174.
محمود نامه	122.
محمود و آیاز	317, 376.
مختار نامه	236 I.
مخزن الاسرار	225–9, 233.
مخزن الغرائب	117.
مخزن المحمود	122.
مدائح المعتمدیه	127–8.
مراد نامه	353.
مرآة الاحوال	131.
مرآة الاولیاء	85.
مرآة القاسان	99.
مرآة المحققین	418 III.
مرآة النجاة	257.
مرآة الهند	83.
مرزبان نامه	382-3.
مرصاد العباد	17.
مشارب التجارب	80.
مصیبت نامه	235 IV., 236 IV.
مطلع الانوار	255.
مطلع الشمس	74.
المعجم فی معاییر اشعار العجم	190.
المعجم فی ملوك العجم	257.
معراج الخیال مجلی	376.
معراج الخیال نظام	419 XIII.
معیار الاشعار	190.
معیار جمالی	167.
مفاتیح الفضائل	163.
مفتاح الفتوح	235 VI.
مفتاح الفضلاء	163.
مفتاح الفلاح	8.
مفتاح الكنوز	221 II.
مفرح القلوب	397.
مقامات العارفین	417 I.
المقصد الاقصی	149.
مكاتبات ابو الفضل	169 II., IV.
مناجاة عبد الله انصاری	16 II.
مناهج الشارعین	10.
منتخب المحمود	122.
منطق الطیر	235 II., 236 III.
مواهب الهی	50.
مواهب علیه	1.
مهابهارت	24.
مهر خاوری	71.

مهمات الاسنوی	80.
میخانه	107.
میخانه و بتخانه	107.
میزان طبائع	379.
ناظر و منظور	376.
نامهٔ خاقان	71.
نان و حلوا	419 xx., 376.
نخبة التواریخ	41.
نرکـدان	376.
نزهة الارواح	100 I.
نزهة القلوب	136-7.
نژاد نامهٔ پادشاهان	42.
نسب نامهٔ میکالیه	80.
نسخهٔ احوال شاهی	130.
نصاب انکلیسی	187.
نصائح المحمود	122.
نصیحت نامهٔ شاهی	149.
نظم السلوك	425.
نکارستان دارا	123.
نکارستان معینی	394.
نوادر الامثال	264 III.
نور نامه	85.
واقعات بابری	75.
واقعات درانی	74.
واقعات کشمیر	85.
واله و سلطان	343.
وامق و عذرا	348-9.
وسط الحیوة	220 IV.
وصلت نامه	236 VI.
هدایت نامه	364 I.
هدایة السعدا	6.
هدیة الاحباب	376.
هشت بهشت	376.
هفت اقلیم	138.
هفت اورنك	289-90.
هفت بهشت	255.
هفت پیکر کاشف	396.
هفت پیکر نظامی	225—30, 376.
هفت منظر	295, 305 II.
(ترجمه) یمینی	215 IV., 382.
یوسف و زلیخای جامی	289-94.
——— شهاب	353.
——— فردوسی	200.

INDEX OF PERSONS' NAMES.

NUMERALS in parenthesis are Hijrah dates. Coming after a man's name they are precise or approximate obituary dates; when following the title of a work, they relate to its composition. Other numerals are references to the Nos. of the Supplement. Muḥ. is short for Muḥammad; *t.* for 'takhalluṣ,' or poetical surname.

SCHEME OF TRANSCRIPTION.

ث s̱, ح ḥ, خ kh, ذ ẕ, ژ zh, ص ṣ, ض ẓ, ط ṭ, ظ ẕ, ع ', غ gh, ق ḳ, و v, medial hamzah '.

Ibn 'Abbād (385) 88.
'Abbās I., 402, 417 n.
'Abbās II., 402.
'Abbās Mirza, Vali-'ahd, 121, 170, 408 s.
'Abdullah Anṣāri (481) 16 n., 108.
'Abdullah Khān Uzbek, 411, 417 n.
'Abdullah Mirza, 121.
'Abdullah B. Muḥ. Āḳā, t. Raunaḳ. *Ḥadīḳat Amānullāhi* (1265) 129.
'Abdullah B. Muḥ. 'Ali, Lisān ul-Ḥaḳḳ, t. Mahram. *Farhang i Khulāparasti* (1277).
'Abdullah B. Ni'mat-ullah Shūshtari (1173). *Taẕkirah i Shūshtariyyah*, 98.
'Abd ul-'Ali Birjindi. *Sharḥ Bīst Bāb*, 155 v.
'Abd ul-Bāsiṭ, Shaikh, 169.
'Abd ul-Ḥasīb, v. Muḥ. B. Sayyid Aḥmad al-'Āmili, 10.
'Abd ul-Ḥayy, Khwājah, 353 n.
'Abd ul-Ḥayy Tafrishi, t. Sarkhwush (1131) 400.
'Abd ul-Jalīl B. 'Abd ur-Raḥmān Masīḥi (c. 1050) 162 n.
'Abd ul-Ḳādir (Muhyi ud-Dīn) 408 n.
'Abd ul-Ḳādir Ḳhān. *Ḥishmat i Kashmīr* (1245) 86.
'Abd ul-Karīm Ḳazvīni. *Jung* (1126) 400.
'Abd ul-Laṭīf Shūshtari (1220). *Tuḥfat ul-'Ālam*, 84 n.
'Abd ur-Raḥīm Kāshāni. *Mir'āt ul-Ḳāsān* (1288) 99.
'Abd ur-Raḥīm Khān (1036) 75.
'Abd ur-Raḥīm al-Mūsavi, t. Munṣif. *Badī' ul-Afkār* (1239) 378.
'Abd ur-Raḥmān B. Muḥ. an-Naishābūri, 87.
'Abd ur-Rashīd, calligrapher, 408.
'Abd ur-Razzāḳ Lābiji, t. Fayyāẓ (c. 1060). *Gauhar i Murād*, 9. *Divan*, 324.
'Abd ur-Razzāḳ B. Najaf Ḳuli (1243). *Baṣīrat Nāmah*, 63. *Ma'āṣir i Sulṭāniyyah*, 68-9. *Nigāristān i Dārā*, 123. *Tajribat ul-Aḥrār*, 132.
'Abd ul-Vahhāb B. 'Ali Ashraf Shīrāzi. *Nukhbat ul-akhbār* (1257) 41.
'Abd ul-Vahhāb Iṣfahāni, t. Nashāṭ (1244) 188 n. *Divan*, 362-3.—118, 119, 120, 122-4, 132.
'Abd ul-Vāsi' Jabali (555). *Divan*, 217.—105 t., 107, 115.
'Abdi, formerly Nuvīdi (988). *Būstān i Khayāl*, *Khazā'in ul-Malakūt*, 307.

Abshār Marghazi, 107.
Abu 'l-'Alā Ganjavi, 115.
Abu 'Ali Ḳalandar, 111.
Abu 'l Baḳā Mūsavi, 411.
Abu Bakr B. Sa'd, 190.
Abu Dulaf, 201 I.
Abu 'l-Faraj Rūni (c. 500). *Divan*, 211 I.—105, 107, 115, 190, 378.
Abu 'l-Faraj Sīstāni, 107, 108 I.
Abu 'l-Fatḥ Busti, 106, 107.
Abu 'l-Fatḥ B. Sulṭān Ḥusain (907) 268.
Abu 'l-Fazl 'Allāmi, 169 II., IV.
Abu 'l-Fazl Gulpāigāni, 15.
Abu Ḥanīfah, 107.
Abu 'l-Ḥasan Balkhi, 106, 107.
Abu 'l-Ḥasan Farāhāni, 219, 419 X.
Abu 'l-Ḥasan Ghaffāri. *Gulshan i Murād*, 66.
Abu 'l-Ḥasan Jafāni, 107.
Abu 'l-Ḥasan B. Muḥ. Kāẓim Jājarmi. *Akhlāḳ ul-Auliyā* (1239) 360.
Abu 'l-Ḳāsim Beg Aivaghli. *Majma' ul-Inshā*, 398.
Abu 'l-Ḳāsim Kāzarūni, 108.
Abu 'l-Muayyad, 107, 200.
Abu 'l-Muḥaḳḳiḳ, 107.
Abu 'l-Muẓaffar Ṭāhir, 107.
Abu Naṣr Aḥmad al-Ḳubāvi. *Ta'rīkh i Bukhārā*, (322) 87.
Abu Rajā, 107.
Abu Rajā Aḥmad B. 'Abd uṣ-ṣamad 'Ābidi, 390.
Abu Sa'īd Abu 'l-Khair, 108, 116.
Abu Salīḳ, 107.
Abu Sarāḳab, 107.
Abu Ṭāhir Ṭarasūsi. *Dārāb Nāmah*, 384-5.
Abu Ṭālib al-Ḥusaini. *Tuzūk i Tīmūri* (1047) 51.
Abu Ṭālib Khān I'timād ud-Daulah, 417 II.
Abu Ṭālib Tabrīzi (1221). *Khulāṣat ul-Afkār. Lubb us-Siyar*, 110.
Abu Turāb Beg (1026). *Divan*, 318 I.—108.
Abu Yazīd Basṭāmi, 107, 108.
Adab, 127.
Adīb, 127.
Adīb Ṣābir (540). *Divan*, 239 II.—105, 107, 115.
'Ādil, 123, 124.
Aflāṭūn, Mulla, 66.
Afsar, 111, 120.
Afshān, 127.
Afẓal ud-Dīn Kirmāni. *'Iḳd ul-'Ula* (584) 90, 91.
Agasi (Mirza) 412.
Ahli Shīrāzi, or Turshīzi. *Siḥri Ḥalāl*, 419 VII.—108, 375, 378.
Ahli Khurāsāni, 108.
Aḥmad or Aḥmadi. *Shāhanshāh Nāmah* (738) 201 II.
Aḥmad 'Ali Hāshimi. *Makhzan ul-Gharā'ib* (1218) 117.
Aḥmad 'Ali Mirza, 121, 123.
Aḥmad 'Allūmah, 85.
Aḥmad B. Muḥ. Bahbahāni. *Mir'āt ul-Aḥvāl* (1225) 131.
Aḥmad Rūmi (c. 720). *Daḳā'iḳ ul-Ḥaḳā'iḳ*, 18.
Aḥmad Shāh, 411.
Aḥmadi, 111.
Aḥsan, 111.
'Ājiz, 124.
Ajri, 111.
Aḳā Khān (Mirza) 412, 404.
Akbar Pādishāh, 408, 411, 417 II.
Akbar, Mirza 'Ali Akbar, 124.
Akhgar, 127.
Akhtar, 124.
'Alā ud-Daulah Simnāni (736). *Al-'Urvah*, 19.
'Alā ud-Dīn Ḥusain Jahānsūz (556) 390.
'Ālamgīr, 408, 411.
'Ālī, 124, 127.
'Ali B. Abu Ṭālib, 124, 419 XIX.
'Ali 'Ādilshāh, 411.
'Ali B. Aḥmad, 195.
'Ali Akbar Shīrāzi, t. Bismil (c. 1280). *Baḥr ul-La'āli*, 48.—120, 123, 127, 412.
'Ali Aṣghar Amīn uṣ-Sultān, 403 16.
'Ali Aṣghar B. 'Ali Akbar, t. Nayyir. *Ẓiyā un-Nār* (c. 1263) 368.
'Ali Aṣghar B. Yūsuf Ḳazvini (1100) 400.
'Ali Hamadāni, Sayyid (786). *Aurād*, 20.
'Ali B. Ḥusain Kāshifi (939). *Laṭā'if uṭ-ṭavā'if*, 100 III.

'Alī Ibrāhīm Khān (1208) 405.
'Ali Ḳuli Beg Mūsavi, 412.
'Ali Ḳuli Khān t. Vālih (1169). *Riyāẓ ush-shu'arā,* 112.—343-4.
'Ali Ḳuli Mirza, 74, 121, 123, 412.
'Ali Ḳushji (879). *Sharḥ Zij,* 156.
'Ali Khān, 121.
'Ali B. Maḥmūd Ḥusaini. *Bazm-ārāi* (1000) 106.
'Ali Mardān Khān, 411.
'Ali (Mīr), calligrapher, 408.
'Ali B. Muḥ. 'Āmili (1103) 400.
'Ali Murād Khān Zand (1198) 352.
'Ali Naḳi Kamara'i (1030). *Divan,* 320, 419 v.—108.
'Ali Rashti, 127.
'Ali Riẓa Mirza, 121.
'Ali Shāh Mirza, 121.
'Alīshīr, Mīr, t. Navā'i (906). *Majālis un-Nafā'is,* 104.—375.
Allahḳuli, 111.
Allahvirdi Mirza, 121, 123.
Allahyār Khān, 123.
Alvand Beg Aḳ-ḳuyunlu (907) 401 II.
A'ma, 127.
'Am'aḳ, 105, 107, 115.
Amāni (c. 1016). *Divan,* 312.—111.
Amān-ullah Khān, 129.
'Amīd Lūnaki, 374.
'Āmil ud-Dīn Muḥ. Ṭāhir. *Divan* (1298) 373.
Amīn Aḥmad Rāzi. *Haft Iḳlīm* (1002) 138.
Amīnā Mudaḳḳiḳ Yazdi, 376.
Amir Beg, v. Mirza Beg, 58.
Amīr Khān, 111.
'Andalīb, 123, 124, 127.
Anīsi Shāmlu. *Maḥmūd u Āyāz,* 376.
Anjum, 128.
Anjuman, 127.
'Anḳā, 127.
Anvari (587). *Divan,* 211 v., 215 v., 218-20.—105, 107, 115, 190, 374, 378-9, 419 xxi.
'Ārifi (853). *Ḥāl Nāmah,* 283.—286 v.
Arshad (c. 1084). *Divan,* 330.
Ārzū, Sirāj ud-Dīn 'Ali Khān (1169) 232.
Asad, 111.
Asadi, 105, 106-8, 115, 124.
Asadi. *Garshāsp Nāmah* (458) 195 I., 196 I., 201 I., 202.
Asad-ullah Khān, 124, 412.
Āṣaf, 111.
Āṣaf Khān, 417 II.
Āṣaf ud-Daulah (1212) 81-2, 408.
Āṣafi, 128, 375.
Āṣafjāh, 411.
Aṣālat Khān, 411.
Aṣar, Shafī'ā, 376.
'Āshiḳ (1181). *Divan,* 340-41.—132.
Ashki (972). *Divan,* 306.
Āshnā, 111.
Ashraf, of Azarbaijan, 123-4.
Ashraf Samarḳandi (854) 286 a.—107, 115.
Ashraf Kāshāni, 107.
Āshuftah, 128.
Asīr, 111.—123-4.
Aṡīr Akhsikati, 107, 115.
Aṡīr Aumāni (665). *Divan,* 239 I.—107, 115.
Asīri, 132.
'Asjadi, 106, 108, 115.
Aslam, v. Badī' uz-zamān Abu 'l-Ḳāsim, 85.
'Aṭā-ullah B. Maḥmūd (920) 191 III., 192, 421 IV.
'Atīḳi (744). *Divan,* 260.
'Aṭṭār, Farīd ud-Dīn (627). *Kulliyāt,* 235-7.—107, 115, 376.
'Aufi, Muḥ. *Jāmi' ul-Ḥikāyāt* (625) 391-2.
Auḥad ud-Dīn Gurgānji, 107.
Auḥad ud-Dīn Kirmāni, 240.
Auḥad ud-Dīn Māmarghi, 107.
Auḥadi (738). *Divan, Jām i Jam, Dah Nāmah,* 258-9.—111, 115.
Aumāni, Aṡīr ud-Dīn (665). *Divan,* 239.—107, 115.
Āzād, 111.—123-4.
Āzād, Mīr Ghulām 'Ali (or rather Muḥ. Muḳīm of Kashmīr, who died A.H. 1150; v. Ṣuḥḥ i Gulshan, p. 6, and the Persian Catalogue, p. 1092a). *Continuation of Ḥamlah i Ḥaidari,* 336.
Āẓari (866) 201 III.—107.
Azhari, 106.

Aẕhari, 111.
'Azīz, 123.
'Azīz-ullah B. Asad-ullah. *Durr i Maknūn* (1151) 21.
'Azīz-ullah Zāhidi. *Rauẓat ul-'Āshiḳīn* (820) 278.
Azraḳi (526). *Divan*, 211 III., 213 I., 224 III., 234 III.—105, 107, 108, 115, 190.
'Aẓud ud-Daulah Sulṭān Aḥmad. *Ta'rīkh i 'Aẓudi* (1304) 72.
Āẕur, v. Luṭf 'Ali Beg.
Bāb, 'Ali Muḥ. Shīrāzi (1266). *Bayān i Fārsi*, 12.
Bābar. *Vāḳi'āt i Bābari*, 75.
Ibn Bābavaih (321). *Ḳiṣṣah i Bilauhar*, 380, 36.—23.
Badī' Tabrīzi, v. Minuchihr.
Badī' ud-Dīn Abu 'l-Ḳāsim Muḥ. Aslam. *Gauhar i 'Alam* (c. 1200), 85, 86.
Badī' Muḥ. Yazdi. A collection of Masnavis (1170) 376.
Badī' uz-Zamān Rashīd Khān (1107). *Laṭā'if ul-Akhbār*, 78.
Badīhi, 107, 390.
Bahā Imāmi, 412.
Bahā ud-Dīn al-'Amili (1030). *Miftāḥ ul-Falāḥ*, 8. *Nān u Ḥalvā*, 376. *Shīr u Shakar*, 419 IX.—400, 403 IS.
Bahā ud-Dīn Marghīnāni, 107.
Bahā ud-Dīn B. Ṣāḥibḳirān, 107.
Bahā ud-Dīn Zanjāni, 107.
Bahā-ullah, Ḥusain 'Ali (1309). *Letters*, 13-14, 403 IS.
Bahādur Shāh, 411.
Bahār, Muḥ. 'Ali, 127-8.
Bahjat, 127.
Bahman Mirza (c. 1300). *Taẕkirah i Muhammad-shāhi*, 124.—121, 171, 402 XXVII.
Bahrām Mirza, 121.
Baihaḳi, Abu 'l-Ḥasan 'Ali. *Ta'rīkh i Baihaḳ* (563) 89.
Baisunghar, Mirza (837) 196.
Baiẓā, 123.
Bakhtiyāri, 200.
Bāḳi, 120, 124.
Bandah, Muḥ. Raẓi (1228). *Zīnat ut-Tavārīkh*.—120, 123-4.
Barīdi Pādishāh, 411.
Barkyāruḳ, 197 II.
Baṣīr, 127.
Bayāni, 'Abdullah Marvārīd (922) 268.
Bāẕil (1124). *Ḥamlah i Ḥaidari*, 336.
Bazmi, 118.
Bidarbakht, 411.
Bīdil, 'Abd ul-Ḳādir (1133) 338.
Bīdil, Muḥ. Raḥīm, 120, 123-4, 127.
Bijai Singh, Rājah, 411.
Binā'i, 108, 115, 375.
Bīnavā, 120, 124.
Bishan La'l, t. Nāẓir. *Ḳaiṣari Nāmah* (1297) 372.
Bismil, 'Ali Akbar (c. 1280) 48.—120, 123, 127, 412.
Burhāni, 107.
Buzurg, Mirza, 120, 122-4.
Castries (Maréchal de) 407.
Chākar, 123, 127.
Chand Bibi, 411.
Daḳīḳi, 190.
Dārā, 120, 123-4.
Dārā-shikūh, 411.
Darvīsh, 132.
Darvīzah Ningarhāri. *Taẕkirat ul-Abrār* (1021) 5.
Daryā, 127.
Dā'ūd Mustaufi (1133) 400.
Dā'ūd Mutavalli, 376.
Dā'ūd Pasha, 356.
Daulat, 119-20, 123-4.
Davā'i, 106.
Dāvari, 370.
Dīn Muḥammad (1006) 104.
Diyānat Khān, 162.
Durri Shushtari (c. 1241) 111.
Efendi, 124.
Elchi i Niẓāmshāh, v. Khwurshāh B. Ḳubād, 32.
Faiẓ, v. Muḥ. Muḥsin B. Murtaẓa.
Faiẓi, 108, 127.
Fakhr ud-Dīn B. Aḥmad Rūdbāri. *Kanz ul-Hidāyah* (1253) 161.
Fakhr ud-Dīn Ibrāhīm (825) 88.

Fakhr ud-Din Mas'ūd (Malik) 390.
Fakhr ud-Din Rāzi (606). *Jāmi' ul-'Ulūm*, 142. *Ḥadā'iḳ ul-Anvār*, 143.
Fakhrī B Muḥ. Amīri. *Tuḥfat ul-Ḥabīb* (c. 930) 375.
Faḳir 'Abbāsi (1199). *Vālih u Sulṭān*, 343.
Falaki, 105, 115, 374.
Fanā, 127.
Faraj-ullah Shūshtari (c. 1080). *Divan*, 327.
Fardi, 124.
Farhād Mirza (1305). *Niṣāb Ingilisi*, 187.—418 II., 400.
Farhang, Abu 'l-Ḳāsim, 370.
Farīd ud-Din Aḥval (c. 680). *Divan*, 213 III.—115.
Fāris. *Divan* (hof. 1087) 271 IV.
Farrukh, Muḥ. Ḥasan Khān (1287). *Divan*, 355.—119, 122-3.
Farrukhi (429). *Divan*, 203-4.—105 I., 106, 108 I., 115, 190, 390.
Faṣiḥi, 108.
Fatḥ 'Ali Khān, t. Ṣabā, 66, 118-20, 122, 124, 127, 188 II., 379.
Fatḥ 'Ali Shāh, t. Khāḳān, 118-124, 188 II., 378, 402 XXV.
Fatḥ-ullah Khān, 411.
Fatḥ-ullah Mirza, 121.
Fauḳi. *Farhād u Shīrīn*, 376, 419 IV.
Fayyāẓ, v. 'Abd ur-Razzāḳ Lāhiji, 324.
Faẓl-ullah Ḳazvini (c. 740). *Works*, 257.—107.
Faẓl-ullah Shīrāzi, t. Khāvari. *Ta'rīkh i Ẕulḳarnain* (1251) 71. *Divan*, 358.—120, 123, 124, 127, 379.
Faẓl-ullah B. Shaikh ul-Mulūk. *Ẓiyā ul-'Ārifīn* (1272) 102.
Fidā, 127.
Fighāni (925). *Divan*, 258 IV.—108.
Fikrat, 120, 123-4.
Fili, 127.
Firdausi. *Shāhnāmah*, 195-9, 263. *Yūsuf u Zulaikhā*, 200.—106-8, 115, 390.
Firībi, 132.
Firishtah (c. 1033). *Dustūr ul-Aṭibbā*, 160.
Furūgh, 127.
Furūghi, 403 II.
Fuẓūli (963). *Rind u Zāhid*, *Divan*, 304-5, 422 IV. *Laili Majnūn*, 261 I. *Ḥusn u 'Ishḳ*, 422 II.
Ghā'ib, 127.
Ghālib, 132.
Ghamāmi. *Divan* (1268) 366.
Ghaughā, 127.
Ghaẓā'iri, 108 I., 190.
Ghazāl, 127.
Ghazāli, 128.
Ghiyāṣ ud-Din (c. 750) 162 V.
Ghiyāṣ ud-Din Manṣūr (948). *Akhlāḳ i Manṣūri*, 150.
Ghulām Bāsiṭ. *Ta'rīkh Mamālik i Hind* (1196) 83 II.
Ghulām Jilāni Rāmpūri. *Jangnāmah* (c. 1213) 351.
Ghulām Muḥammad Khān (c. 1213) 351.
Gulandāni (c. 791) 207, 271.
Hādi Sabzavāri, Mulla (1295) 403 II.
Ḥāfiẓ (791). *Divan*, 267-75.—115, 374, 417.
Ḥāfiẓ i Abrū (834). *Zubdat ut-Tavārīkh*, 27.—423.
Ḥāfiẓ Tanish. *Sharafnāmah i Shāhi* (997) 73.
Ḥafiẓ ud-Din Aḥmad. *Inscriptions of Delhi* (1232) 415.
Ḥaidar Rāzi. *Ta'rīkh* (1028) 33.
Ḥaidar Ḳuli Mirza, t. Khāvar. *Divan* (1238) 359. *Mīzān i Ṭabā'i'* (1242) 379.—120, 123.
Ḥaidar Tūniyāni, 162 IV.
Ḥairati (961). *Kitāb i Mu'jizāt*, 303.
Ḥājat, 132.
Ḥājib, 120, 123-4.
Ḥakīm, Muḥ. Yūsuf, 127.
Ḥakīm, Maḥmūd (1268) 370.
Ḥāli, 108, 123.
Ḥāli, 'Abdullah Karbalā'i (1090) 400.
Ḥalīmi. *Lughāt*, 164-5.
Ḥamd-ullah Mustaufi. *Ẓafar Nāmah* (735) 263. *Nuzhat ul-Ḳulūb* (740) 136-7.
Hamgar, v. Majd ud-Din Hamgar.
Ḥamīd Ḳalandar, 374.
Ḥāmid Khān, 411.
Ḥamīd ud-Din Balkhi, 107.
Ḥamīd ud-Din. *Mir'āt ul-Muḥaḳḳiḳīn*, 418 III.
Ḥarīf, 119, 124.

Hārūn (c. 700). *Divan*, 254.
Ḥasan 'Ali Mirza, 121.
Ḥasan, Amīr (727) 286 +, 107.
Ḥasan Beg Rūmlū. *Aḥsan ut-tavārīkh* (985) 55.
Ḥasan Chelebi, t. Shaidā. *Durrat ut-tāj* (1237) 356.
Ḥasan Ghaznavi (565). *Divan*, 215 vi.—105, 107, 115, 190.
Ḥasan B. Luṭf-ullah Ṭihrāni. *Maikhānah* (1040) 107.
Ḥasan, Mulla, 348 iii., 123-4.
Ḥasan Mutakallim, 107.
Ḥasan Yazdi, t. Vāhib, 376.
Ḥasrat, 120, 123-4.
Hastings (Warren), 405.
Hātif, 132, 378-9.
Hātifi (927). *Khamsah*, 295, 305 ii.—108, 275.
Ḥayāt, 128.
Ḥāziḳ Gilāni (1068). *Divan*, 325.
Hidāyat, v. Riẓa Ḳuli Khān.
Hidāyat-ullah B. Mirza Aḥmad (1253) 161.
Hijrān, 128.
Hijri, 132, 378.
Hilāl, 127.
Hilāli (935). *Ṣifāt ul-'Āshiḳīn*. *Shāh u Darvīsh*, 302.—108, 375.
Himmatyār Khān (1204) 411.
Ibn Hindūshāh, v. Muḥ. B. Hindūshāh, 189.
Ḥishmat, 120, 123.
Ḥubaish B. Ibrāhīm Tiflisi. *Ḳānūn ul-Adab*, 425.
Humā, v. Muḥ. Ṣādiḳ Marvazi, 118.
Humām, 374-5.
Humāyūn Iṣfahāni, 378.
Humāyūn Mirza, 121, 123.
Humāyūn Pādishāh, 411, 417 ii.
Hurmuz Mirza, 121.
Ḥusain, 124.
Ḥusain, of Sāri, 120.
Ḥusain 'Aḳīli Rustamdāri. *Riyāẓ ul-Abrār* (979) 144.
Ḥusain 'Ali Mirza (1251) 45, 120, 121.
Ḥusain B. Ghiyāṣ ud-Dīn. *Iḥyā ul-Mulūk* (1028) 97. *Khair ul-Bayān* (1035) 108-9.
Ḥusain Hamadāni (1299). *Ta'rīkh i Jadīd*, 15.
Ḥusain Kāshifi (910). *Anvār i Suhaili*, 381. *Mavāhib 'Aliyyah*, 1. *Lubb i Lubāb i Ma'navi*, 241-2.
Ḥusain Khwānsāri, Aḳa, 376.
Ḥusain B. Muḥ., Mīr. *Risālah i Mu'amma*, 192 v., 194.
Ḥusain Shīrāzi Karbalā'i. *Ta'rīkh i Aḥmad Shāh* (1305) 74.
Ḥusaini Sādāt, 115.
Ḥusām ud-Dīn 'Ali B. Mas'ūd (Malik) 390.
Ḥusām ud-Dīn Bukhāri, 107.
Ḥusām ud-Dīn Nakhshabi, 107.
Ibrāhīm Hamadāni, 417 ii.
Ibrāhīm Khān, 123.
Ibrāhīm Shāh Afshār, 402 xviii.
Ibrāhīm Sultan B. Shāhmelik, 149.
Ibrāhīm Sultan B. Shāhrukh, 193.
Idrāki, 108.
Īmā, Ismā'īl (1132) 400.
'Imād (Mīr) 408.
Ibn 'Imād (800). *Dah Nāmah*, 348 ii.
'Imād ud-Daulah, 412.
'Imād ud-Dīn B. Naṣīr (774) 43.
'Imādi, 105 i., 115, 190.
Imāmi (686). *Divan*, 213 ii., iv., 245 i.—107, 115.
Imāmvirdi Mirza, 120-1, 123-4.
'Ināyat Khān Rāsikh, 76.
'Ināyat-ullah B. Muḥibb 'Ali. *Tatimmah i Akbar-nāmah*, 76.
Īraj Mirza, 121.
'Irāḳi, Fakhr ud-Dīn, 374.
Ibn Isfandiyār. *Ta'rīkh i Ṭabaristān* (613) 92.
Ishrāḳ, 123.
'Ishrat, 120, 123.
Iskandar Munshi. *'Ālam-ārāi 'Abbāsi*, 59.
Ismā'īl Mirza, 121.
Ismā'īl, Shāh, 401 iii.
'Iṣmat Bukhāri (840). *Divan*, 282.—108.
Al-Isnawi, 89.
Istighnā, 111.
I'timād us-Salṭanah Mirza Muḥ. Ḥasan, 72.
I'tiẓād us-Salṭanah, v. 'Ali Ḳuli Mirza, 74.

'Izzat, 120, 123.
'Izzat-ullah. *Travels* (1228) 133.
Ja'far Beg, Āṣaf Khān (1021). *Divan*, 314 II. *Khusrau Shīrīn*, 314 I., 315.
Ja'far Ja'fari. *Sharḥ ul-Aurād*, 20.
Ja'far Khān Zand, 402 XXII.
Ja'fari, 107.
Jahān, 123.
Jahāngīr. *Jahāngīr Nāmah*, 77.—408, 417 II.
Jahānshāh Mirza, 121, 123.
Jaisingh Savāi, 411.
Jājarmi, Badr ud-Dīn, 107.
Ibn Jājarmi, 107.
Jalāl ud-Dīn Mirza, Iḥtishām ul-Mulk, 99.
Jalāl ud-Dīn Rūmi (672). *Masnavi*, 240-1. *Divan*, 243-4.—18, 115.
Jalāl Munajjim. *Ta'rikh i Shāh 'Abbās* (1020) 57.
Jamāl ud-Dīn Ashhari, 107.
Jamāl ud-Dīn Ḥusain Injū. *Farhang i Jahāngīri*, (1017) 168.
Jamāl ud-Dīn Iṣfahāni (588). *Divan*, 224 IV.—115.
Jamāl ud-Dīn Khwānsāri (1125). *Miftāḥ ul-Falāḥ*, 8.—400.
Jamāl ud-Dīn Samarḳandi, 107.
Jamāli Mihrījirdi. *Bahman Nāmah* (c. 502) 201 III.
Jāmi (898). *Divan*, 287-8. *Haft Aurang*, 289-94. *Treatise on rhyme*, 192 IV. *Lavā'iḥ*, 419 I.—107, 108, 275, 286.
Jāni, Ḥāji Mirza (1268) 15.
Jānsipār Khān, 411.
Jauhari Zargar, 107.
Javād Karbalā'i (c. 1301) 15.
Javāhir Raḳam, 408.
Ḳā'āni (1270). *Divan*, 367.—127, 348 IV.
Ḳābil, 123-4.
Ḳādiri, 107.
Kāhi, Ḳāsim, 417 II.
Kaikā'ūs B. Iskandar. *Ḳābūs Nāmah* (475) 145.
Kaikā'ūs Mirza, 121.
Kaikhusrau Mirza, 121.
Kaiḳubād Mirza, 121.
Kalīm, 376, 417 II., 419 X.
Kamāl Iṣfahāni (635) 107, 115, 374.
Kamāl Khujandi (803). *Divan*, 275-6.—286, 420 II.
Kamāl ud-Dīn Ḥusain Khwārazmi (833). *Naṣīḥat-nāmah i Shāhi*, 149.
Kamāl ud-Dīn Ḥusain Ṭabīb (c. 990) 159.
Kāmi, 109, 128.
Karīm Khān Zand, 412, 402 XX., XXI.
Kāshif, v. Muḥ. Sharīf, 396.
Ḳāsim 'Ali Khān, Navvāb, 409.
Ḳāsim ul-Anvār (837). *Divan*, 280-81. *Anīs ul-'Ārifīn*, 280 II. *Risālat ul-Amānah*, 280 III.—275.
Ḳāsim B. Dūst 'Ali Bukhāri (c. 1000). *Kashf ul-Auṭār*, 162 IV.
Ḳāsim Junābadi, 106.
Ḳāsim 'Ali Khān, Stowe, Or. 18.
Ḳaṭarān (c. 450). *Divan*, 204 III., 207-8, 245 II.—105, 107, 115, 374.
Kātibi (838) 275.
Ḳaṭrah, Mirza 'Abd ul-Vahhāb. *Divan* (1235) 357.—127.
Kaukab, 120, 123-4, 127.
Kauṣar, 123-4.
Kayūmarṣ Mirza, 121.
Ḳazvīni (682). *'Ajā'ib ul-Makhlūḳāt*, 135.
Khādim, Bābā Ḳāsim, 376.
Khādim, of Isfahan, 128.
Khādim, Sayyid Isma'īl of Ḳum, 127.
Khāḳān, v. Fatḥ 'Ali Shāh.
Khāḳāni. *Tuḥfat ul-'Irāḳain*, 221. *Divan*, 221 II.—105, 107, 115, 190, 374, 379.
Khālid, Shams ud-Dīn, 107.
Khalīl Ḳazvīni (1089) 400.
Khān Aḥmad of Gīlān, 106.
Khāndanrān (1167) 51.
Ibn Khaṭīb, 107.
Khāvar, v. Ḥaidar Ḳuli Mirza.
Khāvar, Maḥmūd Khān, 120, 123, 127.
Khāvari, v. Faẓl-ullah Shīrāzi, 71.
Khāvari, Ma'ṣūm, 118, 119.
Khāvari, Muḥ. Bāḳir, 127.
Khurram, 124, 127.
Khusrau Dihlavi, Amīr (725). *Divan*, 220 IV.

Khamsah, 255. *Ḳirān us-Sa'dain*, 256.—107, 275, 376.
Khusrau Khān (1250) 129.
Khusrau Khān Kirmāni, 412.
Khusravi, Muḥ. Ḳuli Mirza, 120, 121, 123, 124, 379.
Al-Khuwāri, 'Ali B. 'Abi Ṣāliḥ, 89.
Khwāju (c. 750). *Divan*, 262.—196 II., 374.
Khwānd-amir (941). *Ma'āṣir ul-Mulūk*, 29. *Khulāṣat ul-Akhbār*, 30. *Ḥabīb us-Siyar*, 31.
Khwurshāh B. Ḳubād, Elchi o Niẓāmshāh (972). *Ta'rīkh*, 32.
Khwushḥālchand. *Ta'rīkh i Muḥammadshāhi*, 37.
Kisā'i, 106, 108, 115.
Ḳivām ud-Dīn Niẓām ul-Mulk (892) 101.
Krusinski. *Afghan invasion*, 63.
Kūchak, Sayyid (c. 1200). *Divan*, 345.
Ḳudrat, 128.
Ḳudsi (1056). *Divan*, 323.
Kūhi, 'Ali Bābā (442). *Divan*, 271 II.
Ḳummi, Ḥasan B. Muḥ. *Kitāb Ḳumm* (378) 88.
Ḳummi, Ḥasan B. al-Ḥasan (825) 88.
Ḳushairi, 'Abd ul-Karīm (465). *Risālah*, 16.
Ḳutb ud-Dīn Bakhtiyār Kāki (633) 238.
Ḳuṭubshāh, Muḥ., 146, 237.
Lāmi'i (c. 550). *Divan*, 212 II.—105, 115.
Lisān ul-Ḥaḳḳ, v. 'Abdullah B. Muḥ. 'Ali, 371.
Lisāni, 108.
Luṭf 'Ali Beg, t. Āẕur (1195). *Ātashkadah*, 114.
Madhūsh, 379.
Maftūn, 'Abd ur-Razzāḳ, 118, 120, 124.
Maghribi (809). *Divan*, 277 I.
Mahd Auliya, 403 I.
Mahdi, Mirza. *Ta'rīkh i Nādiri*, 65. *Sanglākh*, 176.
Maḥjūb, 127.
Mahjūr, 127.
Maḥmūd Khān, Malik ush-Shu'arā, 412.
Maḥmūd B. Khwāndamir, *Hist. of Shah Ismā'īl and Tahmāsp* (955-57) 53.
Maḥmūd Mirza. *Ta'rīkh i Ṣāḥibḳirāni* (1248) 70. *Gulshan i Maḥmūd* (1236) 121. *Safīnat ul-Maḥmūd* (1240) 122. *Bayān ul-Maḥmūd* (1240) 377. *Maḥmūd ul-Lughah*, 174.—120, 123-4.
Maḥmūd B. Muḥ. al-Īji, called Najīb, *Hist. of Muḥ.* (c. 850) 43.
Maḥmūd Shihābi, 411.
Maḥram, v. 'Abdullah B. Muḥ. 'Ali, 371.
Maḥram, Muḥ. 'Ali, 127.
Maḥram, Aḳa Ḥusain 'Ali, 123.
Maḥrūm, 120.
Mā'il, 118, 120, 123-4.
Maimandi, 107.
Majd ud-Dīn Hamgar (686). *Rubā'īs*, 211 II., IV., VII.—115.
Majd ud-Dīn Muḥ. Majdi. *Zīnat ul-Majālis* (1004) 395.
Majnūn, 127.
Majẕūb (1093). *Divan*, 331.
Majẕūb 'Ali Shāh, 387.
Maktabi (c. 900). *Laili u Majnūn*, 298-9.—108.
Maktūm, 128.
Malik Ḳāsim Mirza, 121, 124.
Malik Ḳummi, 108.
Malik, Muḥ. Mahdi, 128.
Malik Manṣūr, 121.
Al-Malik al-Mujāhid Ali (764) 161.
Mānakji Līmji (c. 1308) 15, 42, 99.
Manṣūr, 120, 123-4.
Manẓar, 127.
Mauẓūr, 120, 123.
Marvārīd, 'Abdullah, t. Bayāni (922) 268.
Marzabān B. Rustam. *Marzabān Nāmah*, 392-3.
Mashrab, 127.
Mashriḳi, 107-8.
Mashriḳi, Shams. *Divan*, 277 II.
Masīḥ, Rukn ud-Dīn Kāshi (1066) 108, 376.
Masīḥ uz-Zamān (1061) 162 II.
Mas'ūd i Sa'd, 105, 107, 108, 115, 190.
Maṭlab, Mirza, 412.
Maẓhar, 128.
Mazlām, 127.
Mihri, 376.
Mijmar, Sayyid Ḥasan, 107.
Mijmar, Sayyid Ḥusain (1225). *Kulliyāt*, 354.—118-19, 120, 123-4, 379.
Minūchihr, Badi' Tabrīzi. *Al-Iḥyā fil-Mu'amma* (c. 800) 420 II.

Minûchihr Khān (1203) 127.
Minūchihr Mirza, 121.
Minūchihri (432). *Divan*, 206, 212 v., 2244.—105, 107-8, 115, 190, 374.
Mīr Aḥmad Khān, 411.
Mīr 'Ālam. *Ḥadīḳat ul-'Ālam*, 84 i.
Mīr Jumlah, 411.
Mīrak Naḳḳāsh. *Divan* (1053) 322.
Mīram Siyāh (c. 960). *Divan*, 358 ii.
Mīrzā Beg B. Ḥasan. *Rauẓat uṣ-Ṣafaviyyah* (1038) 58.
Miskīn, 127.
Mu'ayyad Nasafi, 107.
Mubāriz Khān, 411.
Mughīṣ Hānsavi, 374.
Muḥ. B. 'Abd ul-Fattāḥ Tanakābuni (1124) 400.
Muḥ. 'Abd ur-Raḥmān B. Rūshan Khān, 74.
Muḥ. 'Ali, t. Bahār. *Madā'iḥ Mu'tamadiyyah* (1059-1063) 127-8.
Muḥ. 'Ali B. Iskandar Shīrvāni. *Ḥaḳīḳat ul-Ḥaḳā'iḳ* (1252) 387.
Muḥ. 'Ali Khān Shīrāzi (1210) 66.
Muḥ. 'Ali Mirza, t. Daulat, 119-21, 123.
Muḥ. Amīn Mirza, 121.
Muḥ. Amīn Vaḳūri. *Guldastah i Andīshah* (c. 1090) 399.
Muḥ. B. Amīr Faẓl-ullah, 423.
Muḥ. A'ẓam Dīdahmari, 85.
Muḥ. Bāḳir B. Ghāzi Ḳazvīni (1080) 400.
Muḥ. Bāḳir Majlisi (1110). *Zā'idah Zād ul-Ma'ād*, 11. *Taẕkirat ul-A'immah*, 44. *Ḥilyat ul-Muttaḳīn*, 153.—380, 400.
Muḥ. B. Dā'ūd Shādiyābādi. *Miftāḥ ul-Fuẓalā* (873) 163.
Muḥ. Fāẓil, t. Rāvi (1252). *Anjuman i Khāḳān*, 120.—123-4.
Muḥ. Hādi B. Muḥ. Ṣāliḥ Māzandarāni (1088) 400.
Muḥ. Hāshim. *Zīvar i Āl i Dā'ūd* (1226) 64.
Muḥ. Ḥasan B. Ma'ṣūm Ḳazvīni (c. 1250). *Riyāẓ ush-Shahādah*, 45.
Muḥ. B. Hindūshāh. *Dustūr ul-Kātib*, 189.—167.
Muḥ. Ḥusain, Adīb, 212 v.
Muḥ. Ḥusain Mirza, t. Ḥishmat, 123.
Muḥ. Ḥusain B. Ṣāliḥ Māzandarāni (1088) 400.
Muḥ. Ḥusain Tafrishi, 107.
Muḥ. Ibrāhīm Naṣiri. *Dastūr i Shahriyārān* (1110) 62.
Muḥ. B. Jalāl Riẓavi (1028) 162 i.
Muḥ. Jūibāri, Khwājah, 73.
Muḥ. Karīm B. Mahdi Ḳuli. *Farhang i Muḥammadshāhi* (c. 1250) 171.
Muḥ. Ḳāsim Khān Ḳajar, 140.
Muḥ. Ḳāsim Khān, t. Shaukat, 120, 123, 127.
Muḥ Kāẓim Vālih, 403 16.
Muḥ. Khān Ḳājār, 412, 403 9.
Muḥ. Khān (Mirza), 127.
Muḥ. Khān (Sharaf ud-Dīn Ughli) (955) 53.
Muḥ. B. Ḳivām Balkhi, 233.
Muḥ. Ḳuli Ḳājār. *Lubb ul-Lubāb* (1097) 38.
Muḥ. Ḳuli Mirza, v. Khusravi.
Muḥ. Laṭīf. *Mir'āt ul-Hind*, 83.
Muḥ. Mahdi Ḳā'ini, t. Ḥayāt, 128.
Muḥ. Mahdi Mirza, 121.
Muḥ. B. Manṣūr. *Javāhir Nāmah*, 158.
Muḥ. B. Mas'ūd Mas'ūdi. *Jahān Dānish* (643) 154.
Muḥ. Ma'ṣūm Ḳazvīni (1091) 400.
Muḥ. B. Muḥ. Dārābi. *Laṭīfah i Ghaibi* (1087) 417 i.
Muḥ. Muḥsin B. Murtaẓa, t. Faiẓ (1091) 400.
Muḥ. Muḥsin Mustaufi. *Zubdat ut-Tavārīkh* (1154) 86.
Muḥ. Muḥsin Sāvi (1080) 400.
Muḥ. B. Murtaẓa Hādi (1096) 400.
Muḥ. B. Mu'tamad Khān, 76.
Muḥ. Naṣīr Tabrīzi, 403 ii.
Muḥ. Raẓi Tabrīzi, t. Bandah (1223). *Zīnat ut-tavārīkh*, 39.—120, 123-24.
Muḥ. Riẓa Mirza, t. Afsar, 120-21, 130.
Muḥ. Sa'd, t. Ghālib. *Sharḥ i Shāfiyah*, 175.
Muḥ. Ṣādiḳ Marvazi, t. Humā. *Zīnat ul-Madā'iḥ* (1223) 118-19.—71, 120, 214, 127, 403 18.
Muḥ. Ṣādiḳ Mūsavi, t. Nāmi (1204). *Khusrau Shīrīn*, 346-7. *Vāmiḳ u 'Azrā*, 348-9.
Muḥ. Ṣāliḥ Ḳazvīni, t. Raughani, 400.
Muḥ. B. Sayyid Aḥmad 'Āmili, 'Abd ul-Ḥasīb. *Taḳdīs ul-Anbiyā*, 10.

Muḥ. Shāh of India, 411.
Muḥ. Shāh Ḳājār, 387, 402 xxvii., 403 3, 4.
Muḥ. Shāh Saljūḳ, 201 iii.
Muḥ. Sharīf, t. Kāshif. *Sirāj ul-Munīr* (1030) 419 ii., 422 i. *Khazān u Bahār* (1060) 396.
Muḥ. Ṭāhir Naṣrābādi. *Tazkirah* (1083) 110.
Muḥ. Taḳi Majlisi (1070). *Lavāmi'*, 23.
Muḥ. Taḳi Mirza, t. Shaukat, 120, 121, 123.
Muḥ. Vali Mirza, 121.
Muḥ. Zamān Khān, 417 ii.
Muḥ. B. Zufar. *Ta'rīkh i Bukhārā* (574) 87.
Muḥīṭ, Ma'ṣūm, 120.
Muḥyi. *Futūḥ ul-Ḥaramain*, 301.—275.
Mu'īn Yazdi. *Mavāhib i Ilāhi*, 50.
Mu'īn Zamji Asfizāri. *Rauḍāt ul-Jannāt* (897) 94.
Mu'īn ud-Dīn Shahristāni, 107.
Mu'īni Juvaini. *Nigāristān*, 394.
Mu'izzi, 105, 107, 108, 115, 190, 374, 379, 390.
Mujīr Bailaḳāni, 107, 115, 190.
Mu'jiz-Ḳalam, 411.
Mukhtāri (554). *Divan*, 211 vi., 215 vii., 216.—105, 107, 115, 190.
Mulhimi, 108.
Mumtāz Maḥall (1040) 413.
Mūnis, 120, 123.
Munshi, 127.
Munṣif. *Badī' ul-Afkār* (1239) 378.
Munṣif, Muḥ. Ismā'īl (1060) 396.
Murtaẓa 'Alam ul-Huda (c. 658). *Tabṣirat ul-'Avām*, 7.
Murtaẓa Ḳuli Khān Shāmlu, 400.
Murtaẓa B. Muḥ. Mu'min, 400.
Mūsa B. Ayyūb Naṣrapūri. *Shir'at ul-Islām*, 4.
Mushfiḳi, 108.
Mushīr, 120.
Mushkīn-Ḳalam, 411.
Mushtāḳ, 132.
Mu'tamad Khān, 76 ii.
Muṭī', 127.
Muvāli. *Divan* (850) 285 iii.
Muẓaffar, t. Shifā'i (963). *Akhlāḳ i Shifā'i*, 151.
Muẓaffar ud-Dīn Mirza, Vali-'ahd, 412.
Muẓuib, 124.
Nabīl, Mirza Muḥ., 12.
Nadīm, 'Ali Akbar, 127.
Nadīm, Muḥ. of Barfurūsh (1241). *Mufarriḥ ul-Ḳulūb*, 397.—120, 123.
Nādir Shāh, 402 xvi., xvii.
Naghmah, 127.
Naḥḥās Rāzi, 107.
An-Naishābūri al-Ḥākim (405) 89.
Najābat Khān, 411.
Najāt, Mīr (c. 1126). *Gul i Kushti*, 387, 376.
Najib, v. Maḥmūd B. Muḥ. 43.
Najīb Jurpādaḳāni (625). *Divan*, 234 i.—108 i.
Najm ud-Dīn Dāyah (654). *Mirṣād ul-'Ibād*, 17.
Najm ud-Dīn Kubra. *Ṣifat ul-ādāb*, 154.—108.
Nāmi, v. Muḥ. Ṣādiḳ Mūsavi, 316.
Narshakhi (348). *Ta'rīkh i Bukhārā*, 87.
Nashāṭ, v. 'Abd ul-Vahhāb Iṣfahāni, 188 ii.
Nashāṭi, 119, 120, 123, 127.
Naṣīb, 124, 132.
Naṣībi, 108.
Nāṣiḥ B. Ẓafar, 215 iv.
Naṣir Adīb, 107.
Nāṣir 'Ali (1108) 169, 376.
Nāṣir Hamadāni (1030). *Divan*, 318 ii.—376, 417 ii.
Nāṣir Jang, 411.
Nāṣir i Khusrau (481). *Divan*, 209-10.—105, 107, 115, 419 xv.
Nāṣir ud-Dīn Shāh, 412, 402 xxviii.-xxxi., 403 5, 6.
Naṣīr ud-Dīn Ṭūsi (672). *Akhlāḳ i Nāṣiri*, 147-8. *Bist Bāb*, 155 ii. *Tansūḳ Nāmah*, 157.—107.
Naṣīri, v. Muḥ. Ibrāhīm, 62.
Naṣr-ullah, 124.
Ibn Naṣūḥ, 111.
Nāṭiḳ, 119, 127.
Nau'i. *Sūz u Gudāz*, 313, 376, 419 x.—108, 376.
Nauras, Muḥ. Ḥusain (c. 1100). *Divan*, 333.
Navā, Darvīsh Ḥusain. *Tazkirah* (c. 1253) 115.—124.
Navā'i, v. 'Alīshīr.
Navā'i, Muḥ. Taḳi, 123.
Nayyir, v. 'Ali Aṣghar, 308.
Naẓr 'Ali Mirza, 123-4.

Nāẓir, v. Bishan Laʻl, 372.
Naẓīri (1022). *Divan*, 316.—108.
Niʻmat-ullah Vali (834). *Divan*, 279.
Niʻmat-ullah Yazdi, 159.
Niyāzi, 132.
Niẓām Dust i Ghaib (1029). *Divan*, 319.
Niẓāmi ʻArūẓi. *Chahār Maḳālah* (552-6) 390, 418.
Niẓāmi Ganjavi (c. 610). *Khamsah*, 225-9.—107, 115, 374.
Nujūmi Harawi, 56.
Nūr ud-Dīn Rāzi, 107.
Nūr ud-Dīn Vali, 85.
Nūri, Nūr ud-Dīn Iṣfahāni (1000). *Divan*, 224 v., 422 vi.
Nūrjahān Bīgam, 411.
Nuṣrat, Sulṭān Ḥusain, 120, 123.
Nuṣrat ud-Dīn Atābak, 257.
Navidi, v. ʻAbdi.
Partav, ʻAli Riẓa, 127.
Parvānah, Muḥ. Ṣādiḳ, 120, 127.
Pindār Rāzi, 108 i.
Pūr Bahā, 107.
Pūr Ḥasan, 107.
Rabīb ud-Dīn Abu 'l-Ḳāsim Hārūn (c. 610) 382.
Rafīʻ ud-Dīn Ibrāhīm Shīrāzi. *Taẕkirat ul-Mulūk* (c. 1020) 83 iii.
Rafīʻ ud-Dīn Lunbāni (603). *Divan*, 239 iv.—107.
Rafīʻ ud-Dīn Vāʻiẓ (c. 1105). *Abwāb ul-Jinān*, 152. *Divan*, 334.—400.
Rafīʻ i Naishāpūri, 107, 111.
Rafīḳ (1212). *Divan*, 340.—132.
Rāghib Iṣfahāni (c. 500). *Zarīʻah*, 146.
Raḥīm, ʻAli Beg, 412.
Rāḳim, Saʻd ud-Dīn Muḥ. (c. 1090). *Divan*, 332.
Rakhshān, 128.
Rām Mohan Rāi (1240). *Tuḥfat ul-Muvaḥḥidīn*, 22.
Ramzi Iṣfahāni, 106.
Ranvar Singh, 411.
Rashīd Vaṭvāṭ (578). *Ḥadā'iḳ us-Siḥr*, 188, 420 i. *Divan*, 212 iv., 234 ii. *On metre*, 191 ii.—105, 107, 115, 190, 379.
Rashīd ud-Dīn Faẓl-ullah (718). *Jāmiʻ ut-tawārīkh*, 25-6.
Rashīdi Samarḳandi, 107.
Raunaḳ, v. ʻAbdullah B. Muḥ. Aḳā, 129.
Raunaḳ, Muh. Hāshim, 127.
Rāvi, v. Muḥ. Fāẓil, 120.
Raẓī Artīmāni, 376.
Raẓī B. Mirza Muḥ. Shafīʻ, 118-19.
Raẓī ud-Dīn Khashshāb, 107.
Raẓī ud-Dīn Muḥ. B. Ḥasan (1096) 400.
Raẓī ud-Dīn Naishāpūri, 107, 115.
Redhouse. *Thesaurus*, 177-86.
Revari (Rājah of), 184.
Rifʻat, Fatḥ-ullah, 127.
Riyāẓi Samarḳandi (884). *Divan*, 285 ii.—275.
Riẓa B. Raẓī Tabrīzi, 124.
Riẓa Ḳuli of Hamadān, 127.
Riẓa Ḳuli Khān, t. Hidāyat (1288). *Nizhād Nāmah*, 42. *Majmaʻ ul-Fuṣaḥā*, 125. *Riyāẓ ul-ʻĀrifīn*, 126. *Miftāḥ ul-Kunūz*, 221 ii. *Hidāyat Nāmah*, 364 i. *Anīs ul-ʻĀshiḳīn*, 364 ii. *Divan*, 365.—93, 212 v., 412.
Rūdagi, 106, 107, 108, 115, 204 iii., 390.
Rūḥ-ullah Khān, 411.
Rūḥi, 107.
Rūʻi, 106.
Rukn ud-Dīn Kāshi, v. Masīḥ.
Rūshan, 127.
Rūshan-ḳalam, 411.
Saʻādat-ullah Khān, 411.
Ṣabā, v. Fatḥ ʻAli Khān.
Ṣabāḥi, Sulaimān, 118, 132, 379.
Ṣabūr, Aḥmad, 118-120, 123-4.
Saʻd al-Varāvīni. *Marzubān Nāmah* (c. 610) 382-3.
Saʻd ud-Dīn Saʻīd, 107.
Saʻd-ullah Khān, 411.
Saʻd ud-Dīn Shūshtari, 107.
Saʻdi (690). *Kulliyyāt*, 246-8. *Gulistān*, 249-50. *Būstān*, 251. *Pand Nāmah*, 252-3.—115, 374.
Ṣadr ud-Dīn Muḥ. Kazvīni (1080) 400.
Ṣadr ud-Dīn Muh. Shīrāzi (1050) 417 ii., 123.
Ṣadr ud-Dīn Tabrīzi. *Farhang i ʻAbbāsi* (1225) 170.

Ṣafā, 'Abd ul-Vāsi', 127.
Ṣafā'i, Aḥmad Narāḳi, 123.
Safā'i, Mulla Muḥ., 127.
Ṣāfi, Aḥmad of Narāḳ, 124, 132.
Ṣafi, Shāh, 402 vi.
Sāghar, Muḥ. of Shirāz, 124.
Sāghar, Muḥ. Ibrāhīm of Isfahan, 127.
Saḥāb, Sayyid Muḥ., 118-20, 123-4, 379.
Ṣahbā, Aḳa Muḥ. Taḳi, 132.
Ṣāḥib, daughter of Shahbāz Khān, 119.
Ṣāḥib, Muḥ. Taḳi, 120, 123, 127.
Sāḥiri, 108 a.
Ṣā'ib (1088). *Divan*, 328-9.—376, 419 x., xii.
Sa'īd B. As'ad, 212 i.
Sa'īd B. Muḥ. al-Ḳaṭṭān. *Sirāj ul-Ḳulūb*, 3.
Ṣaidi (1060). *Divan*, 422, vii.
Saif ud-Dīn Akhsīkati, 107.
Saif ud-Dīn Ḥāji. *Āṣār ul-Vuzarā* (883) 101.
Saif ud-Dīn Isfarangi (666). *Divan*, 220 ii.—115.
Saif-ullah Mirza, 121.
Saifi (c. 910). *'Arūẓ*, 101 i.
Saifi, Yādgār Beg (870) 275 ii.
Ṣā'in ud-Dīn Shirāzi, 107.
Sāḳi, Musta'idd Khān (1136) 335.
Ṣāḳib, 127.
Sālim, Salīm 'Aṭṭār Yazdi, 376.
Salim, Muḥ. Ḳuli, 376.
Salmān Sāvaji (779). *Divan*, 220 iii., 265-6. *Khurshid u Jamshid*, 265 v., 266. *Firāḳ Nāmah*, 265 vi., 266.—374, 379.
Sām Mirza. *Tuḥfah i Sāmi*, 103.
Sanā'i, Ḥakīm (c. 545). *Divan*, 214, 215 iii. *Ḥadīḳah*, 215 i.—105, 107, 115, 190.
Ṣanā'i Mashhadi (996). *Divan*, 300 i.
Sangīn Beg, 415.
Ṣanī' ul-Mulk, 412.
Sarshār Najaf Ḳuli Khān, 123-4.
Sarv i Āzād, 196 v.
Sayyid Kūchak (c. 1200). *Divan*, 345.
Sha'af, 'Abdullah Ḳummi, 376.
Shāh (Mulla) (1072) 130.
Shāh 'Ālam, 411.
Shāh 'Ali B. 'Abd ul-'Ali. *Majālis un-Nafā'is*, 104.
Shāh Malik, Amīr (829) 149.
Shāh Shujā' Muẓaffari, 146.
Shāh Shujā', of Afghanistan (1258). *Divan*, 361.
Shāhid Ṭihrāni, 376.
Shahidi, 108.
Shāhīn, 127.
Shāhjahān, 411, 413.
Shāhḳuli Mirza, 121.
Shāhpūr Mirza, 121.
Shahrazūri. *Ta'rīkh ul-Ḥukamā* (c. 600) 100 i.
Shāhrukh, 402 xix.
Shaidā (c. 1080). *Divan*, 326.
Shaidā, v. Ḥasan Chelebi, 356.
Shā'iḳ, 124, 128.
Shaikh 'Ali Mirza, 121, 123-4.
Shams i Fakhri, 167.
Shams i Ḳais. *Al-Mu'ajjam* (c. 630) 190.
Shams i Mashriḳi. *Divan*, 277 ii.
Shams i Tabrīz. *Divan*, 243-4.
Shams ud-Dīn Muḥ. Kashmiri, 167.
Shāpūr (c. 1030). *Divan*, 321.—108.
Shāpūr, Shaikh 'Ali Mirza, 120, 123-4.
Sharaf Rāmi (795). *Anīs ul-'Ushshāḳ*, 420 iii., 421 iii. *Ḥadīḳat ul-Ḥaḳā'iḳ*, 421 v.
Sharaf ud-Dīn Khān Bitlīsi. *Sharaf Nāmah* (1005) 95-6.
Sharaf ud-Dīn Faẓl-ullah Kazvīni (c. 740). *Works*, 257.—107.
Sharaf ud-Dīn Shufurvah (c. 600). *Divan*, 239 iii.—107, 118, 190.
Sharaf ud-Dīn Yazdi (858). *Ḥulal i Muṭarraz*, 193.
Sharaf Shāh, 107.
Sharar, Ḥusain 'Ali Beg, 118.
Sharīf Tabrīzi, 108.
Sharīf Iṣfahāni, 108.
Shaukat, Muḥ. Taḳi Mirza, 120, 123-4.
Shaukat, Muḥ. Ḳāsim, 120, 123.
Shauḳi (c. 800) 286 7.
Shifā, 123.
Shifā'i, v. Muẓaffar, 151.
Shihāb, 'Abdullah Turshīzi (1215). *Khusrau Shīrīn*, 352 i. *Hist. of 'Ali Murād Khān*, 352 ii. *Divan*, 353.

Shihāb, Naṣr-ullah, 127.
Shiḥnah, 120, 123-4.
Shujā', son of Shāhjahān, 411.
Shujā', Shāh (1258). *Divan*, 361.
Shukr-ullah B. Shihāb ud-Dīn. *Bahjat ut-tavārīkh* (861) 28.
Sīmā, 127.
Sipihr, 123, 377.
Sīrāf, Ḥusām ud-Dīn, 392.
Sirāj ud-Dīn Sijistāni, 107.
Sūdi. *Sharḥ Divan Ḥāfiẓ*, 274.
Ṣūfī Māzandarāni, 107.
Suhaili (907) 275.
Sulaimān Khān, 123.
Sulaimān Mirza, 121.
Sulaimān Ṣafavī, Shāh, 402 IX.
Sulṭān Aḥmad Mirza, 121.
Sulṭān Aḥmad, Sardār, 403 II.
Sulṭān Ḥamzah Mirza, 121.
Sulṭān Ḥusain Baiḳarā. *Divan*, 300.—417 II.
Sulṭān Ḥusain Ṣafavi, 402 XII.-XIV., 403 I.
Sulṭān Ibrāhīm Mirza, 121.
Sulṭān Muḥammad Mirza, 121.
Sulṭān Muṣṭafa Mirza, 121.
Sulṭān Salīm Mirza, 121.
Sulṭāni, 120.
Surūr, 123.
Surūri. *Sharḥ i Ḥāfiẓ*, 273.
Surūri, Sikandar. *Divan* (1114) 335.
Sūzani, 105 I., 108, 115.
Ṭabīb, 'Abd ul-Bāḳi (1168). *Divan*, 339.
Ṭabīb, Muḥ. of Burūjird, 124, 132.
Ṭāhir, Ḥasan Khān, 120.
Ṭāhir, of Hamadān, 127.
Ṭāhir Naṣrābādi. *Taẕkirah* (1083) 110.—376.
Ṭāhir Vaḥīd. *Hist. of 'Abbās II.*, 60, 61.—34.
Ṭahmāsp I., Shāh, 402 I.-III.
Ṭahmāsp II., Shāh, 402 XV.
Ṭahmāsp B. Daulatshāh (1279) 400.
Ṭahmāsp Mirza, 123.
Ṭahmūraṣ Mirza, 121.
Ṭā'ir, 123-4.
Tajalli, 376.
Taḳi, 124.
Taḳi ud-Dīn Kāshāni. *Khulāṣat ul-Ash'ār* (996) 105.
Ṭālib Āmuli, 108, 376.
Ṭāli'i (858) 286 v.
Ṭarab, 120, 123.
Tārāj, 127.
Ta'ṣīr, Muḥ. Muḥsin (1091) 400.
Taslīm. *Ḳaẓā u Ḳadar*, 419 XVII.
Tauḥīd, Muḥ. Ismā'īl, 370.
Tavakkul Beg Kulali. *Nuskhah i Aḥvāl i Shāhi* (1077) 130.
Taẕarv, 128.
Tīmūr, Amīr. *Tuzūk i Tīmūri*, 51.—411.
Tipu Sulṭān, 406.
Tishnah, 127.
Ṭūba, 128.
Ṭūfān (1190). *Divan*, 342.—132.
Ṭughrā, Mulla, 323, 376, 419 XVIII.
Ṭughrul, 120, 123-4.
Ṭūsi (869) 286 I.
Ṭūṭi, 123-4.
'Ubaid Zākāni (772). *Kulliyyāt*, 264.—374.
Ulfat, 111.
Ulfati, 111.
Ulugh Beg (853). *Zīj*, 156.
Ibn Umailah al-Marāghi (778) 43.
'Umar Khayyām (517) 390.
'Umdat ul-Mulk, 411.
Ummīd, 123, 127.
Ummīdi (930). *Divan*, 422 VIII.
'Unṣuri (431). *Divan*, 204 II., 205, 212 III.—105, 106, 108, 115, 190, 390.
'Urfī (999). *Divan*, 310. *Farhād u Shīrīn*, 310 v, 311 II.—108, 309 II., 311, 419 XII., XIV., 376.
'Uẓri, 132.
Vafā (1200). *Divan*, 344.—123, 127.
Vafā'i, 120, 123.
Vafā'i, Ḥusain. *Risālah*, 167.
Vāhib, Ḥasan Yazdi, 376.
Vaḥīd, v. Ṭāhir Vaḥīd.
Vaḥshi (991). *Farhād u Shīrīn*, 303, 376, 418 II., 419 III.—376, 419 VI.

Vā'iẓ, v. Rafī' ud-Dīn Vā'iẓ, 152.
Vaḳār, Aḥmad. *Bahrām u Bihrūz* (c. 1274) 369.—370.
Vaḳāri, v. Muḥ. Amīn, 399.
Vālā, 123-4.
Vālih, 124.
Vālih, v. 'Ali Ḳuli Khān, 112.
Vaṣṣāf. *Ta'rīkh ul-Vaṣṣāf*, 49.
Viṣāl Shīrāzi (1263). *Farhād u Shīrīn*, 308, 418 II.—107, 127, 403 20.
Yaghmā, 123, 403 10.
Yaḥya Lāhiji, 108.
Yaḥya, Mīr, 376.
Yaḥya Mirza, 121.
Ya'ḳūb Beg Aḳ-ḳuyunlu (896) 401.
Ibn Yamīn (745) 261 II., 107.
Yamīn ud-Dīn Tughrā'i, 378.
Yamīni, 124.
Yūsuf Amīri, 378.
Yūsuf Beg Istājlu, 378.
Yūsuf Khān, 411.
Ẕabīḥi, 127, 376.
Ẓafar Khān, 419 x.
Ẓāfir, Shams ud-Dīn Ḥasan, 146.
Ẓahīr ud-Daulah Ibrāhīm Khān, 123-4.
Ẓahīr ud-Dīn Mar'ashi. *Ta'rīkh i Ṭabaristān* (881) 93.
Ẓahīr Fāriyābi (598). *Divan*, 222-24.—107, 115, 190, 374, 379.
Zain ul-'Ābidīn B. Sayyid Razī. *Fatḥ ul-Mujāhidīn*, 406.
Zain ul-'Ābidīn Shīrvāni. *Riyāẓ us-Siyāḥat* (1242). *Bustān us-Siyāḥat* (1248) 140-41.—387, 403 17.
Zain ud-Dīn Sijzi, 107.
Zaini 'Alavi, 107.
Ẓamīri, 108.
Zakariyyā Mirza, 121.
Zargar, 127.
Zāri', 128.
Ẓarīf, 120.
Ẓarrah, 124.
Zarrīn Raḳam, Hidāyat-ullah, 408, 411.
Ẕauḳi, 127.
Ẓiyā, 123, 127, 376.
Ẓuhūri (1025) 422 III., 419 x., 108, 376.
Zulāli (c. 1025). *Maḥmūd u Āyāz*, 317.—376.
Ẕulfaḳār Shīrvāni, 115.

CLASSED INDEX OF WORKS.

The works are arranged, as far as possible, under each heading in chronological order. Numerals in parenthesis are Hijrah dates relating to the composition of the works or to the death of the authors. Other numerals refer to the nos. under which the MSS. are described.

THEOLOGY.

Mavāhib i 'Aliyyah (899) 1.
Anonymous Tafsīr (before 1085) 2.
Sirāj ul-Ḳulūb, 3.
Shir'at ul-Islām (573) 4.
Tazkirat ul-Abrār (1021) 5.
Hidāyat us-Su'adā, 6.
Tuḥfat ul-Muvaḥḥidīn by Rām Mohan Rāi (1249) 22.

Shī'ah Works.

Tabṣirat ul-'Avām (c. 653) 7.
Miftāḥ ul-Falāḥ (1030) 8.
Gauhar i Murād (c. 1060) 9.
Taḳdīs ul-Anbiyā (before 1073) 10.
Zā'idah i Zād ul-Ma'ād (1110) 11.

Bābī Books.

Bayān i Fārsi (before 1266) 12.
Īḳān. Letters of Bahā (c. 1280) 13, 403 II.
Bahā's letter to the Shāh (1285) 14.
Ta'rīkh i Jadīd (before 1298) 15.

Sufism and Asceticism.

Risālat ul-Ḳushairi (465) 16.
Anecdotes of saints (c. 500) 393.
Mirṣād ul-'Ibād (654) 17.
Daḳā'iḳ ul-Ḥaḳā'iḳ (720) 18.
Al-'Urvah li-ahli 'l-khalwah (736) 19.
Sharḥ i Aurād i Sayyid 'Ali Hamadāni (786) 20.
Khazā'in ul-Malakūt by 'Abdi (968) 307 II.
Abvāb ul-Jinān by Rafī' Vā'iẓ (1105) 152.
Ḥilyat ul-Muttaḳīn by Muḥ. Bāḳir (1110) 153.
Durr i Maknūn (1151) 21.
Mir'āt ul-Muḥaḳḳiḳīn by Ḥamīd ud-Dīn, 418 III.

LAW.

Lavāmi' i Ṣāḥibḳirāni (1065) 23.

HINDUISM.

Asvamedha Parva of Mahābhārata, 24.

HISTORY.

General History.

Jāmi' ut-Tavārīkh by Rashīd ud-Dīn (704) 25-6.
Ẓafar Nāmah by Ḥamdullah Mustaufi (735) 263.
Zubdat ut-Tavārīkh by Ḥāfiẓ i Abrū (830) 27.
Ta'rīkh i Khairāt (850) 423.
Bahjat ut-Tavārīkh by Shukr-ullah (855) 28.
Ma'āṣir ul-Mulūk by Khwāndamīr (c. 900) 29.
Khulāṣat ul-Akhbār by the same (905) 30.
Ḥabīb us-Siyar by the same (930) 31.
Ta'rīkh i Elchi i Niẓāmshāh (972) 32.
Ta'rīkh i Alfi (997) 424.

Majma' ut-Tavārīkh by Ḥaidar Rāzi (1028) 33.
Khuld i Barīn (1071) 34-5.
Lubb ul-Lubāb by Muḥ. Ḳuli Ḳājār (1097) 38.
Zubdat ut-Tavārīkh by Muḥ. Muḥsin (1154) 36.
Ta'rīkh Muḥammadshāhi by Khushḥālchand (1154) 37.
Zīnat ut-Tavārīkh by Muḥ. Raẓī (1220) 39.
Khulāṣat i Ta'rīkh, anonymous (1250) 40.
Nukhbat ul-Akhbār by 'Abd ul-Vahhāb (1257) 41.
Nizhād Nāmah i Pādishāhān by Riẓa Ḳuli Khān (c. 1280) 42.

Muḥammad, Khalifs and Imams.

Hist. of Muḥ. and the Khalifs by Najīb (c. 850) 43.
Kitāb i Mu'jizāt by Ḥairati (961) 303.
Taẕkirat ul-A'immah by Muḥ. Bāḳir Majlisī (d. 1110) 44.
Ḥamlah i Ḥaidari by Bāẕil (1124) 336.
Riyāẓ ush-Shahādah by Muḥ. Ḥasan Ḳazvīni (1227) 45-7.
Baḥr ul-La'āli by 'Ali Akbar Shīrāzi (1257) 48.
Farhang i Khudāparastī (1277) 371.

Special Dynasties.

Moghols.

Ta'rīkh ul-Vaṣṣāf (712) 49.
Shāhanshāh Nāmah (738) 201 II.
Hist. of Uljā'itu and Abu Sa'īd (c. 820) 26 II.

Muẓaffaris.

Mavāhib i Ilāhi by Mu'īn Yazdi (767) 50.

Timur.

Tuzūk i Tīmūri (1047) 51.

Safavis.

Hist. of Shāh Ismā'īl (c. 940) 52.
Hist. of Ismā'īl and Ṭahmāsp by Amīr Maḥmūd (957) 53-4.
Aḥsan ut-Tavārīkh by Ḥasan Beg (985) 55.
Afẓal ut-Tavārīkh (c. 1020) 56.
Ta'rīkh i Jalāl Munajjim (1020) 57.
Rauẓat uṣ-Ṣafaviyyah (1028-35) 58.
'Ālam-ārāi 'Abbāsi (1038) 59.
Khuld i Barīn (1071) 34-5.
Ta'rīkh i Ṭāhir Vaḥīd (1074) 60-61.
Dastūr i Shahriyārān (1110) 62.
Afghan invasion by Krusinski (c. 1140) 65.
Zīvar i Āl i Dā'ūd (1226) 65.

Nādir Shah.

Ta'rīkh i Jahāngushāi Nādiri (1161) 65.

Zands.

Gulshan i Murād (1198-1210) 66.
Hist. of 'Ali Murād Khān (c. 1198) 352 II.

Ḳajars.

Ta'rīkh i Muḥammadi (1211) 67.
Mufarriḥ ul-Ḳulūb, by Nadīm (c. 1220) 397.
Ma'āṣir i Sulṭāniyyah (1229) 68-9.
Ta'rīkh i Ṣāḥibḳirāni (1248) 70.
Ta'rīkh i Ẕulḳarnain (1262) 71.
Memoirs of Fatḥ 'Ali Shāh's Court by 'Aẓud ud-Daulah (1304) 72.

Uzbeks.

Sharaf Nāmah i Shāhi (997) 73.

Afghans.

Ta'rīkh i Aḥmad Shāh (1257) 74.

India.

Vāḳi'āt i Bābari (936) 75.
Tatimmah i Akbar Nāmah, 76 I.
Jahāngīr Nāmah (1033) 77.
Early history of Shāhjahān (1037) 76 II.
Laṭā'if ul-Akhbār (1063) 78.
Fragments relating to Jahāndār Shāh (1124) 79.
Hist. of Muḥammad Shāh (1144) 80.
Akhbār (1210) 81-2.

Deccan.

Taẕkirat ul-Mulūk (c. 1020) 83 III.
Ḥadīḳat ul-'Ālam (c. 1218) 84.

Kashmir.

Gauhar i 'Ālam (c. 1200) 85.
Ḥishmat i Kashmīr (1245) 86.

Local Histories.

Ta'rīkh i Bukhārā (348) 87.
Kitāb i Ḳum (378) 88.
Ta'rīkh i Baihaḳ (563) 89.
Conquest of Kirman by Malik Dīnār (584) 90-91.
Ta'rīkh i Ṭabaristān by Ibn Isfandiyār (750) 92.
Ta'rīkh i Ṭabaristān by Ẓahīr ud-Dīn (881) 93.
Rauẓāt ul-Jannāt, a hist. of Herat (897) 94.
Sharaf Nāmah, a hist. of the Kurds (1005) 95-6.
Iḥyā ul-Mulūk, a hist. of Sīstān (1028) 97.
Taẕkirah i Shushtariyyah (1169) 98.
Tuḥfat ul-'Ālam, a hist. of Shushtar (1216) 84 II.
Mir'āt ul-Ḳāsān (1288) 99.

BIOGRAPHY.

Ta'rīkh i Ḥukamā by Shahrazūrī (c. 600) 100 I.
Āsār ul-Vuzarā (883) 101.
Haft Iḳlīm by Amīn Rāzi (1002) 138.
Ziyā ul-'Ārifīn by Faẓl-ullah (1272) 102.

Tazkirahs.

Majālis un-Nafā'is (896) 104.
Tuḥfah i Sāmi (987) 103.
Khulāṣat ul-Ash'ār (996) 105.
Bazm-ārāi by Sayyid 'Ali (1000) 106.
Khair ul-Bayān by Mīr Ḥusain (1019-36) 108-9.
Maikhānah by Ḥasan Ṭihrāni (1040) 107.
Taẕkirah i Ṭāhir Naṣrābādi (1083) 110.
Safīnah i Khushgū (1137-47) 111.
Riyāẓ ush-Shu'arā by Vālih (1161) 112-13.
Ātashkadah by Āẕur (1193) 114.
Khulāṣat ul-Afkār by Abu Ṭālib (1207) 116.
Makhzan ul-Gharā'ib by Aḥmad 'Ali (1218) 117.
Zīnat ul-Madā'iḥ by Humā (1218-23) 118-19.
Anjuman i Khāḳān by Fāẓil (1234) 120.
Gulshan i Maḥmūd by Maḥmūd Mirza (1235) 121.
Safīnat ul-Maḥmūd by the same (1240) 122.
Nigāristān i Dārā by 'Abd ur-Razzāḳ (1241) 123.
Taẕkirah i Muḥammadshāhi by Bahman (1249) 124.
Taẕkirah i Darvīsh Navā (c. 1250) 115.
Majma' ul-Fuṣaḥā by Riẓa Ḳuli Khān (c. 1250) 125.
Riyāẓ ul-'Ārifīn by the same (1260) 126.
Madā'iḥ ul-Mu'tamadiyyah by Bahār (1259-63) 127-8.
Ḥadīḳat Amānullāhi by Raunaḳ (1265) 129.

Memoirs and Travels.

Aḥvāl i Shāhi by Tavakkul Beg (1077) 130.
Jangnāmah i Navvāb Ghulām Muḥammad Khān (1213) 351.
Mir'āt ul-Aḥvāl by Aḥmad Bahbahāni (1225) 131.
Tajribat ul-Aḥrār by 'Abd ur-Razzāḳ (1228) 132.
Travels of 'Izzat-ullah (1227-8) 133.
Hist. of Dā'ūd Pasha of Bagdad (1237) 356.
Statement of the Raja of Revari (c. 1270) 134.

COSMOGRAPHY AND GEOGRAPHY.

'Ajā'ib ul-Makhlūḳāt by Ḳazvīni (682) 135.
Nuzhat ul-Ḳulūb by Ḥamd-ullah (740) 136-7.
Haft Iḳlīm by Amīn Rāzi (1002) 138.
Riyāẓ us-Siyāḥat by Zain ul-'Ābidīn (1242) 139.
Ḥadā'iḳ us-Siyāḥat by the same (1242) 141.
Bustān us-Siyāḥat by the same (1247) 140.

SCIENCES.

Encyclopædias.

Jāmi' ul-'Ulūm by Fakhr ud-Dīn Rāzi (574) 142-3.
Riyāẓ ul-Abrār by Ḥusain 'Aḳīli (979) 144.

Ethics and Politics.

Ḳābūs Nāmah by Kaikā'ūs (475) 145.
Az-Zarī'ah by Rāghib Isfahāni (c. 500) 146.
Akhlāḳ i Nāṣiri by Naṣīr ud-Dīn Ṭūsi (672) 147-8.
Naṣīḥat Nāmah i Shāhi by Ḥusain Khwārazmi (829) 149.
Akhlāḳ i Manṣūri by Ghiyāṣ ud-Dīn (948) 150.
Akhlāḳ i Shifā'i by Muẓaffar (963) 151.
Abvāb ul-Jinān by Rafī' Vā'iẓ (1105) 152.
Mufarriḥ ul-Ḳulūb by Nadīm (1241) 397.

Astronomy.

Jahān Dānish by Sharaf ud-Dīn Mas'ūdi (643) 154.
Bīst Bāb by Naṣīr ud-Dīn Ṭūsi (672) with comm., 155.
'Alī Ḳūshji's comm. on Zīj i Ulugh Beg (c. 850) 156.

Mineralogy.

Tansūḳ Nāmah by Naṣīr ud-Dīn Ṭūsi (672) 157.
Javāhir Nāmah by Muḥ. B. Manṣūr (c. 880) 158.

Medicine.

Risālah i Tiryāḳ i Fārūḳ by Kamāl ud-Dīn (c. 950) 159.
Dustūr ul-Aṭibbā by Firishtah (1033) 160.

Farriery.

Translation of al-Aḳwāl al-Kāfiyah (c. 750) 161.

Music.

Treatises on music (collected A.H. 1075) 162.
On musical moods, 191 VII.

PHILOLOGY.

Persian Lexicography.

Miftāḥ ul-Fuẓalā by Muḥ. Shādiyābādi (873) 163.
Lughāt i Ḥalīmī (c. 886) 164-5.
Tuḥfah i Shāhidi (920) 166.
Risālah i Ḥusain Vafā'i (933) 167.
Farhang i Jahāngīrī (1017) 168.
Treatise of 'Abd ul-Bāsiṭ (c. 1150) 169.
Farhang i 'Abbāsi (1225) 170.
Farhang i Muḥammadshāhi (1249) 171.

Arabic Lexicography and Grammar.

Ḳānūn ul-Adab by Ḥubaish Tiflīsi (c. 600) 425.
Dustūr ul-Ikhwān (c. 822) 172.
Kanz ul-Lughah (c. 880) 173.
Maḥmūd ul-Lughah (bef. 1131) 174.
Comm. on the Shāfiyah, 175.

Varia.

Sanglākh, a Turki-Persian Dictionary (1173) 176.
Redhouse's Thesaurus, 177-86.
Niṣāb i Ingilīsi by Farhād Mirza (1269) 187.

Rhetoric, Inshā and Poetical Figures.

Ḥadā'iḳ us-Siḥr by Rashīd Vaṭvāṭ (c. 550) 188.
Tarassul un-Nuṣriyyah by Faẓl-ullah (c. 732) 257 II.
Dustūr ul-Kātib by Ibn Hindūshāh (c. 770) 189.
Anīs ul-'Ushshāḳ by Sharaf Rāmī (795) 420 III.
Ḥadīḳat ul-Ḥaḳā'iḳ by the same, 421 V.

Prosody.

Al-Mu'ajjam by Shams i Ḳais (c. 620) 190.
'Arūẓ i Saifī (896) 191 I.
Treatise on rhyme by 'Aṭā'ullah (929) 191 III., 192.

Riddles.

Al-Iḥyā fi'l Mu'ammā by Minūchihr (c. 800) 420 II.
Ḥulal i Muṭarraz by 'Ali Yazdi (858) 193.
Treatise by Mīr Ḥusain (904) 191 V., 194.

POETRY.

Firdausi (411). Shahnāmah, 195-8, 269. Yūsuf u Zulaikhā, 200.
Barzū Nāmah, 195 II., 196 VIII.
Farāmurz Nāmah, 196 VI., 199 II.
Āzarbarzīn Nāmah, 197 I.
Farrukhi (429) 203-4.
'Unṣuri (431) 204 II., 205, 212 III.
Minūchihri (432) 206, 212 V., 224 II.
Asadi. Garshāsp Nāmah (458) 195 I., 196 I., 201 I., 202.
Ḳaṭarān (465) 204 III., 207-8, 245 II.
Nāṣir i Khusrau (481) 209-10.
Jamāli. Bahman Nāmah, 197 II., 201 III. Kūsh Nāmah, 201 IV.
Abu'l-Faraj Rūni (c. 500) 210 I.
Lāmi'ī (c. 520) 212 I.
Azraḳi (526) 211 III., 213 I., 224 III., 234 III.
Adīb Ṣābir (540) 239 II.
Sanā'i (c. 542) 214-15.
Mukhtāri (544) 211 VI., 215 VII., 216.
'Abd ul-Vāsi' Jabali (555) 217.
Ḥasan Ghaznavi (565) 215 VI.

Rashīd Vaṭvāṭ (578) 212 iv., 234 ii.
Anvari (587) 211 v., 218-19.
Jamāl Iṣfahāni (588) 224 iv.
Khāḳāni (595) 221.
Ẓahīr Fāriyābi (598) 222-24.
Sharaf Shufurvah (c. 600) 230 iii.
Rafī' Lunbāni (603) 230 iv.
Niẓāmi Ganjavi (c. 607) 225-33.
Najīb Jurpādaḳāni (625) 234.
Farīd ud-Dīn 'Aṭṭār (627) 235-7.
Ḳuṭb ud-Dīn (633?) 238.
Aṣīr Aumāni (665) 239 i.
Saif Isfarangi (666) 220 ii.
Jalāl ud-Dīn Rūmi (672) 240-44.
Imāmi Haravi (686) 213 ii., 245 i.
Majd ud-Dīn Hamgar (686) 211 ii., iv., vii.
Farīd ud-Dīn Aḥval (c. 686) 213 iii.
Sa'di (691) 246-53.
Hārūn (c. 700) 254.
Khusrau Dihlavi (725) 220 iv., 255.
Amīr Ḥasan (727) 286 4.
Faẓl-ullah Ḳazvīni (c. 732) 257.
Auḥadi (738) 258-59.
Aḥmad Tabrīzi. Shahanshāh Nāmah (738) 201 ii.
Ḥamd-ullah Mustaufi (c. 740). Ẓafar Nāmah, 263.
'Atīḳi (744) 260.
Ibn Yamīn (745) 261 ii.
Khwājū (c. 750) 262. Sām Nāmah, 196 ii.
'Ubaid Zākāni (772) 264.
Salmān Sāvaji (779) 220 iii., 265-66.
Ḥāfiẓ (791) 267-74.
Ibn 'Imād (c. 800) 348 ii.
Kamāl Khujandi (803) 275-76, 286 6.
Maghribi (809) 277 i.
Shams Mashriḳi (c. 800) 277 ii.
'Azīz-ullah. Rauẓat ul-'Āshiḳīn (820) 278.
Ni'mat-ullah Vali (834) 279.
Muvāli (c. 834) 285 iii.
Ḳāsim ul-Anvār (837) 280-81.
Kātibi (838) 275 ii.
'Iṣmat (840) 282.
'Ārifi (853) 283, 286 7.
Ashraf (854) 286 3.
Shāhi (857) 284-85.
Ṭāli'i (858) 286 8.
Ṭūsi (869) 286 1.
Saifi (870) 275 ii.
Riyāẓi (884) 285 ii., 275 ii
Jāmi (898) Divan, 287-88; Haft Aurang, 289-93.
Maktabi (c. 900) 298.
Suhaili (907) 275 ii.
Hātifi (927) 295-97, 305 ii., 275 ii.
Ummīdi (930) 422 viii.
Muḥyi (933) 301, 275 ii.
Hilāli (935) 302.
Mīram Siyāh (c. 960) 353 ii.
Ḥairati (961) 303.
Fuẓūli (963) 304-5, 422 ii.
Ashki (972) 306.
'Abdi (961-68) 307.
Vaḥshi (991) 308.
Ṣanā'i (996) 309 i.
'Urfi (999) 309 ii., 310-11.
Nūri Iṣfahāni (1000) 224 v. 422 vi.
Amāni (c. 1016) 312.
Nau'i (1019) 313.
Ja'far (1021) 314-15.
Naẓīri (1022) 316.
Zulāli (c. 1025) 317.
Abu Turāb Beg (1026) 318 i.
Niẓām Dast i Ghaib (1029) 319.
Naṣīr Hamadāni (1030) 318 ii.
'Ali Naḳi Kamara'i (1030) 320.
Shāpūr (c. 1030) 321.
Mīrak (c. 1053) 322.
Ḳudsi (1056) 323.
Fayyāẓ Lāhiji (c. 1060) 324.
Ḥāziḳ (1068) 325.
Ṣaidi (1069) 422 vii.
Shaidā (c. 1080) 327.
Rāḳim (c. 1084) 332.
Ṣā'ib (1088) 326-29.
Arshad (c. 1089) 330.
Majẕūb (1093) 331.
Nauras (c. 1105) 333.
Rafī' Vā'iẓ (c. 1105) 334.

Surûri (c. 1114) 335.
Bâzil (1124) 336.
Mîr Najât (c. 1126) 337.
Bîdil (1133) 338.
Ṭabîb (1168) 339.
'Âshiḳ (1181) 340-41.
Ṭûfân (1190) 342.
Faḳîr 'Abbâsi (c. 1199) 343.
Vafâ (1200) 344.
Sayyid Kûchak (c. 1200) 345.
Nâmi (1204) 346-49.
Rafîḳ (1212) 350.
Ghulâm Jîlâni, Jangnâmah (1213) 351.
Shihâb (1215) 352-53.
Mijmar (1225) 354.
Ḳaṭrah (1235) 357.
Farrukh (1237) 355.
Shaidâ, Ḥasan Chelebi (c. 1237) 356.
Khâvari (1237) 358.
Khâvar (1238) 359.
Abu 'l-Ḥasan Jâjarmi (1239) 360.
Shâh Shujâ' (1240) 361.
Nashâṭ (1244) 362-3.
Hidâyat (1253-83) 364-5.
Viṣâl (1263) 308.
Nayyir (1263) 368.
Ghamâmi (1269) 366.
Ḳâ'âni (1270) 367.
Vaḳâr (1274) 369-70.
Maḥram (1277) 371.
Nâẓir (1297) 372.
'Âmil (1298) 373.

Anthologies.

Dustûr ush-Shu'arâ, an anonymous anthology of Persian and Indian poets (803) 374.
Tuḥfat ul-Ḥabîb by Fakhri (c. 930) 375.
Collection of Masnavis by Badî' Muḥ. (1170) 376.
Badî' ul-Afkâr by Munṣif (1239) 378.
Maḥmûd ul-Bayân by Maḥmûd Mirza (1240) 377.
Mizân i Ṭabâ'i', by Khâvar (1242) 379.

TALES AND FABLES.

Ḳiṣṣah i Bilauhar by Ibn Bâbavaih (321) 380.
Marzabân Nâmah (c. 610) 382-3.
Anvâr i Suhaili by Ḥusain Kâshifi (910) 381.
Dârâb Nâmah by Abu Ṭâhir Ṭarasûsi, 384-5.
Ḥaḳîkat ul-Ḥaḳâ'iḳ by Muḥ. 'Ali Shîrvâni (1252) 387.
Ḳiṣṣah i Mas'ûd Shâh, 388.

Collections of Anecdotes.

Al-Faraj ba'd ash-Shiddah, 389.
Anecdotes of Saints, anonymous (c. 500) 393.
Chahâr Maḳâlah by Niẓâmi (c. 552) 390.
Jâmi' ul-Ḥikâyât by 'Aufi (625) 391-2.
Nigâristân i Mu'îni (735) 394.
Zînat ul-Majâlis by Majdi (1004) 395.
Historical anecdotes, anonymous (c. 1000) 102.
Sirâj ul-Munîr by Kâshif (1030) 419 II., 422.
Khazân u Bahâr by the same (1060) 396.
Mufarriḥ ul-Ḳulûb by Nadîm (1241) 397.

LETTERS, STATE PAPERS, AND AUTOGRAPHS.

Majma' ul-Inshâ by Abu 'l-Ḳâsim Beg (c. 1052) 398.
Guldastah i Andîshah by Vaḳâri (c. 1081) 399.
Anonymous collection of royal letters (c. 1100) 417 II.
Autographs compiled by 'Abd ul-Karîm Ḳazvîni (1080-1126) 400.
Firmans of the Shahs (884-1283) 401-2.
Collection of autographs, 403.
Copies of treaties (1224-72) 404.
Addresses to Warren Hastings, 405.
Military rules of Tipu Sultan, 406.
A Letter from Deccan to Maréchal de Castries, 407.

PAINTINGS.

Album of Âṣaf ud-Daulah, 408.
Album of Himmat-yâr Khân (1204) 411.
Portraits of Persian princes and ministers, 412.

Inscriptions.

Inscriptions of Tâj Maḥall and Delhi, 413-15.
Inscription of Khwâjah Khiẓr, 416.

NUMERICAL INDEX.

SHOWING THE CORRESPONDENCE OF THE NUMBERS BY WHICH THE MANUSCRIPTS ARE DESIGNATED WITH THE NUMBERS UNDER WHICH THEY ARE DESCRIBED IN THE PRESENT SUPPLEMENT.

Oriental.	Supplement.	Oriental.	Supplement.	Oriental.	Supplement.
2676 .	391	2819 .	12	2876 .	70
2677	31	2833	263	2877	118
2692 .	84	2834 .	225	2878 .	202
2693	112	2837	41	2879	208
2694 .	329	2838 .	297	2880 .	224
2699	86	2839	313	2881	45
2710 .	267	2841 .	156	2862 .	46
2739	152	2842	4	2883	47
2743 .	217	2843 .	205	2885 .	26
2747	236	2844	206	2886	50
2769 .	133	2845 .	209	2887 .	90
2774	27	2846	239	2888	237
2775 .	28	2847 .	245	2889 .	212
2776	54	2848	303	2892	176
2777 .	87	2849 .	326	2926 .	196
2778	92	2850	342	2927	25
2779 .	97	2851 .	345	2928 .	30
2780	201	2852	417	2929	114
2781 .	384	2862 .	93	2930 .	200
2787	411	2863	148	2931	226
2799 .	381	2864 .	157	2932 .	227
2812	8	2865	160	2933	231
2813 .	11	2866 .	243	2934 .	233
2814	190	2867	295	2935	290
2815 .	265	2868 .	343	2936 .	336
2816	241	2869	341	2937	168
2817 .	352	2870 .	304	2939 .	53
2818 .	155	2872	312	2940 . .	60

Oriental.	Supplement.	Oriental.	Supplement.	Oriental.	Supplement.
2941	62	3000	368	3271	76
2942	15	3115	14	3272	59
2943	129	3116	13	3273	172
2944	188	3202	39	3274	314
2945	203	3203	130	3275	315
2946	199	3204	311	3276	77
2947	264	3205	274	3277	158
2948	246	3206	273	3278	68
2949	255	3207	393	3279	69
2950	275	3208	3	3280	298
2951	281	3216	168	3281	80
2952	317	3223	388	3282	328
2953	349	3233	218	3283	284
2954	369	3234	324	3284	361
2955	418	3235	358	3285	335
2956	382	3236	340	3286	339
2957	396	3237	366	3287	78
2959-68	177-86	3238	238	3288	37
2969	48	3239	344	3299	163
2970	49	3240	367	3300	170
2971	7	3241	194	3301	223
2972	142	3242	17	3302	214
2973	383	3243	372	3303	276
2974	394	3244	375	3304	280
2975	419	3245	360	3305	286
2976	197	3246	204	3306	283
2979	310	3247	268	3307	420
2980	191	3248	52	3308	143
2983	2	3249	192	3312	219
2984	356	3250	124	3313	277
2985	299	3251	371	3314	422
2986	308	3252	145	3315	154
2993	9	3253	240	3316	296
2994	43	3254	373	3317	207
2995	213	3255	316	3318	353
2996	150	3256	370	3319	323
2997	278	3260	406	3320	217
2998	319	3261	252	3321	347
2999	346	3262	253	3322	257

Oriental.	Supplement.	Oriental.	Supplement.	Oriental.	Supplement.
3323	210	3501	387	3589	116
3324	321	3504	307	3590	389
3325	222	3505	320	3592	66
3332	61	3506	105	3600	386
3333	40	3507	390	3602	64
3334	285	3508	123	3603	99
3344	189	3509	193	3604	378
3374	216	3512	23	3610	79
3375	262	3513	232	3632	146
3376	234	3514	242	3633	301
3377	365	3515	175	3634	331
3378	42	3516	153	3641	44
3379	300	3517	169	3642	422
3386	115	3520	174	3643	29
3387	260	3521	167	3644	333
3388	58	3522	102	3647	254
3389	106	3523	132	3648	144
3390	120	3524	125	3649	19
3391	88	3527	71	3653	165
3396	104	3528	364	3666	141
3397	108	3529	380	3667	318
3398	164	3535	32	3668	337
3399	119	3536	126	3677	140
3400	38	3537	107	3713	211
3401	221	3541	330	3714	75
3402	399	3542	338	4106	94
3481	35	3543	354	4107	101
3482	398	3544	355	4108	72
3483	161	3545	122	4109	149
3484	359	3546	151	4110	374
3486	220	3547	18	4118	16
3487	332	3549	57	4119	147
3488	350	3550	74	4120	249
3489	357	3551	67	4121	251
3490	108	3552	377	4122	291
3497	73	3553	121	4123	287
3498	36	3584	91	4124	302
3499	397	3587	89	4132	34
3500	262	3588	271	4133	10

Oriental.	Supplement.
4134	55
4135	279
4151	235
4195	173
4238	351
4379	1
4380	6
4381	20
4382	21
4383	135
4384	198
4385	228
4386	229
4387	250
4388	270
4389	293
4390	294
4391	325
4392	392
4482	258
4507	5
4508	33
4509	63
4510	109
4511	127
4512	128
4513	289
4514	215
4515	348
4516	362
4535	402 2
4543	407
4561	24
4595	415

Oriental.	Supplement.
4608	82
4600	81
4610	117
4615	385
4616	306
4617	139
4658	100
4671	110
4672	111
4673	379
4678	56
4679	404
4680	171
4681	288
4688	85
4689	244
4691	159
4709	113
4722	51
4730	230
4733	131
4738	22
4745	272
4768	416
4772	376
4773	269
4774	334
4775	65
4776	83
4779	248
4836	95
4898	423
4900	424
4900	96

Oriental.	Supplement.
4901	98
4902	138
4903	136
4904	137
4905	187
4906	195
4907	395
4908	134
4909	266
4910	261
4911	305
4912	322
4913	309
4914	363
4932	259
4934	401
4935	402
4936	403
4937	400
4938	412
4948	425

Stowe Or.	Supplement.
14	256
15	327
16	403
17	413-14
18	409
19	410

Add.	
20,217	405

www.ingramcontent.com/pod-product-compliance
Lightning Source LLC
Chambersburg PA
CBHW022023240426
43667CB00042B/1067
9783337310882